ADVANCED VISUAL BASIC 4.0
PROGRAMMING

ADVANCED VISUAL BASIC 4.0 PROGRAMMING

Steven Holzner

M&T BOOKS

M&T Books
A Division of MIS:Press, Inc.
A Subsidiary of Henry Holt and Company, Inc.
115 West 18th Street
New York, New York 10011

Limits of Liability and Disclaimer of Warranty

The Author and Publisher of this book have used their best efforts in preparing the book and the programs contained in it. These efforts include the development, research, and testing of the theories and programs to determine their effectiveness.

The Author and Publisher make no warranty of any kind, expressed or implied, with regard to these programs or the documentation contained in this book. The Author and Publisher shall not be liable in any event for incidental or consequential damages in connection with, or arising out of, the furnishing, performance, or use of these programs.

All products, names and services are trademarks or registered trademarks of their respective companies.

ISBN: 1-55851-474-0

10 9 8 7 6 5 4 3 2 1

Associate Publisher: Paul Farrell
Managing Editor: Cary Sullivan
Development Editor: Michael Sprague
Copy Edit Manager: Shari Chappell
Copy Editor: Betsy Hardinger
Production Editor: Stephanie Doyle

DEDICATION

This book is dedicated to Nancy Conner, computer expert,
for hundreds and hundreds of reasons. And she knows them all.

CONTENTS

CHAPTER 5:

USING VISUAL BASIC'S CUSTOM OCX CONTROLS 215

x

CHAPTER 9:

CONNECTING VISUAL BASIC TO WINDOWS AND C++ 403

CHAPTER 10:

CREATING WINDOWS HELP FILES AND SETUP PROGRAMS 455

CHAPTER 11:

INTRODUCING DATABASES 485

CHAPTER 12:
CREATING AND FILLING DATABASES 523

CHAPTER 13
USING DATABASES IN CODE 569

APPENDIX A:

ISSUES OF 16-BIT VS. 32-BIT PROGRAMMING

APPENDIX B:

VISUAL BASIC, ENTERPRISE EDITION

APPENDIX C:

ABOUT THE DISKETTE

INDEX

ACKNOWLEDGMENTS

I'd like to thank the people at M&T Books for making writing for and working with them such a smooth process, especially Michael Sprague and Stephanie Doyle. Thanks to you all, and good work.

INTRODUCTION

When Visual Basic first appeared, it produced a revolution in Windows programming, a revolution that continues to this day. Never before had Windows programming been so easy and so quick. Before, programmers had to use C to create Windows programs, and the process was a long one, the learning curve steep. Just a simple program that put a window on the screen—nothing more—took five pages of C code. And C programming was not like DOS programming; it was completely different. But the options were clear: learn C and C Windows programming, or forget it.

Then came Visual Basic. To produce a fully working window in Visual Basic, you only have to do one thing: select the Run menu's **Start** item. That's it—a fully working (although blank) window appears on the screen. It's all been done for you. This caused a sensation: Windows programming without the torture! Accessible programming for everyone: revolutionary! Visual Basic may have been the first programming environment that was so easy to use that it was actually enjoyable.

The idea behind Visual Basic is to make programming as visual as possible: if you want a button in your Visual Basic program, you just draw it there. If you want a new menu in your program, you just use the menu editor and type the new menu's name—and there it is. The Visual Basic programmer is freed from the tyranny of resource files, DEF files, and trying to figure out what the program you've just written in code will look like on the screen. Current C++ programming environments have made Windows programming much easier, but they still can't compare to Visual Basic. In C++, controls such as buttons and text boxes are programming constructs: C++ objects. Yet Visual Basic is ahead of that: in Visual Basic, these objects are visual objects. They're visible on the screen—just as they will be when the program is running—and working with them is just that easy.

C and C++ programmers sometimes deride Visual Basic as being too elementary, too limited—in a word, too basic. Yet the unexpected truth is that Visual Basic can do many, even most, of the things that Visual C++ can. And with Visual Basic's built-in tools, it takes only minutes, and not days, to get powerful programs working. In fact, that's the subject of this book—pushing the Visual Basic envelope. We pick up where the introductory books finish, and we keep moving, far into the uncharted territories. We'll see what Visual Basic can really do (and, for that matter, how to connect it to Visual C++).

OUR APPROACH

This is a book for programmers, so we include a lot of examples, ready to run. That's the best way for programming books to work: filled with bite-sized, useful examples. You can actually see the code and run it. Later, if you need to know how something works you can refer to the example in the book and examine the working code.

And because this is a book for programmers, we'll stick as close to the code as we can. We'll develop our examples line by line, in context, all the way through this book. Then we'll run the finished program, and you'll see what's going on immediately. You don't learn to fly by reading aircraft parts manuals—you learn to fly by getting into the plane and trying it out. Similarly, you don't learn to program through dry, detached discussions of programming constructs—you learn to program by getting in there and making it work. Together, we'll do just that; we'll develop the code and see it in action.

In addition, we want to fill this book with utility, with programming power—so we include topics such as how to work with the entire screen at once and how to read the mouse position even though it's outside our window. How to add toolbars to our programs and use OLE automation to execute code across program boundaries. How to program databases and use the new Windows 95 custom controls. And much more—as much as we could, we packed this book with programming power.

The style we use is informal. We're not interested in working through long tables of Basic instructions or abstract descriptions of data structures. We're interested in producing results that you can use. Although we'll follow good programming practices, our major purpose is to get the most out of Visual Basic and to put it to work for ourselves. We'll keep that goal in mind.

That's the idea, then: to give you an edge—something special, something added. We want to move your programs from standard to powerful, from professional to legendary.

WHAT'S IN THIS BOOK

In this book, we'll range as far as Visual Basic can take us. There is a great deal of power in Visual Basic, and we want to get as much of it for ourselves as we can. Here are some of the topics we'll cover:

- Advanced graphics
- MDI programming and coordinating multiple views
- Adding toolbars to programs
- Using the mouse anywhere on the screen
- OLE automation
- OLE containers
- Adding status bars to programs
- Creating Windows help files
- Creating a professional installation program: **SETUP.EXE**
- Advanced control handling
- Database programming
- Multimedia programming
- Passing forms to functions
- Interfacing Visual Basic directly to Windows functions
- Interfacing Visual Basic directly to C++
- Using arrays of forms
- Using Visual Basic's OCX controls
- Using the new Windows 95 super-controls

In addition, we'll see powerful programming techniques and inside Visual Basic tips. The idea is to get into as many areas of Visual Basic as we can and see what they can do for us. Visual Basic is a wonderful program, full of powerful code and methods, and we'll see a great deal of it in this book.

What You'll Need

To use this book profitably, you'll need a running version of Visual Basic 4.0 or later (16- or 32-bit version, Standard, Professional, or Enterprise edition) and some knowledge of how to use it. This is not an introductory book; you should have used Visual Basic before tackling the subjects we'll cover. On the other hand, if you can read through the review in Chapter 1 without difficulty, this book is for you. If that chapter gives you trouble, it might be wise to explore an introductory Visual Basic book first.

The material in the body of this book will work with either the 16- or the 32-bit version of Visual Basic 4.0. On the other hand, there are differ-

4

ences between these two versions, and we'll talk about them in the book and in Appendix A. Except for that, however, you can use the body of this book no matter which version you have.

That's really it—Visual Basic is self-contained enough so that it's almost all we'll need. If you want to explore the world of OLE automation fully in Chapter 8, it would help to have an OLE automation server program such as the latest version of Microsoft Excel or Word for Windows. (Yet not even these are necessary, because we'll build our own OLE automation server.) In addition, if you want to produce Windows help files as we do in Chapter 10, you should have a word processor that can produce rich text files; we'll use Microsoft Word for Windows. (We'll see in Chapter 5 that the new RichTextBox Windows 95 control also lets us produce rich text files.)

With all this in mind, then, let's turn to Chapter 1, where we begin our guided tour of advanced Visual Basic with a review of Visual Basic itself.

REVIEWING VISUAL BASIC

Welcome to *Advanced Visual Basic 4.0 Programming*. This is the book that's going to carry us beyond the ordinary in Visual Basic, into the realms of powerful code and truly professional applications. And this is the programming package to let us do it. With each new version, Visual Basic becomes more and more powerful and encapsulates more and more functionality. The fact that it's easy to use and easy to create programs with makes many people (especially C and C++ programmers) mistake it for a low-level product. The truth is that Visual Basic—in addition to being easy and forgiving to work with—is one of the most powerful Windows programming environments around.

Programming in Visual Basic is a joy, especially if you know what you're missing. In most C or C++ packages, you have to create your visual objects (i.e., controls such as buttons or text boxes—we will not use the word *object* in the C++ sense here) in code and hope they look the way you want them to. In Visual Basic, by contrast, you simply draw what you want and then add perhaps a few lines of code. What could be easier or more appropriate?

Yet Visual Basic has a coding side, too, and what we can do there is powerful. In fact, we'll show how to connect Visual Basic to the same Windows functions that C++ programmers use. These functions are stored in Windows dynamic link libraries such as **SHELL.DLL**, **SHELL32.DLL**, or **COMMDLG.DLL** in WINDOWS\SYSTEM, which means that you can take over much of the functionality and nitty-gritty of any C++ program in Visual Basic. You can connect Visual Basic to C++ or even assembly language routines directly, and we'll see how to do that, too.

All in all, Visual Basic provides an enormous, powerful set of resources and tools for us to explore. In this chapter, we'll start our exploration of Visual Basic by reviewing some of its elementary concepts to bring us up to speed for the following chapters. We'll begin by starting with a review of Windows terminology.

AN OVERVIEW OF WINDOWS

You may be surprised to learn that Microsoft started working on Windows in 1983, when the PC was all of two years old. The original version, Windows 1.01, didn't ship until 1985, however, and windows could be placed only like tiles on the screen and could not overlap. Anyone who has seen the original Windows knows that Microsoft still had far to go; the interface felt flat (both in perceived depth on the screen and in power) and lost few opportunities to crash.

Next came Windows 2, but that product could run only in 80x86 real mode, hobbling it in a total of 1MB of memory. For a while, Windows even split into two products—Windows 386 and Windows 286—to take advantage of the new memory modes offered by the then-new 80386.

In May 1990, Microsoft introduced the first product that people think of as Windows: Windows 3.0. This was a revolutionary step: not only was the feel of the program far stronger, but also it could handle as much as 16MB of real memory, and a total of 64MB if virtual memory was enabled(in virtual memory, sections of memory can be stored on disk). Next came Windows 3.1, with TrueType fonts and a common set of dialog boxes that helped unify the user interface. By this time, Windows had become the fastest-selling software package in history (3,000,000 copies of Windows 3.0 were sold in the first nine months).

But, predictably, the memory boundaries began to chafe more and more programs as computers became more powerful. Now Microsoft has introduced its Windows NT and Windows 95 products, and the limits are off—true 32-bit programming has arrived. Windows 95, in particular, has been a tremendous success. The Task Manager of Windows 3 has become the Taskbar in Windows 95. The cumbersome File Manager has been replaced by the Explorer. Windows 95 is also much more robust (resistant to crashing) than Windows 3, and Windows 95 supports true multitasking. The successor to DOS has finally come into its own.

Windows Terminology

Because this is a book about Windows programming, we'll include a brief review of Windows and Windows terminology here. You should certainly be a Windows user before you proceed with this book, because we'll take for granted most of the basic Windows terminology such as menu, dialog box, menu bar, toolbar, and so on.

A typical 16-bit window appears in Figure 1.1, and a 32-bit one in Figure 1.2. We should note the various parts of these windows. At the top of the window is the title bar, which typically displays the name of the program. The title bar also contains buttons at the extreme right: the first box on the left minimizes the window, the next maximizes it; the last button closes it. Under the title bar comes the menu bar, and the names of the available menus appear in this bar. To open a menu, a user simply moves the mouse cursor to the menu bar and presses the left mouse button when the cursor is over the menu. Because all Windows operations are also (theoretically) supposed to be possible with the keyboard, the user can also press the **Alt** key to highlight the first menu item in the menu bar (thus moving the input *focus*—the target of key strokes and mouse clicks—to the menu bar) and then press the first letter of the item to open. We'll review menus further in a moment.

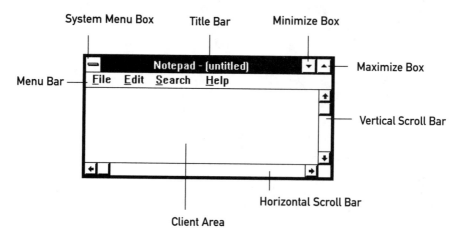

FIGURE 1.1 WHAT A 16-BIT WINDOW LOOKS LIKE.

Under the menu bar is the toolbar. Here you see a series of buttons corresponding to menu items; connecting these menu items to buttons in the toolbar allows the user to select them rapidly without having to open a menu. Under the toolbar is the *client area* of the window. In our programs, we'll be responsible for working with the client area of the program's window (or windows), and the rest of Visual Basic will normally maintain the nonclient area for us; the *nonclient area* includes the title bar, toolbar, menu bar, scroll bars if they exist on the sides of the client area, the border of the window, and everything else not in the client area. The last part of the window we might point out in Figures 1.1 and 1.2 is the status bar; this bar displays comments explaining what various menu items (or toolbar buttons) do; the status bar can also indicate the status of keyboard "modes" such as Caps Lock and Num Lock.

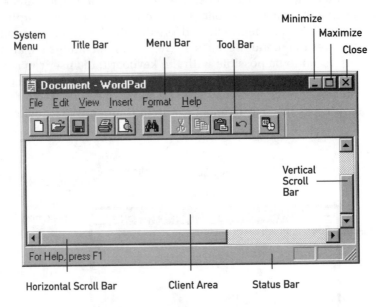

FIGURE 1.2 WHAT A 32-BIT WINDOW LOOKS LIKE.

In Figure 1.3, you see a typical Windows menu. In this case, we've opened the File menu, which is almost always the first menu on the left in the menu bar. Programs almost always have a File menu even if they don't handle files, because users have come to expect it. Each menu carries menu items that the user may select; the last menu item in the File menu is the **Exit** item, which is the usual way you exit a program in Windows. Your program should always have an **Exit** item, and it should usually be the last item in the File menu. Users expect this item to be there.

In addition to menus, there are many other ways of interacting with Windows programs. Such ways include text boxes for users to type text into, list boxes that list a number of choices for users to select from, buttons that users can click, and scroll bars. Scroll bars can be positioned either vertically or horizontally in a window, and they're used to position the document you're working on in the window; the small box you move inside a scroll bar is called the *thumb*. Such items—text boxes, scroll bars, buttons, and so on—are called *controls* in Windows. Much of our programming will have to do with adding controls to windows or dialog boxes and connecting them to our program. Controls typically appear in dialog boxes and not in main windows; in the dialog box in Figure 1.4, you see a text box, list boxes, and buttons.

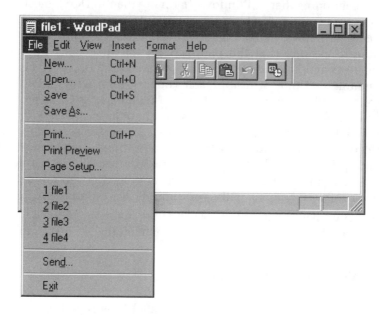

FIGURE 1.3 WHAT A WINDOWS MENU LOOKS LIKE.

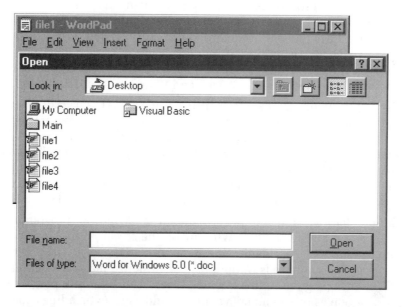

FIGURE 1.4 WHAT A DIALOG BOX LOOKS LIKE.

The Windows "Feel"

It's worth mentioning that in Windows (far more than in DOS), most programs should share a common "feel" in their user interfaces. You get to know this feel by using Windows, by reading about Windows conventions, or both. It's reasonable to assume that the people who will use your programs are Windows users and have used Windows programs before, so it's also reasonable to assume that they will approach your program with certain expectations. For example, they will expect a File menu whose last menu item is **Exit**. In most cases, your main window should not be crowded with controls; controls should be reserved for dialog boxes in most cases. The user often expects certain key combinations to do certain things—for example, **Ctrl-X** quits an application and **Ctrl-I** switches to italics. There are dozens of Windows conventions, which we won't review here. If you are planning to release your software commercially, you should become familiar with them.

Now that we have reviewed the background environment we'll be working in, let's take a look at the programming environment that will concern us most.

ABOUT WINDOWS PROGRAMMING

When Microsoft introduced Windows, it created little sensation. Few people held Windows conferences, and few people published magazines about Windows. But Microsoft stuck to it, perhaps realizing that graphical user interfaces (GUIs) would eventually be the wave of the future. And so it proved. Although Windows did not become popular until version 3.0, with that version came a steadily rising tide of interest. It was robust, offered real utility, and helped PC users break the 640KB memory barrier. Windows 3.1 became the fastest-selling software product ever, and Windows 95 also broke records.

The original programs for Windows were written exclusively by Microsoft. After Windows caught on, however, other programmers also wanted to write Windows programs. Microsoft evidently saw the wisdom in this, and it released the Windows Software Development Kit (SDK)—but programmers were dismayed. The SDK was a mass of uncoordinated functions, thousands of them, interacting in unpredictable and inconsistent ways. The C programming techniques used in Windows programs were also confusing.

The problem was the amount of material the Windows programmer had to master before putting a single window on the screen. It took a five-page C program to simply place a blank window in front of the user. The programmer had to select from hundreds of options and initialize many mysterious parts of the Windows program in unexplained ways. And Windows programs grew quickly. As soon as programmers wanted to add, say, text-reading capabilities or file handling, they found themselves working with pages and pages of code. In C, Windows programming was unwieldy.

Introducing Visual Basic

The first major breakthrough in Windows programming was Visual Basic. (The second was the application of C++ to Windows programming, which also solved many problems.) Visual Basic came on the scene like a thunderbolt—here was Windows programming as it should be. Visually oriented—like the program you're creating—easy to use, even fun. If you want a window a certain size, just stretch it. If you want a list box, just draw it in. Visual Basic was an overnight success. And with it, Windows programming truly became popular, no longer the esoteric pursuit of a handful of programmers.

OUR FIRST PROGRAM

Our first task in this book is to review Visual Basic and bring ourselves up to speed, so let's see Visual Basic in action now. Start it up, as shown in Figure 1.5. As you can see, we already have a window under design, called a *form*, ready for us in Visual Basic.

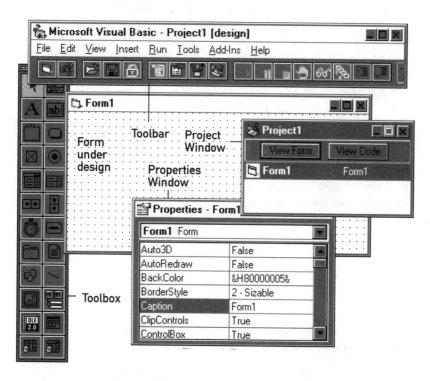

FIGURE 1.5 THE VISUAL BASIC ENVIRONMENT.

We can run this program as it stands by selecting **Start** in the Run menu. If we do so, we'll get the blank window shown in Figure 1.6. Nothing appears in this window, but the maximize and minimize buttons are active, as is the system menu. You can resize this window with the mouse simply by dragging the lower-right corner to the new position you'd like. You can move the window around the screen and use it to cover other windows.

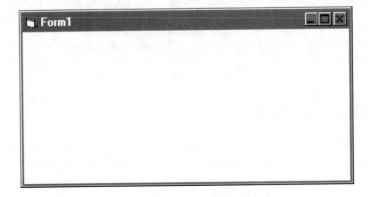

FIGURE 1.6 RUNNING THE DEFAULT VISUAL BASIC FORM.

Our program offers us a lot of support, but there's not much of interest to a user here. Let's start by personalizing our window. End the running program now by selecting **Close** in its System menu.

We might begin our first Visual Basic program by printing out the phrase "No problem." in our window. That's easy enough—simply return to Visual Basic and double-click the main form to open the associated subroutine, Form_Load(), as shown in Figure 1.7. We get at code in Visual Basic by double-clicking the form to open the code window. Form_Load() is an event-handling subroutine. Because this event occurs when the form is first loaded, Form_Load() is called then. Inside Form_Load() is where we will perform the initialization associated with the form. In this case, we simply want to print the words "No problem." so we add that to the Form_Load event by adding this code (as also shown in Figure 1.7):

```
        Private Sub Form_Load()
-->         Print "No problem."
        End Sub
```

In addition, we have to set the form's AutoRedraw property to True in the properties window, as shown in Figure 1.8. Find the line labeled **AutoRedraw** in the properties window, click it, and set it to True using the drop-down list box that appears. This property is important in Visual Basic, and, unless otherwise stated, we'll set it to True in all our programs. AutoRedraw handles the following situation: when you've placed your window on the screen and have filled it with the graphics you want, it becomes vulnerable. The user may place another window on top of yours or may minimize your window. When your window is reopened or uncovered, it must reproduce the graphics that it originally held. This redrawing is quite a bother in C or C++ programs, where you must redraw everything in that window yourself. In Visual Basic, however, the AutoRedraw event handles this chore entirely for us. If we set it to True, our program will automatically redraw (hence AutoRedraw) the window any time such redrawing is required. Our window will not display the initial text we place in it ("No problem.") unless we set the AutoRedraw property to True, so we set it to True as shown in Figure 1.8.

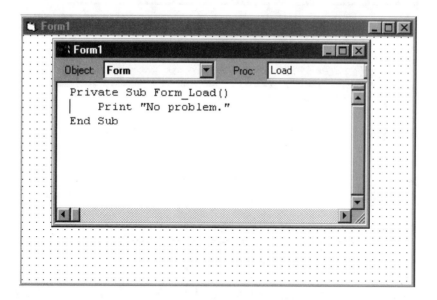

FIGURE 1.7 ADDING CODE TO THE FORM_LOAD() EVENT.

In addition, we can give our program's window the caption "No Problem." simply by setting the form's Caption property to that string in the properties window. Click the line labeled **Caption** and type in the new caption: **No Problem.**. That's all it takes. Now we run our program, as shown in Figure 1.9.

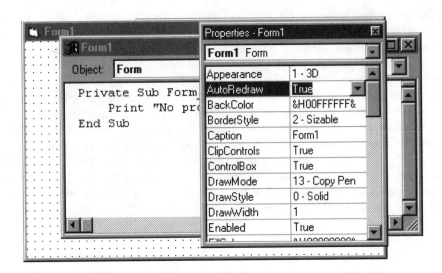

FIGURE 1.8 SETTING A FORM'S AUTOREDRAW PROPERTY TO TRUE.

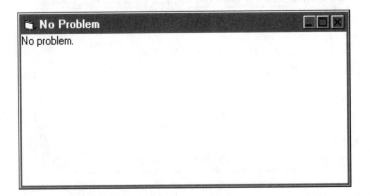

FIGURE 1.9 OUR FIRST PROGRAM AT WORK.

This window can be resized, closed and opened, covered and uncovered, and so on—it's fully functional.

Visual Basic Projects

Now that we've created our first program, let's store it and its code on disk. We will store this program in a directory named NOPROB. Visual Basic programs under development are stored as *projects*. After you create a directory named NOPROB, select the form by clicking it and then select the **Save File As...** menu item in Visual Basic's File menu. This opens the Save File As dialog box; using this box, save the form as **NOPROB\FORM1.FRM**. Next, save the project file itself (the project file keeps track of the files associated with the project) as **NOPROB\NOPROB.VBP** (.VBP = Visual Basic project) using the **Save Project As...** menu item in Visual Basic's File menu. That's it—now we've stored our project on disk. The code for **FORM1.FRM** appears in Listing 1.1, and for **NOPROB.VBP** in Listing 1.2.

LISTING 1.1 (NOPROB) FORM1.FRM

```
VERSION 4.00
Begin VB.Form Form1
    AutoRedraw      =     --1    'True
    Caption         =     "Form1"
    ClientHeight    =     4095
    ClientLeft      =     1095
    ClientTop       =     1515
    ClientWidth     =     6225
    BeginProperty Font
        name            =     "MS Sans Serif"
        charset         =     1
        weight          =     400
        size            =     8.25
        underline       =     0    'False
        italic          =     0    'False
        strikethrough   =     0    'False
    EndProperty
    Height          =     4500
    Left            =     1035
    LinkTopic       =     "Form1"
    ScaleHeight     =     4095
    ScaleWidth      =     6225
    Top             =     1170
    Width           =     6345
End
Attribute VB_Name = "Form1"
Attribute VB_Creatable = False
Attribute VB_Exposed = False
Private Sub Form_Load()
    Print "No problem."
End Sub
```

LISTING 1.2 NOPROB.VBP

```
FORM1.FRM
Object={F9043C88--F6F2--101A--A3C9--08002B2F49FB}#1.0#0; COMDLG16.OCX
Object={FAEEE763--117E--101B--8933--08002B2F4F5A}#1.0#0; DBLIST16.OCX
ProjWinSize=124,339,202,94
ProjWinShow=2
ExeName="Project1.exe"
Path="D:\VB"
```

```
Command=""
Name="Project1"
HelpContextID="0"
StartMode=0
VersionCompatible="0"
MajorVer=1
MinorVer=0
RevisionVer=0
AutoIncrementVer=0
VersionCompanyName=""
Reference=*\G{00025E01--0000--0000--C000--
        000000000046}#0.0#0#DAO2516.DLL#Microsoft DAO 2.5 Object
        Library
```

VISUAL BASIC CONTROLS

This is fine as far as it goes, but what about something interactive, something the user can click or type? Most Windows programs use controls (such as text boxes) of some kind, and we'll look into controls in our next program. In reality, these controls are windows unto themselves. They are typically called *child windows* because they are basically children of the main window. In this case, we might add a text box and a command button (the kind of button you click) to our No Problem program so that it looks like this:

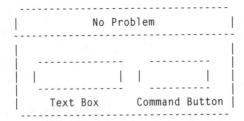

We might give the button the caption **Click Me**:

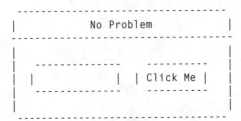

When the user clicks this button, we can place the "No Problem." message into the text box:

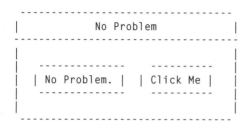

Let's put this to work now as we review how Windows controls work and how to use them in our programs. Return to our NOPROB project in Visual Basic and double-click the text box button in the Visual Basic toolbox (second button down on the right in the toolbox). A new text box, with the text Text1 already in it, appears in the center of the form, surrounded by small black squares called *sizing handles*. Using the mouse, move the text box to the left of the form and stretch it to roughly the size shown in Figure 1.10; to stretch it, press the mouse button when the mouse cursor is over a sizing handle and drag that sizing handle to the desired position.

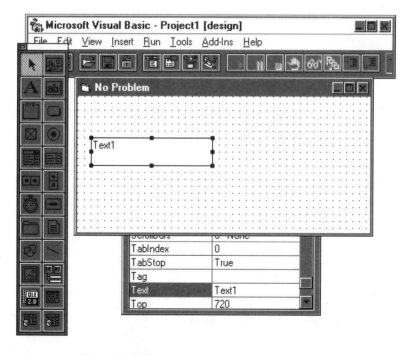

FIGURE 1.10 WE CREATE AND POSITION A NEW TEXT BOX.

Next, erase the text in the text box by selecting the text box with the mouse: click the text box, making sure that the sizing handles appear. Delete the text in its Text property in the properties window: select the line labeled **Text** in the properties window and delete the text there. Now create a new command button by selecting the command button tool in the toolbox (third tool down on the right) and clicking it twice. A new button appears on the form; move it to the right of the form, as shown in Figure 1.11. Set the new button's Caption property to "Click Me" in the properties window, making that string appear in the button, as also shown in Figure 1.11. In addition, set the button's TabIndex property to 0 in the properties window; this makes sure that this button has the input focus (i.e., is surrounded by a black border and responds to keyboard input) when we start our program. (This step is optional, but it gives the program a nicer feel.)

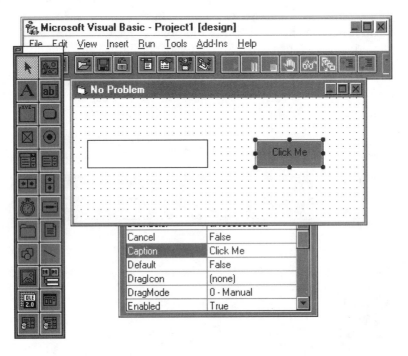

FIGURE 1.11 WE CREATE AND POSITION A NEW COMMAND BUTTON.

When the user clicks this new command button, Command1, we want to display the string "No Problem." in the text box, Text1. Double-click the command button, opening the subroutine Command1_Click() as shown in Figure 1.12. That subroutine looks like this:

```
Private Sub Command1_Click()

End Sub
```

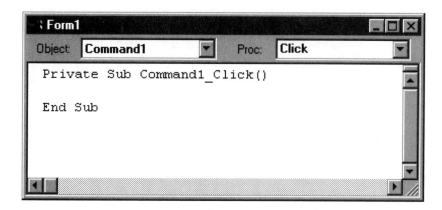

FIGURE 1.12 OPENING THE COMMAND1_CLICK() SUBROUTINE.

Our program will call this subroutine when the user clicks the command button. We want the string "No Problem." to appear in the text box. To do so, we must set the text box's Text property to that string in our code.

Visual Basic Properties in Code

As far as Visual Basic is concerned, our program is made up of a collection of *objects*. The form itself is a program object, the text box is an object, and so is the command button; in fact, there is also an Application object representing the entire program. Each of these objects has associated with it both properties and methods. A *property* holds data (such as the string "No Problem."), and a *method* is either a function or a subroutine built into the object (such as the Move method, which allows you to move windows and controls around when your program runs). You refer to a property like this: object.property; a method looks like this: object.method(). (Note that although the use of the word *object* here does not correspond exactly to the idea of an object in object-oriented programming, it is pretty close.) To set the Text property of the text box to the string "No Problem." we execute this code in Command1_Click():

```
        Private Sub Command1_Click()
-->         Text1.Text = "No Problem."
        End Sub
```

Place this line of code into the subroutine Command1_Click() and run the program. When you do, and when you click the button, our text string is placed into the text box's Text property. That's how we display it, as shown in Figure 1.13.

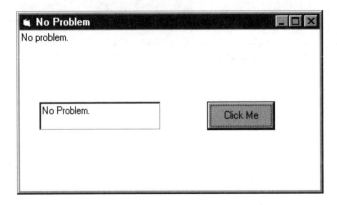

FIGURE 1.13 OUR **NOPROB** PROGRAM WITH WORKING BUTTON AND TEXT BOX.

Note that the text in the text box is now vulnerable—users can change it any way they want it. To avoid this, you should use a label control instead of a text box. Label controls (second tool down on the left in the toolbox) will allow you to display text without letting the user change it.

This is getting better—now the user can interact with our program. The new version of **FORM1.FRM** appears in Listing 1.3. However, that's just the beginning. What if we wanted to display a dialog box when the user clicks the **Click Me** button? It's easy to do that in Visual Basic, and it will be our next review topic.

LISTING 1.3 (NOPROB VERSION 2) FORM1.FRM

```
VERSION 4.00
Begin VB.Form Form1
    AutoRedraw      =   --1   'True
    Caption         =   "No Problem"
    ClientHeight    =   2505
    ClientLeft      =   1095
    ClientTop       =   1515
    ClientWidth     =   5370
    BeginProperty Font
        name        =   "MS Sans Serif"
        charset     =   1
        weight      =   400
        size        =   8.25
        underline   =   0     'False
        italic      =   0     'False
```

```
        strikethrough   =    0      'False
   EndProperty
   Height          =    2910
   Left            =    1035
   LinkTopic       =    "Form1"
   ScaleHeight     =    2505
   ScaleWidth      =    5370
   Top             =    1170
   Width           =    5490
   Begin VB.CommandButton Command1
      Caption       =    "Click Me"
      Height        =    495
      Left          =    3360
      TabIndex      =    0
      Top           =    960
      Width         =    1215
   End
   Begin VB.TextBox Text1
      Height        =    495
      Left          =    360
      TabIndex      =    1
      Top           =    960
      Width         =    2175
   End
End
Attribute VB_Name = "Form1"
Attribute VB_Creatable = False
Attribute VB_Exposed = False
Private Sub Command1_Click()
   Text1.Text = "No Problem."
End Sub

Private Sub Form_Load()
   Print "No problem."
End Sub
```

MULTIFORM VISUAL BASIC PROGRAMS

Let's redesign our program so that when the user clicks the **Click Me** button, a dialog box opens. First, we start with the program as it stands now:

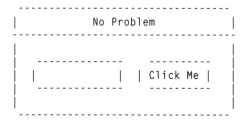

But when the user clicks the **Click Me** button, a dialog box opens that has a button with the caption **Click Me Too**:

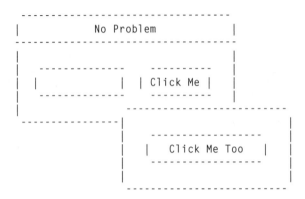

When the user clicks this new button, the program places our text message into the text box in the main window and removes the dialog box from the screen:

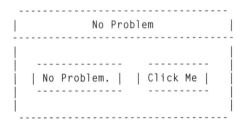

Let's see this in action. Open the NOPROB project. We want to add a new dialog box to our program. Select the Insert menu's **Form** item, creating a new form, as shown in Figure 1.14. This new form has the name Form2 (just as our text box was named Text1, our command button Button1, and so on). Give Form2 a new caption by selecting the **Caption** property in the properties window; set the caption to **Click Me Too**, as also shown in Figure 1.14.

Now return to Form1, the main form. When the user clicks the **Click Me** button, we used to place our message directly into the text box Text1:

```
       Private Sub Command1_Click()
-->        Text1.Text = "No Problem."
       End Sub
```

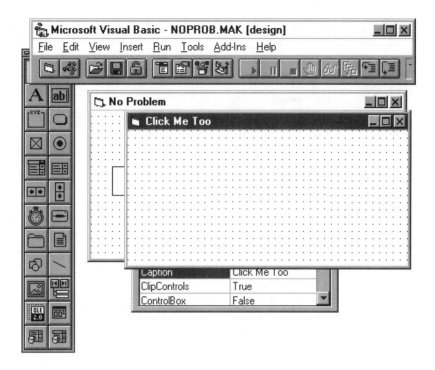

FIGURE 1.14 CREATING A NEW FORM IN VISUAL BASIC.

Now we want to display our new dialog box, Form2, instead. We can display it with the Show method this way: Form2.Show. Place that line into Command1_Click(), replacing the earlier code:

```
        Private Sub Command1_Click()
-->         Form2.Show
        End Sub
```

When the user clicks the **Click Me** button, the dialog box will appear on the screen. Return to the dialog box, Form2, now. Add a new command button to that form, giving it the caption **Click Me Too** by setting its Caption property in the properties window, as shown in Figure 1.15.

Now double-click this new button, opening the associated click event handler, which looks like this:

```
        Private Sub Command1_Click()

        End Sub
```

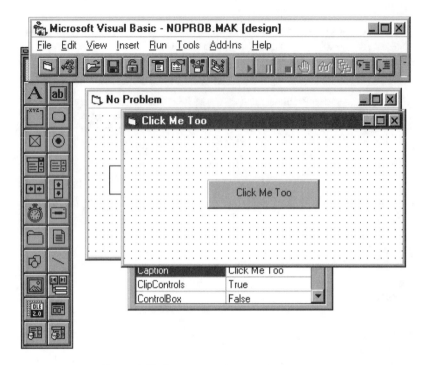

FIGURE 1.15 ADDING A BUTTON TO OUR DIALOG BOX.

When the user clicks the **Click Me Too** button, we want to display our message in the text box Text1 (in Form1) and to hide the dialog box again. We start by placing the string "No Problem." into the Text property of the control Text1 in Form1. We've already seen that properties can be reached using object.property. If the object is a control, like Text1, we can elaborate that into form.object.property. We usually skip the first part, the name of the form, when we refer to a property, because the controls we deal with are usually on the same form that we're working with. Here, however, the property we want to access—Text1.Text—is connected to a form on another form, so we can reach it this way: Form1.Text1.Text. We set that property to our string by adding this code to Command1_Click():

```
        Private Sub Command1_Click()
-->         Form1.Text1.Text = "No Problem."
                .
                .
                .
        End Sub
```

Next, we have to make sure that the dialog box disappears from the screen, and we do that with the Hide method (which applies to forms) by adding this code:

```
      Private Sub Command1_Click()
          Form1.Text1.Text = "No Problem."
  -->       Form2.Hide
      End Sub
```

Now the code for our **Click Me Too** button is complete. To make Form2 into a dialog box, we also remove its maximize button by setting its MaxButton property to False and remove its minimize button by setting its MinButton property to False; we remove its system menu by setting its ControlBox property to False. We also give it a rigid, nonsizable border by setting its BorderStyle to 3, Fixed Double.

Now let's run the program. First, our main window appears by itself:

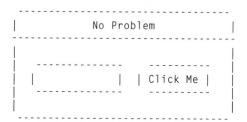

When the user clicks **Click Me**, our dialog box opens and displays the **Click Me Too** button, as also shown in Figure 1.16:

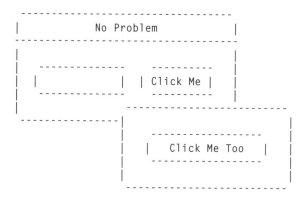

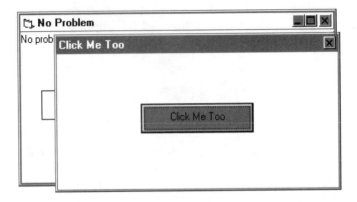

FIGURE 1.16 OUR DIALOG BOX IN OPERATION.

When the user clicks the dialog box's button, we place our text message into the text box in the main window and hide the dialog box:

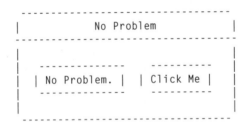

Our dialog box program is now fully functional, and we've seen how to handle multiple forms in our programs. The new version of **FORM1.FRM** appears in Listing 1.4, **FORM2.FRM** appears in Listing 1.5, and the new **NOPROB.VBP** appears in Listing 1.6.

LISTING 1.4 (NOPROB VERSION 3) FORM1.FRM

```
VERSION 4.00
Begin VB.Form Form1
    AutoRedraw      =    --1  'True
    Caption         =    "No Problem"
    ClientHeight    =    2505
    ClientLeft      =    1095
    ClientTop       =    1515
    ClientWidth     =    5370
    BeginProperty Font
        name        =    "MS Sans Serif"
        charset     =    1
        weight      =    400
```

```
            size            =    8.25
            underline       =    0     'False
            italic          =    0     'False
            strikethrough   =    0     'False
        EndProperty
        Height          =    2910
        Left            =    1035
        LinkTopic       =    "Form1"
        ScaleHeight     =    2505
        ScaleWidth      =    5370
        Top             =    1170
        Width           =    5490
        Begin VB.CommandButton Command1
            Caption         =    "Click Me"
            Height          =    495
            Left            =    3360
            TabIndex        =    0
            Top             =    960
            Width           =    1215
        End
        Begin VB.TextBox Text1
            Height          =    495
            Left            =    360
            TabIndex        =    1
            Top             =    960
            Width           =    2175
        End
    End
Attribute VB_Name = "Form1"
Attribute VB_Creatable = False
Attribute VB_Exposed = False
Private Sub Command1_Click()
    Form2.Show
End Sub

Private Sub Form_Load()
    Print "No problem."
End Sub
```

LISTING 1.5 (NOPROB VERSION 3) FORM2.FRM

```
VERSION 4.00
Begin VB.Form Form2
    BorderStyle     =    3   'Fixed Double
    Caption         =    "Click Me Too"
    ClientHeight    =    2265
    ClientLeft      =    2025
    ClientTop       =    2400
    ClientWidth     =    4815
    ControlBox      =    0    'False
```

```
    BeginProperty Font
        name              =    "MS Sans Serif"
        charset           =    1
        weight            =    400
        size              =    8.25
        underline         =    0     'False
        italic            =    0     'False
        strikethrough     =    0     'False
    EndProperty
    Height            =    2670
    Left              =    1965
    LinkTopic         =    "Form2"
    MaxButton         =    0     'False
    MinButton         =    0     'False
    ScaleHeight       =    2265
    ScaleWidth        =    4815
    Top               =    2055
    Width             =    4935
    Begin VB.CommandButton Command1
        Caption           =    "Click Me Too"
        Height            =    495
        Left              =    1440
        TabIndex          =    0
        Top               =    840
        Width             =    1935
    End
End
Attribute VB_Name = "Form2"
Attribute VB_Creatable = False
Attribute VB_Exposed = False
Private Sub Command1_Click()
    Form1.Text1.Text = "No Problem."
    Form2.Hide
End Sub
```

LISTING 1.6 (NOPROB VERSION 3) NOPROB.VBP

```
FORM1.FRM
FORM2.FRM
Object={F9043C88--F6F2--101A--A3C9--08002B2F49FB}#1.0#0; COMDLG16.OCX
Object={FAEEE763--117E--101B--8933--08002B2F4F5A}#1.0#0; DBLIST16.OCX
ProjWinSize=124,339,202,94
ProjWinShow=1
IconForm="Form1"
ExeName="Project1.exe"
Path="D:\VB"
Command=""
Name="Project1"
HelpContextID="0"
```

```
StartMode=0
VersionCompatible="0"
MajorVer=1
MinorVer=0
RevisionVer=0
AutoIncrementVer=0
VersionCompanyName=""
Reference=*\G{00025E01--0000--0000--C000--
000000000046}#0.0#0#DAO2516.DLL#Microsoft DAO 2.5 Object Library
```

We've taken another important step by reviewing dialog boxes. Next, we'll look at the process of adding a new menu system to our program.

MENUS

We can add a menu to our program and let the user display our message by making a selection in that menu. For example, we might add a File menu to our program. (The File menu has become so common that even programs that do not handle files often have one.)

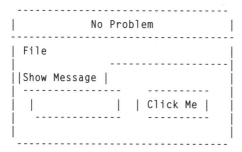

We can give that menu one item—Show Message—so that users see that item when they open the menu:

```
-----------------------------------------
|              No Problem              |
-----------------------------------------
| File                                 |
|         -------------------|
||Show Message |                        |
|  ---------------     ----------       |
|  |             |   | Click Me |      |
|  ---------------     ----------       |
|                                      |
-----------------------------------------
```

After users select the **Show Message** item, we can display our message in the text box:

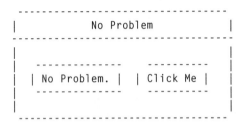

In fact, let's add a second items to the File menu: **Exit**. Users expect **Exit** to be the last item in the File menu, which is why the File menu is so popular even if the program doesn't handle files. We will include **Exit** in our File menu, too:

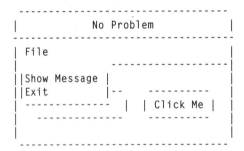

Let's see this in action. Load the NOPROB project into Visual Basic if it's not already there. Next, select **Form1** with the mouse (we will add our menu system to Form1) and start the menu creation process by selecting the **Menu Editor** item in the Visual Basic Tools menu. The Visual Basic Menu Editor opens, as shown in Figure 1.17.

We begin the creation of our new menu simply by typing the name of that menu, **File**, into the box labeled **Caption** at the top of the Menu Editor, as shown in Figure 1.18. That's the name of the menu that will appear in the menu bar. (Although Visual Basic does not limit you to one-word menu names, it's a good convention to follow. Menus with two or more words in the menu bar sometimes look as if they represent two or more separate menus, one belonging to each word.) In addition to the caption, we need a way of referring to our menu in code, and we specify this name by typing it into the **Name** box just below the **Caption** box in the Menu Editor. In this case, we will use the name **File**, as also shown in Figure 1.18.

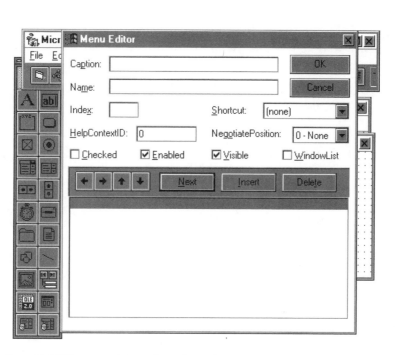

FIGURE 1.17 WE USE THE VISUAL BASIC MENU EDITOR TO CREATE AND MODIFY MENUS.

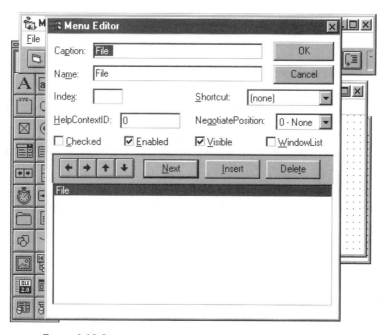

FIGURE 1.18 CREATING A NEW MENU IS AS EASY AS TYPING ITS NAME.

So far, then, we have specified the name of our new menu in the Menu Editor. If we were to quit the Menu Editor now, we'd have that menu in our program:

```
-------------------------------------
|              No Problem           |
-------------------------------------
| File                              |
|-----------------------------------|
|                                   |
|    ---------------   ----------   |
|    |             |   | Click Me |  |
|    ---------------   ----------   |
|                                   |
-------------------------------------
```

However, we also want two menu items in the menu—**Show Message** and **Exit**:

```
-------------------------------------
|              No Problem           |
-------------------------------------
| File                              |
|            -------------------|    |
||Show Message |                |    |
||Exit         |--  ----------  |    |
|  -------------  | | Click Me | |   |
|    -------------   ----------  |   |
|                                |   |
-------------------------------------
```

Now let's add the **Show Message** menu item. First, click the **Next** button in the Menu Editor to indicate that we want to create another entry in the menu system. The highlighted bar in the large box below the **Next** button moves to the next line, indicating that the Menu Editor is ready for the next entry. Type the caption **Show Message** for this new menu item, and give it the name ShowMessage, as shown in Figure 1.19.

We're not finished. If we left our new entry, **Show Message**, as it is, it would be a new menu and not a new menu item. But **Show Message** is supposed to be the first item in the File menu, so we have to indicate that to the Menu Editor by *indenting* **Show Message** underneath the entry for **File**. Click the arrow that points to the right (in the group of four such buttons near the **Next** button). When you click the arrow button, the entry for the menu item **Show Message** appears indented under the entry for the File menu, as shown in Figure 1.19, and four dots appear before this new menu item:

```
File
....Show Message
```

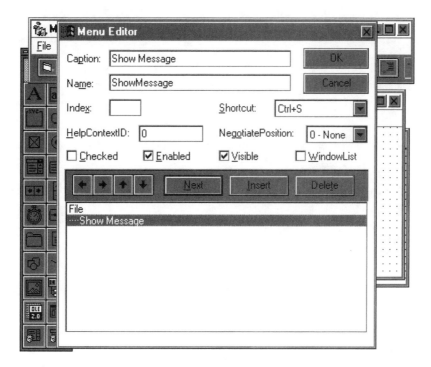

File
Show Message

FIGURE 1.19 CREATING A MENU ITEM IS AS EASY AS TYPING IT IN THE MENU EDITOR.

This is the way you create a menu system in the Menu Editor: place a new entry in it corresponding to a new menu, and follow that by indented entries corresponding to the items in the menu. Now we can add the final item in the File menu: **Exit**. Click **Next** in the Menu Editor again. Move the highlighted bar down one level, indicating that the editor is ready for a new entry. Give this new item the name **Exit** and the caption **Exit**, and indent it under the File menu using the right-pointing arrow button. Our menu system appears like this, as also shown in Figure 1.20:

```
File
....Show Message
....Exit
```

Now our menu system is complete. Click the **OK** button in the Menu Editor to close the Menu Editor and to install the new menu system in our form, as shown in Figure 1.21.

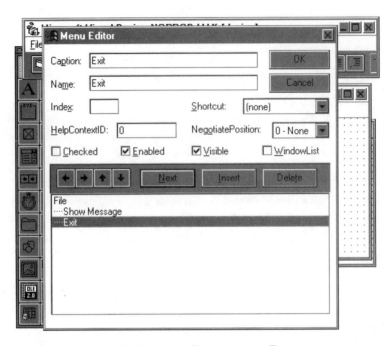

FIGURE 1.20 WE ADD AN EXIT ITEM TO OUR FILE MENU.

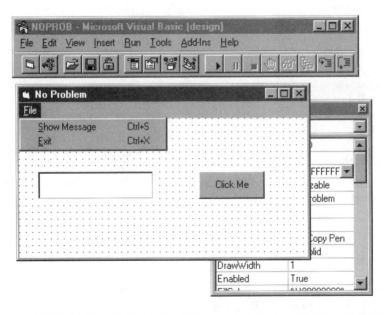

FIGURE 1.21 A FORM CAN DISPLAY ITS ASSOCIATED MENU SYSTEM WHILE UNDER DESIGN.

The next step is to add the code to these menu items that will make them active. Visual Basic treats menu items as controls just as it treats text boxes as controls. Click the **Show Message** item in the File menu, opening the corresponding event handler, ShowMessage_Click(), which our program calls when the user clicks that item:

```
Private Sub ShowMessage_Click()

End Sub
```

When the user clicks this item, we want to display the message "No problem." in the text box Text1. We do that as we've done before, by adding this text:

```
Private Sub ShowMessage_Click()
    Text1.Text = "No problem."          <--
End Sub
```

That's it for ShowMessage_Click(). The next step is to make the **Exit** item active, so click that item now, opening the associated event handler, Exit_Click():

```
Private Sub Exit_Click()

End Sub
```

If the user clicks the **Exit** item, we want to end the program. We do that with the Visual Basic End command:

```
Private Sub Exit_Click()
    End                     <--
End Sub
```

And that's it—our program is ready to run. Select **Start** in the Run menu to execute the program. Our menu appears as in Figure 1.22, with both menu items active.

When you click the **Show Message** menu item, our message is displayed in the text box as before. Our program is a success. The new version of **FORM1.FRM** appears in Listing 1.7, and **NOPROB.VBP** appears in Listing 1.8.

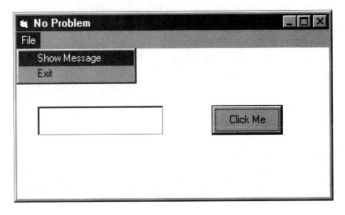

FIGURE 1.22 OUR FIRST WORKING VISUAL BASIC MENU.

LISTING 1.7 (NOPROB VERSION 4) FORM1.FRM

```
VERSION 4.00
Begin VB.Form Form1
   AutoRedraw       =    --1  'True
   Caption          =    "No Problem"
   ClientHeight     =    2505
   ClientLeft       =    1095
   ClientTop        =    1800
   ClientWidth      =    5370
   BeginProperty Font
      name          =    "MS Sans Serif"
      charset       =    1
      weight        =    400
      size          =    8.25
      underline     =    0    'False
      italic        =    0    'False
      strikethrough =    0    'False
   EndProperty
   Height           =    3195
   Left             =    1035
   LinkTopic        =    "Form1"
   ScaleHeight      =    2505
   ScaleWidth       =    5370
   Top              =    1170
   Width            =    5490
   Begin VB.CommandButton Command1
      Caption       =    "Click Me"
      Height        =    495
      Left          =    3360
      TabIndex      =    0
```

```
        Top           =    960
        Width         =    1215
     End
     Begin VB.TextBox Text1
        Height        =    495
        Left          =    360
        TabIndex      =    1
        Top           =    960
        Width         =    2175
     End
     Begin VB.Menu File
        Caption        =    "File"
        Begin VB.Menu ShowMessage
           Caption     =    "Show Message"
        End
        Begin VB.Menu Exit
           Caption     =    "Exit"
        End
     End
  End
End
Attribute VB_Name = "Form1"
Attribute VB_Creatable = False
Attribute VB_Exposed = False
Private Sub Command1_Click()
    Form2.Show
End Sub

Private Sub Exit_Click()
    End
End Sub

Private Sub Form_Load()
    Print "No problem."
End Sub

Private Sub ShowMessage_Click()
    Text1.Text = "No problem."
End Sub
```

LISTING 1.8 (NOPROB VERSION 4) NOPROB.VBP

```
FORM1.FRM
FORM2.FRM
Object={F9043C88--F6F2--101A--A3C9--08002B2F49FB}#1.0#0; COMDLG16.OCX
Object={FAEEE763--117E--101B--8933--08002B2F4F5A}#1.0#0; DBLIST16.OCX
ProjWinSize=431,10,202,94
ProjWinShow=2
IconForm="Form1"
ExeName="Project1.exe"
```

```
Path="D:\VB"
Command=""
Name="Project1"
HelpContextID="0"
StartMode=0
VersionCompatible="0"
MajorVer=1
MinorVer=0
RevisionVer=0
AutoIncrementVer=0
VersionCompanyName=""
Reference=*\G{00025E01--0000--0000--C000--
000000000046}#0.0#0#DAO2516.DLL#Microsoft DAO 2.5 Object Library
```

It is also possible to add shortcuts and accelerator keys to a menu. A *short-cut* is a key or key combination that you can use at any time to select the corresponding menu item even if the menu that holds it is not open. For example, **Exit** is usually given the shortcut **Alt+F4** in a Windows program; if you want to exit a Windows program, you can simply type that combination at any time. An *accelerator* key is a key you can use with the **Alt** key to select a menu or menu item; the menu or menu item must be on the screen (its menu must be open) when you do so. For example, we might give our **Show Message** item the accelerator character *S*, in which case the user can select that item by typing **Alt+S** if the File menu is already open. Let's add a few shortcut and accelerator keys to our program now.

Menu Shortcuts and Accelerator Keys

It's easy to add shortcut keys to a Visual Basic program. Using the Menu Editor, you simply highlight the menu item you want to give a shortcut to, and select the shortcut you want from the **Shortcut** box in the Menu Editor (see Figure 1.20). For example, we select **Show Message** in the Menu Editor and give it the shortcut **Ctrl+S** in this way. Similarly, we can give the short-cut **Ctrl+X** to the **Exit** item. When we run the program, the new shortcut keys appear in the File menu, as shown in Figure 1.23.

Unfortunately, Visual Basic reserves the **Alt+F4** key, which is a standard way of exiting Windows programs, so we cannot give that shortcut to the **Exit** item in our File menu. On the other hand, **Alt+F4** already works in our program, because it is associated with the **Close** item in our system menu. We can also give our menu items accelerator keys. For example, we can make the *F* in File, the *S* in **Show Message**, and the *E* in **Exit** into accelerator keys. To do that, just place an ampersand (&) in front of those characters in the Caption property of each menu item, using the Menu Editor. Our new menu system looks like this:

```
&File
....&Show Message
....&Exit
```

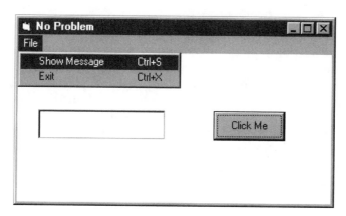

FIGURE 1.23 WE CAN ADD SHORTCUT KEYS TO OUR FILE MENU.

Now run the program. You'll see that each of the accelerator keys is underlined. They can be selected by typing **Alt** together with the key. The result appears in Figure 1.24.

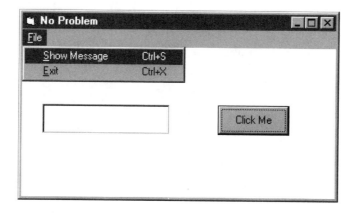

FIGURE 1.24 WE CAN ADD ACCELERATOR KEYS TO OUR FILE MENU.

So far, we've reviewed forms and controls such as text boxes, menu items, and command buttons. However, there is more to Visual Basic than simply forms and controls—we also have to interact with devices such as the mouse and keyboard. We'll take a look at the mouse first, when we develop a drawing program named SCRIBBLE.

THE MOUSE AND SCRIBBLE

Start a new Visual Basic project named **SCRIBBLE.VBP** now, placing it in its own directory, SCRIBBLE. (This is optional but recommended: if you don't rename all your project's files, such as **FORM1.FRM**, before saving them, you might conflict with files from other projects unless you save them in different subdirectories.) The idea of this program is simply to let users draw with the mouse. When they press the mouse button, we will assume that they want to start drawing from that point, which we can store as (xpos, ypos):

Then the user moves the mouse to a new position, whose coordinates, (x, y), will be passed to us in a MouseMove event:

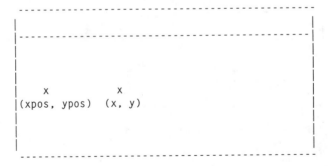

We'll draw a line between our first point (xpos, ypos) and the new location of the mouse, (x, y):

```
 ---------------------------------------------------------
|                                                         |
| ------------------------------------------------------- |
|                                                         |
|                                                         |
|                                                         |
|     x-----------x                                       |
|(xpos, ypos)  (x, y)                                     |
|                                                         |
|                                                         |
|                                                         |
 ---------------------------------------------------------
```

You may wonder why we draw a line between successive mouse locations. Why don't we simply draw dots for each mouse location? The answer is that only a limited number of MouseMove events are generated each second. If we drew only single points each time such an event was generated, we would leave only unconnected dots on the screen. By connecting successive mouse locations with (short) lines, we give the illusion of continuous drawing.

Next, we update our line origin location, (xpos, ypos), in preparation for the next mouse movement. We simply set xpos to our new location x and ypos to the new location y:

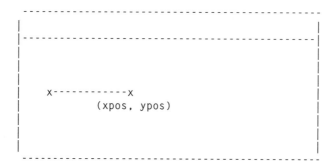

```
 ---------------------------------------------------------
|                                                         |
| ------------------------------------------------------- |
|                                                         |
|                                                         |
|     x------------x                                      |
|            (xpos, ypos)                                 |
|                                                         |
|                                                         |
|                                                         |
 ---------------------------------------------------------
```

Now the process is ready to be repeated as often as required. Let's see this in code. First, give the name **Scribble** to the form (Form1) in our program. Next, double-click that form to open the code window. When you type text in the code window outside any subroutine or function, that text goes into the *general* object of the program, and variables entered here are accessible to subroutines and functions throughout the form. We'll enter variables here in a moment. First, make sure that the **Form** object in the code window's Object box is selected so that we can connect subroutines to our form. Next, select the MouseDown event in the code window's Proc box (at the top right of the code window), creating the function Form_MouseDown():

```
Private Sub Form_MouseDown(Button As Integer, Shift As Integer, x As
Single, y As Single)


End Sub
```

When the program calls this subroutine, the user has pressed the mouse button. We want to do two things here: indicate that the mouse button has gone down (we shouldn't draw before the mouse button has been pressed) and store the location where the button has gone down so that we can start drawing from there. To indicate that the mouse button is down, we can create a new Boolean (i.e., True or False values only) variable named MouseDown. Click the top of the code window (outside the Form_MouseDown() subroutine) and enter this variable in the (general) object simply by typing it:

```
Dim MouseDown As Boolean
```

By adding this code, we can set MouseDown to True in Form_MouseDown(), indicating that the mouse button has been pressed:

```
Private Sub Form_MouseDown(Button As Integer, Shift As Integer, x As
Single, y As Single)

--> MouseDown = True
         .
         .
         .

End Sub
```

Note, however, that we should start the program with MouseDown set to False. To do that, use the Proc box in the code window to create a new subroutine, Form_Load():

```
Private Sub Form_Load()

End Sub
```

By adding this code, we set our variable MouseDown to False when the program first loads the form:

```
Private Sub Form_Load()

--> MouseDown = False

End Sub
```

Next, in Form_MouseDown(), we store the original location of the mouse position so that we can start drawing from there:

Place this code in Form_MouseDown() to store this point in (xpos, ypos):

```
Private Sub Form_MouseDown(Button As Integer, Shift As Integer, x As
Single, y As Single)

    MouseDown = True
--> xpos = x
--> ypos = y

End Sub
```

In addition, we add these two new variables as Singles (i.e., single-precision variables) to the (general) object at the top of the code window. (We place them here so that various subroutines will have access to them. Usually, however, it is good programming practice to keep (general) as unclogged as possible, to avoid confusion.)

```
Dim MouseDown As Boolean
Dim xpos As Single              <--
Dim ypos As Single              <--
```

Now we've processed the Form_MouseDown() event by setting MouseDown correctly and storing the mouse location in (xpos, ypos). The next step happens when the user moves the mouse. When that happens, we want to connect the new location of the mouse with the one we've already stored with a line. To do so, add a new function, Form_MouseMove(), to our program using the Proc box:

```
Private Sub Form_MouseMove(Button As Integer, Shift As Integer, x As
Single, y As Single)


End Sub
```

We'll draw in this subroutine. We start by making sure that the mouse button is actually down. We check our Boolean variable MouseDown using this new code:

```
Private Sub Form_MouseMove(Button As Integer, Shift As Integer, x As
Single, y As Single)

--> If (MouseDown) Then


--> End If

End Sub
```

If the mouse button has been pressed, we want to draw, because now the mouse has been moved. In particular, we have the new location of the mouse, because that point's coordinates are passed to us as (x, y) in Form_MouseMove(). Our job here is to connect our original point, (xpos, ypos), and the current location, (x, y):

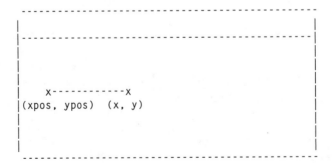

Drawing the line is simple:

```
Private Sub Form_MouseMove(Button As Integer, Shift As Integer, x As
Single, y As Single)

    If (MouseDown) Then
-->     Line (x, y)--(xpos, ypos)
            .
            .
            .
    End If

End Sub
```

Now we need to update xpos and ypos so that they'll be ready for next time. We move the beginning of the next line—stored in (xpos, ypos)—to the end of the current line (now stored in (x, y)):

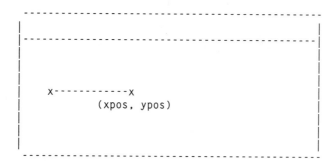

In code, that looks like this:

```
Private Sub Form_MouseMove(Button As Integer, Shift As Integer, x As
Single, y As Single)

    If (MouseDown) Then
        Line (x, y)--(xpos, ypos)
-->     xpos = x
-->     ypos = y
    End If

End Sub
```

Finally, we need to set MouseDown to False if the user releases the mouse button. We add a new subroutine, Form_MouseUp(), to our program using the Proc box:

```
Private Sub Form_MouseUp(Button As Integer, Shift As Integer, x As
Single, y As Single)
```

```
End Sub
```

And we set MouseDown to False in that subroutine:

```
Private Sub Form_MouseUp(Button As Integer, Shift As Integer, x As
Single, y As Single)

--> MouseDown = False

End Sub
```

That's all there is to SCRIBBLE. Run the program at this point. As you can see in Figure 1.25, SCRIBBLE allows you to draw using the mouse. The program is a success—now we're handling the mouse.

FIGURE 1.25 SCRIBBLE LETS THE USER DRAW WITH THE MOUSE.

The form's code for this program, **FORM1.FRM**, is in Listing 1.9, and the project file, **SCRIBBLE.VBP**, is in Listing 1.10.

LISTING 1.9 (SCRIBBLE) FORM1.FRM

```
VERSION 4.00
Begin VB.Form Form1
   AutoRedraw    =    --1   'True
   Caption       =    "Scribble"
```

```
    ClientHeight    =    4230
    ClientLeft      =    1095
    ClientTop       =    1515
    ClientWidth     =    6720
    BeginProperty Font
        name            =    "MS Sans Serif"
        charset         =    1
        weight          =    400
        size            =    8.25
        underline       =    0    'False
        italic          =    0    'False
        strikethrough   =    0    'False
    EndProperty
    Height          =    4635
    Left            =    1035
    LinkTopic       =    "Form1"
    ScaleHeight     =    4230
    ScaleWidth      =    6720
    Top             =    1170
    Width           =    6840
End
Attribute VB_Name = "Form1"
Attribute VB_Creatable = False
Attribute VB_Exposed = False
Dim MouseDown As Boolean
Dim xpos As Single
Dim ypos As Single

Private Sub Form_Load()

    MouseDown = False

End Sub

Private Sub Form_MouseDown(Button As Integer, Shift As Integer, x As
Single, y As Single)

    MouseDown = True
    xpos = x
    ypos = y

End Sub

Private Sub Form_MouseMove(Button As Integer, Shift As Integer, x As
Single, y As Single)

    If (MouseDown) Then
        Line (x, y)--(xpos, ypos)
        xpos = x
        ypos = y
    End If

End Sub
```

```
Private Sub Form_MouseUp(Button As Integer, Shift As Integer, x As
Single, y As Single)

    MouseDown = False

End Sub
```

LISTING 1.10 SCRIBBLE.VBP

```
FORM1.FRM
Object={F9043C88--F6F2--101A--A3C9--08002B2F49FB}#1.0#0; COMDLG16.OCX
Object={FAEEE763--117E--101B--8933--08002B2F4F5A}#1.0#0; DBLIST16.OCX
ProjWinSize=386,373,202,94
ProjWinShow=2
IconForm="Form1"
ExeName="Project1.exe"
Path="D:\VB"
Command=""
Name="Project1"
HelpContextID="0"
StartMode=0
VersionCompatible="0"
MajorVer=1
MinorVer=0
RevisionVer=0
AutoIncrementVer=0
VersionCompanyName=""
Reference=*\G{00025E01--0000--0000--C000--
000000000046}#0.0#0#DAO2516.DLL#Microsoft DAO 2.5 Object Library
```

Now we've reviewed the use of the mouse as an I/O device. Another significant I/O device that we deal with often in our programs is the keyboard. We'll take a look at keyboard handling next.

THE READER KEYBOARD PROGRAM

Usually, we let text boxes or other controls handle keys typed at the keyboard. But sometimes, it's more useful to handle keys from the keyboard yourself, especially in longer applications where you do significant text handling (e.g., one special key might format your text, another might spellcheck it). There are three main keyboard events: KeyDown, KeyPress, and KeyUp. Here are the arguments passed to their event handlers:

```
Sub KeyDown(KeyCode As Integer, Shift As Integer)

Sub KeyPress(KeyAscii As Integer)

Sub KeyUp(KeyCode As Integer, Shift As Integer)
```

The KeyCode parameter passed to KeyDown() and KeyUp() does not hold the standard character constants that we normally use when we read keys; instead, it holds key codes, such as this one for **F1**: vbKeyF1. To read the state of the **Shift**, **Ctrl**, and **Alt** keys, you have to examine the Shift parameter. For these reasons, we usually use the KeyPress() subroutine. This subroutine is passed the KeyAscii parameter, which holds a character we can use directly. To see how, create a new Visual Basic project named READER, and store it in its own directory. In this program, we'll read typed keys and display them.

Double-click Form1 in READER, opening the code window. Next, select **KeyPress** in the Proc box, and the subroutine Form_KeyPress() appears:

```
Private Sub Form_KeyPress(KeyAscii As Integer)

End Sub
```

When the user types a key, the program will place the the matching character into the argument KeyAscii and pass it to us. Let's create a new string named datastring to hold the typed keys. Add datastring to the program's (general) object; click outside Form_KeyPress() at the top of the code window and add the following code:

```
Dim datastring As String
```

We can clear datastring (set it to an empty string, "") when the form loads. Add a FormLoad event and initialize datastring this way:

```
Private Sub Form_Load()
--> datastring = ""
End Sub
```

Our goal is to store the typed characters in our string datastring. In Form_KeyPress(), we concatenate (i.e., add) the just-typed character to datastring:

```
Private Sub Form_KeyPress(KeyAscii As Integer)
--> datastring = datastring + Chr$(KeyAscii)
        .
        .
        .
End Sub
```

To view datastring as characters are added to it, we print it:

```
Private Sub Form_KeyPress(KeyAscii As Integer)
    datastring = datastring + Chr$(KeyAscii)
```

```
--> Print datastring
End Sub
```

That's all there is to it. Now run the program and type a few keys. You'll be able to watch our datastring growing larger and larger, as in Figure 1.26. READER is a success.

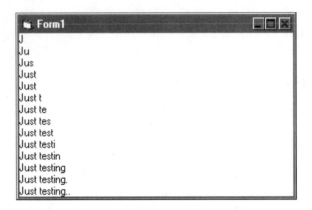

FIGURE 1.26 THE READER PROGRAM READS KEYS FROM THE KEYBOARD.

The listing for READER's **FORM1.FRM** is in Listing 1.11, and **READER.VBP** is in Listing 1.12.

LISTING 1.11 (READER) FORM1.FRM

```
VERSION 4.00
Begin VB.Form Form1
    Caption         =   "Form1"
    ClientHeight    =   4230
    ClientLeft      =   1095
    ClientTop       =   1515
    ClientWidth     =   6720
    BeginProperty Font
        name            =   "MS Sans Serif"
        charset         =   1
        weight          =   400
        size            =   8.25
        underline       =   0   'False
        italic          =   0   'False
        strikethrough   =   0   'False
    EndProperty
    Height          =   4635
    Left            =   1035
```

```
    LinkTopic        =     "Form1"
    ScaleHeight      =     4230
    ScaleWidth       =     6720
    Top              =     1170
    Width            =     6840
End
Attribute VB_Name = "Form1"
Attribute VB_Creatable = False
Attribute VB_Exposed = False
Dim datastring As String

Private Sub Form_KeyPress(KeyAscii As Integer)
    datastring = datastring + Chr$(KeyAscii)
    Print datastring
End Sub

Private Sub Form_Load()
    datastring = ""
End Sub
```

LISTING 1.12 READER.VBP

```
FORM1.FRM
Object={F9043C88--F6F2--101A--A3C9--08002B2F49FB}#1.0#0; COMDLG16.OCX
Object={FAEEE763--117E--101B--8933--08002B2F4F5A}#1.0#0; DBLIST16.OCX
ProjWinSize=386,373,202,94
ProjWinShow=2
IconForm="Form1"
ExeName="Project1.exe"
Path="D:\VB"
Command=""
Name="Project1"
HelpContextID="0"
StartMode=0
VersionCompatible="0"
MajorVer=1
MinorVer=0
RevisionVer=0
AutoIncrementVer=0
VersionCompanyName=""
Reference=*\G{00025E01--0000--0000--C000--
000000000046}#0.0#0#DAO2516.DLL#Microsoft DAO 2.5 Object Library
```

That's it for keyboard handling—and that's it for our review of Visual Basic. If you had trouble with unfamiliar ideas and concepts here, it is a good idea to work through an introductory Visual Basic book before continuing. Otherwise, let's move on to Chapter 2 and start working with multiple document interface (MDI) programs.

ADVANCED MDI PROGRAMMING

In this chapter, we'll examine the ins and outs of the multiple document interface (MDI) in Visual Basic, including MDI itself, multiple views, tooltips, status bars, and more. Let's take a moment to understand these concepts before digging into the programming.

So far, our programs have contained only one window:

```
-------------------------------------------
|File    Edit    Help                      |
|------------------------------------------|
|Here's the text...                        |
|                                          |
|                                          |
|                                          |
|                                          |
|                                          |
|                                          |
-------------------------------------------
```

However, MDI programs are multiple-window programs; not multiple windows in the sense that there might be five windows of equal size in different parts of the screen, but rather multiple windows enclosed by a single, larger-frame window. Such a program might start by displaying the enclosing (MDI) window first:

```
-------------------------------------------
|File    Edit    Window    Help            |
|------------------------------------------|
|                                          |
|                                          |
|                                          |
|                                          |
|                                          |
|                                          |
|                                          |
|                                          |
-------------------------------------------
```

To create or open a new document—and therefore to create a new window inside the MDI frame window—in our program, the user could select **New** in the File menu (to create a new document) or **Open** (to open an existing one):

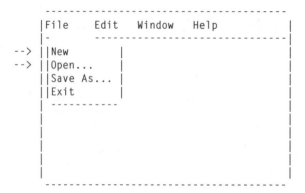

This opens a new window inside the main MDI window, and this new window corresponds to its own document. If this were a word-processing program, the user could place his or her own text into the new document:

Using the **New** and/or **Open** menu item, the user could also open another document in the main window:

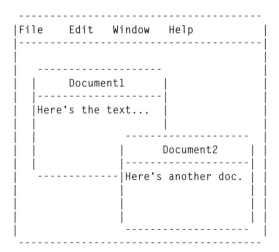

These windows are called *MDI children*. The documents can then be edited independently in their own windows, but both of them are still "corralled" in the larger MDI window, making the entire application one neat package. If required, the user can maximize (usually temporarily) one of the documents so that its window takes over the entire main window's client area. In addition, MDI programs can provide multiple views of documents.

A *view* works like this: suppose we opened a document named Document1 in our MDI program, and suppose it's a very long document—too long to fit into one window. In that case, the user will be able to see only a part of the document in an MDI child window. To alleviate that problem, MDI programs often allow the user to open another view into the document, that is, another window that can show another part of the same document.

This is what Document1 might look like, and these are the sections our two views, View 1 and View 2, might show:

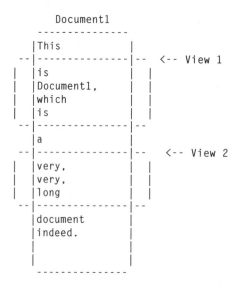

```
        Document1
        - - - - - - - - - - - - - - -
        |This           |
    - - |- - - - - - - - - - - - - - -|- -   <-- View 1
       |  |is          |  |
       |  |Document1,   |  |
       |  |which        |  |
       |  |is           |  |
    - - |- - - - - - - - - - - - - - -|- -
       |  |a           |
    - - |- - - - - - - - - - - - - - -|- -   <-- View 2
       |  |very,        |  |
       |  |very,        |  |
       |  |long         |  |
    - - |- - - - - - - - - - - - - - -|- -
       |document        |
       |indeed.         |
       |                |
       |                |
        - - - - - - - - - - - - - - -
```

Those views would appear this way in the MDI program; although there are two windows open, they correspond to the same document and display different parts of that document. (Note the nomenclature for the captions of these windows: Document1:1, indicating view 1, and Document1:2, indicating 2.)

```
    - - - - - - - - - - - - - - - - - - - - - - - - - - - - - - - - -
    |File     Edit    Window     Help                    |
    |- - - - - - - - - - - - - - - - - - - - - - - - - - - - - - - - -|
    |                                                    |
    |                                                    |
    |     - - - - - - - - - - - - - - - - - -            |
    |    |      Document1:1        |                     |
    |    |- - - - - - - - - - - - - - - - - -|            |
    |    |is                       |                     |
    |    |Document1,                |                     |
    |    |which           - - - - - - - - - - - - - - - - - -  |
    |    |is             |        Document1:2     |  |  |
    |     - - - - - - - - - - - - -|- - - - - - - - - - - - - - -|  |
    |                   |very,                    |  |
    |                   |very                     |  |
    |                   |long                     |  |
    |                    - - - - - - - - - - - - - - - - - -   |
    - - - - - - - - - - - - - - - - - - - - - - - - - - - - - - - - -
```

Each of these views provides just that—a view into the document. Each view is independently scrollable and editable. However, there is a problem: Visual

Basic supports MDI windows and not MDI views, although many users have come to expect them. We'll solve that problem in this chapter. From a Visual Basic point of view, the problem we have to solve is this: if a user has two views open in the same document and edits in one of the views, the other view must be updated as well, but that doesn't happen in Visual Basic! The user may enter some text in one view, and it won't appear in the other:

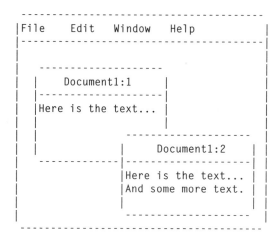

Obviously, this is a problem, and one we'll solve here. When we're finished, the user will be able to enter text in one view and see it updated automatically in the other views as well:

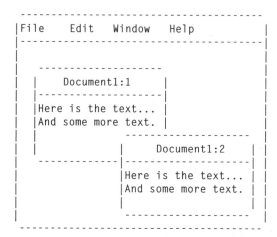

In addition, many MDI programs use toolbars at the top of their client areas and status bars at the bottom; the toolbar, like the one in Visual Basic itself, gives the user quick access to menu items with a simple mouse click, and the status bar at the bottom indicates program status, such as the "Ready" message here:

```
-------------------------------------------
|File    Edit    Window    Help           |
|-----------------------------------------|
|  Tool1 |  Tool2 |  Tool 3  |            |   <-- Toolbar
|-----------------------------------------|
|                                         |
|     --------------------                |
|    |    Document1:1     |               |
|    |--------------------|               |
|    |Here is the text... |               |
|    |And some more text. |               |
|    |                --------------------|
|    |               |    Document1:2     | |
|     ---------------|--------------------| |
|                   |Here is the text... | |
|                   |And some more text. | |
|                   |                    | |
|                    --------------------  |
|-----------------------------------------|
|Ready                                    |   <-- Status bar
-------------------------------------------
```

We'll see how to create and use toolbars and status bars in this chapter with the standard Visual Basic method of using picture boxes. If you are using Windows 95, you can also use the special Toolbar and StatusBar 32-bit controls for this purpose, as we'll see in Chapter 5. In addition, Windows now uses *tooltips*, small pop-up boxes that appear when the mouse cursor is on a tool in the toolbar and indicate what the tool does (e.g., draw or paste). This is to prompt the user, because the hieroglyphics that appear in a toolbar's buttons may be confusing. Visual Basic supports tooltips for the Windows 95 Toolbar and StatusBar controls (as we'll see in Chapter 5), but not otherwise. However, here, we'll add them to our programs ourselves, regardless of Visual Basic or Windows version. Let's get started now with MDI basics.

OUR FIRST MDI PROGRAM

Start Visual Basic now. We'll create our first MDI program rather easily. Open the Visual Basic Insert menu and select **MDI Form**. A new MDI form appears, named MDIForm1, as shown in Figure 2.1; this will be our main MDI window. This form acts much like a normal form in our program, except that we can have only one MDI form per program. Using the properties window, give the MDI form the caption MDI (i.e., set its Caption property to **MDI**), as also shown in Figure 2.1.

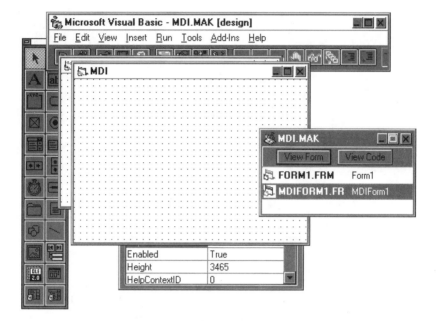

FIGURE 2.1 WE USE VISUAL BASIC TO CREATE A NEW MDI MAIN WINDOW.

Now move back to Form1, the original startup form that normally appears in a Visual Basic program. Because this is an MDI program, Form1 must become a child window of the main MDI window. To make Form1 into an MDI child window, just set its MDIChild property to True in the properties window: click the line labeled **MDIChild** in the properties window and set this property to True. Also, give Form1 the caption **MDI Child** by setting its Caption property to **MDI Child**. To make this new window more interesting, we might add some appealing graphics, so add this code to Form1's Form_Load() event. To bring up the Form_Load() event, just double-click the form.

```
Private Sub Form_Load()
--> For loop_index% = 1 To 10
-->      DrawWidth = loop_index%
```

```
-->     Line (0, loop_index% * ScaleHeight / 11)-(ScaleWidth,
-->       loop_index% * ScaleHeight / 11)
--> Next loop_index%
--> DrawMode = 6
--> DrawWidth = 10
--> Line (0, ScaleHeight)-(ScaleWidth, 0)
--> Line (0, 0)-(ScaleWidth, ScaleHeight)
End Sub
```

This code displays some graphics for us. Now run the program, as shown in
Figure 2.2. Our first MDI program is a success, but a limited one. We can see
that the MDI child window appears inside the main window, and we can
even move the child window around, maximize it (so that it takes up the
whole client area), and minimize it (so that it appears as an icon in the
lower-left area of the main MDI window)—but there's only one child window. How do we add others? We'll look into that in our first major MDI program, coming next.

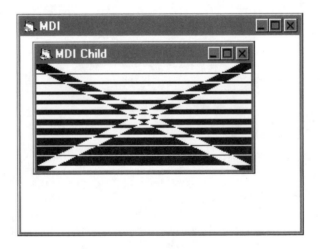

FIGURE 2.2 WE RUN OUR FIRST MDI PROGRAM SUCCESSFULLY.

The code for Form1 appears in **FORM1.FRM** (Listing 2.1), **MDIFORM1.FRM**
appears in Listing 2.2, and **MDI.VBP** appears in Listing 2.3.

LISTING 2.1 (MDI) FORM1.FRM

```
VERSION 4.00
Begin VB.Form Form1
    AutoRedraw      =     -1   'True
    Caption         =     "MDI Child"
```

```
    ClientHeight    =    3720
    ClientLeft      =    1095
    ClientTop       =    1515
    ClientWidth     =    6090
    BeginProperty Font
        name            =    "MS Sans Serif"
        charset         =    1
        weight          =    400
        size            =    8.25
        underline       =    0    'False
        italic          =    0    'False
        strikethrough   =    0    'False
    EndProperty
    Height          =    4125
    Left            =    1035
    LinkTopic       =    "Form1"
    MDIChild        =    -1    'True
    ScaleHeight     =    3720
    ScaleWidth      =    6090
    Top             =    1170
    Width           =    6210
End
Attribute VB_Name = "Form1"
Attribute VB_Creatable = False
Attribute VB_Exposed = False
Private Sub Form_Load()
    For loop_index% = 1 To 10
        DrawWidth = loop_index%
        Line (0, loop_index% * ScaleHeight / 11)-(ScaleWidth,
        loop_index% * ScaleHeight / 11)
    Next loop_index%
    DrawMode = 6
    DrawWidth = 10
    Line (0, ScaleHeight)-(ScaleWidth, 0)
    Line (0, 0)-(ScaleWidth, ScaleHeight)
End Sub
```

LISTING 2.2 (MDI) MDIFORM1.FRM

```
VERSION 4.00
Begin VB.MDIForm MDIForm1
    BackColor       =    &H8000000C&
    Caption         =    "MDI"
    ClientHeight    =    4230
    ClientLeft      =    1095
    ClientTop       =    1515
    ClientWidth     =    6720
    Height          =    4635
    Left            =    1035
```

```
    LinkTopic      =    "MDIForm1"
    Top            =    1170
    Width          =    6840
End
Attribute VB_Name = "MDIForm1"
Attribute VB_Creatable = False
Attribute VB_Exposed = False
```

LISTING 2.3 MDI.VBP

```
FORM1.FRM
MDIFORM1.FRM
Object={F9043C88-F6F2-101A-A3C9-08002B2F49FB}#1.0#0; COMDLG16.OCX
Object={FAEEE763-117E-101B-8933-08002B2F4F5A}#1.0#0; DBLIST16.OCX
ProjWinSize=345,402,202,111
ProjWinShow=2
ExeName="Project1.exe"
Path="D:\VB"
Command=""
Name="Project1"
HelpContextID="0"
StartMode=0
VersionCompatible="0"
MajorVer=1
MinorVer=0
RevisionVer=0
AutoIncrementVer=0
VersionCompanyName=""
Reference=*\G{00025E01-0000-0000-C000-
000000000046}#0.0#0#DAO2516.DLL#Microsoft DAO 2.5 Object Library
VERSION 4.00
```

THE WRITER PROGRAM

At the beginning of this chapter, we discussed an MDI program that allows the user to edit multiple documents. Thanks to Visual Basic text box controls, such a program is not hard to write. We'll work on creating our text-editing program, called WRITER, now. When we're finished, we'll have a toolbar and a status bar, and we'll be able to edit multiple documents (but not yet multiple views into those documents). We'll base our MDI child windows on the Visual Basic text box control for easy text handling. Functions such as word wrap, text entry, and selecting text are already built into text boxes, so they'll be built into our MDI child windows, too.

```
----------------------------------------
|                  Writer                |
|----------------------------------------|
|File    Edit    Window    Help          |
|----------------------------------------|
|  Tool1 |  Tool2  |  Tool 3 |           |     <-- Toolbar
|----------------------------------------|
|     --------------------                |
|     | Write Document 1 |                |
|     |------------------|                |
|     |Here is the text...|               |
|     |And some more text. |              |
|     |                                   |
|     |          --------------------     |
|     |          | Writer Document 2 |  | |
|     -----------|------------------ |  | |
|                |Here is the text... |  | |
|                |And some more text. |  | |
|                |                    |  | |
|                 --------------------     |
|----------------------------------------|
|Ready                                   |     <-- Status bar
----------------------------------------
```

Start a new project in Visual Basic and name it **WRITER.VBP**. We'll start with Form1, which will become our MDI child form. Add a text box to Form1 (the size of the text box doesn't matter, because we will set that in code). Using the properties window, remove the default text in the text box: edit the Text property and set it to an empty string, "". Set the text box's MultiLine property to True (so that we can handle multiple lines of text), and set the ScrollBars property to 2 (giving the text box a vertical scrollbar). Next, give Form1 the caption **Writer Document** using the Caption property in the properties window, and set Form1's MDIChild property to True. This sets up Form1 the way we want it. The next-to-last step is to resize the text box, Text1, so that it covers the form's client area, and we do that in Form_Load() in **WRITER.FRM** by adding the following code. (Double-click Form1 to bring up Form_Load() in the code window.)

```
Private Sub Form_Load()
--> Text1.Height = Form1.ScaleHeight
--> Text1.Width = Form1.ScaleWidth
End Sub
```

The last step is to add the same code to the Form_Resize event; in case our form is resized at any time (i.e., in case our MDI child window is resized), we still want the text box to cover the window's client area. We do that by selecting Form_Resize in the code window's Proc box to open that subroutine and place this code in it (from **WRITER.FRM**):

```
Private Sub Form_Resize()
--> Text1.Height = Form1.ScaleHeight
--> Text1.Width = Form1.ScaleWidth
End Sub
```

Now insert a new MDI form into the program as before, using the **Insert | MDIForm** menu item to create MDIForm1. Give this new form the caption **Writer** (by setting its Caption property in the properties window), and add a File menu to MDIForm1. (Select **Menu Editor...** in the Tools menu and add the menu as we reviewed in the last chapter.) Give this menu just two menu items: **New Document** (set this item's Name property to **New** in the Menu Editor) and **Exit** (set this item's Name property to **Exit** in the Menu Editor).

We can add the code for the **Exit** item easily enough. Close the Menu Editor by clicking **OK** and click that menu item to open Exit_Click() this way (from **MDIFORM1.FRM**):

```
Private Sub Exit_Click()

End Sub
```

We need an End statement here to terminate the program, so add that now:

```
Private Sub Exit_Click()
--> End
End Sub
```

Next, click the **New Document** menu item, opening the subroutine New_Click() (from **MDIFORM1.FRM**):

```
Private Sub New_Click()

End Sub
```

When this menu item is clicked, we want to add a new document to our program. However, this takes a little thought. We will also add a menu system to Form1, the MDI child. And here's the interesting part: when an MDI child is present, its menu system will take over the main MDI window's menu system. If there are no child windows, we'll see the menu system we just designed, with only one menu, File:

```
----------------------------------------
|                 Writer                 |
|----------------------------------------|
|File                                    |
|----------------------------------------|
|                                        |
|                                        |
|                                        |
|                                        |
|                                        |
|                                        |
|                                        |
|                                        |
|                                        |
|                                        |
----------------------------------------
```

Yet if the program is displaying child windows inside the main MDI window, the child windows' menus will take over the main menu bar; in our case, the child windows will have three menus: File, Window, and Edit:

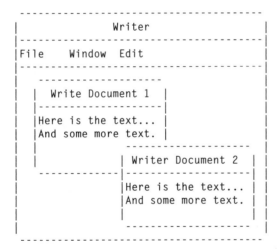

What we must realize here is that the user can create a new document by clicking **New Document** in either the main MDI window's File menu or in the MDI children's File menu. For that reason, we won't place the code that creates and displays a new document window in the main MDI window's New_Click() subroutine. Instead, we'll just call a subroutine that we can also call from the MDI children's menu. Let's name that subroutine AddADocument() and add the call to it in New_Click():

```
Private Sub New_Click()
--> AddADocument
End Sub
```

We'll call this subroutine, AddADocument(), from our MDI form and from our MDI children forms, so it has to be accessible to both forms. Sharing code and data is a recurring problem in multiwindow Visual Basic programs, because each window usually holds its own self-sufficient code. To support this subroutine and make it accessible to all forms, we will place it into a new *module*. Select Visual Basic's **Insert | Module** menu item to create a new module, which Visual Basic names **MODULE1.BAS**. Open that module from the project window (double-click it) and create the skeleton of our subroutine AddADocument() by adding this code by hand to **MODULE1.BAS**:

```
Public Sub AddADocument()        <--

End Sub                          <--
```

Note that we declare AddADocument() Public so that procedures in all forms and modules may call it.

The program calls this subroutine when the user wants to create and display a new document window. We can keep track of our windows by setting up a new variable—an integer named NumberDocuments—to hold the number of documents we have displayed. Add NumberDocuments to **MODULE1.BAS**:

```
Public NumberDocuments As Integer       <--

Public Sub AddADocument()

End Sub
```

Note that we have declared NumberDocuments as Public, which means that all forms and procedures throughout the program will have access to this universal number, the number of documents in the MDI window. When our program loads, it will immediately open a default MDI child window inside the main MDI window, so the number of documents starts at 1. We can initialize NumberDocuments to 1 when the MDI form loads in the MDIForm_Load() event (in **MDIFORM1.FRM**) by adding the following code. (Double-click the MDI form MDIForm1 to bring up MDIForm_Load().)

```
Private Sub MDIForm_Load()
--> NumberDocuments = 1
End Sub
```

It is not necessary to start with an open MDI child window. At least one Form1 window is displayed in the main MDI window, because we have left Form1 as the startup form in the Project Options box. (You reach this box with the **Tools | Project Options** menu item.) If we had instead set the startup form to MDIForm1, the program would start without an open MDI child window.

At this point, then, the variable NumberDocuments is set up and initialized. Now let's write the subroutine AddADocument(). In this subroutine, we want to create a new MDI child and add it to our MDI main window. In AddADocument(), we want to add a new document, so we increment NumberDocuments first, letting us keep track of the number of open MDI child windows (from **MODULE1.BAS**):

```
Public NumberDocuments As Integer

Public Sub AddADocument()
--> NumberDocuments = NumberDocuments + 1
        .
        .
        .
End Sub
```

Now we want to create and display a new MDI child. Note that we might add a number of new MDI child windows; how do we keep track of them? Instead of giving them names such as Form1, Form2, Form3, and so on, one good solution is to store these windows in a *form array*. We can set aside an array of, say, 10 such windows and fill it with new document windows (restricting us in this example program to 10 document windows). Each time a new MDI child is created, we can add it to the form array, allowing us to reference each window easily with an array index instead of giving a separate name to each window.

We declare our form array by adding this code to **MODULE1.BAS**:

```
Public NumberDocuments As Integer
Dim Documents(10) As Form                    <--

Public Sub AddADocument()
    NumberDocuments = NumberDocuments + 1
        .
        .
        .
End Sub
```

Note that we did not declare Documents, the array of forms, as Public for two reasons: there is no need to do so, because this array will be handled by the code internal to Module1, and you can't declare arrays Public in Visual Basic anyway. (If you want to give code in other parts of the program access to an array like this, you must do it through Public subroutines or functions you place in the module.)

Now we can add a new form of type Form1—our MDI child window—to the Documents array using the Set and New keywords (if there is space in the form array). We need to use the Set and New keywords because forms are Visual Basic objects and not simply variables; New creates a new Visual Basic object, and Set places it in the Documents array. The code looks like this (from **MODULE1.BAS**):

```
Public NumberDocuments As Integer
Dim Documents(10) As Form

Public Sub AddADocument()
    NumberDocuments = NumberDocuments + 1
--> If NumberDocuments <= 10 Then
-->     Set Documents(NumberDocuments) = New Form1
          .
          .
          .

End Sub
```

This code creates a new window of class Form1 and installs it into our array of forms after checking to make sure that we haven't exceeded the maximum number of windows we have storage for (10). All that's left is to show this new form on the screen, and we do that with the Show method (as we've seen for dialog boxes in the last chapter):

```
Public NumberDocuments As Integer
Dim Documents(10) As Form

Public Sub AddADocument()
    NumberDocuments = NumberDocuments + 1
    If NumberDocuments <= 10 Then
        Set Documents(NumberDocuments) = New Form1
-->     Documents(NumberDocuments).Show
--> End If
End Sub
```

This completes the code for our main MDI window and module for the moment. Let's turn now to Form1, our MDI child window. Note that none of our MDI child forms knows where it is in the form array (e.g., form number 1, number 2 and so on). We should change this so that each MDI child form can display a title such as "Writer Document 3" as well as store its data in a file such as **WRITER3.TXT**. We can do this by storing each form's location in the form array in a local (i.e., local to the form) variable, which we might call MyDocumentNumber. Add that variable to Form1 now (from **WRITER.FRM**):

```
Dim MyDocumentNumber As Integer <--

Private Sub Form_Load()
    Text1.Height = Form1.ScaleHeight
    Text1.Width = Form1.ScaleWidth
End Sub
```

When this new Form1 object is loaded, we set that variable in the MDI child form's Form_Load() event (also from **WRITER.FRM**):

```
Dim MyDocumentNumber As Integer

Private Sub Form_Load()
--> MyDocumentNumber = NumberDocuments
    Text1.Height = Form1.ScaleHeight
    Text1.Width = Form1.ScaleWidth
        .
        .
        .
End Sub
```

In this way, we'll be able to store the index of each Form1 object inside that object itself so that it becomes aware of its own document number. We can also have that document number appear in the MDI child's caption:

```
    ------------------------------------------
    |                   Writer                |
    |-----------------------------------------|
    |File     Window   Edit                   |
    |-----------------------------------------|
    |   --------------------                   |
--->|   Write Document 1  |                    |
    |   |------------------|                   |
    |   |Here is the text... |                 |
    |   |And some more text. |                 |
    |   |         --------------------         |
    |   |         | Writer Document 2  |<---    |
    |   ----------|--------------------| |      |
    |             |Here is the text... | |      |
    |             |And some more text. | |      |
    |             |                    | |      |
    |             -------------------- |        |
    ------------------------------------------
```

The code to display the document number is in the Form_Load() event (in **WRITER.FRM**):

```
Dim MyDocumentNumber As Integer

Private Sub Form_Load()
    MyDocumentNumber = NumberDocuments
    Text1.Height = Form1.ScaleHeight
    Text1.Width = Form1.ScaleWidth
--> Caption = "Writer Document " + Str$(MyDocumentNumber)
        .
        .
        .

End Sub
```

There is one last step to take in Form_Load(). When we start, our program has already placed an MDI child window inside the main MDI frame—but that first, default MDI child window is not part of our array of forms. To install it in that array, we have to add some code. Note, however, that the form array is internal to the module, and because we are working with code in the MDI child form, we will have to reach that array by setting up in the module a new subroutine that we can call from the MDI child. We will name the new module subroutine AttachWindow(). We have to specifically call AttachWindow() only for the first, default MDI child window (i.e., when NumberDocuments = 1). After that, we'll call the module subroutine we already have, AddADocument(), to create and add new windows to the form array in the module.

This is the right way to do things. Because the form array is internal to the module, we use subroutines to let forms outside the module manipulate the data in that form array (in this way, the internal data of the module stays internal):

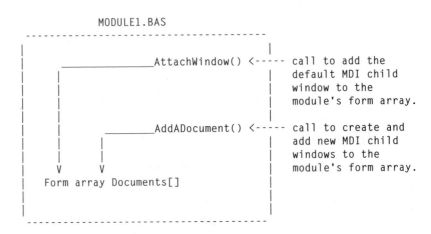

Now let's write AttachWindow(), allowing us to place the default MDI child window in the form array. We will call AttachWindow() only for the first MDI child window, so we place this code in Form1's Form_Load() event (in **WRITER.FRM**) to see whether this current window is the first, default MDI child. (The ellipsis, "...", indicates that there is more code to come—don't add it to the code.)

```
Private Sub Form_Load()
    MyDocumentNumber = NumberDocuments
    Text1.Height = Form1.ScaleHeight
    Text1.Width = Form1.ScaleWidth
    Caption = "Writer Document " + Str$(MyDocumentNumber)
--> If NumberDocuments = 1...
End Sub
```

If the current window is the default MDI child window, we want to pass it to the AttachWindow() subroutine. How do we pass the current form to AttachWindow()? We do that by using the Me keyword as the argument we pass to that subroutine. When we are inside the current form's code, the Visual Basic keyword Me is the name we can use to reference that form, and we can pass it to AttachWindow() with this new code in **WRITER.FRM**:

```
Private Sub Form_Load()
    MyDocumentNumber = NumberDocuments
    Text1.Height = Form1.ScaleHeight
    Text1.Width = Form1.ScaleWidth
    Caption = "Writer Document " + Str$(MyDocumentNumber)
--> If NumberDocuments = 1 Then AttachWindow Me
End Sub
```

That's it for our call to AttachWindow(); now add the subroutine AttachWindow() to **MODULE1.BAS** by placing this code in the module by hand:

```
Public Sub AttachWindow(TheForm As Form)      <--

End Sub                                        <--
```

Note that we've declared the parameter passed to AttachWindow() to be a form; it will be the Me parameter of the first, default MDI child window. We can place that form in our array of forms by adding this code:

```
Public Sub AttachWindow(TheForm As Form)
    Set Documents(NumberDocuments) = TheForm       <--
End Sub
```

That's it—AttachWindow() is complete. We have now installed the default MDI child window in our form array. At this point, we're able to store the default MDI child window in the form array. If the user closes all MDI child windows, the user can even create a new window by clicking the **New Window** menu item in our main window's File menu.

The next step is to create and implement the MDI children's menu system (the one that will take over the menu bar when MDI child windows are present). Using this menu system, the user will be able to add new windows to our MDI main window when other MDI child windows are present.

The MDI Child's Menu

The MDI child window's menu is the menu that will take over the main window's menu when child windows are present. We can give our MDI child form, Form1, three menus—File, Window, and Edit—using the Menu Editor as we have before. Also using the Menu Editor, give the File menu these items:

```
File
    New Document
    Save
    Read
    Exit
```

Do not give the Window menu any items at all:

```
File
    New Document
    Save
    Read
    Exit

-->  Window
```

Instead, select the Window menu in the Menu Editor (highlight the line corresponding to that menu) and click the box marked **WindowList**. This is a special type of menu designed expressly for MDI programs. Now when our program runs, Visual Basic will attach menu items to the Window menu itself, and each of these items will correspond to an open window:

```
--------------------------------------------
|                  Writer                    |
|--------------------------------------------|
|File    Window  Edit                        |
|---------        _____  --------------  |
|          |Write Document 1|                |
|          |Write Document 2|                |
|           ----------------                 |
|       ----------------------               |
|       |  Write Document 1  |               |
|       |--------------------|               |
|       |Here is the text... |               |
|       |And some more text. |               |
|       |                     ----------------- |
|       |          | Writer Document 2   | |
|        -------------|--------------------| |
|       |            |Here is the text... | |
|       |            |And some more text. | |
|       |            |                    | |
|       |             --------------------  |
--------------------------------------------
```

The user can use this menu to select which MDI child window is active. Finally, using the Menu Editor, add an Edit menu with one token item: **Cut**.

```
File
      New Document
      Save
      Read
      Exit

Window

-->   Edit
-->       Cut
```

As usual, the **Exit** item is the easiest to code; leave the Menu Editor by clicking **OK** and double-click that item now, opening Exit_Click(). Add this line of code to Exit_Click() (in **WRITER.FRM**):

```
Private Sub Exit_Click()
--> End
End Sub
```

We also will set up our program so that it's easy to add a new document when the user selects the **New Window** menu item. We will add a new window simply by calling the subroutine AddADocument(), so add that call now to the **New Document** item's click event handler, New_Click(), in **WRITER.FRM**. (Select the **New Document** menu item with the mouse to open New_Click().)

```
Private Sub New_Click()
--> AddADocument
End Sub
```

When the user selects the **New Window** item, the program will add a new MDI child window to the main MDI window.

The last two items in the File menu are **Save** and **Read**. We won't do anything elaborate here; we'll add more power to WRITER in Chapter 5, allowing users to specify the name of the file they wish to save. If the user wants to save a document—say, document 3—we will simply write the contents of the text box to the file **WRITER3.TXT**. We do that first by creating the file and using the variable MyDocumentNumber, which holds the index of the current document in the form array. We use the Open statement, passing it the name of the output file and indicating that this will be file number 1 (from **WRITER.FRM**):

```
Private Sub Save_Click()
--> Open "Write" + Format(MyDocumentNumber) + ".txt" For Output As #1
        .
        .
        .
End Sub
```

Next, we copy into the file the text from the text box that covers the client area of this MDI child window. We add a Print statement, printing to this file:

```
Private Sub Save_Click()
    Open "Write" + Format(MyDocumentNumber) + ".txt" For Output As #1
--> Print #1, Text1.Text
        .
        .
        .
End Sub
```

Ignoring any errors for the moment (Chapter 6 will add file error-handling code to WRITER), we indicate with a message box that the file was saved and then close the file:

```
Private Sub Save_Click()
    Open "Write" + Format(MyDocumentNumber) + ".txt" For Output As #1
    Print #1, Text1.Text
--> MsgBox ("Saved")
--> Close #1
End Sub
```

To read a file into a document's window, we'll open the corresponding document with Open in Read_Click() (from **WRITER.FRM**):

```
Private Sub Read_Click()
--> Open "Write" + Format(MyDocumentNumber) + ".txt" For Input As #1

        .
        .
        .

End Sub
```

Next, we read the text, place it into the text box, and close the file:

```
Private Sub Read_Click()
    Open "Write" + Format(MyDocumentNumber) + ".txt" For Input As #1
--> Text1.Text = Input$(LOF(1), #1)
--> Close #1
End Sub
```

Now our WRITER program can read from and save to the disk. Let's give all this a try. Start WRITER from Visual Basic. As you can see in Figure 2.3, the program starts with one MDI child window visible, and its caption is Writer Document 1.

As you can also see in Figure 2.3, the active menu system is the menu system of Form1 and not of MDIForm1; this is because an MDI child window is visible. Using the **New Document** menu item, the user can create and edit new documents, as shown in Figure 2.4.

In addition, our Window menu is now active and holds a list of the MDI child windows, as you see in Figure 2.5.

If we were to close all MDI child windows, the menu system would change to that of the MDI window itself, with just a File menu, as shown in Figure 2.6. If users wanted to open a document window, they could use the **New Document** item in that menu.

WRITER is a success so far. However, there's more to add here—let's look into toolbars and status bars next.

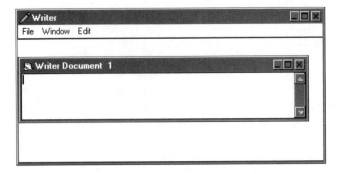

FIGURE 2.3 OUR WRITER PROGRAM OPENS WITH ONE MDI CHILD WINDOW.

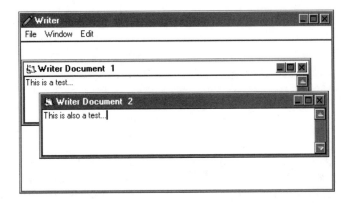

FIGURE 2.4 OUR WRITER PROGRAM ALLOWS THE USER TO EDIT MULTIPLE DOCUMENTS AT ONCE.

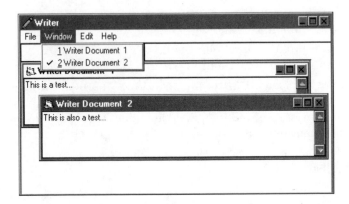

FIGURE 2.5 OUR WRITER PROGRAM'S WINDOW MENU KEEPS TRACK OF THE MDI CHILD WINDOWS.

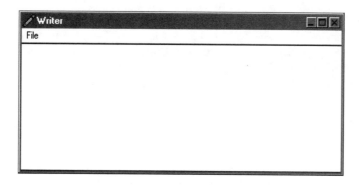

FIGURE 2.6 WITH ALL CHILD WINDOWS CLOSED, WRITER USES THE MDI MAIN MENU SYSTEM.

TOOLBARS AND STATUS BARS

One of the assets of writing MDI programs in Visual Basic is that we can add toolbars and status bars to them:

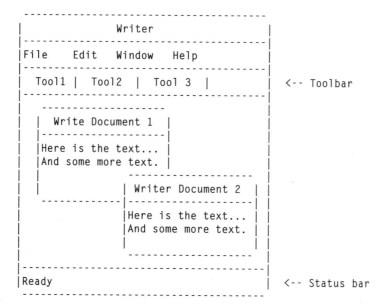

This is easy to do in Visual Basic using picture box controls. Open Visual Basic and select the MDIForm1 of the WRITER project. Next, double-click the PictureBox tool (the top tool on the right in the toolbox). A new picture box (Visual Basic names it Picture1) appears at the top of the MDI form, covering the top of the client area. Visual Basic has placed the picture box in the exact location we need to use it as a toolbar. The only way you can add a picture box to an MDI form is by aligning the picture box on the top, left, right, or bottom of the client area.

Next, double-click the picture box tool again, creating a second picture box (Visual Basic will give it the name Picture2). Set this second picture box's Align property to 2 (Align Bottom) to place this new picture box at the bottom of our client area, where we can use it as a status bar. The new MDI form appears in Figure 2.7.

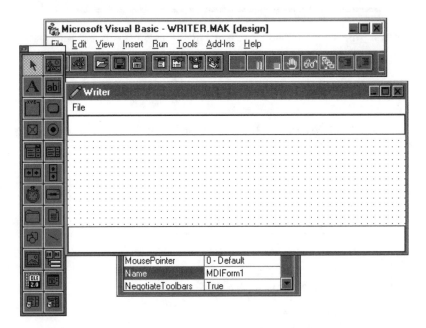

FIGURE 2.7 OUR NEW TOOLBAR AND STATUS BAR IN THE WRITER PROGRAM.

Next, we add two command buttons to the toolbar. Select the toolbar picture box (make sure that it appears with black sizing handles) and draw a new command button in it. You must select the toolbar picture box first because Visual Basic does not allow buttons directly on an MDI form.) Repeat the procedure, drawing a second command button in the toolbar. Give the first command button the caption **New Document** by setting its Caption property in the properties window and give the second button the caption **Close**, as shown in Figure 2.8.

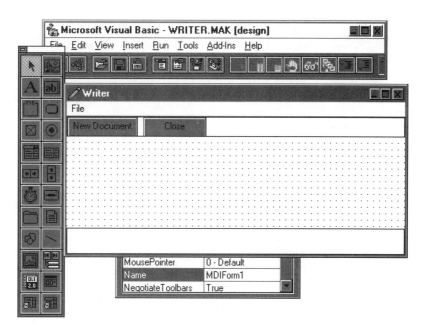

FIGURE 2.8 WE ADD BUTTONS TO THE NEW TOOLBAR.

Now double-click the button **New Document**, opening the associated click event handler, Command1_Click() (from **MDIFORM1.FRM**):

```
Private Sub Command1_Click()

End Sub
```

When the user clicks the **New Document** button, we want to add a new document to the program, and we do that by calling the AddADocument() subroutine:

```
Private Sub Command1_Click()
-->  AddADocument
      .
      .
      .
End Sub
```

We can also place a message into our status bar (the picture box control named Picture2 at the bottom of the client area) by using the picture box Print method. In this case, we can display the message "Ready" this way:

```
Private Sub Command1_Click()
    AddADocument
--> Picture2.Print "Ready"
End Sub
```

Next, open the **Close** button's click event handler, Command2_Click() (from **MDIFORM1.FRM**):

```
Private Sub Command2_Click()

End Sub
```

When users select the **Close** button, they want to close the currently active MDI child window. We determine which window is the active one by using the MDI form's property ActiveForm. We hide the active window using the following code. (Note that in this simple example, we will not remove the closed window from the array of forms, but in a fully finished program we should do so.)

```
Private Sub Command2_Click()
--> MDIForm1.ActiveForm.Hide
        .
        .
        .
End Sub
```

We can also place a "Ready" message into the status bar:

```
Private Sub Command2_Click()
    MDIForm1.ActiveForm.Hide
--> Picture2.Print "Ready"
End Sub
```

That's it—now we're using buttons in our toolbar and using a status bar. (We'll see how to design our button's images soon.) The WRITER program appears in Figure 2.9.

The code for this project appears in these listings: Listing 2.4 (**WRITER.FRM**), Listing 2.5 (**MDIFORM1.FRM**), Listing 2.6 (**MODULE1.BAS**), and Listing 2.7 (**WRITER.VBP**).

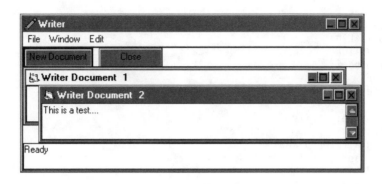

FIGURE 2.9 OUR **WRITER** PROGRAM CAN BE USED TO EDIT MULTIPLE DOCUMENTS
AND SUPPORTS BOTH A TOOLBAR AND A STATUS BAR.

LISTING 2.4 (WRITER) WRITER.FRM

```
VERSION 4.00
Begin VB.Form Form1
    Caption         =    "Writer Document"
    ClientHeight    =    2445
    ClientLeft      =    1695
    ClientTop       =    2055
    ClientWidth     =    5475
    BeginProperty Font
        name            =    "MS Sans Serif"
        charset         =    1
        weight          =    400
        size            =    8.25
        underline       =    0     'False
        italic          =    0     'False
        strikethrough   =    0     'False
    EndProperty
    Height          =    3135
    Left            =    1635
    LinkTopic       =    "Form1"
    MDIChild        =    -1    'True
    ScaleHeight     =    2445
    ScaleWidth      =    5475
    Top             =    1425
    Width           =    5595
    Begin VB.TextBox Text1
```

```
          Height          =    1935
          Left            =    0
          MultiLine       =    -1   'True
          ScrollBars      =    2    'Vertical
          TabIndex        =    0
          Top             =    0
          Width           =    5175
       End
       Begin VB.Menu File
          Caption         =    "File"
          Begin VB.Menu New
             Caption          =    "New Document"
          End
          Begin VB.Menu Save
             Caption          =    "Save"
          End
          Begin VB.Menu Read
             Caption          =    "Read"
          End
          Begin VB.Menu Exit
             Caption          =    "Exit"
          End
       End
       Begin VB.Menu Window
          Caption         =    "Window"
          WindowList      =    -1   'True
       End
       Begin VB.Menu Edit
          Caption         =    "Edit"
          Begin VB.Menu Cut
             Caption          =    "Cut"
          End
       End
    End
End
Attribute VB_Name = "Form1"
Attribute VB_Creatable = False
Attribute VB_Exposed = False
Dim MyDocumentNumber As Integer

Private Sub Exit_Click()
    End
End Sub

Private Sub Form_Load()
    MyDocumentNumber = NumberDocuments
    Text1.Height = Form1.ScaleHeight
    Text1.Width = Form1.ScaleWidth
    Caption = "Writer Document " + Str$(MyDocumentNumber)
    If NumberDocuments = 1 Then AttachWindow Me
End Sub
```

```
Private Sub Form_Resize()
    Text1.Height = Form1.ScaleHeight
    Text1.Width = Form1.ScaleWidth
End Sub

Private Sub New_Click()
    AddADocument
End Sub

Private Sub Read_Click()
    Open "Write" + Format(MyDocumentNumber) + ".txt" For Input As #1
    Text1.Text = Input$(LOF(1), #1)
    Close #1
End Sub

Private Sub Save_Click()
    Open "Write" + Format(MyDocumentNumber) + ".txt" For Output As #1
    Print #1, Text1.Text
    MsgBox ("Saved")
    Close #1
End Sub
```

LISTING 2.5 (WRITER) MDIFORM1.FRM

```
VERSION 4.00
Begin VB.MDIForm MDIForm1
    BackColor       =   &H8000000C&
    Caption         =   "Writer"
    ClientHeight    =   4230
    ClientLeft      =   1260
    ClientTop       =   1830
    ClientWidth     =   6720
    Height          =   4920
    Left            =   1200
    LinkTopic       =   "MDIForm1"
    Top             =   1200
    Width           =   6840
    Begin VB.PictureBox Picture2
        Align           =   2  'Align Bottom
        BeginProperty Font
            name            =   "MS Sans Serif"
            charset         =   1
            weight          =   400
            size            =   8.25
            underline       =   0   'False
            italic          =   0   'False
            strikethrough   =   0   'False
        EndProperty
        Height          =   495
```

```
            Left            =    0
            ScaleHeight     =    465
            ScaleWidth      =    6690
            TabIndex        =    3
            Top             =    3735
            Width           =    6720
      End
      Begin VB.PictureBox Picture1
         Align           =    1  'Align Top
         BeginProperty Font
            name            =    "MS Sans Serif"
            charset         =    1
            weight          =    400
            size            =    8.25
            underline       =    0    'False
            italic          =    0    'False
            strikethrough   =    0    'False
         EndProperty
         Height          =    375
         Left            =    0
         ScaleHeight     =    345
         ScaleWidth      =    6690
         TabIndex        =    0
         Top             =    0
         Width           =    6720
         Begin VB.CommandButton Command2
            Caption         =    "Close"
            BeginProperty Font
               name            =    "MS Sans Serif"
               charset         =    1
               weight          =    400
               size            =    8.25
               underline       =    0    'False
               italic          =    0    'False
               strikethrough   =    0    'False
            EndProperty
            Height          =    375
            Left            =    1440
            TabIndex        =    2
            Top             =    0
            Width           =    1215
         End
         Begin VB.CommandButton Command1
            Caption         =    "New Document"
            BeginProperty Font
               name            =    "MS Sans Serif"
               charset         =    1
               weight          =    400
```

```
            size            =    8.25
            underline       =    0      'False
            italic          =    0      'False
            strikethrough   =    0      'False
         EndProperty
         Height          =    375
         Left            =    0
         TabIndex        =    1
         Top             =    0
         Width           =    1335
      End
   End
   Begin VB.Menu File
      Caption          =    "File"
      Begin VB.Menu New
         Caption       =    "New Document"
      End
      Begin VB.Menu Exit
         Caption       =    "Exit"
      End
   End
End
Attribute VB_Name = "MDIForm1"
Attribute VB_Creatable = False
Attribute VB_Exposed = False

Private Sub Command1_Click()
    AddADocument
    Picture2.Print "Ready"
End Sub

Private Sub Command2_Click()
    MDIForm1.ActiveForm.Hide
    Picture2.Print "Ready"
End Sub

Private Sub Exit_Click()
    End
End Sub

Private Sub MDIForm_Load()
    NumberDocuments = 1
End Sub

Private Sub New_Click()
    AddADocument
End Sub
```

LISTING 2.6 (WRITER) MODULE1.BAS

```
Attribute VB_Name = "Module1"
Public NumberDocuments As Integer
Dim Documents(10) As Form

Public Sub AddADocument()
    NumberDocuments = NumberDocuments + 1
    If NumberDocuments <= 10 Then
        Set Documents(NumberDocuments) = New Form1
        Documents(NumberDocuments).Show
    End If
End Sub

Public Sub AttachWindow(TheForm As Form)
    Set Documents(NumberDocuments) = TheForm
End Sub
```

LISTING 2.7 (WRITER) WRITER.VBP

```
WRITER.FRM
MODULE1.BAS
MDIFORM1.FRM
Object={F9043C88-F6F2-101A-A3C9-08002B2F49FB}#1.0#0; COMDLG16.OCX
Object={FAEEE763-117E-101B-8933-08002B2F4F5A}#1.0#0; DBLIST16.OCX
ProjWinSize=345,402,202,111
ProjWinShow=2
IconForm="MDIForm1"
HelpFile=""
ExeName="Project1.exe"
Path="D:\VB"
Command=""
Name="Project1"
HelpContextID="0"
StartMode=0
VersionCompatible="0"
MajorVer=1
MinorVer=0
RevisionVer=0
AutoIncrementVer=0
VersionCompanyName=""
Reference=*\G{00025E01-0000-0000-C000-
000000000046}#0.0#0#DAO2516.DLL#Microsoft DAO 2.5 Object Library
```

We've come far in WRITER. We've seen how to handle multiple documents, how to create, display, and store MDI child windows, and how to use toolbars and status bars. Next, we'll augment our MDI knowledge by learning how to maintain multiple MDI views in a program.

MAINTAINING MULTIPLE VIEWS

The next step in our MDI exploration is to examine the idea of MDI views. An MDI program can maintain several documents open at once. Most MDI programs also allow the user to open several views into a document. These views provide portals into the document, and these portals can be moved around at will. If we have a number of views into, say, Document1, all these views will display the same document, although perhaps different parts of it:

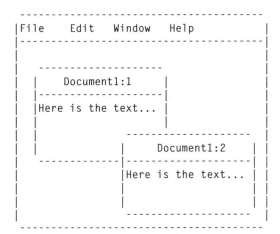

It is not difficult to display such multiple views in Visual Basic. The problem comes when the user enters something in one view and not the other. There is no provision in Visual Basic to update other views into the same document in such cases (there is in such packages as Visual C++). If the user adds text to one view, it does not appear in another view:

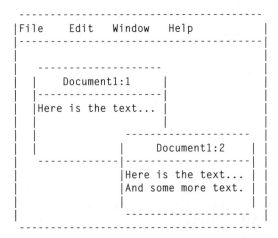

Our next goal, therefore, will be to create a multiview program that solves this problem. When the user enters text in one view, it automatically appears in the others, too (even though they do not have the input focus):

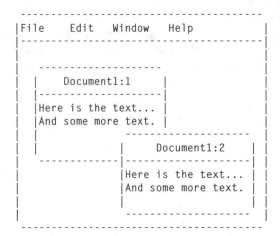

```
-------------------------------------------
|File    Edit    Window    Help           |
|-----------------------------------------|
|                                         |
|    --------------------                 |
|    |    Document1:1    |                |
|    |-------------------|                |
|    |Here is the text...|                |
|    |And some more text.|                |
|    |                   --------------------  |
|    |                   |   Document1:2    | |
|    --------------|-------------------|  |
|                  |Here is the text...|  |
|                  |And some more text.|  |
|                  |                   |  |
|                  --------------------   |
-------------------------------------------
```

Let's set up a multiview program now. To keep our example programs simple, this new program will maintain only one document, but it will allow us multiple views into that document. (We won't add multiple views to WRITER, because WRITER is a multidocument program. Adding multiple views into each of those documents would mean adding many extraneous bookkeeping details, obscuring the main MDI programming points.)

Start Visual Basic and create a new project named **MULTVIEW.VBP**. In this program, we'll see how to maintain multiple views into a single document. Some of the fundamentals of this program can be transferred whole from our WRITER program; for example, give the default form, Form1, a similar menu system using the Menu Editor. But note that we have changed the **New Document** entry into a **New View** entry (and that we're omitting file handling here):

```
File
    New View
    Exit

Window

Edit
    Cut
```

In addition, set Form1's MDIChild property to True. We can fill in Form1's Exit_Click() subroutine in **MULTVIEW.FRM** first with the following code. (Select **Exit** to open Exit_Click().)

```
Private Sub Exit_Click()
--> End
End Sub
```

Next, add a text box, Text1, to Form1. We can write Form1's Form_Load() and Form_Resize() subroutines now; as we did in WRITER, we stretch the text box Text1 to cover the MDI child's client area. We also supply a caption to our new form (Multiview Document : 1 for the first view, Multiview Document : 2 for the second, and so on). And, as in WRITER, we have to place the first (default) MDI child window into our array of forms using the subroutine AttachWindow(). When the program starts, it places a new MDI child in the main MDI window, and we have to add that new MDI child to our form array, which we do in AttachWindow(); add this code to Form_Load() and Form_Resize() (from **MULTVIEW.FRM**):

```
Private Sub Form_Load()
--> Text1.Height = Form1.ScaleHeight
--> Text1.Width = Form1.ScaleWidth
--> Caption = "MultiView Document :" + Str$(NumberViews)
--> If NumberViews = 1 Then AttachWindow Me
End Sub

Private Sub Form_Resize()
--> Text1.Height = Form1.ScaleHeight
--> Text1.Width = Form1.ScaleWidth
End Sub
```

As in WRITER, add a new module, **MODULE1.BAS**, to this program using the Visual Basic **Insert | Module** menu item. We can define AttachWindow() in this module. First, declare the public variable NumberViews (which will store the number of views) and the form of arrays (which we'll call Views here) this way:

```
Public NumberViews As Integer          <--
Dim Views(10) As Form                  <--
        .
        .
        .
```

Next, add the AttachWindow() subroutine to the module; here, we install the first MDI child window in the form array, Views, much as we did in WRITER:

```
Public NumberViews As Integer
Dim Views(10) As Form

Public Sub AttachWindow(TheForm As Form)    <--
    Set Views(NumberViews) = TheForm        <--
End Sub                                      <--
```

So far we've been able to handle the first, default MDI child. If the user wants another view into the document, however, we have to pop another window into the MDI main window. To do so, we will create a new subroutine named, say, NewView(), which adds a new view into the document. We will call that subroutine when the user clicks Form1's New View menu item. Open that menu item's click event handler, New_Click(), and add the call to NewView() there (from **MULTVIEW.FRM**):

```
Private Sub New_Click()
--> NewView
End Sub
```

As we did in WRITER, we add new MDI child windows with a subroutine (NewView() here) in the module, because we have to be able to add a new child window from both MDIForm1 and Form1. We can write NewView() very simply in **MODULE1.BAS**. Create that subroutine there by adding this code by hand:

```
Public NumberViews As Integer
Dim Views(10) As Form

Public Sub NewView()            <--

End Sub                         <--
```

We increment the number of views (NumberViews) first and then create a new MDI child window (of type Form1) and install it in our array of forms by adding this code to **MODULE1.BAS**:

```
Public NumberViews As Integer
Dim Views(10) As Form

Public Sub NewView()
--> NumberViews = NumberViews + 1
--> If NumberViews <= 10 Then
-->     Set Views(NumberViews) = New Form1
         .
         .
         .
End Sub
```

Finally, we show the new view window with the Show method as we've used it earlier in this chapter:

```
Public NumberViews As Integer
Dim Views(10) As Form

Public Sub NewView()
    NumberViews = NumberViews + 1
    If NumberViews <= 10 Then
        Set Views(NumberViews) = New Form1
-->     Views(NumberViews).Show
--> End If
End Sub
```

That's it—we've allowed the user to open multiple view windows in the MDI frame:

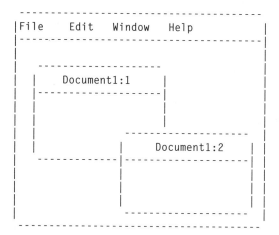

We haven't yet tied these views together. We want them to share the same data, because they're supposed to be displaying the same single document. This means that when something is typed in one view, we'll have to communicate the new text to the other views. To start that process, select the Text1 text box in Form1 and double-click it to open the code window, which displays the subroutine Text1_Change() (from **MULTVIEW.FRM**):

```
Sub Text1_Change()

End Sub
```

This subroutine is called when the user changes the text in our text box. We can communicate with the other views, setting the same text in them, by calling a subroutine we might name SetChars() and passing it the (changed) text in our text box, Text1.Text:

```
Sub Text1_Change()
    SetChars (Text1.Text)          <--
End Sub
```

We set up SetChars() in our module **MODULE1.BAS**:

```
Public NumberViews As Integer
Dim Views(10) As Form
        .
        .
        .
Public Sub SetChars(TheData As String)  <--

End Sub                                  <--
```

First, in SetChars(), we store the newly updated text, which is passed to us in a public string that we name Data:

```
Public NumberViews As Integer
Public Data As String                    <--
Dim Views(10) As Form
        .
        .
        .
Public Sub SetChars(TheData As String)
    Data = TheData                       <--
        .
        .
        .
End Sub
```

This is where we store the document's data (in this example program, we'll maintain only one document). Now we must update the other views; we have obtained and stored the new text, but we have not yet transferred it to the other views. We do that by looping over all views and filling their text boxes with the new text. (We can loop over the other views easily, because they are simply elements in the form array, which we can reference with a single array index.)

```
Public NumberViews As Integer
Public Data As String
Dim Views(10) As Form
        .
        .
        .
Public Sub SetChars(TheData As String)
    Data = TheData
```

```
--> For loop_index% = 1 To NumberViews
-->     Views(loop_index%).Text1.Text = TheData
--> Next loop_index%
End Sub
```

Transferring the entire text from view to view this way could be a problem if the document were very long. In such cases, you write additional code to do the text handling in a smart way. For example, you can use the text box methods GetSel(), SetSel(), ReplaceSel(), and so on to update only the changed data, or you can omit using text boxes and design your own text handling.

That completes the update process; when the user types something in one view, we will automatically transfer it to the others. Our views are now coordinated.

Note that when a new view window is created, we should also initialize it with the current document data, which we have stored in the module's public string named Data. We initialize new view windows in the Form1 Form_Load() event with this code (from **MULTVIEW.FRM**):

```
Private Sub Form_Load()
    Text1.Height = Form1.ScaleHeight
    Text1.Width = Form1.ScaleWidth
--> Text1.Text = Data
    Caption = "MultiView Document :" + Str$(NumberViews)
    If NumberViews = 1 Then AttachWindow Me
End Sub
```

This way, if the user asks for a new view, the data in the document also appears in the new view.

At this stage, then, we're using multiple views, all of which are coordinated:

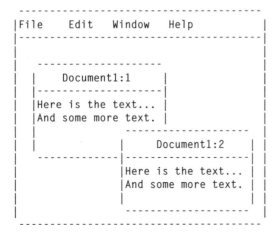

All that remains in this program is to add the code for the main MDI window. As before, we can give this window a toolbar—this time, with two buttons: **New View** (Name property = Command1) and **Close** (Name property = Command2).

```
       ----------------------------------------
       |File    Edit    Window    Help         |
       |---------------------------------------|
 -->   | New View |   Close  |                 |
       |---------------------------------------|
       |    --------------------               |
       |    |    Document1:1    |               |
       |    |------------------ |               |
       |    |Here is the text...|               |
       |    |And some more text.|               |
       |    |                 --------------------|
       |    |                 |    Document1:2    | |
       |    -------------- |------------------ | |
       |                   |Here is the text...| |
       |                   |And some more text.| |
       |                   |                   | |
       |                   -------------------- |
       |                                        |
       ----------------------------------------
```

Now we add code to Command1_Click() and Command2_Click(); in Command1_Click() (corresponding to the **New View** button), we request a new view, and in Command2_Click() (corresponding to the **Close** button), we hide the currently active MDI child (from **MDIFORM1.FRM**):

```
Private Sub Command1_Click()
--> NewView
End Sub

Private Sub Command2_Click()
--> ActiveForm.Hide
End Sub
```

In addition, we give the MDI form a menu system with one menu—File— which has two menu items: **New View** and **Exit**. We add the required code to those menu items' event handlers (from **MDIFORM1.FRM**):

```
Private Sub New_Click()
    NewView                      <--
End Sub
```

```
Private Sub Exit_Click()
    End                          <--
End Sub
```

The last step is to initialize the entire program in MDIForm_Load() in **MDI-FORM1.FRM**, which the program calls when it first runs. In our case, all we have to do is to initialize the number of views to 1 (because the program places a default MDI child in the main MDI window):

```
Private Sub MDIForm_Load()
--> NumberViews = 1
End Sub
```

Now run the program and create a few view windows. When you type something in one view, it is shared in the others, as shown in Figure 2.10. In addition, these views are independently scrollable, and you can scroll through the document at will. MULTVIEW is a success. Users have come to expect multiple views into documents in MDI programs, and now we've seen how to support such views.

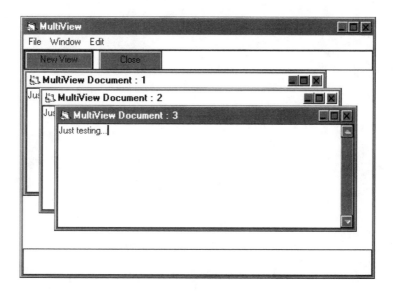

FIGURE 2.10 MULTIVIEW ALLOWS THE USER TO USE DIFFERENT VIEWS IN THE SAME DOCUMENT.

The code for this program appears in these listings: Listing 2.8 (**MULTVIEW FRM**), Listing 2.9 (**MDIFORM1.FRM**), Listing 2.10 (**MODULE1.BAS**), and Listing 2.11 (**MULTVIEW.VBP**).

LISTING 2.8 (MULTIVIEW) MULTVIEW.FRM

```
VERSION 4.00
Begin VB.Form Form1
   Caption         =    "MultiView Document"
   ClientHeight    =    2445
   ClientLeft      =    1695
   ClientTop       =    2055
   ClientWidth     =    5475
   BeginProperty Font
      name               =    "MS Sans Serif"
      charset            =    1
      weight             =    400
      size               =    8.25
      underline          =    0    'False
      italic             =    0    'False
      strikethrough      =    0    'False
   EndProperty
   Height          =    3135
   Left            =    1635
   LinkTopic       =    "Form1"
   MDIChild        =    -1 'True
   ScaleHeight     =    2445
   ScaleWidth      =    5475
   Top             =    1425
   Width           =    5595
   Begin VB.TextBox Text1
      Height       =    1935
      Left         =    0
      MultiLine    =    -1 'True
      ScrollBars   =    2    'Vertical
      TabIndex     =    0
      Top          =    0
      Width        =    5175
   End
   Begin VB.Menu File
      Caption      =    "File"
      Begin VB.Menu New
         Caption   =    "New View"
      End
      Begin VB.Menu Exit
         Caption   =    "Exit"
      End
   End
   Begin VB.Menu Window
```

```
        Caption        =    "Window"
        WindowList     =    -1   'True
   End
   Begin VB.Menu Edit
      Caption          =    "Edit"
      Begin VB.Menu Cut
         Caption       =    "Cut"
      End
   End
End
Attribute VB_Name = "Form1"
Attribute VB_Creatable = False
Attribute VB_Exposed = False

Private Sub Exit_Click()
    End
End Sub

Private Sub Form_Load()
    Text1.Height = Form1.ScaleHeight
    Text1.Width = Form1.ScaleWidth
    Text1.Text = Data
    Caption = "MultiView Document :" + Str$(NumberViews)
    If NumberViews = 1 Then AttachWindow Me
End Sub

Private Sub Form_Resize()
    Text1.Height = Form1.ScaleHeight
    Text1.Width = Form1.ScaleWidth
End Sub

Private Sub New_Click()
    NewView
End Sub

Sub Text1_Change()
    SetChars (Text1.Text)
End Sub
```

LISTING 2.9 (MULTIVIEW) MDIFORM1.FRM

```
VERSION 4.00
Begin VB.MDIForm MDIForm1
   BackColor        =    &H8000000C&
   Caption          =    "MultiView"
   ClientHeight     =    4230
   ClientLeft       =    1350
   ClientTop        =    1920
   ClientWidth      =    6720
```

```
Height          =    4920
Left            =    1290
LinkTopic       =    "MDIForm1"
Top             =    1290
Width           =    6840
Begin VB.PictureBox Picture2
    Align             =    2 'Align Bottom
    BeginProperty Font
        name              =    "MS Sans Serif"
        charset           =    1
        weight            =    400
        size              =    8.25
        underline         =    0    'False
        italic            =    0    'False
        strikethrough     =    0    'False
    EndProperty
    Height          =    495
    Left            =    0
    ScaleHeight     =    465
    ScaleWidth      =    6690
    TabIndex        =    3
    Top             =    3735
    Width           =    6720
End
Begin VB.PictureBox Picture1
    Align             =    1 'Align Top
    BeginProperty Font
        name              =    "MS Sans Serif"
        charset           =    1
        weight            =    400
        size              =    8.25
        underline         =    0    'False
        italic            =    0    'False
        strikethrough     =    0    'False
    EndProperty
    Height          =    375
    Left            =    0
    ScaleHeight     =    345
    ScaleWidth      =    6690
    TabIndex        =    0
    Top             =    0
    Width           =    6720
    Begin VB.CommandButton Command2
        Caption           =    "Command2"
        BeginProperty Font
            name              =    "MS Sans Serif"
            charset           =    1
            weight            =    400
            size              =    8.25
            underline         =    0    'False
```

```
            italic          =   0    'False
            strikethrough   =   0    'False
         EndProperty
         Height          =   375
         Left            =   1440
         TabIndex        =   2
         Top             =   0
         Width           =   1215
      End
      Begin VB.CommandButton Command1
         Caption         =   "New View"
         BeginProperty Font
            name            =   "MS Sans Serif"
            charset         =   1
            weight          =   400
            size            =   8.25
            underline       =   0    'False
            italic          =   0    'False
            strikethrough   =   0    'False
         EndProperty
         Height          =   375
         Left            =   0
         TabIndex        =   1
         Top             =   0
         Width           =   1335
      End
   End
   Begin VB.Menu File
      Caption         =   "File"
      Begin VB.Menu New
         Caption         =   "New View"
      End
      Begin VB.Menu Exit
         Caption         =   "Exit"
      End
   End
End
Attribute VB_Name = "MDIForm1"
Attribute VB_Creatable = False
Attribute VB_Exposed = False

Private Sub Command1_Click()
    NewView
End Sub

Private Sub Command2_Click()
    ActiveForm.Hide
End Sub

Private Sub Exit_Click()
```

```
        End
    End Sub

    Private Sub MDIForm_Load()
        NumberViews = 1
    End Sub

    Private Sub New_Click()
        NewView
    End Sub
```

LISTING 2.10 (MULTIVIEW) MODULE1.BAS

```
Attribute VB_Name = "Module1"
Public NumberViews As Integer
Public Data As String
Dim Views(10) As Form

Public Sub NewView()
    NumberViews = NumberViews + 1
    If NumberViews <= 10 Then
        Set Views(NumberViews) = New Form1
        Views(NumberViews).Show
    End If
End Sub

Public Sub SetChars(TheData As String)
    Data = TheData
    For loop_index% = 1 To NumberViews
        Views(loop_index%).Text1.Text = TheData
    Next loop_index%
End Sub

Public Sub AttachWindow(TheForm As Form)
    Set Views(NumberViews) = TheForm
End Sub
```

LISTING 2.11 MULTVIEW.VBP

```
MULTVIEW.FRM
MODULE1.BAS
MDIFORM1.FRM
Object={F9043C88-F6F2-101A-A3C9-08002B2F49FB}#1.0#0; COMDLG16.OCX
Object={FAEEE763-117E-101B-8933-08002B2F4F5A}#1.0#0; DBLIST16.OCX
ProjWinSize=345,402,202,111
ProjWinShow=2
IconForm="MDIForm1"
```

```
HelpFile=""
ExeName="Project1.exe"
Path="D:\VB"
Command=""
Name="Project1"
HelpContextID="0"
StartMode=0
VersionCompatible="0"
MajorVer=1
MinorVer=0
RevisionVer=0
AutoIncrementVer=0
VersionCompanyName=""
Reference=*\G{00025E01-0000-0000-C000-
000000000046}#0.0#0#DAO2516.DLL#Microsoft DAO 2.5 Object Library
```

We've covered many of the fundamentals of MDI programming, but there is more. Next, we'll add tooltips and use bitmapped toolbar controls.

TOOLTIPS AND TOOLBAR IMAGES

So far, we have used only command buttons in our toolbars, but they are not the only controls we can use; we can use any controls that have a Click event. For example, we can load our own bitmaps into image controls and use them in our toolbars. In addition, we'll install tooltips (the small yellow prompts that appear when the mouse cursor is over a button in the toolbar). Let's see how this works.

Bitmap Toolbar Buttons

In our next example, we'll place bitmapped graphics images into our toolbar, allowing us to give the tools in the toolbar any appearance we wish (as opposed to the standard push-buttons we have been using until now). This capability is useful if you have, say, a drawing tool that you would like to show as a pencil in the toolbar and not just as a button labeled Draw.

Start a new Visual Basic project named **TIPS.VBP**. Add a new MDI form and place in it a toolbar (a picture box aligned at the top of the client area). Next, add two image controls to the toolbar. (The image control tool is the 10th tool down on the left in the Visual Basic toolbox.)

We will use some of the icons that come with Visual Basic as our bitmaps here; in particular, we'll assume that our first toolbar button is a drawing tool named **Draw** and that our second button is an erasing tool named **Erase**. The icon we'll use for the **Draw** tool is a pencil, **VB\ICONS\WRITING\PENCIL01.ICO**. For the erase tool, we'll show a pencil eraser, **VB\ICONS\WRITING\ERASE01.ICO**.

Find the Picture property of the new image controls in the properties window and set the Picture property of Image1 to **C:\VB\ICONS\WRITING\PENCIL01.ICO**, and the Picture property of Image2 to **C:\VB\ICONS\WRITING\ERASE01.ICO**. (Use the drive and path appropriate to your installation of Visual Basic.)

Now double-click the Image controls, opening the corresponding Click event handlers (from **MDIFORM1.FRM**):

```
Private Sub Image1_Click()

End Sub

Private Sub Image2_Click()

End Sub
```

In each case, we'll indicate with a message box which tool was chosen. We add this code (from **MDIFORM1.FRM**):

```
Private Sub Image1_Click()
--> MsgBox ("You clicked the Draw tool")
End Sub

Private Sub Image2_Click()
--> MsgBox ("You clicked the Erase tool")
End Sub
```

Finally, we use the properties window to set the BackColor property of the toolbar to the usual color for toolbars—a neutral gray—by setting that property to &H00C0C0C0 in the properties window. Now run the program, as in Figure 2.11.

Our bitmapped tool images appear as expected. When you click a tool, a message box appears, telling you which tool you selected. If you want each toolbar image to appear as its own button, you can do one of two things: either set the BorderStyle property of Image1 and Image2 to Fixed Single or draw your own bitmaps to look like buttons. (You can use the Visual Basic tool ImageEdit, which we'll mention in Chapter 3.)

Now let's add tooltips.

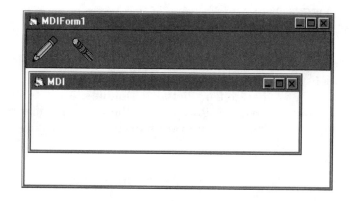

FIGURE 2.11 OUR TIPS PROGRAM USES BITMAP ICONS IN THE TOOLBAR.

Tooltips

Next, we will create and display tooltips. Visual Basic supports tooltips in its Windows 95 controls, such as the Toolbar and StatusBar controls, but only if you are running Windows 95 and the 32-bit version of Visual Basic. Here, however, we'll see how to add tooltips for the 16-bit version of Visual Basic and for any Windows version, not just Windows 95. A *tooltip* is the small yellow window that appears over a tool when you position the mouse over it. For example, if we positioned the mouse over the Draw tool in our program, we would want a small yellow tooltip to appear with the caption **Draw**. This helps the user remember what each tool is for.

We'll base our tooltips on a timer control, Timer1, and on a label control, Label1. When the mouse is on a tool in the toolbar, we'll enable the timer, which means that the program will call the subroutine Timer_Timer() repeatedly. In that subroutine, we'll configure a label control as a tooltip and display it. We'll also check to see whether the mouse has moved away, in which case we should stop displaying the tooltip.

In the TIPS project, create a new timer control (the Timer tool is the seventh tool down on the left in Visual Basic's toolbox) and give it an Interval property of 100 (i.e., 100 milliseconds) in the properties window. Set its Enabled property to False so that we do not display any tooltips when the program first starts.

In addition, create a new label control (the second tool on the left in the Visual Basic toolbox) named Label1, and make it small enough to hold the single word **Draw** or **Erase**. Set the label's BackColor property to light yellow.

(Type **&H0080FFFF** for this property or, if you prefer, look at the tooltips in Visual Basic's toolbox and match them with the pop-up palette for Label1's BackColor property in the properties window.) Set the label's BorderStyle property to 1, Fixed Single.

Next, open the code window and add MouseMove event handlers to Image1, Image2, and the toolbar, Picture1. Double-click a control to open the code window and use the Proc box in the code window as we have before to add these mouse move event-handling subroutines (from **MDI-FORM1.FRM**):

```
Private Sub Image1_MouseMove(Button As Integer, Shift As Integer, X As
        Single, Y As Single)

End Sub

Private Sub Image2_MouseMove(Button As Integer, Shift As Integer, X As
        Single, Y As Single)

End Sub

Private Sub Picture1_MouseMove(Button As Integer, Shift As Integer, X
        As Single, Y As Single)

End Sub
```

In these subroutines, we will set a form-wide variable named Tool to indicate which tool, if any, the mouse cursor is currently on top of; this variable will tell us which tooltip to display. We can set Tool to 0 if the mouse cursor is not over a tool, to 1 if it is over Image1 (the Draw tool), and to 2 if it is over Image2 (the Erase tool). Note also that we set Tool to 0 when we first load the MDI form in MDIForm_Load():

```
Dim Tool As Integer     <--

Private Sub Image1_MouseMove(Button As Integer, Shift As Integer, X As
        Single, Y As Single)
--> Tool = 1
End Sub

Private Sub Image2_MouseMove(Button As Integer, Shift As Integer, X As
        Single, Y As Single)
--> Tool = 2
End Sub

Private Sub Picture1_MouseMove(Button As Integer, Shift As Integer, X
        As Single, Y As Single)
--> Tool = 0
End Sub
```

```
Private Sub MDIForm_Load()
--> Tool = 0
End Sub
```

When the mouse cursor is over a tool, we display the tooltip simply by enabling our timer control (because we'll show the tooltip in Timer1_Timer()) by adding this code (from **MDIFORM1.FRM**):

```
Dim Tool As Integer

Private Sub Image1_MouseMove(Button As Integer, Shift As Integer, X As
        Single, Y As Single)
    Tool = 1
--> Timer1.Enabled = True
End Sub

Private Sub Image2_MouseMove(Button As Integer, Shift As Integer, X As
        Single, Y As Single)
    Tool = 2
--> Timer1.Enabled = True
End Sub

Private Sub Picture1_MouseMove(Button As Integer, Shift As Integer, X
        As Single, Y As Single)
--> Timer1.Enabled = False
    Tool = 0
End Sub

Private Sub MDIForm_Load()
    Tool = 0
End Sub
```

Now create Timer1_Timer() by double-clicking the **Timer** control to open the code window (from **MDIFORM1.FRM**):

```
Private Sub Timer1_Timer()

End Sub
```

If the mouse cursor is not over a tool (i.e., Tool = 0), we should make sure that the tooltip is not visible by adding this code:

```
Private Sub Timer1_Timer()
--> If Tool = 0 Then
-->     Label1.Visible = False
--> End If
        .
        .
        .
End Sub
```

On the other hand, if Tool = 1, the mouse cursor is over the Draw tool and we can flash the correct tooltip on the screen. (Note that we move the tooltip using its Left and Top properties so that it appears over the correct tool.)

```
Private Sub Timer1_Timer()
    If Tool = 0 Then
        Label1.Visible = False
    End If
--> If Tool = 1 Then
-->     Label1.Caption = "Draw"
-->     Label1.Left = Image1.Left
-->     Label1.Top = Image1.Top
-->     Label1.Visible = True
--> End If
         .
         .
         .
End Sub
```

If Tool = 2, the mouse cursor is over the Erase tool, and we draw that tooltip:

```
Private Sub Timer1_Timer()
    If Tool = 0 Then
        Label1.Visible = False
    End If           /
    If Tool = 1 Then
        Label1.Caption = "Draw"
        Label1.Left = Image1.Left
        Label1.Top = Image1.Top
        Label1.Visible = True
    End If
--> If Tool = 2 Then
-->     Label1.Caption = "Erase"
-->     Label1.Left = Image2.Left
-->     Label1.Top = Image2.Top
-->     Label1.Visible = True
--> End If
End Sub
```

Finally, when the user moves the mouse cursor away from the tools (and therefore over the picture box), we make sure that the tooltip is hidden in Picture1_MouseMove() (from **MDIFORM1.FRM**):

```
Private Sub Picture1_MouseMove(Button As Integer, Shift As Integer, X
        As Single, Y As Single)
    Timer1.Enabled = False
    Tool = 0
--> Label1.Visible = False
End Sub
```

Give the new program a try. As you can see in Figure 2.12, it supports tooltips even though we had to program them from scratch. The TIPS program is a success; now we're able to support tooltips and bitmapped tool icons in the toolbar.

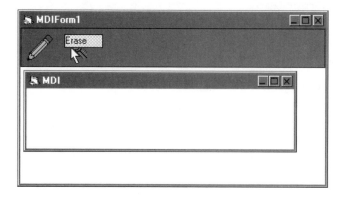

FIGURE 2.12 OUR TIPS PROGRAM SUPPORTS TOOLBAR TOOLTIPS.

The code for this program appears in these listings: Listing 2.12 (**FORM1.FRM**), Listing 2.13 (**MDIFORM1.FRM**), and Listing 2.14 (**TIPS.VBP**).

LISTING 2.12 (TIPS) FORM1.FRM

```
VERSION 4.00
Begin VB.Form Form1
   Caption         =   "MDI"
   ClientHeight    =   4230
   ClientLeft      =   1095
   ClientTop       =   1515
   ClientWidth     =   6720
   BeginProperty Font
      name         =   "MS Sans Serif"
      charset      =   1
      weight       =   400
      size         =   8.25
      underline    =   0   'False
      italic       =   0   'False
      strikethrough =  0   'False
   EndProperty
   Height          =   4635
   Left            =   1035
   LinkTopic       =   "Form1"
   MDIChild        =   -1  'True
   ScaleHeight     =   4230
   ScaleWidth      =   6720
   Top             =   1170
```

```
   Width            =    6840
End
Attribute VB_Name = "Form1"
Attribute VB_Creatable = False
Attribute VB_Exposed = False
VERSION 4.00
Begin VB.MDIForm MDIForm1
   BackColor       =    &H8000000C&
   Caption         =    "MDIForm1"
   ClientHeight    =    4230
   ClientLeft      =    1530
   ClientTop       =    2115
   ClientWidth     =    6720
   Height          =    4635
   Left            =    1470
   LinkTopic       =    "MDIForm1"
   Top             =    1770
   Width           =    6840
   Begin VB.PictureBox Picture1
      Align          =    1  'Align Top
      AutoRedraw     =    -1  'True
      BackColor      =    &H00C0C0C0&
      BeginProperty Font
         name          =    "MS Sans Serif"
         charset       =    1
         weight        =    400
         size          =    8.25
         underline     =    0   'False
         italic        =    0   'False
         strikethrough =    0   'False
      EndProperty
      Height         =    495
      Left           =    0
      ScaleHeight    =    495
      ScaleWidth     =    6720
      TabIndex       =    0
      Top            =    0
      Width          =    6720
      Begin VB.Timer Timer1
         Interval       =    100
         Left           =    5760
         Top            =    0
      End
      Begin VB.Label Label1
         BackColor      =    &H0080FFFF&
         BorderStyle    =    1  'Fixed Single
         BeginProperty Font
            name          =    "MS Sans Serif"
            charset       =    1
            weight        =    400
```

```
            size            =    8.25
            underline       =    0    'False
            italic          =    0    'False
            strikethrough   =    0    'False
         EndProperty
         Height          =    255
         Left            =    1560
         TabIndex        =    1
         Top             =    240
         Visible         =    0    'False
         Width           =    735
      End
      Begin VB.Image Image2
         Height          =    480
         Left            =    840
         Picture         =    "MDIFORM1.frx":0000
         Top             =    0
         Width           =    480
      End
      Begin VB.Image Image1
         Height          =    480
         Left            =    120
         Picture         =    "MDIFORM1.frx":030A
         Top             =    0
         Width           =    480
      End
   End
End
```

LISTING 2.13 (TIPS) MDIFORM1.FRM

```
Attribute VB_Name = "MDIForm1"
Attribute VB_Creatable = False
Attribute VB_Exposed = False
Dim Tool As Integer

Private Sub Image1_Click()
    MsgBox ("You clicked the Draw tool")
End Sub

Private Sub Image1_MouseMove(Button As Integer, Shift As Integer, X As
        Single, Y As Single)
    Tool = 1
    Timer1.Enabled = True
End Sub

Private Sub Image2_Click()
    MsgBox ("You clicked the Erase tool")
End Sub
```

```
Private Sub Image2_MouseMove(Button As Integer, Shift As Integer, X As
        Single, Y As Single)
    Tool = 2
    Timer1.Enabled = True
End Sub

Private Sub MDIForm_Load()
    Tool = 0
End Sub

Private Sub Picture1_MouseMove(Button As Integer, Shift As Integer, X
        As Single, Y As Single)
    Timer1.Enabled = False
    Tool = 0
    Label1.Visible = False
End Sub

Private Sub Timer1_Timer()
    If Tool = 0 Then
        Label1.Visible = False
    End If
    If Tool = 1 Then
        Label1.Caption = "Draw"
        Label1.Left = Image1.Left
        Label1.Top = Image1.Top
        Label1.Visible = True
    End If
    If Tool = 2 Then
        Label1.Caption = "Erase"
        Label1.Left = Image2.Left
        Label1.Top = Image2.Top
        Label1.Visible = True
    End If
End Sub
```

LISTING 2.14 TIPS.VBP

```
TIPS.FRM
MDIFORM1.FRM
Object={F9043C88-F6F2-101A-A3C9-08002B2F49FB}#1.0#0; COMDLG16.OCX
Object={FAEEE763-117E-101B-8933-08002B2F4F5A}#1.0#0; DBLIST16.OCX
ProjWinSize=345,402,202,111
ProjWinShow=2
ExeName="Project1.exe"
Path="D:\VB"
Command=""
Name="Project1"
HelpContextID="0"
StartMode=0
```

```
VersionCompatible="0"
MajorVer=1
MinorVer=0
RevisionVer=0
AutoIncrementVer=0
VersionCompanyName=""
Reference=*\G{00025E01-0000-0000-C000-
000000000046}#0.0#0#DAO2516.DLL#Microsoft DAO 2.5 Object Library
```

That's it for our coverage of MDI programs. We've seen a great deal in this chapter, from simply supporting MDI to coordinating multiple views, from toolbars with and without bitmap buttons to status bars and more. In the next chapter, we'll continue our exploration of advanced Visual Basic when we begin working with a favorite programming topic—graphics.

## CHAPTER 3

ADVANCED GRAPHICS

In this chapter, we'll examine the process of creating graphics in Visual Basic. Creating graphics is always a popular topic with programmers, and the results are (often) visible and pleasing. We'll begin by examining the ways Visual Basic allows programmers to draw in windows. Next, we'll examine the processes of loading bitmaps into a program, creating animation, customizing a form's dimensions to fit our own desired scale, drawing fonts, using "inside" lines, and more. (As we'll see, inside lines help when we draw a figure with heavy lines and want to avoid overrunning the figure's boundaries.) Let's begin with a discussion of some of the most important Visual Basic drawing properties.

DRAWING WITH PENS

The first three drawing properties we will examine are the drawing properties DrawWidth, DrawMode, and DrawStyle. These properties affect how the image we draw is displayed in Visual Basic, and the results can be impressive. We will start with the DrawWidth property.

The DrawWidth Property

Objects that support drawing (such as forms and picture boxes) maintain a "pen"—a fictitious drawing tool of a certain width, color, and "style" (dotted, solid, and so on) that acts much as an actual pen might. When you draw lines in Visual Basic, the program acts as though you are using the current pen, and the program draws lines in the pen's color, drawing width, and so on.

The color of the current pen is held in its ForeColor property, and we set that color with the RGB() function. This function takes three color values (ranging from 0 to 255) that represent the red, green, and blue values in the color we want to create, and it returns a 32-bit color. For example, setting the pen's color in Form1 to a neutral gray (red = green = blue = 128) looks like this:

```
Form1.ForeColor = RGB(128, 128, 128)
```

One of the drawing properties that we can use with pens in forms and picture boxes (as well as OLE containers and the Printer object) is DrawWidth, the width of the drawing pen. To see this in action, start a new project and open the Form_Load() event: double-click **Form1**. Also, set AutoRedraw to True in the properties window to make sure that what we draw in Form_Load() stays on the screen:

```
Private Sub Form_Load()

End Sub
```

We'll draw 10 lines here of steadily increasing width by steadily increasing the DrawWidth setting. DrawWidth is measured in pixels, and the default setting is 1 pixel wide. The maximum setting is 32,767 (although it's hard to imagine a line 32,767 pixels wide).

Set up a loop to draw the 10 lines by adding this code to Form1's Form_Load() event:

```
Private Sub Form_Load()
--> For loop_index% = 1 To 10

--> Next loop_index%
End Sub
```

Our variable loop_index% varies from 1 to 10, and we can simply set the form's DrawWidth property to that value:

```
Private Sub Form_Load()
    For loop_index% = 1 To 10
-->     DrawWidth = loop_index%
          .
          .
          .
    Next loop_index%
End Sub
```

Next, we draw a line 1/11th of the way down the window (if there are 10 lines, we have to make them all visible), and we draw the following lines another 1/11th farther down:

```
Private Sub Form_Load()
    For loop_index% = 1 To 10
```

```
        DrawWidth = loop_index%
-->     Line (0, loop_index% * ScaleHeight / 11)-(ScaleWidth,
            loop_index% * ScaleHeight / 11)
    Next loop_index%
End Sub
```

If we run the program now, we see the result shown in Figure 3.1, where the lines we draw steadily increase in width as we work our way down the form.

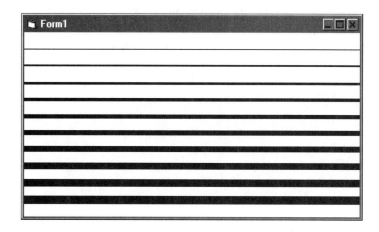

FIGURE 3.1 OUR PROGRAM INCREASES THE DRAWWIDTH PROPERTY TO PRODUCE THIS RESULT.

This is straightforward enough, and it points out one aspect of drawing with pens in Visual Basic. Now that we have set *what* we will draw with a pen, let's take a look at *how* we will draw it, using the DrawMode property.

The DrawMode Property

A pen's DrawMode property controls the way a pen draws on the screen. For example, the default value for DrawMode, 13, is the "copy pen" setting, in which the pen merely draws in the selected forecolor with the selected DrawWidth. On the other hand, if we set DrawMode to 1, the pen is set to "blackness," which means that it simply draws in black. Setting DrawMode to 16 means that it will draw in "whiteness" (sometimes good for erasing).

There are many variations for the DrawMode setting, and they appear in Table 3.1.

TABLE 3.1 DRAWMODE PROPERTY SETTINGS.

DrawMode	Means
1	Blackness—draws black.
2	Not Merge Pen—the inverse of setting 15 (Merge Pen).
3	Mask Not Pen—the combination of the colors in both the background color and the inverse of the pen.
4	Not Copy Pen—the inverse of the Copy pen.
5	Mask Pen Not—the combination of the colors in both the pen and the inverse of the display.
6	Invert—the inverse of the display.
7	Xor Pen—the combination of colors in the pen and in the display color, but not in both (i.e., Xored).
8	Not Mask Pen—this is the inverse of the Mask Pen.
9	Mask Pen—a combination of the colors in both the pen and the display.
10	Not Xor Pen—this is the inverse of the Xor Pen.
11	Nop—no operation is performed. This setting turns drawing off.
12	Merge Not Pen—a combination of the display color and the color inverse of the pen color.
13	Copy Pen (Default)—draws color specified by the ForeColor property.
14	Merge Pen Not—a combination of the pen color and the inverse of the display.
15	Merge Pen—a simple combination of the pen color and the display color.
16	Whiteness—draws white.

Some of the more interesting DrawMode settings are 4, the Not Copy pen, which draws in the color inverse of the current forecolor; setting 6, which simply inverts what's on the screen as the pen draws over it; and setting 7, the Xor pen. When you use the Xor DrawMode—that is, use the Xor pen, DrawMode = 7—the drawing color and whatever's on the screen are Xored together as the pen draws. Xor stands for exclusive Or, and it works just like the logical Or operator does, except that when the two values it's Xoring together are both 1, the result is 0 and not 1 as it would be with Or. Here's how Xor works compared with Or and And (all values in binary):

```
   0101           1111           1111
Or 1010       And 1010       Xor 1010
   ----           ----           ----
   1111           1010           0101
```

The interesting thing about Xor is that if you Xor value A with value B, you get a certain result—and if you Xor it with B again, you get A back. This makes it useful for screen pens, because it means that if you draw something with the Xor pen, it will appear on the screen, but if you draw it again in the same place, the original screen will reappear. In other words, you don't have to store the part of the screen that you overwrite in order to restore it later; if you use the Xor pen, just draw the same image again, and the original screen will appear. Bit by bit, it might look like this if we have a certain original value:

```
    1111    Original
```

Now we Xor this value with, say, 1010:

```
    1111    Original
Xor 1010    Xor with 1010
    ----
    0101    Result
```

The result is 0101. We then Xor this result with 1010 again, and we get back our original value:

```
    1111    Original
Xor 1010    Xor with 1010
    ----
    0101    Result
Xor 1010    Xor with 1010 again
    ----
--> 1111    Get back original after second Xor
```

We might add that Xor is often used in encryption for just this reason; it's easy to get the original value back, provided that you know what you Xored it with the first time. In other words, if you bitwise Xor a text document with a password, you will have encrypted it; to recover the original document, just Xor it with the password again.

Now let's put the Xor pen to use. Open the program's Form_Load() event and set DrawMode to 7, the Xor pen:

```
Private Sub Form_Load()
    For loop_index% = 1 To 10
        DrawWidth = loop_index%
        Line (0, loop_index% * ScaleHeight / 11)-(ScaleWidth,
        loop_index% * ScaleHeight / 11)
    Next loop_index%
--> DrawMode = 7
        .
        .
        .
```

We also will select a new DrawWidth; here, we'll start with a constant value
of 10 pixels wide:

```
Private Sub Form_Load()
    For loop_index% = 1 To 10
        DrawWidth = loop_index%
        Line (0, loop_index% * ScaleHeight / 11)-(ScaleWidth,
        loop_index% * ScaleHeight / 11)
    Next loop_index%
    DrawMode = 7
--> DrawWidth = 10
        .
        .
        .
```

Now let's let our Xor pen interact with the steadily thickening horizontal
lines we've already drawn by drawing some vertical lines (and therefore
Xoring them with the horizontal lines where they intersect):

```
Private Sub Form_Load()
    For loop_index% = 1 To 10
        DrawWidth = loop_index%
        Line (Q, loop_index% * ScaleHeight / 11)-(ScaleWidth,
        loop_index% * ScaleHeight / 11)
    Next loop_index%
    DrawMode = 7
    DrawWidth = 10
--> For loop_index% = 1 To 10
-->     Line (loop_index% * ScaleWidth / 11, 0)-(loop_index% *
-->     ScaleWidth / 11, ScaleHeight)
--> Next loop_index%
        .
        .
        .
```

For an interesting graphics effect, we'll let the lines get thinner and thinner
as we move from left to right:

```
Private Sub Form_Load()
    For loop_index% = 1 To 10
        DrawWidth = loop_index%
        Line (0, loop_index% * ScaleHeight / 11)-(ScaleWidth,
        loop_index% * ScaleHeight / 11)
    Next loop_index%
    DrawMode = 7
    DrawWidth = 10
    For loop_index% = 1 To 10
-->     DrawWidth = 11 - loop_index%
        Line (loop_index% * ScaleWidth / 11, 0)-(loop_index% *
        ScaleWidth / 11, ScaleHeight)
    Next loop_index%
        .
        .
        .
```

Finally, we reset DrawMode to its original value, 13 (the default value), with this code:

```
Private Sub Form_Load()
    For loop_index% = 1 To 10
        DrawWidth = loop_index%
        Line (0, loop_index% * ScaleHeight / 11)-(ScaleWidth,
        loop_index% * ScaleHeight / 11)
    Next loop_index%
    DrawMode = 7
    DrawWidth = 10
    For loop_index% = 1 To 10
        DrawWidth = 11 - loop_index%
        Line (loop_index% * ScaleWidth / 11, 0)-(loop_index% *
        ScaleWidth / 11, ScaleHeight)
    Next loop_index%
--> DrawMode = 13
End Sub
```

We run the program, producing exactly the same result as in Figure 3.1. Our vertical Xor lines don't appear at all! Why not? The answer is that our default color is black, RGB(0, 0, 0), and Xoring 0 with anything yields the original value, unchanged. When we draw a black line (RGB(0, 0, 0)) on a white window (RGB(255, 255, 255)), the result is simply the white window again (RGB(255, 255, 255)). Even when we go through a black line (RGB(0, 0, 0)) the result is still the same: a black line (still RGB(0, 0, 0)).

To change this, we will draw with a white line and not a black one. The reason is that white, RGB(255, 255, 255), has all bits set, so we'll end up logically inverting (0's become 1's and 1's become 0's) whatever is on the screen now when we Xor it to our white pen. Add this code, changing the pen to white:

```
Private Sub Form_Load()
    For loop_index% = 1 To 10
        DrawWidth = loop_index%
        Line (0, loop_index% * ScaleHeight / 11)-(ScaleWidth,
        loop_index% * ScaleHeight / 11)
    Next loop_index%
    DrawMode = 7
    DrawWidth = 10
--> ForeColor = RGB(255, 255, 255)
    For loop_index% = 1 To 10
        DrawWidth = 11 - loop_index%
        Line (loop_index% * ScaleWidth / 11, 0)-(loop_index% *
        ScaleWidth / 11, ScaleHeight)
    Next loop_index%
    DrawMode = 13
End Sub
```

Change the pen back to the default black before we leave:

```
Private Sub Form_Load()
    For loop_index% = 1 To 10
        DrawWidth = loop_index%
        Line (0, loop_index% * ScaleHeight / 11)-(ScaleWidth,
        loop_index% * ScaleHeight / 11)
    Next loop_index%
    DrawMode = 7
    DrawWidth = 10
    ForeColor = RGB(255, 255, 255)
    For loop_index% = 1 To 10
        DrawWidth = 11 - loop_index%
        Line (loop_index% * ScaleWidth / 11, 0)-(loop_index% *
        ScaleWidth / 11, ScaleHeight)
    Next loop_index%
    DrawMode = 13
--> ForeColor = RGB(0, 0, 0)
End Sub
```

Now run the program, generating the result you see in Figure 3.2. This is much better. We've managed to invert everything as we draw over it with our white Xor line.

We can also place the same code in the Form_Resize() event handler so that when a user resizes our window, the program will correctly redisplay our graphics. (Find the Form_Resize() event in the code window's Proc box and select it to open this function.)

```
Private Sub Form_Resize()
--> Cls
--> For loop_index% = 1 To 10
```

```
-->      DrawWidth = loop_index%
-->      Line (0, loop_index% * ScaleHeight / 11)-(ScaleWidth,
-->      loop_index% * ScaleHeight / 11)
--> Next loop_index%
--> DrawMode = 7
--> DrawWidth = 10
--> ForeColor = RGB(255, 255, 255)
--> For loop_index% = 1 To 10
-->      DrawWidth = 11 - loop_index%
-->      Line (loop_index% * ScaleWidth / 11, 0)-(loop_index% *
-->      ScaleWidth / 11, ScaleHeight)
--> Next loop_index%
--> DrawMode = 13
--> ForeColor = RGB(0, 0, 0)
End Sub
```

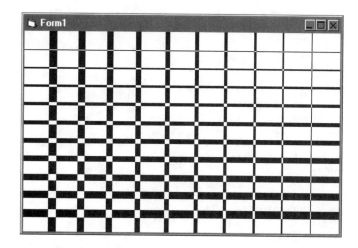

FIGURE 3.2 DRAWING VERTICAL LINES WITH A WHITE XOR PEN.

Note that we started Form_Resize() with the Cls method, which clears our client area of whatever was left there from the window before it was resized. (The term *Cls* originally meant "clear screen" in DOS BASIC.)

Save this program as **XOR.VBP** and **XOR.FRM**. **XOR.FRM** appears in Listing 3.1, and **XOR.VBP** in Listing 3.2.

LISTING 3.1 XOR.FRM

```
VERSION 4.00
Begin VB.Form Form1
   AutoRedraw      =    -1  'True
   Caption         =    "Form1"
```

```
      ClientHeight    =    4230
      ClientLeft      =    1095
      ClientTop       =    1515
      ClientWidth     =    6720
      BeginProperty Font
         name         =    "MS Sans Serif"
         charset      =    1
         weight       =    400
         size         =    8.25
         underline    =    0    'False
         italic       =    0    'False
         strikethrough =   0    'False
      EndProperty
      Height          =    4635
      Left            =    1035
      LinkTopic       =    "Form1"
      ScaleHeight     =    4230
      ScaleWidth      =    6720
      Top             =    1170
      Width           =    6840
   End
   Attribute VB_Name = "Form1"
   Attribute VB_Creatable = False
   Attribute VB_Exposed = False
   Private Sub Form_Load()
       For loop_index% = 1 To 10
           DrawWidth = loop_index%
           Line (0, loop_index% * ScaleHeight / 11)-(ScaleWidth,
           loop_index% * ScaleHeight / 11)
       Next loop_index%
       DrawMode = 7
       DrawWidth = 10
       ForeColor = RGB(255, 255, 255)
       For loop_index% = 1 To 10
           DrawWidth = 11 - loop_index%
           Line (loop_index% * ScaleWidth / 11, 0)-(loop_index% *
           ScaleWidth / 11, ScaleHeight)
       Next loop_index%
       DrawMode = 13
       ForeColor = RGB(0, 0, 0)
   End Sub

   Private Sub Form_Resize()
       Cls
       For loop_index% = 1 To 10
           DrawWidth = loop_index%
           Line (0, loop_index% * ScaleHeight / 11)-(ScaleWidth,
           loop_index% * ScaleHeight / 11)
       Next loop_index%
```

```
        DrawMode = 7
        DrawWidth = 10
        ForeColor = RGB(255, 255, 255)
        For loop_index% = 1 To 10
            DrawWidth = 11 - loop_index%
            Line (loop_index% * ScaleWidth / 11, 0)-(loop_index% *
            ScaleWidth / 11, ScaleHeight)
        Next loop_index%
        DrawMode = 13
        ForeColor = RGB(0, 0, 0)
End Sub
```

LISTING 3.2 XOR.VBP

```
XOR.FRM
Object={F9043C88-F6F2-101A-A3C9-08002B2F49FB}#1.0#0; COMDLG16.OCX
Object={FAEEE763-117E-101B-8933-08002B2F4F5A}#1.0#0; DBLIST16.OCX
ProjWinSize=345,402,202,111
ProjWinShow=2
IconForm="Form1"
ExeName="Project1.exe"
Path="D:\VB"
Command=""
Name="Project1"
HelpContextID="0"
StartMode=0
VersionCompatible="0"
MajorVer=1
MinorVer=0
RevisionVer=0
AutoIncrementVer=0
VersionCompanyName=""
Reference=*\G{00025E01-0000-0000-C000-
000000000046}#0.0#0#DAO2516.DLL#Microsoft DAO 2.5 Object Library
```

So far, we've gained a good idea of how to use the Xor pen—drawing with white allows us to color invert what's already there. If we were to draw in blue with the Xor pen on a white background, for example, blue would end up turned off in the result, which would be a mixture only of red and green. In this way, you can make objects that you Xor over in white on the screen seem highlighted, and this is often what programs do.

There's one last pen property to examine: the DrawStyle property. If DrawMode sets how we draw something and DrawWidth determines how widely we draw it, DrawStyle determines much more *what* we are actually drawing.

The DrawStyle Property

The DrawStyle property allows us to change the way we draw—up to a point. Using DrawStyle, we can draw lines that are made up of dotted, dashed, or dashed *and* dotted lines. However, there is a serious limitation: when DrawWidth is greater than 1, all the DrawStyle settings 1–4 simply produce solid lines. We can draw dashed or dotted lines only if they have a width of one pixel! The various settings for DrawStyle appear in Table 3.2, and you can see how they look in Figure 3.3.

TABLE 3.2 DRAWSTYLE PROPERTY SETTINGS.

DrawStyle	Meaning
0	Solid (the default)
1	Dash (DrawWidth = 1 only)
2	Dot (DrawWidth = 1 only)
3	Dash-dot (DrawWidth = 1 only)
4	Dash-dot-dash (DrawWidth = 1 only)
5	Transparent (do not draw) (DrawWidth = 1 only)
6	Inside line (DrawWidth = 1 only)

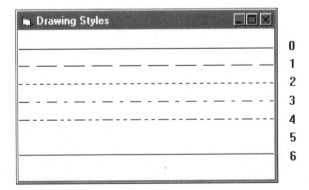

FIGURE 3.3 HERE ARE THE SEVEN DRAWSTYLE SETTINGS POSSIBLE IN VISUAL BASIC.

We can modify our XOR program so that it displays dashed lines. For example, we might change the DrawStyle property for the horizontal lines from 0 to 1. (We also leave the width of those lines at 1, because we cannot draw dashed lines that are thicker than that.)

```
Private Sub Form_Load()
--> DrawStyle = 1
    For loop_index% = 1 To 10
-->     ' taken out for DrawStyle setting... DrawWidth = loop_index%
        Line (0, loop_index% * ScaleHeight / 11)-(ScaleWidth,
        loop_index% * ScaleHeight / 11)
    Next loop_index%
    DrawMode = 7
    DrawWidth = 10
--> DrawStyle = 0
    ForeColor = RGB(255, 255, 255)
    For loop_index% = 1 To 10
        DrawWidth = 11 - loop_index%
        Line (loop_index% * ScaleWidth / 11, 0)-(loop_index% *
        ScaleWidth / 11, ScaleHeight)
    Next loop_index%
    DrawMode = 13
    ForeColor = RGB(0, 0, 0)
End Sub

Private Sub Form_Resize()
    Cls
--> DrawStyle = 1
    For loop_index% = 1 To 10
-->     ' taken out for DrawStyle setting... DrawWidth = loop_index%
        Line (0, loop_index% * ScaleHeight / 11)-(ScaleWidth,
        loop_index% * ScaleHeight / 11)
    Next loop_index%
    DrawMode = 7
    DrawWidth = 10
--> DrawStyle = 0
    ForeColor = RGB(255, 255, 255)
    For loop_index% = 1 To 10
        DrawWidth = 11 - loop_index%
        Line (loop_index% * ScaleWidth / 11, 0)-(loop_index% *
        ScaleWidth / 11, ScaleHeight)
    Next loop_index%
    DrawMode = 13
    ForeColor = RGB(0, 0, 0)
End Sub
```

The result appears in Figure 3.4. The new version of **XOR.FRM** appears in Listing 3.3.

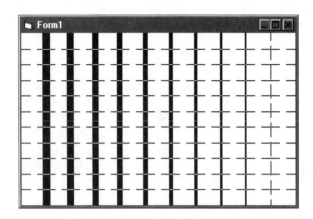

FIGURE 3.4 HERE WE SET THE DRAWSTYLE PROPERTY OF
THE HORIZONTAL LINES TO 1, MAKING THEM DASHED.

LISTING 3.3 XOR.FRM

```
VERSION 4.00
Begin VB.Form Form1
   AutoRedraw        =    -1   'True
   Caption           =    "Form1"
   ClientHeight      =    4230
   ClientLeft        =    1095
   ClientTop         =    1515
   ClientWidth       =    6720
   BeginProperty Font
      name           =    "MS Sans Serif"
      charset        =    1
      weight         =    400
      size           =    8.25
      underline      =    0    'False
      italic         =    0    'False
      strikethrough  =    0    'False
   EndProperty
   Height            =    4635
   Left              =    1035
   LinkTopic         =    "Form1"
   ScaleHeight       =    4230
   ScaleWidth        =    6720
   Top               =    1170
   Width             =    6840
End
Attribute VB_Name = "Form1"
Attribute VB_Creatable = False
```

```
Attribute VB_Exposed = False
Private Sub Form_Load()
    DrawStyle = 1
    For loop_index% = 1 To 10
        ' taken out for DrawStyle setting... DrawWidth = loop_index%
        Line (0, loop_index% * ScaleHeight / 11)-(ScaleWidth,
        loop_index% * ScaleHeight / 11)
    Next loop_index%
    DrawMode = 7
    DrawWidth = 10
    DrawStyle = 0
    ForeColor = RGB(255, 255, 255)
    For loop_index% = 1 To 10
        DrawWidth = 11 - loop_index%
        Line (loop_index% * ScaleWidth / 11, 0)-(loop_index% *
        ScaleWidth / 11, ScaleHeight)
    Next loop_index%
    DrawMode = 13
    ForeColor = RGB(0, 0, 0)
End Sub

Private Sub Form_Resize()
    Cls
    DrawStyle = 1
    For loop_index% = 1 To 10
        ' taken out for DrawStyle setting... DrawWidth = loop_index%
        Line (0, loop_index% * ScaleHeight / 11)-(ScaleWidth,
        loop_index% * ScaleHeight / 11)
    Next loop_index%
    DrawMode = 7
    DrawWidth = 10
    DrawStyle = 0
    ForeColor = RGB(255, 255, 255)
    For loop_index% = 1 To 10
        DrawWidth = 11 - loop_index%
        Line (loop_index% * ScaleWidth / 11, 0)-(loop_index% *
        ScaleWidth / 11, ScaleHeight)
    Next loop_index%
    DrawMode = 13
    ForeColor = RGB(0, 0, 0)
End Sub
```

You may wonder what the "inside line" DrawStyle setting, setting 6, is all about (see Table 3.2). To demonstrate, let's create a new project, **INSIDE.VBP**.

We will first work in **INSIDE.VBP** without inside lines to demonstrate the graphics problem that inside lines are meant to solve. Let's say that we want to enclose the top half of the client area in a box drawn with a width of, say, 18 pixels. We might start by setting DrawWidth to 18 in INSIDE's Form1 Form_Load() event handler:

```
Private Sub Form_Load()
--> DrawWidth = 18
            .
            .
            .
End Sub
```

Then we would draw our box, using the Line method with the "B" parameter (for box) specified in this code:

```
Private Sub Form_Load()
    DrawWidth = 18
--> Line (0, 0)-(ScaleWidth, ScaleHeight / 2), , B
End Sub
```

We can also add this code (with an additional Cls instruction at the beginning) to Form1's Form_Resize() event:

```
Private Sub Form_Load()
    DrawWidth = 18
    Line (0, 0)-(ScaleWidth, ScaleHeight / 2), , B
End Sub

Private Sub Form_Resize()
--> Cls
--> DrawWidth = 18
--> Line (0, 0)-(ScaleWidth, ScaleHeight / 2), , B
End Sub
```

Now we run the program, generating the result shown in Figure 3.5. As you can see, there is a problem: the box's sides are the full thickness only at the bottom and not on the top and sides. On the top and sides, we appear to have only half of the correct thickness for our lines.

The reason is that Visual Basic draws thick lines such that the middle of the thick line corresponds to the line that we pass to the Line method. Suppose we passed this line to the Line method:

```
- - - - - - - - - - - - - -Line actually passed to Line Method- -
```

But also suppose that we asked for this line to be 18 pixels thick. The thick line would be drawn using the given line as its middle:

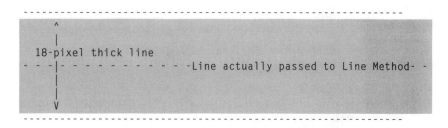

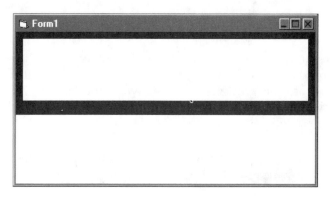

FIGURE 3.5 THE INSIDE PROGRAM, FIRST TRY, WITH UNEQUAL THICKNESSES OF THE BOX'S SIDES.

An inside line is different. When we indicate that we want to draw an enclosed figure such as a box, Visual Basic will draw inside lines so that they appear entirely inside the given boundaries. For example, if the thick line we're currently drawing makes up the top of the box, all the pixels we draw will be inside that box:

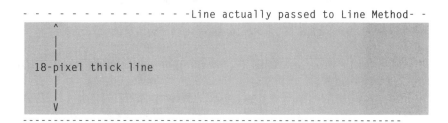

We can change the code in INSIDE to match this by setting the DrawStyle property to 6, the inside line setting, in Form1's Form_Load() and Form_Resize() event handlers:

```
Private Sub Form_Load()
    DrawWidth = 18
--> DrawStyle = 6
    Line (0, 0)-(ScaleWidth, ScaleHeight / 2), , B
End Sub

Private Sub Form_Resize()
    Cls
    DrawWidth = 18
--> DrawStyle = 6
    Line (0, 0)-(ScaleWidth, ScaleHeight / 2), , B
End Sub
```

The new result appears in Figure 3.6; the full width of our thick lines now lies inside our box, which means that the lines are not cut off at the edges of the client area. In this way, you can also avoid interfering with other graphics in your window by using nonoverlapping inside lines that restrict themselves to their own territory.

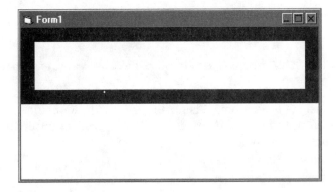

FIGURE 3.6 ▪ DRAWING AN ENCLOSED BOX WITH INSIDE LINES.

The code for this program, **INSIDE.FRM**, appears in Listing 3.4. **INSIDE.VBP** appears in Listing 3.5.

LISTING 3.4 ▪ INSIDE.FRM

```
VERSION 4.00
Begin VB.Form Form1
    AutoRedraw      =   -1  'True
    Caption         =   "Form1"
    ClientHeight    =   4230
    ClientLeft      =   1095
    ClientTop       =   1515
```

```
    ClientWidth     =    6720
    BeginProperty Font
       name            =    "MS Sans Serif"
       charset         =    1
       weight          =    400
       size            =    8.25
       underline       =    0    'False
       italic          =    0    'False
       strikethrough   =    0    'False
    EndProperty
    Height          =    4635
    Left            =    1035
    LinkTopic       =    "Form1"
    ScaleHeight     =    4230
    ScaleWidth      =    6720
    Top             =    1170
    Width           =    6840
End
Attribute VB_Name = "Form1"
Attribute VB_Creatable = False
Attribute VB_Exposed = False

Private Sub Form_Load()
    DrawWidth = 18
    DrawStyle = 6
    Line (0, 0)-(ScaleWidth, ScaleHeight / 2), , B
End Sub

Private Sub Form_Resize()
    Cls
    DrawWidth = 18
    DrawStyle = 6
    Line (0, 0)-(ScaleWidth, ScaleHeight / 2), , B
End Sub
```

LISTING 3.5 INSIDE.VBP

```
INSIDE.FRM
Object={F9043C88-F6F2-101A-A3C9-08002B2F49FB}#1.0#0; COMDLG16.OCX
Object={FAEEE763-117E-101B-8933-08002B2F4F5A}#1.0#0; DBLIST16.OCX
ProjWinSize=345,402,202,111
ProjWinShow=2
ExeName="Project1.exe"
Path="D:\VB"
Command=""
Name="Project1"
HelpContextID="0"
StartMode=0
VersionCompatible="0"
```

```
MajorVer=1
MinorVer=0
RevisionVer=0
AutoIncrementVer=0
VersionCompanyName=""
Reference=*\G{00025E01-0000-0000-C000-
000000000046}#0.0#0#DAO2516.DLL#Microsoft DAO 2.5 Object Library
```

Having mastered some of the drawing properties (DrawStyle, DrawMode, and so on), let's take a look at working with graphics when you don't draw anything—that is, when you simply load in bitmapped files.

USING BITMAPPED GRAPHICS

Using bitmaps to display graphics figures is often a good idea in Visual Basic—for example, it helps a great deal in graphics animation. You might assume that creating working animation means that you would draw a picture, erase it, and draw it again, perhaps in a new location. Regrettably, Visual Basic is not up to that task. The only method you have of truly drawing pixel-by-pixel graphics in Visual Basic is the impossibly slow PSet() (pixel set) method. You have to draw your image pixel by pixel and then erase the whole image, redrawing it elsewhere. PSet() is so slow, however, that it produces noticeable lag at each step. It turns out that a far better way to produce animation in Visual Basic is to load previously drawn bitmaps and work with them, as we'll see how to do soon.

If you are set on the idea of drawing your own pixel-by-pixel graphics for animation and don't want to use PSet(), you can use the Windows (not Visual Basic) function BitBlt(), and we'll see how to call that function when we learn how to interface directly to Windows in Chapter 9. BitBlt() is fast enough for animation.

Let's examine some of the ways of loading bitmapped graphics in Visual Basic. Create a new project, **LOADBMP.VBP**, and open the Form1 Form_Load() event handler by double-clicking **Form1**:

```
Private Sub Form_Load()

End Sub
```

We can load graphics files into forms, picture boxes, or image controls in Visual Basic. For example, we might load into our form the file **ARCHES.BMP**, which comes with Windows. The file is C:**WINDOWS\ARCHES.BMP**.

```
Private Sub Form_Load()
--> Picture = LoadPicture("c:\windows\arches.bmp")
End Sub
```

Note that to correctly install the graphics image, we had to assign the return value from LoadPicture() to the form's Picture property.

133

Run the program now; it loads the file **arches.bmp** and displays it starting at (0, 0) in the form, as shown in Figure 3.7. As you can see, it is easy to load a bitmap and display it.

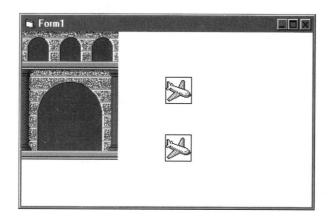

FIGURE 3.7 WE LOAD A BITMAPPED FILE INTO OUR FORM IN THE LOADBMP PROGRAM.

In addition to **.BMP** files, we can load **.ICO** (icon) files and **.WMF** (Windows metafile) files. You might wonder what a Windows metafile is. Like Visual Basic, Windows has its own set of drawing functions, usually called from a C or C++ program. A Windows metafile is a stored set of calls to such functions; the file reproduces the desired graphics simply by passing arguments to those functions.

In addition to forms, picture boxes and image controls can load and display graphics files. Let's add a new image control, Image1, and a new picture box, Picture1, to our LOADBMP program. Although we can use the LoadPicture method with Picture1 and Image1, we can also load images into them at design time by setting their Picture properties. For example, let's load an icon, **C:\VB\ICONS\INDUSTRY\PLANE.ICO**, which comes with Visual Basic and displays a small airplane. In the properties window, set the Picture property of both Image1 and Picture1 to **C:\VB\ICONS\INDUS-TRY\PLANE.ICO** before running the program. Now run the program as shown in Figure 3.8; here, Image1 is on top, Picture1 on the bottom.

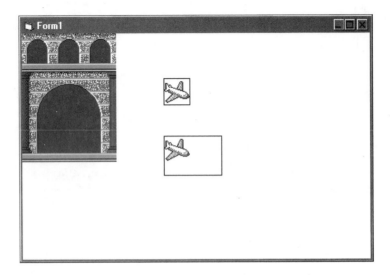

FIGURE 3.8 USING THE PICTURE PROPERTY OF IMAGE CONTROLS AND PICTURE BOXES.

Note that the image control has automatically reshaped itself to the size of the icon, but the picture box has not; this is one of the differences between image controls and picture boxes (the others are coming up in the next paragraph). We can set the picture box's AutoSize property to True, and Picture1 will also resize itself automatically to fit the icon, as shown in Figure 3.9.

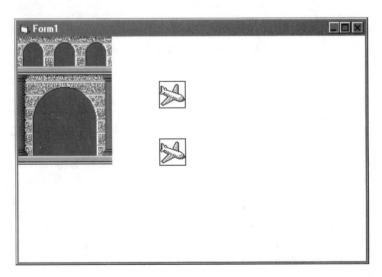

FIGURE 3.9 AFTER WE SET THE PICTURE BOX'S AUTOSIZE PROPERTY TO TRUE,
IT SHAPES ITSELF TO FIT THE ICON.

You may wonder what the difference is between image controls and picture boxes. Although picture boxes have many more methods and properties than image controls, picture boxes also take up more memory and perform actions slower. Image controls support only the following methods. (Refresh redisplays the graphics image, and ZOrder determines how this control will be overlapped by other controls.)

```
Image controls:
Drag, Move, Refresh, ZOrder
```

Picture boxes support all the following methods. (The Link methods have to do with DDE—dynamic data exchange—between programs.)

```
Picture boxes:
Circle, Cls, Drag, Line, LinkExecute, LinkPoke, LinkRequest, LinkSend,
Move, PaintPicture, Point, Print, PSet, Refresh, Scale, SetFocus,
TextHeight, TextWidth, ZOrder
```

We've reviewed the fundamentals of loading bitmapped graphics into a Visual Basic program. The file **LOADBMP.FRM** appears in Listing 3.6, and **LOADBMP.VBP** in Listing 3.7.

LISTING 3.6 LOADBMP.FRM

```
VERSION 4.00
Begin VB.Form Form1
   AutoRedraw         =    -1   'True
   Caption            =    "Form1"
   ClientHeight       =    4230
   ClientLeft         =    1095
   ClientTop          =    1515
   ClientWidth        =    6720
   BeginProperty Font
      name                 =    "MS Sans Serif"
      charset              =    1
      weight               =    400
      size                 =    8.25
      underline            =    0    'False
      italic               =    0    'False
      strikethrough        =    0    'False
   EndProperty
   Height             =    4635
   Left               =    1035
   LinkTopic          =    "Form1"
   ScaleHeight        =    4230
   ScaleWidth         =    6720
   Top                =    1170
   Width              =    6840
```

```
    Begin VB.PictureBox Picture1
        AutoSize        =   -1  'True
        Height          =   510
        Left            =   2760
        Picture         =   "LOADBMP.frx":0000
        ScaleHeight     =   480
        ScaleWidth      =   480
        TabIndex        =   0
        Top             =   1920
        Width           =   510
    End
    Begin VB.Image Image1
        BorderStyle     =   1   'Fixed Single
        Height          =   510
        Left            =   2520
        Picture         =   "LOADBMP.frx":030A
        Top             =   1320
        Width           =   510
    End
End
Attribute VB_Name = "Form1"
Attribute VB_Creatable = False
Attribute VB_Exposed = False

Private Sub Form_Load()
    Picture = LoadPicture("c:\windows\arches.bmp")
End Sub
```

LISTING 3.7 LOADBMP.VBP

```
..\LOADBMP\LOADBMP.FRM
Object={F9043C88-F6F2-101A-A3C9-08002B2F49FB}#1.0#0; COMDLG16.OCX
Object={FAEEE763-117E-101B-8933-08002B2F4F5A}#1.0#0; DBLIST16.OCX
ProjWinSize=345,402,202,111
ProjWinShow=2
IconForm="Form1"
ExeName="Project1.exe"
Path="D:\VB"
Command=""
Name="Project1"
HelpContextID="0"
StartMode=0
VersionCompatible="0"
MajorVer=1
MinorVer=0
RevisionVer=0
AutoIncrementVer=0
VersionCompanyName=""
Reference=*\G{00025E01-0000-0000-C000-
000000000046}#0.0#0#DAO2516.DLL#Microsoft DAO 2.5 Object Library
```

Now that we have the appropriate tools for it, let's take a look at creating graphics animation in a Visual Basic program.

CREATING GRAPHICS ANIMATION

In our next example, we're going to create and display working graphics animation. Suppose we have a picture box, Picture1, that displays some graphics:

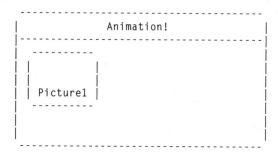

To move this image around the window, animating it, we can simply use the picture box's Move method:

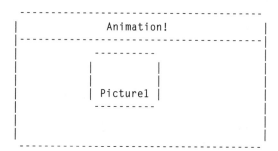

For example, we might draw a car using the Windows Paint program and save it to a **.BMP** file. (Or we could use the handy Visual Basic tool ImageEdit, which is in the **VB\TOOLS\IMAGEDIT** directory. This tool lets us create bitmaps and icons.) Then we can load this file into a picture box using the LoadPicture() method and animate it by sending it across the client area with the Move method.

We start the Windows Paint program, as shown in Figure 3.10, and we draw a car as also shown in that figure. Save this image to a file named **ANIMATE.BMP**.

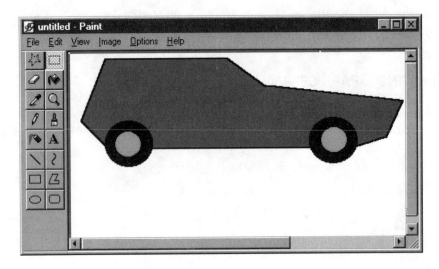

FIGURE 3.10 WE CREATE A NEW .BMP FILE WITH THE IMAGE OF A CAR.

Next, create a new Visual Basic program named **ANIMATE.VBP** and place a picture box, Picture1, on the form. We can load our new .BMP file into this picture box simply by setting its Picture property correctly; set that property to **ANIMATE.BMP**. Now double-click the form to open the code window, and create the subroutine Form_Click() by selecting it in the code window's Proc box:

```
Private Sub Form_Click()

End Sub
```

Here, we'll animate our car by using the Move method to move it across the screen:

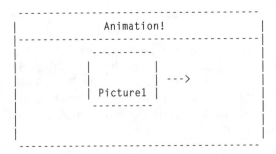

Begin by setting up a loop:

```
Private Sub Form_Click()
--> For loop_index% = 1 To 100
         .
         .
         .
--> Next loop_index%
End Sub
```

Next, place this code inside the loop:

```
Private Sub Form_Click()
    For loop_index% = 1 To 100
-->      Picture1.Move Picture1.Left + loop_index%, Picture1.Top,
-->      Picture1.Width, Picture1.Height
    Next loop_index%
End Sub
```

Now run the program, as shown in Figure 3.11. When you click the form, you'll see the car drive across it. The motion is smooth, without jerks. Our animation program is a success.

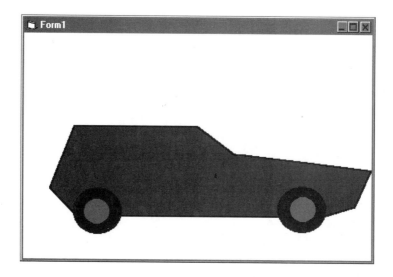

FIGURE 3.11 OUR ANIMATE PROGRAM MOVES AN IMAGE OF A CAR ACROSS THE SCREEN.

The code for **ANIMATE.FRM** appears in Listing 3.8, and **ANIMATE.VBP** appears in Listing 3.9.

Listing 3.8 ANIMATE.FRM

```
VERSION 4.00
Begin VB.Form Form1
    AutoRedraw      =   -1  'True
    Caption         =   "Form1"
    ClientHeight    =   4230
    ClientLeft      =   1095
    ClientTop       =   1515
    ClientWidth     =   6720
    BeginProperty Font
        name            =   "MS Sans Serif"
        charset         =   1
        weight          =   400
        size            =   8.25
        underline       =   0   'False
        italic          =   0   'False
        strikethrough   =   0   'False
    EndProperty
    Height          =   4635
    Left            =   1035
    LinkTopic       =   "Form1"
    ScaleHeight     =   4230
    ScaleWidth      =   6720
    Top             =   1170
    Width           =   6840
    Begin VB.PictureBox Picture1
        AutoSize        =   -1  'True
        BorderStyle     =   0   'None
        Height          =   2340
        Left            =   120
        Picture         =   "ANIMATE.frx":0000
        ScaleHeight     =   2340
        ScaleWidth      =   6720
        TabIndex        =   0
        Top             =   1560
        Width           =   6720
    End
End
Attribute VB_Name = "Form1"
Attribute VB_Creatable = False
Attribute VB_Exposed = False
Private Sub Form_Click()
    For loop_index% = 1 To 100
        Picture1.Move Picture1.Left + loop_index%, Picture1.Top,
        Picture1.Width, Picture1.Height
    Next loop_index%
End Sub
```

LISTING 3.9 ANIMATE.VBP

```
ANIMATE.FRM
Object={F9043C88-F6F2-101A-A3C9-08002B2F49FB}#1.0#0; COMDLG16.OCX
Object={FAEEE763-117E-101B-8933-08002B2F4F5A}#1.0#0; DBLIST16.OCX
ProjWinSize=378,439,202,111
ProjWinShow=2
ExeName="Project1.exe"
Path="D:\VB"
Command=""
Name="Project1"
HelpContextID="0"
StartMode=0
VersionCompatible="0"
MajorVer=1
MinorVer=0
RevisionVer=0
AutoIncrementVer=0
VersionCompanyName=""
Reference=*\G{00025E01-0000-0000-C000-
000000000046}#0.0#0#DAO2516.DLL#Microsoft DAO 2.5 Object Library
```

There are additional powerful graphics techniques available in Visual Basic. One such technique is the use of customized graphics scales, which let us readjust the coordinate system of our window to suit our needs. We'll explore this process next.

CUSTOMIZED GRAPHICS SCALES

Visual Basic contains a great deal of support for customized scale handling. This means that when you draw in Visual Basic, you use a certain coordinate system to specify where you want your graphics. We'll examine the process of modifying that coordinate system, including using properties and methods such as Scale, ScaleHeight, ScaleWidth, ScaleX, ScaleY, ScaleMode, and more. Of all the methods of setting a graphics scale, setting the ScaleMode property is probably the easiest. We'll take a look at that first.

The ScaleMode Property

ScaleMode is a property of forms, picture boxes, and the Printer object. You use ScaleMode to change the system of measurement used in those objects. The default unit of measurement in Visual Basic is *twips*, which is 1/1440th of an inch. (*Twip* is short for twentieth of a point, and a point is 1/72nd of an inch). For example, a window may be 4000 twips high and 6000 twips wide:

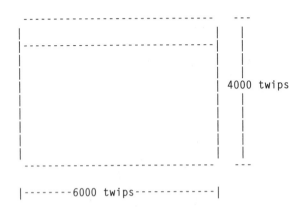

Using ScaleMode, however, we can change the measurement system from twips to, say, centimeters. Or to millimeters. Or, if we wish, to pixels; this is useful for drawing graphics if you want to work pixel by pixel on the screen. The possible ScaleMode values appear in Table 3.3.

TABLE 3.3 SCALEMODE VALUES.

ScaleMode	Meaning
0	Indicates that one or more of the ScaleHeight, ScaleWidth, ScaleLeft, and ScaleTop properties have been set to custom values
1	(Default) Twip (1440 twips per logical inch; 567 twips per logical centimeter)
2	Point (72 points in a logical inch)
3	Pixel (the smallest unit of monitor or printer resolution)
4	Character (horizontal = 120 twips per unit, and vertical = 240 twips per unit)
5	Inch
6	Millimeter
7	Centimeter

Experienced Windows programmers might expect that changing the scale would also change the direction of the positive Y axis from pointing downward (as it does in the Windows MM_TEXT mode) to upward, because this is what happens in C and C++ programs. In fact, that does not happen in Visual Basic programs. The positive Y axis remains downward for all the ScaleMode values 1–7. (Value 0 indicates a custom scale, in which the positive Y axis may point up.)

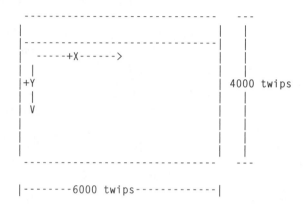

This means that it's easy to change from twips to, say, inches with the simple instruction ScaleMode = 5. From that point on, all measurements will be made in inches when you plot points. For example, the instruction PSet(1440, 1440) with ScaleMode 1 will plot the same point as PSet(1, 1) when the ScaleMode setting is 5 (inches).

Although setting alternative scales can be useful, translating between scales can become confusing if you switch between them often. Visual Basic supplies the ScaleX and ScaleY methods to help programmers here.

The ScaleX and ScaleY Methods

The ScaleX and ScaleY methods allow you to translate measurements from one scale to another. You specify the width or height you want to convert from one scale to another and call ScaleX (for X measurements) or ScaleY (for Y measurements):

```
object.ScaleX (width, FromScale, ToScale)
object.ScaleY (height, FromScale, ToScale)
```

The FromScale and ToScale parameters are constants that represent the scales you want to change from and to, and these constants appear in Table 3.4.

TABLE 3.4 SCALEX AND SCALEY CONSTANTS.

ScaleX/ScaleY Constant	Value	Meaning
vbUser	0	User-defined: indicates that the width or height of object is set to a custom value
vbTwips	1	Twip (1440 twips per logical inch; 567 twips per logical centimeter)
vbPoints	2	Point (72 points per logical inch)
vbPixels	3	Pixel (smallest unit of monitor or printer resolution)
vbCharacters	4	Character (horizontal = 120 twips per unit; vertical = 240 twips per unit)
vbInches	5	Inch
vbMillimeters	6	Millimeter
vbCentimeters	7	Centimeter

We'll have occasion to use ScaleX and ScaleY later in the book when we draw outside our program's window in Chapter 9 and have to translate between our window's twip scale and the screen's pixel scale. Now we'll look into ScaleHeight and ScaleWidth.

ScaleHeight and ScaleWidth

We already know what ScaleHeight and ScaleWidth signify—the internal dimensions of the client area of our window:

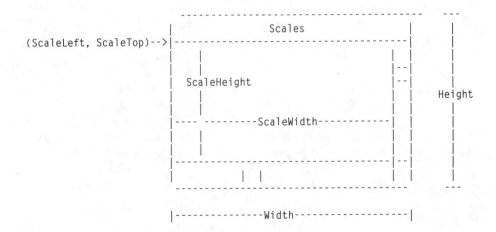

The Width and Height properties of our window give us the external dimensions including scrollbars, toolbars, status bars, and title bars—that is, the external width and height of our window. ScaleWidth and ScaleHeight work differently from Width and Height; when you set the Width and Height properties of a window, you can change its dimensions (the window changes size), but when you change the ScaleWidth and ScaleHeight properties, you're resetting the number of units that the client area is wide or high (the window does not change shape), as we'll see in a moment.

Let's look at an example of using a custom scale to make it clearer why this is useful. The Scale method allows us to change both ScaleWidth and ScaleHeight at the same time, and we'll use that method next.

The Scale Method

Let's say that we're in charge of tracking the fish consumption of a local restaurant by month and that this is the data we want to plot:

```
Month       Fish Consumption (kilos)
-----       ------------------
January     12
February    5
March       17
April       23
May         17
June        9
July        10
August      22
September   5
October     18
November    12
December    14
```

We might start with a program in Visual Basic. Our default window might look like the following, where the Y axis points downward and the unit of measurement (twips) makes the range of our window extend to the thousands:

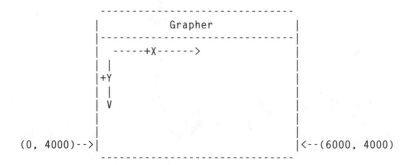

It would be much easier to graph the fish consumption if we had our window set up as shown next. The Y axis points upward, and the window is measured in 12 units horizontally (corresponding to the 12 months) and 25 vertically (allowing us to fit in the entire fish-consumption range, which goes from 5 to 23):

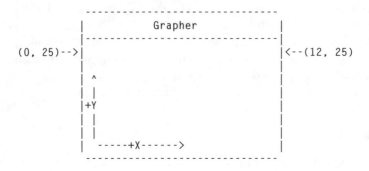

As you can see, plotting fish consumption would be far easier with the second scale than with the first one. We can set the scale this way using the Scale method.

Start a new Visual Basic project named GRAPHER and open the Form_Load event by double-clicking **Form1**. (Also, set AutoRedraw to True.)

```
Private Sub Form_Load()

End Sub
```

First, we'll store our data in an array named FishConsumption:

```
Dim FishConsumption(12) As Integer       <--

Private Sub Form_Load()
--> FishConsumption(1) = 12
--> FishConsumption(2) = 5
--> FishConsumption(3) = 17
--> FishConsumption(4) = 23
--> FishConsumption(5) = 17
--> FishConsumption(6) = 9
--> FishConsumption(7) = 10
--> FishConsumption(8) = 22
--> FishConsumption(9) = 5
--> FishConsumption(10) = 18
--> FishConsumption(11) = 12
--> FishConsumption(12) = 14
          .
          .
          .
```

Next, we can draw axes for our graph and label it "Fish Consumption." (We'll see more about fonts in a moment.)

```
Dim FishConsumption(12) As Integer

Private Sub Form_Load()
    FishConsumption(1) = 12
    FishConsumption(2) = 5
    FishConsumption(3) = 17
    FishConsumption(4) = 23
    FishConsumption(5) = 17
    FishConsumption(6) = 9
    FishConsumption(7) = 10
    FishConsumption(8) = 22
    FishConsumption(9) = 5
    FishConsumption(10) = 18
    FishConsumption(11) = 12
    FishConsumption(12) = 14

--> Line (0.05 * ScaleWidth, 0)-(0.05 * ScaleWidth, 0.9 * ScaleHeight)
--> Line (0.05 * ScaleWidth, 0.9 * ScaleHeight)-(0.95 * ScaleWidth,
-->     0.9 * ScaleHeight)

--> FontSize = 20
--> FontName = "Times New Roman"
--> CurrentX = 0.25 * ScaleWidth
--> CurrentY = 0.9 * ScaleHeight
--> Print ("Consumption of Fish")
        .
        .
        .
```

We already know that our X axis should be able to hold values from 1 to 12 (corresponding to the months). To find our Y range, we find the maximum y value, MaxY%:

```
Const NumberEntries = 12              <--
Dim FishConsumption(12) As Integer

Private Sub Form_Load()
    FishConsumption(1) = 12
        .
        .
        .
    Line (0.05 * ScaleWidth, 0)-(0.05 * ScaleWidth, 0.9 * ScaleHeight)
    Line (0.05 * ScaleWidth, 0.9 * ScaleHeight)-(0.95 * ScaleWidth,
        0.9 * ScaleHeight)

    FontSize = 20
    FontName = "Times New Roman"
```

```
      CurrentX = 0.25 * ScaleWidth
      CurrentY = 0.9 * ScaleHeight
      Print ("Consumption of Fish")

--> MaxY% = 0

--> For loop_index% = 1 To NumberEntries
-->     If FishConsumption(loop_index%) > MaxY% Then
-->         MaxY% = FishConsumption(loop_index%)
-->     End If
--> Next loop_index%
          .
          .
          .
```

Now we're ready to customize the scale of our window. In general, we use the Scale method this way:

```
            Scale (left, top) - (right, bottom)
```

Here, left, top, right, and bottom are the new internal dimensions we want:

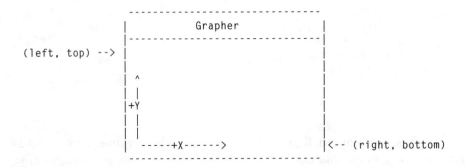

We'll inflate the actual dimensions by 10% to give us an empty border around our graph so that we don't end up plotting points on the extreme edge of the client area:

```
Const NumberEntries = 12
Dim FishConsumption(12) As Integer

Private Sub Form_Load()
    FishConsumption(1) = 12
    FishConsumption(2) = 5

        .
        .
        .

    For loop_index% = 1 To NumberEntries
        If FishConsumption(loop_index%) > MaxY% Then
```

```
          MaxY% = FishConsumption(loop_index%)
      End If
   Next loop_index%

--> Scale (0, 1.1 * MaxY%)-(1.1 * NumberEntries, 0)
       .
       .
       .
```

At this point, our window is set up as shown next, which is much more amenable to the task of plotting fish consumption. (Note that the Y axis points upward.)

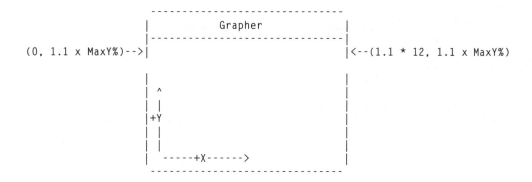

Now that our scale is set up, we put tick marks on our graph's axes and move to the location of our first data point. Setting CurrentX and CurrentY sets the *graphics output position*, and the line that we draw to the next point will begin from that position.

```
Const NumberEntries = 12
Dim FishConsumption(12) As Integer

Private Sub Form_Load()
    FishConsumption(1) = 12
    FishConsumption(2) = 5
       .
       .
       .
--> For loop_index% = 1 To NumberEntries
-->     Line (loop_index%, 0.1 * MaxY%)-(loop_index%, 0.12 * MaxY%)
--> Next loop_index%

--> CurrentX = 1
--> CurrentY = FishConsumption(1)
       .
       .
       .
```

Now we can simply loop over data points, plotting them with the Line method. Using Line as we do next causes it to draw a line from the last graphics output position to the new location we specify, which is exactly what we want as we draw our graph from point to point.

```
Const NumberEntries = 12
Dim FishConsumption(12) As Integer

Private Sub Form_Load()
    FishConsumption(1) = 12
    FishConsumption(2) = 5
        .
        .
        .
    For loop_index% = 1 To NumberEntries
        Line (loop_index%, 0.1 * MaxY%)-(loop_index%, 0.12 * MaxY%)
    Next loop_index%

    CurrentX = 1
    CurrentY = FishConsumption(1)

--> For loop_index% = 1 To NumberEntries
-->     Line -(loop_index%, FishConsumption(loop_index%))
--> Next loop_index%

End Sub
```

Our custom scale program is working. The results appear in Figure 3.12.

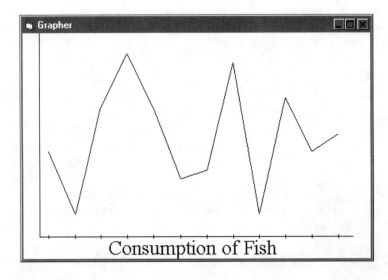

FIGURE 3.12 DRAWING GRAPHS IS EASIER WITH A CUSTOMIZED SCALE OF MEASUREMENT.

GRAPHER.FRM appears in Listing 3.10, and **GRAPHER.VBP** in Listing 3.11.

LISTING 3.10 GRAPHER.FRM

151

```
VERSION 4.00
Begin VB.Form Form1
    AutoRedraw       =   -1   'True
    Caption          =   "Grapher"
    ClientHeight     =   4230
    ClientLeft       =   1095
    ClientTop        =   1515
    ClientWidth      =   6720
    BeginProperty Font
        name         =   "MS Sans Serif"
        charset      =   1
        weight       =   400
        size         =   8.25
        underline    =   0   'False
        italic       =   0   'False
        strikethrough =  0   'False
    EndProperty
    Height           =   4635
    Left             =   1035
    LinkTopic        =   "Form1"
    ScaleHeight      =   4230
    ScaleWidth       =   6720
    Top              =   1170
    Width            =   6840
End
Attribute VB_Name = "Form1"
Attribute VB_Creatable = False
Attribute VB_Exposed = False
Const NumberEntries = 12
Dim FishConsumption(12) As Integer

Private Sub Form_Load()
    FishConsumption(1) = 12
    FishConsumption(2) = 5
    FishConsumption(3) = 17
    FishConsumption(4) = 23
    FishConsumption(5) = 17
    FishConsumption(6) = 9
    FishConsumption(7) = 10
    FishConsumption(8) = 22
    FishConsumption(9) = 5
    FishConsumption(10) = 18
    FishConsumption(11) = 12
    FishConsumption(12) = 14

    Line (0.05 * ScaleWidth, 0)-(0.05 * ScaleWidth, 0.9 * ScaleHeight)
    Line (0.05 * ScaleWidth, 0.9 * ScaleHeight)-(0.95 * ScaleWidth,
        0.9 * ScaleHeight)
```

```
FontSize = 20
FontName = "Times New Roman"
CurrentX = 0.25 * ScaleWidth
CurrentY = 0.9 * ScaleHeight
Print ("Consumption of Fish")

MaxY% = 0

For loop_index% = 1 To NumberEntries
    If FishConsumption(loop_index%) > MaxY% Then
        MaxY% = FishConsumption(loop_index%)
    End If
Next loop_index%

Scale (0, 1.1 * MaxY%)-(1.1 * NumberEntries, 0)

For loop_index% = 1 To NumberEntries
    Line (loop_index%, 0.1 * MaxY%)-(loop_index%, 0.12 * MaxY%)
Next loop_index%

CurrentX = 1
CurrentY = FishConsumption(1)

For loop_index% = 1 To NumberEntries
    Line -(loop_index%, FishConsumption(loop_index%))
Next loop_index%

End Sub
```

LISTING 3.11 GRAPHER.VBP

```
GRAPHER.FRM
Object={F9043C88-F6F2-101A-A3C9-08002B2F49FB}#1.0#0; COMDLG16.OCX
Object={FAEEE763-117E-101B-8933-08002B2F4F5A}#1.0#0; DBLIST16.OCX
ProjWinSize=345,402,202,111
ProjWinShow=2
IconForm="Form1"
ExeName="Project1.exe"
Path="D:\VB"
Command=""
Name="Project1"
HelpContextID="0"
StartMode=0
VersionCompatible="0"
MajorVer=1
MinorVer=0
RevisionVer=0
AutoIncrementVer=0
VersionCompanyName=""
Reference=*\G{00025E01-0000-0000-C000-
000000000046}#0.0#0#DAO2516.DLL#Microsoft DAO 2.5 Object Library
```

Now let's look at another aspect of graphics: fonts.

USING FONTS

In Windows, printing text is treated as producing any other kind of graphics, so let's take a look at some of the graphics techniques used. Create a new project named **FONT.VBP**. If we wanted to fill FONT's window with the message "No Problem.", we could start by placing this code in Form1's Form_Load() event handler:

```
Private Sub Form_Load()
--> data_string$ = "No Problem."
        .
        .
        .
```

All objects that can display text, from text boxes to forms to the Printer object to picture boxes, have a Font property. We'll set the form's Font property to the name of the font we want, Times New Roman:

```
Private Sub Form_Load()
    data_string$ = "No Problem."
--> Font = "Times New Roman"
        .
        .
        .
```

Font sizes are measured in points (1/72nd of an inch), so now we loop over point sizes, selecting for our string the largest point size that will fit into the window horizontally. To determine the width of the string, we use the TextWidth() method:

```
Private Sub Form_Load()
    data_string$ = "No Problem."
    Font = "Times New Roman"
--> For loop_index = 20 To 100
-->     FontSize = loop_index
-->     If TextWidth(data_string$) > ScaleWidth Then
-->         FontSize = loop_index - 1
-->         Exit For
-->     End If
--> Next loop_index
        .
        .
        .
```

Now we've set the font size. Next, we can adjust the height of our window so that it just encloses our text vertically. To do that, we set the Height property of our window (which will resize it). First, we find the height of our window's title bar, then add that to the height of the text (found with the TextHeight method), and finally readjust the window's height accordingly:

```
PrivateHeight = Height - ScaleHeight
--> Height = TextHeight(data_string$) + TitleHeight
        .
        .
        .
```

The last step, now that our window is adjusted, is to print the data string in the window:

```
Private Sub Form_Load()
    data_string$ = "No Problem."
    Font = "Times New Roman"
    For loop_index = 20 To 100
        FontSize = loop_index
        If TextWidth(data_string$) > ScaleWidth Then
            FontSize = loop_index - 1
        Exit For
        End If
    Next loop_index
    TitleHeight = Height - ScaleHeight
    Height = TextHeight(data_string$) + TitleHeight
--> Print data_string$
End Sub
```

The result appears in Figure 3.13. **FONT.FRM** is in Listing 3.12, and **FONT.VBP** is in Listing 3.13. With this program, we've seen how to set a font, determine its height and width, and make our program's window match.

FIGURE 3.13 OUR FONT PROGRAM SHOWS HOW TO SET THE FONT AND DETERMINE ITS WIDTH AND HEIGHT.

LISTING 3.12 FONT.FRM

```
VERSION 4.00
Begin VB.Form Form1
    AutoRedraw      =    -1   'True
    Caption         =    "Form1"
    ClientHeight    =    4230
    ClientLeft      =    1095
    ClientTop       =    1515
    ClientWidth     =    6720
    BeginProperty Font
        name        =    "MS Sans Serif"
        charset     =    1
        weight      =    400
        size        =    8.25
        underline   =    0    'False
        italic      =    0    'False
        strikethrough =  0    'False
    EndProperty
    Height          =    4635
    Left            =    1035
    LinkTopic       =    "Form1"
    ScaleHeight     =    4230
    ScaleWidth      =    6720
    Top             =    1170
    Width           =    6840
End
Attribute VB_Name = "Form1"
Attribute VB_Creatable = False
Attribute VB_Exposed = False
Private Sub Form_Load()
    data_string$ = "No Problem."
    Font = "Times New Roman"
    For loop_index = 20 To 100
        FontSize = loop_index
        If TextWidth(data_string$) > ScaleWidth Then
            FontSize = loop_index - 1
        Exit For
        End If
    Next loop_index
    TitleHeight = Height - ScaleHeight
    Height = TextHeight(data_string$) + TitleHeight
    Print data_string$
End Sub
```

LISTING 3.13 FONT.VBP

```
FONT.FRM
Object={F9043C88-F6F2-101A-A3C9-08002B2F49FB}#1.0#0; COMDLG16.OCX
Object={FAEEE763-117E-101B-8933-08002B2F4F5A}#1.0#0; DBLIST16.OCX
ProjWinSize=345,402,202,111
ProjWinShow=2
ExeName="Project1.exe"
Path="D:\VB"
Command=""
Name="Project1"
HelpContextID="0"
StartMode=0
VersionCompatible="0"
MajorVer=1
MinorVer=0
RevisionVer=0
AutoIncrementVer=0
VersionCompanyName=""
Reference=*\G{00025E01-0000-0000-C000-
000000000046}#0.0#0#DAO2516.DLL#Microsoft DAO 2.5 Object Library
```

JUST FOR FUN

No chapter on graphics would be complete without a figure such as Figure 3.14, which we include just for fun. With some care, you can produce interesting graphics in Visual Basic, and often that process amounts to little more than combining simple elements. This example is just a simple collection of circles, drawn so their centers fall on a single larger circle.

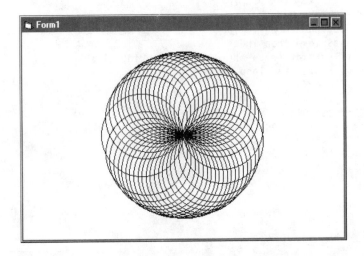

FIGURE 3.14 SOME GRAPHICS FOR FUN.

Here's the code that produces this graphics example:

```
Private Sub Form_Load()
    xorg = ScaleWidth / 2
    yorg = ScaleHeight / 2
    radius = ScaleHeight / 5

    Scale (0, ScaleHeight)-(ScaleWidth, 0)

    For loop_index = -radius To radius Step ScaleWidth / 80
        Circle (loop_index + xorg, (radius ^ 2 - loop_index ^ 2) ^ 0.5
            + yorg), radius, RGB(0, 0, 0)

        Circle (loop_index + xorg, -(radius ^ 2 - loop_index ^ 2) ^ 0.5
            + yorg), radius, RGB(0, 0, 0)
    Next loop_index
End Sub
```

In this way, you can take the simple drawing elements that Visual Basic provides and combine them into an image with powerful impact. Often the best way to create good graphics programming is simply to keep at it. Use the techniques we've learned in this chapter: try different drawing modes, different drawing elements. You can produce extraordinary results. Good luck with your graphics programming.

The code for this example, **FUN.FRM**, is in Listing 3.14; **FUN.VBP** is in Listing 3.15.

LISTING 3.14 FUN.FRM

```
VERSION 4.00
Begin VB.Form Form1
    AutoRedraw      =    -1   'True
    Caption         =    "Form1"
    ClientHeight    =    4230
    ClientLeft      =    1095
    ClientTop       =    1515
    ClientWidth     =    6720
    BeginProperty Font
        name            =    "MS Sans Serif"
        charset         =    1
        weight          =    400
        size            =    8.25
        underline       =    0    'False
        italic          =    0    'False
        strikethrough   =    0    'False
    EndProperty
    Height          =    4635
    Left            =    1035
    LinkTopic       =    "Form1"
```

```
      ScaleHeight    =    4230
      ScaleWidth     =    6720
      Top            =    1170
      Width          =    6840
End
Attribute VB_Name = "Form1"
Attribute VB_Creatable = False
Attribute VB_Exposed = False

Private Sub Form_Load()
    xorg = ScaleWidth / 2
    yorg = ScaleHeight / 2
    radius = ScaleHeight / 5

    Scale (0, ScaleHeight)-(ScaleWidth, 0)

    For loop_index = -radius To radius Step ScaleWidth / 80
        Circle (loop_index + xorg, (radius ^ 2 - loop_index ^ 2) ^ 0.5
        + yorg), radius, RGB(0, 0, 0)

        Circle (loop_index + xorg, -(radius ^ 2 - loop_index ^ 2) ^
        0.5 + yorg), radius, RGB(0, 0, 0)
    Next loop_index
End Sub
```

LISTING 3.15 FUN.VBP

```
FUN.FRM
Object={F9043C88-F6F2-101A-A3C9-08002B2F49FB}#1.0#0; COMDLG16.OCX
Object={FAEEE763-117E-101B-8933-08002B2F4F5A}#1.0#0; DBLIST16.OCX
ProjWinSize=345,402,202,111
ProjWinShow=2
ExeName="Project1.exe"
Path="D:\VB"
Command=""
Name="Project1"
HelpContextID="0"
StartMode=0
VersionCompatible="0"
MajorVer=1
MinorVer=0
RevisionVer=0
AutoIncrementVer=0
VersionCompanyName=""
Reference=*\G{00025E01-0000-0000-C000-
000000000046}#0.0#0#DAO2516.DLL#Microsoft DAO 2.5 Object Library
```

That's it for our graphics chapter. In the next chapter, we turn to another popular Visual Basic topic: advanced form and control handling.

## CHAPTER 4

ADVANCED FORM
AND CONTROL HANDLING

In this chapter, we'll see how to work with forms and controls in ways that surpass the ordinary, giving us a great deal of programming power. For example, we'll pass forms and controls as arguments to subroutines, allowing us the capability of working with them flexibly in code (for example, we might need to write only one subroutine to handle many windows). We'll see how to let the user drag controls around the window using the mouse—in particular, we'll see how to create a puzzle in which the user can reassemble the pieces of an image of a fish. We'll see how to create and display new controls as a program is running. No longer will we have to design all our controls before the program runs: now we'll be able to add controls as needed. If we need text input, for example, we can simply create and display a new text box. We'll see how to determine a control's type in code. We'll also see how to create pop-up menus. And more. Let's begin by passing forms as arguments to subroutines.

PASSING FORMS TO SUBROUTINES

Let's say that we have a program that maintains four windows:

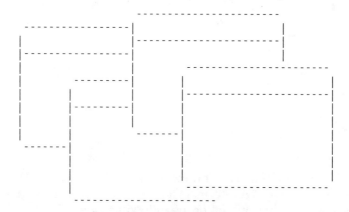

And let's say that we want to draw in each of these windows. We might want to draw a grid in each window, giving the windows the appearance of being tiled. To draw a grid in each window, we might write a single subroutine, named Tile(), that will draw the grid in any form we pass to it. In this way, we need only one subroutine to handle all the windows, an improvement over having to duplicate the subroutine in each of the windows separately.

Start Visual Basic and create a new project named **TILER.VBP**. Select the **Insert | New Form** menu item three times, adding the new forms Form2, Form3, and Form4 to our program. Now open Form1's code window and open the Form_Click() event handler from the code window's Proc box (from **FORM1.FRM**):

```
Private Sub Form_Click()

End Sub
```

When the user clicks our first window (which is the only one visible when the program starts), we will display the other three windows:

```
Private Sub Form_Click()
--> Form2.Show
--> Form3.Show
--> Form4.Show
        .
        .
        .
End Sub
```

Next, we can tile all the windows by creating a new subroutine named Tile(). We will add this new subroutine to Form1 only. To use Tile(), we'll add this code to pass all our forms to that subroutine so that it can draw in them:

```
Private Sub Form_Click()
    Form2.Show
    Form3.Show
    Form4.Show
--> Tile Form1
--> Tile Form2
--> Tile Form3
--> Tile Form4
End Sub
```

Now, in the Form1 (general) area of the code window create Tile() and give it one parameter, declared "As Form." Click outside the Form_Click() subroutine in the code window and enter the following code:

```
Sub Tile(AForm As Form)          <--

End Sub                          <--
```

Inside Tile(), we will now be able to refer to the form passed to us as AForm (the name we've given Tile()'s parameter). For example, we might tile each window with a grid of lines one centimeter apart, in which case we will set the form's ScaleMode to 7, the Centimeters ScaleMode, using this new code (after first saving its original ScaleMode):

```
Sub Tile(AForm As Form)
--> old_scalemode = AForm.ScaleMode
--> AForm.ScaleMode = 7
        .
        .
        .
End Sub
```

Next, we simply draw the grid, tiling the form passed to us. To do that, we use the form's ScaleHeight and ScaleWidth properties as discussed in the last chapter, and we use the form's Line method to draw the grid:

```
Sub Tile(AForm As Form)
    old_scalemode = AForm.ScaleMode
    AForm.ScaleMode = 7
--> For loop_index% = 1 To AForm.ScaleHeight
-->     AForm.Line (0, loop_index%)-(AForm.ScaleWidth, loop_index%)
--> Next loop_index%
--> For loop_index% = 1 To AForm.ScaleWidth
-->     AForm.Line (loop_index%, 0)-(loop_index%, AForm.ScaleHeight)
--> Next loop_index%
        .
        .
        .
End Sub
```

Finally, we reset the form's ScaleMode to its original value:

```
Sub Tile(AForm As Form)
    old_scalemode = AForm.ScaleMode
    AForm.ScaleMode = 7
    For loop_index% = 1 To AForm.ScaleHeight
        AForm.Line (0, loop_index%)-(AForm.ScaleWidth, loop_index%)
    Next loop_index%
    For loop_index% = 1 To AForm.ScaleWidth
        AForm.Line (loop_index%, 0)-(loop_index%, AForm.ScaleHeight)
    Next loop_index%
--> AForm.ScaleMode = old_scalemode
End Sub
```

That's it—we've completed our Tile() subroutine, which takes forms as arguments. Run the program and click **Form1** when it appears, displaying and tiling the other forms, as shown in Figure 4.1. The TILER program is a success—now we can pass forms as arguments to subroutines.

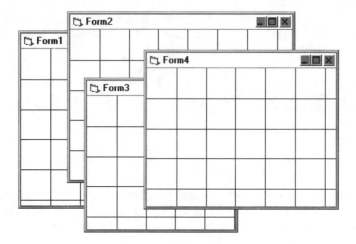

FIGURE 4.1 THE TILE() SUBROUTINE TAKES FORMS AS ARGUMENTS AND DRAWS A GRID IN EACH OF THEM.

The code for **FORM1.FRM** appears in Listing 4.1, and the code for **TILER.VBP** in Listing 4.2.

LISTING 4.1 (TILER) FORM1.FRM

```
VERSION 4.00
Begin VB.Form Form1
   AutoRedraw      =    -1   'True
   Caption         =    "Form1"
   ClientHeight    =    4230
   ClientLeft      =    1095
   ClientTop       =    1515
   ClientWidth     =    6720
   BeginProperty Font
      name              =    "MS Sans Serif"
      charset           =    1
      weight            =    400
      size              =    8.25
      underline         =    0    'False
      italic            =    0    'False
      strikethrough     =    0    'False
   EndProperty
   Height          =    4635
   Left            =    1035
```

```
   LinkTopic        =    "Form1"
   ScaleHeight      =    4230
   ScaleWidth       =    6720
   Top              =    1170
   Width            =    6840
End
Attribute VB_Name = "Form1"
Attribute VB_Creatable = False
Attribute VB_Exposed = False

Sub Tile(AForm As Form)
    old_scalemode = AForm.ScaleMode
    AForm.ScaleMode = 7
    For loop_index% = 1 To AForm.ScaleHeight
        AForm.Line (0, loop_index%)-(AForm.ScaleWidth, loop_index%)
    Next loop_index%
    For loop_index% = 1 To AForm.ScaleWidth
        AForm.Line (loop_index%, 0)-(loop_index%, AForm.ScaleHeight)
    Next loop_index%
    AForm.ScaleMode = old_scalemode
End Sub

Private Sub Form_Click()
    Form2.Show
    Form3.Show
    Form4.Show
    Tile Form1
    Tile Form2
    Tile Form3
    Tile Form4
End Sub
```

LISTING 4.2 TILER.VBP

```
FORM1.FRM
FORM2.FRM
FORM3.FRM
FORM4.FRM
Object={F9043C88-F6F2-101A-A3C9-08002B2F49FB}#1.0#0; COMDLG16.OCX
Object={FAEEE763-117E-101B-8933-08002B2F4F5A}#1.0#0; DBLIST16.OCX
ProjWinSize=345,402,202,111
ProjWinShow=2
ExeName="Project1.exe"
Path="D:\VB"
Command=""
Name="Project1"
HelpContextID="0"
StartMode=0
VersionCompatible="0"
MajorVer=1
MinorVer=0
```

```
RevisionVer=0
AutoIncrementVer=0
VersionCompanyName=""
Reference=*\G{00025E01-0000-0000-C000-
000000000046}#0.0#0#DAO2516.DLL#Microsoft DAO 2.5 Object Library
```

PASSING CONTROLS AS ARGUMENTS

In our next example, we'll pass controls as arguments to a subroutine. In this case, our example will be an MDI tic-tac-toe game for two players. When you start the game, an MDI child window appears with nine command buttons corresponding to the nine positions in tic-tac-toe:

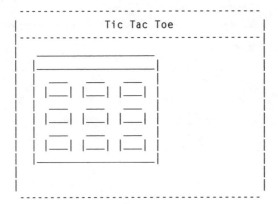

When users click a button, we'll pass the entire button to a subroutine named SetXO(), which will set alternating *x*'s and *o*'s as the clicked button's captions:

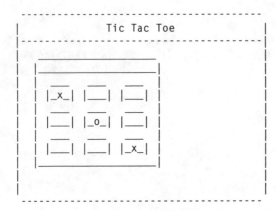

Passing the entire button to a subroutine that sets its caption this way means that we don't have to duplicate the subroutine in each button's code. Instead, all we need is one subroutine.

Start this project now, calling it **TICTAC.VBP**. Insert a new MDI Form (MDIForm1) using the **Insert MDI Form** menu item, and set Form1's MDIChild property to True in the properties window. Next, draw the nine command buttons in Form1, as shown in Figure 4.2, and set their Caption properties to empty strings, "".

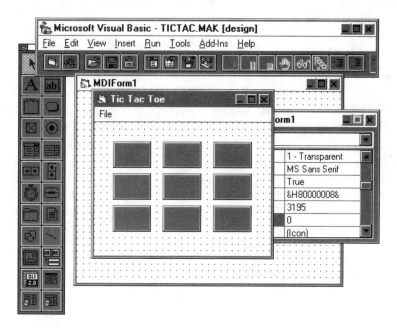

FIGURE 4.2 WE DESIGN OUR **TICTAC** GAME.

In addition, select each of the nine buttons and change their Name property in the properties window from Button1, Button2, Button3, and so on to TicTac. As soon as you try to name two or more buttons TicTac, Visual Basic will display a message box asking whether you want to set up a control array. Answer **yes**.

Control Arrays

Because control arrays come under the heading of advanced control handling, we will review them here. When you give all nine command buttons the same Name property (TicTac), Visual Basic places them in a control array and assigns each of them an Index property in that array. If there were only one button named TicTac, its Click event handler subroutine would look like this:

```
Private Sub TicTac_Click()

End Sub
```

However, because there are nine buttons named TicTac, Visual Basic also passes an Index parameter to TicTac_Click() to indicate which of the nine buttons was clicked:

```
Private Sub TicTac_Click(Index As Integer)        <--

End Sub
```

We'll use this Index parameter in a minute, when we pass the clicked button to the subroutine SetXO(), which will set its Caption property to **x** or **o**.

Now that our control array of buttons is ready, use the Menu Editor to add a File menu to Form1 and place two items in it: **New Window** (Name property: New) and **Exit** (Name property: Exit). We can add the correct code for these two menu items immediately: when users select **Exit**, they want to quit. When users select **New Window**, we should pop up a new MDI child window on the screen, as we've seen how to do in Chapter 2. The following code comes from **TICTAC.FRM**.

```
Private Sub Exit_Click()
    End
End Sub

Private Sub New_Click()
--> Dim NewTicTacForm As New Form1
--> NewTicTacForm.Show
End Sub
```

Now let's look at the process of setting alternating **x**'s and **o**'s in our buttons as they're clicked. To toggle between **x** and **o**, we set up a Boolean flag named XFlag and set it to True when this window loads in the Form_Load() event. Click **Form1** to bring up the Form_Load() event (from **TICTAC.FRM**):

```
Dim XFlag As Boolean             <--

Private Sub Exit_Click()
    End
End Sub
```

```
Private Sub Form_Load()          <--
    XFlag = True                 <--
End Sub                          <--

Private Sub New_Click()
    Dim NewTicTacForm As New Form1
    NewTicTacForm.Show
End Sub
```

Because we can have open a number of tic-tac-toe MDI child windows, we leave XFlag as a private variable in each window. In window 1, the next character to display may be **x**, and in window 2, the next character to display may be **o**, so each MDI child window should have its own XFlag variable to keep track of which letter, **x** or **o**, to draw next:

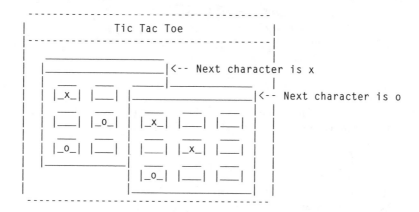

When the user clicks a button, the associated Click subroutine is called. Create that subroutine in Form1's code window using the Proc box:

```
Dim XFlag As Boolean

Private Sub Exit_Click()
    End
End Sub

Private Sub Form_Load()
    XFlag = True
End Sub

Private Sub New_Click()
    Dim NewTicTacForm As New Form1
    NewTicTacForm.Show
End Sub
```

```
Private Sub TicTac_Click(Index As Integer)      <--

End Sub                                         <--
```

At this point, we want to set the caption of the clicked button to **x** (if XFlag = True) or to **o** (if XFlag = False). We do that by passing to the subroutine SetXO() the current button, which is TicTac(Index) (a member of our control array), as well as the current setting of XFlag. The subroutine SetXO() sets the button's caption:

```
Private Sub New_Click()
    Dim NewTicTacForm As New Form1
    NewTicTacForm.Show
End Sub

Private Sub TicTac_Click(Index As Integer)
--> SetXO TicTac(Index), XFlag

        .
        .
        .

End Sub
```

Finally, we toggle XFlag using the Not operator (which toggles Boolean variables between True and False) so that we'll draw the other character (**x** or **o**) next time:

```
Private Sub New_Click()
    Dim NewTicTacForm As New Form1
    NewTicTacForm.Show
End Sub

Private Sub TicTac_Click(Index As Integer)
    SetXO TicTac(Index), XFlag
--> XFlag = Not XFlag
End Sub
```

To let all MDI child windows reach the code in the SetXO() subroutine, we place it in a new module, **MODULE1.BAS**. Create that module using the **Insert | Module** menu item, and create SetXO() in it by typing the following code in **MODULE.BAS**. (Note that we declare this subroutine Public to make it accessible from each MDI child window.)

```
Public Sub SetXO(AControl As Control, XFlag As Boolean)

End Sub
```

Here we are informing Visual Basic that we expect a parameter to be passed to us here that represents a control—that is, AControl is declared "As Control." Inside our subroutine, we'll be able to refer to the button passed to us as AControl. We first check to see whether that button has already been clicked (in which case we should not change its Caption property again):

```
Public Sub SetXO(AControl As Control, XFlag As Boolean)
--> If AControl.Caption <> "" Then Exit Sub
          .
          .
          .
End Sub
```

If the button's Caption property has not yet been set, we set it according to whether XFlag is True:

```
Public Sub SetXO(AControl As Control, XFlag As Boolean)
    If AControl.Caption <> "" Then Exit Sub
--> If XFlag Then
-->     AControl.Caption = "x"
          .
          .
          .
End Sub
```

or False:

```
Public Sub SetXO(AControl As Control, XFlag As Boolean)
    If AControl.Caption <> "" Then Exit Sub
    If XFlag Then
        AControl.Caption = "x"
--> Else
-->     AControl.Caption = "o"
--> End If
End Sub
```

We've passed a control as a parameter to this subroutine and have worked with it in code. Run the program and click a few buttons, as shown in Figure 4.3. The appropriate characters—**x**'s and **o**'s—will appear. We're passing controls to subroutines, and TICTAC is a success.

The code for **TICTAC.FRM** appears in Listing 4.3, **MODULE1.BAS** appears in Listing 4.4, and **TICTAC.VBP** appears in Listing 4.5.

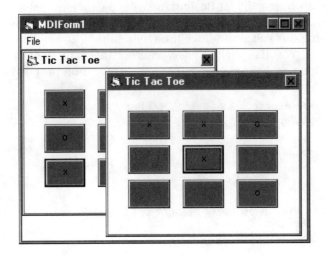

FIGURE 4.3 OUR TICTAC PROGRAM PASSES CONTROLS TO A SUBROUTINE TO SET THE BUTTONS TO X OR O.

LISTING 4.3 TICTAC.FRM

```
VERSION 4.00
Begin VB.Form Form1
    BorderStyle     =   3   'Fixed Double
    Caption         =   "Tic Tac Toe"
    ClientHeight    =   2505
    ClientLeft      =   1095
    ClientTop       =   1800
    ClientWidth     =   3390
    BeginProperty Font
        name            =   "MS Sans Serif"
        charset         =   1
        weight          =   400
        size            =   8.25
        underline       =   0   'False
        italic          =   0   'False
        strikethrough   =   0   'False
    EndProperty
    Height          =   3195
    Left            =   1035
    LinkTopic       =   "Form1"
    MDIChild        =   -1  'True
    ScaleHeight     =   2505
    ScaleWidth      =   3390
    Top             =   1170
```

```
Width            =    3510
Begin VB.CommandButton TicTac
   Height        =    495
   Index         =    1
   Left          =    1320
   TabIndex      =    8
   Top           =    360
   Width         =    735
End
Begin VB.CommandButton TicTac
   Height        =    495
   Index         =    8
   Left          =    2280
   TabIndex      =    7
   Top           =    1560
   Width         =    735
End
Begin VB.CommandButton TicTac
   Height        =    495
   Index         =    7
   Left          =    1320
   TabIndex      =    6
   Top           =    1560
   Width         =    735
End
Begin VB.CommandButton TicTac
   Height        =    495
   Index         =    6
   Left          =    360
   TabIndex      =    5
   Top           =    1560
   Width         =    735
End
Begin VB.CommandButton TicTac
   Height        =    495
   Index         =    5
   Left          =    2280
   TabIndex      =    4
   Top           =    960
   Width         =    735
End
Begin VB.CommandButton TicTac
   Height        =    495
   Index         =    4
   Left          =    1320
   TabIndex      =    3
   Top           =    960
   Width         =    735
End
```

```
Begin VB.CommandButton TicTac
    Height          =   495
    Index           =   3
    Left            =   360
    TabIndex        =   2
    Top             =   960
    Width           =   735
End
Begin VB.CommandButton TicTac
    Height          =   495
    Index           =   2
    Left            =   2280
    TabIndex        =   1
    Top             =   360
    Width           =   735
End
Begin VB.CommandButton TicTac
    Height          =   495
    Index           =   0
    Left            =   360
    TabIndex        =   0
    Top             =   360
    Width           =   735
End
Begin VB.Menu File
    Caption         =   "File"
    Begin VB.Menu New
        Caption         =   "New Window"
    End
    Begin VB.Menu Exit
        Caption         =   "Exit"
    End
End
End
Attribute VB_Name = "Form1"
Attribute VB_Creatable = False
Attribute VB_Exposed = False
Dim XFlag As Boolean

Private Sub Exit_Click()
    End
End Sub

Private Sub Form_Load()
    XFlag = True
End Sub
```

```
Private Sub New_Click()
    Dim NewTicTacForm As New Form1
    NewTicTacForm.Show
End Sub

Private Sub TicTac_Click(Index As Integer)
    SetXO TicTac(Index), XFlag
    XFlag = Not XFlag
End Sub
```

173

Listing 4.4 MODULE1.BAS

```
Attribute VB_Name = "Module1"

Public Sub SetXO(AControl As Control, XFlag As Boolean)
    If AControl.Caption <> "" Then Exit Sub
    If XFlag Then
        AControl.Caption = "x"
    Else
        AControl.Caption = "o"
    End If
End Sub
```

Listing 4.5 TICTAC.VBP

```
TICTAC.FRM
MDIFORM1.FRM
MODULE1.BAS
Object={F9043C88-F6F2-101A-A3C9-08002B2F49FB}#1.0#0; COMDLG16.OCX
Object={FAEEE763-117E-101B-8933-08002B2F4F5A}#1.0#0; DBLIST16.OCX
ProjWinSize=345,402,202,111
ProjWinShow=2
ExeName="Project1.exe"
Path="D:\VB"
Command=""
Name="Project1"
HelpContextID="0"
StartMode=0
VersionCompatible="0"
MajorVer=1
MinorVer=0
RevisionVer=0
AutoIncrementVer=0
VersionCompanyName=""
Reference=*\G{00025E01-0000-0000-C000-
000000000046}#0.0#0#DAO2516.DLL#Microsoft DAO 2.5 Object Library
```

Next, we'll see how to determine which control is active, or has the input focus, in a Visual Basic program. Recall from Chapter 1 that the control that has the input focus is the target of key strokes.

DETERMINING CONTROL TYPE AND DETERMINING WHICH CONTROL IS ACTIVE

In our next program, we'll see how to work with controls outside their Click() or Change() events. For example, suppose we have a program, named RESET, that contains a number of text boxes and command buttons:

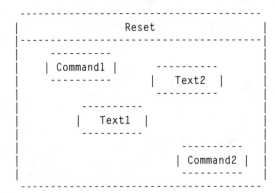

We might let the user "reset" the Caption or Text properties of these controls to "", clearing the text in them. That is straightforward in, say, a click event, which might look like this:

```
Private Sub Command1_Click()
    Text = ""
End Sub
```

When the user clicks this button, its Caption will be cleared. However, what if we wanted to let the user clear the text in a control by selecting a menu item? For example, the user could give the focus to one of the controls (making it the currently active control) and select a **Reset Control** menu item:

```
-----------------------------------------
|                  Reset                  |
|-----------------------------------------|
| File                                    |
|-----       -------------------------    |
  -->   ||Reset Control |                 |
        ||End           |    ----------   |
        | ------------          | Text2 |  |
        |                       ----------  |
        |          ----------               |
        |         |  Text1  |               |
        |          ----------               |
        |                   ----------      |
        |                  | Command2 |  |  |
        |                   ----------      |
-----------------------------------------
```

To clear the text in the control, we'll first have to determine which control has the focus. In addition to clearing the Caption property of the control buttons, we have to clear the Text property of the text boxes' so in addition to determining which control is active, we have to determine what type of control it is before clearing its text. Let's see how this works in code.

Create a new program named RESET. Give this program a File menu with two items: **Reset Control** (Name property: Reset) and **End** (Name property: End). We will make this an MDI program; set Form1's MDIChild property to True and insert a new MDI form.

Open the **Exit** menu item's Click event handler in the code window and add the required End statement as we always do for this item (from **RESET.FRM**):

```
Private Sub Exit_Click()
    End           <--
End Sub
```

Next, open the **Reset Control** menu item's Click event handler in the code window by clicking that menu item (from **RESET.FRM**):

```
Private Sub Reset_Click()

End Sub
```

Because this is an MDI program, the subroutine that clears the text is placed in a control in a shared module; name that subroutine ResetControl(). In Reset_Click(), we call that subroutine:

```
Private Sub Reset_Click()
--> ResetControl
End Sub
```

Next, insert a new module (**MODULE1.BAS**) into the program and add it to the Public subroutine ResetControl() by typing in this code (from **MODULE1.BAS**):

```
Public Sub ResetControl()        <--

End Sub                          <--
```

When we reach this subroutine, our task is to clear the text in the control that has the focus. At any one time, only one control is active on the screen (there is only one input focus), and we can determine which control it is by referring to it as Screen.ActiveControl. Here we use the Visual Basic Screen object (a useful object, especially if you want to determine the screen dimension in pixels) and check its ActiveControl property. That property holds the control with the active focus.

We still need to know whether we should clear the control's Caption property (for command buttons) or its Text property (for text boxes). We can determine the type of control with the TypeOf keyword. We add this code to check whether the type of the active control is a text box:

```
Public Sub ResetControl()
--> If TypeOf Screen.ActiveControl Is TextBox Then
        .
        .
        .
End Sub
```

We can use the Is keyword in Visual Basic to compare two objects:

```
        If First_Object Is Second_Object Then
            MsgBox("The objects are the same")
        End If
```

In our ResetControl() subroutine, we check to see whether the type of the active control equals TextBox. We can compare the type of that control to other types, such as ListBox, PictureBox, CommandButton, and so on. In our case, if the active control is a text box, we can reset its Text property to the empty string:

```
Public Sub ResetControl()
    If TypeOf Screen.ActiveControl Is TextBox Then
-->     Screen.ActiveControl.Text = ""
    End If
End Sub
```

On the other hand, if the control is a command button, we reset its Caption property by adding this code:

```
Public Sub ResetControl()
    If TypeOf Screen.ActiveControl Is TextBox Then
        Screen.ActiveControl.Text = ""
    End If

--> If TypeOf Screen.ActiveControl Is CommandButton Then
-->     Screen.ActiveControl.Caption = ""
--> End If
End Sub
```

That's it—now we can work with controls outside their own event handlers (and even outside the window that contains them). Run the program and select a control. Next, select **Reset Control**. The program will clear the selected control's text, as shown in Figure 4.4.

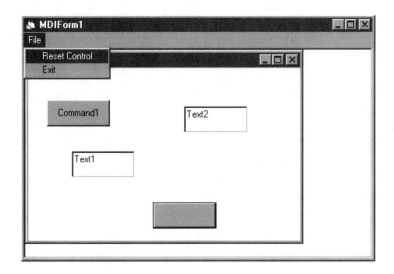

FIGURE 4.4 THE RESET PROGRAM DETERMINES WHICH CONTROL IS ACTIVE
AND WHAT ITS TYPE IS AND THEN CLEARS ITS TEXT.

The code for this program appears in these listings: Listing 4.6 (**RESET.FRM**), Listing 4.7 (**MODULE1.BAS**), Listing 4.8 (**MDIFORM1.FRM**), and Listing 4.9 (**RESET.VBP**).

LISTING 4.6 RESET.FRM

```
VERSION 4.00
Begin VB.Form Form1
   Caption          =    "Reset"
   ClientHeight     =    4230
   ClientLeft       =    1095
   ClientTop        =    1800
   ClientWidth      =    6720
   BeginProperty Font
      name             =    "MS Sans Serif"
      charset          =    1
      weight           =    400
      size             =    8.25
      underline        =    0      'False
      italic           =    0      'False
      strikethrough    =    0      'False
   EndProperty
   Height           =    4920
   Left             =    1035
   LinkTopic        =    "Form1"
   MDIChild         =    -1     'True
   ScaleHeight      =    4230
   ScaleWidth       =    6720
   Top              =    1170
   Width            =    6840
   Begin VB.TextBox Text2
      Height           =    495
      Left             =    3000
      TabIndex         =    3
      Text             =    "Text2"
      Top              =    480
      Width            =    1215
   End
   Begin VB.CommandButton Command2
      Caption          =    "Command2"
      Height           =    495
      Left             =    2760
      TabIndex         =    2
      Top              =    1920
      Width            =    1215
   End
   Begin VB.TextBox Text1
      Height           =    495
      Left             =    1440
      TabIndex         =    1
      Text             =    "Text1"
      Top              =    1800
      Width            =    1215
   End
```

```
    Begin VB.CommandButton Command1
        Caption         =   "Command1"
        Height          =   495
        Left            =   1080
        TabIndex        =   0
        Top             =   840
        Width           =   1215
    End
    Begin VB.Menu File
        Caption         =   "File"
        Begin VB.Menu Reset
            Caption         =   "Reset Control"
        End
        Begin VB.Menu Exit
            Caption         =   "Exit"
        End
    End
End
Attribute VB_Name = "Form1"
Attribute VB_Creatable = False
Attribute VB_Exposed = False
Private Sub Exit_Click()
    End
End Sub


Private Sub Reset_Click()
    ResetControl
End Sub
```

LISTING 4.7 (RESET) MODULE1.BAS

```
Attribute VB_Name = "Module1"
Public Sub ResetControl()
    If TypeOf Screen.ActiveControl Is TextBox Then
        Screen.ActiveControl.Text = ""
    End If

    If TypeOf Screen.ActiveControl Is CommandButton Then
        Screen.ActiveControl.Caption = ""
    End If
End Sub
```

LISTING 4.8 (RESET) MDIFORM1.FRM

```
VERSION 4.00
Begin VB.MDIForm MDIForm1
    BackColor       =   &H8000000C&
    Caption         =   "MDIForm1"
    ClientHeight    =   4230
    ClientLeft      =   1095
    ClientTop       =   1515
```

```
ClientWidth    =   6720
Height         =   4635
Left           =   1035
LinkTopic      =   "MDIForm1"
Top            =   1170
Width          =   6840
End
Attribute VB_Name = "MDIForm1"
Attribute VB_Creatable = False
Attribute VB_Exposed = False
```

LISTING 4.9 RESET.VBP

```
RESET.FRM
MODULE1.BAS
MDIFORM1.FRM
Object={F9043C88-F6F2-101A-A3C9-08002B2F49FB}#1.0#0; COMDLG16.OCX
Object={FAEEE763-117E-101B-8933-08002B2F4F5A}#1.0#0; DBLIST16.OCX
ProjWinSize=345,402,202,111
ProjWinShow=2
IconForm="Form1"
ExeName="Project1.exe"
Command=""
Name="Project1"
HelpContextID="0"
StartMode=0
VersionCompatible="0"
MajorVer=1
MinorVer=0
RevisionVer=0
AutoIncrementVer=0
VersionCompanyName=""
Reference=*\G{00025E01-0000-0000-C000-
000000000046}#0.0#0#DAO2516.DLL#Microsoft DAO 2.5 Object Library
```

Next, we'll take a look at letting the user drag and drop controls in our program as it is running.

DRAGGING AND DROPPING CONTROLS

Our next program will allow the user to drag controls around on the screen. We'll create a puzzle in which the user can drag the pieces into position using the mouse. Create the project **PUZZLE.VBP**. Using Windows Paint, we draw a picture of a fish and divide it into four pieces, storing them as **FISH1.BMP**, **FISH2.BMP**, **FISH3.BMP**, and **FISH4.BMP**. Next, create four picture boxes in the PUZZLE program's Form1: Picture1, Picture2, Picture3, and Picture4. Load the **.BMP** files into those picture boxes, as shown in Figure 4.5. Set their Picture properties to **FISH1.BMP**, **FISH2.BMP**, and so on as we saw in the last chapter.

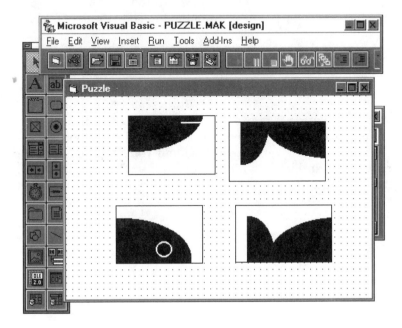

FIGURE 4.5 OUR PUZZLE PROGRAM IS A PUZZLE OF A FISH.

Like many other controls, picture boxes have a DragMode property. If we set that property to 1, Automatic DragDrop, the user will be able to drag and drop the picture box using the mouse. This sounds like that we want, except for one thing: when you set a control's DragMode property to Automatic, it can no longer respond to mouse events. This is a problem, because it means that we cannot determine where in the puzzle piece the mouse cursor was when the button was pressed. The user can drag a puzzle piece and then drop it, and we'll get the location of the drop point, but then we'll have no option except to set the upper-left corner of the puzzle piece to the mouse location when the puzzle piece is dropped (because we don't know where the mouse cursor was inside the puzzle piece). For example, if the user placed the mouse cursor in the middle of the puzzle piece, moved it, and then dropped it, he or she would see the piece jump so that the upper-left corner of the piece appears under the mouse cursor. The user expected the middle of the piece to remain there.

This problem is solved if we record the location in the puzzle piece at which the mouse button was pressed. To do that, we need to use the puzzle piece's MouseDown() event handler. This means that we have to leave mouse events enabled, which in turn means that we have to leave the DragDrop property at 0 (manual dragging). In the code window, create the subroutine Picture1_MouseDown() from the Proc box (from **PUZZLE.FRM**):

```
Private Sub Picture1_MouseDown(Button As Integer, Shift As Integer, x
        As Single, y As Single)

End Sub
```

When the mouse button is clicked in a puzzle piece, we'll record the offset of the mouse position with respect to the upper-left corner of the puzzle piece by adding the new variables xoffset and yoffset. (The X and Y coordinates passed to us in Picture1_MouseDown() are with respect to the upper-left corner of Picture1.)

```
Dim xoffset As Integer          <--
Dim yoffset As Integer          <--

Private Sub Picture1_MouseDown(Button As Integer, Shift As Integer, x
        As Single, y As Single)
--> xoffset = x
--> yoffset = y
        .
        .
        .
End Sub
```

Next, we enable dragging, just as if the DragDrop property had been set to Automatic, by calling the picture box's Drag method with an argument of 1 (which enables dragging):

```
Dim xoffset As Integer
Dim yoffset As Integer

Private Sub Picture1_MouseDown(Button As Integer, Shift As Integer, x
        As Single, y As Single)
    xoffset = x
    yoffset = y
--> Picture1.Drag 1
End Sub
```

Now users can move the puzzle piece around with the mouse. When they drop the piece, a DragDrop event occurs. For example, the user may drop the piece on the form, which we can handle with a Form_DragDrop() event handler. Using the code window's Proc box, add this subroutine to Form1 (from **PUZZLE.FRM**):

```
Dim xoffset As Integer
Dim yoffset As Integer

Private Sub Picture1_MouseDown(Button As Integer, Shift As Integer, x
        As Single, y As Single)
    xoffset = x
    yoffset = y
    Picture1.Drag 1
End Sub

Private Sub Form_DragDrop(Source As Control, x As Single, y As Single) <--

End Sub                 <--
```

The location where the user dropped the puzzle piece is passed to us as (x, y), and the picture box that was dragged is passed to us as the argument Source. We can move the picture box to its new location using the Move method. (Note: although the user has dragged the picture box and dropped it, the program does not automatically move the picture box to its new location. That action is left to us, because the user may have moved the picture box to a location we consider forbidden.)

```
Private Sub Form_DragDrop(Source As Control, x As Single, y As Single)
--> Source.Move x - xoffset, y - yoffset
End Sub
```

We did not simply move the picture box to the location of the drop: (x, y). Instead, we took into account the fact that the mouse cursor was probably not at the exact upper-left corner of the puzzle piece when the drag began; it was actually at the location in the piece we stored as (xoffset, yoffset). We correct for the mouse offset inside the puzzle piece by dropping the piece at (x – xoffset, y – yoffset).

If the user drops a picture box on another picture box, it's slightly more complicated. The (x, y) location we get in, say, Picture1_DragDrop() is the location of the drop point inside the picture box—relative to the upper-left corner of the picture box, and not to the form. This means that before setting the new location of the dropped picture box in the form as a whole, we have to add Picture1.Left to the X coordinate we get, and Picture1.Top to the Y coordinate. (Create Picture1_DragDrop() from the code window's Proc box.)

```
Private Sub Picture1_DragDrop(Source As Control, x As Single, y As Single)
--> Source.Move Picture1.Left + x - xoffset, Picture1.Top + y - yoffset
End Sub
```

All we have to do now is to repeat the code we've developed for Picture1 for the other picture boxes (from **PUZZLE.FRM**):

```
Dim xoffset As Integer
Dim yoffset As Integer

Private Sub Picture1_DragDrop(Source As Control, x As Single, y As
Single)
    Source.Move Picture1.Left + x - xoffset, Picture1.Top + y - yoffset
End Sub

Private Sub Picture1_MouseDown(Button As Integer, Shift As Integer, x
        As Single, y As Single)
    xoffset = x
    yoffset = y
    Picture1.Drag 1
End Sub

Private Sub Picture2_DragDrop(Source As Control, x As Single, y As
Single)
    Source.Move Picture2.Left + x - xoffset, Picture2.Top + y - yoffset
End Sub

Private Sub Picture2_MouseDown(Button As Integer, Shift As Integer, x
        As Single, y As Single)
    xoffset = x
    yoffset = y
    Picture2.Drag 1
End Sub

Private Sub Picture3_DragDrop(Source As Control, x As Single, y As
Single)
    Source.Move Picture3.Left + x - xoffset, Picture3.Top + y - yoffset
End Sub

Private Sub Picture3_MouseDown(Button As Integer, Shift As Integer, x
        As Single, y As Single)
    xoffset = x
    yoffset = y
    Picture3.Drag 1
End Sub

Private Sub Picture4_DragDrop(Source As Control, x As Single, y As
Single)
    Source.Move Picture4.Left + x - xoffset, Picture4.Top + y - yoffset
End Sub

Private Sub Picture4_MouseDown(Button As Integer, Shift As Integer, x
        As Single, y As Single)
    xoffset = x
    yoffset = y
    Picture4.Drag 1
End Sub
```

When users run this program, they will be able to drag and drop the puzzle pieces using the mouse, as shown in Figure 4.6. At this point, then, we're able to drag and drop controls at run time (most controls have a DragDrop method). PUZZLE is a success.

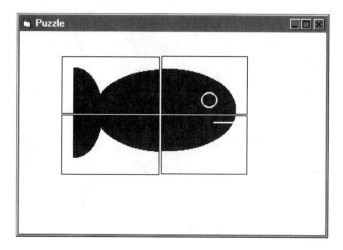

FIGURE 4.6 OUR PUZZLE PROGRAM LETS THE USER USE THE MOUSE TO REARRANGE PUZZLE PIECES.

The code for this program, **PUZZLE.FRM**, appears in Listing 4.10, and **PUZZLE.VBP** appears in Listing 4.11.

LISTING 4.10 PUZZLE.FRM

```
VERSION 4.00
Begin VB.Form Form1
    Caption         =   "Puzzle"
    ClientHeight    =   3795
    ClientLeft      =   1170
    ClientTop       =   1875
    ClientWidth     =   5880
    BeginProperty Font
        name            =   "MS Sans Serif"
        charset         =   1
        weight          =   400
        size            =   8.25
        underline       =   0   'False
        italic          =   0   'False
        strikethrough   =   0   'False
    EndProperty
    Height          =   4200
    Left            =   1110
    LinkTopic       =   "Form1"
    ScaleHeight     =   3795
```

```
ScaleWidth      =    5880
Top             =    1530
Width           =    6000
Begin VB.PictureBox Picture4
   AutoSize        =    -1  'True
   Height          =    1110
   Left            =    1200
   Picture         =    "PUZZLE.frx":0000
   ScaleHeight     =    1080
   ScaleWidth      =    1635
   TabIndex        =    3
   Top             =    360
   Width           =    1665
End
Begin VB.PictureBox Picture3
   AutoSize        =    -1  'True
   Height          =    1095
   Left            =    960
   Picture         =    "PUZZLE.frx":1042
   ScaleHeight     =    1065
   ScaleWidth      =    1635
   TabIndex        =    2
   Top             =    2040
   Width           =    1665
End
Begin VB.PictureBox Picture2
   AutoSize        =    -1  'True
   Height          =    1125
   Left            =    3120
   Picture         =    "PUZZLE.frx":204C
   ScaleHeight     =    1095
   ScaleWidth      =    1845
   TabIndex        =    1
   Top             =    480
   Width           =    1875
End
Begin VB.PictureBox Picture1
   AutoSize        =    -1  'True
   Height          =    1080
   Left            =    3240
   Picture         =    "PUZZLE.frx":330E
   ScaleHeight     =    1050
   ScaleWidth      =    1845
   TabIndex        =    0
   Top             =    2040
   Width           =    1875
End
   End
End
Attribute VB_Name = "Form1"
Attribute VB_Creatable = False
Attribute VB_Exposed = False
```

```
Dim xoffset As Integer
Dim yoffset As Integer

Private Sub Form_DragDrop(Source As Control, x As Single, y As Single)
    Source.Move x - xoffset, y - yoffset
End Sub

Private Sub Picture1_DragDrop(Source As Control, x As Single, y As Single)
    Source.Move Picture1.Left + x - xoffset, Picture1.Top + y - yoffset
End Sub

Private Sub Picture1_MouseDown(Button As Integer, Shift As Integer, x
        As Single, y As Single)
    xoffset = x
    yoffset = y
    Picture1.Drag 1
End Sub

Private Sub Picture2_DragDrop(Source As Control, x As Single, y As Single)
    Source.Move Picture2.Left + x - xoffset, Picture2.Top + y - yoffset
End Sub

Private Sub Picture2_MouseDown(Button As Integer, Shift As Integer, x
        As Single, y As Single)
    xoffset = x
    yoffset = y
    Picture2.Drag 1
End Sub

Private Sub Picture3_DragDrop(Source As Control, x As Single, y As Single)
    Source.Move Picture3.Left + x - xoffset, Picture3.Top + y - yoffset
End Sub

Private Sub Picture3_MouseDown(Button As Integer, Shift As Integer, x
        As Single, y As Single)
    xoffset = x
    yoffset = y
    Picture3.Drag 1
End Sub

Private Sub Picture4_DragDrop(Source As Control, x As Single, y As Single)
    Source.Move Picture4.Left + x - xoffset, Picture4.Top + y - yoffset
End Sub

Private Sub Picture4_MouseDown(Button As Integer, Shift As Integer, x
        As Single, y As Single)
    xoffset = x
    yoffset = y
    Picture4.Drag 1
End Sub
```

LISTING 4.11 PUZZLE.VBP

```
PUZZLE.FRM
Object={F9043C88-F6F2-101A-A3C9-08002B2F49FB}#1.0#0; COMDLG16.OCX
Object={FAEEE763-117E-101B-8933-08002B2F4F5A}#1.0#0; DBLIST16.OCX
ProjWinSize=345,402,202,111
ProjWinShow=2
ExeName="Project1.exe"
Path="D:\VB"
Command=""
Name="Project1"
HelpContextID="0"
StartMode=0
VersionCompatible="0"
MajorVer=1
MinorVer=0
RevisionVer=0
AutoIncrementVer=0
VersionCompanyName=""
Reference=*\G{00025E01-0000-0000-C000-
000000000046}#0.0#0#DAO2516.DLL#Microsoft DAO 2.5 Object Library
```

There is far more that we can do with controls and forms. For example, we've seen that it's possible to create new forms at run time—but it's also possible to create new controls. Let's look into that next.

CREATING NEW CONTROLS AT RUN TIME

Suppose we have a program with two option buttons—Option0 and Option1—in our main window:

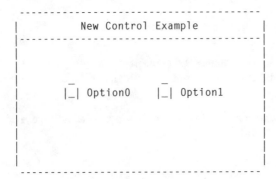

Next, let's say that we decide that we need another option button, one that was not created at design time. It turns out that we can add controls at run time. It's easiest to do that in Visual Basic if the new control is part of a control array. Our two existing option buttons might be part of a control array named OptButton; the two buttons might be OptButton(0) and OptButton(1):

```
----------------------------------------
|           New Control Example        |
|--------------------------------------|
|                                      |
|                                      |
|    _           _                     |
|   |_| OptButton(0) |_| OptButton(1)  |
|                                      |
|                                      |
|                                      |
|                                      |
 ----------------------------------------
```

It's simple to create and display a new control that is part of a control array, and we might place that new control—OptButton(2)—at location (0, 0) in our form:

```
 ----------------------------------------
|           New Control Example        |
|--------------------------------------|
||_| OptButton(2)                       |
|                                      |
|                                      |
|    _           _                     |
|   |_| OptButton(0) |_| OptButton(1)  |
|                                      |
|                                      |
|                                      |
 ----------------------------------------
```

Let's see how this works in code. Create a new program named **NEWC-TRL.VBP**. Create two option buttons: Option1 and Option2. (The Option button tool is the fourth tool down on the right in the Visual Basic toolbox.) Next, give Option1 the new Name property **OptButton** in the properties window, and do the same to Option2. Answer **Yes** when Visual Basic asks whether you want to create a control array. This produces a control array with two controls: OptButton(0) and OptButton(1). This is how those controls are stored in **NEWCTRL.FRM**:

```
Begin VB.OptionButton OptButton
    Caption         =   "OptButton(0)"
    Height          =   495
    Index           =   0
    Left            =   1440
    TabIndex        =   0
    Top             =   1200
    Width           =   1215
End
Begin VB.OptionButton OptButton
    Caption         =   "OptButton(1)"
    Height          =   495
    Index           =   1
    Left            =   3600
    TabIndex        =   1
    Top             =   1200
    Width           =   1215
End
```

When the program first runs, it will display the two option buttons. When the user clicks the form, we might create and display a new option button, OptButton(2). Create the subroutine Form_Click() in the code window by clicking **Form1** to bring up this subroutine (from **NEWCTRL.FRM**):

```
Private Sub Form_Click()

End Sub
```

To add a new option button to our program, we merely have to use the Load statement, indicating that we want to add a new option button to our option button array:

```
Private Sub Form_Click()
--> Load OptButton(2)
        .
        .
        .
End Sub
```

Next, we position that button with its Move method so that it doesn't cover any other option buttons by placing it at (0,0) in the form. (OptButton(2) is originally positioned over the first option button in the control array, OptButton(0).)

```
Private Sub Form_Click()
    Load OptButton(2)
--> OptButton(2).Move 0, 0
        .
        .
        .
End Sub
```

Now we can give OptButton(2) a new caption, showing that it is a new member of the control array:

```
Private Sub Form_Click()
    Load OptButton(2)
    OptButton(2).Move 0, 0
--> OptButton(2).Caption = "OptButton(2)"

        .
        .
        .

End Sub
```

Finally, we display the new option button this way, setting its Visible property to True:

```
Private Sub Form_Click()
    Load OptButton(2)
    OptButton(2).Move 0, 0
    OptButton(2).Caption = "OptButton(2)"
--> OptButton(2).Visible = True
End Sub
```

That's it—the NEWCTRL program is complete. Run it and click the form to create and display a new option button, as shown in Figure 4.7. Our program is a success: at this point, we're able to create new controls and add them to our programs.

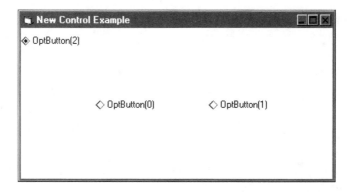

FIGURE 4.7 WITH THE NEWCTRL PROGRAM, WE CAN CREATE
NEW VISUAL BASIC CONTROLS ON DEMAND.

The code for this program, **NEWCTRL.FRM**, appears in Listing 4.12, and **NEWCTRL.VBP** appears in Listing 4.13.

LISTING 4.12 NEWCTRL.FRM

```
VERSION 4.00
Begin VB.Form Form1
   Caption         =    "New Control Example"
   ClientHeight    =    4230
   ClientLeft      =    1095
   ClientTop       =    1515
   ClientWidth     =    6720
   BeginProperty Font
      name              =    "MS Sans Serif"
      charset           =    1
      weight            =    400
      size              =    8.25
      underline         =    0      'False
      italic            =    0      'False
      strikethrough     =    0      'False
   EndProperty
   Height          =    4635
   Left            =    1035
   LinkTopic       =    "Form1"
   ScaleHeight     =    4230
   ScaleWidth      =    6720
   Top             =    1170
   Width           =    6840
   Begin VB.OptionButton OptButton
      Caption         =    "OptButton(1)"
      Height          =    495
      Index           =    1
      Left            =    3600
      TabIndex        =    1
      Top             =    1200
      Width           =    1215
   End
   Begin VB.OptionButton OptButton
      Caption         =    "OptButton(0)"
      Height          =    495
      Index           =    0
      Left            =    1440
      TabIndex        =    0
      Top             =    1200
      Width           =    1215
   End
End
Attribute VB_Name = "Form1"
Attribute VB_Creatable = False
Attribute VB_Exposed = False
Private Sub Form_Click()
   Load OptButton(2)
   OptButton(2).Move 0, 0
   OptButton(2).Caption = "OptButton(2)"
   OptButton(2).Visible = True
End Sub
```

LISTING 4.13 NEWCTRL.VBP

```
NEWCTRL.FRM
Object={F9043C88-F6F2-101A-A3C9-08002B2F49FB}#1.0#0; COMDLG16.OCX
Object={FAEEE763-117E-101B-8933-08002B2F4F5A}#1.0#0; DBLIST16.OCX
ProjWinSize=345,402,202,111
ProjWinShow=2
ExeName="Project1.exe"
Path="D:\VB"
Command=""
Name="Project1"
HelpContextID="0"
StartMode=0
VersionCompatible="0"
MajorVer=1
MinorVer=0
RevisionVer=0
AutoIncrementVer=0
VersionCompanyName=""
Reference=*\G{00025E01-0000-0000-C000-
        000000000046}#0.0#0#DAO2516.DLL#Microsoft DAO 2.5 Object
        Library
VERSION 4.00
```

That's it for creating new controls. We might note that it's also easy to remove controls from our program using the Unload statement. On the other hand, there are times when you don't want to get rid of a control, but you don't want to make it accessible to the user either. In that case, we will simply disable the control, and we'll look into how that works next.

DISABLING CONTROLS

Although the specialty of Windows programs usually is to keep as many options before the user as possible, there are times when some options should simply not be available, such as a **Paste** menu choice when no control is selected that can accept a paste operation. In such cases, we can disable controls, which usually means "graying" their captions and no longer allowing them to accept the input focus.

Let's take a look at this process. Create a new Visual Basic program called **GRAYOUT.VBP** and place an option button, a command button, and a text box in the default form, as shown in Figure 4.8.

When the user clicks or makes changes to any of these controls, we can place a message box on the screen and then disable the control. For example, open the option button's click event handler, Option1_Click(), by double-clicking that control (from **GRAYOUT.FRM**):

```
Private Sub Option1_Click()

End Sub
```

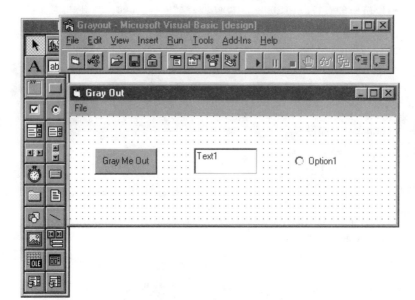

FIGURE 4.8 WE DESIGN OUR **GRAYOUT** PROGRAM.

First, we display the message box with the warning:

```
Private Sub Option1_Click()
--> MsgBox ("The option button is about to be disabled.")
        .
        .
        .
End Sub
```

Next, we disable the option button. We set the button's Enabled property to False:

```
Private Sub Option1_Click()
    MsgBox ("The option button is about to be disabled.")
--> Option1.Enabled = False
End Sub
```

At this point, the option button will turn gray and will no longer respond to the mouse. We can do the same thing for our command button, Command1.

Double-click Command1 to create and open Command1_Click(), and add
this code to it (from **GRAYOUT.FRM**):

```
Private Sub Command1_Click()
--> MsgBox ("The command button is about to be disabled.")
--> Command1.Enabled = False
End Sub
```

Text boxes also have Click events, and we can do the same for Text1 (from
GRAYOUT.FRM):

```
Private Sub Text1_Click()
--> MsgBox ("The text box is about to be disabled.")
--> Text1.Enabled = False
End Sub
```

We can also add a File menu to our GRAYOUT program, as also shown in
Figure 4.8. Give that menu two items: **Gray Me Out...** (Name property: Gray)
and **Exit** (Name property: Exit). We can gray out menu items as easily as we
can other controls, of course:

```
Private Sub Gray_Click()
--> MsgBox ("The menu item is about to be disabled.")
--> Gray.Enabled = False
End Sub
```

When we execute the line Gray.Enabled = False, the menu item becomes
grayed out and the user can no longer select it.

We can even disable the entire form! All we have to do is to set the
form's Enabled property to False when the form is clicked:

```
Private Sub Form_Click()
--> MsgBox ("The form is about to be disabled.")
--> Form1.Enabled = False
End Sub
```

After we execute the line Form1.False, the form can no longer receive the
input focus; when the user clicks it again with the mouse, the program simply beeps.

Now run the GRAYOUT program and click a control; when you do, a
message box appears to inform you that the control is about to be disabled.
When you click **OK**, the control is disabled, as was shown in Figure 4.9. (To
enable the control again in code, simply reset its Enabled property to True.)

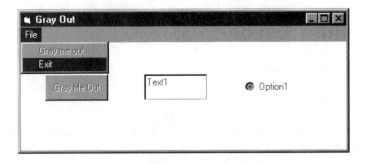

FIGURE 4.9 OUR GRAYOUT PROGRAM SHOWS HOW TO DISABLE CONTROLS.

The code for this program, **GRAYOUT.FRM**, appears in Listing 4.14.
GRAYOUT.VBP appears in Listing 4.15.

LISTING 4.14 GRAYOUT.FRM

```
Begin VB.Form Form1
    Caption         =   "Gray Out"
    ClientHeight    =   4230
    ClientLeft      =   1095
    ClientTop       =   1800
    ClientWidth     =   6720
    BeginProperty Font
        name            =   "MS Sans Serif"
        charset         =   1
        weight          =   400
        size            =   8.25
        underline       =   0   'False
        italic          =   0   'False
        strikethrough   =   0   'False
    EndProperty
    Height          =   4920
    Left            =   1035
    LinkTopic       =   "Form1"
    ScaleHeight     =   4230
    ScaleWidth      =   6720
    Top             =   1170
    Width           =   6840
    Begin VB.TextBox Text1
        Height          =   495
        Left            =   2760
        TabIndex        =   2
        Text            =   "Text1"
        Top             =   960
        Width           =   1215
    End
    Begin VB.OptionButton Option1
        Caption         =   "Option1"
        Height          =   495
```

```
            Left            =    2760
            TabIndex        =    1
            Top             =    1920
            Width           =    1215
        End
        Begin VB.CommandButton Command1
            Caption         =    "Gray Me Out"
            Height          =    495
            Left            =    480
            TabIndex        =    0
            Top             =    600
            Width           =    1215
        End
        Begin VB.Menu File
            Caption         =    "File"
            Begin VB.Menu Gray
                Caption         =    "Gray me out..."
            End
            Begin VB.Menu Exit
                Caption         =    "Exit"
            End
        End
    End
End
Attribute VB_Name = "Form1"
Attribute VB_Creatable = False
Attribute VB_Exposed = False
Private Sub Command1_Click()
    MsgBox ("The command button is about to be disabled.")
    Command1.Enabled = False
End Sub

Private Sub Exit_Click()
    End
End Sub

Private Sub Form_Click()
    MsgBox ("The form is about to be disabled.")
    Form1.Enabled = False
End Sub

Private Sub Gray_Click()
    MsgBox ("The menu item is about to be disabled.")
    Gray.Enabled = False
End Sub

Private Sub Option1_Click()
    MsgBox ("The option button is about to be disabled.")
    Option1.Enabled = False
End Sub

Private Sub Text1_Click()
    MsgBox ("The text box is about to be disabled.")
    Text1.Enabled = False
End Sub
```

LISTING 4.15 GRAYOUT.VBP

```
GRAYOUT.FRM
Object={F9043C88-F6F2-101A-A3C9-08002B2F49FB}#1.0#0; COMDLG16.OCX
Object={FAEEE763-117E-101B-8933-08002B2F4F5A}#1.0#0; DBLIST16.OCX
ProjWinSize=345,402,202,111
ProjWinShow=2
ExeName="Project1.exe"
Path="D:\VB"
Command=""
Name="Project1"
HelpContextID="0"
StartMode=0
VersionCompatible="0"
MajorVer=1
MinorVer=0
RevisionVer=0
AutoIncrementVer=0
VersionCompanyName=""
Reference=*\G{00025E01-0000-0000-C000-
         000000000046}#0.0#0#DAO2516.DLL#Microsoft DAO 2.5 Object
         Library
```

Our next topic in advanced control handling is how to change the tab order of controls at run time.

CHANGING TAB ORDER

Although Windows programs are supposed to be entirely usable with just a keyboard and without a mouse, this is the case more often in theory than in practice. The keyboard is especially important for navigating around a window when there are many text boxes to fill with data. It is difficult for the user to type in a text box, use the mouse to move to the next text box, type there, use the mouse to move to the next one, and so on. In Windows, the user is supposed to be able to move from control to control with the **Tab** key, and that's what most people do when entering data in many text boxes.

The TabIndex property of most controls indicates where it stands in the tab order. The first control you put on a Visual Basic form gets the TabIndex 0, which means that this control will receive the default focus—it will get the focus when the form first appears. The next control has its TabIndex property set to 1, the next to 2, and so on. In this way, the user can tab from control to control. When the program starts, the first control will have the focus; pressing the **Tab** key moves the focus to the second control, and so on. If you ever want to change the tab order, you need only change the TabIndex property of the controls you want to work with.

It is sometimes desirable to change the tab order while a program is running. To demonstrate this, we might write a program that will draw both rectangles and circles. The user first clicks a button marked **Rectangle** to draw a rectangle or **Circle** to draw a circle. If the user clicks **Rectangle**, we'll need to read four parameters—(x1, y1) and (x2, y2)—for the upper-left and lower-right corners of the rectangle. Let's arrange the **Rectangle** and **Circle** buttons and the text boxes for the parameter values this way:

```
-----------------------------------------------------------------
|                        Tab Order Example                      |
|---------------------------------------------------------------|
|                                                               |
|  ---------                                                    |
| |Rectangle|    x1         y1         x2         y2            |
|  ---------     --------   --------   --------   --------   -------- |
|  ---------    |      |   |      |   |      |   |      |   | Draw | |
| | Circle  |    --------   --------   --------   --------   -------- |
|  ---------                                                    |
|                                                               |
|                                                               |
-----------------------------------------------------------------
```

The user can click **Rectangle** and then enter the first parameter, x1, in the correct box. The user presses **Tab** to move to the y1 box, **Tab** again to move to x2 box, and **Tab** once more to move to the y2 box. We will add a command button marked **Draw** as shown, and pressing **Tab** a final time moves the input focus to that button so that the user can draw the rectangle simply by pressing **Enter**.

On the other hand, if the user clicks the **Circle** button, we need only three parameters: the center of the circle (x, y) and the radius of the circle:

```
-----------------------------------------------------------------
|                        Tab Order Example                      |
|---------------------------------------------------------------|
|                                                               |
|  ---------                                                    |
| |Rectangle|    x          y          radius                  |
|  ---------     --------   --------   --------   --------   -------- |
|  ---------    |      |   |      |   |      |   |      |   | Draw | |
| | Circle  |    --------   --------   --------   --------   -------- |
|  ---------                                                    |
|                                                               |
|                                                               |
-----------------------------------------------------------------
```

This means that we should change the tab order so that we skip the fourth parameter box. After the user has entered a value in the radius box, pressing the **Tab** key should move the input focus directly to the **Draw** button, skipping the (unnecessary) fourth parameter box.

Let's see this in code. Create a new program, **TABINDEX**, and place the controls we'll need on the form as shown. Working from left to right, here are the control's TabIndex properties:

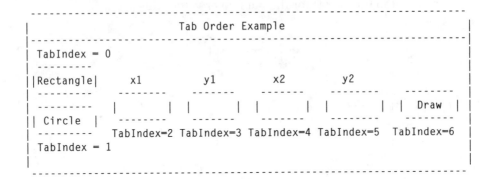

```
-----------------------------------------------------------------
|                        Tab Order Example                      |
|---------------------------------------------------------------|
| TabIndex = 0                                                  |
| ---------                                                     |
||Rectangle|    x1          y1          x2          y2          |
| ---------   --------    --------    -------    --------    -------- |
| ---------    |     |  |     |  |     |  |      | |  | Draw |  |
|| Circle  |   --------    -------    -------    --------    -------- |
| ---------   TabIndex=2 TabIndex=3 TabIndex=4 TabIndex=5 TabIndex=6 |
| TabIndex = 1                                                  |
|                                                               |
-----------------------------------------------------------------
```

Place four labels—Label1 to Label4—one above each of the parameter text boxes so that we can label those text boxes correctly. Double-click the form to open TABINDEX's code window. Here, we set up two Boolean variables: RectFlag and CircFlag. (Place them outside any subroutines.) These variables will indicate which type of figure we are to draw (from **TABORDER.FRM**):

```
Dim RectFlag As Boolean
Dim CircFlag As Boolean
```

In addition, we set these two flags to False when the form loads in the Form_Load() event. Double-click the form to create and open the Form_Load() event.

```
Dim RectFlag As Boolean
Dim CircFlag As Boolean

Private Sub Form_Load()
--> RectFlag = False
--> CircFlag = False
End Sub
```

Our Rectangle command button is Command1. When the user clicks this button, we will prepare to receive the four parameters we need for a rectangle: (x1, y1) and (x2, y2). We first set RectFlag to True and CircFlag to False in Command1_Click(). Double-click **Rectangle** to open this subroutine (from **TABORDER.FRM**):

```
Private Sub Command1_Click()
--> RectFlag = True
--> CircFlag = False
         .
         .
         .
```

Next, we label the four parameter text boxes correctly for a rectangle, indicating that we require the two coordinate locations (x1, y1) and (x2, y2) to draw a rectangle:

```
Private Sub Command1_Click()
    RectFlag = True
    CircFlag = False
--> Label1.Caption = "x1"
--> Label2.Caption = "y1"
--> Label3.Caption = "x2"
--> Label4.Caption = "y2"
         .
         .
         .
```

Finally, we set up the tab order of our controls. We set the first parameter text box to TabIndex 1, the next one to TabIndex 2, and so on up to the last text box, TabIndex 4. After entering the last parameter, the user will probably want to **Tab** to the **Draw** button, Command3, so we give it a TabIndex property of 5:

```
Private Sub Command1_Click()
    RectFlag = True
    CircFlag = False
    Label1.Caption = "x1"
    Label2.Caption = "y1"
    Label3.Caption = "x2"
    Label4.Caption = "y2"
--> Text1.TabIndex = 1
--> Text2.TabIndex = 2
--> Text3.TabIndex = 3
--> Text4.TabIndex = 4
--> Command3.TabIndex = 5
End Sub
```

That's it for the **Rectangle** button. Double-click **Circle** to open Command2_Click() (from **TABORDER.FRM**):

```
Private Sub Command2_Click()

End Sub
```

Now that the user has selected the **Circle** command button, Command2, we will set CircFlag to True and RectFlag to False by adding this code:

```
Private Sub Command2_Click()
--> CircFlag = True
--> RectFlag = False
           .
           .
           .
End Sub
```

To draw a circle, we need only three parameters—the center of the circle (x, y) and its radius—so we label the text boxes accordingly. We set the label of the fourth parameter box to the empty string, "":

```
Private Sub Command2_Click()
--> CircFlag = True
--> RectFlag = False
--> Label1.Caption = "x"
--> Label2.Caption = "y"
--> Label3.Caption = "radius"
--> Label4.Caption = ""
           .
           .
           .
```

Now we set the tab order. In this case, we'll simply skip the fourth parameter text box, moving directly from the text box marked **radius** to the **Draw** button (Command3), as discussed previously:

```
Private Sub Command2_Click()
    CircFlag = True
    RectFlag = False
    Label1.Caption = "x"
    Label2.Caption = "y"
    Label3.Caption = "radius"
    Label4.Caption = ""
--> Command2.TabIndex = 0
--> Text1.TabIndex = 1
--> Text2.TabIndex = 2
--> Text3.TabIndex = 3
--> Command3.TabIndex = 4
    End Sub
```

All that remains is to do the actual drawing. We do that in the **Draw** button's Click event handler, Command3_Click(). Open it by double-clicking **Draw** (from **TABORDER.FRM**):

```
Private Sub Command3_Click()

End Sub
```

If RectFlag = True, we take the required four parameters and draw the rectangle:

```
Private Sub Command3_Click()
--> If RectFlag Then
-->     Line (Val(Text1.Text), Val(Text2.Text))-(Val(Text3.Text),
-->     Val(Text4.Text)), , B
--> End If
        .
        .
        .
```

If CircFlag is True, on the other hand, we take the required three parameters and draw the circle:

```
Private Sub Command3_Click()
    If RectFlag Then
        Line (Val(Text1.Text), Val(Text2.Text))-(Val(Text3.Text),
        Val(Text4.Text)), , B
    End If

--> If CircFlag Then
-->     Circle (Val(Text1.Text), Val(Text2.Text)), Val(Text3.Text)
--> End If
End Sub
```

Now our program is complete. Run it and click **Rectangle**. When you do, the labels of the four text boxes will change to **x1**, **y1**, **x2**, and **y2**. Fill in those parameters, tabbing from one box to the next. Finally, tab to the **Draw** button and press **Enter**, drawing the rectangle as shown in Figure 4.10.

Next, click **Circle**. The parameter box labels change to **x**, **y**, and **radius**. Enter those values now; press **Tab** again after entering the radius, and the focus skips the unnecessary fourth parameter to the **Draw** button. Click **Draw** by pressing **Enter**, drawing the circle as shown in Figure 4.11. Our program is a success.

The code for **TABORDER.FRM** is in Listing 4.16, and **TABORDER.VBP** is in Listing 4.17.

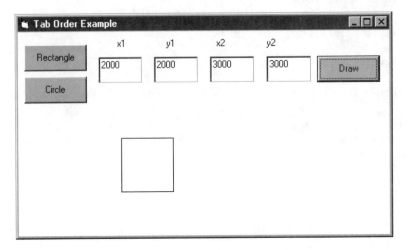

FIGURE 4.10 OUR TABORDER PROGRAM LETS THE USER TAB FROM CONTROL TO CONTROL.

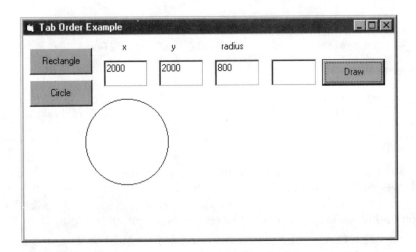

FIGURE 4.11 OUR TABORDER PROGRAM MAKES THE FOCUS SKIP UNNEEDED CONTROLS.

LISTING 4.16 TABORDER.FRM

```
VERSION 4.00
Begin VB.Form Form1
   Caption         =    "Tab Order Example"
   ClientHeight    =    3825
   ClientLeft      =    1095
   ClientTop       =    1515
   ClientWidth     =    7155
   BeginProperty Font
      name           =    "MS Sans Serif"
      charset        =    1
      weight         =    400
      size           =    8.25
      underline      =    0      'False
      italic         =    0      'False
      strikethrough  =    0      'False
   EndProperty
   Height          =    4230
   Left            =    1035
   LinkTopic       =    "Form1"
   ScaleHeight     =    3825
   ScaleWidth      =    7155
   Top             =    1170
   Width           =    7275
   Begin VB.CommandButton Command3
      Caption         =    "Draw"
      Height          =    495
      Left            =    5760
      TabIndex        =    6
      Top             =    480
      Width           =    1215
   End
   Begin VB.TextBox Text4
      Height          =    495
      Left            =    4800
      TabIndex        =    5
      Top             =    480
      Width           =    855
   End
   Begin VB.TextBox Text3
      Height          =    495
      Left            =    3720
      TabIndex        =    4
      Top             =    480
      Width           =    855
   End
```

```
Begin VB.TextBox Text2
   Height          =    495
   Left            =    2640
   TabIndex        =    3
   Top             =    480
   Width           =    855
End
Begin VB.TextBox Text1
   Height          =    495
   Left            =    1560
   TabIndex        =    2
   Top             =    480
   Width           =    855
End
Begin VB.CommandButton Command2
   Caption         =    "Circle"
   Height          =    495
   Left            =    120
   TabIndex        =    1
   Top             =    840
   Width           =    1215
End
Begin VB.CommandButton Command1
   Caption         =    "Rectangle"
   Height          =    495
   Left            =    120
   TabIndex        =    0
   Top             =    240
   Width           =    1215
End
Begin VB.Label Label4
   Height          =    255
   Left            =    4800
   TabIndex        =    10
   Top             =    120
   Width           =    615
End
Begin VB.Label Label3
   Caption         =    "radius"
   Height          =    255
   Left            =    3840
   TabIndex        =    9
   Top             =    120
   Width           =    615
End
Begin VB.Label Label2
   Caption         =    "y"
   Height          =    255
   Left            =    2880
   TabIndex        =    8
```

```
            Top            =    120
            Width          =    255
        End
        Begin VB.Label Label1
            Caption        =    "x"
            Height         =    255
            Left           =    1920
            TabIndex       =    7
            Top            =    120
            Width          =    135
        End
    End
End
Attribute VB_Name = "Form1"
Attribute VB_Creatable = False
Attribute VB_Exposed = False
Dim RectFlag As Boolean
Dim CircFlag As Boolean

Private Sub Command1_Click()
    RectFlag = True
    CircFlag = False
    Label1.Caption = "x1"
    Label2.Caption = "y1"
    Label3.Caption = "x2"
    Label4.Caption = "y2"
    Text1.TabIndex = 1
    Text2.TabIndex = 2
    Text3.TabIndex = 3
    Text4.TabIndex = 4
    Command3.TabIndex = 5
End Sub

Private Sub Command2_Click()
    CircFlag = True
    RectFlag = False
    Label1.Caption = "x"
    Label2.Caption = "y"
    Label3.Caption = "radius"
    Label4.Caption = ""
    Command2.TabIndex = 0
    Text1.TabIndex = 1
    Text2.TabIndex = 2
    Text3.TabIndex = 3
    Command3.TabIndex = 4
End Sub

Private Sub Command3_Click()
    If RectFlag Then
        Line (Val(Text1.Text), Val(Text2.Text))-(Val(Text3.Text),
        Val(Text4.Text)), , B
```

```
    End If

    If CircFlag Then
        Circle (Val(Text1.Text), Val(Text2.Text)), Val(Text3.Text)
    End If
End Sub

Private Sub Form_Load()
    RectFlag = False
    CircFlag = False
End Sub
```

LISTING 4.17 TABORDER.VBP

```
TABORDER.FRM
Object={F9043C88-F6F2-101A-A3C9-08002B2F49FB}#1.0#0; COMDLG16.OCX
Object={FAEEE763-117E-101B-8933-08002B2F4F5A}#1.0#0; DBLIST16.OCX
ProjWinSize=345,402,202,111
ProjWinShow=2
ExeName="Project1.exe"
Path="D:\VB"
Command=""
Name="Project1"
HelpContextID="0"
StartMode=0
VersionCompatible="0"
MajorVer=1
MinorVer=0
RevisionVer=0
AutoIncrementVer=0
VersionCompanyName=""
Reference=*\G{00025E01-0000-0000-C000-
000000000046}#0.0#0#DAO2516.DLL#Microsoft DAO 2.5 Object Library
```

Our last topic will be pop-up menus, and we'll turn to that now.

CREATING POP-UP MENUS

You may be surprised to find pop-up menus in a chapter on control handling, but menus are controls just like any other controls. Pop-up menus can appear anywhere in a form, as shown in Figure 4.12, and are activated with the right mouse button.

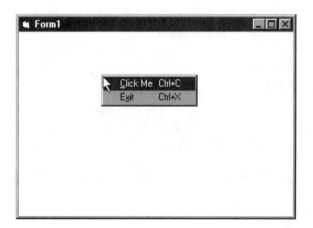

FIGURE 4.12 OUR POP-UP MENU AT WORK.

To create the pop-up menu in Figure 4.12, create a new project, calling it
POPUP.VBP. Now we have only to create a new menu control, calling it
Menu1. To create a new menu control, we use the Menu Editor. Using that
editor, set the Name property of the new menu to Menu1 (by typing that into
the Name box in the Menu Editor) and give the menu the caption Popup (by
typing that into the Caption box). The caption of the pop-up menu does not
matter, because it is not displayed, but the menu items in that menu certainly are. Add two menu items, giving them the captions **Click Me** (Name =
ClickMe) and **Exit** (Name = Exit). Then make sure that you click the **Visible**
box in the Menu Editor so that it is *unchecked*, making this menu invisible.
The result appears in the Menu Editor and in Figure 4.13.

Here is how the new menu control, Menu1, is specified in **POPUP.FRM**:

```
Begin VB.Menu Menu1
   Caption         =   "Popup"
   Visible         =   0   'False
   Begin VB.Menu ClickMe
      Caption      =   "&Click Me"
      Shortcut     =   ^C
   End
   Begin VB.Menu Exit
      Caption      =   "E&xit"
      Shortcut     =   ^X
   End
End
```

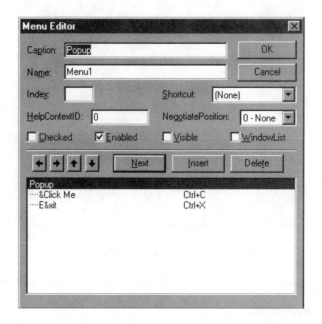

FIGURE 4.13 DESIGNING OUR POP-UP MENU IN THE MENU EDITOR

To activate the pop-up menu as shown in Figure 4.12, we will use the PopupMenu method in the Form_MouseDown() event, which is triggered when the user presses the mouse button. Open that event now:

```
Private Sub Form_MouseDown(Button As Integer, Shift As Integer, X As
        Single, Y As Single)

End Sub
```

First we check to make sure that the right mouse button was pressed. We check the Button parameter passed to us in the subroutine:

```
Private Sub Form_MouseDown(Button As Integer, Shift As Integer, X As
        Single, Y As Single)
--> If Button = 2 Then                 'Right mouse button?
        .
        .
        .
--> End If
End Sub
```

If the button was pressed, we display our pop-up menu, Menu1, with the PopupMenu method:

```
Private Sub Form_MouseDown(Button As Integer, Shift As Integer, X As
        Single, Y As Single)
    If Button = 2 Then                      'Right mouse button?
-->     PopupMenu Menu1
    End If
End Sub
```

At this point, the pop-up menu appears on the screen, as shown in Figure 4.12. (If you want a different pop-up menu for a control in our form, just use that control's MouseDown event and display the desired menu control in that event.)

One question remains: how do we add code to the **Click Me** and **Exit** pop-up menu items? The answer is that we simply need to look for those items in the code window and add code to their click events, as with any other menu item. For example, we can make the computer beep when the user selects **Click Me** and end the program when he or she selects **Exit**. We add this code to the two menu items' click events:

```
Private Sub ClickMe_Click()
--> Beep
End Sub
```

```
Private Sub Exit_Click()
--> End
End Sub
```

Now we have created and used pop-up menus. This program appears in Listing 4.18 (**POPUP.FRM**) and Listing 4.19 (**POPUP.VBP**).

LISTING 4.18 POPUP.FRM

```
VERSION 4.00
Begin VB.Form Form1
   BackColor       =    &H00FFFFFF&
   Caption         =    "Form1"
   ClientHeight    =    3450
   ClientLeft      =    1590
   ClientTop       =    1920
   ClientWidth     =    5265
   Height          =    3855
   KeyPreview      =    -1   'True
   Left            =    1530
   LinkTopic       =    "Form1"
   ScaleHeight     =    3450
   ScaleWidth      =    5265
   Top             =    1575
   WhatsThisButton =    -1   'True
```

```
    WhatsThisHelp    =    -1   'True
    Width            =    5385
    Begin VB.Menu Menu1
       Caption          =    "Popup"
       Visible          =    0    'False
       Begin VB.Menu ClickMe
          Caption          =    "&Click Me"
          Shortcut         =    ^C
       End
       Begin VB.Menu Exit
          Caption          =    "E&xit"
          Shortcut         =    ^X
       End
    End
End
Attribute VB_Name = "Form1"
Attribute VB_Creatable = False
Attribute VB_Exposed = False

Private Sub ClickMe_Click()
    Beep
End Sub

Private Sub Exit_Click()
    End
End Sub

Private Sub Form_MouseDown(Button As Integer, Shift As Integer, X As
        Single, Y As Single)
    If Button = 2 Then
        PopupMenu Menu1
    End If
End Sub
```

LISTING 4.19 POPUP.VBP

```
Form=popup.Frm
Reference=*\G{BEF6E001-A874-101A-8BBA-
        00AA00300CAB}#2.0#0#C:\WINDOWS\SYSTEM\OLEPRO32.DLL#Standard
        OLE Types
ProjWinSize=175,396,202,111
ProjWinShow=2
Name="Project1"
HelpContextID="0"
StartMode=0
VersionCompatible32="0"
MajorVer=1
MinorVer=0
RevisionVer=0
```

```
AutoIncrementVer=0
ServerSupportFiles=0
```

We've come far in this chapter, from creating new controls at run time to passing forms as arguments to subroutines, from dragging and dropping controls to determining which control is active and using pop-up menus. In the next chapter, we'll turn to another popular topic for professional Visual Basic programming: Visual Basic's custom controls.

## CHAPTER 5

USING VISUAL BASIC'S
CUSTOM OCX CONTROLS

In this chapter, we will explore some of the custom controls that come with Visual Basic—new controls that will add advanced power to our programs. The Grid control will give us the power to create spreadsheet-like programs easily by displaying text and numbers in a grid of cells. The Graph control will allow us to quickly and easily graph numerical data in a variety of attractive formats. The CommonDialog control supports all the common dialog boxes that Windows programs use to present the user with a familiar interface. These dialog boxes include the Windows Save As dialog box (gets from the user the name of a file in which to save data), the Open dialog box (gets the name of a file to open), the Print dialog box (lets the user select the number of copies of a document to print, which pages to print, which printer to use, and so on), and more. We'll also look at the Multimedia control and at animation buttons—which let you display graphics animation—as well as other new and powerful controls. We will start with one of the most popular: the Grid control.

THE GRID CONTROL

The Grid control presents us with a spreadsheet-like display; we can place text and graphics in each cell. For example, we might place a Grid control in one of our programs:

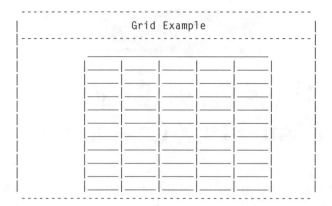

To become familiar with this control, we might make this example a spread-sheet, allowing the user to enter data into the grid simply by typing it. However, the grid control cannot respond directly to key press events, so we will enter our data in a separate text box, making our example look some-thing like this:

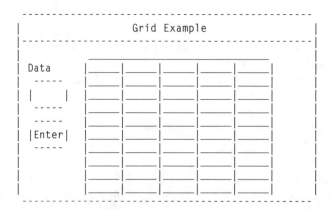

The user can click the grid, highlighting a cell, and then type the data for that cell into the Data text box above. When the data is ready to be trans-ferred to the highlighted cell, the user can click the **Enter** control button.

This is a common way of entering data into a grid control. (We'll see in Chapter 11 that a new type of grid, the DBGrid control, allows us to auto-matically display data from a database.) Another, more complicated way is to place code in a Grid_MouseDown() event handler so that when the user clicks a certain cell, you position a borderless text box exactly over that cell and make it visible. Users then get the impression that entering text directly into the grid is possible. After they press, say, the **Enter** key, you can enter the text from the text box into the underlying grid cell and hide the text box once again.

In addition to allowing the user to enter data into the grid, we might label the first row and the first column of cells just as they might appear in a spreadsheet:

```
-------------------------------------------------
|                   Grid Example                 |
|------------------------------------------------|
|                                                |
| Data     |_____|_A__|_B__|_C__|_D__|           |
|  -----   |_1__|____|____|____|____|            |
| |     |  |_2__|____|____|____|____|            |
|  -----   |_3__|____|____|____|____|            |
|  -----   |_4__|____|____|____|____|            |
| |Enter|  |_5__|____|____|____|____|            |
|  -----   |_6__|____|____|____|____|            |
|          |_7__|____|____|____|____|            |
|          |_8__|____|____|____|____|            |
|          |_9__|____|____|____|____|            |
-------------------------------------------------
```

Let's give this a try. Create a new Visual Basic project named **GRID.VBP** and give the default form (Form1) the caption Grid Example. We load the Grid control next; the custom controls we discuss in this chapter are supported by OCX files (the former VBX custom controls are no longer supported by Visual Basic), and we have to load such files into Visual Basic before using them. In particular, the Grid control is supported by the two files **GRID16.OCX** and **GRID32.OCX**, and Visual Basic will have loaded the correct 16- or 32-bit version into your Windows System directory. To add the Grid control, then, all we have to do is to select the **Custom Controls** item in the Visual Basic Tools menu.

Select that menu item now, opening the Custom Controls dialog box, as shown in Figure 5.1.

To add the Grid control to our new project, find the checkbox marked **Microsoft Grid Control** in the Available Controls box, click that checkbox, and then click the Custom Control box's **OK** button. The Grid control is added as a new tool in the Visual Basic toolbox (and shows a small grid on the associated command button in the toolbox).

Double-click the **Grid** tool, adding a new Grid control, Grid1, to our project. Stretch that Grid control so that it covers most of the form's client area, as shown in Figure 5.2. In addition, use the properties window to set the Grid control's Rows property to 21 and its Cols property to 11, giving our new Grid 21 rows and 11 columns.

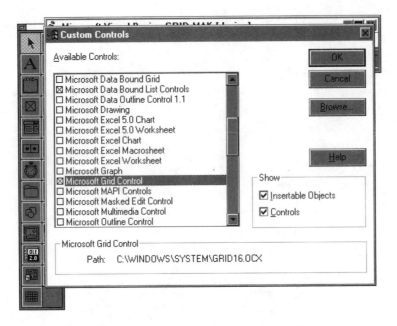

FIGURE 5.1 USE THE CUSTOM CONTROLS DIALOG BOX
TO ADD CUSTOM CONTROLS TO A VISUAL BASIC PROJECT.

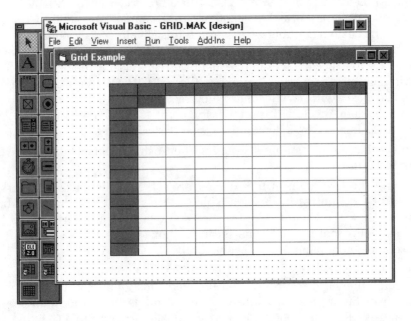

FIGURE 5.2 WE CREATE AND POSITION A NEW GRID CONTROL.

Next, add a text box, Text1, to our window, clearing the default text in the text box. Add a label above the text box with the caption **Data**, and a command button, Command1, changing the button's caption to **Enter**. The result appears in Figure 5.3.

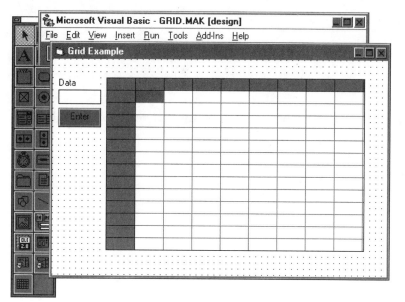

FIGURE 5.3 WE ADD A TEXT BOX AND COMMAND BUTTON
TO ALLOW EASY DATA ENTRY INTO OUR GRID CONTROL.

Our next step will be to prepare the Grid by labeling the first row with the letters **A**, **B**, **C**, and so on, and the first column with the numbers **1**, **2**, **3**, and so forth. By default, the first row and column of a Grid control appear gray and are usually used to label the cells; such labeling rows and columns are called *fixed* rows and columns and are controlled by the FixedRows and FixedCols properties. If you do not want to label the cells, simply set FixedRows and FixedCols to 0 in the properties window. To label our cells, double-click the form to open the Form_Load() event handler (from **GRID.FRM**):

```
Private Sub Form_Load()

End Sub
```

Each Grid control has both a Row and a Col property, and these properties hold the (Row, Col) location of the currently active cell. (Don't confuse the Row and Col properties with the Rows and Cols properties, which hold the *total* number of rows and columns in the Grid.) When we transfer data to the Grid control, that data will appear in the cell at the location (Row, Col). To label the first column, column 0, with numbers, we start by setting Grid1's Col property to 0 with this new code (from **GRID.FRM**):

```
Private Sub Form_Load()
-->      Grid1.Col = 0
            .
            .
            .
End Sub
```

Next, we loop over all rows, setting the Row property accordingly (note that we start at Row 1):

```
Private Sub Form_Load()
         Grid1.Col = 0
--> For loop_index% = 1 To 20
-->      Grid1.Row = loop_index%
            .
            .
            .
--> Next loop_index%
            .
            .
            .
End Sub
```

Now that we've set the Row and Col properties of the Grid, we are free to enter text in the Grid's Text property. That text will appear in the cell at the current (Row, Col) location. We can place ascending numbers in the first column like this:

```
Private Sub Form_Load()
         Grid1.Col = 0
    For loop_index% = 1 To 20
         Grid1.Row = loop_index%
-->      Grid1.Text = Str$(loop_index%)
    Next loop_index%
            .
            .
            .
End Sub
```

Now we can label the first row with letters. To do that, we set Row to 0 and loop over the columns:

```
Private Sub Form_Load()
        Grid1.Col = 0
    For loop_index% = 1 To 20
        Grid1.Row = loop_index%
        Grid1.Text = Str$(loop_index%)
    Next loop_index%
-->     Grid1.Row = 0
--> For loop_index% = 1 To 10
-->     Grid1.Col = loop_index%
             .
             .
             .
--> Next loop_index%
End Sub
```

All we have to do is to convert the loop index into a character starting at **A** and place it into the Grid's Text property:

```
Private Sub Form_Load()
        Grid1.Col = 0
    For loop_index% = 1 To 20
        Grid1.Row = loop_index%
        Grid1.Text = Str$(loop_index%)
    Next loop_index%
        Grid1.Row = 0
    For loop_index% = 1 To 10
        Grid1.Col = loop_index%
-->     Grid1.Text = Chr$(Asc("A") + loop_index% - 1)
    Next loop_index%
End Sub
```

Now our Grid control's cells are labeled. The next step is to allow the user to enter data. When the user clicks the Grid control, the Grid's Row and Col properties are automatically set to the location of the clicked cell. After that, the user enters the data for that cell in the text box Text1 and clicks the command button marked **Enter**. When that button is clicked, we need only transfer the data from the text box to the currently active cell in the Grid control and clear the text box. Double-click **Enter** to bring up Command1_Click() and place this code in it (from **GRID.FRM**):

```
Private Sub Command1_Click()
--> Grid1.Text = Text1.Text
--> Text1.Text = ""
End Sub
```

Our Grid example is complete. Run it as shown in Figure 5.4. Enter data by clicking the correct cell with the mouse, typing into the text box, and clicking **Enter**. The GRID program is a success.

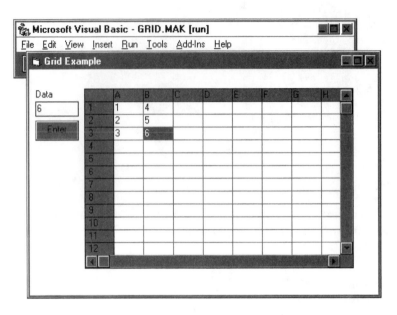

FIGURE 5.4 OUR GRID CONTROL ALLOWS THE USER TO ENTER AND DISPLAY DATA.

If you were creating a spreadsheet and the cells were tied together in some manner (for example, if you wanted to keep a running sum at the bottom of every column), you could perform any required operations (such as adding the column) when the new data was entered into the cell.

The code for this program, **GRID.FRM**, appears in Listing 5.1, and **GRID.VBP** appears in Listing 5.2.

LISTING 5.1 GRID.FRM

```
VERSION 4.00
Begin VB.Form Form1
   Caption         =    "Grid Example"
   ClientHeight    =    4230
   ClientLeft      =    1095
   ClientTop       =    1515
   ClientWidth     =    6720
   BeginProperty Font
      name         =       "MS Sans Serif"
      charset      =       1
      weight       =       400
      size         =       8.25
      underline    =       0      'False
      italic       =       0      'False
```

```
            strikethrough   =    0    'False
      EndProperty
      Height          =    4635
      Left            =    1035
      LinkTopic       =    "Form1"
      ScaleHeight     =    4230
      ScaleWidth      =    6720
      Top             =    1170
      Width           =    6840
      Begin VB.CommandButton Command1
         Caption      =    "Enter"
         Height       =    375
         Left         =    120
         TabIndex     =    3
         Top          =    960
         Width        =    855
      End
      Begin VB.TextBox Text1
         Height       =    285
         Left         =    120
         TabIndex     =    1
         Top          =    600
         Width        =    855
      End
      Begin VB.Label Label1
         Caption      =    "Data"
         Height       =    255
         Left         =    120
         TabIndex     =    2
         Top          =    360
         Width        =    735
      End
      Begin MSGrid.Grid Grid1
         Height       =    3375
         Left         =    1080
         TabIndex     =    0
         Top          =    360
         Width        =    5175
         _version     =    65536
         _extentx     =    9128
         _extenty     =    5953
         _stockprops  =    77
         forecolor    =    16777215
         rows         =    21
         cols         =    11
      End
End
Attribute VB_Name = "Form1"
Attribute VB_Creatable = False
Attribute VB_Exposed = False
```

```
Private Sub Command1_Click()
    Grid1.Text = Text1.Text
    Text1.Text = ""
End Sub

Private Sub Form_Load()
        Grid1.Col = 0
    For loop_index% = 1 To 20
        Grid1.Row = loop_index%
        Grid1.Text = Str$(loop_index%)
    Next loop_index%
        Grid1.Row = 0
    For loop_index% = 1 To 10
        Grid1.Col = loop_index%
        Grid1.Text = Chr$(Asc("A") + loop_index% - 1)
    Next loop_index%
End Sub
```

LISTING 5.2 GRID.VBP

```
GRID.FRM
Object={F9043C88-F6F2-101A-A3C9-08002B2F49FB}#1.0#0; COMDLG16.OCX
Object={FAEEE763-117E-101B-8933-08002B2F4F5A}#1.0#0; DBLIST16.OCX
Object={A8B3B723-0B5A-101B-B22E-00AA0037B2FC}#1.0#0; GRID16.OCX
ProjWinSize=323,395,198,111
ProjWinShow=2
IconForm="Form1"
ExeName="Project1.exe"
Path="D:\VB"
Command=""
Name="Project1"
HelpContextID="0"
StartMode=0
VersionCompatible="0"
MajorVer=1
MinorVer=0
RevisionVer=0
AutoIncrementVer=0
VersionCompanyName=""
Reference=*\G{00025E01-0000-0000-C000-
000000000046}#0.0#0#DAO2516.DLL#Microsoft DAO 2.5 Object Library
```

That's it for our coverage of the Grid control. In Chapter 11, we'll see the DBGrid control, which we can connect to databases. The next custom control we'll cover is also an extremely popular one: the Graph control.

THE GRAPH CONTROL

As you may recall, we created a graph of fish consumption in Chapter 3. That task involved graphing the individual points:

```
CurrentX = 1
CurrentY = FishConsumption(1)

For loop_index% = 1 To NumberEntries
    Line -(loop_index%, FishConsumption(loop_index%))
Next loop_index%
```

In that case, we drew the graph of fish consumption, including the axes and labeling, and graphed the data ourselves. There is an easier way to do this—we can simply use the Graph control.

To use the Graph control, you first add it to a Visual Basic project. Create a new Visual Basic project named **GRAPH.VBP**. Add a Graph control to Form1 as we added the Grid control above: find the Graph control in the Custom Controls dialog box, select its checkbox, and then click **OK**. Now draw a new Graph control in the form, as shown in Figure 5.5. The Graph control already graphs random data. Give the form the caption **Graph Control Example** by setting its Caption property in the properties window.

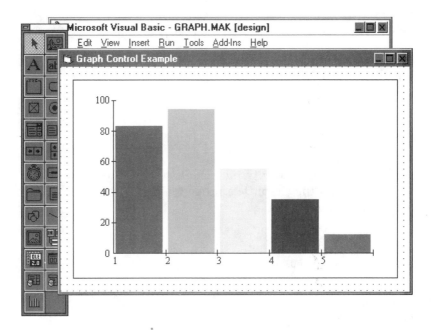

FIGURE 5.5 OUR NEW GRAPH CONTROL ALREADY DISPLAYS DATA.

The name of this Graph control is Graph1. Let's say that we have this data to plot:

Point	Value
1	50
2	60
3	30
4	40
5	60
6	70

We can plot it by repeatedly filling the Graph control's GraphData property with these values. We place the first value in GraphData with this new code in the Form_Load() event handler (from **GRAPH.FRM**):

```
Private Sub Form_Load()
--> Graph1.GraphData = 50
        .
        .
        .
End Sub
```

Next, we fill GraphData with the next data point to graph:

```
Private Sub Form_Load()
    Graph1.GraphData = 50
--> Graph1.GraphData = 60
        .
        .
        .
End Sub
```

The Graph control automatically increments our position along the X axis every time we (re)fill the GraphData property. In this way, we can place all our data into the graph:

```
Private Sub Form_Load()
    Graph1.GraphData = 50
    Graph1.GraphData = 60
--> Graph1.GraphData = 30
--> Graph1.GraphData = 40
--> Graph1.GraphData = 60
--> Graph1.GraphData = 70
        .
        .
        .
End Sub
```

And filling our graph with our data is that easy.

The GraphType Property

Next, we select a graph type. The available selections for this property, the GraphType property, appear in Table 5.1.

TABLE 5.1 THE GRAPH CONTROL'S GRAPHTYPE PROPERTY.

GraphType	Type of Graph
0	None
1	2D pie
2	3D pie
3	(Default) 2D bar
4	3D bar
5	Gantt
6	Line
7	Log/Lin
8	Area
9	Scatter
10	Polar
11	HLC

We'll start with a simple line chart, GraphType = 6. Add this code to Form_Load():

```
Private Sub Form_Load()
    Graph1.GraphData = 50
    Graph1.GraphData = 60
    Graph1.GraphData = 30
    Graph1.GraphData = 40
    Graph1.GraphData = 60
    Graph1.GraphData = 70
--> Graph1.GraphType = 6
End Sub
```

In addition, we might label our graph. For example, we can use the GraphTitle to add a title, "Fish Consumption," by adding this code:

```
Private Sub Form_Load()
--> Graph1.GraphTitle = "Fish Consumption"
    Graph1.GraphData = 50
    Graph1.GraphData = 60
    Graph1.GraphData = 30
```

```
      Graph1.GraphData = 40
      Graph1.GraphData = 60
      Graph1.GraphData = 70
      Graph1.GraphType = 6
End Sub
```

And we might add more explanation at the bottom—a label reading "Measured in Tons"—by placing that string in the BottomTitle property. (In addition to BottomTitle, LeftTitle is also available for labeling the Y axis.)

```
Private Sub Form_Load()
      Graph1.GraphTitle = "Fish Consumption"
--> Graph1.BottomTitle = "Measured in Tons"
      Graph1.GraphData = 50
      Graph1.GraphData = 60
      Graph1.GraphData = 30
      Graph1.GraphData = 40
      Graph1.GraphData = 60
      Graph1.GraphData = 70
      Graph1.GraphType = 6
End Sub
```

Now run the program, producing the graph shown in Figure 5.6. As you can see, our data appears in the graph as a line graph, and our titles appear at the top and the bottom of the graph. So far, the program is a success.

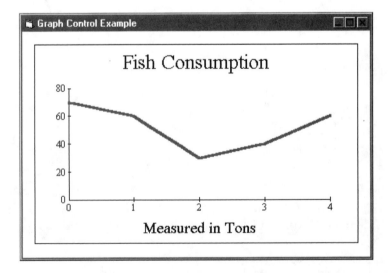

FIGURE 5.6 OUR FIRST GRAPH DISPLAYS ITS DATA AS A LINE GRAPH.

Let's try another type of graph. We can change our graph into a 3-D pie chart simply by changing the GraphType property from 6 (line chart) to 2 (3-D pie chart) this way:

```
Private Sub Form_Load()
    Graph1.GraphTitle = "Fish Consumption"
    Graph1.BottomTitle = "Measured in Tons"
    Graph1.GraphData = 50
    Graph1.GraphData = 60
    Graph1.GraphData = 30
    Graph1.GraphData = 40
    Graph1.GraphData = 60
    Graph1.GraphData = 70
--> Graph1.GraphType = 2
End Sub
```

We can do more with pie charts. For example, we can "explode" one of the pie slices to draw attention to it; it will be drawn slightly separated from the rest of the pie. To explode our first data point, we must set that data point's ExtraData property to 1. Each data point has an ExtraData property, which means different things for different GraphType settings; when we're drawing a 3-D pie chart, setting a point's ExtraData property to 1 explodes that pie piece.

The ThisPoint Property

To work with an individual data point, we use the ThisPoint property. This property selects the current point in the Graph control; to select our first data point, we set Graph1.ThisPoint to 1:

```
Private Sub Form_Load()
    Graph1.GraphTitle = "Fish Consumption"
    Graph1.BottomTitle = "Measured in Tons"
    Graph1.GraphData = 50
    Graph1.GraphData = 60
    Graph1.GraphData = 30
    Graph1.GraphData = 40
    Graph1.GraphData = 60
    Graph1.GraphData = 70
    Graph1.GraphType = 2
--> Graph1.ThisPoint = 1
        .
        .
        .
End Sub
```

Now that we've selected the data point to explode, we set its ExtraData property to 1:

```
Private Sub Form_Load()
    Graph1.GraphTitle = "Fish Consumption"
    Graph1.BottomTitle = "Measured in Tons"
    Graph1.GraphData = 50
    Graph1.GraphData = 60
    Graph1.GraphData = 30
    Graph1.GraphData = 40
    Graph1.GraphData = 60
    Graph1.GraphData = 70
    Graph1.GraphType = 2
    Graph1.ThisPoint = 1
--> Graph1.ExtraData = 1
End Sub
```

The new graph appears in Figure 5.7.

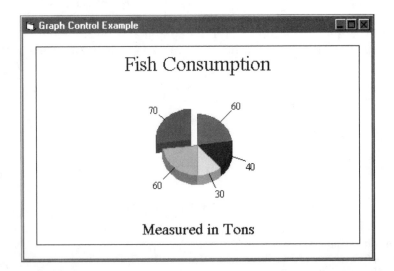

FIGURE 5.7 OUR GRAPH CONTROL DISPLAYS OUR DATA AS A 3-D PIE CHART WITH ONE EXPLODED SLICE.

Of course, not all data will appear neatly at X positions 1, 2, 3, 4, and so on. Usually, we have to set the X data just as we've set the Y data. To set the X position of a point, we first select that point with the ThisPoint property and then set its XPosData property to the correct X value. Using this property (which cycles just as the GraphData property cycles), we can specify the X locations of our data points as well as the Y values.

That's it for the Graph control. As you can see, using it makes graphing numerical data easy. **GRAPH.FRM** appears in Listing 5.3, and **GRAPH.VBP** is in Listing 5.4.

LISTING 5.3 GRAPH.FRM

```
VERSION 4.00
Begin VB.Form Form1
   Caption          =    "Graph Control Example"
   ClientHeight     =    4230
   ClientLeft       =    1095
   ClientTop        =    1665
   ClientWidth      =    6720
   BeginProperty Font
      name          =    "MS Sans Serif"
      charset       =    1
      weight        =    400
      size          =    8.25
      underline     =    0      'False
      italic        =    0      'False
      strikethrough =    0      'False
   EndProperty
   Height           =    4635
   Left             =    1035
   LinkTopic        =    "Form1"
   ScaleHeight      =    4230
   ScaleWidth       =    6720
   Top              =    1320
   Width            =    6840
   Begin GraphLib.Graph Graph1
      Height        =    3735
      Left          =    240
      TabIndex      =    0
      Top           =    240
      Width         =    6255
      _version      =    65536
      _extentx      =    11033
      _extenty      =    6588
      _stockprops   =    96
      borderstyle   =    1
      randomdata    =    1
      colordata     =    0
      extradata     =    0
      extradata[]   =    0
      fontfamily    =    4
      fontsize      =    4
      fontsize[0]   =    200
      fontsize[1]   =    150
      fontsize[2]   =    100
      fontsize[3]   =    100
```

```
        fontstyle       =   4
        graphdata       =   0
        graphdata[]     =   5
        labeltext       =   0
        legendtext      =   0
        patterndata     =   0
        symboldata      =   0
        xposdata        =   0
        xposdata[]      =   0
     End
End
Attribute VB_Name = "Form1"
Attribute VB_Creatable = False
Attribute VB_Exposed = False
Private Sub Form_Load()
    Graph1.GraphTitle = "Fish Consumption"
    Graph1.BottomTitle = "Measured in Tons"
    Graph1.GraphData = 50
    Graph1.GraphData = 60
    Graph1.GraphData = 30
    Graph1.GraphData = 40
    Graph1.GraphData = 60
    Graph1.GraphData = 70
    Graph1.GraphType = 2       'Change for diff graphs
    Graph1.ThisPoint = 1
    Graph1.ExtraData = 1
End Sub
```

LISTING 5.4 GRAPH.VBP

```
GRAPH.FRM
Object={F9043C88-F6F2-101A-A3C9-08002B2F49FB}#1.0#0; COMDLG16.OCX
Object={FAEEE763-117E-101B-8933-08002B2F4F5A}#1.0#0; DBLIST16.OCX
Object={0842D103-1E19-101B-9AAF-1A1626551E7C}#1.0#0; GRAPH16.OCX
ProjWinSize=345,402,202,111
ProjWinShow=2
ExeName="Project1.exe"
Path="D:\VB"
Command=""
Name="Project1"
HelpContextID="0"
StartMode=0
VersionCompatible="0"
MajorVer=1
MinorVer=0
RevisionVer=0
AutoIncrementVer=0
VersionCompanyName=""
Reference=*\G{00025E01-0000-0000-C000-
000000000046}#0.0#0#DAO2516.DLL#Microsoft DAO 2.5 Object Library
```

The Graph control is a useful control that is also easy to use. The next custom control we turn to will be the common dialog boxes—also useful, and (relatively!) easy to use.

THE COMMONDIALOG CONTROL

You might recall from Chapter 2, where we developed our MDI WRITER program, that we simply chose an arbitrary name for the disk file when it came time to save the user's text to the disk (from **WRITER.FRM**):

```
Private Sub Save_Click()
    Open "Write" + Format(MyDocumentNumber) + ".txt" For Output As #1
    Print #1, Text1.Text
    MsgBox ("Saved")
    Close #1
End Sub
```

This is rudimentary programming. Far better would be to ask users what name to give to the file they are saving to disk. However, to do that, we would have to pop a full Save As dialog box on the screen. Putting together all the controls in such a dialog box—including making the controls display the files in the current subdirectory, allowing the user to change directories, and getting all the click events right—is quite a chore. That's why we didn't do it in Chapter 2. In this chapter, however, we'll add that dialog box. It will be simple to do, because we're going to use the predefined dialog boxes in the Visual Basic CommonDialog control.

We will use several of the most popular dialog boxes contained in the CommonDialog control: color selection, open a file, save a file, and print. We'll begin with the Save As dialog box. We should note that these dialog boxes are the same ones used by other Windows programs (hence the word *common* in the name of this control), and using these dialogs promotes a unified and well-integrated feel to our program.

The File Save As Dialog Box

Our task is to modify our WRITER program so that we pop the common dialog Save As dialog box on the screen when the user decides to save the text in a file. Open **WRITER.VBP** in Visual Basic. We start by clearing the code in WRITER's Save_Click() event handler in **WRITER.FRM**, which the program calls when the user selects the **Save** item in the File menu. In addition, change WRITER's File menu item named **Save** to **Save As**.

```
Private Sub Save_Click()

End Sub
```

Now add common dialogs to the WRITER project by using the Visual Basic **Tools | Custom Controls** menu item as we've done for the Graph and Grid controls. Draw a new CommonDialog control in WRITER's **WRITER.FRM** form; Visual Basic gives this control the name CommonDialog1. To pop the Save As dialog box on the screen, it's necessary only to execute CommonDialog1's ShowSave method with this new code (from **WRITER.FRM**):

```
Private Sub Save_Click()
--> CommonDialog1.ShowSave
        .
        .
        .
End Sub
```

At this point, the Save As dialog box appears on the screen, and the user selects or types in a new file name. That name is returned to us in the FileName property of CommonDialog1, and we can use that name to open the file. (Note that there will be an error if the user did not specify a file name; we will fix this problem in the next chapter.)

```
Private Sub Save_Click()
    CommonDialog1.ShowSave
--> Open CommonDialog1.FileName For Output As #1
        .
        .
        .
End Sub
```

Then we save the data to that file as before and close the file:

```
Private Sub Save_Click()
    CommonDialog1.ShowSave
    Open CommonDialog1.FileName For Output As #1
--> Print #1, Text1.Text
--> MsgBox ("Saved")
--> Close #1
End Sub
```

Before running the program, let's add one or two details. For example, we can specify a default file extension in the CommonDialog DefaultExt property. This file extension will be used as the file's extension if the user does not specify an extension:

```
Private Sub Save_Click()
--> CommonDialog1.DefaultExt = ".txt"
    CommonDialog1.ShowSave
    Open CommonDialog1.FileName For Output As #1
    Print #1, Text1.Text
    MsgBox ("Saved")
    Close #1
End Sub
```

In addition, the Save As dialog box includes a small list box at lower left labeled Save File as Type and lists possible extensions. Let's place the extension **.TXT** in that box by placing that extension in the Filter property:

```
Private Sub Save_Click()
    CommonDialog1.DefaultExt = ".txt"
--> CommonDialog1.Filter = "*.txt"
    CommonDialog1.ShowSave
    Open CommonDialog1.FileName For Output As #1
    Print #1, Text1.Text
    MsgBox ("Saved")
    Close #1
End Sub
```

Now run WRITER and select the **Save As** menu item. Doing so pops our Save As dialog box on the screen, as shown in Figure 5.8. The new version of WRITER is a success.

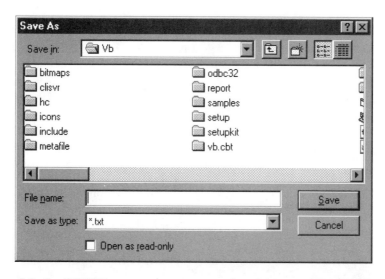

FIGURE 5.8 OUR WRITER PROGRAM NOW INCLUDES A SAVE AS DIALOG BOX FOR SAVING FILES.

In addition to the FileName, DefaultExt, and Filter properties, CommonDialog1 includes a Flags property, allowing you to specify whether the file must already exist before we save to it, whether its path must exist, and many more options, as shown in Table 5.2.

TABLE 5.2 COMMON DIALOG FILE FLAGS SETTINGS

Flags Property	Meaning
vbOFNAllowMultiselect	Specifies that the File Name list box allows multiple selections. The user can select more than one file at run time. The FileName property returns a string containing the names of all selected files, delimited by spaces.
vbOFNCreatePrompt	Specifies that the dialog box prompts the user to create a file that doesn't currently exist.
vbOFNExtensionDifferent	Indicates that the extension of the returned file name must be different from the extension specified by the DefaultExt property.
vbOFNFileMustExist	Specifies that the user can enter only names of existing files in the File Name text box.
vbOFNHideReadOnly	Hides the Read Only checkbox.
vbOFNNoChangeDir	Forces the dialog box to set the current directory to what it was when the dialog box was opened.
vbOFNNoReadOnlyReturn	Specifies that the returned file won't have the Read Only attribute set and won't be in a write-protected directory.
vbOFNNoValidate	Specifies that the common dialog box allows invalid characters in the file name.
vbOFNOverwritePrompt	Causes the Save As dialog box to generate a message box if the selected file already exists.
vbOFNPathMustExist	Specifies that the user can enter only valid paths.
vbOFNReadOnly	Causes the Read Only checkbox to be initially checked when the dialog box is created. This flag also indicates the state of the Read Only checkbox when the dialog box is closed.
vbOFNShareAware	Specifies that sharing violation errors will be ignored.
vbOFNShowHelp	Causes the dialog box to display the Help button.

Now that we've saved our data to disk using the File Save As dialog box, the next step is to read data from the disk. We will open files using the Open dialog box next.

The File Open Dialog Box

Currently, we can read files only in a rudimentary way in the WRITER program. We simply read in the current document using the code in **WRITER.FRM**, assuming that it has a particular name (**WRITE#.TXT**, where # is the document number):

```
Private Sub Read_Click()
    Open "Write" + Format(MyDocumentNumber) + ".txt" For Input As #1
    Text1.Text = Input$(LOF(1), #1)
    Close #1
End Sub
```

Let's improve this. First, clear the code in Read_Click() (from **WRITER.FRM**):

```
Private Sub Read_Click()

End Sub
```

We begin by using the common dialog Open dialog box to get from the user the name of the file to open. Just as we used the ShowSave method of our CommonDialog1 control to display the Save As dialog box, so we can use the ShowOpen method to display the Open dialog box; note that we first set CommonDialog1's FileName property to "*.*" so that all files will be displayed:

```
Private Sub Read_Click()
--> CommonDialog1.FileName = "*.*"
--> CommonDialog1.ShowOpen
        .
        .
        .
End Sub
```

The flags in Table 5.2 apply to both file dialog boxes: Save As and Open. This means that, for example, you can set the Read Only box in the Open dialog box by setting the vbOFNReadOnly flag, and so on. After the user closes the Open dialog box, we can open the required file as shown next. (Again, there will be an error if the user did not specify a file name, and we will fix that problem in the next chapter.)

```
Private Sub Read_Click()
    CommonDialog1.FileName = "*.*"
    CommonDialog1.ShowOpen
--> Open CommonDialog1.FileName For Input As #1
        .
        .
        .
End Sub
```

Finally, we read the data from the text file and display it in the program's text box:

```
Private Sub Read_Click()
    CommonDialog1.FileName = "*.*"
    CommonDialog1.ShowOpen
    Open CommonDialog1.FileName For Input As #1
--> Text1.Text = Input$(LOF(1), #1)
--> Close #1
End Sub
```

Now we display the Open dialog box when the user selects the matching menu item, as shown in Figure 5.9.

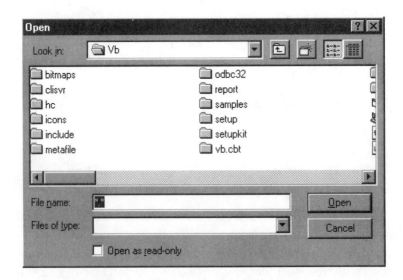

FIGURE 5.9 OUR **WRITER** PROGRAM NOW USES THE COMMON DIALOG OPEN DIALOG BOX.

The next common dialog box we'll cover is the Color dialog box, which allows the user to select a drawing color.

The Color Dialog Box

Using the Color dialog box is easy. Using the Menu Editor as we have many times before, add a new menu item to WRITER's File menu, naming it **Color**, and open the corresponding Click event handler by clicking that new menu item (from **WRITER.FRM**):

```
Private Sub Color_Click()

End Sub
```

We set CommonDialog1's Color property to the current forecolor of the text box by adding this code:

```
Private Sub Color_Click()
--> CommonDialog1.Color = Text1.ForeColor
       .
       .
       .
End Sub
```

Next, we use CommonDialog1's ShowColor method to pop the Color dialog box on the screen:

```
Private Sub Color_Click()
    CommonDialog1.Color = Text1.ForeColor
--> CommonDialog1.ShowColor
       .
       .
       .
End Sub
```

After the user is finished with the Color dialog box, we can set the forecolor of the text box to the new color selected:

```
Private Sub Color_Click()
    CommonDialog1.Color = Text1.ForeColor
    CommonDialog1.ShowColor
--> Text1.ForeColor = CommonDialog1.Color
End Sub
```

Give this new version of the WRITER program a try. Select the **Color** menu item, opening the Color dialog box, as shown in Figure 5.10. Using this dialog box, you can set the new text color of WRITER's text boxes.

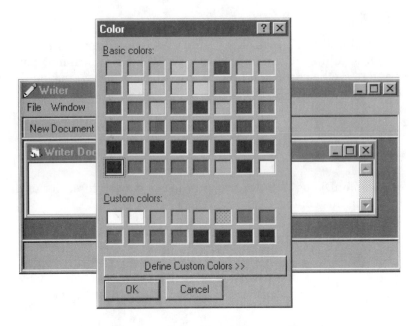

FIGURE 5.10 THE WRITER PROGRAM NOW USES THE
COMMON DIALOG COLOR DIALOG BOX TO SELECT TEXT COLOR.

The last common dialog box we'll cover is the Print dialog box.

The Print Dialog Box

Using the Print dialog box, the user can print a document. To display this dialog box, we use the CommonDialog1 control's ShowPrinter method. Using the Menu Editor, add a new menu item to WRITER's File menu, and give it the name **Print**; next, open the associated Click event handler by clicking that new menu item (from **WRITER.FRM**):

```
Private Sub Print_Click()

End Sub
```

To show the Print dialog box, we execute the ShowPrinter method by adding this new code:

```
Private Sub Print_Click()
--> CommonDialog1.ShowPrinter
        .
        .
        .
End Sub
```

After the user closes this dialog box, we can see the pages specified to print, if any, by examining the CommonDialog1.FromPage and CommonDialog1.ToPage properties. In addition, the user may have set, say, the Copies property of the CommonDialog1 control, indicating that more than one copy of the document are to be printed. We can take advantage of that fact by looping over the number of copies requested:

```
Private Sub Print_Click()
    CommonDialog1.ShowPrinter
--> NumberCopies% = CommonDialog1.Copies
--> For loop_index% = 1 To NumberCopies%
        .
        .
        .
--> Next loop_index%
End Sub
```

To print the document on the printer, we use the Printer object's Print method. Note that after each document is printed, we use the Printer object's EndDoc method to make sure that the last page of the document is ejected from the printer before continuing:

```
Private Sub Print_Click()
    CommonDialog1.ShowPrinter
    NumberCopies% = CommonDialog1.Copies
    For loop_index% = 1 To NumberCopies%
-->     Printer.Print Text1.Text
-->     Printer.EndDoc
    Next loop_index%
End Sub
```

Run WRITER now. When you do, place some text in the document and select **Print** in the File menu. The Print dialog box appears, as in Figure 5.11, allowing you to print your document as many times as you wish.

The new version of **WRITER.FRM**, with all the common dialogs installed, appears in Listing 5.5.

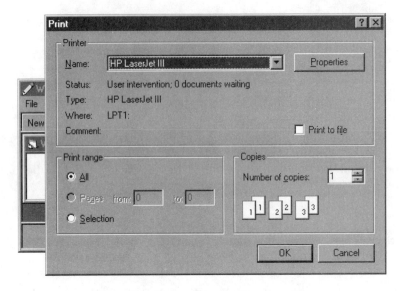

FIGURE 5.11 THE **WRITER** PROGRAM NOW INCLUDES A
PRINT DIALOG BOX TO PRINT DOCUMENTS ON THE PRINTER.

LISTING 5.5 WRITER.FRM WITH PRINT DIALOG BOX

```
VERSION 4.00
Begin VB.Form Form1
    Caption         =   "Writer Document"
    ClientHeight    =   2445
    ClientLeft      =   1695
    ClientTop       =   2055
    ClientWidth     =   5475
    BeginProperty Font
        name            =   "MS Sans Serif"
        charset         =   1
        weight          =   400
        size            =   8.25
        underline       =   0   'False
        italic          =   0   'False
        strikethrough   =   0   'False
    EndProperty
    Height          =   3135
    Left            =   1635
    LinkTopic       =   "Form1"
    MDIChild        =   -1   'True
    ScaleHeight     =   2445
    ScaleWidth      =   5475
    Top             =   1425
```

```
Width           =    5595
Begin VB.TextBox Text1
   Height       =    1935
   Left         =    0
   MultiLine    =    -1  'True
   ScrollBars   =    2   'Vertical
   TabIndex     =    0
   Top          =    0
   Width        =    5055
End
Begin MSComDlg.CommonDialog CommonDialog1
   Left         =    3240
   Top          =    1920
   _version     =    65536
   _extentx     =    847
   _extenty     =    847
   _stockprops  =    0
End
Begin VB.Menu File
   Caption         =    "File"
   Begin VB.Menu New
      Caption      =    "New Document"
   End
   Begin VB.Menu Save
      Caption      =    "Save As..."
   End
   Begin VB.Menu Read
      Caption      =    "Read..."
   End
   Begin VB.Menu Font
      Caption      =    "Font..."
   End
   Begin VB.Menu Color
      Caption      =    "Color..."
   End
   Begin VB.Menu Print
      Caption      =    "Print..."
   End
   Begin VB.Menu Exit
      Caption      =    "Exit"
   End
End
Begin VB.Menu Window
   Caption      =    "Window"
   WindowList   =    -1  'True
End
Begin VB.Menu Edit
   Caption      =    "Edit"
   Begin VB.Menu Cut
      Caption      =    "Cut"
   End
```

```
        End
    End
    Attribute VB_Name = "Form1"
    Attribute VB_Creatable = False
    Attribute VB_Exposed = False
    Dim MyDocumentNumber As Integer

    Private Sub Color_Click()
        CommonDialog1.Color = Text1.ForeColor
        CommonDialog1.ShowColor
        Text1.ForeColor = CommonDialog1.Color
    End Sub

    Private Sub Exit_Click()
        End
    End Sub

    Private Sub Font_Click()
        CommonDialog1.FontName = Text1.FontName
        CommonDialog1.Color = Text1.ForeColor
        CommonDialog1.FontItalic = Text1.FontItalic
        CommonDialog1.FontStrikethru = Text1.FontStrikethru
        CommonDialog1.FontSize = Text1.FontSize
        CommonDialog1.FontUnderline = Text1.FontUnderline
        CommonDialog1.Flags = vbCFBoth
        CommonDialog1.ShowFont
        Text1.FontName = CommonDialog1.FontName
        Text1.FontSize = CommonDialog1.FontSize
    End Sub

    Private Sub Form_Load()
        MyDocumentNumber = NumberDocuments
        Text1.Height = Form1.ScaleHeight
        Text1.Width = Form1.ScaleWidth
        Caption = "Writer Document " + Str$(MyDocumentNumber)
        If NumberDocuments = 1 Then AttachWindow Me
    End Sub

    Private Sub Form_Resize()
        Text1.Height = Form1.ScaleHeight
        Text1.Width = Form1.ScaleWidth
    End Sub

    Private Sub New_Click()
        AddADocument
    End Sub

    Private Sub Print_Click()
        CommonDialog1.ShowPrinter
```

```
    NumberCopies% = CommonDialog1.Copies
    For loop_index% = 1 To NumberCopies%
        Printer.Print Text1.Text
        Printer.EndDoc
    Next loop_index%
End Sub

Private Sub Read_Click()
    CommonDialog1.FileName = "*.*"
    CommonDialog1.ShowOpen
    Open CommonDialog1.FileName For Input As #1
    Open "Write" + Format(MyDocumentNumber) + ".txt" For Input As #1
    Text1.Text = Input$(LOF(1), #1)
    Close #1
End Sub

Private Sub Save_Click()
    CommonDialog1.DefaultExt = ".txt"
    CommonDialog1.Filter = "*.txt"
    CommonDialog1.ShowSave
    Open CommonDialog1.FileName For Output As #1
    Open "Write" + Format(MyDocumentNumber) + ".txt" For Output As #1
    Print #1, Text1.Text
    MsgBox ("Saved")
    Close #1
End Sub
```

That's it for the most popular common dialog boxes: Color, Print, File Open, and File Save. Before leaving the topic of custom controls, let;s look at a few more controls, including keyboard state indicators, Gauge controls, and 3-D controls.

KEYBOARD STATE INDICATOR CONTROLS

Keyboard state indicators are easy to use. These controls indicate the state of various keyboard modes, including **Caps Lock**, **Num Lock**, the **Ins** key, and **Scroll Lock**. Let's add the Key State controls to a new project, which we'll call **CUSTOM.VBP**.

Create four new key state controls, which Visual Basic will call MhState1–MhState4. Next, find each control's Custom property in the properties window. Set the first one's Style property to 0 (**Caps Lock** indicator), the next control's Style property to 1 (**Num Lock** indicator), the next control's Style property to 2 (**Insert** state indicator), and the final control's Style property to 3 (**Scroll Lock** indicator).

When you run the program, as shown in Figure 5.12, the state of these various keyboard modes appears in the key state controls.

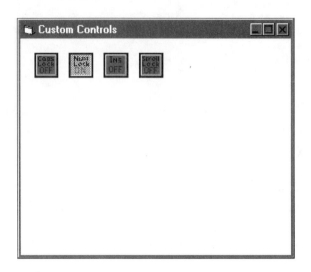

FIGURE 5.12 OUR CUSTOM PROGRAM SHOWS THE STATE OF VARIOUS KEYBOARD MODES.

Some of the OCX custom controls are specially designed to produce a three-dimensional appearance. Let's add these 3-D controls to **CUSTOM.VBP**.

3-D CONTROLS

Some of the more interesting custom controls available are the 3-D controls, which include 3-D buttons, 3-D panels, and 3-D checkboxes. Add the 3-D controls to our CUSTOM program by clicking the 3-D controls entry in the box that opens when you select the **Tools | Custom Controls** menu item. Find the new 3-D command button tool in the toolbox (the tooltip will read "SSCommand" for this tool) and create a new 3-D button in CUSTOM's default form. In the properties window, set this 3-D button's Font3D property to 2, making the button caption's appear in a raised font. In addition, click the 3-D button to open its Click event handler, and add this code so that we'll see a message box each time we click the 3-D button:

```
Private Sub SSCommand1_Click()
--> MsgBox ("You pressed the 3D button")
End Sub
```

Now run the program, displaying our 3-D button as shown in Figure 5.13. As you can see, the button's caption appears raised, as if it were three-dimensional. The new version of **CUSTOM.VBP** is a success.

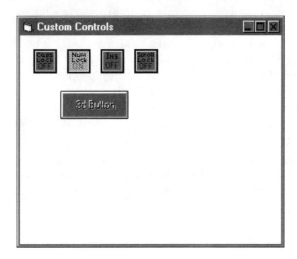

FIGURE 5.13 OUR CUSTOM PROGRAM NOW INCLUDES A 3-D BUTTON CONTROL.

The final custom control we'll expore is the Windows Gauge control. You are probably familiar with gauge controls from using Windows installation programs. Typically, these white horizontal bars fill up with blue as files are installed on your hard disk. Another such example is the Windows 95 progress bar, which we look at later in this chapter.

GAUGE CONTROLS

Visual Basic offers Gauge controls for us to use; let's add them to our CUSTOM program by clicking the Gauge control entry in the box that opens when you select Visual Basic's **Tools | Custom Controls** menu item. Now use the new Gauge control in the toolbox to create a new Gauge control, which Visual Basic will call Gauge1, in CUSTOM's default form.

The value displayed by the Gauge control is held in Gauge1.Value, and that value may range from the minimum, Gauge1.Min (gauge appears empty), to the maximum possible value (gauge appears full), Gauge1.Max. The default for the Min property is 0, and the default for the Max property is 100. We can change that Max property to, say, 80 by resetting that value in the properties window; do that now.

A Gauge control by itself appears merely as a bar or a rotating needle. We can set it to these Styles in the properties window: 0, a vertical bar; 1, a horizontal bar; 2, a "semi" needle (travels in a semicircle); and 3, a "full" needle (travels in a full circle). In addition, we can add a bitmap to surround the Gauge and give it the appearance of a common gauge such as a speedometer; the Gauge control comes with a number of bitmaps, which we can load into Gauge1's Picture property. In this case, we will use the bitmap file **C:\VB\BITMAPS\GAUGE\VERT.BMP** (use the drive and path appropriate to your installation of Visual Basic). Set the Picture property of Gauge1 to that file name in the properties window. This will give our gauge the appearance of a vertical thermometer. Finally, set the Value property of Gauge1 to 50 (of a maximum possible value of 80) in the properties window, so that it appears as a mostly full gauge.

Gauge controls also have Click events; double-click the gauge to open Gauge1_Click(). When the user clicks **Gauge1**, we can change its reading from 50 to 20 by adding this code to Gauge1_Click() (in **CUSTOM.FRM**):

```
Private Sub Gauge1_Click()
--> Gauge1.Value = 20
End Sub
```

Run the program now. Our Windows gauge appears as a nearly full vertical gauge. Next, click the **Gauge** control. You'll see the reading in that control drop from 50 to 20, as shown in Figure 5.14.

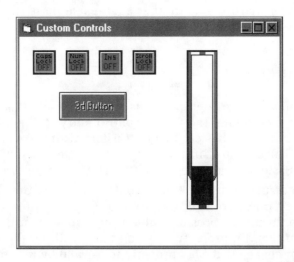

FIGURE 5.14 OUR CUSTOM PROGRAM NOW INCLUDES A GAUGE CONTROL.

CUSTOM.FRM appears in Listing 5.6, and **CUSTOM.VBP** is in Listing 5.7.

LISTING 5.6 CUSTOM.FRM

```
VERSION 4.00
Begin VB.Form Form1
   Caption         =   "Custom Controls"
   ClientHeight    =   3630
   ClientLeft      =   1095
   ClientTop       =   1515
   ClientWidth     =   4650
   BeginProperty Font
      name         =   "MS Sans Serif"
      charset      =   1
      weight       =   400
      size         =   8.25
      underline    =   0    'False
      italic       =   0    'False
      strikethrough =  0    'False
   EndProperty
   Height          =   4035
   Left            =   1035
   LinkTopic       =   "Form1"
   ScaleHeight     =   3630
   ScaleWidth      =   4650
   Top             =   1170
   Width           =   4770
   Begin GaugeLib.Gauge Gauge1
      Height       =   2760
      Left         =   3000
      TabIndex     =   5
      Top          =   240
      Width        =   540
      _version     =   65536
      _extentx     =   953
      _extenty     =   4868
      _stockprops  =   73
      max          =   80
      value        =   50
      style        =   1
      needlewidth  =   1
      picture      =   "CUSTOM.frx":0000
   End
   Begin Threed.SSCommand SSCommand1
      Height       =   495
      Left         =   720
      TabIndex     =   4
      Top          =   960
      Width        =   1215
      _version     =   65536
      _extentx     =   2143
```

```
            _extenty        =    873
            _stockprops     =    78
            caption         =    "3d Button"
            font3d          =    2
        End
        Begin KeyStatLib.MhState MhState4
            Height          =    420
            Left            =    2040
            TabIndex        =    3
            Top             =    240
            Width           =    420
            _version        =    65536
            _extentx        =    741
            _extenty        =    741
            _stockprops     =    65
            style           =    3
        End
        Begin KeyStatLib.MhState MhState3
            Height          =    420
            Left            =    1440
            TabIndex        =    2
            Top             =    240
            Width           =    420
            _version        =    65536
            _extentx        =    741
            _extenty        =    741
            _stockprops     =    65
            style           =    2
        End
        Begin KeyStatLib.MhState MhState2
            Height          =    420
            Left            =    840
            TabIndex        =    1
            Top             =    240
            Width           =    420
            _version        =    65536
            _extentx        =    741
            _extenty        =    741
            _stockprops     =    65
            style           =    1
        End
        Begin KeyStatLib.MhState MhState1
            Height          =    420
            Left            =    240
            TabIndex        =    0
            Top             =    240
            Width           =    420
            _version        =    65536
            _extentx        =    741
```

```
        _extenty        =    741
        _stockprops     =    65
    End
End
Attribute VB_Name = "Form1"
Attribute VB_Creatable = False
Attribute VB_Exposed = False


Private Sub Gauge1_Click()
    Gauge1.Value = 20
End Sub


Private Sub SSCommand1_Click()
    MsgBox ("You pressed the 3D button")
End Sub
```

LISTING 5.7 CUSTOM.VBP

```
CUSTOM.FRM
Object={F9043C88-F6F2-101A-A3C9-08002B2F49FB}#1.0#0; COMDLG16.OCX
Object={FAEEE763-117E-101B-8933-08002B2F4F5A}#1.0#0; DBLIST16.OCX
Object={B9D22273-0C24-101B-AEBD-04021C009402}#1.0#0; KEYSTA16.OCX
Object={0BA686C6-F7D3-101A-993E-0000C0EF6F5E}#1.0#0; THREED16.OCX
Object={C932BA88-4374-101B-A56C-00AA003668DC}#1.0#0; MSMASK16.OCX
Object={7A080CC8-26E2-101B-AEBD-04021C009402}#1.0#0; GAUGE16.OCX
ProjWinSize=345,402,202,111
ProjWinShow=2
IconForm="Form1"
ExeName="Project1.exe"
Path="D:\VB"
Command=""
Name="Project1"
HelpContextID="0"
StartMode=0
VersionCompatible="0"
MajorVer=1
MinorVer=0
RevisionVer=0
AutoIncrementVer=0
VersionCompanyName=""
Reference=*\G{00025E01-0000-0000-C000-
000000000046}#0.0#0#DAO2516.DLL#Microsoft DAO 2.5 Object Library
```

Next, we'll look at an exciting new technology that we can add to our programs: multimedia.

THE MULTIMEDIA CONTROL

Multimedia is certainly a hot topic. It lets us create an integrated environment of video, sound, still pictures, and text. Video Basic gives us access to multimedia through custom controls such as the Media Control Interface (MCI) Multimedia control, the Video Clip control, and the Media Clip control. Let's take advantage of this and create a new project, **MULTIMED.VBP**. We'll integrate both sound and video in this project. The result we are aiming for appears in Figure 5.15, where users can see video and listen to CD audio.

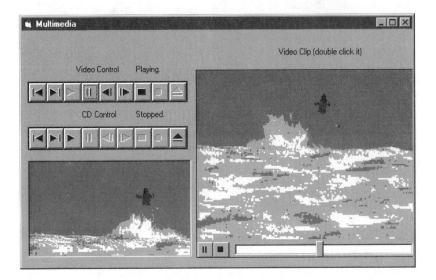

FIGURE 5.15 OUR MULTIMEDIA PROJECT.

To create this program, from the Tools menu add two new control types to the project: the Microsoft Multimedia control and the Video Clip control. First, double-click the **Video Clip** control, opening its control panel as shown in Figure 5.16. This control is particularly easy to use, and we can use it to play **.AVI** file video pictures. The **.AVI** format is the way video sequences are stored in Windows, and a sample **.AVI** file, **SKIING.AVI**, comes with Windows in the **WINDOWS\MEDIA** directory.

When we first place a Video Clip control in our program—the name of this control will be AVIFile1—the Video Clip control panel opens, giving us the chance to connect an **.AVI** file to the Video Clip control. (The Media Clip control works in much the same way except that it also allows us to use CD audio.)

Use the File menu in the Video Clip's control panel to open the **SKIING.AVI** file; then select the **Exit & return to client document** item, also in the File menu. That's all there is to it. Our Video Clip control is installed, and it displays the first frame of the skiing video. When the user double-clicks the control, the skiing video will play.

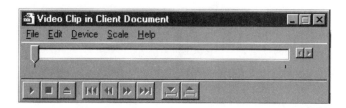

FIGURE 5.16 THE VIDEO CLIP CONTROL PANEL.

The Multimedia control, which appears in Figure 5.17, is more advanced. This control consists of a set of buttons much like those you would see on a CD player. With these buttons, we can control the operation of our multimedia devices.

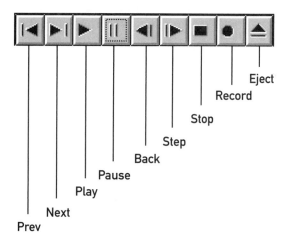

FIGURE 5.17 THE MULTIMEDIA CONTROL.

Let's see how to use this control with both video and audio. Double-click the **Multimedia** control tool in the toolbox, creating a new control,

MMControl1. To use this control to play video, we set its DeviceType property to AVIFILE in the properties window. The different device types that the Multimedia control can work with are shown in Table 5.3.

TABLE 5.3 MMCONTROL DEVICE TYPES.

Name	Type of Device
Animation	Plays animation
CDAudio	Plays CD audio
AVIVideo	Plays **.AVI** files video
Other	Device is not defined
Overlay	Plays analog video
Sequencer	The Musical Instrument Digital Interface (MIDI)
VideoDisc	Plays video discs
WaveAudio	Plays **.WAV** sound files

Multimedia controls do not display video themselves; rather, they only control the action. To actually see anything, we must add a picture control, Picture1, to our program, so do that now. All that remains before we can see video in the picture box is to set up the Multimedia control, including connecting its output to the picture box. We'll do that in the Form_Load() event:

```
Private Sub Form_Load()

End Sub
```

The first thing we do is to set the Multimedia control's *time format*. The available time formats appear in Table 5.4. The one that is appropriate for a particular Multimedia control depends on the type of device that it is controlling. In our case, we're dealing with **.AVI** video, and the correct format is the track/minute/second/frame time format, mciFormatTmsf, so we begin by setting MMControl1's TimeFormat property to mciFormatTmsf:

```
Private Sub Form_Load()
    MMControl1.TimeFormat = mciFormatTmsf
        .
        .
        .
End Sub
```

TABLE 5.4 MULTIMEDIA TIME FORMATS.

Constant	Time Format
mciFormatMilliseconds	Milliseconds format
mciFormatHms	Hours, seconds, and minutes format
mciFormatMsf	Minutes, seconds, and frames format
mciFormatFrames	Frames format
mciFormatSmpte24	24-frame SMPTE format
mciFormatSmpte25	25-frame SMPTE format
mciFormatSmpte30	30-frame SMPTE format
mciFormatSmpte30Drop	30-drop-frame SMPTE format
mciFormatBytes	Bytes format
mciFormatSamples	Samples format
mciFormatTmsf	Tracks minutes, seconds, and frames format

We must still connect MMControl1 to the skiing video and to the picture box. To connect it to the skiing video, we simply set its filename property to **C:\windows\media\skiing.avi**. Now we'll be able to run the video using our Multimedia control. To connect the control to the picture box (so that we actually see something), we set the control's hWndDisplay property to the *Windows handle* of the picture box, which is stored in the Picture1.hWnd property. (As we'll see in Chapter 9, a Windows handle is the unique identifier that Windows uses to keep track of each window. Because each control is a window, its Windows handle is stored in its hWnd property.)

```
Private Sub Form_Load()
    MMControl1.TimeFormat = mciFormatTmsf
--> MMControl1.filename = "C:\windows\media\skiing.avi"
--> MMControl1.hWndDisplay = Picture1.hWnd
        .
        .
        .
End Sub
```

Finally, we open the file, making the buttons in the Multimedia control active, by using the Multimedia control's Command property:

```
Private Sub Form_Load()
    MMControl1.TimeFormat = mciFormatTmsf
    MMControl1.filename = "C:\windows\media\skiing.avi"
    MMControl1.hWndDisplay = Picture1.hWnd
```

```
--> MMControl1.Command = "Open"
        .
        .
        .
End Sub
```

Now the buttons (Play, Stop, Pause, and so on) in our MMControl1 will control the display of the skiing video; it's that simple. Now let's turn to CD audio.

We will add another Multimedia control, MMControl2, to play CD audio. Add that control and set its DeviceType property to CDAUDIO. Next, we set its time format to track/minute/second/frame (as with the video multimedia control we just set up) in the Form_Load() event:

```
Private Sub Form_Load()
    MMControl1.TimeFormat = mciFormatTmsf
    MMControl1.filename = "C:\windows\media\skiing.avi"
    MMControl1.hWndDisplay = Picture1.hWnd
    MMControl1.Command = "Open"
--> MMControl2.TimeFormat = mciFormatTmsf
        .
        .
        .
End Sub
```

There is no **.AVI** file to open here, of course—setting the control's DeviceType to CDAudio tells it all it needs to know. When we execute the **Open** command, the buttons in MMControl2 will control the computer's CD-ROM drive, allowing you to play music:

```
Private Sub Form_Load()
    MMControl1.TimeFormat = mciFormatTmsf
    MMControl1.filename = "C:\windows\media\skiing.avi"
    MMControl1.hWndDisplay = Picture1.hWnd
    MMControl1.Command = "Open"
    MMControl2.TimeFormat = mciFormatTmsf
--> MMControl2.Command = "Open"
End Sub
```

The program is functional at this point. However, we can also do more with the Multimedia control by using its StatusUpdate event, which is called when it switches modes, for example, from Stop to Play. The mode of the Multimedia control is stored in its Mode property, and the available settings appear in Table 5.5.

TABLE 5.5 MULTIMEDIA MODES.

Constant	Meaning
mciModeOpen	Device not open
mciModeStop	Device stop
mciModePlay	Device play
mciModeRecord	Device record
mciModeSeek	Device seek
mciModePause	Device pause
mciModeReady	Device ready

If we add labels to our program, we can indicate the status of both multimedia controls (see Figure 5.15). We can indicate whether the control is playing video or audio, or is paused, or whatever condition it is in. We will display the status of MMControl1 (the video player) using this code:

```
Private Sub MMControl1_StatusUpdate()
    ModeString = ""
    Select Case MMControl1.Mode

    Case mciModeReady
        ModeString = "Ready."

    Case mciModeStop
        ModeString = "Stopped."

    Case mciModeSeek
        ModeString = "Seeking."

    Case mciModePlay
        ModeString = "Playing."

    Case mciModePause
        ModeString = "Paused."

    End Select
    Label4.Caption = ModeString

End Sub
```

Similarly, we can display the status of MMControl2 (the CD player) using this code:

```
Private Sub MMControl2_StatusUpdate()
    ModeString = ""
    Select Case MMControl2.Mode

    Case mciModeReady
        ModeString = "Ready."

    Case mciModeStop
        ModeString = "Stopped."

    Case mciModeSeek
        ModeString = "Seeking."

    Case mciModePlay
        ModeString = "Playing."

    Case mciModePause
        ModeString = "Paused."

    End Select
    Label5.Caption = ModeString

End Sub
```

Now our multimedia program is set. Run it as shown in Figure 5.15. Double-click the **Video Clip** control to see the skiing video, or use the Video Multimedia control to see the same thing in the picture box. If you place a music CD in your CD-ROM drive, you can use the CD Multimedia control to control it, playing music. (Even if you don't have a sound card, CD-ROM drives often have earphone jacks for just this purpose.) In addition, the status of each multimedia device is shown, as in Figure 5.15. Our program is a success. **MULTIMED.FRM** appears in Listing 5.8, and **MULTIMED.VBP** is in Listing 5.9.

LISTING 5.8 MULTIMED.FRM

```
VERSION 4.00
Begin VB.Form Form1
    Caption         =   "Multimedia"
    ClientHeight    =   5010
    ClientLeft      =   795
    ClientTop       =   1305
    ClientWidth     =   8565
    Height          =   5415
    Left            =   735
    LinkTopic       =   "Form1"
    ScaleHeight     =   5010
    ScaleWidth      =   8565
    Top             =   960
    Width           =   8685
```

```
Begin VB.PictureBox Picture1
   Height          =   2055
   Left            =   120
   ScaleHeight     =   1995
   ScaleWidth      =   3555
   TabIndex        =   4
   Top             =   2760
   Width           =   3615
End
Begin VB.Label Label5
   Height          =   255
   Left            =   2520
   TabIndex        =   8
   Top             =   1680
   Width           =   1215
End
Begin VB.Label Label4
   Height          =   255
   Left            =   2520
   TabIndex        =   7
   Top             =   720
   Width           =   1215
End
Begin VB.Label Label3
   Caption         =   "CD Control"
   Height          =   255
   Left            =   1320
   TabIndex        =   6
   Top             =   1680
   Width           =   1215
End
Begin VB.Label Label2
   Caption         =   "Video Control"
   Height          =   255
   Left            =   1200
   TabIndex        =   5
   Top             =   720
   Width           =   1455
End
Begin VB.Label Label1
   Caption         =   "Video Clip (double click it)"
   Height          =   255
   Left            =   5640
   TabIndex        =   3
   Top             =   360
   Width           =   1815
End
Begin avifileCtl.avifile avifile1
   Height          =   4005
   Left            =   3840
   OleObjectBlob   =   "multimed.frx":0000
```

```
            TabIndex      =   2
            Top           =   840
            Width         =   4800
        End
        Begin MCI.MMControl MMControl2
            Height        =   495
            Left          =   120
            TabIndex      =   1
            Top           =   2040
            Width         =   3540
            _Version      =   65536
            DeviceType    =   "CDAudio"
            _ExtentX      =   6244
            _ExtentY      =   873
            _StockProps   =   32
            BorderStyle   =   1
        End
        Begin MCI.MMControl MMControl1
            Height        =   450
            Left          =   120
            TabIndex      =   0
            Top           =   1080
            Width         =   3540
            _Version      =   65536
            DeviceType    =   "AVIVIDEO"
            _ExtentX      =   6244
            _ExtentY      =   794
            _StockProps   =   32
            BorderStyle   =   1
        End
    End
End
Attribute VB_Name = "Form1"
Attribute VB_Creatable = False
Attribute VB_Exposed = False
Function ReturnModeString(Mode As Long) As String

End Function

Private Sub Form_Load()
    MMControl1.TimeFormat = mciFormatTmsf
    MMControl1.filename = "C:\windows\media\skiing.avi"
    MMControl1.hWndDisplay = Picture1.hWnd
    MMControl1.Command = "Open"
    MMControl2.TimeFormat = mciFormatTmsf
    MMControl2.Command = "Open"
End Sub

Private Sub MMControl1_StatusUpdate()
    ModeString = ""
    Select Case MMControl1.Mode

    Case mciModeReady
```

```
        ModeString = "Ready."

    Case mciModeStop
        ModeString = "Stopped."

    Case mciModeSeek
        ModeString = "Seeking."

    Case mciModePlay
        ModeString = "Playing."

    Case mciModePause
        ModeString = "Paused."

    End Select
    Label4.Caption = ModeString

End Sub

Private Sub MMControl2_StatusUpdate()
    ModeString = ""
    Select Case MMControl2.Mode

    Case mciModeReady
        ModeString = "Ready."

    Case mciModeStop
        ModeString = "Stopped."

    Case mciModeSeek
        ModeString = "Seeking."

    Case mciModePlay
        ModeString = "Playing."

    Case mciModePause
        ModeString = "Paused."

    End Select
    Label5.Caption = ModeString

End Sub
```

LISTING 5.9 MULTIMED.VBP

```
Form=multimed.Frm
Object={F9043C88-F6F2-101A-A3C9-08002B2F49FB}#1.0#0; COMDLG32.OCX
Object={6B7E6392-850A-101B-AFC0-4210102A8DA7}#1.0#0; COMCTL32.OCX
Reference=*\G{BEF6E001-A874-101A-8BBA-
        00AA00300CAB}#2.0#0#C:\WINDOWS\SYSTEM\OLEPRO32.DLL#Standard
        OLE Types
Reference=*\G{EE008642-64A8-11CE-920F-
```

```
        08002B369A33}#1.0#0#C:\WINDOWS\SYSTEM\MSRDO32.DLL#Microsoft
        Remote Data Object 1.0
Object={C1A8AF28-1257-101B-8FB0-0020AF039CA3}#1.0#0; MCI32.OCX
Object=avifile; avi
ProjWinSize=383,372,202,94
ProjWinShow=2
IconForm="Form1"
Name="Project1"
HelpContextID="0"
StartMode=0
VersionCompatible32="0"
MajorVer=1
MinorVer=0
RevisionVer=0
AutoIncrementVer=0
ServerSupportFiles=0
```

The last set of custom controls we will look at are the new Windows 95 controls.

THE WINDOWS 95 CUSTOM CONTROLS

A special set of 32-bit controls comes with Visual Basic for use with Windows 95. They will work only in 32-bit systems. These controls are Toolbar, StatusBar, TabStrip, ImageList, RichTextBox, ProgressBar, Slider, ListView, and TreeView. We will take a look at those controls with a special project, **WIN95.VBP**, which is shown in Figure 5.18. Let's take a look at each of the controls, starting with the Toolbar control.

The Toolbar Control

We discussed how to use toolbars in Chapter 2. In that rudimentary project, we simply made toolbars from command buttons and picture boxes. Now we can use the Win95 Toolbar tool to add real toolbars to our program, and they even support tooltips. (As we noted in Chapter 2, tooltips are the little yellow help prompts that appear over a tool when you rest the mouse cursor on that tool in the toolbar.)

Create the Win95 project now. To add a toolbar to this project, double-click the **Toolbar** tool; a new, empty toolbar appears in the top of Form1. As you can see in Figure 5.18, the Win95 program has three buttons in its toolbar, and they are easy to add. To see how this works, click the right mouse button on the new toolbar and select **Properties** in the pop-up menu that appears. This opens the Toolbar Control Properties dialog box, as shown in Figure 5.19. Select the **Buttons** tab in that dialog box. To add a new button, we simply click **Insert Button** in the dialog box. For each new button, we fill in the button's caption and its tooltip text—it's that easy. After creating three buttons, close the Toolbar Control Properties dialog box and run the program. You'll find the three new buttons visible in the toolbar, as in Figure 5.18, with the captions and tooltips you gave them.

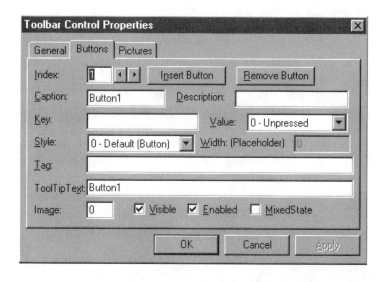

FIGURE 5.18 OUR WIN95 PROJECT.

FIGURE 5.19 THE TOOLBAR CONTROL PROPERTIES DIALOG BOX.

That's all very well, but how do we use these buttons? How do we know when the user clicks them? That also turns out to be easy: just double-click the toolbar to open the Toolbar1_ButtonClick() event:

```
Private Sub Toolbar1_ButtonClick(ByVal Button As Button)

End Sub
```

This is the event handler that is called when the user clicks a button in the toolbar. Those buttons are treated as a control array, which means that we get the index (starting with 1) of the button that was clicked. In this case, we can simply have the computer beep whenever the user clicks any of the buttons (from **WIN95.FRM**):

```
Private Sub Toolbar1_ButtonClick(ByVal Button As Button)
--> Beep
End Sub
```

Designing and implementing a toolbar using the Toolbar control is easy. Let's take a look at status bars next.

The StatusBar Control

The StatusBar control functions very much like the Toolbar control; double-click the **StatusBar** control now, causing a new status bar to appear at the bottom of our form, as in Figure 5.18. A toolbar is divided into buttons, and a status bar is divided into *panels*. Panels can function in a similar way.

Let's add three panels to the status bar. Click it with the right mouse button and select **Properties** in the pop-up menu to open the StatusBar Control Properties dialog box, as shown in Figure 5.20.

Click the **Panels** tab in the StatusBar Control Properties dialog box. Add three panels to the status bar by clicking the **Insert Panel** button three times, giving each button its own text. Like the buttons in the toolbar, the panels in a status bar make up a control array and can be reached with an index. Double-click the status bar now, opening the StatusBar1_PanelClick() event handler:

```
Private Sub StatusBar1_PanelClick(ByVal Panel As Panel)

End Sub
```

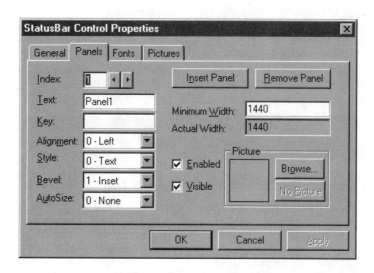

FIGURE 5.20 THE STATUSBAR CONTROL PROPERTIES DIALOG BOX.

If the user clicks the status bar, we might display the text "Status Bar clicked" in the first panel. To do that, we can refer to that panel as StatusBar1.Panels(1) (the next panel is StatusBar1.Panels(2), and so on), and the text in it as StatusBar1.Panels(1).Text. We can set that text to "Status Bar clicked":

```
Private Sub StatusBar1_PanelClick(ByVal Panel As Panel)
    StatusBar1.Panels(1).Text = "Status Bar clicked"
End Sub
```

When the user clicks the status bar, we change the text in the first panel from "Panel1" to "Status Bar clicked." In this way, we can change and update any panel in the status bar at any time we wish.

Next, let's look at the TabStrip Win95 control.

The TabStrip Control

In the StatusBar and Toolbar Control Properties windows we've just seen, we used tabs to select the "page" of information we wanted. When we wanted to work with panels in the StatusBar Control Properties window, we clicked the **Panels** tab, opening that page, as shown in Figure 5.20. In this way, tabs in a tab strip work much like the tabs in a notebook, helping you to find the page you want quickly.

In fact, *page* is the term that Visual Basic uses, and we can set up a tabbed set of pages in our Win95 project, as shown in Figure 5.18, using the TabStrip control. Double-click the **TabStrip** tool now to create a new TabStrip, TabStrip1. Then use the right mouse button to open the TabStrip Control Properties dialog box, as shown in Figure 5.21.

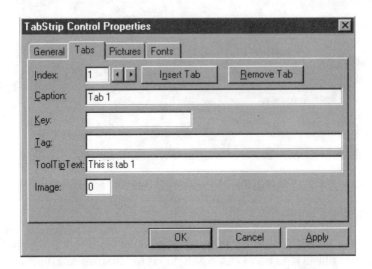

FIGURE 5.21 THE TABSTRIP CONTROL PROPERTIES DIALOG BOX.

Next, select the **Tabs** tab in that dialog box and insert two tabs, giving them the captions **Tab 1** and **Tab 2**. Then click **OK**, closing the dialog box. At this point, the tabstrip, TabStrip1, is almost ready to go.

It turns out that a tabstrip operates much like an array of buttons. It doesn't manipulate the contents of each page, bringing the appropriate page to the top by itself—that is up to us. For that reason, we create a new picture box, Picture1, and position it below the tab strip, as shown in Figure 5.18. Now create another picture box, giving it the same name, Picture1. When Visual Basic asks whether you want to set up a control array, answer **yes**, creating the picture box array Picture1(). Make sure that these two picture boxes are the same size and that one is on top of the other; now, when the tabstrip selects a particular page, we can place the matching picture box on top of the other picture box to give the impression that we are leafing through a folder of tabbed pages. To distinguish between the picture boxes in the picture box array, we can set the BackColor properties to different colors; in the Win95 project, we use red and blue.

We set up our picture boxes by making sure that the first picture box, Picture1(0), is on the top by setting its ZOrder property to 0 in the Form_Load() event:

```
Private Sub Form_Load()
--> Picture1(0).ZOrder 0
       .
       .
       .
End Sub
```

When the user clicks the tabstrip, we can bring the appropriate picture box to the front using the TabStrip1_Click() event. Double-click the tabstrip now to open that event in the code window; when the user clicks a tab in the tabstrip, we can find out which tab was clicked by checking the property TabStrip1.SelectedItem.Index. If tab 1 was clicked, we can place Picture1(0) on the screen; if tab 2 was clicked, we can display Picture1(1) instead:

```
Private Sub TabStrip1_Click()
    Picture1(TabStrip1.SelectedItem.Index - 1).ZOrder 0
End Sub
```

That's all there is to it. Now our tabstrip helps give the impression that we have a tabbed set of pages.

Our next control, the ImageList control, is somewhat similar. This control will also allow us to keep track of a list of items, but, in this case, those items are images.

The ImageList Control

An ImageList control is a repository for a set of images, somewhat like the array of picture boxes we just created. An ImageList control does not display the images but rather holds them in a list for us, ready to use. On the other hand, other Windows 95 controls can use the images stored in our ImageList control (such as the ListView and TreeView controls we'll look at). Let's install an image list in our program.

Create a new ImageList control using the ImageList tool in the toolbar; Visual Basic gives this control the name ImageList1. Using the right mouse button, open the ImageList's ImageList Control Properties dialog box and select the **Images** tab, as shown in Figure 5.22.

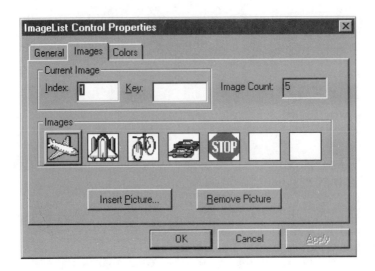

FIGURE 5.22 THE IMAGELIST CONTROL PROPERTIES DIALOG BOX.

Using the **Insert Picture** button, you can browse through your disk, finding the images you want to install in the ImageList. In our case, we have chosen several icons from the Visual Basic icon library, as shown in Figure 5.22. Next, click **OK** in the ImageList Control Properties dialog box to close it and place our images into that list.

To display the images in this image list, we can add a new picture box, Picture2, to our Win95 project. In addition, we place three command buttons, with the captions **1**, **2**, and **3**, above that picture box, as shown in Figure 5.18. When the user clicks button **1**, we can show image 1 from the ImageList control, button **2** displays image 2, and so on. Let's see how to support this in code. Open the click event handler for the first command button, Command1:

```
Private Sub Command1_Click()

End Sub
```

When we click this button, marked **1**, we want to display the first image from the image list:

```
Private Sub Command1_Click()
    Set Picture2.Picture = ImageList1.ListImages(1).Picture ' Set
Picture.
End Sub
```

(As usual, we have to use the **Set** command to set a picture box's Picture property.) We can do the same for the other two command buttons, displaying image 2 when **Command2** is clicked, and image 3 when **Command3** is clicked:

```
Private Sub Command2_Click()
    Set Picture2.Picture = ImageList1.ListImages(2).Picture ' Set
Picture.
End Sub

Private Sub Command3_Click()
    Set Picture2.Picture = ImageList1.ListImages(3).Picture ' Set
Picture.
End Sub
```

In this way, we are able to reach the images inside our image list. That's it for the ImageList control for now; let's move on to the RichTextBox control.

The RichTextBox Control

The RichTextBox control is an especially easy one to use; all we have to do is to create that control and set its FileName property. Rich text is a special format that we will learn about in detail in Chapter 10. In a rich text file, we can mark text as hidden, footnoted, underlined, and more (rich text is supported by such word processors as Microsoft Word for Windows 95). To create a rich text box, double-click the **RichTextBox** control, creating the control RichTextBox1. In this case, we place the name of the rich text file we will create in Chapter 10, **WRITER.RTF**, in the new text box's FileName property. This displays the text in that file, as shown at right in Figure 5.18.

This control is like a normal text box but with several important differences: it does not have the same 64KB text size limit that a text box has, and you can drag and drop text into it from another word processor (which must also support drag and drop) or even whole files from the Windows Explorer. And it supports rich text. To use the rich text features, you select the text you want to make, say, italic or to underline, and then use the SelItalic or SelUnderline properties. In this way, you can support all the features of rich text in your programs. That's all there is to using a rich text box; if the text is too large for the control, scroll bars will automatically appear.

The ProgressBar Control

As with the Gauge control, we usually use a progress bar when we want to keep the user apprised of the progress of an operation that takes time. For example, when our program is involved in a lengthy disk operation, we can use the progress bar to indicate how close we are to completion. And like the Gauge control, this control works something like a thermometer, extending a colored bar in a gauge; when the colored bar reaches the end, the operation is complete. In Figure 5.18, the ProgressBar control is just below the TabStrip control.

Let's see this in code. We set the limits of the progress bar by setting its Min and Max properties, which are set to 0 and 100, respectively, by default. The length of the color bar in the progress bar is set in the Value property; if ProgressBar1.Value = ProgressBar1.Max, the color bar fills the progress bar. For that reason, we set the progress bar's Value property to 0 when our program first loads:

```
Private Sub Form_Load()
    Picture1(0).ZOrder 0
--> ProgressBar1.Value = 0
        .
        .
        .
End Sub
```

Now we can increment the progress bar as we like—say, every time the user clicks it. To do that, double-click the progress bar now, opening its click event, and place this line of code there, simply incrementing the progress bar by one each time it is clicked:

```
Private Sub ProgressBar1_MouseDown(Button As Integer, Shift As
        Integer, x As Single, y As Single)
--> ProgressBar1.Value = ProgressBar1.Value + 1
End Sub
```

Now the user can adjust the progress bar as desired, simply by clicking it. It would take a lot of clicks to reach the maximum possible value (Value = Max), and there are other ways of reaching the maximum than by simply clicking the progress bar. For example, we might use a Slider control.

The Slider Control

The Slider control looks rather like the volume adjustment on a stereo; it appears to the right of the progress bar in Figure 5.18. In fact, we can connect the Slider control and the progress bar easily; each time the user moves the slider in the Slider control, a click event is generated, and we can set the progress bar's setting to match the new setting of the Slider control. Double-click the **Slider** control now to open its click handler:

```
Private Sub Slider1_Click()

End Sub
```

The Slider control is similar to the ProgressBar control (and to scrollbars) in that the Slider control has the three properties Min, Max, and Value. By default, Min = 0 and Max = 100; Value is the value between those two extremes set by the user by moving the slider in the Slider control. This means that we can adjust the setting in the ProgressBar to match the setting of the Slider control:

```
Private Sub Slider1_Click()
    ProgressBar1.Value = Slider1.Value
End Sub
```

That's it—we've added a working Slider control to our program. Using the Slider control, the user can now reset the progress bar as desired.

The next Windows 95 custom control we'll take a look at is the ListView control.

The ListView Control

We're all familiar with windows filled with icons—that's how we manage files in Windows 95. The Visual Basic window is filled with icons corresponding to the programs and files that come with Visual Basic. Clicking one of these icons opens the corresponding program or document.

A ListView control allows us to present the same icon-oriented overview of files. Our ListView appears at the lower right in Figure 5.18, where we display the icons in our ImageList control. To create that ListView control, double-click the **ListView** tool and use the right mouse button to open the ListView Control Properties dialog box, as shown in Figure 5.23.

Select the **Images** tab in the Properties dialog box. The ListView control needs a source of icons to display, and because we have already loaded icons into our ImageList control, ImageList1, we will use that; place the name of that control in both boxes in the ListView Control Properties dialog box, as in Figure 5.23, and click **OK**.

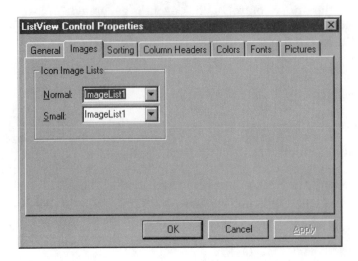

FIGURE 5.23 THE LISTVIEW CONTROL PROPERTIES DIALOG BOX.

Now we have installed the icons in the ImageList1 control into the ListView1 control. We also need to add these icons to the ListView's internal list, and we do that by looping over the icons, adding a new list item each time and setting its Icon property to the position of that icon in the ImageList control We also set the text that will appear under the icon in the ListView control in Form_Load():

```
Private Sub Form_Load()
    Picture1(0).ZOrder 0
    ProgressBar1.Value = 0
--> For loop_index = 1 To 3
-->     Set theItem = ListView1.ListItems.Add()
-->     theItem.Icon = loop_index
-->     theItem.Text = "ListItem " & loop_index
--> Next loop_index
        .
        .
        .
End Sub
```

Now the ListView displays our icons. Using the ListView's View property, you can switch between a display of icons, small icons, and a list of items with text placed to the right of each item. In addition, when the user clicks or double-clicks an icon, you can add code to the ListView control's Click()

or DblClick() events; the icon that the user clicked is stored in the ListView's SelectedItem property.

The TreeView Control

The last Windows 95 custom control we will look at is the TreeView control. Just as the ListView control allowed us to present icons much like a window in Windows 95, the TreeView control allows us to present a "tree" of nodes, just as the Windows 95 Explorer does. The overall directory structure of a disk is presented as a tree, and we can expand or contract each item—called a *node*—in that tree by clicking it. After creating a TreeView control, we fill it with Node objects, and we can navigate through a tree's nodes in code with each node's Root, Parent, Child, FirstSibling, Next, Previous, and LastSibling properties. Our TreeView control appears at bottom right in Figure 5.18.

To create our TreeView control, TreeView1, double-click the **TreeView** tool in the toolbox. In our case, we will set up a root node with four children, as shown in Figure 5.18, in the Form_Load() event. We begin by creating a new Node object in that event:

```
Private Sub Form_Load()
    Picture1(0).ZOrder 0
    ProgressBar1.Value = 0
    For loop_index = 1 To 3
        Set theItem = ListView1.ListItems.Add()
        theItem.Icon = loop_index
        theItem.Text = "ListItem " & loop_index
    Next loop_index
--> Dim theNode As Node
         .
         .
         .
End Sub
```

Inside our TreeView control, TreeView1, there is a collection of nodes named Nodes. As we will see in Chapter 11, a *collection* of objects acts much like an array or list of objects. We will add the desired nodes to this collection using its Add method. In this case, we want to add a root node and four child nodes. In general, the Add method for a Nodes collection looks like this:

```
Nodes.Add(relative, relationship, key, text, image, selectedimage)
```

The parameters in this call are as follows:

- relative: Optional; this is the index number or key of a preexisting Node object. The relationship between the new node and this preexisting node is found in the next argument, relationship.

- relationship: Optional; this indicates the relative placement of the Node object. The possible settings are as follows:

tvwLast:	Node is placed after all other same-level nodes.
tvwNext:	Node is placed after the node named in relative.
tvwPrevious:	Node is placed before the node named in relative.
tvwChild:	Node is a child node of node named in relative.

- key: Optional; a string used to retrieve the Node.

- text: Required; the text string that appears in the Node.

- image: Optional; the index of an image in an associated ImageList control.

- selectedimage: Optional; this is the index of an image in an associated ImageList control shown when the Node is selected.

We can associate the images in our ImageList control with the TreeView control—giving each node its own icon in the ImageList—by opening the TreeView Control Properties dialog box with the right mouse button, as shown in Figure 5.24. We place the name of our ImageList control, ImageList1, into the ImageList box, as shown in Figure 5.24, and click **OK**. Now we can add the root of our tree, giving it the internal name theRoot in the Nodes collection and the label **Root** in the TreeView control. We associate the first icon in the ImageList with it:

```
Private Sub Form_Load()
    Picture1(0).ZOrder 0
    ProgressBar1.Value = 0
    For loop_index = 1 To 3
        Set theItem = ListView1.ListItems.Add()
        theItem.Icon = loop_index
        theItem.Text = "ListItem " & loop_index
    Next loop_index
    Dim theNode As Node
--> Set theNode = TreeView1.Nodes.Add( , , "theRoot", "Root", 1)
        .
        .
        .
End Sub
```

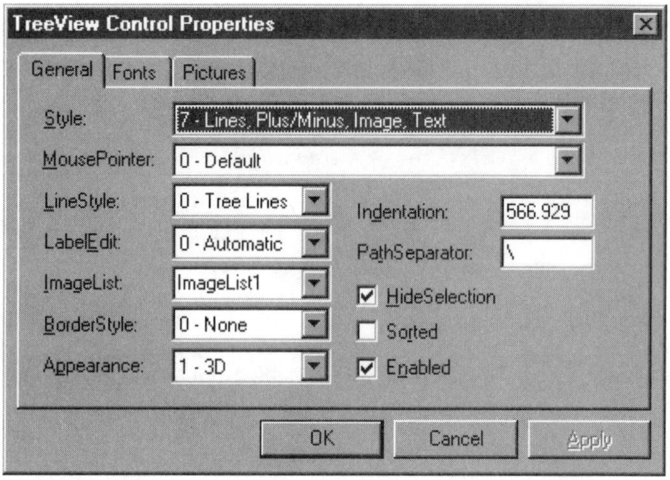

FIGURE 5.24 THE TREEVIEW CONTROL PROPERTIES DIALOG BOX.

Next, we add the four child nodes, indicating that they are child nodes of the node we have named theRoot. We give them the names Child 1 to Child 4 and associate them with icons 2–5 in the ImageList control:

```
Private Sub Form_Load()
    Picture1(0).ZOrder 0
    ProgressBar1.Value = 0
    For loop_index = 1 To 3
        Set theItem = ListView1.ListItems.Add()
        theItem.Icon = loop_index
        theItem.Text = "ListItem " & loop_index
    Next loop_index
    Dim theNode As Node
    Set theNode = TreeView1.Nodes.Add(, , "theRoot", "Root", 1)
--> Set theNode = TreeView1.Nodes.Add("theRoot", tvwChild, , "Child 1", 2)
--> Set theNode = TreeView1.Nodes.Add("theRoot", tvwChild, , "Child 2", 3)
--> Set theNode = TreeView1.Nodes.Add("theRoot", tvwChild, , "Child 3", 4)
--> Set theNode = TreeView1.Nodes.Add("theRoot", tvwChild, , "Child 4", 5)
        .
        .
        .

End Sub
```

At this point, we are ready to set the node's EnsureVisible property, making sure that our full tree (not just the root) is visible when we start the program:

```
Private Sub Form_Load()
    Picture1(0).ZOrder 0
    ProgressBar1.Value = 0
    For loop_index = 1 To 3
        Set theItem = ListView1.ListItems.Add()
        theItem.Icon = loop_index
        theItem.Text = "ListItem " & loop_index
    Next loop_index
    Dim theNode As Node
    Set theNode = TreeView1.Nodes.Add(, , "theRoot", "Root", 1)
    Set theNode = TreeView1.Nodes.Add("theRoot", tvwChild, , "Child 1",
2)
    Set theNode = TreeView1.Nodes.Add("theRoot", tvwChild, , "Child 2",
3)
    Set theNode = TreeView1.Nodes.Add("theRoot", tvwChild, , "Child 3",
4)
    Set theNode = TreeView1.Nodes.Add("theRoot", tvwChild, , "Child 4",
5)
--> theNode.EnsureVisible
--> TreeView1.Style = tvwTreelinesPictureText
--> TreeView1.BorderStyle = vbFixedSingle
End Sub
```

In addition, we set the TreeView control's BorderStyle property to fixed single with the constant vbFixedSingle, and we make the TreeView display our icons as well as the lines of the tree by setting its style to tvwTreelinesPictureText. The available TreeView styles appear in Table 5.6.

TABLE 5.6 TREESTYLE CONSTANTS.

Constant	Meaning
tvwTextOnly	Text only
tvwPictureText	Picture and text
tvwPlusMinusText	Plus/minus and text
tvwPlusPictureText	Plus/minus, picture, and text
tvwTreelinesText	Treelines and text
tvwTreelinesPictureText	Treelines, picture, and text
tvwTreelinesPlusMinusText	Treelines, plus/minus, and text
tvwTreelinesPlusMinusPictureText	Treelines, plus/minus, picture, and text

Now our TreeView control displays a tree that consists of one root and three child nodes, each with an icon from our ImageList control. You can see this new control in operation in Figure 5.18.

That's it for our Win95 project. As you can see, there is a great deal of power in these new controls, ready for you to use. The program appears in Listing 5.10 (**WIN95.FRM**) and Listing 5.11 (**WIN95.VBP**).

LISTING 5.10 WIN95.FRM

```
VERSION 4.00
Begin VB.Form Form1
   Caption         =   "Form1"
   ClientHeight    =   4890
   ClientLeft      =   1635
   ClientTop       =   1500
   ClientWidth     =   6855
   Height          =   5295
   Left            =   1575
   LinkTopic       =   "Form1"
   ScaleHeight     =   4890
   ScaleWidth      =   6855
   Top             =   1155
   Width           =   6975
   Begin VB.CommandButton Command3
      Caption      =   "3"
      Height       =   495
      Left         =   1320
      TabIndex     =   10
      Top          =   720
      Width        =   375
   End
   Begin VB.CommandButton Command2
      Caption      =   "2"
      Height       =   495
      Left         =   720
      TabIndex     =   9
      Top          =   720
      Width        =   375
   End
   Begin VB.CommandButton Command1
      Caption      =   "1"
      Height       =   495
      Left         =   120
      TabIndex     =   8
      Top          =   720
      Width        =   375
   End
   Begin VB.PictureBox Picture2
      Height       =   975
      Left         =   120
      ScaleHeight  =   915
      ScaleWidth   =   1515
      TabIndex     =   7
```

```
         Top             =    1320
         Width           =    1575
      End
      Begin VB.PictureBox Picture1
         BackColor       =    &H000000FF&
         Height          =    1095
         Index           =    1
         Left            =    2040
         ScaleHeight     =    1035
         ScaleWidth      =    1875
         TabIndex        =    4
         Top             =    1080
         Width           =    1935
      End
      Begin VB.PictureBox Picture1
         BackColor       =    &H00FFFFC0&
         FillColor       =    &H00FFFF80&
         ForeColor       =    &H00FFFF80&
         Height          =    1095
         Index           =    0
         Left            =    2040
         ScaleHeight     =    1035
         ScaleWidth      =    1875
         TabIndex        =    3
         Top             =    1080
         Width           =    1935
      End
      Begin ComctlLib.TreeView TreeView1
         Height          =    1095
         Left            =    3600
         TabIndex        =    13
         Top             =    2880
         Width           =    3015
         _Version        =    65536
         _ExtentX        =    5318
         _ExtentY        =    1931
         _StockProps     =    196
         Appearance      =    1
         ImageList       =    "ImageList1"
         PathSeparator   =    "\"
         Style           =    7
      End
      Begin ComctlLib.Slider Slider1
         Height          =    495
         Left            =    5160
         TabIndex        =    12
         Top             =    2280
         Width           =    1215
         _Version        =    65536
         _ExtentX        =    2143
```

```
   _ExtentY          =    873
   _StockProps       =    64
   Max               =    100
   TickFrequency     =    10
End
Begin ComctlLib.ListView ListView1
   Height            =    1095
   Left              =    480
   TabIndex          =    11
   Top               =    2880
   Width             =    2895
   _Version          =    65536
   _ExtentX          =    5106
   _ExtentY          =    1931
   _StockProps       =    205
   ForeColor         =    -2147483640
   BackColor         =    -2147483643
   Appearance        =    1
   Icons             =    "ImageList1"
   SmallIcons        =    "ImageList1"
   NumItems          =    1
   i1                =    "win95.frx":0000
End
Begin ComctlLib.ImageList ImageList1
   Left              =    720
   Top               =    1560
   _Version          =    65536
   _ExtentX          =    1005
   _ExtentY          =    1005
   _StockProps       =    1
   BackColor         =    -2147483643
   ImageWidth        =    32
   ImageHeight       =    32
   NumImages         =    5
   i1                =    "win95.frx":008C
   i2                =    "win95.frx":0583
   i3                =    "win95.frx":0A7A
   i4                =    "win95.frx":0F71
   i5                =    "win95.frx":1468
End
Begin ComctlLib.ProgressBar ProgressBar1
   Height            =    255
   Left              =    360
   TabIndex          =    6
   Top               =    2400
   Width             =    4335
   _Version          =    65536
   _ExtentX          =    7646
   _ExtentY          =    450
   _StockProps       =    192
```

```
      Appearance      =    1
End
Begin RichtextLib.RichTextBox RichTextBox1
      Height          =    1455
      Left            =    4320
      TabIndex        =    5
      Top             =    720
      Width           =    2295
      _Version        =    65536
      _ExtentX        =    4048
      _ExtentY        =    2566
      _StockProps     =    69
      BackColor       =    -2147483643
      ScrollBars      =    3
      TextRTF         =    $"win95.frx":195F
      Filename        =    "C:\VBOOK\WRITER\Writer.rtf"
End
Begin ComctlLib.TabStrip TabStrip1
      Height          =    1575
      Left            =    1920
      TabIndex        =    2
      Top             =    720
      Width           =    2175
      _Version        =    65536
      _ExtentX        =    3836
      _ExtentY        =    2778
      _StockProps     =    68
      ImageList       =    ""
      NumTabs         =    2
      i1              =    "win95.frx":2117
      i2              =    "win95.frx":2262
End
Begin ComctlLib.StatusBar StatusBar1
      Align           =    2    'Align Bottom
      Height          =    495
      Left            =    0
      TabIndex        =    1
      Top             =    4395
      Width           =    6855
      _Version        =    65536
      _ExtentX        =    12091
      _ExtentY        =    873
      _StockProps     =    68
      AlignSet        =    -1   'True
      SimpleText      =    ""
      NumPanels       =    3
      i1              =    "win95.frx":23AD
      i2              =    "win95.frx":2482
      i3              =    "win95.frx":2557
End
```

```
Begin ComctlLib.Toolbar Toolbar1
   Align          =   1  'Align Top
   Height         =   600
   Left           =   0
   TabIndex       =   0
   Top            =   0
   Width          =   6855
   _Version       =   65536
   _ExtentX       =   12091
   _ExtentY       =   1058
   _StockProps    =   96
   ImageList      =   ""
   MouseIcon      =   "win95.frx":262C
   ButtonWidth    =   1164
   ButtonHeight   =   953
   NumButtons     =   3
   i1             =   "win95.frx":2648
   i2             =   "win95.frx":27EF
   i3             =   "win95.frx":2992
   AlignSet       =   -1  'True
   End
End
Attribute VB_Name = "Form1"
Attribute VB_Creatable = False
Attribute VB_Exposed = False
Private Sub Command1_Click()
Set Picture2.Picture = ImageList1.ListImages(1).Picture ' Set Picture.
End Sub

Private Sub Command2_Click()
Set Picture2.Picture = ImageList1.ListImages(2).Picture ' Set Picture.

End Sub


Private Sub Command3_Click()
Set Picture2.Picture = ImageList1.ListImages(3).Picture ' Set Picture.

End Sub


Private Sub Form_Load()
    Picture1(0).ZOrder 0
    ProgressBar1.Value = 0
    For loop_index = 1 To 3
        Set theItem = ListView1.ListItems.Add()
        theItem.Icon = loop_index
        theItem.Text = "ListItem " & loop_index
    Next loop_index
    Dim theNode As Node
```

```
    Set theNode = TreeView1.Nodes.Add(, , "theRoot", "Root", 1)
    Set theNode = TreeView1.Nodes.Add("theRoot", tvwChild, , "Child 1",
2)
    Set theNode = TreeView1.Nodes.Add("theRoot", tvwChild, , "Child 2",
3)
    Set theNode = TreeView1.Nodes.Add("theRoot", tvwChild, , "Child 3",
4)
    Set theNode = TreeView1.Nodes.Add("theRoot", tvwChild, , "Child 4",
5)
    theNode.EnsureVisible
    TreeView1.Style = tvwTreelinesPictureText
    TreeView1.BorderStyle = vbFixedSingle
End Sub

Private Sub ProgressBar1_MouseDown(Button As Integer, Shift As
        Integer, x As Single, y As Single)
    ProgressBar1.Value = ProgressBar1.Value + 1
End Sub

Private Sub Slider1_Click()
    ProgressBar1.Value = Slider1.Value
End Sub

Private Sub StatusBar1_PanelClick(ByVal Panel As Panel)
    StatusBar1.Panels(1).Text = "Status Bar clicked"
End Sub

Private Sub TabStrip1_Click()
Picture1(TabStrip1.SelectedItem.Index - 1).ZOrder 0
End Sub

Private Sub Toolbar1_ButtonClick(ByVal Button As Button)
    Beep
End Sub
```

LISTING 5.11 WIN95.VBP

```
Form=win95.Frm
Object={F9043C88-F6F2-101A-A3C9-08002B2F49FB}#1.0#0; COMDLG32.OCX
Object={BDC217C8-ED16-11CD-956C-0000C04E4C0A}#1.0#0; TABCTL32.OCX
Object={3B7C8863-D78F-101B-B9B5-04021C009402}#1.0#0; RICHTX32.OCX
Object={6B7E6392-850A-101B-AFC0-4210102A8DA7}#1.0#0; COMCTL32.OCX
Reference=*\G{BEF6E001-A874-101A-8BBA-
        00AA00300CAB}#2.0#0#C:\WINDOWS\SYSTEM\OLEPRO32.DLL#Standard
        OLE Types
ProjWinSize=442,469,202,94
ProjWinShow=2
IconForm="Form1"
Name="Project1"
HelpContextID="0"
```

```
StartMode=0
VersionCompatible32="0"
MajorVer=1
MinorVer=0
RevisionVer=0
AutoIncrementVer=0
ServerSupportFiles=0
```

We've completed our exploration of the custom controls that come with Visual Basic. As you can see, there is a great deal of programming capability here, especially when it comes to working with graphs, grids, common dialog boxes, and the Windows 95 controls. In the next chapter, we'll start to examine another important Visual Basic topic: how to handle run-time errors.

## CHAPTER 6

HOW TO HANDLE RUN-TIME ERRORS

One important aspect of professional applications is how well they handle errors. It's all very well to design your programs carefully, but the toughest test is in the field, where, many things can go wrong even if your program is debugged. For example, a user may not have loaded a diskette with a required file into a drive, or there may be memory allocation errors when you load a new form into your program, or a file you're looking for may not exist. It is these *run-time* errors—errors that can occur even for fully debugged programs—that we'll take a look at in this chapter. Knowing how to handle run-time errors is vital to producing applications for the real world. We'll gain that skill in this chapter.

Run-time errors are also called *trappable* errors. Note that these errors are not the same as bugs, which are logic errors. (We'll assume that the logic errors have been eliminated from the programs we discuss here.) Trappable errors are those errors that can occur long after a program is tested and distributed, because they occur only when the program is running. They have to do with the environment that the program runs in, something the program has little control over. Professional programs almost always have a way of handling run-time errors, which is why we'll cover the subject here. The run-time error handling in Visual Basic is quite good, but if you don't make use of it, the person who uses your program may be left staring at cryptic messages in message boxes reminiscent of the infamous DOS Basic error message: "?Redo from start." Adding run-time error handling to your programs will give them a reputation for robustness and will make them into tools the user can believe in.

Because file handling is one of the most notorious error-generating operations, we'll start our run-time error discussion by taking a new look at our WRITER program.

How to Use On Error GoTo

As it stands now, our WRITER program reads files and simply hopes for the best. Take a look at the code in WRITER with which we read a file (from **WRITER.FRM**):

```
Private Sub Read_Click()
    CommonDialog1.FileName = "*.*"
    CommonDialog1.ShowOpen
    Open CommonDialog1.FileName For Input As #1
    Text1.Text = Input$(LOF(1), #1)
    Close #1
End Sub
```

Here, we display the File Open common dialog box, hope that the user selects or types a file name, and then try to open the matching file. Two things might go wrong here: the user may click **Cancel** in the File Open dialog box, meaning that he or she doesn't want to open a file after all, or the file may not exist (for example, the user may have mistyped its name). We are not yet prepared for either problem. How do we handle such errors? This is where run-time error handling comes in; to intercept, or trap, the error, we use the Visual Basic On Error GoTo statement. Add this code to **WRITER.FRM**.

```
Private Sub Read_Click()
--> On Error GoTo OpenError
    CommonDialog1.FileName = "*.*"
    CommonDialog1.CancelError = True
    CommonDialog1.ShowOpen
    Open CommonDialog1.FileName For Input As #1
    Text1.Text = Input$(LOF(1), #1)
    Close #1
End Sub
```

Here, we indicate that if an error occurs, program control should jump to the label OpenError. (Note: to turn error handling off, use the instruction On Error GoTo 0.) Let's place that label at the end of our subroutine. Also note that we place an Exit Sub instruction above it so that if there was no error, the code following the OpenError label is not executed during normal subroutine execution:

```
Private Sub Read_Click()
    On Error GoTo OpenError
    CommonDialog1.FileName = "*.*"
    CommonDialog1.ShowOpen
    Open CommonDialog1.FileName For Input As #1
```

```
    Text1.Text = Input$(LOF(1), #1)
    Close #1
    Exit Sub     <--
OpenError:       <--
End Sub
```

The code following the OpenError label is called an *error handler*. In this case, we'll simply place a message box on the screen explaining that there was an error. (Here, we pass the text for the message box—the value 48 causes an exclamation point to appear in the message box—and the caption we want the message box to have: "Writer.")

```
Private Sub Read_Click()
    On Error GoTo OpenError
    CommonDialog1.FileName = "*.*"
    CommonDialog1.ShowOpen
    Open CommonDialog1.FileName For Input As #1
    Text1.Text = Input$(LOF(1), #1)
    Close #1
    Exit Sub
OpenError:
--> MsgBox "Open Error", 48, "Writer"
End Sub
```

The result of this operation appears in Figure 6.1.

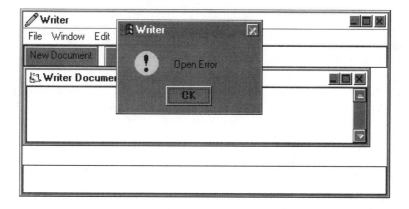

FIGURE 6.1 OUR FIRST ERROR-HANDLING ATTEMPT.

This works, but although it prevents Visual Basic from placing its own error-handling message boxes on the screen, this solution is far from satisfactory—the user is left wondering: what was the specific problem? And if the user wants to retry the operation, we should place the File Open dialog box back on the screen; but if he or she pressed **Cancel**, we should just exit the subroutine. We'll look into these aspects of our program next.

We'll determine exactly what error occurred and how to better suit the remedy to the problem. We'll start by treating the case in which the user clicked **Cancel**.

HOW TO USE ERR AND ERL

Our first task will be to determine whether the user clicked **Cancel** in the File Open dialog box. To check that, we will use CancelError, a property of the File Open dialog box. We set it True:

```
Private Sub Read_Click()
    On Error GoTo OpenError
    CommonDialog1.FileName = "*.*"
--> CommonDialog1.CancelError = True
    CommonDialog1.ShowOpen
    Open CommonDialog1.FileName For Input As #1
    Text1.Text = Input$(LOF(1), #1)
    Close #1
End Sub
```

Our program will now generate an error when the user clicks **Cancel**.

In the error handler section of our code, we can check to see whether the generated error was caused by the **Cancel** button. There is an error code for each trappable error, and some of the more common ones appear in Table 6.1. If the error code, which is stored in the Visual Basic Err object (and which we will check in the error handler), equals 32755, then the user clicked the **Cancel** button and we should exit the subroutine. We do that with this new code (from **WRITER.FRM**):

```
Private Sub Read_Click()
    On Error GoTo OpenError
    CommonDialog1.FileName = "*.*"
    CommonDialog1.CancelError = True
    CommonDialog1.ShowOpen
    Open CommonDialog1.FileName For Input As #1
    Text1.Text = Input$(LOF(1), #1)
    Close #1
    Exit Sub
OpenError:
--> If Err = 32755 Then Exit Sub
End Sub
```

TABLE 6.1 SOME TRAPPABLE ERRORS.

Error Number	Meaning
5	Illegal function call occurred
6	Overflow error
7	Program is out of memory
9	Subscript was out of legal range
10	There was a duplicate definition
11	Division by zero occurred
13	Type mismatch occurred
14	Program is out of string space
19	No RESUME statement found
20	RESUME statement without error found
51	Internal error occurred
52	Bad file name or file number
53	File Not found error occurred
54	Bad file mode error occurred
55	File is already open
57	Device I/O error occurred
58	File already exists error
59	Record length is bad
61	Disk is full error
62	Input past the end of file
63	Record number is bad
64	File name is bad
65	File was previously loaded
67	Too many files open
68	Device is unavailable error
70	Permission was denied
71	Disk(ette) is not ready
72	Disk-media error occurred
75	Path/File access error occurred
76	Path was not found
323	Incompatible Visual Basic version
340	Control array element nonexistent
341	Control array index out of bounds

(continued...)

Error Number	Meaning
342	Insufficient room to allocate control array
343	Object referenced is not an array
344	No index specified when using control array
360	Object already loaded
361	Only forms or control array members can be loaded or unloaded
362	Design-time controls cannot be unloaded
380	Property value illegal
381	Property array index illegal
384	Property cannot be changed when form is minimized or maximized
420	Object reference invalid
421	Method selected is not applicable for this object
422	Property not found
423	Property or control referenced not found
424	Object is required error
425	Object used illegally
427	Object is not the Printer object error
428	Object is not a control error
429	Object is not a form error occurred
430	No currently active control
431	No currently active form
461	Given format does not match format of data
480	Cannot create AutoRedraw bitmap

Now we've handled the case in which the user clicks the File Open dialog box's **Cancel** button. So far, then, error handling has been quite useful for our WRITER program.

There are other types of errors we might run into when trying to open a file, and we'll handle them next. For example, if the file we are trying to open does not exist, a specific error code is generated, and we could print that error code. But that helpful to the user—how does it help to know that error 53 occurred? It's far better to print the English explanation of that error—"File Not Found"—and we can do that with the Visual Basic Error$() function, which returns an English string explaining the error when we use it this way:

```
Private Sub Read_Click()
    On Error GoTo OpenError
    CommonDialog1.FileName = "*.*"
    CommonDialog1.CancelError = True
    CommonDialog1.ShowOpen
    Open CommonDialog1.FileName For Input As #1
    Text1.Text = Input$(LOF(1), #1)
    Close #1
    Exit Sub
OpenError:
    If Err = 32755 Then Exit Sub
--> MsgBox Error$(Err), 48, "Writer"
End Sub
```

This kind of error handling is more useful, and the result appears in Figure 6.2. In this way, we can handle the **Cancel** button if users want to stop the file-reading operation, and we can also inform them what went wrong if they did attempt to read a file but that operation failed.

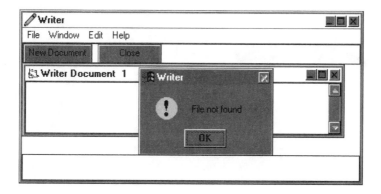

FIGURE 6.2 ERROR HANDLING WITH EXPLANATORY MESSAGES.

For debugging purposes, we can also print the line number at which the error occurred. Line numbers are used infrequently in Visual Basic except in error handling (although they were standard in early BASIC). However, we can number each line as we like and then use the Visual Basic Erl object to determine the line at which the error occurred and display the correct line number. We can print the error number using Str$(Err) and print the matching line number this way:

```
Private Sub Read_Click()
1    On Error GoTo OpenError
```

```
2    CommonDialog1.FileName = "*.*"
3    CommonDialog1.CancelError = True
4    CommonDialog1.ShowOpen
5    Open CommonDialog1.FileName For Input As #1
6    Text1.Text = Input$(LOF(1), #1)
7    Close #1
8    Exit Sub
OpenError:
     If Err = 32755 Then Exit Sub
--> MsgBox "Open Error" + Str$(Err) + " in line " + Str$(Erl), 48,
"Writer"
End Sub
```

If, for example, the file that the user requested us to open does not exist, we would see that error 53 (File Not Found) occurred in line 5 (the Open statement), as shown in Figure 6.3. The program now indicates what error occurred and in which line number. (Line numbers are of much greater use to programmers than to users.)

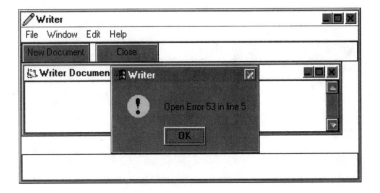

FIGURE 6.3 WE MAKE USE OF ERROR NUMBER AND LINE NUMBER.

The new version of **WRITER.FRM** appears in Listing 6.1.

LISTING 6.1 WRITER.FRM

```
VERSION 4.00
Begin VB.Form Form1
    Caption         =   "Writer Document"
    ClientHeight    =   2445
    ClientLeft      =   1695
    ClientTop       =   2055
    ClientWidth     =   5475
    BeginProperty Font
```

```
        name              =     "MS Sans Serif"
        charset           =     1
        weight            =     400
        size              =     8.25
        underline         =     0      'False
        italic            =     0      'False
        strikethrough     =     0      'False
EndProperty
Height            =     3135
Left              =     1635
LinkTopic         =     "Form1"
MDIChild          =     -1    'True
ScaleHeight       =     2445
ScaleWidth        =     5475
Top               =     1425
Width             =     5595
Begin VB.TextBox Text1
    Height            =     1935
    Left              =     0
    MultiLine         =     -1    'True
    ScrollBars        =     2     'Vertical
    TabIndex          =     0
    Top               =     0
    Width             =     5055
End
Begin MSComDlg.CommonDialog CommonDialog1
    Left              =     3240
    Top               =     1920
    _version          =     65536
    _extentx          =     847
    _extenty          =     847
    _stockprops       =     0
End
Begin VB.Menu File
    Caption           =     "File"
    Begin VB.Menu New
        Caption           =     "New Document"
    End
    Begin VB.Menu Save
        Caption           =     "Save As..."
    End
    Begin VB.Menu Read
        Caption           =     "Open..."
    End
    Begin VB.Menu Font
        Caption           =     "Font..."
    End
    Begin VB.Menu Color
        Caption           =     "Color..."
    End
```

```
        Begin VB.Menu Print
            Caption         =   "Print..."
        End
        Begin VB.Menu Exit
            Caption         =   "Exit"
        End
    End
    Begin VB.Menu Window
        Caption         =   "Window"
        WindowList      =   -1  'True
    End
    Begin VB.Menu Edit
        Caption         =   "Edit"
        Begin VB.Menu Cut
            Caption     =   "Cut"
        End
    End
End
Attribute VB_Name = "Form1"
Attribute VB_Creatable = False
Attribute VB_Exposed = False
Dim MyDocumentNumber As Integer

Private Sub Color_Click()
    CommonDialog1.Color = Text1.ForeColor
    CommonDialog1.ShowColor
    Text1.ForeColor = CommonDialog1.Color
End Sub

Private Sub Exit_Click()
    End
End Sub

Private Sub Font_Click()
    CommonDialog1.FontName = Text1.FontName
    CommonDialog1.Color = Text1.ForeColor
    CommonDialog1.FontItalic = Text1.FontItalic
    CommonDialog1.FontStrikethru = Text1.FontStrikethru
    CommonDialog1.FontSize = Text1.FontSize
    CommonDialog1.FontUnderline = Text1.FontUnderline
    CommonDialog1.Flags = vbCFBoth
    CommonDialog1.ShowFont
    Text1.FontName = CommonDialog1.FontName
    Text1.FontSize = CommonDialog1.FontSize
End Sub

Private Sub Form_Load()
    MyDocumentNumber = NumberDocuments
    Text1.Height = Form1.ScaleHeight
    Text1.Width = Form1.ScaleWidth
```

```
    Caption = "Writer Document " + Str$(MyDocumentNumber)
    If NumberDocuments = 1 Then AttachWindow Me
End Sub

Private Sub Form_Resize()
    Text1.Height = Form1.ScaleHeight
    Text1.Width = Form1.ScaleWidth
End Sub

Private Sub New_Click()
    AddADocument
End Sub

Private Sub Print_Click()
    CommonDialog1.ShowPrinter
    NumberCopies% = CommonDialog1.Copies
    For loop_index% = 1 To NumberCopies%
        Printer.Print Text1.Text
        Printer.EndDoc
    Next loop_index%
End Sub

Private Sub Read_Click()
1   On Error GoTo OpenError
2   CommonDialog1.FileName = "*.*"
3   CommonDialog1.CancelError = True
4   CommonDialog1.ShowOpen
5   Open CommonDialog1.FileName For Input As #1
6   Text1.Text = Input$(LOF(1), #1)
7   Close #1
8   Exit Sub
OpenError:
    If Err = 32755 Then Exit Sub
    'MsgBox Error$(Err), 48, "Writer"
    MsgBox "Open Error" + Str$(Err) + " in line " + Str$(Erl), 48,
"Writer"
End Sub

Private Sub Save_Click()
    CommonDialog1.DefaultExt = ".txt"
    CommonDialog1.Filter = "*.txt"
    CommonDialog1.ShowSave
    Open CommonDialog1.FileName For Output As #1
    Print #1, Text1.Text
    MsgBox ("Saved")
    Close #1
End Sub
```

We've talked about the rudiments of error handling; now it's time to develop that knowledge as we elaborate on our error-handling code.

ERROR HANDLERS

In Visual Basic, error handlers are often quite involved, usually taking the form of a Visual Basic Select Case series of statements or staggered If...Then...Else statements. (Don't worry if you're not familiar with Select Case. We'll see how it works in a minute.)

For example, we might use the current error's error message (Error$(Err)) as the default error message but substitute our own, customized error message for selected errors. We might want to handle error 55 ourselves, customizing the error message to read, "File is already open." Let's look into such customized error handling now. We start by adding this Select Case statement to Read_Click() in **WRITER.FRM**:

```
Private Sub Read_Click()
    On Error GoTo OpenError
    CommonDialog1.FileName = "*.*"
    CommonDialog1.CancelError = True
    CommonDialog1.ShowOpen
    Open CommonDialog1.FileName For Input As #1
    Text1.Text = Input$(LOF(1), #1)
    Close #1
    Exit Sub
OpenError:
--> ErrMsg$ = Error$(Err)
--> Select Case Err
        .
        .
        .
--> End Select
--> MsgBox ErrMsg$, 48, "Writer"
End Sub
```

Here, we've defined a Select Case block:

```
    Select Case Err
        .
        .
        .
    End Select
```

Inside this block, we can specify what code to execute, depending on the value in Err. For example, where Err = 1, we could execute specific code:

```
    Select Case Err
--> Case 1
-->     [Code if Err = 1]
        .
        .
        .
    End Select
```

On the other hand, if Err = 2, we could execute other code:

```
    Select Case Err
    Case 1
        [Code if Err = 1]
--> Case 2
-->     [Code if Err = 2]
         .
         .
         .
    End Select
```

In this way, we can handle a range of values for the Err object. Let's see this in WRITER. If the error code, Err, equals 32755, the user clicked **Cancel** and we want to quit the subroutine, which we do using this new code:

```
Private Sub Read_Click()
    On Error GoTo OpenError
    CommonDialog1.FileName = "*.*"
    CommonDialog1.CancelError = True
    CommonDialog1.ShowOpen
    Open CommonDialog1.FileName For Input As #1
    Text1.Text = Input$(LOF(1), #1)
    Close #1
    Exit Sub
OpenError:
    ErrMsg$ = Error$(Err)
    Select Case Err
--> Case 32755
-->     Exit Sub
         .
         .
         .
    End Select
    MsgBox ErrMsg$, 48, "Writer"
End Sub
```

Now we can customize the error message in those cases we want to handle specially:

```
Private Sub Read_Click()
    On Error GoTo OpenError
    CommonDialog1.FileName = "*.*"
    CommonDialog1.CancelError = True
    CommonDialog1.ShowOpen
    Open CommonDialog1.FileName For Input As #1
    Text1.Text = Input$(LOF(1), #1)
    Close #1
    Exit Sub
```

297

```
OpenError:
    ErrMsg$ = Error$(Err)
    Select Case Err
    Case 32755
        Exit Sub
--> Case 55
-->     ErrMsg$ = "File is already open."
--> Case 57, 68, 71
-->     ErrMsg$ = "Check the disk."
    End Select
    MsgBox ErrMsg$, 48, "Writer"
End Sub
```

Here we handle several errors—numbers 55, 57, 68, and 71—by ourselves, setting the error message as we require. This technique gives us a greater measure of control, and it is more like a real error handler in Visual Basic. The new version of **WRITER.FRM** appears in Listing 6.2. So far, our run-time error handling is a success.

LISTING 6.2 WRITER.FRM, SECOND VERSION

```
VERSION 4.00
Begin VB.Form Form1
    Caption         =   "Writer Document"
    ClientHeight    =   2445
    ClientLeft      =   1695
    ClientTop       =   2055
    ClientWidth     =   5475
    BeginProperty Font
        name            =   "MS Sans Serif"
        charset         =   1
        weight          =   400
        size            =   8.25
        underline       =   0   'False
        italic          =   0   'False
        strikethrough   =   0   'False
    EndProperty
    Height          =   3135
    Left            =   1635
    LinkTopic       =   "Form1"
    MDIChild        =   -1  'True
    ScaleHeight     =   2445
    ScaleWidth      =   5475
    Top             =   1425
    Width           =   5595
    Begin VB.TextBox Text1
        Height          =   1935
        Left            =   0
        MultiLine       =   -1  'True
```

```
      ScrollBars      =    2   'Vertical
      TabIndex        =    0
      Top             =    0
      Width           =    5055
   End
   Begin MSComDlg.CommonDialog CommonDialog1
      Left            =    3240
      Top             =    1920
      _version        =    65536
      _extentx        =    847
      _extenty        =    847
      _stockprops     =    0
   End
   Begin VB.Menu File
      Caption         =    "File"
      Begin VB.Menu New
         Caption       =    "New Document"
      End
      Begin VB.Menu Save
         Caption       =    "Save As..."
      End
      Begin VB.Menu Read
         Caption       =    "Open..."
      End
      Begin VB.Menu Font
         Caption       =    "Font..."
      End
      Begin VB.Menu Color
         Caption       =    "Color..."
      End
      Begin VB.Menu Print
         Caption       =    "Print..."
      End
      Begin VB.Menu Exit
         Caption       =    "Exit"
      End
   End
   Begin VB.Menu Window
      Caption         =    "Window"
      WindowList      =    -1   'True
   End
   Begin VB.Menu Edit
      Caption         =    "Edit"
      Begin VB.Menu Cut
         Caption       =    "Cut"
      End
   End
End
Attribute VB_Name = "Form1"
Attribute VB_Creatable = False
Attribute VB_Exposed = False
```

```
Dim MyDocumentNumber As Integer

Private Sub Color_Click()
    CommonDialog1.Color = Text1.ForeColor
    CommonDialog1.ShowColor
    Text1.ForeColor = CommonDialog1.Color
End Sub

Private Sub Exit_Click()
    End
End Sub

Private Sub Font_Click()
    CommonDialog1.FontName = Text1.FontName
    CommonDialog1.Color = Text1.ForeColor
    CommonDialog1.FontItalic = Text1.FontItalic
    CommonDialog1.FontStrikethru = Text1.FontStrikethru
    CommonDialog1.FontSize = Text1.FontSize
    CommonDialog1.FontUnderline = Text1.FontUnderline
    CommonDialog1.Flags = vbCFBoth
    CommonDialog1.ShowFont
    Text1.FontName = CommonDialog1.FontName
    Text1.FontSize = CommonDialog1.FontSize
End Sub

Private Sub Form_Load()
    MyDocumentNumber = NumberDocuments
    Text1.Height = Form1.ScaleHeight
    Text1.Width = Form1.ScaleWidth
    Caption = "Writer Document " + Str$(MyDocumentNumber)
    If NumberDocuments = 1 Then AttachWindow Me
End Sub

Private Sub Form_Resize()
    Text1.Height = Form1.ScaleHeight
    Text1.Width = Form1.ScaleWidth
End Sub

Private Sub New_Click()
    AddADocument
End Sub

Private Sub Print_Click()
    CommonDialog1.ShowPrinter
    NumberCopies% = CommonDialog1.Copies
    For loop_index% = 1 To NumberCopies%
        Printer.Print Text1.Text
        Printer.EndDoc
    Next loop_index%
End Sub
```

```
Private Sub Read_Click()
    On Error GoTo OpenError
    CommonDialog1.FileName = "*.*"
    CommonDialog1.CancelError = True
    CommonDialog1.ShowOpen
    Open CommonDialog1.FileName For Input As #1
    Text1.Text = Input$(LOF(1), #1)
    Close #1
    Exit Sub
OpenError:
    ErrMsg$ = Error$(Err)
    Select Case Err
    Case 32755
        Exit Sub
    Case 55
        ErrMsg$ = "File is already open."
    Case 57, 68, 71
        ErrMsg$ = "Check the disk."
    End Select
    MsgBox ErrMsg$, 48, "Writer"
End Sub

Private Sub Save_Click()
    CommonDialog1.DefaultExt = ".txt"
    CommonDialog1.Filter = "*.txt"
    CommonDialog1.ShowSave
    Open CommonDialog1.FileName For Output As #1
    Print #1, Text1.Text
    MsgBox ("Saved")
    Close #1
End Sub
```

But, what if the user wants to retry the operation? For example, he or she may not have inserted the correct disk. As our subroutine stands now, the user would have to use WRITER's File menu all over again, selecting the **Open** item to try to reopen the file. Instead, we can offer the option of retrying the operation when we display the error message, as we'll see next.

HOW TO USE THE RESUME STATEMENT

When there is an error, we can offer the user the option of correcting the problem and retrying the operation. For example, if the disk drive where the file was supposed to be actually contained no disk, we could place a message box on the screen like this:

In this case, the user has two buttons—**OK** and **Cancel**—and the user can place a disk in the drive and click **OK** if he or she wishes. Clicking **OK** means that the program should retry the reading operation.

To check whether **OK** has been clicked, we examine the return value from the message box function, MsgBox(); a return value of 1 means that **OK** has been clicked. We now add the following code to pop up our message box on the screen. Note that we pass MsgBox() a value of 49, which means we want a message box with an exclamation point, an **OK** button, and a **Cancel** button.

```
Private Sub Read_Click()
    On Error GoTo OpenError
    CommonDialog1.FileName = "*.*"
    CommonDialog1.CancelError = True
    CommonDialog1.ShowOpen
    Open CommonDialog1.FileName For Input As #1
    Text1.Text = Input$(LOF(1), #1)
    Close #1
    Exit Sub
OpenError:
    ErrMsg$ = Error$(Err) + " Try again?"
    Select Case Err
    Case 32755
        Exit Sub
    Case 55
        ErrMsg$ = "File is already open. Try Again?"
    Case 57, 68, 71
        ErrMsg$ = "Check the disk. Try again?"
    End Select
--> If MsgBox(ErrMsg$, 49, "Writer") = 1 Then
        .
        .
        .
    End If
End Sub
```

If the return value from MsgBox() is 1, the user clicked the **OK** button. To retry the file-opening operation, we use the Visual Basic Resume statement:

```
Private Sub Read_Click()
    On Error GoTo OpenError
    CommonDialog1.FileName = "*.*"
    CommonDialog1.CancelError = True
    CommonDialog1.ShowOpen
    Open CommonDialog1.FileName For Input As #1
    Text1.Text = Input$(LOF(1), #1)
    Close #1
    Exit Sub
OpenError:
    ErrMsg$ = Error$(Err) + " Try again?"
    Select Case Err
    Case 32755
        Exit Sub
    Case 55
        ErrMsg$ = "File is already open. Try Again?"
    Case 57, 68, 71
        ErrMsg$ = "Check the disk. Try again?"
    End Select
    If MsgBox(ErrMsg$, 49, "Writer") = 1 Then
-->     Resume
    End If
End Sub
```

The Resume statement causes program control to return to the line that
caused the error—in this case, the Open statement. The user wants to retry
the file-reading operation, so we jump back to that line with the Resume
statement and try reading the file again.

Give this program a try and request the program to open a file from a
disk drive without a diskette in it; the "Check the disk. Try again?" message
will appear, as shown in Figure 6.4. If you place the correct diskette in the
drive and click **OK**, WRITER will be able to open the file.

FIGURE 6.4 WE CUSTOMIZE OUR ERROR HANDLER AND ALLOW THE USER TO RECOVER FROM THE ERROR.

The new version of **WRITER.FRM** appears in Listing 6.3.

LISTING 6.3 WRITER.FRM, THIRD VERSION

```
VERSION 4.00
Begin VB.Form Form1
    Caption         =   "Writer Document"
    ClientHeight    =   2445
    ClientLeft      =   1695
    ClientTop       =   2055
    ClientWidth     =   5475
    BeginProperty Font
        name            =   "MS Sans Serif"
        charset         =   1
        weight          =   400
        size            =   8.25
        underline       =   0   'False
        italic          =   0   'False
        strikethrough   =   0   'False
    EndProperty
    Height          =   3135
    Left            =   1635
    LinkTopic       =   "Form1"
    MDIChild        =   -1   'True
    ScaleHeight     =   2445
    ScaleWidth      =   5475
    Top             =   1425
    Width           =   5595
    Begin VB.TextBox Text1
        Height          =   1935
        Left            =   0
        MultiLine       =   -1   'True
        ScrollBars      =   2    'Vertical
        TabIndex        =   0
        Top             =   0
        Width           =   5055
    End
    Begin MSComDlg.CommonDialog CommonDialog1
        Left            =   3240
        Top             =   1920
        _version        =   65536
        _extentx        =   847
        _extenty        =   847
        _stockprops     =   0
    End
    Begin VB.Menu File
        Caption         =   "File"
        Begin VB.Menu New
            Caption         =   "New Document"
        End
        Begin VB.Menu Save
```

```
                Caption         =    "Save As..."
            End
            Begin VB.Menu Read
                Caption         =    "Open..."
            End
            Begin VB.Menu Font
                Caption         =    "Font..."
            End
            Begin VB.Menu Color
                Caption         =    "Color..."
            End
            Begin VB.Menu Print
                Caption         =    "Print..."
            End
            Begin VB.Menu Exit
                Caption         =    "Exit"
            End
        End
        Begin VB.Menu Window
            Caption         =    "Window"
            WindowList      =    -1    'True
        End
        Begin VB.Menu Edit
            Caption         =    "Edit"
            Begin VB.Menu Cut
                Caption         =    "Cut"
            End
        End
    End
End
Attribute VB_Name = "Form1"
Attribute VB_Creatable = False
Attribute VB_Exposed = False
Dim MyDocumentNumber As Integer

Private Sub Color_Click()
    CommonDialog1.Color = Text1.ForeColor
    CommonDialog1.ShowColor
    Text1.ForeColor = CommonDialog1.Color
End Sub

Private Sub Exit_Click()
    End
End Sub

Private Sub Font_Click()
    CommonDialog1.FontName = Text1.FontName
    CommonDialog1.Color = Text1.ForeColor
    CommonDialog1.FontItalic = Text1.FontItalic
    CommonDialog1.FontStrikethru = Text1.FontStrikethru
    CommonDialog1.FontSize = Text1.FontSize
    CommonDialog1.FontUnderline = Text1.FontUnderline
    CommonDialog1.Flags = vbCFBoth
```

```vb
    CommonDialog1.ShowFont
    Text1.FontName = CommonDialog1.FontName
    Text1.FontSize = CommonDialog1.FontSize
End Sub

Private Sub Form_Load()
    MyDocumentNumber = NumberDocuments
    Text1.Height = Form1.ScaleHeight
    Text1.Width = Form1.ScaleWidth
    Caption = "Writer Document " + Str$(MyDocumentNumber)
    If NumberDocuments = 1 Then AttachWindow Me
End Sub

Private Sub Form_Resize()
    Text1.Height = Form1.ScaleHeight
    Text1.Width = Form1.ScaleWidth
End Sub

Private Sub New_Click()
    AddADocument
End Sub

Private Sub Print_Click()
    CommonDialog1.ShowPrinter
    NumberCopies% = CommonDialog1.Copies
    For loop_index% = 1 To NumberCopies%
        Printer.Print Text1.Text
        Printer.EndDoc
    Next loop_index%
End Sub

Private Sub Read_Click()
    On Error GoTo OpenError
    CommonDialog1.FileName = "*.*"
    CommonDialog1.CancelError = True
    CommonDialog1.ShowOpen
    Open CommonDialog1.FileName For Input As #1
    Text1.Text = Input$(LOF(1), #1)
    Close #1
    Exit Sub
OpenError:
    ErrMsg$ = Error$(Err) + " Try again?"
    Select Case Err
    Case 32755
        Exit Sub
    Case 55
        ErrMsg$ = "File is already open. Try Again?"
    Case 57, 68, 71
        ErrMsg$ = "Check the disk. Try again?"
    End Select
```

```
        If MsgBox(ErrMsg$, 49, "Writer") = 1 Then
            Resume
        End If
    End Sub
```

```
    Private Sub Save_Click()
        CommonDialog1.DefaultExt = ".txt"
        CommonDialog1.Filter = "*.txt"
        CommonDialog1.ShowSave
        Open CommonDialog1.FileName For Output As #1
        Print #1, Text1.Text
        MsgBox ("Saved")
        Close #1
    End Sub
```

However, it's not always appropriate to resume at the line that caused the error. In some cases, it is better to skip the current error-producing line and move on to the next line or even an entirely different line. We'll examine this process next.

HOW TO USE RESUME NEXT AND RESUME LINE#

Two powerful error-handling statements in Visual Basic are Resume Next and Resume Line#, where Line# is the number of the line to which program control should return when the error-handling code is completed. With both of these statements, we can resume program operation after an error occurred without re-executing the line of code that produced the error.

Let's put together a program to examine the use of Resume Next and Resume Line#. (We'll come back to WRITER later in the chapter.) Call this program **ERRORS.VBP**. Using the Menu Editor, give the default form a menu named File with two menu items: **Create Errors** and **Exit**. As we normally do, add the End statement to the **Exit** menu item's click event handler (Exit_Click()). Now open the **Create Errors** menu item's click event handler in **ERRORS.FRM**. (Click that menu item with the mouse.)

```
Private Sub CreateErrors_Click()

End Sub
```

Since we will use an error-handler here, we add that part of the code first:

```
Private Sub CreateErrors_Click()
    On Error GoTo ErrorHandler      <--
```

```
         .
         .
         .
    Exit Sub                        <--
ErrorHandler:                       <--

End Sub
```

We'll examine the use of Resume Line# first. In particular, we might try to open a file that simply doesn't exist. We start by determining which file number is the next free file number (using the FreeFile keyword) and then trying to open a nonexistent file by passing Visual Basic the filename **EXIST.NOT** (assuming you have no such file on your disk):

```
Private Sub CreateErrors_Click()
    On Error GoTo ErrorHandler

--> FreeFileNumber = FreeFile
--> Open "exist.not" For Input As #FreeFileNumber
--> Text$ = Input(LOF(FreeFileNumber), FreeFileNumber)
--> Close #FileNumber
         .
         .
         .

    Exit Sub
ErrorHandler:

End Sub
```

This generates an error: error number 53, File Not Found. We can test for this error in the error handler. If that was the error that caused us to enter the error handler, we display a message box explaining what the error was by using the Description property of the Err object (which is the same as using Error$(Err)). Next, we abandon the file-opening attempt by moving to the line we label as line 1 by executing the instruction Resume 1:

```
Private Sub CreateErrors_Click()
    On Error GoTo ErrorHandler

    FreeFileNumber = FreeFile
    Open "exist.not" For Input As #FreeFileNumber
    Text$ = Input(LOF(FreeFileNumber), FreeFileNumber)
    Close #FileNumber

    Exit Sub
ErrorHandler:
```

```
--> If Err.Number = 53 Then              'File not found
-->      MsgBox (Err.Description)
-->         Resume 1
--> End If
End Sub
```

Now we have to create a line labeled 1. This will be a few lines past the Open statement, skipping the Input and Close statements:

```
Private Sub CreateErrors_Click()
    On Error GoTo ErrorHandler

    FreeFileNumber = FreeFile
    Open "exist.not" For Input As #FreeFileNumber
    Text$ = Input(LOF(FreeFileNumber), FreeFileNumber)
    Close #FileNumber

1   For loop_index = -10 To 10               <--

        .
        .
        .

    Exit Sub
ErrorHandler:
    If Err.Number = 53 Then                  'File not found
        MsgBox (Err.Description)
        Resume 1
    End If
End Sub
```

In this way, we skip all the file-handling code. That's how Resume Line# works: using that instruction lets you skip past error-producing sections of code after the program generated an error.

Now we'll look at Resume Next, which is also a common instruction. Resume Next is a popular statement to use with error-prone loops, where it allows the programmer to continue loop iteration after skipping the specific loop iteration that caused the problem. For example, we'll set up a loop that prints the reciprocals of the numbers −10 to 10:

```
Private Sub CreateErrors_Click()
    On Error GoTo ErrorHandler

    FreeFileNumber = FreeFile
    Open "exist.not" For Input As #FreeFileNumber
    Text$ = Input(LOF(FreeFileNumber), FreeFileNumber)
    Close #FileNumber

1   For loop_index = -10 To 10
```

```
-->     Print "Reciprocal of " & Str(loop_index) & " = " & Str(1 /
loop_index)
--> Next loop_index

    Exit Sub
ErrorHandler:
    If Err.Number = 53 Then                 'File not found
        MsgBox (Err.Description)
        Resume 1
    End If
End Sub
```

Clearly, there is going to be a problem when we try to find the reciprocal of 0. Checking Table 6.1, we see that an error of type 11, Division by 0, will occur. We trap that error this way:

```
Private Sub CreateErrors_Click()
    On Error GoTo ErrorHandler

    FreeFileNumber = FreeFile
    Open "exist.not" For Input As #FreeFileNumber
    Text$ = Input(LOF(FreeFileNumber), FreeFileNumber)
    Close #FileNumber

1   For loop_index = -10 To 10
        Print "Reciprocal of " & Str(loop_index) & " = " & Str(1 /
loop_index)
    Next loop_index

    Exit Sub
ErrorHandler:
    If Err.Number = 53 Then                 'File not found
        MsgBox (Err.Description)
        Resume 1
    End If
--> If Err.Number = 11 Then                 'Divide by 0
        .

        .
--> End If
End Sub
```

In this case, we can skip the line with the error-producing division instruction by using Resume Next. Resume Next simply causes program execution to begin again at the line after the line that caused the error. In this case, we will resume program execution with the line Next loop_index, moving us to the next iteration of the loop, after safely handling the division by zero. We add Resume Next to our program this way. (Note that we also display a message box with the error message.)

```
Private Sub CreateErrors_Click()
    On Error GoTo ErrorHandler

    FreeFileNumber = FreeFile
    Open "exist.not" For Input As #FreeFileNumber
    Text$ = Input(LOF(FreeFileNumber), FreeFileNumber)
    Close #FileNumber

1   For loop_index = -10 To 10
        Print "Reciprocal of " & Str(loop_index) & " = " & Str(1 /
loop_index)
    Next loop_index

    Exit Sub
ErrorHandler:
    If Err.Number = 53 Then              'File not found
        MsgBox (Err.Description)
        Resume 1
    End If
    If Err.Number = 11 Then              'Divide by 0
-->     MsgBox (Err.Description)
-->     Resume Next
    End If
End Sub
```

When we reach the division by 0, we simply create an error, as shown in Figure 6.5, and skip that iteration of the loop by executing Resume Next. As you can see, Resume Next and Resume Line# are powerful error-recovery instructions.

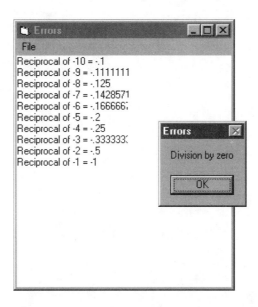

FIGURE 6.5 HANDLING AN ERROR WITHOUT ENDING THE PROGRAM.

ERRORS.FRM appears in Listing 6.4, and **ERRORS.VBP** is in Listing 6.5.

LISTING 6.4 ERRORS.FRM

```
VERSION 4.00
Begin VB.Form Form1
   Caption          =    "Errors"
   ClientHeight     =    4230
   ClientLeft       =    1080
   ClientTop        =    2310
   ClientWidth      =    6720
   BeginProperty Font
      name          =    "MS Sans Serif"
      charset       =    1
      weight        =    400
      size          =    8.25
      underline     =    0    'False
      italic        =    0    'False
      strikethrough =    0    'False
   EndProperty
   Height           =    4920
   Left             =    1020
   LinkTopic        =    "Form1"
   ScaleHeight      =    4230
   ScaleWidth       =    6720
   Top              =    1680
   Width            =    6840
   Begin VB.Menu File
      Caption       =    "File"
      Begin VB.Menu CreateErrors
         Caption    =    "Create Errors"
      End
      Begin VB.Menu Exit
         Caption    =    "Exit"
      End
   End
End
Attribute VB_Name = "Form1"
Attribute VB_Creatable = False
Attribute VB_Exposed = False
Private Sub CreateErrors_Click()
   On Error GoTo ErrorHandler

   FreeFileNumber = FreeFile
   Open "exist.not" For Input As #FreeFileNumber
   Text$ = Input(LOF(FreeFileNumber), FreeFileNumber)
   Close #FileNumber
```

```
1    For loop_index = -10 To 10
         Print "Reciprocal of " & Str(loop_index) & " = " & Str(1 /
loop_index)
     Next loop_index

     Exit Sub
ErrorHandler:
     If Err.Number = 53 Then                'File not found
         MsgBox (Err.Description)
         Resume 1
     End If
     If Err.Number = 11 Then                'Divide by 0
         MsgBox (Err.Description)
         Resume Next
     End If
End Sub

Private Sub Exit_Click()
     End
End Sub
```

LISTING 6.5 ERRORS.VBP

```
ERRORS.FRM
Object={F9043C88-F6F2-101A-A3C9-08002B2F49FB}#1.0#0; COMDLG16.OCX
Object={FAEEE763-117E-101B-8933-08002B2F4F5A}#1.0#0; DBLIST16.OCX
ProjWinSize=276,510,205,115
ProjWinShow=2
IconForm="Form1"
HelpFile=""
ExeName="Project1.exe"
Path="D:\VB"
Command=""
Name="Errors"
HelpContextID="0"
StartMode=0
VersionCompatible="0"
MajorVer=1
MinorVer=0
RevisionVer=0
AutoIncrementVer=0
VersionCompanyName=""
Reference=*\G{00025E01-0000-0000-C000-
000000000046}#0.0#0#DAO2516.DLL#Microsoft DAO 2.5 Object Library
```

Next, we'll add Resume Line# to **WRITER.FRM**, producing a new version of that program.

THE WRITER PROGRAM WITH RESUME LINE#

We can make use of Resume Line# in **WRITER.FRM** to allow the user to start the whole file-opening process over again if desired. As the program stands now, we allow the user to try again but do not display the File Open message box on the screen before trying to open the file a second time. This is fine if the error was caused by a missing diskette, but if the user misspelled the file name or wanted to open a different file in the second attempt, we should show the File Open dialog box again. We can do that with Resume Line#. In particular, we skip back to the beginning of the code that attempts to open the file, repeating the entire process from the File Open dialog box to the Open statement (and not to just the Open statement, as we did earlier with the simple Resume statement).

```
Private Sub Read_Click()
    On Error GoTo OpenError
1   CommonDialog1.FileName = "*.*"                          <--
    CommonDialog1.CancelError = True
    CommonDialog1.ShowOpen
    Open CommonDialog1.FileName For Input As #1
    Text1.Text = Input$(LOF(1), #1)
    Close #1
    Exit Sub
OpenError:
    ErrMsg$ = Error$(Err) + ". Try again?"
    Select Case Err
    Case 32755
        Exit Sub
    Case 55
        ErrMsg$ = "File is already open. Try Again?"
    Case 57, 68, 71
        ErrMsg$ = "Check the disk. Try again?"
    End Select
    If MsgBox(ErrMsg$, 49, "Writer") = 1 Then
        Resume 1                                            <--
    End If
End Sub
```

That's it—we've allowed the user to respecify the file name. When opening a file creates an error, we allow the user two options: cancel the operation with the **Cancel** button or try the whole operation again (from start to finish) by clicking **OK**. This is the essence of good error handling—allowing the user as many options as possible in recovery. The final version of **WRITER.FRM** appears in Listing 6.6.

LISTING 6.6 FINAL VERSION OF **WRITER.FRM**

```
VERSION 4.00
Begin VB.Form Form1
   Caption         =   "Writer Document"
   ClientHeight    =   2445
   ClientLeft      =   1695
   ClientTop       =   2055
   ClientWidth     =   5475
   BeginProperty Font
      name         =   "MS Sans Serif"
      charset      =   1
      weight       =   400
      size         =   8.25
      underline    =   0   'False
      italic       =   0   'False
      strikethrough =  0   'False
   EndProperty
   Height          =   3135
   Left            =   1635
   LinkTopic       =   "Form1"
   MDIChild        =   -1  'True
   ScaleHeight     =   2445
   ScaleWidth      =   5475
   Top             =   1425
   Width           =   5595
   Begin VB.TextBox Text1
      Height       =   1935
      Left         =   0
      MultiLine    =   -1  'True
      ScrollBars   =   2   'Vertical
      TabIndex     =   0
      Top          =   0
      Width        =   5055
   End
   Begin MSComDlg.CommonDialog CommonDialog1
      Left         =   3240
      Top          =   1920
      _version     =   65536
      _extentx     =   847
      _extenty     =   847
      _stockprops  =   0
   End
   Begin VB.Menu File
      Caption      =   "File"
      Begin VB.Menu New
         Caption   =   "New Document"
      End
      Begin VB.Menu Save
```

```
                  Caption          =    "Save As..."
               End
               Begin VB.Menu Read
                  Caption          =    "Open..."
               End
               Begin VB.Menu Font
                  Caption          =    "Font..."
               End
               Begin VB.Menu Color
                  Caption          =    "Color..."
               End
               Begin VB.Menu Print
                  Caption          =    "Print..."
               End
               Begin VB.Menu Exit
                  Caption          =    "Exit"
               End
            End
            Begin VB.Menu Window
               Caption          =    "Window"
               WindowList       =    -1    'True
            End
            Begin VB.Menu Edit
               Caption          =    "Edit"
               Begin VB.Menu Cut
                  Caption          =    "Cut"
               End
            End
         End
Attribute VB_Name = "Form1"
Attribute VB_Creatable = False
Attribute VB_Exposed = False
Dim MyDocumentNumber As Integer

Private Sub Color_Click()
    CommonDialog1.Color = Text1.ForeColor
    CommonDialog1.ShowColor
    Text1.ForeColor = CommonDialog1.Color
End Sub

Private Sub Exit_Click()
    End
End Sub

Private Sub Font_Click()
    CommonDialog1.FontName = Text1.FontName
    CommonDialog1.Color = Text1.ForeColor
    CommonDialog1.FontItalic = Text1.FontItalic
    CommonDialog1.FontStrikethru = Text1.FontStrikethru
    CommonDialog1.FontSize = Text1.FontSize
```

```
    CommonDialog1.FontUnderline = Text1.FontUnderline
    CommonDialog1.Flags = vbCFBoth
    CommonDialog1.ShowFont
    Text1.FontName = CommonDialog1.FontName
    Text1.FontSize = CommonDialog1.FontSize
End Sub

Private Sub Form_Load()
    MyDocumentNumber = NumberDocuments
    Text1.Height = Form1.ScaleHeight
    Text1.Width = Form1.ScaleWidth
    Caption = "Writer Document " + Str$(MyDocumentNumber)
    If NumberDocuments = 1 Then AttachWindow Me
End Sub

Private Sub Form_Resize()
    Text1.Height = Form1.ScaleHeight
    Text1.Width = Form1.ScaleWidth
End Sub

Private Sub New_Click()
    AddADocument
End Sub

Private Sub Print_Click()
    CommonDialog1.ShowPrinter
    NumberCopies% = CommonDialog1.Copies
    For loop_index% = 1 To NumberCopies%
        Printer.Print Text1.Text
        Printer.EndDoc
    Next loop_index%
End Sub

Private Sub Read_Click()
    On Error GoTo OpenError
1   CommonDialog1.FileName = "*.*"
    CommonDialog1.CancelError = True
    CommonDialog1.ShowOpen
    Open CommonDialog1.FileName For Input As #1
    Text1.Text = Input$(LOF(1), #1)
    Close #1
    Exit Sub
OpenError:
    ErrMsg$ = Error$(Err) + " Try again?"
    'ErrMsg$ = Err.Source + " Try again?"
    Select Case Err
    Case 32755
        Exit Sub
    Case 55
        ErrMsg$ = "File is already open. Try Again?"
```

```
      Case 57, 68, 71
          ErrMsg$ = "Check the disk. Try again?"
      End Select
      If MsgBox(ErrMsg$, 49, "Writer") = 1 Then
          Resume 1
      End If
End Sub

Private Sub Save_Click()
    CommonDialog1.DefaultExt = ".txt"
    CommonDialog1.Filter = "*.txt"
    CommonDialog1.ShowSave
    Open CommonDialog1.FileName For Output As #1
    Print #1, Text1.Text
    MsgBox ("Saved")
    Close #1
End Sub
```

This completes our coverage of error handling. We've seen that we can trap errors with the On Error GoTo statement, use Erl and Err to determine the line number and error type, and recover from errors using Resume, Resume Next, and Resume Line#. In the next chapter, we'll dig further into Visual Basic when we see how to work with OLE programming.

## CHAPTER 7

CREATING OLE PROGRAMS

One of Windows' most exciting aspects currently is Object Linking and Embedding (OLE), and Visual Basic supports it. Using OLE, a user can embed part of a document from another program (called an *OLE item*) into a program that's running. In this way, users can embed spreadsheet sections in a word-processing document, MS Paintbrush pictures in that same word-processing document, and perhaps a graph of data from yet another program. One program can display a composite of many programs, integrating those programs into one powerful package.

As you can imagine, the potential here is great. And in addition to displaying the data, the user can also double-click embedded OLE items to edit them *in-place*: if you are working in a word processor and have embedded an OLE item from a painting program and want to redraw the item, you need only double-click it; when you do, the item opens for editing right there and then. With in-place editing, you can work with and change the picture right there in the word-processing program. The menu system of the painting program takes over the menu system of your word processor so that you can use the necessary painting tools.

Programs that can hold and display OLE items are called OLE *containers*, and programs that can create the OLE items for insertion into a container are called *servers*. Visual Basic provides support for OLE container (not server) programs, and in this chapter we'll examine that support, which is in the Visual Basic OLE control. In a beginning book, we might see a container program that supported a single OLE item that you could open with a double-click—and that's it. Here, however, our container program will support in-place editing, multiple OLE items, moving and resizing OLE items, double-click opening of OLE items, item selection in our container program, zooming (i.e., enlarging) the OLE item, and more. Let's create that program now.

ALL ABOUT OLE CONTAINER PROGRAMS

Let's say that we have an OLE container program named **CONTAIN.EXE**:

```
------------------------
|         Contain        |
|------------------------|
|File Edit               |
|------------------------|
|                        |
|                        |
|                        |
|                        |
|                        |
|                        |
 ------------------------
```

To insert OLE items (from servers such as MS Paintbrush or MS Word for Windows) into our container program, we use the **Insert New Object** menu item in the Edit menu:

```
------------------------
|         Contain        |
|------------------------|
|File Edit View Help     |
|----------------------|_
|        |             | |
|        |             | |
|        |Insert New Object...|
|        |             | |
|         -------------------
|                        |
|                      |
|                      |
 ------------------------
```

This opens the Insert New Object dialog box, which lists the available OLE servers (all servers must register with Windows). We might choose Microsoft Excel for Windows, in which case part of a spreadsheet opens in the OLE item in our container program:

Now we can move that item around, placing it in our document as desired:

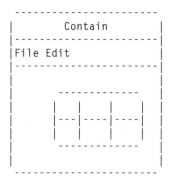

For servers that support in-place editing, we can simply double-click the OLE item, and **CONTAIN.EXE**'s menu system is taken over by the server's menus so that we can edit using the server's tools. Once we are finished, we have only to click outside our OLE item to close the in-place editing session.

As the name object linking and embedding implies, there are two ways to work with OLE items: embedding them and linking them. When we *embed* an OLE item in our program, the item's data is stored with our program's own internal data. On the other hand, if we *link* to an object, that object's data is stored in an external file. For example, we might link to an Excel worksheet file that already exists on disk. We will work mostly with the more popular embedding process here.

Let's put some of this to use now as we create our first OLE container program.

OUR FIRST OLE CONTAINER

Start Visual Basic now and select the OLE container tool, marked **OLE 2.0**, in the toolbox. Double-click that tool, creating a new OLE control named OLE1 in Form1. When you do, the Insert Object dialog box appears, as shown in Figure 7.1.

In this case, we will insert a Microsoft Excel OLE item. (If you do not have Microsoft Excel, you might use one of the programs that come with Windows, such as Microsoft WordPad.) We select Microsoft Excel Worksheet in the Insert Object box and click **OK**. This inserts a blank Excel worksheet in the OLE1 control.

That's almost all that's necessary to create an OLE container program. Run the program and double-click the OLE control. Excel displays its worksheet in

OLE1, as shown in Figure 7.2. Because Excel supports in-place editing, Excel itself does not appear, but the worksheet becomes active. As we'll see in a minute, when we add a menu system and toolbar to our program, Excel takes over both menu and toolbar systems.

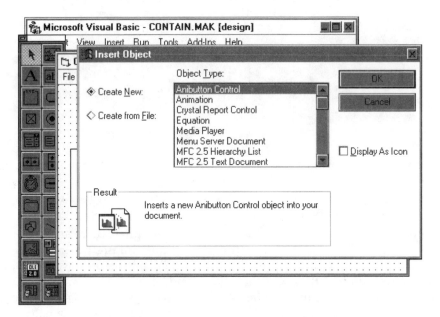

FIGURE 7.1 VISUAL BASIC'S INSERT OBJECT DIALOG BOX.

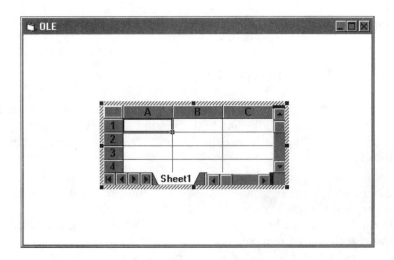

FIGURE 7.2 OUR FIRST ATTEMPT AT EMBEDDING AN OLE ITEM.

That's all there is to creating our first container program—it's that quick and easy to embed our first OLE item. The code for **OLE.FRM** appears in Listing 7.1, and **OLE.VBP** appears in Listing 7.2.

LISTING 7.1 OLE.FRM

```
VERSION 4.00
Begin VB.Form Form1
   Caption         =   "OLE"
   ClientHeight    =   4230
   ClientLeft      =   1095
   ClientTop       =   1515
   ClientWidth     =   6720
   BeginProperty Font
      name         =   "MS Sans Serif"
      charset      =   1
      weight       =   400
      size         =   8.25
      underline    =   0   'False
      italic       =   0   'False
      strikethrough =  0   'False
   EndProperty
   Height          =   4635
   Left            =   1035
   LinkTopic       =   "Form1"
   ScaleHeight     =   4230
   ScaleWidth      =   6720
   Top             =   1170
   Width           =   6840
   Begin VB.OLE OLE1
      Class        =   "Excel.Sheet.5"
      Height       =   1095
      Left         =   1920
      OleObjectBlob =  "OLE.frx":0000
      TabIndex     =   0
      Top          =   1560
      Width        =   3015
   End
End
Attribute VB_Name = "Form1"
Attribute VB_Creatable = False
Attribute VB_Exposed = False
```

LISTING 7.2 OLE.VBP

```
OLE.FRM
Object={F9043C88-F6F2-101A-A3C9-08002B2F49FB}#1.0#0; COMDLG16.OCX
Object={FAEEE763-117E-101B-8933-08002B2F4F5A}#1.0#0; DBLIST16.OCX
ProjWinSize=216,289,250,185
```

```
ProjWinShow=2
ExeName="Project1.exe"
Path="D:\VB"
Command=""
Name="Project1"
HelpContextID="0"
StartMode=0
VersionCompatible="0"
MajorVer=1
MinorVer=0
RevisionVer=0
AutoIncrementVer=0
VersionCompanyName=""
Reference=*\G{00025E01-0000-0000-C000-
000000000046}#0.0#0#DAO2516.DLL#Microsoft DAO 2.5 Object Library
```

Our first OLE program shows how to create an embedded OLE item at design time, but there are many other options. Let's look at the other side of OLE programming for a moment as we see how to link an OLE item into a program in code.

PROGRAMS THAT SUPPORT OLE LINKS

As we've seen, it's easy to create an embedded OLE item. We can also create linked items. Start a new project, **LINK.VBP**, in Visual Basic and add an OLE container control, OLE1, to Form1 (by double-clicking the **OLE** tool in the toolbox as before). Set OLE1's SizeMode to 2, AutoSize. This means that the OLE container will automatically resize itself to fit the OLE item it contains. Using the Menu Editor, give Form1 a File menu with one item, **Exit**, and add an Edit menu with one item: **Paste Special**. We add the code for Exit_Click(), as we have before (from **LINK.FRM**):

```
Private Sub Exit_Click()
--> End
End Sub
```

Next, open the PasteSpecial_Click() event handler by clicking the **Paste Special** menu item (from **LINK.FRM**):

```
Private Sub PasteSpecial_Click()

End Sub
```

Here's how users can create an OLE link in our program: in the OLE server (here we'll use Excel), they can create and edit a document. Next, they save the document to a file on disk. Still in the OLE server program, they now select the range of data they are interested in embedding in the LINK program, and, in the server's Edit menu, they choose **Copy**. If the server supports OLE links, it will copy into the clipboard all the information needed for an OLE link. Then, in our new LINK program, users select our **Paste Special** menu item. If the information in the clipboard is complete, our program will create an OLE link and display the OLE item, establishing the OLE link.

Let's see this in code. When users select LINK's **Paste Special** menu item, they should have already copied the necessary OLE data from the server program. To check that in the PasteSpecial_Click() subroutine, we test to see that the data in the clipboard is in the right format for an OLE link by using the OLE control's PasteOK method. We use this new code (from **LINK.FRM**):

```
Private Sub PasteSpecial_Click()
--> If OLE1.PasteOK Then

         .
         .
         .
--> End If
End Sub
```

If OLE1.PasteOK returns True, we can create an OLE link using the information in the clipboard. To do that, we display the Paste Special dialog box, allowing the user to select which link (if there are more than one) to paste from the clipboard. To display that dialog box, we use OLE1's PasteSpecialDlg method:

```
Private Sub PasteSpecial_Click()
    If OLE1.PasteOK Then
-->      OLE1.PasteSpecialDlg
    End If
End Sub
```

When the user selects an item, the program creates an OLE link to that file on disk and displays the item's data in OLE1, as shown in Figure 7.3.

As you can see, in just a few lines of code we're supporting OLE links. **LINK.FRM** appears in Listing 7.3, and **LINK.VBP** is in Listing 7.4.

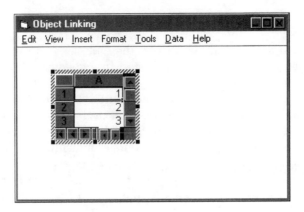

FIGURE 7.3 THE LINK PROGRAM CREATES AN OLE LINK USING A PASTE SPECIAL MENU ITEM.

LISTING 7.3 LINK.FRM

```
VERSION 4.00
Begin VB.Form Form1
    Caption         =   "Object Linking"
    ClientHeight    =   4230
    ClientLeft      =   1095
    ClientTop       =   1800
    ClientWidth     =   6720
    BeginProperty Font
        name        =   "MS Sans Serif"
        charset     =   1
        weight      =   400
        size        =   8.25
        underline   =   0    'False
        italic      =   0    'False
        strikethrough =  0    'False
    EndProperty
    Height          =   4920
    Left            =   1035
    LinkTopic       =   "Form1"
    ScaleHeight     =   4230
    ScaleWidth      =   6720
    Top             =   1170
    Width           =   6840
    Begin VB.OLE OLE1
        Height      =   1095
        Left        =   1920
        TabIndex    =   0
        Top         =   1320
        Width       =   3015
```

```
      End
      Begin VB.Menu File
         Caption         =   "File"
         Begin VB.Menu Exit
            Caption       =   "Exit"
         End
      End
      Begin VB.Menu Edit
         Caption         =   "Edit"
         Begin VB.Menu PasteSpecial
            Caption       =   "Paste Special"
         End
      End
   End
Attribute VB_Name = "Form1"
Attribute VB_Creatable = False
Attribute VB_Exposed = False
Private Sub Exit_Click()
    End
End Sub


Private Sub PasteSpecial_Click()
    If OLE1.PasteOK Then
        OLE1.PasteSpecialDlg
    End If
End Sub
```

Listing 7.4 LINK.VBP

```
LINK.FRM
Object={F9043C88-F6F2-101A-A3C9-08002B2F49FB}#1.0#0; COMDLG16.OCX
Object={FAEEE763-117E-101B-8933-08002B2F4F5A}#1.0#0; DBLIST16.OCX
ProjWinSize=216,289,250,185
ProjWinShow=2
ExeName="Project1.exe"
Path="D:\VB"
Command=""
Name="Project1"
HelpContextID="0"
StartMode=0
VersionCompatible="0"
MajorVer=1
MinorVer=0
RevisionVer=0
AutoIncrementVer=0
VersionCompanyName=""
Reference=*\G{00025E01-0000-0000-C000-
000000000046}#0.0#0#DAO2516.DLL#Microsoft DAO 2.5 Object Library
```

You might notice in Figure 7.3 that the menu system has many more items than we have placed there. We placed only a File and an Edit menu in our program, but now it has Edit, View, Insert, Format, Tools, Data, and Help menus when the Excel OLE item has been double-clicked, opening it for in-place editing. This is because Excel has taken over our menu system and has substituted its menus for our own. We will take a closer look at this aspect of in-place editing and at how the server can take over a status bar next, when we examine MDI OLE programs.

MDI OLE PROGRAMS

Now let's take a look at MDI OLE programs. We'll use both a menu system and a toolbar so that we can see how an OLE server such as Excel can take over that part of our program.

Create a new Visual Basic project named **MDIOLE.VBP**, set Form1's MDIChild property to True, and insert a new MDI form, MDIForm1, into the project using the Visual Basic **Insert | MDI Form** menu item. Now add an OLE container control, OLE1, to Form1, but do not set its SizeMode property to AutoSize. We will do something different this time: we will stretch our OLE control until it covers the client area of our MDI child window. In Form1, open the Form_Load() event handler (from **MDIOLE.FRM**) by double-clicking Form1:

```
Private Sub Form_Load()

End Sub
```

Here, we size our OLE1 control with this new code, covering the MDI child's client area with that control:

```
Private Sub Form_Load()
--> OLE1.Top = 0
--> OLE1.Left = 0
--> OLE1.Width = ScaleWidth
--> OLE1.Height = ScaleHeight
End Sub
```

In addition, use the Menu Editor to add two menus to Form1: File, with one menu item, **Exit**, and Edit, with one item, **Insert New Object**. We add code to the **Exit** item first as we have done so often:

```
Private Sub Exit_Click()
--> End
End Sub
```

In InsertNewObject_Click(), we display the Insert New Object dialog box
and let OLE1 do the rest. (Insert the new OLE item in the OLE1 control.)

```
Private Sub InsertNewObject_Click()
--> OLE1.InsertObjDlg
End Sub
```

Finally, add a toolbar to the MDI form in the same way we did in Chapter 2:
by adding a picture box and setting its Align property to 1, Align Top. Now
run the program and use the Edit menu's **Insert New Object** item to place a
new OLE item in the MDI child window, as shown in Figure 7.4. As you can
see, the Excel worksheet has taken over not only our menu system but also
our toolbar. The program is a success.

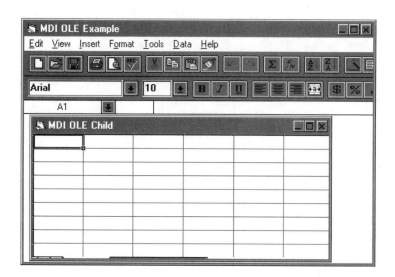

FIGURE 7.4 OUR MDIOLE PROGRAM SHOWS HOW TO CREATE MDI OLE PROGRAMS
THAT CAN TAKE OVER OUR MENU BAR AND TOOLBAR.

MDIOLE.FRM appears in Listing 7.5, **MDIFORM1.FRM** in Listing 7.6, and
MDIOLE.VBP in Listing 7.7.

LISTING 7.5 MDIOLE.FRM

```
VERSION 4.00
Begin VB.Form Form1
   Caption          =    "MDI OLE Child"
   ClientHeight     =    4230
   ClientLeft       =    1095
   ClientTop        =    1800
   ClientWidth      =    6720
   BeginProperty Font
      name          =    "MS Sans Serif"
      charset       =    1
      weight        =    400
      size          =    8.25
      underline     =    0    'False
      italic        =    0    'False
      strikethrough =    0    'False
   EndProperty
   Height           =    4920
   Left             =    1035
   LinkTopic        =    "Form1"
   MDIChild         =    -1   'True
   ScaleHeight      =    4230
   ScaleWidth       =    6720
   Top              =    1170
   Width            =    6840
   Begin VB.OLE OLE1
      Height        =    2895
      Left          =    480
      SizeMode      =    2    'AutoSize
      TabIndex      =    0
      Top           =    480
      Width         =    5655
   End
   Begin VB.Menu File
      Caption        =    "File"
      Begin VB.Menu Exit
         Caption     =    "Exit"
      End
   End
   Begin VB.Menu Edit
      Caption        =    "Edit"
      Begin VB.Menu InsertNewObject
         Caption      =    "Insert New Object..."
      End
   End
End
Attribute VB_Name = "Form1"
Attribute VB_Creatable = False
Attribute VB_Exposed = False
```

```
Private Sub Exit_Click()
    End
End Sub

Private Sub Form_Load()
    OLE1.Top = 0
    OLE1.Left = 0
    OLE1.Width = ScaleWidth
    OLE1.Height = ScaleHeight
End Sub

Private Sub InsertNewObject_Click()
    OLE1.InsertObjDlg
End Sub
```

LISTING 7.6 MDIFORM1.FRM

```
VERSION 4.00
Begin VB.MDIForm MDIForm1
   BackColor       =   &H8000000C&
   Caption         =   "MDI OLE Example"
   ClientHeight    =   4230
   ClientLeft      =   1095
   ClientTop       =   1515
   ClientWidth     =   6720
   Height          =   4635
   Left            =   1035
   LinkTopic       =   "MDIForm1"
   Top             =   1170
   Width           =   6840
   Begin VB.PictureBox Picture2
      Align        =   2 'Align Bottom
      BeginProperty Font
         name          =   "MS Sans Serif"
         charset       =   1
         weight        =   400
         size          =   8.25
         underline     =   0    'False
         italic        =   0    'False
         strikethrough =   0    'False
      EndProperty
      Height       =   495
      Left         =   0
      ScaleHeight  =   465
      ScaleWidth   =   6690
      TabIndex     =   1
      Top          =   3735
      Width        =   6720
   End
```

```
    Begin VB.PictureBox Picture1
        Align              =   1   'Align Top
        BeginProperty Font
       ·    name           =   "MS Sans Serif"
            charset        =   1
            weight         =   400
            size           =   8.25
            underline      =   0   'False
            italic         =   0   'False
            strikethrough  =   0   'False
        EndProperty
        Height         =   495
        Left           =   0
        ScaleHeight    =   465
        ScaleWidth     =   6690
        TabIndex       =   0
        Top            =   0
        Width          =   6720
    End
End
Attribute VB_Name = "MDIForm1"
Attribute VB_Creatable = False
Attribute VB_Exposed = False
```

LISTING 7.7 MDIOLE.VBP

```
MDIOLE.FRM
MDIFORM1.FRM
Object={F9043C88-F6F2-101A-A3C9-08002B2F49FB}#1.0#0; COMDLG16.OCX
Object={FAEEE763-117E-101B-8933-08002B2F4F5A}#1.0#0; DBLIST16.OCX
ProjWinSize=216,289,250,185
ProjWinShow=2
IconForm="Form1"
ExeName="Project1.exe"
Path="D:\VB"
Command=""
Name="Project1"
HelpContextID="0"
StartMode=0
VersionCompatible="0"
MajorVer=1
MinorVer=0
RevisionVer=0
AutoIncrementVer=0
VersionCompanyName=""
Reference=*\G{00025E01-0000-0000-C000-
000000000046}#0.0#0#DAO2516.DLL#Microsoft DAO 2.5 Object Library
```

That's it for our MDI OLE program. Our next project will be to construct a general-purpose OLE container program.

OUR SERIOUS OLE CONTAINER PROGRAM

Now let's work on creating an OLE container program that will show many of the features that OLE container programs are expected to have. For example, how do we stop an in-place editing session? If you place an Excel OLE item in an OLE control and open it for in-place editing, Excel takes over the menu system but does not display a File menu. This means that the user has no way of quitting Excel in our program. (In the worst case, he or she can select **Close** from the control box, but that closes our entire program.) It is usual for OLE containers to deactivate an open OLE item when the user clicks anywhere in the client area outside that item, and we'll do so here.

Here's what our general, multiple-item container might look like:

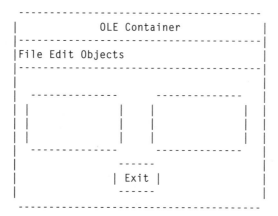

Container programs should give users maximum flexibility and power, and that can include letting them drag the OLE controls to positions they prefer. For example, if you have embedded a Paint picture inside text, the user will want to position that picture in the text properly. We'll implement dragging here, allowing the user to move the OLE items around:

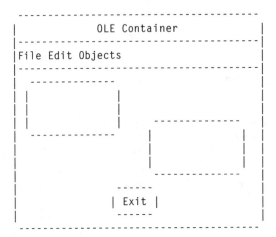

Now that we're working with multiple OLE items, we need a way of letting the user select which one to work with, and we usually do that by moving the focus from item to item. Here, we will also add an Objects menu that lets users move the focus to the next OLE item (they can also just click the item), open the currently selected item, or delete it. (Note that we mean deleting the OLE item and not deleting the OLE control.)

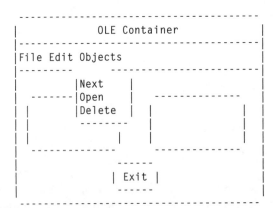

In addition, we should not restrict users to the OLE controls we've already supplied. If they want to insert a new object into our program, we should create a new OLE control and fill it with the item they want to display. We'll position our new OLE items at location (0, 0).

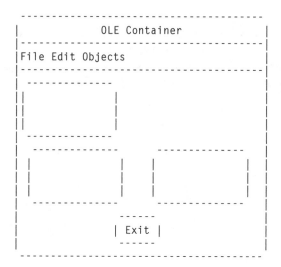

Let's get started now.

Starting the CONTAIN Program

Start the **CONTAIN.VBP** project and give Form1 the caption **OLE Container**. Next, add a File menu with one item: **Exit** (Name property: Exit), placing the usual End statement in Exit_Click() (from **CONTAIN.FRM**):

```
Private Sub Exit_Click()
--> End
End Sub
```

Next, add an Edit menu with one item: **Insert New Object**. (Give this menu item the Name property InsertNewObject in the properties window.), Now add an Objects menu with three items: **Next**, **Open**, and **Delete** (Name properties: Next, Open, and Delete). Add a command button, Command1, to Form1, giving it the caption **Exit**. This will allow users an easy exit if they want to quit while another program has control of the menu system. Place the End statement in Command1_Click():

```
Private Sub Command1_Click()
--> End
End Sub
```

Finally, add two OLE controls to Form1 (do not place any OLE items into the controls), set their SizeMode to AutoSize, and set both their Name properties to OLEOBJ in the properties window. When you do, Visual Basic asks whether you want to create a control array; answer **yes**. This leaves us with two members of that control array: OLEOBJ(0) and OLEOBJ(1).

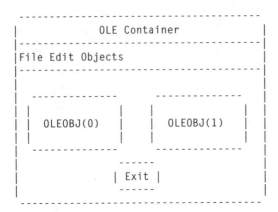

Now we can make the Edit menu's **Insert New Object** item active. Open the associated Click event handler by clicking that menu item (from **CON-TAIN.FRM**):

```
Private Sub InsertNewObject_Click()

End Sub
```

If the user has selected one of our two OLE controls, we should insert an OLE item into it when he or she clicks **Insert New Object**. First, let's make sure that the active control (the one with the focus) is an OLE control:

```
Private Sub InsertNewObject_Click()
--> If TypeOf ActiveControl Is OLE Then
         .
         .
         .
--> End If
End Sub
```

If the active control is an OLE control, we can execute its InsertObjDlg method to insert an OLE item into it. This opens the Insert OLE Object dialog box, lets the user select an OLE item to insert, and inserts that item in the active OLE control:

```
Private Sub InsertNewObject_Click()
    If TypeOf ActiveControl Is OLE Then
-->     ActiveControl.InsertObjDlg
            .
            .
            .
    End If
End Sub
```

We can also check to see whether that operation worked by examining the OLEType property of the active OLE control; if the value in that property is equal to the predefined constant NONE, the insertion of the OLE item failed, and we can have the program beep:

```
Private Sub InsertNewObject_Click()
    If TypeOf ActiveControl Is OLE Then
        ActiveControl.InsertObjDlg
-->     If ActiveControl.OLEType = None Then
-->         Beep
-->     End If
    End If
End Sub
```

We've started our CONTAIN program, and we've been able to insert OLE items. The functioning program so far appears in Figure 7.5.

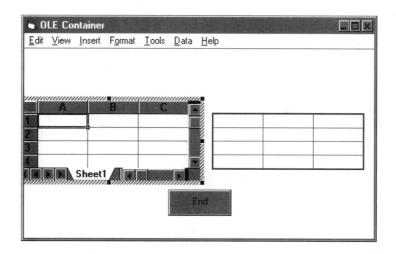

Figure 7.5 Our CONTAIN program can handle several OLE items.

CONTAIN.FRM appears in Listing 7.8, and **CONTAIN.VBP** is in Listing 7.9.

LISTING **7.8** CONTAIN.FRM, FIRST VERSION

```
VERSION 4.00
Begin VB.Form Form1
    Caption         =   "OLE Container"
    ClientHeight    =   3555
    ClientLeft      =   1095
    ClientTop       =   1800
    ClientWidth     =   6720
    BeginProperty Font
        name            =   "MS Sans Serif"
        charset         =   1
        weight          =   400
        size            =   8.25
        underline       =   0   'False
        italic          =   0   'False
        strikethrough   =   0   'False
    EndProperty
    Height          =   4245
    Left            =   1035
    LinkTopic       =   "Form1"
    ScaleHeight     =   3555
    ScaleWidth      =   6720
    Top             =   1170
    Width           =   6840
    Begin VB.CommandButton Command1
        Caption         =   "End"
        Height          =   495
        Left            =   2760
        TabIndex        =   2
        Top             =   2640
        Width           =   1215
    End
    Begin VB.OLE OLEOBJ
        Height          =   1095
        Index           =   1
        Left            =   3600
        TabIndex        =   1
        Top             =   1200
        Width           =   3015
    End
    Begin VB.OLE OLEOBJ
        Height          =   1095
        Index           =   0
        Left            =   240
        TabIndex        =   0
        Top             =   1200
        Width           =   3015
    End
    Begin VB.Menu File
        Caption         =   "File"
```

```
        Begin VB.Menu Exit
            Caption         =   "Exit"
        End
    End
    Begin VB.Menu Edit
        Caption         =   "Edit"
        Begin VB.Menu InsertNewObject
            Caption         =   "Insert New Object..."
        End
    End
    Begin VB.Menu Objects
        Caption         =   "Objects"
        Begin VB.Menu Next
            Caption         =   "Next"
        End
        Begin VB.Menu Open
            Caption         =   "Open"
        End
        Begin VB.Menu DeleteObject
            Caption         =   "Delete"
        End
    End
End
Attribute VB_Name = "Form1"
Attribute VB_Creatable = False
Attribute VB_Exposed = False

Private Sub Command1_Click()
    End
End Sub


Private Sub Exit_Click()
    End
End Sub


Private Sub InsertNewObject_Click()
    If TypeOf ActiveControl Is OLE Then
        ActiveControl.InsertObjDlg
        If ActiveControl.OLEType = None Then
            Beep
        End If
    End If
End Sub
```

LISTING 7.9 CONTAIN.VBP

```
CONTAIN.FRM
Object={F9043C88-F6F2-101A-A3C9-08002B2F49FB}#1.0#0; COMDLG16.OCX
Object={FAEEE763-117E-101B-8933-08002B2F4F5A}#1.0#0; DBLIST16.OCX
ProjWinSize=324,337,202,111
ProjWinShow=2
```

```
IconForm="Form1"
ExeName="Project1.exe"
Path="D:\VB"
Command=""
Name="Project1"
HelpContextID="0"
StartMode=0
VersionCompatible="0"
MajorVer=1
MinorVer=0
RevisionVer=0
AutoIncrementVer=0
VersionCompanyName=""
Reference=*\G{00025E01-0000-0000-C000-
000000000046}#0.0#0#DAO2516.DLL#Microsoft DAO 2.5 Object Library
```

Deactivating OLE Items

One of the things we want to do to support multiple OLE items is to let the user deactivate an OLE item by clicking the client area outside that item. This gives users more control: if they double-click an OLE item, it opens for editing; if they click outside an OLE item, that item should deactivate (i.e., present its default appearance, no longer open for in-place editing).

When the user clicks the form, then, we want to deactivate the active OLE item if there is one. We can loop over our control array, deactivating the OLE controls one by one. First, however, let's keep track of the number of OLE controls we have, because that number will increase as the user adds new ones. We store the number of OLE controls in the variable NumberOLEObjs by adding it to **CONTAIN.FRM**'s code window:

```
Dim NumberOLEObjs As Integer
```

We can set that variable to 2 for our first two OLE controls in the Form_Load() event. (Click **Form1** to add this event to the code window.)

```
Dim NumberOLEObjs As Integer

Private Sub Form_Load()
--> NumberOLEObjs = 2
End Sub
```

When users click the form, they want to deactivate the OLE objects, and we do that by looping over our OLE control array in Form_Click():

```
Dim NumberOLEObjs As Integer

Private Sub Form_Click()
```

```
    For loop_index = 1 To NumberOLEObjs        <--
        .
        .
        .
    Next loop_index                            <--
End Sub
```

To deactivate an OLE item (e.g., close an in-place editing session), we set the item's AppIsRunning property to False:

```
Private Sub Form_Click()
    For loop_index = 1 To NumberOLEObjs
-->     OLEOBJ(loop_index - 1).AppIsRunning = False
        .
        .
        .
    Next loop_index
End Sub
```

We also make sure that it remains visible by setting its Visible property to True:

```
Private Sub Form_Click()
    For loop_index = 1 To NumberOLEObjs
        OLEOBJ(loop_index - 1).AppIsRunning = False
-->     OLEOBJ(loop_index - 1).Visible = True
    Next loop_index
End Sub
```

Now we've looped over all the OLE items, deactivating them. We can also shift the focus away from the OLE controls by giving it to the **Exit** button on the form, which we do by deselecting all OLE items:

```
Private Sub Form_Click()
    For loop_index = 1 To NumberOLEObjs
        OLEOBJ(loop_index - 1).AppIsRunning = False
        OLEOBJ(loop_index - 1).Visible = True
    Next loop_index
--> Command1.SetFocus
End Sub
```

At this point, we've allowed the user to click an OLE item to open it and to click the form to close it. This capability is useful because the menu system will usually not offer a way of closing an OLE item when it's being edited in-place.

There's more to managing multiple OLE items. If the user selects **Insert New Object** but has not selected an OLE control (i.e., given it the focus) to receive the new OLE item, we should create a new OLE control and place the new OLE item in it. We will do that now.

Creating New OLE Items

Let's say the user has selected **Insert New Object**, which currently inserts an OLE item into the selected OLE control in InsertNewObject_Click() (from **CONTAIN.FRM**):

```
Private Sub InsertNewObject_Click()
    ActiveControl.InsertObjDlg
    If ActiveControl.OLEType = None Then
        Beep
    End If
End Sub
```

This is fine if an OLE control is the currently active control; but if it is not, we can create an entirely new OLE control and insert the new OLE item into it. First, we'll check to see whether the currently active control in our program is an OLE control in InsertNewObject_Click(). If it is not an OLE control, we will create a new OLE control:

```
Private Sub InsertNewObject_Click()
--> If TypeOf ActiveControl Is OLE Then
        ActiveControl.InsertObjDlg
        If ActiveControl.OLEType = None Then
            Beep
        End If
--> Else
        .
        .
    [Create new OLE control]
        .
        .
--> End If
End Sub
```

We discussed how to create new controls in Chapter 4. In this case, we start by incrementing the number of OLE controls, NumberOLEObjs:

```
Private Sub InsertNewObject_Click()
    If TypeOf ActiveControl Is OLE Then
        ActiveControl.InsertObjDlg
        If ActiveControl.OLEType = None Then
            Beep
```

```
            End If
        Else
-->         NumberOLEObjs = NumberOLEObjs + 1
                .
                .
                .
        End If
    End Sub
```

Next, we use Load to load in a new member of the OLE control array. This new OLE control will have its Index property set to NumberOLEObjs – 1:

```
Private Sub InsertNewObject_Click()
    If TypeOf ActiveControl Is OLE Then
        ActiveControl.InsertObjDlg
        If ActiveControl.OLEType = None Then
            Beep
        End If
    Else
        NumberOLEObjs = NumberOLEObjs + 1
-->     Load OLEOBJ(NumberOLEObjs - 1)
            .
            .
            .
    End If
End Sub
```

Next, we position the new OLE control at (0, 0) in CONTAIN's window so that it doesn't appear on top of the OLE control OLEOBJ(0), as it would otherwise. We insert the new OLE item by executing its InsertObjDlg method:

```
Private Sub InsertNewObject_Click()
    If TypeOf ActiveControl Is OLE Then
        ActiveControl.InsertObjDlg
        If ActiveControl.OLEType = None Then
            Beep
        End If
    Else
        NumberOLEObjs = NumberOLEObjs + 1
        Load OLEOBJ(NumberOLEObjs - 1)
-->     OLEOBJ(NumberOLEObjs - 1).Move 0, 0
-->     OLEOBJ(NumberOLEObjs - 1).InsertObjDlg
            .
            .
            .
    End If
End Sub
```

As before, if the insertion was not successful, we have the program beep:

```
Private Sub InsertNewObject_Click()
    If TypeOf ActiveControl Is OLE Then
        ActiveControl.InsertObjDlg
        If ActiveControl.OLEType = None Then
            Beep
        End If
    Else
        NumberOLEObjs = NumberOLEObjs + 1
        Load OLEOBJ(NumberOLEObjs - 1)
        OLEOBJ(NumberOLEObjs - 1).Move 0, 0
        OLEOBJ(NumberOLEObjs - 1).InsertObjDlg
-->     If OLEOBJ(NumberOLEObjs - 1).OLEType = None Then
-->         Beep
-->     End If
    End If
End Sub
```

Now the user can activate or deactivate any of our multiple OLE items as well as add entirely new OLE controls to the program, as shown in Figure 7.6.

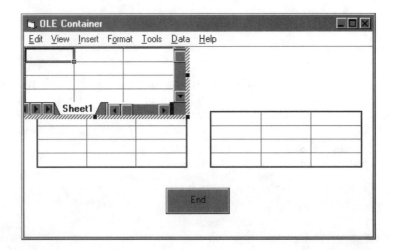

FIGURE 7.6 THE USER CAN CREATE AND ADD NEW OLE CONTROLS TO OUR CONTAIN PROGRAM.

Next, we'll take a look at CONTAIN's Objects menu. We've placed three items in the Object menu: **Next**, **Open**, and **Delete**. We'll implement them one by one, starting with **Next**.

The Objects Menu

Our next task is to make the menu items in the Objects menu active, and we'll start with **Next**. Only one OLE control can have the focus at any one time in our program. (In fact, only one control can have the focus at all, because there is only one focus—keyboards are not multitasking.) The user can use the mouse to select which of the OLE controls has the focus simply by clicking it, which makes the control's border appear as a thick black line, and we can do the same thing with a menu item. When the user selects **Next**, we will move the focus from the current OLE item to the next one. This will select the OLE item for such operations as inserting a new OLE item (with our Edit menu's **Insert New Object** menu item) or opening that OLE item for editing with **Open**.

Open Next_Click now (from **CONTAIN.FRM**):

```
Private Sub Next_Click()

End Sub
```

In this subroutine, we want to check which OLE item currently has the focus and then move the focus to the next OLE item in the control array. If no OLE item has the focus currently, we'll return without doing anything. We start by determining which, if any, OLE item has the focus, and we'll store that OLE item's control array index in the variable ActiveIndex, which we initialize to −1. This impossible value indicates that no OLE control has the focus.

```
Private Sub Next_Click()
--> ActiveIndex = -1
          .
          .
          .
End Sub
```

Next, we loop over all the elements of the OLE control array, checking to see which of these elements, if any, is the active control. Keep in mind that the control array OLEOBJ is 0-based.

```
Private Sub Next_Click()
    ActiveIndex = -1
--> For loop_index = 1 To NumberOLEObjs
-->     If OLEOBJ(loop_index - 1) Is ActiveControl Then
```

```
-->            ActiveIndex = loop_index - 1
-->            Exit For
-->        End If
--> Next loop_index
            .
            .
            .

End Sub
```

If none of the OLE items is active, ActiveIndex will still be set to −1 after we have looped over all OLE controls, and we can quit the subroutine:

```
Private Sub Next_Click()
    ActiveIndex = -1
    For loop_index = 1 To NumberOLEObjs
        If OLEOBJ(loop_index - 1) Is ActiveControl Then
            ActiveIndex = loop_index - 1
            Exit For
        End If
    Next loop_index
--> If ActiveIndex = -1 Then Exit Sub
        .
        .
        .

End Sub
```

On the other hand, if one of the OLE items is active, then we want to move the focus to the next OLE item in the control array. We check first to make sure that we're not moving past the end of the control array, and then we fill the variable NextIndex with the index of the OLE item that will receive the focus:

```
Private Sub Next_Click()
    ActiveIndex = -1
    For loop_index = 1 To NumberOLEObjs
        If OLEOBJ(loop_index - 1) Is ActiveControl Then
            ActiveIndex = loop_index - 1
            Exit For
        End If
    Next loop_index
    If ActiveIndex = -1 Then Exit Sub
--> If ActiveIndex + 1 <= NumberOLEObjs - 1 Then
-->     NextIndex = ActiveIndex + 1
        .
        .
        .

    End If
    OLEOBJ(NextIndex).SetFocus
End Sub
```

If the OLE item currently having the focus is the last item in the control array, however, we can set the focus to the first element in the array:

```
Private Sub Next_Click()
    ActiveIndex = -1
    For loop_index = 1 To NumberOLEObjs
        If OLEOBJ(loop_index - 1) Is ActiveControl Then
            ActiveIndex = loop_index - 1
            Exit For
        End If
    Next loop_index
    If ActiveIndex = -1 Then Exit Sub
    If ActiveIndex + 1 <= NumberOLEObjs - 1 Then
        NextIndex = ActiveIndex + 1
--> Else
-->     NextIndex = 0
--> End If
        .
        .
        .
End Sub
```

All that remains is to set the focus to element NextIndex in the control array:

```
Private Sub Next_Click()
    ActiveIndex = -1
    For loop_index = 1 To NumberOLEObjs
        If OLEOBJ(loop_index - 1) Is ActiveControl Then
            ActiveIndex = loop_index - 1
            Exit For
        End If
    Next loop_index
    If ActiveIndex = -1 Then Exit Sub
    If ActiveIndex + 1 <= NumberOLEObjs - 1 Then
        NextIndex = ActiveIndex + 1
    Else
        NextIndex = 0
    End If
--> OLEOBJ(NextIndex).SetFocus
End Sub
```

Now we can let the user cycle through our OLE items using **Next**.

The item following **Next** in our Objects menu is **Open**, so let's take a look at its Click event handler (from **CONTAIN.FRM**):

```
Private Sub Open_Click()

End Sub
```

In this subroutine, we want to open the currently active OLE item for editing. We can do that with the OLE control's DoVerb method, which executes an OLE verb. OLE *verbs* tell the OLE server what action to take with the OLE item (for example, open it for in-place editing). They are listed in Table 7.1.

TABLE 7.1 OLE VERBS.

OLE Verb	Meaning
0	The default action for the object.
−1	Activates object for editing. If the application that created the object supports in-place editing, object is activated in the OLE container control.
−2	Opens object in a separate application window. If the application that created the object supports in-place editing, object is activated in its own window.
−3	For embedded objects, this verb hides the application that created the object.
−4	If the object supports in-place editing, activates the object for in-place editing and shows any user-interface tools. If the object doesn't support in-place editing, the object doesn't activate, and an error occurs.
−5	If the user moves the focus to the OLE container control, creates a window for the object and prepares the object to be edited. An error occurs if the object doesn't support activation on a single mouse click.
−6	Used when the object is activated for editing to discard all record of changes that the object's application can undo.

Here, we'll use OLE verb 0, the default OLE verb for the item (usually opening the item for in-place editing). After checking to make sure that the currently active control is an OLE item, we use this code:

```
Private Sub Open_Click()
--> If TypeOf ActiveControl Is OLE Then
-->      ActiveControl.DoVerb 0
         .
         .
         .
End Sub
```

Otherwise, if the active control is not an OLE item, we beep and quit:

```
Private Sub Open_Click()
    If TypeOf ActiveControl Is OLE Then
        ActiveControl.DoVerb 0
--> Else
-->     Beep
--> End If
End Sub
```

Our final item in the Objects menu is **Delete**, with which we can delete OLE items (but not the OLE controls they are embedded in). Open the Click event handler associated with the **Delete** menu item (from **CONTAIN.FRM**):

```
Private Sub DeleteObject_Click()

End Sub
```

Here, the user wants to delete the OLE item in the currently selected OLE control—if an OLE control is currently selected. We check that first:

```
Private Sub DeleteObject_Click()
--> If TypeOf ActiveControl Is OLE Then
        .
        .
        .
--> End If
End Sub
```

If the currently selected control is an OLE control, we delete the item in it using the OLE control Delete method:

```
Private Sub DeleteObject_Click()
    If TypeOf ActiveControl Is OLE Then
-->     ActiveControl.Delete
    End If
End Sub
```

That's all there is to it. We've activated all three menu items in the Objects menu: **Next**, **Open**, and **Delete**. The new version of **CONTAIN.FRM** appears in Listing 7.10.

LISTING 7.10 CONTAIN.FRM, SECOND VERSION

```
VERSION 4.00
Begin VB.Form Form1
    Caption         =   "OLE Container"
    ClientHeight    =   3555
```

```
ClientLeft      =   1095
ClientTop       =   1800
ClientWidth     =   6720
BeginProperty Font
   name         =   "MS Sans Serif"
   charset      =   1
   weight       =   400
   size         =   8.25
   underline    =   0    'False
   italic       =   0    'False
   strikethrough =  0    'False
EndProperty
Height          =   4245
Left            =   1035
LinkTopic       =   "Form1"
ScaleHeight     =   3555
ScaleWidth      =   6720
Top             =   1170
Width           =   6840
Begin VB.CommandButton Command1
   Caption      =   "End"
   Height       =   495
   Left         =   2760
   TabIndex     =   2
   Top          =   2640
   Width        =   1215
End
Begin VB.OLE OLEOBJ
   Height       =   1095
   Index        =   1
   Left         =   3600
   TabIndex     =   1
   Top          =   1200
   Width        =   3015
End
Begin VB.OLE OLEOBJ
   Height       =   1095
   Index        =   0
   Left         =   240
   TabIndex     =   0
   Top          =   1200
   Width        =   3015
End
Begin VB.Menu File
   Caption      =   "File"
   Begin VB.Menu Exit
      Caption   =   "Exit"
   End
End
Begin VB.Menu Edit
```

```
        Caption         =   "Edit"
        Begin VB.Menu InsertNewObject
            Caption       =   "Insert New Object..."
        End
    End
    Begin VB.Menu Objects
        Caption         =   "Objects"
        Begin VB.Menu Next
            Caption       =   "Next"
        End
        Begin VB.Menu Open
            Caption       =   "Open"
        End
        Begin VB.Menu DeleteObject
            Caption       =   "Delete"
        End
    End
End
Attribute VB_Name = "Form1"
Attribute VB_Creatable = False
Attribute VB_Exposed = False
Dim NumberOLEObjs As Integer
Dim xoffset
Dim yoffset

Private Sub Command1_Click()
    End
End Sub

Private Sub DeleteObject_Click()
    If TypeOf ActiveControl Is OLE Then
        ActiveControl.Delete
    End If
End Sub

Private Sub Exit_Click()
    End
End Sub

Private Sub Form_Click()
    For loop_index = 1 To NumberOLEObjs
        OLEOBJ(loop_index - 1).AppIsRunning = False
        OLEOBJ(loop_index - 1).Visible = True
    Next loop_index
    Command1.SetFocus
End Sub

Private Sub Form_Load()
    NumberOLEObjs = 2
End Sub
```

```vb
Private Sub InsertNewObject_Click()
    If TypeOf ActiveControl Is OLE Then
        ActiveControl.InsertObjDlg
        If ActiveControl.OLEType = None Then
            Beep
        End If
    Else
        NumberOLEObjs = NumberOLEObjs + 1
        Load OLEOBJ(NumberOLEObjs - 1)
        OLEOBJ(NumberOLEObjs - 1).Move 0, 0
        OLEOBJ(NumberOLEObjs - 1).InsertObjDlg
        If OLEOBJ(NumberOLEObjs - 1).OLEType = None Then
            Beep
        End If
    End If

End Sub

Private Sub Next_Click()
    ActiveIndex = -1
    For loop_index = 1 To NumberOLEObjs
        If OLEOBJ(loop_index - 1) Is ActiveControl Then
            ActiveIndex = loop_index - 1
            Exit For
        End If
    Next loop_index
    If ActiveIndex = -1 Then Exit Sub
    If ActiveIndex + 1 <= NumberOLEObjs - 1 Then
        NextIndex = ActiveIndex + 1
    Else
        NextIndex = 0
    End If
    OLEOBJ(NextIndex).SetFocus

End Sub

Private Sub OLEOBJ_MouseDown(Index As Integer, Button As Integer, _
        Shift As Integer, x As Single, y As Single)
    xoffset = x
    yoffset = y
    OLEOBJ(Index).Drag 1
End Sub

Private Sub OLEOBJ_Updated(Index As Integer, Code As Integer)
    OLEOBJ(Index).SizeMode = vbOLESizeAutoSize
End Sub

Private Sub Open_Click()
    If TypeOf ActiveControl Is OLE Then
        ActiveControl.DoVerb 0
```

```
        Else
                Beep
        End If
End Sub
```

```
Private Sub Form_DragDrop(Source As Control, x As Single, y As Single)
        Source.Move x - xoffset, y - yoffset
End Sub
```

Dragging OLE Items

We can also enable dragging of our OLE items. We've seen how to drag controls in Chapter 4: when the mouse button is pressed inside an OLE control, we'll enable dragging. We start by adding the MouseDown event handler, OLEOBJ_MouseDown(), to CONTAIN using the Proc box of the code window:

```
Private Sub OLEOBJ_MouseDown(Index As Integer, Button As Integer,
        Shift As Integer, x As Single, y As Single)
            .
            .
            .
End Sub
```

As we've done before, we simply store the (x, y) offset of the mouse pointer with respect to the upper-left corner of the control (the location of the mouse cursor inside the OLE control):

```
Dim NumberOLEObjs As Integer
Dim xoffset        <--
Dim yoffset        <--

Private Sub OLEOBJ_MouseDown(Index As Integer, Button As Integer,
        Shift As Integer, x As Single, y As Single)
--> xoffset = x
--> yoffset = y
            .
            .
            .
End Sub
```

Then we enable dragging using the Drag method:

```
Dim NumberOLEObjs As Integer
Dim xoffset
Dim yoffset
```

```
Private Sub OLEOBJ_MouseDown(Index As Integer, Button As Integer,
        Shift As Integer, x As Single, y As Single)
    xoffset = x
    yoffset = y
--> OLEOBJ(Index).Drag 1
End Sub
```

Now the user can drag the OLE control as desired. When the user drops it on the form, we execute the control's Move method to move it to its new location (taking into account the mouse cursor's offset inside the control, as we did in Chapter 4). We add the Form_DragDrop() subroutine from the Proc box in the code window and place in it this line of code (from **CONTAIN.FRM**):

```
Private Sub Form_DragDrop(Source As Control, x As Single, y As Single)
--> Source.Move x - xoffset, y - yoffset
End Sub
```

Now the user can place the OLE controls on the form as desired, as shown in Figure 7.7. CONTAIN is complete, and **CONTAIN.FRM** appears in Listing 7.11.

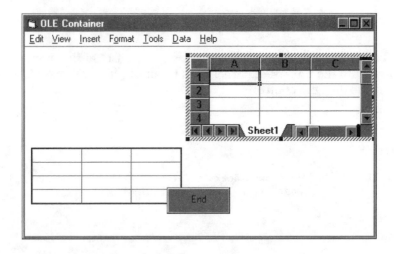

FIGURE 7.7 OUR CONTAIN PROGRAM ALLOWS THE USER TO DRAG AND DROP OLE CONTROLS.

LISTING 7.11 CONTAIN.FRM, FINAL VERSION

```
VERSION 4.00
Begin VB.Form Form1
    Caption         =   "OLE Container"
    ClientHeight    =   3555
    ClientLeft      =   1095
    ClientTop       =   1800
```

```
ClientWidth        =    6720
BeginProperty Font
   name            =    "MS Sans Serif"
   charset         =    1
   weight          =    400
   size            =    8.25
   underline       =    0    'False
   italic          =    0    'False
   strikethrough   =    0    'False
EndProperty
Height          =    4245
Left            =    1035
LinkTopic       =    "Form1"
ScaleHeight     =    3555
ScaleWidth      =    6720
Top             =    1170
Width           =    6840
Begin VB.CommandButton Command1
   Caption         =    "End"
   Height          =    495
   Left            =    2760
   TabIndex        =    2
   Top             =    2640
   Width           =    1215
End
Begin VB.OLE OLEOBJ
   Height          =    1095
   Index           =    1
   Left            =    3600
   TabIndex        =    1
   Top             =    1200
   Width           =    3015
End
Begin VB.OLE OLEOBJ
   Height          =    1095
   Index           =    0
   Left            =    240
   TabIndex        =    0
   Top             =    1200
   Width           =    3015
End
Begin VB.Menu File
   Caption         =    "File"
   Begin VB.Menu Exit
      Caption         =    "Exit"
   End
End
Begin VB.Menu Edit
   Caption         =    "Edit"
   Begin VB.Menu InsertNewObject
      Caption         =    "Insert New Object..."
   End
```

```
        End
        Begin VB.Menu Objects
            Caption        =    "Objects"
            Begin VB.Menu Next
                Caption        =    "Next"
            End
            Begin VB.Menu Open
                Caption        =    "Open"
            End
            Begin VB.Menu DeleteObject
                Caption        =    "Delete"
            End
        End
    End
End
Attribute VB_Name = "Form1"
Attribute VB_Creatable = False
Attribute VB_Exposed = False
Dim NumberOLEObjs As Integer
Dim xoffset
Dim yoffset

Private Sub Command1_Click()
    End
End Sub

Private Sub DeleteObject_Click()
    If TypeOf ActiveControl Is OLE Then
        ActiveControl.Delete
    End If
End Sub

Private Sub Exit_Click()
    End
End Sub

Private Sub Form_Click()
    For loop_index = 1 To NumberOLEObjs
        OLEOBJ(loop_index - 1).AppIsRunning = False
        OLEOBJ(loop_index - 1).Visible = True
    Next loop_index
    Command1.SetFocus
End Sub

Private Sub Form_Load()
    NumberOLEObjs = 2
End Sub

Private Sub InsertNewObject_Click()
    If TypeOf ActiveControl Is OLE Then
        ActiveControl.InsertObjDlg
        If ActiveControl.OLEType = None Then
            Beep
```

```
                End If
        Else
            NumberOLEObjs = NumberOLEObjs + 1
            Load OLEOBJ(NumberOLEObjs - 1)
            OLEOBJ(NumberOLEObjs - 1).Move 0, 0
            OLEOBJ(NumberOLEObjs - 1).InsertObjDlg
            If OLEOBJ(NumberOLEObjs - 1).OLEType = None Then
                Beep
            End If
        End If
    End Sub

Private Sub Next_Click()
    ActiveIndex = -1
    For loop_index = 1 To NumberOLEObjs
        If OLEOBJ(loop_index - 1) Is ActiveControl Then
            ActiveIndex = loop_index - 1
            Exit For
        End If
    Next loop_index
    If ActiveIndex = -1 Then Exit Sub
    If ActiveIndex + 1 <= NumberOLEObjs - 1 Then
        NextIndex = ActiveIndex + 1
    Else
        NextIndex = 0
    End If
    OLEOBJ(NextIndex).SetFocus
End Sub

Private Sub OLEOBJ_MouseDown(Index As Integer, Button As Integer,
        Shift As Integer, x As Single, y As Single)
    xoffset = x
    yoffset = y
    OLEOBJ(Index).Drag 1
End Sub

Private Sub OLEOBJ_Updated(Index As Integer, Code As Integer)
    OLEOBJ(Index).SizeMode = vbOLESizeAutoSize
End Sub

Private Sub Open_Click()
    If TypeOf ActiveControl Is OLE Then
        ActiveControl.DoVerb 0
    Else
        Beep
    End If
End Sub

Private Sub Form_DragDrop(Source As Control, x As Single, y As Single)
    Source.Move x - xoffset, y - yoffset
End Sub
```

The last topic we'll cover here has to do with OLE zooming. This process allows us to enlarge an OLE item so that the user can get a closer look at it.

USING OLE ZOOMING

So far in this chapter, we have set our OLE control's SizeMode to AutoSize, which makes that control grow or shrink to match the OLE item it contains. However, we can also make our OLE item appear large and magnified, and sometimes it's desirable to have it that way. In OLE, this is called *zooming*. When we zoom an OLE item, we magnify it to make more of the details visible. What actually happens is that we no longer match the OLE control's size to the OLE item (the OLE item's size is sent to us from the OLE server); instead, we might double the OLE control's size and pass that size to the OLE server. The choice of OLE control size is up to us—we tell the server what size to draw its item. Let's see how to zoom OLE items.

Start a new Visual Basic project and name it ZOOMER. Create a new OLE control, OLE1, in ZOOMER's form and set the OLE control's SizeMode property to Zoom (value 3). Next, add two command buttons to Form1: **Exit** and **Zoom**. We can add the code for the **Exit** button, Command1, immediately; click that button now to open its click event handler, Command1_Click() (from **ZOOMER.FRM**), and place the End statement in it to end the program:

```
Private Sub Command1_Click()
--> End
End Sub
```

Next, open the **Zoom** button's Click event handler, Command2_Click() (from **ZOOMER.FRM**), by clicking that button:

```
Private Sub Command2_Click()

End Sub
```

Here, we can simply reset the OLE control's size, doubling both its width and height by adding this code:

```
Private Sub Command2_Click()
--> OLE1.Width = 2 * OLE1.Width
--> OLE1.Height = 2 * OLE1.Height
End Sub
```

Now we've zoomed our OLE item in both the X and Y directions by a factor of 2, giving us an area zoom of 400%. That's all there is to it—now we can magnify our OLE items as we wish. Before running the program, let's give ourselves a way to quit; when the server is running it will take over the menu system, and we want to take the menu system back and be able to quit. First, add a File menu to our ZOOMER program and give it one item: **Exit**. We can implement that menu item at once (from **ZOOMER.FRM**):

```
Private Sub Exit_Click()
     End
End Sub
```

In addition, we must have a way of deactivating our OLE item, and we can do that by clicking the form itself in **ZOOMER.FRM**'s Form_Click() event. (Open this event handler from the code window's Proc box.)

```
Private Sub Form_Click()
--> OLE1.AppIsRunning = False
--> Command1.SetFocus
End Sub
```

Finally, give Form1 the new caption Zoomer, and place an OLE item into the OLE control, OLE1. Here, we will simply use an Excel worksheet. Now run the program, as shown in Figure 7.8, displaying the unopened OLE item.

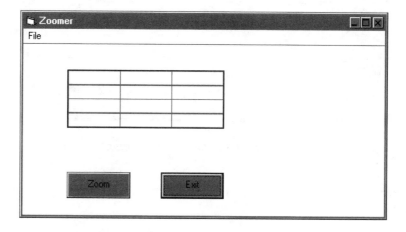

FIGURE 7.8 OUR ZOOMER PROGRAM FIRST DISPLAYS THE OLE ITEM IN ITS NORMAL SIZE.

Next, click the **Zoom** button, zooming the OLE control as shown in Figure 7.9.

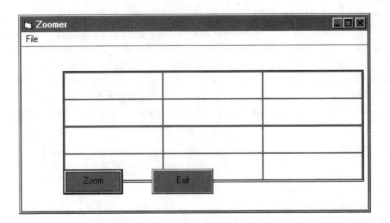

FIGURE 7.9 OUR ZOOMER PROGRAM NEXT DISPLAYS THE OLE ITEM AS ZOOMED BUT UNOPENED.

Finally, double-click the **OLE** control, opening the now-zoomed OLE item, as shown in Figure 7.10.

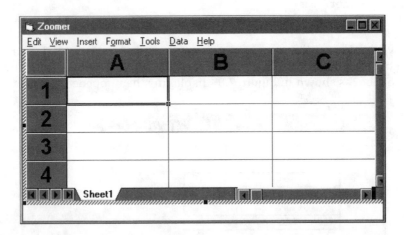

FIGURE 7.10 OUR ZOOMER PROGRAM DISPLAYS A ZOOMED OLE ITEM.

That's it—we've zoomed our OLE item and our program is a success. The listing of **ZOOMER.FRM** appears in Listing 7.12, and **ZOOMER.VBP** appears in Listing 7.13.

LISTING 7.12 ZOOMER.FRM

```
VERSION 4.00
Begin VB.Form Form1
   Caption        =    "Zoomer"
   ClientHeight   =    3210
```

```
    ClientLeft      =    1095
    ClientTop       =    1800
    ClientWidth     =    6945
    BeginProperty Font
        name        =    "MS Sans Serif"
        charset     =    1
        weight      =    400
        size        =    8.25
        underline   =    0    'False
        italic      =    0    'False
        strikethrough =  0    'False
    EndProperty
    Height          =    3900
    Left            =    1035
    LinkTopic       =    "Form1"
    ScaleHeight     =    3210
    ScaleWidth      =    6945
    Top             =    1170
    Width           =    7065
    Begin VB.CommandButton Command2
        Caption     =    "Zoom"
        Height      =    495
        Left        =    840
        TabIndex    =    1
        Top         =    2400
        Width       =    1215
    End
    Begin VB.CommandButton Command1
        Caption     =    "Exit"
        Height      =    495
        Left        =    2640
        TabIndex    =    0
        Top         =    2400
        Width       =    1215
    End
    Begin VB.OLE OLE1
        Class       =    "Excel.Sheet.5"
        Height      =    1095
        Left        =    840
        OleObjectBlob =  "ZOOMER.frx":0000
        SizeMode    =    3 'Zoom
        TabIndex    =    2
        Top         =    480
        Width       =    3015
    End
    Begin VB.Menu File
        Caption     =    "File"
        Begin VB.Menu Exit
            Caption     =    "Exit"
        End
    End
End
```

```
Attribute VB_Name = "Form1"
Attribute VB_Creatable = False
Attribute VB_Exposed = False
Private Sub Command1_Click()
    End
End Sub

Private Sub Command2_Click()
    OLE1.Width = 2 * OLE1.Width
    OLE1.Height = 2 * OLE1.Height
End Sub

Private Sub Exit_Click()
    End
End Sub

Private Sub Form_Click()
    OLE1.AppIsRunning = False
    Command1.SetFocus
End Sub
```

LISTING 7.13 ZOOMER.VBP

```
ZOOMER.FRM
Object={F9043C88-F6F2-101A-A3C9-08002B2F49FB}#1.0#0; COMDLG16.OCX
Object={FAEEE763-117E-101B-8933-08002B2F4F5A}#1.0#0; DBLIST16.OCX
ProjWinSize=216,289,250,185
ProjWinShow=2
IconForm="Form1"
ExeName="Project1.exe"
Path="D:\VB"
Command=""
Name="Project1"
HelpContextID="0"
StartMode=0
VersionCompatible="0"
MajorVer=1
MinorVer=0
RevisionVer=0
AutoIncrementVer=0
VersionCompanyName=""
Reference=*\G{00025E01-0000-0000-C000-
000000000046}#0.0#0#DAO2516.DLL#Microsoft DAO 2.5 Object Library
```

That completes our coverage of OLE containers. We've come far in this chapter, from implementing OLE links to embedding OLE items, from handling multiple OLE items to deleting those items, and from deactivating OLE items to zooming them. In the next chapter, we'll press on with more OLE topics, when we start discussing OLE automation.

## CHAPTER 8

OLE AUTOMATION AND PROGRAMMABLE OBJECTS

In the previous chapter, we saw how to embed OLE items into OLE container controls. Those OLE items were maintained by their respective OLE servers—that is, if we embedded a Microsoft Excel OLE item, Excel was responsible for maintaining that item and letting the user edit it. We had no interaction with the item's data or internal code. How can we interact with other programs and send them commands? The Visual Basic SendKeys method does send keys to the currently active window or application asw though the user were typing the keys themselves, but as useful as that is, it is of coarse limited.

OLE automation lets us go a step further. If we work with an OLE automation object, we'll actually be able to work with its internal data and methods. In other words, we'll be able to cross program boundaries, working with the data and subroutines of another program. This can be very useful if the OLE automation item—called a *programmable object* in Visual Basic—has some capability you'd like to offer in your own program. For example, you might wish to offer the user some of the math capabilities of Microsoft Excel or the spell checking capabilities of Microsoft Word. In this case, Excel or Word makes up the programmable object in our program, and our application, the one that programs Excel or Word, is called the *controlling* application. Using OLE automation, then, you can use the internal power of other programs just as if you had written those programs yourself.

OLE automation is part of Microsoft's vision for the future. The company envisions that some programs will be little more than frameworks for tools that the user may select. The emphasis will be on the document that the user is working with. No longer will it be necessary to buy one huge program to find all the capabilities users require. Instead, they can purchase a modest controlling program and then customize it by buying selected automation tools (i.e., programmable objects).

In this chapter, we'll explore OLE automation. First, we'll see how to create a controlling application, one that works with a programmable object from Microsoft Excel. Next, we'll see how to create our own programmable object; we'll write a program that supports a public property (just like an object's property in Visual Basic) that other programs may read. Maintaining a public property like this is called *exposing* a property in OLE automation terms. Our programmable objects will develop from there, exposing properties (i.e., data) and methods (i.e., subroutines and functions) to controlling applications. Then we'll see how to support a visual interface in our programmable objects as we place a form on the screen when the controlling application requests it.

OUR FIRST OLE AUTOMATION CONTROLLING APPLICATION

In this example, we'll use the math capabilities of Microsoft Excel. Our program will be the controlling application (like an OLE container for the OLE automation item), and we'll use a programmable object supported by Excel (think of Excel as the OLE automation server). For example, we can add the values 1 + 2 + 3 using Excel and display the result in a message box.

Create a new project, calling it **AUTO1.VBP**. We'll perform our addition when the user clicks the form, and we'll print a prompt in our form, telling the user, "Click this form to add 1 + 2 + 3 using Microsoft Excel."

```
--------------------------------------------------------------
|                                                            |
| ---------------------------------------------------------- |
| Click this form to add 1 + 2 + 3 using Microsoft Excel.    |
|                                                            |
|                                                            |
|                                                            |
|                                                            |
|                                                            |
--------------------------------------------------------------
```

We add the code to print this prompt to the Form_Load() event handler in **AUTO1.FRM**. (Double-click the form to open Form_Load().) Also, set AutoRedraw to True so that this text will remain in the form when it is actually displayed.

```
Private Sub Form_Load()
    Print "Click this form to add 1 + 2 + 3 using Microsoft Excel."
End Sub
```

Next, open the Form_Click() event handler by finding it in the code window's Proc box:

```
Private Sub Form_Click()

End Sub
```

When the user clicks the form, we want to create a Microsoft Excel programmable object, use it to perform our math operation, get the result, and display that result in a message box.

We start by declaring the Excel programmable object with the Dim keyword:

```
Private Sub Form_Click()
--> Dim ExcelObj As Object
        .
        .
        .
End Sub
```

Next, we will use the Set keyword to set this object to an Excel worksheet. First, we have to "install" Excel as a programmable object source in our program. Do that by selecting the Visual Basic **Tools | References** menu item, opening the References dialog box, as shown in Figure 8.1.

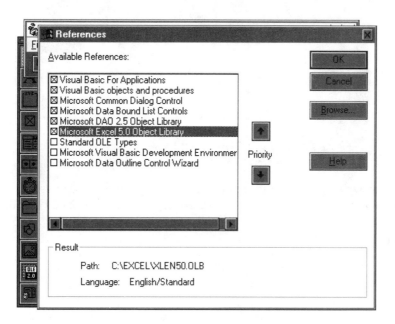

FIGURE 8.1 USE THE REFERENCES DIALOG BOX TO ADD SOURCES OF PROGRAMMABLE OLE AUTOMATION OBJECTS TO OUR PROGRAM.

Click the box marked **Microsoft Excel** in the Available References box and click **OK**, installing Excel as a source of programmable automation objects in our program. Next, select **View | Object Browser** to open the Object Browser (or just press **F2**) as shown in Figure 8.2. When you select Microsoft Excel in the Object Browser, you see a list of the methods and properties of Excel objects, and you can find help on any of these topics by clicking the **?** button in the Object Browser. In this way, you can see what's available in an Excel programmable object to our controlling application.

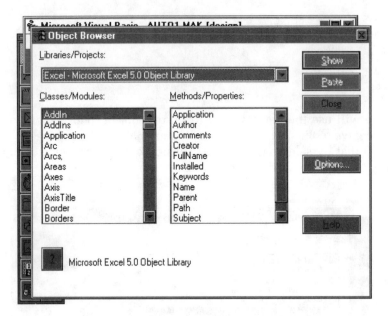

FIGURE 8.2 THE VISUAL BASIC OBJECT BROWSER TELLS YOU ABOUT THE
PROPERTIES AND METHODS OF VARIOUS PROGRAMMABLE OBJECTS.

Now that we've added a reference to Microsoft Excel, we can set a programmable object corresponding to an Excel worksheet in our ExcelObj object:

```
Private Sub Form_Click()
    Dim ExcelObj As Object
--> Set ExcelObj = CreateObject("Excel.Sheet")
        .
        .
        .
End Sub
```

We're free to use ExcelObj as we use any other object in Visual Basic: we can refer to ExcelObj's properties as ExcelObj.property and its methods as ExcelObj.method().

One of the most useful objects in an Excel programmable object is the Application object; a list of this object's properties appears in Table 8.1, and its methods are shown in Table 8.2.

TABLE 8.1 MICROSOFT EXCEL APPLICATION OBJECT PROPERTIES.

ActiveCell	DisplayRecentFiles	Parent
ActiveChart	DisplayScrollBars	Path
ActiveDialog	DisplayStatusBar	PathSeparator
ActiveMenuBar	EditDirectlyInCell	PreviousSelections
ActivePrinter	EnableCancelKey	PromptForSummaryInfo
ActiveSheet	EnableTipWizard	RecordRelative
ActiveWindow	FileConverters	ReferenceStyle
ActiveWorkbook	FixedDecimal	RegisteredFunctions
AlertBeforeOverwriting	FixedDecimalPlaces	ScreenUpdating
AltStartupPath	Height	Selection
Application	IgnoreRemoteRequests	SheetsInNewWorkbook
AskToUpdateLinks	Interactive	ShowToolTips
CalculateBeforeSave	International	StandardFont
Calculation	Iteration	StandardFontSize
Caller	LargeButtons	StartupPath
CanPlaySounds	Left	StatusBar
CanRecordSounds	LibraryPath	ThisWorkbook
Caption	MailSession	Top
CellDragAndDrop	MailSystem	TransitionMenuKey
ClipboardFormats	MathCoprocessorAvailable	TransitionMenuKeyAction
ColorButtons	MaxChange	TransitionNavigKeys
CommandUnderlines	MaxIterations	UsableHeight
ConstrainNumeric	MemoryFree	UsableWidth
CopyObjectsWithCells	MemoryTotal	UserName
Creator	MemoryUsed	Value
CustomListCount	MouseAvailable	Version
CutCopyMode	MoveAfterReturn	Visible
DataEntryMode	Name	Width
DDEAppReturnCode	OnCalculate	WindowsForPens
DefaultFilePath	OnData	WindowState
DisplayAlerts	OnDoubleClick	

(continued...)

DisplayClipboardWindow	OnEntry
DisplayExcel4Menus	OnSheetActivate
DisplayFormulaBar	OnSheetDeactivate
DisplayFullScreen	OnWindow
DisplayInfoWindow	OperatingSystem
DisplayNoteIndicator	OrganizationName

TABLE 8.2 MICROSOFT EXCEL APPLICATION OBJECT METHODS.

ActivateMicrosoftApp	Excel4MacroSheets	Range
AddChartAutoFormat	ExecuteExcel4Macro	RecordMacro
AddCustomList	FindFile	RegisterXLL
AddIns	GetCustomListContents	Repeat
Calculate	GetCustomListNum	ResetTipWizard
Cells	GetOpenFilename	Rows
CentimetersToPoints	GetSaveAsFilename	Run
Charts	Goto	Save
CheckSpelling	Help	SendKeys
Columns	InchesToPoints	SetDefaultChart
ConvertFormula	InputBox	Sheets
DDEExecute	Intersect	ShortcutMenus
DDEInitiate	MailLogoff	Toolbars
DDEPoke	MailLogon	Undo
DDERequest	MenuBars	Union
DDETerminate	Modules	Volatile
DeleteChartAutoFormat	Names	Wait
DeleteCustomList	NextLetter	Windows
Dialogs	OnKey	Workbooks
DialogSheets	OnRepeat	Worksheets
DoubleClick	OnTime	
Evaluate	OnUndo	
Excel4IntlMacroSheets	Quit	

In our case, we will display Excel by setting the Application object's Visible property to True:

```
Private Sub Form_Click()
    Dim ExcelObj As Object
    Set ExcelObj = CreateObject("Excel.Sheet")
```

```
--> ExcelObj.Application.Visible = True
        .
        .
        .
End Sub
```

There are many other objects we can reach in ExcelObj. For example, we install the values we want to add—1, 2, and 3—in the first three cells of the Excel worksheet by referring to ExcelObj.Cells(1, 1), ExcelObj.Cells(2, 1), and so on:

```
Private Sub Form_Click()
    Dim ExcelObj As Object
    Set ExcelObj = CreateObject("Excel.Sheet")

    ExcelObj.Application.Visible = True
--> ExcelObj.Cells(1, 1).Value = "1"
--> ExcelObj.Cells(2, 1).Value = "2"
--> ExcelObj.Cells(3, 1).Value = "3"
        .
        .
        .
End Sub
```

Next, we manipulate the data we have placed in the first three rows of the first column of the spreadsheet by installing an Excel formula in cell (4, 1). This formula will add the values in cells (1, 1), (2, 1), and (3, 1), placing the result in cell (4, 1):

```
Private Sub Form_Click()
    Dim ExcelObj As Object
    Set ExcelObj = CreateObject("Excel.Sheet")

    ExcelObj.Application.Visible = True
    ExcelObj.Cells(1, 1).Value = "1"
    ExcelObj.Cells(2, 1).Value = "2"
    ExcelObj.Cells(3, 1).Value = "3"

--> ExcelObj.Cells(4, 1).Formula = "=R1C1 + R2C1 +R3C1"
        .
        .
        .
End Sub
```

Now the sum of 1 + 2 + 3 is in cell (4, 1). We retrieve that data and display the result in a message box:

```
Private Sub Form_Click()
    Dim ExcelObj As Object
    Set ExcelObj = CreateObject("Excel.Sheet")

    ExcelObj.Application.Visible = True
    ExcelObj.Cells(1, 1).Value = "1"
    ExcelObj.Cells(2, 1).Value = "2"
    ExcelObj.Cells(3, 1).Value = "3"

    ExcelObj.Cells(4, 1).Formula = "=R1C1 + R2C1 +R3C1"
--> MsgBox "1 + 2 + 3 = " & ExcelObj.Cells(4, 1)
    .
    .
    .

End Sub
```

All that remains is to end Excel, which we do with the Application object's Quit method:

```
Private Sub Form_Click()
    Dim ExcelObj As Object
    Set ExcelObj = CreateObject("Excel.Sheet")

    ExcelObj.Application.Visible = True
    ExcelObj.Cells(1, 1).Value = "1"
    ExcelObj.Cells(2, 1).Value = "2"
    ExcelObj.Cells(3, 1).Value = "3"

    ExcelObj.Cells(4, 1).Formula = "=R1C1 + R2C1 +R3C1"
    MsgBox "1 + 2 + 3 = " & ExcelObj.Cells(4, 1)

--> ExcelObj.Application.Quit
End Sub
```

Now run the program and click the form. You'll see the result of our sum (1 + 2 + 3 equals 6), as shown in Figure 8.3. Our program is a success.

The code for this program, **AUTO1.FRM**, appears in Listing 8.1, and **AUTO1.VBP** appears in Listing 8.2.

LISTING 8.1 AUTO1.FRM

```
VERSION 4.00
Begin VB.Form Form1
    AutoRedraw      =    -1  'True
    Caption         =    "OLE Automation"
    ClientHeight    =    4230
    ClientLeft      =    1320
    ClientTop       =    1785
    ClientWidth     =    6720
    BeginProperty Font
```

```
        name            =    "MS Sans Serif"
        charset         =    1
        weight          =    400
        size            =    8.25
        underline       =    0    'False
        italic          =    0    'False
        strikethrough   =    0    'False
    EndProperty
    Height          =    4635
    Left            =    1260
    LinkTopic       =    "Form1"
    ScaleHeight     =    4230
    ScaleWidth      =    6720
    Top             =    1440
    Width           =    6840
End
Attribute VB_Name = "Form1"
Attribute VB_Creatable = False
Attribute VB_Exposed = False
Private Sub Form_Click()
    Dim ExcelObj As Object
    Set ExcelObj = CreateObject("Excel.Sheet")

    ExcelObj.Application.Visible = True
    ExcelObj.Cells(1, 1).Value = "1"
    ExcelObj.Cells(2, 1).Value = "2"
    ExcelObj.Cells(3, 1).Value = "3"

    ExcelObj.Cells(4, 1).Formula = "=R1C1 + R2C1 +R3C1"
    MsgBox "1 + 2 + 3 = " & ExcelObj.Cells(4, 1)

    ExcelObj.Application.Quit
End Sub

Private Sub Form_Load()
    Print "Click this form to add 1 + 2 + 3 using Microsoft Excel."
End Sub
```

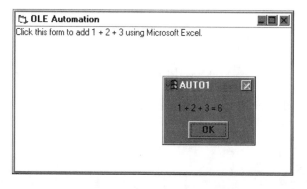

FIGURE 8.3 USING MICROSOFT EXCEL AS A PROGRAMMABLE
OLE AUTOMATION OBJECT, WE ADD THREE NUMBERS.

LISTING 8.2 AUTO1.VBP

```
AUTO1.FRM
Object={F9043C88-F6F2-101A-A3C9-08002B2F49FB}#1.0#0; COMDLG16.OCX
Object={FAEEE763-117E-101B-8933-08002B2F4F5A}#1.0#0; DBLIST16.OCX
ProjWinSize=151,398,205,115
ProjWinShow=2
IconForm="Form1"
ExeName="Project1.exe"
Path="D:\VB"
Command=""
Name="Project1"
HelpContextID="0"
StartMode=0
VersionCompatible="0"
MajorVer=1
MinorVer=0
RevisionVer=0
AutoIncrementVer=0
VersionCompanyName=""
Reference=*\G{00025E01-0000-0000-C000-
        000000000046}#0.0#0#DAO2516.DLL#Microsoft DAO 2.5 Object
        Library
Reference=*\G{00020813-0000-0000-C000-
        000000000046}#1.0#9#C:\EXCEL\XLEN50.OLB#Microsoft Excel 5.0
        Object Library
```

This gives us a good background on how to work with programmable objects. We simply create a programmable object and then use it like this (from our AUTO1 example):

```
Dim ExcelObj As Object
Set ExcelObj = CreateObject("Excel.Sheet")

ExcelObj.Application.Visible = True
    .
    .
    .
```

In an introductory book, you would probably see more examples of controlling applications that make use of programmable objects. But this is advanced Visual Basic, so let's take a look at the process of creating our own programmable objects.

CREATING A PROGRAMMABLE OBJECT

Our first progammable object (an OLE automation server) will be simple: we'll support a single property, which we'll call Is1, that always holds the value 1. We'll call our new project PROP1, and we'll also create a controlling application (an OLE automation client) named PROPTEST:

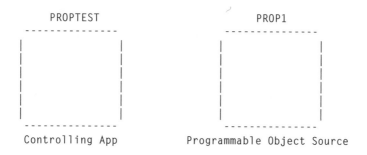

We can name the actual type of our programmable object, called its *class*, PropExampleClass. This means that our application's name is PROP1, and the class of programmable objects that we can create from it is named PropExampleClass:

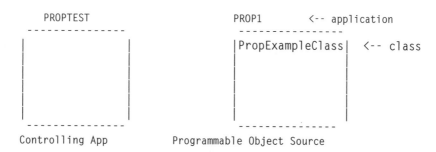

PROP1 is the programmable object's application, and PropExampleClass is our programmable object's class. (In our first example in this chapter, we created an object of type Excel.Sheet, where Excel was the application and Sheet was the class.) In PROPTEST, we will set up a programmable object named PropObj from the PROP1 application of class PropExampleClass (we'll add this code to a program in a minute):

```
Dim PropObj As Object
Set PropObj = CreateObject("Prop1.PropExampleClass")
        .
        .
        .
```

Now the programmable object exists in PROPTEST:

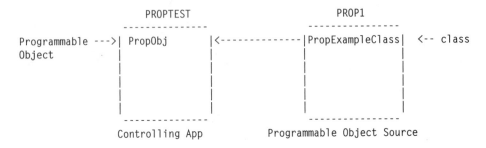

Our single property in the PropExampleClass class is named Is1, and it's always 1:

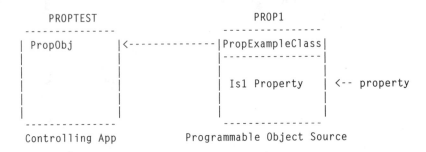

In PROPTEST, we can refer to the Is1 property of the programmable object PropObj as PropObj.Is1 this way:

```
    Dim PropObj As Object
    Set PropObj = CreateObject("Prop1.PropExampleClass")
--> MsgBox "The Is1 property = " & Str(PropObj.Is1)
```

We can now access the Is1 property in PROPTEST:

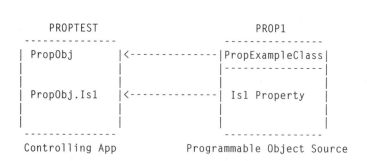

Creating the Object Application PROP1

Let's give this a try. Start Visual Basic and create a new project named PROP1. We will indicate to Visual Basic that we want to make this project an OLE automation server, so select **Options** in the Tools menu, opening the Project Options dialog box, as shown in Figure 8.4.

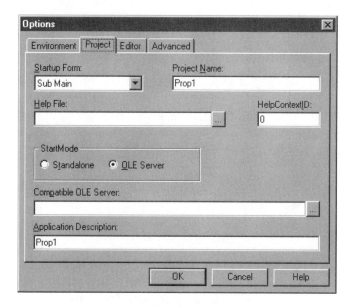

FIGURE 8.4 USING THE OPTIONS DIALOG BOX, WE INDICATE
THAT WE WANT TO CREATE AN OLE AUTOMATION SERVER.

First, change the project name to Prop1, as shown in Figure 8.4. When we need to add a reference to this automation server in the controlling application PROPTEST, we'll see Prop1 in the References dialog box. Next, change the startup form from Form1 to Sub Main, as shown in Figure 8.4. It may surprise you to learn that Visual Basic programs do not need a startup form at all and can run completely invisibly. That is the case if we declare a subroutine named Main() in a module (hence our selection of Sub Main in the Options dialog box), and we'll do that here to avoid popping our automation server on the screen when the controlling application is running.

Set the Application Description in the Options dialog box to Prop1, as also shown in Figure 8.4, and click the **OLE Server** button in the StartMode box as shown in Figure 8.4 to indicate that we want this project to be an OLE automation server. Now click **OK**, closing the Options dialog box.

Our next step is to declare the Main() subroutine, so use **Insert | Module** to insert a new module in our program, and call it **PROP1.BAS**. Declare Main() in this module by typing this code into **PROP1.BAS**:

```
Sub Main()

End Sub
```

We will not place any code in Main() (however, you can put initialization code here if you want). We create this subroutine so that Prop1 will not put any windows on the screen. In addition, place an Option Explicit statement in **PROP1.BAS**:

```
Option Explicit         <--

Sub Main()

End Sub
```

This statement causes the symbols in **PROP1.BAS** to be made public (available outside the module), which is what we want, because Main() is the starting point of our program. Next, use the Visual Basic **Remove File** menu item in the File menu to remove **FORM1.FRM** from the project. Our object application PROP1 will not support forms.

Now we are ready to set up our class, PropExampleClass, in PROP1. This is the class that we will make programmable objects from in PROPTEST. To create a new class, select **Insert | Class Module** in Visual Basic. Using the properties window, set the Name property of this new class to PropExampleClass. In addition, set PropExampleClass's Instancing property to 2 (Creatable MultiUse), and set Public property to True in the properties window so that other applications can create objects of this class. Now open the class by double-clicking its entry in the Project window, which opens the code window.

We start the code of our new class by declaring all symbols Explicit (making them public) with this new code in the code window:

```
Option Explicit        <--
        .
        .
        .
```

Now we declare our property, Is1 (this property can be reached from controlling applications):

```
Option Explicit

Public Is1 As Single    <--
```

In addition, we want to make sure that Is1 is always 1, so we should set it that way when the class is initialized. Add by hand the subroutine Class_Initialize() in the code window (or find it in the Proc box of the code window and click it to open it):

```
Option Explicit

Public Is1 As Single

Private Sub Class_Initialize()  <--

End Sub                         <--
```

Here, we set Is1 to 1:

```
Option Explicit

Public Is1 As Single

Private Sub Class_Initialize()
    Is1 = 1                     <--
End Sub
```

That's it—we've set up our object application and the class PropExample Class, and we've given that class a property that other programs can read. Save the project now, giving the class module the name **PROP1.CLS (.CLS** is the default extension for class modules). **PROP1.CLS** appears in Listing 8.3, **PROP1.BAS** is in Listing 8.4, and **PROP1.VBP** is in Listing 8.5.

LISTING 8.3 PROP1.CLS

```
VERSION 1.0 CLASS
BEGIN
  MultiUse = -1  'True
END
Attribute VB_Name = "PropExampleClass"
Attribute VB_Creatable = True
Attribute VB_Exposed = True
Option Explicit
Public Is1 As Single

Private Sub Class_Initialize()
    Is1 = 1
End Sub
```

LISTING 8.4 PROP1.BAS

```
Attribute VB_Name = "modProp1Main"
Option Explicit

Sub Main()
End Sub
```

LISTING 8.5 PROP1.VBP

```
Module=Module1; Prop1.Bas
Class=PropExampleClass; Prop1.Cls
ProjWinSize=276,510,205,115
ProjWinShow=2
HelpFile=""
Name="Prop1"
HelpContextID="0"
StartMode=1
Description="Prop1"
VersionCompatible32="0"
MajorVer=1
MinorVer=0
RevisionVer=0
AutoIncrementVer=0
ServerSupportFiles=0
```

Our next task is to create the controlling application PROPTEST, which will create programmable objects from the object application PROP1. Run

PROP1 and leave it running, making the PropExampleClass class available to other applications.

Creating the Controlling Application PROPTEST

Now start Visual Basic a *second* time. In this second instance of Visual Basic, we will develop PROPTEST and use it to examine the Is1 property of PROP1's PropExampleClass class. We leave PROP1 running in the first instance of Visual Basic so that we can access its classes from the second instance of Visual Basic—but once your object application is debugged and ready to go, just select Visual Basic's **File | Make EXE File** menu item to create **PROP1.EXE**. When the user runs **PROP1.EXE**, it will register itself as an object application with Windows, and, from then on, it will be available to controlling applications. (On the other hand, when we stop the first instance of Visual Basic here, PROP1 will no longer be available to controlling applications.)

Start a new project in this new instance of Visual Basic, give it the name **PROPTEST.VBP**, and give Form1 the caption **OLE Automation Property** by setting its Caption property in the properties window. Set the form's AutoRedraw property to True and double-click the form, opening the code window. In PROPTEST, our goal is to make a programmable object of class PropExampleClass, and we can name that object PropObj:

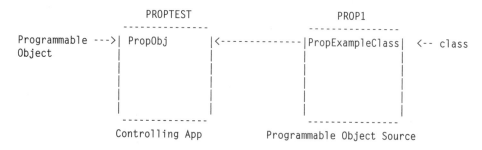

```
                    PROPTEST                      PROP1
                  --------------                --------------
Programmable --->| PropObj      |<-------------|PropExampleClass| <-- class
Object           |              |              |              |
                 |              |              |              |
                 |              |              |              |
                 |              |              |              |
                 |              |              |              |
                  --------------                --------------
               Controlling App          Programmable Object Source
```

We start by declaring PropObj in Form1's code window. Add this line outside any subroutine in the code window (from **PROPTEST.FRM**):

```
Dim PropObj As Object    <--
```

Next, we use CreateObject() (as we have before with Microsoft Excel) to create the actual programmable object when the form loads. Double-click the form to open the Form_Load() event. Here, we will specify the name of the object application, PROP1, and the class of object we want, PropExampleClass (from **PROPTEST.FRM**), to create our programmable object, PropObj:

```
Dim PropObj As Object

Private Sub Form_Load()
--> Set PropObj = CreateObject("Prop1.PropExampleClass")
End Sub
```

Next, we have to make sure that PROPTEST knows about PROP1. Open the References dialog box from the Tools menu and find the box marked Prop1 in the Available References box, as shown in Figure 8.5. Click the **Prop1** box, adding a reference to Prop1 to PROPTEST, as shown in Figure 8.5.

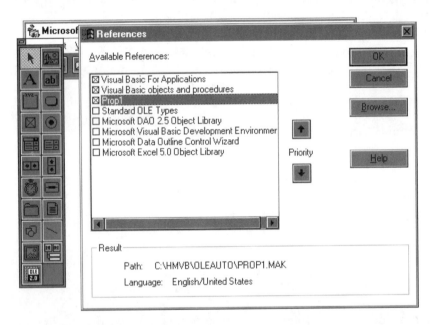

FIGURE 8.5 WE SELECT OUR OBJECT APPLICATION FROM THE CONTROLLING APPLICATION.

We can access the property in PropExampleClass, Is1, when the user clicks a command button. Add a command button now to the middle of Form1 and give it the caption **Click Me**. We can print the prompt "Click the button to read the property value." in the window itself:

```
 ----------------------------------------------------
|                                                    |
| -------------------------------------------------- |
|  Click the button to read the property value.      |
|                                                    |
|                                                    |
|                                                    |
|               - - - - - - - - - -                  |
|               |  Click Me  |                       |
|               - - - - - - - - - -                  |
|                                                    |
 ----------------------------------------------------
```

We print that prompt in the Form_Load() subroutine in **PROPTEST.FRM** (setting AutoRedraw to True so that this prompt appears when the program runs):

```
Dim PropObj As Object

Private Sub Form_Load()
    Set PropObj = CreateObject("Prop1.PropExampleClass")
--> Print "Click the button to read the property value."
End Sub
```

When the user clicks the button, the program calls the Command1_Click() event handler, so open that subroutine now from the Proc box in the code window:

```
Dim PropObj As Object

Private Sub Form_Load()
    Print "Click the button to read the property value."
    Set PropObj = CreateObject("Prop1.PropExampleClass")
End Sub

Private Sub Command1_Click()                 <--

End Sub
```

Here, we want to check and display the value in the Is1 property. We do that by checking PropObj.Is1 and by using a message box:

```
Dim PropObj As Object

Private Sub Form_Load()
```

```
    Print "Click the button to read the property value."
    Set PropObj = CreateObject("Prop1.PropExampleClass")
End Sub

Private Sub Command1_Click()
--> MsgBox "The Is1 property = " & Str(PropObj.Is1)
End Sub
```

PROPTEST is finished. Run the program and click the button marked **Click Me**. We examine PROP1's Is1 property and display the result as shown in Figure 8.6. Is1 = 1, and PROP1 is a success.

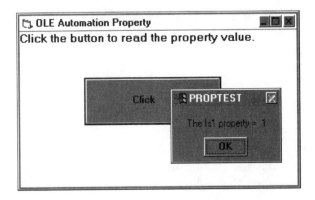

FIGURE 8.6 WE EXAMINE PROP1'S IS1 PROPERTY USING OLE AUTOMATION.

Note that when you run an OLE automation server in the first instance of Visual Basic, Visual Basic registers that server with a unique ID value in Windows. The next time you run the server, it will probably get a different ID number. This means that each time you start the server in Visual Basic and then the controlling application in another instance of Visual Basic, you must add a new reference to the server in the controlling application (and remove the previous reference, which, no longer referring to the server, will cause an error). For this reason, the OLE automation controlling programs on the disk that accompanies this book are shipped without a stored reference to their server programs, and you must add such a reference before running the controlling program. For example, run PROP1 in Visual Basic. Then start a new version of Visual Basic, open PROPTEST in it, and use **Tools | References** to add a reference to the running copy of PROP1 before running PROPTEST.

We have created our own, functional object application. The code for **PROPTEST.FRM** appears in Listing 8.6, and **PROPTEST.VBP** appears in Listing 8.7.

LISTING 8.6 PROPTEST.FRM

```
VERSION 4.00
Begin VB.Form Form1
    AutoRedraw      =    -1   'True
    BackColor       =    &H00FFFFFF&
    Caption         =    "Form1"
    ClientHeight    =    2220
    ClientLeft      =    1770
    ClientTop       =    1635
    ClientWidth     =    3225
    Height          =    2625
    Left            =    1710
    LinkTopic       =    "Form1"
    ScaleHeight     =    2220
    ScaleWidth      =    3225
    Top             =    1290
    Width           =    3345
    Begin VB.CommandButton Command1
        Caption     =    "Click Me"
        Height      =    495
        Left        =    1080
        TabIndex    =    0
        Top         =    840
        Width       =    1215
    End
End
Attribute VB_Name = "Form1"
Attribute VB_Creatable = False
Attribute VB_Exposed = False
Dim PropObj As Object
Private Sub Command1_Click()
    MsgBox Str(PropObj.Is1)
End Sub


Private Sub Form_Load()
    Print "Click the button to read the property value."
    Set PropObj = CreateObject("Prop1.PropExampleClass")
End Sub
```

LISTING 8.7 PROPTEST.VBP

```
Form=proptest.Frm
Reference=*\G{80C7DD57-EF5A-11CE-B01D-
        92668F0CF447}#1.0#0#C:\VBOOK\prop1\prop1.Vbp#Prop1
ProjWinSize=102,9,234,115
```

```
ProjWinShow=2
IconForm="Form1"
Name="Project1"
HelpContextID="0"
StartMode=0
VersionCompatible32="0"
MajorVer=1
MinorVer=0
RevisionVer=0
AutoIncrementVer=0
ServerSupportFiles=0
```

So far, we've managed to support only a single property, Is1, in our object application. Let's take a deeper look at properties and methods next.

SUPPORTING BOTH PROPERTIES AND METHODS

Our next OLE automation example will show how to add methods (functions and subroutines we can call in the controlling application) to our programmable object, as well as illustrate another way to support properties. In particular, we will create a calculator program that will allow us to add two integers we place in test boxes (Text1 and Text2):

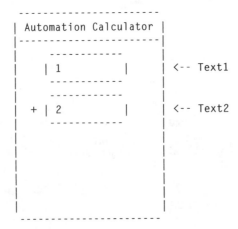

The user clicks the button marked =:

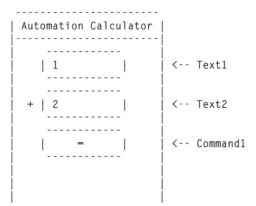

We will send the integer values from Text1 and Text2 to a method in our programmable object—we'll call this method Add()—to add these values and then display the result of that addition in a label, Label2. (Label1 holds the + sign next to Text1.)

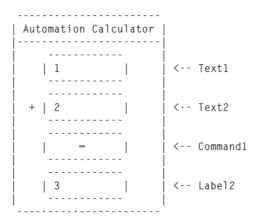

Let's see this program in action.

Creating the Object Application CALCULAT

Create a new Visual Basic project named **CALCULAT.VBP**. This will be our object application (the OLE automation server, our source of programmable objects). Delete Form1 in CALCULAT and replace it with a new module named **CALCULAT.BAS**. (Use the Visual Basic **Insert | Module** menu item.) We add Option Explicit and Main() to **CALCULAT.BAS** by hand:

```
Option Explicit          <--

Sub Main()               <--

End Sub                  <--
```

As with PROP1, open the Options dialog box from the Tools menu, set the Startup Form to Sub Main, and click the **Object Application** button in the StartMode box. Next, set the Project Name to Calculat in the Options dialog box, and set the Application Description to Calculat.

Now use **Insert | Class module** to create a new class module and save it as **CALCULAT.CLS**. Set the Instancing property of this class to 2 (Creatable MultiUse) and the Public property to True in the properties window, and give this class the name Calculator, also in the properties window. This gives our object application the name CALCULAT and our class the name Calculator. Open the class module in the code window and declare all symbols public by adding this code to **CALCULAT.CLS**:

```
Option Explicit          <--
```

This is where we'll write the code for our programmable object. In particular, our programmable object will support a method we've named Add() that will add two values. Here, we can set up the Add() method. We will pass two values from the text boxes in our calculator, so declare Add() by adding this code to **CALCULAT.CLS**, naming these two values X1 and X2:

```
Option Explicit

Public Sub Add(ByVal X1 As Single, ByVal X2 As Single)          <--

End Sub                                                         <--
```

Note that we pass the two parameters, X1 and X2, using the ByVal keyword, which specifies that the program pass these parameters by value (not by reference). There are two ways of passing parameters to subroutines: by value (in which case the actual value of the parameter is passed to the subroutine) and by reference (in which case the address at which the parameter's value may be found is passed). Passing values by value is the standard in Windows. We're working between Windows programs, so we must adhere to that standard.

We can add the two values X1 and X2 and place their sum in a new variable named Sum, which we make public:

```
Option Explicit

Public Sum As Single              <--

Public Sub Add(ByVal X1 As Single, ByVal X2 As Single)
    Sum = X1 + X2                 <--
End Sub
```

Because we've made Sum public, we'll be able to reach it as a property from our controlling application. We'll pass the two values we want to add to Add() and retrieve the sum from the Sum property. (Alternatively, we could have made Add() into a function.)

While we're working on our CALCULAT object application, let's also explore a new way of creating properties for our Calculator class. In particular, note that we've simply declared Sum as a public property (much as we did with the Is1 property):

```
Option Explicit

Public Sum As Single              <--

Public Sub Add(ByVal X1 As Single, ByVal X2 As Single)
    Sum = X1 + X2
End Sub
```

There is another way to set up a property. If we wanted to do some work when the user asked for the property's value—such as averaging an array of scores before passing a value back to the controlling application for a property named ScoreAverage—we could set up a property named, say, Five, using the Property keyword:

```
Option Explicit

Public Sum As Single

Public Sub Add(ByVal X1 As Single, ByVal X2 As Single)
    Sum = X1 + X2
End Sub

Property Get Five() As Double     <--

End Property                      <--
```

Notice the syntax here. We use the Get keyword to indicate that when a controlling application tries to read this property, this is the subroutine that should be called. If we had used the keyword Set, this subroutine would have been called when the controlling application tried to set the property to a specific value.

In this case, we set up the property named Five, which we set to 5 when the controlling application reads it:

```
Option Explicit

Public Sum As Single

Public Sub Add(ByVal X1 As Single, ByVal X2 As Single)
    Sum = X1 + X2
End Sub

Property Get Five() As Double
    Five = 5                    <--
End Property
```

We've seen two ways of supporting properties: by declaring them Public in our class module, and by using the Property Get and Property Set statements. If you want to perform some actions (such as averaging the values in an array) when the controlling application tries to read or change your property, you should use the Property Get and Property Set statements.

We've also set up the Add() method, so that's it for our object application, CALCULAT. **CALCULAT.CLS** appears in Listing 8.8, **CALCULAT.BAS** is in Listing 8.9, and **CALCULAT.VBP** is in Listing 8.10.

LISTING 8.8 CALCULAT.CLS

```
Version 1.0 Class
BEGIN
  MultiUse = -1  'True
END
Attribute VB_Name = "Calculator"
Attribute VB_Creatable = True
Attribute VB_Exposed = True
Option Explicit

Public Sum As Single

Public Sub Add(ByVal X1 As Single, ByVal X2 As Single)
    Sum = X1 + X2
End Sub
```

```
Property Get Five() As Double
    Five = 5
End Property
```

LISTING 8.9 CALCULAT.BAS

```
Attribute VB_Name = "modCalculatMain"
Option Explicit

Sub Main()
End Sub
```

LISTING 8.10 CALCULAT.VBP

```
CALCULAT.CLS
CALCULAT.BAS
ProjWinSize=151,398,205,115
ProjWinShow=2
HelpFile=""
ExeName="CALCULAT.exe"
Command=""
Name="Calculat"
HelpContextID="0"
StartMode=1
Description="Calculat"
VersionCompatible="0"
MajorVer=1
MinorVer=0
RevisionVer=0
AutoIncrementVer=0
VersionCompanyName=" "
```

Now that we've created the CALCULAT object application and the Calculator class, we need a controlling application to make use of it. We'll create that program, CALCTEST, next.

Creating the Controlling Application CALCTEST

Our CALCTEST program will be the controlling application that uses CALCULAT's Calculator class and, in particular, the Add() method in that class. Run CALCULAT in Visual Basic and then start a new, second instance of Visual Basic. Next, add the text boxes, labels, and the command button to the new Form1 that we need in our calculator:

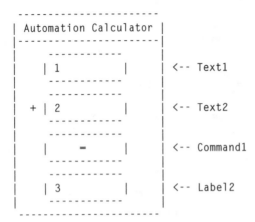

Now use the References dialog box from the Tools menu to add a reference to CALCULAT, as we have already done for our earlier programs AUTO1 and PROP1. Open Form1's code window and set up our programmable object, Calc, by adding this code (from **CALCTEST.FRM**):

```
Dim Calc As Object        <--
```

We can create that programmable object (from the object application CAL-CULAT and the Calculator class in that application) when the form first loads by adding this code to the Form_Load() subroutine:

```
Dim Calc As Object

Private Sub Form_Load()                                    <--
    Set Calc = CreateObject("calculat.calculator")         <--
End Sub                                                    <--
```

We're ready; when the user clicks the = button (Command1), we want to pass the two values in Text1 and Text2 to the Add() method of the Calc object. We do this in Command1_Click() (from **CALCTEST.FRM**):

```
Dim Calc As Object

Private Sub Form_Load()
    Set Calc = CreateObject("calculat.calculator")
End Sub
```

```
Private Sub Command1_Click()
--> Calc.Add Val(Text1), Val(Text2)
          .
          .
          .
```

(Note that in this simple example, we do not provide error checking.) The result of this addition is stored in Calc.Sum, so we place it into Label2 to display it:

```
Dim Calc As Object

Private Sub Form_Load()
    Set Calc = CreateObject("calculat.calculator")
End Sub

Private Sub Command1_Click()
    Calc.Add Val(Text1), Val(Text2)
--> Label2.Caption = Str(Calc.Sum)
          .
          .
          .

End Sub
```

We can test our Calc.Five property at the same time. To do that, we display it in a message box:

```
Dim Calc As Object

Private Sub Form_Load()
    Set Calc = CreateObject("calculat.calculator")
End Sub

Private Sub Command1_Click()
    Calc.Add Val(Text1), Val(Text2)
    Label2.Caption = Str(Calc.Sum)
--> MsgBox "The Five property = " & Str(Calc.Five)
End Sub
```

Now we've seen how to implement methods in OLE automation as well as a new way of implementing properties. Run the program and give it a try—place two numbers in the text boxes and click the = button to see the result:

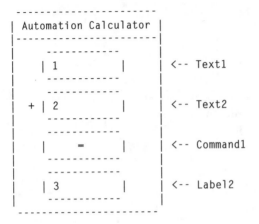

The program is a success, as we see in Figure 8.7.

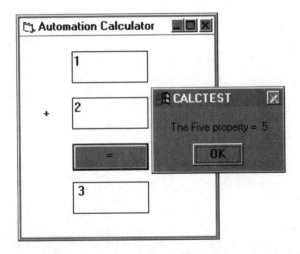

FIGURE 8.7 OUR CALCTEST PROGRAM PASSES VALUES TO THE OLE AUTOMATION SERVER CALCULAT.

The code for **CALCTEST.FRM** appears in Listing 8.11, and **CALCTEST.VBP** is in Listing 8.12.

LISTING 8.11 CALCTEST.FRM

```
VERSION 4.00
Begin VB.Form Form1
   Caption       =   "Automation Calculator"
   ClientHeight  =   3135
```

```
ClientLeft        =    2025
ClientTop         =    1830
ClientWidth       =    3120
BeginProperty Font
   name           =    "MS Sans Serif"
   charset        =    1
   weight         =    700
   size           =    9.75
   underline      =    0    'False
   italic         =    0    'False
   strikethrough  =    0    'False
EndProperty
Height            =    3540
Left              =    1965
LinkTopic         =    "Form1"
ScaleHeight       =    3135
ScaleWidth        =    3120
Top               =    1485
Width             =    3240
Begin VB.TextBox Text2
   Height         =    495
   Left           =    840
   TabIndex       =    2
   Top            =    960
   Width          =    1215
End
Begin VB.TextBox Text1
   Height         =    495
   Left           =    840
   TabIndex       =    1
   Top            =    240
   Width          =    1215
End
Begin VB.Timer Timer1
   Enabled        =    0    'False
   Left           =    315
   Top            =    4200
End
Begin VB.CommandButton Command1
   Caption        =    "="
   BeginProperty Font
      name        =    "MS Sans Serif"
      charset     =    1
      weight      =    700
      size        =    8.25
      underline   =    0    'False
      italic      =    0    'False
      strikethrough =  0    'False
   EndProperty
   Height         =    420
   Left           =    840
   TabIndex       =    0
```

```
            Top              =    1680
            Width            =    1215
         End
         Begin VB.Label Label2
            BorderStyle      =    1  'Fixed Single
            Height           =    495
            Left             =    840
            TabIndex         =    4
            Top              =    2280
            Width            =    1215
         End
         Begin VB.Label Label1
            Caption          =    "+"
            Height           =    255
            Left             =    360
            TabIndex         =    3
            Top              =    1080
            Width            =    255
         End
         Begin VB.Shape Shape1
            BorderStyle      =    3  'Dot
            Height           =    972
            Left             =    120
            Top              =    5400
            Width            =    972
         End
      End
      Attribute VB_Name = "Form1"
      Attribute VB_Creatable = False
      Attribute VB_Exposed = False
      Option Explicit
      Dim Calc As Object

      Private Sub Command1_Click()
          Calc.Add Val(Text1), Val(Text2)
          Label2.Caption = Str(Calc.Sum)
          MsgBox "The Five property = " & Str(Calc.Five)
      End Sub

      Private Sub Form_Load()
          Set Calc = CreateObject("calculat.calculator")
      End Sub
```

LISTING 8.12 CALCTEST.VBP

```
Form=CALCTEST.FRM
Reference=*\G{80C7DD80-EF5A-11CE-B01D-
        92668F0CF447}#1.0#0#C:\VBOOK\calculat\CALCULAT.vbp#Calculat
ProjWinSize=102,9,234,115
```

```
ProjWinShow=0
IconForm="Form1"
HelpFile=""
ExeName="CALCTEST.exe"
Command=""
Name="Project1"
HelpContextID="0"
StartMode=0
VersionCompatible32="0"
VersionCompatible="0"
MajorVer=1
MinorVer=0
RevisionVer=0
AutoIncrementVer=0
ServerSupportFiles=0
VersionCompanyName=" "
```

So far, all our object applications have been invisible. However, it's also possible to display a window from an object application, and we'll examine that process next.

Using Forms in Object Applications

In our object applications until now, we've removed the default form, Form1—but we don't have to do that. Let's leave Form1 in this time and see what happens.

Creating the Object Application OLEPICT

In the next example, let's use the programmable object to display a picture; for example, we can display **PENCIL01.ICO**, one of the icons we saw in Chapter 2. From the controlling application, we will be able to pop the object application on the screen, and the object application will display this icon. To display the icon, we'll use a picture box in the object application.

Start a new project in Visual Basic, giving it the name **OLEPICT.VBP**. Do not remove **FORM1.FRM** from the files in the project; instead, draw a picture box, Picture1, on that form. Next, prepare this program to be an object application, as before, by opening the Options dialog box, setting the Startup Form to Sub Main, and clicking **Object Application** in the StartMode box. Change the project name from Project1 to Olepict, and make that the Application Description as well. Now close the Options box by clicking **OK**.

We've indicated that we will use a startup subroutine, Main(), so add a new module, changing its name from **MODULE1.BAS** to **OLEPICT.BAS**, and place our default subroutine Main() there, along with Option Explicit:

```
Option Explicit      <--

Sub Main()           <--

End Sub              <--
```

Next, use the Visual Basic Insert menu to add a new class module to OLEPICT. In the properties window, set the class's Instancing property to 2 (Creatable MultiUse) and its Public property to True. Set its Name property to Display (i.e., Display will be our programmable object's class name). Open that class module in the code window. We can give this class one method: Show(). When the controlling application calls this method, our OLEPICT object application can display Form1 with its picture box. We give this class the method Show() by declaring it in our class module, **OLEPICT.CLS**:

```
Option Explicit           <--

Public Sub Show()         <--

End Sub                   <--
```

Before displaying Form1, we load the icon we want to display into Form1's Picture1 control. We use the LoadPicture() method with the following new code in **OLEPICT.CLS**. (Use the path and drive appropriate to your installation of Visual Basic.)

```
Option Explicit

Public Sub Show()
--> Form1.Picture1.Picture =
LoadPicture("c:\vb\icons\writing\pencil01.ico")
      .
      .
      .
End Sub
```

When our object application starts, Form1 is not displayed (even though its Visible property is True). To display it, we use the Show method:

```
Option Explicit

Public Sub Show()
    Form1.Picture1.Picture =
LoadPicture("c:\vb\icons\writing\pencil01.ico")
--> Form1.Show
End Sub
```

That's it. Our object application is able to use and display forms. When the controlling application calls our Show() method, we'll pop OLEPICT's Form1 on the screen and display the icon in it. The code for **OLEPICT.CLS** is in Listing 8.13, **OLEPICT.BAS** is in Listing 8.14, and **OLEPICT.VBP** is in Listing 8.15.

LISTING 8.13 OLEPICT.CLS

```
VERSION 1.0 CLASS
BEGIN
  MultiUse = -1  'True
END
Attribute VB_Name = "Display"
Attribute VB_Creatable = True
Attribute VB_Exposed = True
Option Explicit

Public Sub Show()
    Form1.Picture1.Picture =
LoadPicture("c:\vb\icons\writing\pencil01.ico")
    Form1.Show
End Sub
```

LISTING 8.14 OLEPICT.BAS

```
Attribute VB_Name = "modOlepictMain"
Option Explicit

Sub Main()
End Sub
```

LISTING 8.15 OLEPICT.VBP

```
OLEPICT.CLS
OLEPICT.BAS
OLEPICT.FRM
ProjWinSize=336,491,205,115
ProjWinShow=2
```

```
HelpFile=""
ExeName="OLEPICT.exe"
Command=""
Name="Olepict"
HelpContextID="0"
StartMode=1
Description="Olepict"
VersionCompatible="0"
MajorVer=1
MinorVer=0
RevisionVer=0
AutoIncrementVer=0
VersionCompanyName=" "
```

Next, we'll create a controlling application to match OLEPICT and to call the Show() method.

Creating the Controlling Application PICTTEST

As before, run OLEPICT in Visual Basic and start a new instance of Visual Basic. Call the new Visual Basic project (in the second instance of Visual Basic) PICTTEST. Also, as we have done before, add the OLEPICT object application to this new project as a reference using **References** in the Tools menu. Now add a command button, Command1, to Form1 in PICTTEST, and give it the caption **Show Picture**. Finally, open Form1's code window and, in particular, the Form_Load() event handler:

```
Private Sub Form_Load()

End Sub
```

We begin by dimensioning a new object named OleDisp:

```
Dim OleDisp As Object    <--

Private Sub Form_Load()

End Sub
```

In Form_Load(), we can create the object from our OLEPICT object application, making OleDisp an object of our class Display:

```
Dim OleDisp As Object

Private Sub Form_Load()
--> Set OleDisp = CreateObject("olepict.display")
End Sub
```

When the user clicks our **Show Picture** button, Command1, we want to execute our programmable object's Show() method to display the icon in the picture box. We do that by adding this code to Command1_Click():

```
Dim OleDisp As Object

Private Sub Command1_Click()
--> OleDisp.Show
End Sub

Private Sub Form_Load()
    Set OleDisp = CreateObject("olepict.display")
End Sub
```

The program is finished. Run it now and click the **Show Picture** button. We execute the Show() method of our OleDisp object, causing OLEPICT to show its form and the picture box, as shown in Figure 8.8. Our program is a success—now we're able to display windows in our object applications.

FIGURE 8.8 OUR OLEPICT OBJECT APPLICATION CAN DISPLAY A FORM.

PICTTEST.FRM appears in Listing 8.16, and **PICTTEST.VBP** is in Listing 8.17.

LISTING 8.16 PICTTEST.FRM

```
VERSION 4.00
Begin VB.Form Form1
    Caption         =   "OLE Pictures"
    ClientHeight    =   2790
    ClientLeft      =   2025
    ClientTop       =   1830
    ClientWidth     =   2730
    BeginProperty Font
        name            =   "MS Sans Serif"
        charset         =   1
        weight          =   700
        size            =   9.75
        underline       =   0   'False
        italic          =   0   'False
        strikethrough   =   0   'False
    EndProperty
    Height          =   3195
    Left            =   1965
    LinkTopic       =   "Form1"
    ScaleHeight     =   2790
    ScaleWidth      =   2730
    Top             =   1485
    Width           =   2850
    Begin VB.CommandButton Command1
```

```
        Caption          =    "Show Picture"
        BeginProperty Font
            name         =    "MS Sans Serif"
            charset      =    1
            weight       =    700
            size         =    8.25
            underline    =    0    'False
            italic       =    0    'False
            strikethrough =   0    'False
        EndProperty
        Height       =    420
        Left         =    720
        TabIndex     =    0
        Top          =    960
        Width        =    1215
    End
    Begin VB.Shape Shape1
        BorderStyle  =    3  'Dot
        Height       =    972
        Left         =    120
        Top          =    5400
        Width        =    972
    End
End
Attribute VB_Name = "Form1"
Attribute VB_Creatable = False
Attribute VB_Exposed = False
Option Explicit
Dim OleDisp As Object

Private Sub Command1_Click()
    OleDisp.Show
End Sub

Private Sub Form_Load()
    Set OleDisp = CreateObject("olepict.display")
End Sub
```

LISTING 8.17 OLEPICT.VBP

```
PICTTEST.FRM
PICTTEST.BAS
ProjWinSize=102,9,234,115
ProjWinShow=2
IconForm="Form1"
HelpFile=""
ExeName="PICTTEST.exe"
Command=""
Name="Project1"
```

```
HelpContextID="0"
StartMode=0
VersionCompatible="0"
MajorVer=1
MinorVer=0
RevisionVer=0
AutoIncrementVer=0
VersionCompanyName=" "
Reference=*\G{FF95E821-CAF5-101B-B0A0-
8D46BE1650FF}#1.0#409#C:\VBOOK\OLEPICT\OLEPICT.VBP#Olepict
```

That's it for our coverage of OLE automation. In this chapter, we've seen how to create both OLE automation controlling applications and automation object applications. We've seen how to support properties and methods in object applications and how to use them in controlling applications. And we've seen how to make our object application display a window. All in all, we've gained an enormous amount of OLE programming power in this chapter. In the next chapter, we'll add even more power to our arsenal when we see how to connect Visual Basic directly to Windows.

## CHAPTER 9

CONNECTING VISUAL BASIC
TO WINDOWS AND C++

In this chapter, we'll pursue some advanced Visual Basic techniques by connecting Visual Basic to Windows and to C++ code directly. We'll use the low-level Windows graphics routines (instead of relying on Visual Basic to call them for us) to see how to write powerful code—code you can't write in Visual Basic alone. Our example will be a screen capture program, something you can't do in Visual Basic without accessing the Windows routines directly. Next, we'll see how to connect C++ code to a Visual Basic program. Many programmers already have long routines written in C or C++ and would like to connect these routines to Visual Basic. In addition, many routines are provided in the libraries that accompany C++ packages (such as Microsoft Visual C++'s quick-sorting routines) that we just don't have in Visual Basic, and we'll be extending our power significantly by connecting those routines to our programs.

THE SCREENER PROGRAM

Our screen capture program shows some of the advantages of accessing Windows routines directly. This program allows us to use the mouse anywhere on the screen, draw anywhere on the screen, read graphics anywhere on the screen, and copy graphics from one location to another using the low-level fast bitmap functions built into Windows.

Windows has thousands of routines available for us to use. In fact, Visual Basic calls these routines to work with Windows. But we can also call these Windows routines ourselves: they reside in the Windows libraries in the **WINDOWS\SYSTEM** directory.

We'll use the Windows routines in our screen capture program. In that program, users will select the Capture menu in our menu bar to start the screen capture process. Next, they can move the mouse as they wish on the screen and draw a rectangle outlining the area they want to capture. When they release the mouse button, we can capture the outlined area of the screen and copy it to our program's client area. That's the way our capture process will work: we'll allow the user to draw a rectangle on the screen, and we'll copy the graphics in that rectangle to our own program's window.

Until this point in the book, it has not mattered which version of Visual Basic we use—the 16-bit or the 32-bit version. However, now that we will call the Windows routines directly, it does matter. For maximum compatibility, we will primarily use the 16-bit version of Visual Basic in this chapter, and the resulting program will function as written under Windows 3.1, Windows NT, and Windows 95. However, the differences between versions turn out not to be very significant. We will point out the differences between the 16-bit and 32-bit versions of Visual Basic as we develop our programs here, and we'll list both 16-bit and 32-bit final versions of all programs. No matter what version you are using, you can follow along.

There are a few differences between 16-bit and 32-bit Windows to keep track of as we enter into our discussion: Windows uses numbers to keep track of individual windows, and these numbers are called *handles*. In 16-bit Windows, handles are 16 bits, but in 32-bit Windows, handles are 32 bits. In a 16-bit program, therefore, handles are declared as Integer (i.e., 16 bits); in a 32-bit program, handles are declared as Long (i.e., 32 bits) instead. In addition, we will use two Windows libraries here. The 16-bit names for these libraries are **USER.DLL** and **GDI.DLL**, whereas the 32-bit versions are **USER32.DLL** and **GDI32.DLL**. Also, when a Windows function returns an Integer in 16-bit Windows, it will return a Long in 32-bit Windows. (All the 16-bit details can be found in the file **VB\WINAPI\WIN31API.TXT**, and the 32-bit details are in **VB\WINAPI\WIN32API.TXT**. These files come with Visual Basic and list the declaration of each Windows call in Visual Basic terms.) Finally, MoveTo(), one of the functions we will use, does not exist in 32-bit Windows; there, it is called MoveToEx().

With this in mind, it should be easy for 32-bit programmers to follow along, even as we discuss a 16-bit version of SCREENER. And we will also include SCREEN32, the 32-bit version of SCREENER. (For more information on the differences between 16-bit and 32-bit Windows programming, see Appendix B.)

Start a new Visual Basic project named **SCREENER.VBP**. Set the form's ScaleMode to Pixels (ScaleMode = 3) in the properties window, because we'll do all our drawing using pixel measurements. Next, use the Menu Editor to add a menu bar with one menu: Capture. Don't give this menu any menu items; when the user clicks the menu's name, we will begin the capture process and so we need not include any menu items. Open Capture_Click(), the subroutine associated with our Capture menu (from **SCREENER.FRM**):

```
Private Sub Capture_Click()

End Sub
```

When users click this menu, they want to start the screen capture process, so we should set a flag. We do not want to start the screen capture yet, however, because we have to wait for the mouse to go down (as the user outlines the area to capture). We set to True a flag named CaptureNext to capture the next mouse down event:

```
Private Sub Capture_Click()
--> CaptureNext = True
        .
        .
        .
End Sub
```

In addition, we dimension that variable as Boolean in the code window, placing it outside our Capture_Click() subroutine (from **SCREENER.FRM**):

```
Dim CaptureNext As Boolean        <--

Private Sub Capture_Click()
    CaptureNext = True
        .
        .
        .
End Sub
```

We set it False when the program starts, by adding code to the Form_Load() event to **SCREENER.FRM**. (Click the form to open the Form_Load() event.)

```
Dim CaptureNext As Boolean

Private Sub Form_Load()
    CaptureNext = False        <--
End Sub

Private Sub Capture_Click()
    CaptureNext = True
        .
        .
        .
End Sub
```

Because the region of the screen the user wants to capture may lie outside our window, we want to capture the mouse so that we can handle mouse events that occur outside our window.

Capturing the Mouse

Capturing the mouse means maintaining control of it as it passes over other program's windows; we will use the Windows SetCapture() function to do that. We have to pass that function hWnd, a handle to our window. (A window handle is the value Windows assigns to that window in its index of windows. We can refer to that window with its handle.) hWnd is a property of each window in Visual Basic. To make sure that we get all the mouse events that occur, we execute this line:

```
Private Sub Capture_Click()
    CaptureNext = True
--> RetVal = SetCapture(hWnd)
End Sub
```

We have to tell Visual Basic where this function is. It turns out to be in the Windows USER library (32-bit version: USER32), and we can declare this function in a new module. Using **Insert | Module**, insert a new module into the project, calling it **SCREENER.BAS**, and place the following line in it. (Note that in 32-bit programming, all Windows handles are Longs and not Integers.)

```
Declare Function SetCapture Lib "User" (ByVal hWnd As Integer) As Integer
```

The 32-bit declaration is as follows:

```
Declare Function SetCapture Lib "user32" (ByVal hwnd As Long) As Long
```

In SCREENER, we are indicating to Visual Basic that the function SetCapture is in the USER library, it takes an Integer argument, and it returns an Integer value. Note also that we use the ByVal keyword here, indicating that we want to pass the hWnd argument to SetCapture() by value and not by reference. As we saw in the last chapter, parameters we pass to subroutines and functions may be passed by reference (where we pass the address of the parameter) or by value (where we pass its actual value). The Windows convention is to pass by value, which we indicate to Visual Basic here. That's it—now we've called and made use of a low-level Windows function to capture the mouse. Wherever the mouse goes on the screen, Windows will pass mouse messages to our program.

The next step is to handle the mouse down event. When users press the left mouse button, we should begin the capture process; they've started to outline the area of the screen they wish to capture. Open the mouse down subroutine from the code window's Proc box (from **SCREENER.FRM**):

```
Dim CaptureNext As Boolean

Private Sub Form_Load()
    CaptureNext = False
End Sub
```

```
--> Private Sub Form_MouseDown(Button As Integer, Shift As Integer, X As
        Single, Y As Single)

    End Sub
```

Here we can record the location of the first corner of the target area. The user then drags the mouse to the other corner and releases the mouse button, and we will capture the graphics in the rectangle that has been outlined. First, we check whether we are supposed to start capturing by testing the CaptureNext flag:

```
Private Sub Form_MouseDown(Button As Integer, Shift As Integer, X As
        Single, Y As Single)
--> If CaptureNext Then
        .
        .
        .
--> End If
End Sub
```

If we are to begin the capture process, we can set another flag to True, indicating that we are now capturing. Let's call that flag Capturing. We declare it in the code window and initialize it to False in the Form_Load() event (from **SCREENER.FRM**):

```
Dim CaptureNext As Boolean
Dim Capturing As Boolean          <--
        .
        .
        .
Private Sub Form_Load()
    CaptureNext = False
--> Capturing = False
End Sub
```

In Form_MouseDown(), we set the flag Capturing to True, indicating to the other mouse events that capturing is in progress:

```
Private Sub Form_MouseDown(Button As Integer, Shift As Integer, X As
        Single, Y As Single)
    If CaptureNext Then
-->     Capturing = True
        .
        .
        .
    End If
End Sub
```

To work with graphics in C and C++ Windows programs, we use a programming construct called a *device context*. It works like this: to draw in a window, we first create a device context for that window—all graphics work in Windows is done in device contexts. After we have a device context, we draw by using the many Windows drawing functions that work with device contexts (some of which we'll see soon). To work with the entire screen, we need a device context for the entire screen, and we create one using the CreateDC() function. First, we add the declaration of this function to **SCREENER.BAS**, our module:

```
    Declare Function SetCapture Lib "User" (ByVal hWnd As Integer) As
        Integer
--> Declare Function CreateDC Lib "GDI" (ByVal lpDriverName As String,
        ByVal lpDeviceName As Any, ByVal lpOutPut As Any, ByVal
        lpInitData As Any) As Integer
```

Now we're free to use CreateDC() in the Form_MouseDown() subroutine in **SCREENER.FRM**. In this case, passing the string "DISPLAY" to CreateDC() returns a device context corresponding to the whole screen. The other parameters in the CreateDC() call are used when we want to create a device context for a general device such as a printer; these parameters include the address of initialization data for that device, the address of the name of the device, and so on. But we need none of that here and so pass zeros for these parameters:

```
Private Sub Form_MouseDown(Button As Integer, Shift As Integer, X As
        Single, Y As Single)
    If CaptureNext Then
        Capturing = True
-->     DisplayHandle = CreateDC("DISPLAY", ByVal 0&, ByVal 0&, ByVal 0&)
        .
        .
        .
    End If
End Sub
```

This code returns a device context handle. We store the handle—an Integer (or Long in 32-bit Windows) referring to the device context—in a new variable named DisplayHandle. Because we'll use DisplayHandle in other event handlers, we make it a form-wide variable by declaring it this way in the code window:

```
Dim CaptureNext As Boolean
Dim Capturing As Boolean
Dim DisplayHandle As Integer      <--
        .
        .
        .
Private Sub Form_Load()
    CaptureNext = False
    Capturing = False
End Sub
```

In Form_MouseDown(), we should store the point at which the mouse button was clicked so that we know where the user started outlining the target area. Because this mouse press marks the first corner of the area we are to capture, we can store it as a point named Origin in two variables—OriginX and OriginY—which we add to the code window's declarations (from **SCREENER.FRM**):

```
Dim CaptureNext As Boolean
Dim Capturing As Boolean
Dim DisplayHandle As Integer
Dim OriginX As Integer            <--
Dim OriginY As Integer            <--
        .
        .
        .
```

We get the location at which the user pressed the mouse button in Form_MouseDown(), but note that the (X, Y) location passed to us there is passed in local coordinates with respect to the upper-left corner of the client area. We want to work with the whole screen, so we transform that location from client coordinates (where the upper-left corner of our client area is (0, 0)) to screen coordinates (where the upper-left corner of the screen is (0, 0)).

We do that by adding the screen coordinates of the client area's upper-left corner to the X and Y values we get in Form_MouseDown(). Visual Basic holds the screen coordinates of the upper-left corner of our window (not the client area) in the Form1.Left and Form1.Top properties, so we add them to the X and Y values we get in Form_MouseDown() to find the screen location at which the mouse button was pressed. Note that we have to change the Form1.Left and Form1.Top properties from twips to pixels before performing the addition. We use the ScaleX and ScaleY methods that we saw in Chapter 3 (add these lines of code to **SCREENER.FRM**):

```
Private Sub Form_MouseDown(Button As Integer, Shift As Integer, X As
        Single, Y As Single)
    If CaptureNext Then
        Capturing = True
        DisplayHandle = CreateDC("DISPLAY", ByVal 0&, ByVal 0&, ByVal 0&)
-->     OriginX = X + Form1.ScaleX(Form1.Left, vbTwips, vbPixels)
-->     OriginY = Y + Form1.ScaleY(Form1.Top, vbTwips, vbPixels) +
BarHeight
    End If
End Sub
```

Because Form1.Left and Form1.Top hold the screen location of the top left portion of the window, and not of our client area, we add the menu and title bar height—stored in our variable named BarHeight—to the Y coordinate. In this way, we are really storing the location of the mouse press with regard to the upper-left corner of our client area:

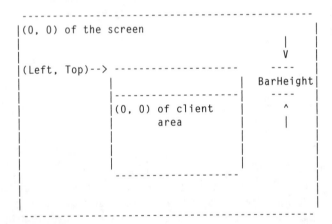

We store BarHeight in the code window's general area (from **SCREENER.FRM**):

```
Dim CaptureNext As Boolean
Dim Capturing As Boolean
Dim DisplayHandle As Integer
Dim BarHeight As Integer         <--
Dim OriginX As Integer
Dim OriginY As Integer
```

We fill BarHeight with the height of the menu bar and title bar by finding the differences between Form1's Height and ScaleHeight properties in Form_Load() (from **SCREENER.FRM**):

```
Dim CaptureNext As Boolean
Dim Capturing As Boolean
Dim DisplayHandle As Integer
Dim BarHeight As Integer
Dim OriginX As Integer
Dim OriginY As Integer

Private Sub Form_Load()
    CaptureNext = False
    Capturing = False
--> BarHeight = Form1.ScaleY(Form1.Height -
        Form1.ScaleY(Form1.ScaleHeight, vbPixels, vbTwips), vbTwips,
        vbPixels)
End Sub
```

Now we have stored in screen coordinates the location at which the mouse button was pressed; the next step occurs when the user moves the mouse. In particular, we can draw a box around the region that's being outlined on the screen as the user moves the mouse. The user presses the mouse button at one location, and we draw a rectangle as he or she moves the mouse, giving the user the impression of stretching the rectangle to cover the area to be captured.

Open the mouse move event handler, Form_MouseMove(), from the Proc box in the code window (from **SCREENER.FRM**):

```
Sub Form_MouseMove(Button As Integer, Shift As Integer, X As Single, Y
        As Single)

End Sub
```

First, we check the Capturing flag to make sure that we are engaged in a screen capture:

```
Sub Form_MouseMove(Button As Integer, Shift As Integer, X As Single, Y
        As Single)
--> If Capturing Then

            .
            .
            .
--> End If
End Sub
```

We have the original location at which the mouse button went down in (OriginX, OriginY); now the user has moved the mouse, and we get the new (X, Y) location in Form_MouseMove() in client coordinates. We transform these coordinates into screen coordinates and store them in a new point (MouseLocationX, MouseLocationY):

```
Sub Form_MouseMove(Button As Integer, Shift As Integer, X As Single, Y
        As Single)
    If Capturing Then
-->     MouseLocationX = X + Form1.ScaleX(Form1.Left, vbTwips, vbPixels)
-->     MouseLocationY = Y + Form1.ScaleY(Form1.Top, vbTwips,
            vbPixels) + BarHeight
                .
                .
                .
    End If
End Sub
```

As the user moves the mouse, we indicate the area being outlined by drawing a box from (OriginX, OriginY) to the new mouse location (MouseLocationX, MouseLocationY). It works like this: the user starts at location (OriginX, OriginY):

```
(OriginX, OriginY) x
```

Then he or she moves the mouse to a new location, (MouseLocationX, MouseLocationY):

```
(OriginX, OriginY) x

                    x (MouseLocationX, MouseLocationY)
```

We draw a box indicating the outlined area:

```
(OriginX, OriginY) x-----
                   |    |
                   -----x (MouseLocationX, MouseLocationY)
```

Then we store the current mouse location as (OldMouseLocationX, OldMouseLocationY) in preparation for the next time the user moves the mouse:

```
(OriginX, OriginY) x-----
                   |    |
                   -----x (OldMouseLocationX, OldMouseLocationY)
```

When the user moves the mouse again, it is moved to a new location (MouseLocationX, MouseLocationY):

```
(OriginX, OriginY) x-----
                   |    |
                   -----x (OldMouseLocationX, OldMouseLocationY)

                        x (MouseLocationX, MouseLocationY)
```

We want to erase the old rectangle before drawing a new one to the new mouse location. We can use the Xor drawing mode and redraw the original rectangle, which erases it:

```
(OriginX, OriginY) x

                        x (OldMouseLocationX, OldMouseLocationY)

                        x (MouseLocationX, MouseLocationY)
```

Then we draw the new rectangle from (OriginX, OriginY) to (MouseLocationX, MouseLocationY):

```
(OriginX, OriginY) x--------
                   |       |
                   |       |
                   |       |
                   --------x (MouseLocationX, MouseLocationY)
```

In code, we start by setting our device context's drawing mode to Xor drawing (as we did in Chapter 3); we use the set binary raster operation function SetROP2(). We pass DisplayHandle, the handle of our device context, to SetROP2(), as well as the drawing mode we wish to set: the Xor drawing mode. For SetROP2(), this is mode number 6 (from **SCREENER.FRM**):

```
Sub Form_MouseMove(Button As Integer, Shift As Integer, X As Single, Y
        As Single)
    If Capturing Then
        MouseLocationX = X + Form1.ScaleX(Form1.Left, vbTwips, vbPixels)
        MouseLocationY = Y + Form1.ScaleY(Form1.Top, vbTwips,
            vbPixels) + BarHeight

-->     RetVal = SetROP2(DisplayHandle, 6)
        .
        .
        .
    End If
End Sub
```

We add SetROP2()'s declaration to our module (from **SCREENER.BAS**):

```
    Declare Function SetCapture Lib "User" (ByVal hWnd As Integer) As
        Integer
    Declare Function CreateDC Lib "GDI" (ByVal lpDriverName As String,
        ByVal lpDeviceName As Any, ByVal lpOutPut As Any, ByVal
        lpInitData As Any) As Integer
--> Declare Function SetROP2 Lib "GDI" (ByVal hDC As Integer, ByVal
        nDrawMode As Integer) As Integer
        .
        .
        .
```

Note that because SetROP2() is a function, we have to use its return value in Visual Basic. We place that value in the variable RetVal, a dummy variable; we will not use the value in RetVal.

Our first action in the mouse move event handler is to erase the old rectangle (drawn when the mouse was moved earlier). The old rectangle stretches from (OriginX, OriginY) to (OldMouseLocationX, OldMouseLocationY), so we'll redraw that rectangle using the Xor drawing mode. Note, however, that when the mouse is moved for the first time, OldMouseLocationX and OldMouseLocationY have nothing stored in them, so we would have a problem trying to redraw this nonexistent rectangle. To overcome this, we fill OldMouseLocationX and OldMouseLocationY initially with OriginX and OriginY in Form_MouseDown() (from **SCREENER.FRM**):

```
Private Sub Form_MouseDown(Button As Integer, Shift As Integer, X As
        Single, Y As Single)
    If CaptureNext Then
        Capturing = True
        DisplayHandle = CreateDC("DISPLAY", ByVal 0&, ByVal 0&, ByVal 0&)
        OriginX = X + Form1.ScaleX(Form1.Left, vbTwips, vbPixels)
        OriginY = Y + Form1.ScaleY(Form1.Top, vbTwips, vbPixels) +
BarHeight
-->     OldMouseLocationX = OriginX
-->     OldMouseLocationY = OriginY
    End If
End Sub
```

Now we're free to erase the old rectangle, which stretches from (OriginX, OriginY) to (OldMouseLocationX, OldMouseLocationY), in Form_MouseMove(). We do that by redrawing the rectangle (we've set the drawing mode to Xor). We use the MoveTo() Windows function, which sets the location where we start drawing, and the LineTo() function, which draws a line. (MoveTo() is called

MoveToEx() in 32-bit Windows, as shown in **SCREEN32.FRM** below.) We pass
MoveTo() the device context handle, followed by the screen location we wish
to move to, and we pass LineTo() the device context handle, followed by the
target point we want to draw a line to from our current position. In code it
looks like this:

```
Sub Form_MouseMove(Button As Integer, Shift As Integer, X As Single, Y
        As Single)
    If Capturing Then
        MouseLocationX = X + Form1.ScaleX(Form1.Left, vbTwips, vbPixels)
        MouseLocationY = Y + Form1.ScaleY(Form1.Top, vbTwips,
            vbPixels) + BarHeight

        RetVal = SetROP2(DisplayHandle, 6)
-->     ReturnVal& = MoveTo(DisplayHandle, OldMouseLocationX,
            OldMouseLocationY)
-->     RetVal = LineTo(DisplayHandle, OriginX, OldMouseLocationY)
-->     RetVal = LineTo(DisplayHandle, OriginX, OriginY)
-->     RetVal = LineTo(DisplayHandle, OldMouseLocationX, OriginY)
-->     RetVal = LineTo(DisplayHandle, OldMouseLocationX,
OldMouseLocationY)
            .
            .
            .
    End If
End Sub
```

We also add these function declarations to our module, **SCREENER.BAS**:

```
    Declare Function SetCapture Lib "User" (ByVal hWnd As Integer) As
        Integer
    Declare Function CreateDC Lib "GDI" (ByVal lpDriverName As String,
        ByVal lpDeviceName As Any, ByVal lpOutPut As Any, ByVal
        lpInitData As Any) As Integer
    Declare Function SetROP2 Lib "GDI" (ByVal hDC As Integer, ByVal
        nDrawMode As Integer) As Integer
--> Declare Function MoveTo Lib "GDI" (ByVal hDC As Integer, ByVal X As
        Integer, ByVal Y As Integer) As Long
--> Declare Function LineTo Lib "GDI" (ByVal hDC As Integer, ByVal X As
        Integer, ByVal Y As Integer) As Integer
```

In preparation for the next mouse move event in Form_MouseMove(), in
which we want to erase the current rectangle before drawing the next one,
we fill the coordinates (OldMouseLocationX, OldMouseLocationY) with the
current mouse location. We add this code to **SCREENER.FRM**:

```
Sub Form_MouseMove(Button As Integer, Shift As Integer, X As Single, Y
        As Single)
    If Capturing Then
        MouseLocationX = X + Form1.ScaleX(Form1.Left, vbTwips, vbPixels)
        MouseLocationY = Y + Form1.ScaleY(Form1.Top, vbTwips,
            vbPixels) + BarHeight

        RetVal = SetROP2(DisplayHandle, 6)
        ReturnVal& = MoveTo(DisplayHandle, OldMouseLocationX,
            OldMouseLocationY)
        RetVal = LineTo(DisplayHandle, OriginX, OldMouseLocationY)
        RetVal = LineTo(DisplayHandle, OriginX, OriginY)
        RetVal = LineTo(DisplayHandle, OldMouseLocationX, OriginY)
        RetVal = LineTo(DisplayHandle, OldMouseLocationX, OldMouseLocationY)
-->     OldMouseLocationX = MouseLocationX
-->     OldMouseLocationY = MouseLocationY
            .
            .
            .

    End If
End Sub
```

Finally, we draw the box from (OriginX, OriginY) to the current mouse location:

```
Sub Form_MouseMove(Button As Integer, Shift As Integer, X As Single, Y
        As Single)
    If Capturing Then
        MouseLocationX = X + Form1.ScaleX(Form1.Left, vbTwips, vbPixels)
        MouseLocationY = Y + Form1.ScaleY(Form1.Top, vbTwips,
            vbPixels) + BarHeight

        RetVal = SetROP2(DisplayHandle, 6)
        ReturnVal& = MoveTo(DisplayHandle, OldMouseLocationX,
            OldMouseLocationY)
        RetVal = LineTo(DisplayHandle, OriginX, OldMouseLocationY)
        RetVal = LineTo(DisplayHandle, OriginX, OriginY)
        RetVal = LineTo(DisplayHandle, OldMouseLocationX, OriginY)
        RetVal = LineTo(DisplayHandle, OldMouseLocationX, OldMouseLocationY)
        OldMouseLocationX = MouseLocationX
        OldMouseLocationY = MouseLocationY
-->     ReturnVal& = MoveTo(DisplayHandle, MouseLocationX, MouseLocationY)
-->     RetVal = LineTo(DisplayHandle, OriginX, MouseLocationY)
-->     RetVal = LineTo(DisplayHandle, OriginX, OriginY)
-->     RetVal = LineTo(DisplayHandle, MouseLocationX, OriginY)
-->     RetVal = LineTo(DisplayHandle, MouseLocationX, MouseLocationY)
    End If
End Sub
```

Now we are able to draw a box on the screen as users move the mouse around. This gives the impression that users are "stretching" the rectangle as they move around the screen, outlining the area they want to capture.

When users release the mouse button, they have outlined the area they want to capture, and now we must capture it. When the mouse button goes up, we'll do this in the Form_MouseUp() subroutine. From the code window's Proc box, open Form_MouseUp() (from **SCREENER.FRM**):

```
Sub Form_MouseUp(Button As Integer, Shift As Integer, X As Single, Y
        As Single)

End Sub
```

First, we make sure that we are engaged in a capture operation by checking the Capturing flag using this new code:

```
Sub Form_MouseUp(Button As Integer, Shift As Integer, X As Single, Y
        As Single)
-->  If Capturing Then
        .
        .
        .
-->  End If
End Sub
```

If we are engaged in a capture operation, then we are supposed to complete the screen capture now. First, we release control of the mouse using the Windows ReleaseCapture() subroutine (this subroutine takes no arguments) and reset our Capturing flags for the next operation:

```
Sub Form_MouseUp(Button As Integer, Shift As Integer, X As Single, Y
        As Single)
     If Capturing Then
-->       ReleaseCapture
-->       CaptureNext = False
-->       Capturing = False
          .
          .
          .
     End If
End Sub
```

Next, we convert the final location of the mouse cursor, as passed to us in the X and Y parameters, into the screen coordinates MouseLocationX and MouseLocationY:

```
Sub Form_MouseUp(Button As Integer, Shift As Integer, X As Single, Y
        As Single)
    If Capturing Then
        ReleaseCapture
        CaptureNext = False
        Capturing = False
-->     MouseLocationX = X + Form1.ScaleX(Form1.Left, vbTwips, vbPixels)
-->     MouseLocationY = Y + Form1.ScaleY(Form1.Top, vbTwips,
            vbPixels) + BarHeight
            .
            .
            .
    End If
End Sub
```

Setting our screen device context's drawing mode to Xor, we erase the final rectangle on the screen (drawn just before the mouse button went up):

```
Sub Form_MouseUp(Button As Integer, Shift As Integer, X As Single, Y
        As Single)
    Dim BitmapWidth As Integer
    Dim BitmapHeight As Integer
    Dim LeftX As Integer
    Dim LeftY As Integer

    If Capturing Then
        ReleaseCapture
        CaptureNext = False
        Capturing = False
        MouseLocationX = X + Form1.ScaleX(Form1.Left, vbTwips, vbPixels)
        MouseLocationY = Y + Form1.ScaleY(Form1.Top, vbTwips,
            vbPixels) + BarHeight
-->     RetVal = SetROP2(DisplayHandle, 6)
-->     ReturnVal& = MoveTo(DisplayHandle, OldMouseLocationX,
-->         OldMouseLocationY)
-->     RetVal = LineTo(DisplayHandle, OriginX, OldMouseLocationY)
-->     RetVal = LineTo(DisplayHandle, OriginX, OriginY)
-->     RetVal = LineTo(DisplayHandle, OldMouseLocationX, OriginY)
-->     RetVal = LineTo(DisplayHandle, OldMouseLocationX, OldMouseLocationY)
            .
            .
            .
    End If
End Sub
```

Now we have the screen coordinates of the area that the user wishes to capture—from (OriginX, OriginY) to (MouseLocationX, MouseLocationY). Getting those two points, the corners of our capture rectangle, was the goal of all our mouse operations. Now we copy into our program's window the screen graphics inside this rectangle.

To perform the capture, we use the Windows function BitBlt() (for "Bit Blast"), which is Windows' fast, low-level bitmap handler. This function is complex to use and has many arguments, as you can see in its declaration, which we add to **SCREENER.BAS**:

```
    Declare Function SetCapture Lib "User" (ByVal hWnd As Integer) As
        Integer
    Declare Function CreateDC Lib "GDI" (ByVal lpDriverName As String,
        ByVal lpDeviceName As Any, ByVal lpOutPut As Any, ByVal
        lpInitData As Any) As Integer
    Declare Function SetROP2 Lib "GDI" (ByVal hDC As Integer, ByVal
        nDrawMode As Integer) As Integer
    Declare Function MoveTo Lib "GDI" (ByVal hDC As Integer, ByVal X As
        Integer, ByVal Y As Integer) As Long
    Declare Function LineTo Lib "GDI" (ByVal hDC As Integer, ByVal X As
        Integer, ByVal Y As Integer) As Integer
    Declare Function DeleteDC Lib "GDI" (ByVal hDC As Integer) As Integer
--> Declare Function BitBlt Lib "GDI" (ByVal hDestDC As Integer, ByVal X
        As Integer, ByVal Y As Integer, ByVal nWidth As Integer, ByVal
        nHeight As Integer, ByVal hSrcDC As Integer, ByVal XSrc As
        Integer, ByVal YSrc As Integer, ByVal dwROP As Long) As
        Integer
    Declare Sub ReleaseCapture Lib "User" ()
```

To copy the outlined area into our program's client area, we pass BitBlt() a number of parameters, starting with the handle to our screen device context and a handle to our program window's device context. The handle to our program window's device context is stored in the Visual Basic property hDC, and we'll pass that to BitBlt(). In addition, we pass the upper-left corner of the screen area to capture to BitBlt(), as well as the width and height of the area, in pixels. The upper-left corner could be either (OriginX, OriginY) or (MouseLocationX, MouseLocationY), depending on how the user outlined the area to be captured on the screen. We explicitly check which point is the upper-left corner and place its coordinates in a new point, (LeftX, LeftY), by adding this code to **SCREENER.FRM**:

```
Sub Form_MouseUp(Button As Integer, Shift As Integer, X As Single, Y
        As Single)
--> Dim LeftX As Integer
--> Dim LeftY As Integer

    If Capturing Then
        ReleaseCapture
        CaptureNext = False
```

```
        Capturing = False
        MouseLocationX = X + Form1.ScaleX(Form1.Left, vbTwips, vbPixels)
        MouseLocationY = Y + Form1.ScaleY(Form1.Top, vbTwips,
            vbPixels) + BarHeight
        RetVal = SetROP2(DisplayHandle, 6)
        ReturnVal& = MoveTo(DisplayHandle, OldMouseLocationX,
            OldMouseLocationY)
        RetVal = LineTo(DisplayHandle, OriginX, OldMouseLocationY)
        RetVal = LineTo(DisplayHandle, OriginX, OriginY)
        RetVal = LineTo(DisplayHandle, OldMouseLocationX, OriginY)
        RetVal = LineTo(DisplayHandle, OldMouseLocationX, OldMouseLocationY)

-->     LeftX = MouseLocationX
-->     If OriginX < MouseLocationX Then LeftX = OriginX
-->     LeftY = MouseLocationY
-->     If OriginY < MouseLocationY Then LeftY = OriginY
            .
            .
            .
    End If
End Sub
```

We can easily find the height and the width of the area to be captured, and we store these values in two new variables: BitmapHeight and BitmapWidth.

```
Sub Form_MouseUp(Button As Integer, Shift As Integer, X As Single, Y
        As Single)
--> Dim BitmapWidth As Integer
--> Dim BitmapHeight As Integer
    Dim LeftX As Integer
    Dim LeftY As Integer

    If Capturing Then
        ReleaseCapture
        CaptureNext = False
        Capturing = False
        MouseLocationX = X + Form1.ScaleX(Form1.Left, vbTwips, vbPixels)
        MouseLocationY = Y + Form1.ScaleY(Form1.Top, vbTwips,
            vbPixels) + BarHeight
        RetVal = SetROP2(DisplayHandle, 6)
        ReturnVal& = MoveTo(DisplayHandle, OldMouseLocationX,
            OldMouseLocationY)
        RetVal = LineTo(DisplayHandle, OriginX, OldMouseLocationY)
        RetVal = LineTo(DisplayHandle, OriginX, OriginY)
        RetVal = LineTo(DisplayHandle, OldMouseLocationX, OriginY)
        RetVal = LineTo(DisplayHandle, OldMouseLocationX, OldMouseLocationY)
```

```
          LeftX = MouseLocationX
          If OriginX < MouseLocationX Then LeftX = OriginX
          LeftY = MouseLocationY
          If OriginY < MouseLocationY Then LeftY = OriginY
-->       BitmapWidth = Abs(OriginX - MouseLocationX)
-->       BitmapHeight = Abs(OriginY - MouseLocationY)
              .
              .
              .
      End If
  End Sub
```

Finally, we are ready to use BitBlt() itself. The last parameter we pass it, with a value of &hCC0020, indicates that we want to copy over the source bitmap (from the screen device context) into our target bitmap (i.e., in our client area device context):

```
Sub Form_MouseUp(Button As Integer, Shift As Integer, X As Single, Y
      As Single)
    Dim BitmapWidth As Integer
    Dim BitmapHeight As Integer
    Dim LeftX As Integer
    Dim LeftY As Integer

    If Capturing Then
        ReleaseCapture
        CaptureNext = False
        Capturing = False
        MouseLocationX = X + Form1.ScaleX(Form1.Left, vbTwips, vbPixels)
        MouseLocationY = Y + Form1.ScaleY(Form1.Top, vbTwips,
            vbPixels) + BarHeight
        RetVal = SetROP2(DisplayHandle, 6)
        ReturnVal& = MoveTo(DisplayHandle, OldMouseLocationX,
            OldMouseLocationY)
        RetVal = LineTo(DisplayHandle, OriginX, OldMouseLocationY)
        RetVal = LineTo(DisplayHandle, OriginX, OriginY)
        RetVal = LineTo(DisplayHandle, OldMouseLocationX, OriginY)
        RetVal = LineTo(DisplayHandle, OldMouseLocationX, OldMouseLocationY)

        LeftX = MouseLocationX
        If OriginX < MouseLocationX Then LeftX = OriginX
        LeftY = MouseLocationY
        If OriginY < MouseLocationY Then LeftY = OriginY
        BitmapWidth = Abs(OriginX - MouseLocationX)
        BitmapHeight = Abs(OriginY - MouseLocationY)
```

```
-->      RetVal = BitBlt(hDC, 0, 0, BitmapWidth, BitmapHeight,
              DisplayHandle, LeftX, LeftY, &hcc0020)
          RetVal = DeleteDC(DisplayHandle)
      End If
  End Sub
```

Note also that we delete the device context when we're finished with it. The last step is to add ReleaseDC()'s declaration to **SCREENER.BAS**:

```
Declare Function SetCapture Lib "User" (ByVal hWnd As Integer) As
        Integer
Declare Function CreateDC Lib "GDI" (ByVal lpDriverName As String,
        ByVal lpDeviceName As Any, ByVal lpOutPut As Any, ByVal
        lpInitData As Any) As Integer
Declare Function SetROP2 Lib "GDI" (ByVal hDC As Integer, ByVal
        nDrawMode As Integer) As Integer
Declare Function MoveTo Lib "GDI" (ByVal hDC As Integer, ByVal X As
        Integer, ByVal Y As Integer) As Long
Declare Function LineTo Lib "GDI" (ByVal hDC As Integer, ByVal X As
        Integer, ByVal Y As Integer) As Integer
Declare Function BitBlt Lib "GDI" (ByVal hDestDC As Integer, ByVal X
        As Integer, ByVal Y As Integer, ByVal nWidth As Integer, ByVal
        nHeight As Integer, ByVal hSrcDC As Integer, ByVal XSrc As
        Integer, ByVal YSrc As Integer, ByVal dwROP As Long) As
        Integer
Declare Sub ReleaseCapture Lib "User" ()
Declare Function DeleteDC Lib "GDI" (ByVal hDC As Integer) As Integer  <-
-
```

Now run the program and click the Capture menu. You'll be able to capture an area of the screen by pressing the mouse button at one corner of the area, outlining it with the mouse (stretch the rectangle you draw on the screen), and releasing the mouse button, as shown in Figure 9.1. When you release the mouse button, the area you have outlined on the screen appears in the program's client area. After much work, the result is worth it: SCREENER is a success.

SCREENER.FRM appears in Listing 9.1, **SCREENER.BAS** is in Listing 9.2, and **SCREENER.VBP** is in Listing 9.3. If you are running 32-bit Windows, the 32-bit versions appear in these listings: **SCREEN32.FRM** in Listing 9.4, **SCREEN32.BAS** in Listing 9.5, and **SCREEN32.VBP** in Listing 9.6.

FIGURE 9.1 OUR SCREEN CAPTURE PROGRAM AT WORK.

LISTING 9.1 **SCREENER.FRM**

```
VERSION 4.00
Begin VB.Form Form1
   Caption        =    "Screener"
   ClientHeight   =    3075
   ClientLeft     =    1425
   ClientTop      =    2460
   ClientWidth    =    4980
   BeginProperty Font
      name        =    "MS Sans Serif"
      charset     =    1
      weight      =    400
      size        =    8.25
      underline   =    0    'False
      italic      =    0    'False
      strikethrough =  0    'False
   EndProperty
   Height         =    3765
   Left           =    1365
   LinkTopic      =    "Form1"
   ScaleHeight    =    205
   ScaleMode      =    3  'Pixel
   ScaleWidth     =    332
   Top            =    1830
```

```
    Width          =    5100
    Begin VB.Menu Capture
       Caption         =    "Capture"
    End
End
Attribute VB_Name = "Form1"
Attribute VB_Creatable = False
Attribute VB_Exposed = False

Dim CaptureNext As Boolean
Dim Capturing As Boolean
Dim DisplayHandle As Integer
Dim BarHeight As Integer
Dim OriginX As Integer
Dim OriginY As Integer
Dim MouseLocationX As Integer
Dim MouseLocationY As Integer
Dim OldMouseLocationX As Integer
Dim OldMouseLocationY As Integer

Private Sub Capture_Click()
    CaptureNext = True
    RetVal = SetCapture(hWnd)
End Sub

Private Sub Form_Load()
    CaptureNext = False
    Capturing = False
    BarHeight = Form1.ScaleY(Form1.Height -
        Form1.ScaleY(Form1.ScaleHeight, vbPixels, vbTwips), vbTwips,
        vbPixels)
End Sub

Private Sub Form_MouseDown(Button As Integer, Shift As Integer, X As
        Single, Y As Single)
    If CaptureNext Then
        Capturing = True
        DisplayHandle = CreateDC("DISPLAY", ByVal 0&, ByVal 0&, ByVal 0&)
        OriginX = X + Form1.ScaleX(Form1.Left, vbTwips, vbPixels)
        OriginY = Y + Form1.ScaleY(Form1.Top, vbTwips, vbPixels) + BarHeight
        OldMouseLocationX = OriginX
        OldMouseLocationY = OriginY
    End If
End Sub

Sub Form_MouseMove(Button As Integer, Shift As Integer, X As Single, Y
        As Single)
    If Capturing Then
```

```
        MouseLocationX = X + Form1.ScaleX(Form1.Left, vbTwips, vbPixels)
        MouseLocationY = Y + Form1.ScaleY(Form1.Top, vbTwips,
            vbPixels) + BarHeight

        RetVal = SetROP2(DisplayHandle, 6)
        ReturnVal& = MoveTo(DisplayHandle, OldMouseLocationX,
            OldMouseLocationY)
        RetVal = LineTo(DisplayHandle, OriginX, OldMouseLocationY)
        RetVal = LineTo(DisplayHandle, OriginX, OriginY)
        RetVal = LineTo(DisplayHandle, OldMouseLocationX, OriginY)
        RetVal = LineTo(DisplayHandle, OldMouseLocationX, OldMouseLocationY)
        OldMouseLocationX = MouseLocationX
        OldMouseLocationY = MouseLocationY
        ReturnVal& = MoveTo(DisplayHandle, MouseLocationX, MouseLocationY)
        RetVal = LineTo(DisplayHandle, OriginX, MouseLocationY)
        RetVal = LineTo(DisplayHandle, OriginX, OriginY)
        RetVal = LineTo(DisplayHandle, MouseLocationX, OriginY)
        RetVal = LineTo(DisplayHandle, MouseLocationX, MouseLocationY)
    End If
End Sub

Sub Form_MouseUp(Button As Integer, Shift As Integer, X As Single, Y
        As Single)
    Dim BitmapWidth As Integer
    Dim BitmapHeight As Integer
    Dim LeftX As Integer
    Dim LeftY As Integer

    If Capturing Then
        ReleaseCapture
        CaptureNext = False
        Capturing = False
        MouseLocationX = X + Form1.ScaleX(Form1.Left, vbTwips, vbPixels)
        MouseLocationY = Y + Form1.ScaleY(Form1.Top, vbTwips,
            vbPixels) + BarHeight
        RetVal = SetROP2(DisplayHandle, 6)
        ReturnVal& = MoveTo(DisplayHandle, OldMouseLocationX,
            OldMouseLocationY)
        RetVal = LineTo(DisplayHandle, OriginX, OldMouseLocationY)
        RetVal = LineTo(DisplayHandle, OriginX, OriginY)
        RetVal = LineTo(DisplayHandle, OldMouseLocationX, OriginY)
        RetVal = LineTo(DisplayHandle, OldMouseLocationX, OldMouseLocationY)

        LeftX = MouseLocationX
        If OriginX < MouseLocationX Then LeftX = OriginX
        LeftY = MouseLocationY
        If OriginY < MouseLocationY Then LeftY = OriginY
        BitmapWidth = Abs(OriginX - MouseLocationX)
```

```
        BitmapHeight = Abs(OriginY - MouseLocationY)

        RetVal = BitBlt(hDC, 0, 0, BitmapWidth, BitmapHeight,
            DisplayHandle, LeftX, LeftY, &hcc0020)
        RetVal = DeleteDC(DisplayHandle)
    End If
End Sub
```

LISTING 9.2 SCREENER.BAS

```
Attribute VB_Name = "Module1"

Declare Function SetCapture Lib "User" (ByVal hWnd As Integer) As
        Integer
Declare Function CreateDC Lib "GDI" (ByVal lpDriverName As String,
        ByVal lpDeviceName As Any, ByVal lpOutPut As Any, ByVal
        lpInitData As Any) As Integer
Declare Function SetROP2 Lib "GDI" (ByVal hDC As Integer, ByVal
        nDrawMode As Integer) As Integer
Declare Function MoveTo Lib "GDI" (ByVal hDC As Integer, ByVal X As
        Integer, ByVal Y As Integer) As Long
Declare Function LineTo Lib "GDI" (ByVal hDC As Integer, ByVal X As
        Integer, ByVal Y As Integer) As Integer
Declare Function DeleteDC Lib "GDI" (ByVal hDC As Integer) As Integer
Declare Function BitBlt Lib "GDI" (ByVal hDestDC As Integer, ByVal X
        As Integer, ByVal Y As Integer, ByVal nWidth As Integer, ByVal
        nHeight As Integer, ByVal hSrcDC As Integer, ByVal XSrc As
        Integer, ByVal YSrc As Integer, ByVal dwROP As Long) As
        Integer
Declare Sub ReleaseCapture Lib "User" ()
```

LISTING 9.3 SCREENER.VBP

```
SCREENER.FRM
SCREENER.BAS
Object={F9043C88-F6F2-101A-A3C9-08002B2F49FB}#1.0#0; COMDLG16.OCX
Object={FAEEE763-117E-101B-8933-08002B2F4F5A}#1.0#0; DBLIST16.OCX
ProjWinSize=96,288,233,185
ProjWinShow=2
IconForm="Form1"
ExeName="Project1.exe"
Path="D:\VB"
Command=""
Name="Project1"
HelpContextID="0"
StartMode=0
VersionCompatible="0"
MajorVer=1
```

```
MinorVer=0
RevisionVer=0
AutoIncrementVer=0
VersionCompanyName=""
Reference=*\G{00025E01-0000-0000-C000-
        000000000046}#0.0#0#DAO2516.DLL#Microsoft DAO 2.5 Object
        Library
```

LISTING 9.4 SCREEN32.FRM

```
VERSION 4.00
Begin VB.Form Form1
    BackColor       =   &H00FFFFFF&
    Caption         =   "Screener"
    ClientHeight    =   3360
    ClientLeft      =   1425
    ClientTop       =   2460
    ClientWidth     =   4980
    Height          =   4050
    Left            =   1365
    LinkTopic       =   "Form1"
    ScaleHeight     =   224
    ScaleMode       =   3   'Pixel
    ScaleWidth      =   332
    Top             =   1830
    Width           =   5100
    Begin VB.Menu Capture
        Caption        =    "Capture"
    End
End
Attribute VB_Name = "Form1"
Attribute VB_Creatable = False
Attribute VB_Exposed = False

Dim CaptureNext As Boolean
Dim Capturing As Boolean
Dim DisplayHandle As Integer
Dim BarHeight As Integer
Dim OriginX As Integer
Dim OriginY As Integer
Dim MouseLocationX As Integer
Dim MouseLocationY As Integer
Dim OldMouseLocationX As Integer
Dim OldMouseLocationY As Integer

Private Sub Capture_Click()
    CaptureNext = True
    RetVal = SetCapture(hwnd)
End Sub
```

```vb
Private Sub Form_Load()
    CaptureNext = False
    Capturing = False
    BarHeight = Form1.ScaleY(Form1.Height -
        Form1.ScaleY(Form1.ScaleHeight, vbPixels, vbTwips), vbTwips,
        vbPixels)
End Sub

Private Sub Form_MouseDown(Button As Integer, Shift As Integer, x As
        Single, y As Single)
    If CaptureNext Then
        Capturing = True
        Dim Dev As DEVMODE
        DisplayHandle = CreateDC("DISPLAY", ByVal 0&, ByVal 0&, Dev)
        OriginX = x + Form1.ScaleX(Form1.Left, vbTwips, vbPixels)
        OriginY = y + Form1.ScaleY(Form1.Top, vbTwips, vbPixels) + BarHeight
        OldMouseLocationX = OriginX
        OldMouseLocationY = OriginY
    End If
End Sub

Sub Form_MouseMove(Button As Integer, Shift As Integer, x As Single, y
        As Single)
    If Capturing Then
        MouseLocationX = x + Form1.ScaleX(Form1.Left, vbTwips, vbPixels)
        MouseLocationY = y + Form1.ScaleY(Form1.Top, vbTwips,
            vbPixels) + BarHeight

        RetVal = SetROP2(DisplayHandle, 6)
        Dim Pt As POINTAPI
        Pt.x = 0
        Pt.y = 0
        ReturnVal& = MoveToEx(DisplayHandle, OldMouseLocationX,
            OldMouseLocationY, Pt)
        RetVal = LineTo(DisplayHandle, OriginX, OldMouseLocationY)
        RetVal = LineTo(DisplayHandle, OriginX, OriginY)
        RetVal = LineTo(DisplayHandle, OldMouseLocationX, OriginY)
        RetVal = LineTo(DisplayHandle, OldMouseLocationX, OldMouseLocationY)
        OldMouseLocationX = MouseLocationX
        OldMouseLocationY = MouseLocationY
        ReturnVal& = MoveToEx(DisplayHandle,MouseLocationX,MouseLocationY, Pt)
        RetVal = LineTo(DisplayHandle, OriginX, MouseLocationY)
        RetVal = LineTo(DisplayHandle, OriginX, OriginY)
        RetVal = LineTo(DisplayHandle, MouseLocationX, OriginY)
        RetVal = LineTo(DisplayHandle, MouseLocationX, MouseLocationY)
    End If
End Sub
```

```
Sub Form_MouseUp(Button As Integer, Shift As Integer, x As Single, y As Single)
    Dim BitmapWidth As Integer
    Dim BitmapHeight As Integer
    Dim LeftX As Integer
    Dim LeftY As Integer

    If Capturing Then
        ReleaseCapture
        CaptureNext = False
        Capturing = False
        MouseLocationX = x + Form1.ScaleX(Form1.Left, vbTwips, vbPixels)
        MouseLocationY = y + Form1.ScaleY(Form1.Top, vbTwips,
            vbPixels) + BarHeight
        RetVal = SetROP2(DisplayHandle, 6) Dim Pt As POINTAPI
        ReturnVal& = MoveToEx(DisplayHandle, OldMouseLocationX,
            OldMouseLocationY, Pt)
        RetVal = LineTo(DisplayHandle, OriginX, OldMouseLocationY)
        RetVal = LineTo(DisplayHandle, OriginX, OriginY)
        RetVal = LineTo(DisplayHandle, OldMouseLocationX, OriginY)
        RetVal = LineTo(DisplayHandle, OldMouseLocationX, OldMouseLocationY)

        LeftX = MouseLocationX
        If OriginX < MouseLocationX Then LeftX = OriginX
        LeftY = MouseLocationY
        If OriginY < MouseLocationY Then LeftY = OriginY
        BitmapWidth = Abs(OriginX - MouseLocationX)
        BitmapHeight = Abs(OriginY - MouseLocationY)

        RetVal = BitBlt(hdc, 0, 0, BitmapWidth, BitmapHeight,
            DisplayHandle, LeftX, LeftY, &HCC0020) RetVal =
        DeleteDC(DisplayHandle)
    End If
End Sub
```

LISTING 9.5 SCREEN32.BAS

```
Attribute VB_Name = "Module1"
Public Const CCHDEVICENAME = 32
Public Const CCHFORMNAME = 32

Type DEVMODE
        dmDeviceName As String * CCHDEVICENAME
        dmSpecVersion As Integer
        dmDriverVersion As Integer
        dmSize As Integer
        dmDriverExtra As Integer
        dmFields As Long
```

429

```
        dmOrientation As Integer
        dmPaperSize As Integer
        dmPaperLength As Integer
        dmPaperWidth As Integer
        dmScale As Integer
        dmCopies As Integer
        dmDefaultSource As Integer
        dmPrintQuality As Integer
        dmColor As Integer
        dmDuplex As Integer
        dmYResolution As Integer
        dmTTOption As Integer
        dmCollate As Integer
        dmFormName As String * CCHFORMNAME
        dmUnusedPadding As Integer
        dmBitsPerPel As Integer
        dmPelsWidth As Long
        dmPelsHeight As Long
        dmDisplayFlags As Long
        dmDisplayFrequency As Long
End Type
Type POINTAPI
        x As Long
        y As Long
End Type

Declare Function SetCapture Lib "user32" (ByVal hwnd As Long) As Long
Declare Function CreateDC Lib "gdi32" Alias "CreateDCA" (ByVal
        lpDriverName As String, ByVal lpDeviceName As String, ByVal
        lpOutput As String, lpInitData As DEVMODE) As Long
Declare Function SetROP2 Lib "gdi32" (ByVal hdc As Long, ByVal
        nDrawMode As Long) As Long
Declare Function MoveToEx Lib "gdi32" (ByVal hdc As Long, ByVal x As
        Long, ByVal y As Long, lpPoint As POINTAPI) As Long
Declare Function LineTo Lib "gdi32" (ByVal hdc As Long, ByVal x As
        Long, ByVal y As Long) As Long
Declare Function DeleteDC Lib "gdi32" (ByVal hdc As Long) As Long
Declare Function BitBlt Lib "gdi32" (ByVal hDestDC As Long, ByVal x As
        Long, ByVal y As Long, ByVal nWidth As Long, ByVal nHeight As
        Long, ByVal hSrcDC As Long, ByVal xSrc As Long, ByVal ySrc As
        Long, ByVal dwRop As Long) As Long
Declare Function ReleaseCapture Lib "user32" () As Long
```

LISTING 9.6 SCREEN32.VBP

```
Form=screen32.Frm
Module=Module1; SCREENER.BAS
Object={F9043C88-F6F2-101A-A3C9-08002B2F49FB}#1.0#0; COMDLG32.OCX
Object={FAEEE763-117E-101B-8933-08002B2F4F5A}#1.0#0; DBLIST32.OCX
Reference=*\G{00025E01-0000-0000-C000-000000000046}#0.0#0#C:\PROGRAM
        FILES\COMMON FILES\MICROSOFT SHARED\DC:\PROGRAM FIL#Microsoft
```

```
        DAO 2.5 Object Library
ProjWinSize=159,173,233,185
ProjWinShow=2
IconForm="Form1"
Title="SCREENER"
ExeName="screener.exe"
Path="D:\VB"
Command=""
Name="Project1"
HelpContextID="0"
StartMode=0
VersionCompatible32="0"
VersionCompatible="0"
MajorVer=1
MinorVer=0
RevisionVer=0
AutoIncrementVer=0
ServerSupportFiles=0
VersionCompanyName="STEVECO"
```

Our next topic concerns connecting Visual Basic to Microsoft Visual C++.
Visual Basic is a powerful package, but sometimes C++ has more to offer us.
For example, Microsoft's Visual C++ comes with a number of libraries filled
with routines that we don't find in Visual Basic. You may also have written
extensive code in C++ and don't want to translate it into Visual Basic.
Instead, you might want to set up an interface between the two languages,
and that is not hard to do.

CONNECTING VISUAL BASIC TO VISUAL C++

If you have routines written in different programming languages and want
to connect them after they have been compiled, usually all you do is to link
the various object (**.OBJ**) files: object files are in binary machine language
and can be connected seamlessly. But Visual Basic doesn't work like that—
there is no linker that we can use to link machine language modules. Yet we
have seen in this chapter that we can call Windows routines outside Visual
Basic. These routines were stored in the dynamic link libraries **USER.DLL**
and **GDI.DLL** (32-bit versions: **USER32.DLL** and **GDI32.DLL**). A *dynamic
link library* (a file with the extension **.DLL**) holds routines that any
Windows program can call, and it turns out that we can call compiled C++
code if we place it in our own dynamic link libraries.

For this purpose, we will use Microsoft's Visual C++. For the rest of this
chapter, if you are writing 16-bit Windows applications, use Visual C++ version 1.5; if you are writing 32-bit Windows applications, use Visual C++ version 2.0 or later. The C++ code is almost the same, and again we will point

out differences and list both the 16-bit and the 32-bit versions of our programs. (Note that you will cause errors if you try to call a 32-bit dynamic
link library from a 16-bit Windows program or vice versa.)

The DYNAM Custom Dynamic Link Library

Our dynamic link library example, which we'll call **DYNAM.DLL**, is relatively short. In it, we'll place a routine named DLLCall(), which we'll be
able to call from Visual Basic programs:

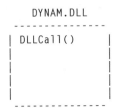

```
DYNAM.DLL
- - - - - - - - - - - - - - -
| DLLCall()       |
|                 |
|                 |
|                 |
|                 |
- - - - - - - - - - - - - -
```

This C++ function will take an Integer value from Visual Basic, double that
value, and return it. In this way, we'll keep the programming details to a
minimum as we see how dynamic link libraries work.

We will use Visual C++ for this example, and if you want to follow along,
we will assume that you have some familiarity with C++ programming. (This
is a book about Visual Basic, after all, and not C++.) In Visual C++, use **File |
New** to create a new text file named **DYNAM.CPP**. This new file opens in the
Visual C++ editor; add the following code to it to include the standard file
AFXWIN.H. This allows us to use the Microsoft Foundation Class library,
which is the basis of much Visual C++ programming (from **DYNAM.CPP**):

```
#include <afxwin.h>      <--
        .
        .
        .
```

Let's define the body of DLLCall() by adding this code to **DYNAM.CPP**,
where we indicate that the DLLCall() function takes a parameter named
value:

```
#include <afxwin.h>

extern "C"                                      <--
int FAR PASCAL _export DLLCall(int value)       <--
{
```

```
}            .
             .
             .
```

In 32-bit Windows programming, omit the FAR keyword and use EXPORT instead of _export:

```
#include <afxwin.h>

extern "C"                                      <--
int PASCAL EXPORT DLLCall(int value)            <--
{

}            .
             .
             .
```

In addition to defining the body of the function, we declare the function to Visual C++ in a file named **DYNAM.H**. Using **File | New**, create **DYNAM.H** in Visual C++. Next, declare DLLCall() in **DYNAM.H** by placing this code in it:

```
extern "C" {                                    <--
int FAR PASCAL _export DLLCall(int value);      <--
}                                               <--
```

In 32-bit programming, use this code:

```
extern "C" {                                    <--
int PASCAL EXPORT DLLCall(int value);           <--
}                                               <--
```

Note that we declare DLLCall() "extern," which means that it will be a public symbol and we can make it available to other programs through our **.DLL** file. Now we include **DYNAM.H** in **DYNAM.CPP** by adding this code to **DYNAM.CPP**:

```
#include <afxwin.h>
#include "dynam.h"              <--

extern "C"
int FAR PASCAL _export DLLCall(int value)
{

}            .
             .
             .
```

Next, we write the code for DLLCall(). The idea is to take an integer in the parameter we've named value, double it, and return the result. We do that in **DYNAM.CPP**:

```
#include <afxwin.h>
#include "dynam.h"

extern "C"
int FAR PASCAL _export DLLCall(int value)
{
--> return 2 * value;
}              .
               .
               .
```

In 32-bit programming, it looks like this:

```
#include <afxwin.h>
#include "dynam.h"

extern "C"
int PASCAL EXPORT DLLCall(int value)
{
--> return 2 * value;
}              .
               .
               .
```

That's it—our function is finished. However, there is more C++ to write. In Visual C++, programs are built around objects based on the CWinApp class, so we will create a class based on CWinApp. When we declare an object of that class, we will create our **.DLL** program. We call the class we create CDynamDLL by adding this code to **DYNAM.CPP**. (This class is the same in 16-bit or 32-bit programming.)

```
#include <afxwin.h>
#include "dynam.h"

extern "C"
int FAR PASCAL _export DLLCall(int value)
{
    return 2 * value;
}

class CDynamDLL : public CWinApp        <--
{                                       <--

};                                      <--
```

We will write three member functions of this class: InitInstance() (where you perform initialization of the dynamic link library), ExitInstance() (where you clean up by deallocating memory before exiting the program), and a default constructor (constructors are called to initialize C++ objects). We include these member functions so that the base class CWinApp's constructor is also called (from **DYNAM.CPP**):

435

```
#include <afxwin.h>
#include "dynam.h"

extern "C"
int FAR PASCAL _export DLLCall(int value)
{
    return 2 * value;
}

class CDynamDLL : public CWinApp
{
public:
--> virtual BOOL InitInstance();
--> virtual int ExitInstance();
--> CDynamDLL(const char* pszAppName) : CWinApp(pszAppName){}
};
```

As you can see, the program body of the default constructor is empty. All we are doing is making sure that the base class's constructor is called. In InitInstance(), we perform the standard action of setting the color for dialog boxes. Although we don't use dialog boxes here, we might add them in the future, and this is a standard action for a DLL's InitInstance() function (from **DYNAM.CPP**):

```
#include <afxwin.h>
#include "dynam.h"

extern "C"
int FAR PASCAL _export DLLCall(int value)
{
    return 2 * value;
}

class CDynamDLL : public CWinApp
{
public:
    virtual BOOL InitInstance();
    virtual int ExitInstance();

    CDynamDLL(const char* pszAppName) : CWinApp(pszAppName){}
};
```

```
BOOL CDynamDLL::InitInstance()          <--
{                                        <--
    SetDialogBkColor();                  <--
    return TRUE;                         <--
}       .                                <--
        .
        .
```

In ExitInstance(), we call CWinApp's ExitInstance() function (although we might want to deallocate memory here in programs that have allocated additional memory):

```
#include <afxwin.h>
#include "dynam.h"

extern "C"
int FAR PASCAL _export DLLCall(int value)
{
    return 2 * value;
}

class CDynamDLL : public CWinApp
{
public:
    virtual BOOL InitInstance();
    virtual int ExitInstance();

    CDynamDLL(const char* pszAppName) : CWinApp(pszAppName){}
};

BOOL CDynamDLL::InitInstance()
{
    SetDialogBkColor();
    return TRUE;
}

int CDynamDLL::ExitInstance()           <--
{                                        <--
    return CWinApp::ExitInstance();      <--
}       .                                <--
        .
        .
```

The last step is to declare an object of our new class, CDynamDLL, using the line

```
CDynamDLL NEAR dyamDLL("dynam.dll")
```

in Visual C++ 1.5. Instead, use the line

```
CDynamDLL dyamDLL("dynam.dll")
```

in Visual C++ 2 or later. (NEAR has no meaning in 32-bit programming.)

```
#include <afxwin.h>
#include "dynam.h"

extern "C"
int FAR PASCAL _export DLLCall(int value)
{
    return 2 * value;
}

class CDynamDLL : public CWinApp
{
public:
    virtual BOOL InitInstance();
    virtual int ExitInstance();

    CDynamDLL(const char* pszAppName) : CWinApp(pszAppName){}
};

BOOL CDynamDLL::InitInstance()
{
    SetDialogBkColor();
    return TRUE;
}

int CDynamDLL::ExitInstance()
{
    return CWinApp::ExitInstance();
}

CDynamDLL  NEAR dyamDLL("dynam.dll");      //Visual C++ 2+: remove NEAR   <--
```

Now our two files—**DYNAM.H** and **DYNAM.CPP**—are ready. There's still more to a Visual C++ program. The next step is to integrate these two files into a Visual C++ project.

Creating a Visual C++ 1.5 Project

Next, we create a Visual C++ project. In Visual C++ 1.5, use the **New** item in the Project menu, opening the New Project dialog box. Give our project the name DYNAM and set the Project Type box to **Windows dynamic link library (.DLL)**. Next, click **OK** to create the project. After it is created, the Project Edit dialog box comes up, letting you add **DYNAM.CPP** to the project. (**DYNAM.H** is included automatically because it is referenced in **DYNAM.CPP**.) In addition, we'll need a **.DEF** file for our project. To indicate that we're creating a Windows library file and not an **.EXE** file, we use this code in **DYNAM.DEF** for Visual C++ 1.5:

```
LIBRARY       DYNAM
DESCRIPTION   'DLL Test'

EXETYPE       WINDOWS

CODE          PRELOAD MOVEABLE DISCARDABLE
DATA          PRELOAD MOVEABLE SINGLE

HEAPSIZE      1024

SEGMENTS
    WEP_TEXT FIXED PRELOAD

EXPORTS
    WEP @1 RESIDENTNAME
```

Add **DYNAM.DEF** to the project in the Project Edit dialog box. The last thing we have to do is to indicate to Visual C++ 1.5 what kind of dynamic link library we're building. There are two kinds of Visual C++ dynamic link libraries, and they are specified by two constants: _USRDLL (standard dynamic link libraries) and _AFXDLL (dynamic link libraries that can use Microsoft Foundation Class Library objects). In this example, we'll stick to the standard _USRDLLs.

Select **Project** in Visual C++ 1.5's Options menu, opening the Project Options dialog box. Select **Compiler**, opening the C/C++ Compiler Options dialog box. Next, select **Preprocessor** in the Category box. In the Symbols and Macros to Define box, add _USRDLL. Click **OK** to close the Compiler Options dialog box, and click **OK** again in the Project Options dialog box. To create **DYNAM.DLL** in 16-bit Visual C++ 1.5, select **Build DYNAM.DLL** in the Project menu.

Creating a Visual C++ 2.0 Project

Setting up the project file **DYNAM.VBP** is a little different in 32-bit Visual C++ 2.0 or later. Here, we select **File | New** and the New dialog box opens. Select

Project in the New dialog box, opening the Project window. Select **Dynamic-Link Library** as the type of project (in the Project Type box). Give the project the name DYNAM and click **Create**.

After the project has been created, the Project Files dialog box comes up, letting you add **DYNAM.CPP** to the project. In addition, we'll need a **.DEF** file for our Visual C++ 2.0 or later project, and a **.DEF** file for such a project looks different from the ones for Visual C++ 1.5. Here, **DYNAM.DEF** looks like this:

```
LIBRARY     DYNAM

CODE        PRELOAD MOVEABLE DISCARDABLE
DATA        PRELOAD SINGLE

EXPORTS
    DLLCall             @2
```

Add **DYNAM.DEF** to the project. The project window opens in Visual C++, indicating that both **DYNAM.CPP** and **DYNAM.DEF** are member files of our project. Finally, use Visual C++ 2.0 or later to build **DYNAM.DLL** with the Project menu's **Build DYNAM.DLL** menu item.

At this point, we've created **DYNAM.DLL**, and it includes our function DLLCall(). Copy this dynamic link library file to **C:\WINDOWS\SYSTEM** = so that our Visual Basic programs can find it. The 16-bit version of **DYNAM.CPP** appears in Listing 9.7, **DYNAM.DEF** is in Listing 9.8, **DYNAM.H** is in Listing 9.9, and **DYNAM.MAK** is in Listing 9.10. For 32-bit Windows, **DYNAM32.CPP** appears in Listing 9.11, **DYNAM32.DEF** is in Listing 9.12, **DYNAM32.H** is in Listing 9.13, and **DYNAM32.MAK** is in Listing 9.14.

LISTING 9.7 DYNAM.CPP

```cpp
#include <afxwin.h>
#include "dynam.h"

extern "C"
int FAR PASCAL _export DLLCall(int value)
{
    return 2 * value;
}

class CDynamDLL : public CWinApp
{
public:
    virtual BOOL InitInstance();
    virtual int ExitInstance();
```

```
    CDynamDLL(const char* pszAppName) : CWinApp(pszAppName){}
};

BOOL CDynamDLL::InitInstance()
{
    SetDialogBkColor();
    return TRUE;
}

int CDynamDLL::ExitInstance()
{
    return CWinApp::ExitInstance();
}

CDynamDLL   NEAR dyamDLL("dynam.dll");
```

LISTING 9.8 DYNAM.DEF

```
LIBRARY        DYNAM
DESCRIPTION    'DLL Test'

EXETYPE        WINDOWS

CODE           PRELOAD MOVEABLE DISCARDABLE
DATA           PRELOAD MOVEABLE SINGLE

HEAPSIZE       1024

SEGMENTS
    WEP_TEXT FIXED PRELOAD

EXPORTS
    WEP @1 RESIDENTNAME
```

LISTING 9.9 DYNAM.H

```
extern "C" {

int FAR PASCAL DLLCall(int value);

}
```

LISTING 9.10 DYNAM.MAK

```
# Microsoft Visual C++ generated build script - Do not modify

PROJ = DYNAM
DEBUG = 1
PROGTYPE = 1
CALLER =
```

```
ARGS =
DLLS =
D_RCDEFINES = -d_DEBUG
R_RCDEFINES = -dNDEBUG
ORIGIN = MSVC
ORIGIN_VER = 1.00
PROJPATH = C:\VBOOK\TIMES2\
USEMFC = 1
CC = cl
CPP = cl
CXX = cl
CCREATEPCHFLAG =
CPPCREATEPCHFLAG =
CUSEPCHFLAG =
CPPUSEPCHFLAG =
FIRSTC =
FIRSTCPP = DYNAM.CPP
RC = rc
CFLAGS_D_WDLL = /nologo /G2 /W3 /Zi /ALw /Od /D "_DEBUG" /D "_USRDLL"
        /FR /GD /GEf /Fd"DYNAM.PDB"
CFLAGS_R_WDLL = /nologo /W3 /ALw /O1 /D "NDEBUG" /D "_USRDLL" /FR /GD
LFLAGS_D_WDLL = /NOLOGO /ONERROR:NOEXE /NOD /PACKC:61440 /CO /NOE
        /ALIGN:16 /MAP:FULL
LFLAGS_R_WDLL = /NOLOGO /ONERROR:NOEXE /NOD /PACKC:61440 /NOE
        /ALIGN:16 /MAP:FULL
LIBS_D_WDLL = lafxdwd oldnames libw commdlg shell olecli olesvr ldllcew
LIBS_R_WDLL = lafxdw oldnames libw commdlg shell olecli olesvr ldllcew
RCFLAGS = /nologo
RESFLAGS = /nologo
RUNFLAGS =
DEFFILE = DYNAM.DEF
OBJS_EXT =
LIBS_EXT =
!if "$(DEBUG)" == "1"
CFLAGS = $(CFLAGS_D_WDLL)
LFLAGS = $(LFLAGS_D_WDLL)
LIBS = $(LIBS_D_WDLL)
MAPFILE = nul
RCDEFINES = $(D_RCDEFINES)
!else
CFLAGS = $(CFLAGS_R_WDLL)
LFLAGS = $(LFLAGS_R_WDLL)
LIBS = $(LIBS_R_WDLL)
MAPFILE = nul
RCDEFINES = $(R_RCDEFINES)
!endif
!if [if exist MSVC.BND del MSVC.BND]
!endif
SBRS = DYNAM.SBR


DYNAM_DEP = c:\vbook\times2\dynam.h
```

```
all:    $(PROJ).DLL $(PROJ).BSC

DYNAM.OBJ:     DYNAM.CPP $(DYNAM_DEP)
    $(CPP) $(CFLAGS) $(CPPCREATEPCHFLAG) /c DYNAM.CPP


$(PROJ).DLL::    DYNAM.OBJ $(OBJS_EXT) $(DEFFILE)
    echo >NUL @<<$(PROJ).CRF
DYNAM.OBJ +
$(OBJS_EXT)
$(PROJ).DLL
$(MAPFILE)
d:\msvc\lib\+
d:\msvc\mfc\lib\+
c:\msvc\lib\+
c:\msvc\mfc\lib\+
c:\msvc\ole2\samples\lib\+
$(LIBS)
$(DEFFILE);
<<
    link $(LFLAGS) @$(PROJ).CRF
    $(RC) $(RESFLAGS) $@
    implib /nowep $(PROJ).LIB $(PROJ).DLL


run: $(PROJ).DLL
    $(PROJ) $(RUNFLAGS)


$(PROJ).BSC: $(SBRS)
    bscmake @<<
/o$@ $(SBRS)
<<
```

LISTING 9.11 DYNAM32.CPP

```cpp
// dynam.cpp

#include <afxwin.h>
#include "dynam.h"

extern "C"
int PASCAL EXPORT DLLCall(int value)
{
    return 2*value;
}

class CDynamDLL : public CWinApp
{
public:
```

```
    virtual BOOL InitInstance();
    virtual int ExitInstance();

    CDynamDLL(LPCTSTR pszAppName) : CWinApp(pszAppName){}
};

BOOL CDynamDLL::InitInstance()
{
    SetDialogBkColor();
    return TRUE;
}

int CDynamDLL::ExitInstance()
{
    return CWinApp::ExitInstance();
}

CDynamDLL dyamDLL("dynam.dll");
```

LISTING 9.12 DYNAM32.DEF

```
LIBRARY        DYNAM

CODE           PRELOAD MOVEABLE DISCARDABLE
DATA           PRELOAD SINGLE

EXPORTS
    DLLCall              @2
```

LISTING 9.13 DYNAM32.H

```
extern "C" {

int PASCAL EXPORT DLLCall(int value);

}
```

LISTING 9.14 DYNAM32.MAK

```
# Microsoft Visual C++ Generated NMAKE File, Format Version 2.00
# ** DO NOT EDIT **

# TARGTYPE "Win32 (x86) Dynamic-Link Library" 0x0102

!IF "$(CFG)" == ""
CFG=Win32 Debug
!MESSAGE No configuration specified.  Defaulting to Win32 Debug.
!ENDIF
```

```
!IF "$(CFG)" != "Win32 Release" && "$(CFG)" != "Win32 Debug"
!MESSAGE Invalid configuration "$(CFG)" specified.
!MESSAGE You can specify a configuration when running NMAKE on this make-
file
!MESSAGE by defining the macro CFG on the command line.  For example:
!MESSAGE
!MESSAGE NMAKE /f "dynam.mak" CFG="Win32 Debug"
!MESSAGE
!MESSAGE Possible choices for configuration are:
!MESSAGE
!MESSAGE "Win32 Release" (based on "Win32 (x86) Dynamic-Link Library")
!MESSAGE "Win32 Debug" (based on "Win32 (x86) Dynamic-Link Library")
!MESSAGE
!ERROR An invalid configuration is specified.
!ENDIF

################################################################################
#####
# Begin Project
# PROP Target_Last_Scanned "Win32 Debug"
MTL=MkTypLib.exe
CPP=cl.exe
RSC=rc.exe


!IF  "$(CFG)" == "Win32 Release"

# PROP BASE Use_MFC 2
# PROP BASE Use_Debug_Libraries 0
# PROP BASE Output_Dir "WinRel"
# PROP BASE Intermediate_Dir "WinRel"
# PROP Use_MFC 2
# PROP Use_Debug_Libraries 0
# PROP Output_Dir ""
# PROP Intermediate_Dir "WinRel"
OUTDIR=.
INTDIR=.\WinRel

ALL : $(OUTDIR)/dynam.dll $(OUTDIR)/dynam.bsc

$(INTDIR) :
    if not exist $(INTDIR)/nul mkdir $(INTDIR)

# ADD BASE MTL /nologo /D "NDEBUG" /win32
# ADD MTL /nologo /D "NDEBUG" /win32
MTL_PROJ=/nologo /D "NDEBUG" /win32
# ADD BASE CPP /nologo /MD /W3 /GX /YX /O2 /D "WIN32" /D "NDEBUG" /D
        "_WINDOWS" /D "_AFXDLL" /D "_MBCS" /FR /c
# ADD CPP /nologo /MD /W3 /GX /YX /O2 /D "WIN32" /D "NDEBUG" /D
        "_WINDOWS" /D "_AFXDLL" /D "_MBCS" /FR /c
CPP_PROJ=/nologo /MD /W3 /GX /YX /O2 /D "WIN32" /D "NDEBUG" /D "_WINDOWS"
/D\
```

```
 "_AFXDLL" /D "_MBCS" /FR$(INTDIR)/ /Fp$(OUTDIR)/"dynam.pch" /Fo$(INT-
DIR)/ /c
CPP_OBJS=.\WinRel/
# ADD BASE RSC /l 0x409 /d "NDEBUG" /d "_AFXDLL"
# ADD RSC /l 0x409 /d "NDEBUG" /d "_AFXDLL"
BSC32=bscmake.exe
# ADD BASE BSC32 /nologo
# ADD BSC32 /nologo
BSC32_FLAGS=/nologo /o$(OUTDIR)/"dynam.bsc"
BSC32_SBRS= \
        $(INTDIR)/DYNAM.SBR

$(OUTDIR)/dynam.bsc : $(OUTDIR)  $(BSC32_SBRS)
    $(BSC32) @<<
  $(BSC32_FLAGS) $(BSC32_SBRS)
<<


LINK32=link.exe
# ADD BASE LINK32 /NOLOGO /SUBSYSTEM:windows /DLL /MACHINE:I386
# ADD LINK32 /NOLOGO /SUBSYSTEM:windows /DLL /MACHINE:I386
LINK32_FLAGS=/NOLOGO /SUBSYSTEM:windows /DLL /INCREMENTAL:no\
 /PDB:$(OUTDIR)/"dynam.pdb" /MACHINE:I386 /DEF:".\dynam.def"\
 /OUT:$(OUTDIR)/"dynam.dll" /IMPLIB:$(OUTDIR)/"dynam.lib"
DEF_FILE=.\dynam.def
LINK32_OBJS= \
        $(INTDIR)/DYNAM.OBJ

$(OUTDIR)/dynam.dll : $(OUTDIR)  $(DEF_FILE) $(LINK32_OBJS)
    $(LINK32) @<<
  $(LINK32_FLAGS) $(LINK32_OBJS)
<<


!ELSEIF  "$(CFG)" == "Win32 Debug"

# PROP BASE Use_MFC 2
# PROP BASE Use_Debug_Libraries 1
# PROP BASE Output_Dir "WinDebug"
# PROP BASE Intermediate_Dir "WinDebug"
# PROP Use_MFC 2
# PROP Use_Debug_Libraries 1
# PROP Output_Dir ""
# PROP Intermediate_Dir "WinDebug"
OUTDIR=.
INTDIR=.\WinDebug

ALL : $(OUTDIR)/dynam.dll $(OUTDIR)/dynam.bsc

$(INTDIR) :
    if not exist $(INTDIR)/nul mkdir $(INTDIR)

# ADD BASE MTL /nologo /D "_DEBUG" /win32
```

```
# ADD MTL /nologo /D "_DEBUG" /win32
MTL_PROJ=/nologo /D "_DEBUG" /win32
# ADD BASE CPP /nologo /MD /W3 /GX /Zi /YX /Od /D "WIN32" /D "_DEBUG"
        /D "_WINDOWS" /D "_AFXDLL" /D "_MBCS" /FR /c
# ADD CPP /nologo /MD /W3 /GX /Zi /YX /Od /D "WIN32" /D "_DEBUG" /D
        "_WINDOWS" /D "_AFXDLL" /D "_MBCS" /FR /c
CPP_PROJ=/nologo /MD /W3 /GX /Zi /YX /Od /D "WIN32" /D "_DEBUG" /D "_WIN-
DOWS"\
 /D "_AFXDLL" /D "_MBCS" /FR$(INTDIR)/ /Fp$(OUTDIR)/"dynam.pch" /Fo$(INT-
DIR)/\
 /Fd$(OUTDIR)/"dynam.pdb" /c
CPP_OBJS=.\WinDebug/
# ADD BASE RSC /l 0x409 /d "_DEBUG" /d "_AFXDLL"
# ADD RSC /l 0x409 /d "_DEBUG" /d "_AFXDLL"
BSC32=bscmake.exe
# ADD BASE BSC32 /nologo
# ADD BSC32 /nologo
BSC32_FLAGS=/nologo /o$(OUTDIR)/"dynam.bsc"
BSC32_SBRS= \
        $(INTDIR)/DYNAM.SBR

$(OUTDIR)/dynam.bsc : $(OUTDIR)   $(BSC32_SBRS)
    $(BSC32) @<<
  $(BSC32_FLAGS) $(BSC32_SBRS)
<<

LINK32=link.exe
# ADD BASE LINK32 /NOLOGO /SUBSYSTEM:windows /DLL /DEBUG /MACHINE:I386
# ADD LINK32 /NOLOGO /SUBSYSTEM:windows /DLL /DEBUG /MACHINE:I386
LINK32_FLAGS=/NOLOGO /SUBSYSTEM:windows /DLL /INCREMENTAL:yes\
 /PDB:$(OUTDIR)/"dynam.pdb" /DEBUG /MACHINE:I386 /DEF:".\dynam.def"\
 /OUT:$(OUTDIR)/"dynam.dll" /IMPLIB:$(OUTDIR)/"dynam.lib"
DEF_FILE=.\dynam.def
LINK32_OBJS= \
        $(INTDIR)/DYNAM.OBJ

$(OUTDIR)/dynam.dll : $(OUTDIR)   $(DEF_FILE) $(LINK32_OBJS)
    $(LINK32) @<<
  $(LINK32_FLAGS) $(LINK32_OBJS)
<<

!ENDIF

.c{$(CPP_OBJS)}.obj:
   $(CPP) $(CPP_PROJ) $<

.cpp{$(CPP_OBJS)}.obj:
   $(CPP) $(CPP_PROJ) $<

.cxx{$(CPP_OBJS)}.obj:
   $(CPP) $(CPP_PROJ) $<

############################################################################
####
```

```
# Begin Group "Source Files"

################################################################################
#####
# Begin Source File

SOURCE=.\DYNAM.CPP
DEP_DYNAM=\
        .\DYNAM.H


$(INTDIR)/DYNAM.OBJ :   $(SOURCE)   $(DEP_DYNAM) $(INTDIR)

# End Source File
################################################################################
#####
# Begin Source File

SOURCE=.\dynam.def
# End Source File
# End Group
# End Project
################################################################################
#####
```

The TIMES2 Visual Basic Dynamic Link Library Connection

The next step is to make use of the C++ code we've placed in **DYNAM.DLL** from a Visual Basic program. In the Visual Basic program, we will send an integer to the DLLCall() function and get it back doubled.

We can call our DLLCall() function when the user clicks a button in a Visual Basic program we'll call TIMES2. The idea is that when the program starts, we will have a text box with an original value in it—say, 1.

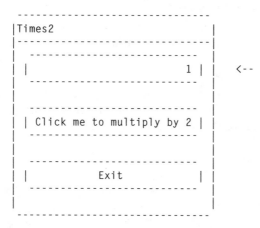

When the user clicks the button **Click Me To Multiply By 2**, we can pass the value in the text box to our DLL function DLLCall(), get the return value, and display that return value in the text box:

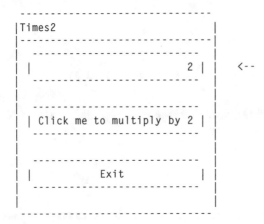

Start Visual Basic and name the Visual Basic project **TIMES2.VBP**. Using **Insert | Module**, insert a new module—**DYNAM.BAS**—in TIMES2 so that we can declare our **DYNAM.DLL** dynamic link library file. Add the following code to **DYNAM.BAS**. (We are already familiar with these kinds of declarations from our work in the first half of this chapter.)

```
Declare Function DLLCall Lib "dynam.dll" (ByVal TheVar As Integer) As
        Integer
```

Now give Form1 the caption **Dynamic Link Library Connection** by setting its Caption property in the properties window, and add two buttons and a text box to Form1, as shown in Figure 9.2.

Give the first command button, Command1, the caption **Click Me To Multiply By 2**, clear the text from the text box, and give the other button the caption **Exit**, as shown in Figure 9.2. Now double-click the default form, Form1, opening the code window.

First, place the usual code in the **Exit** button's click handler, Command2_Click() (open it from the Proc box in the code window), to terminate the program (from **TIMES2.FRM**):

```
Private Sub Command2_Click()
    End         <--
End Sub
```

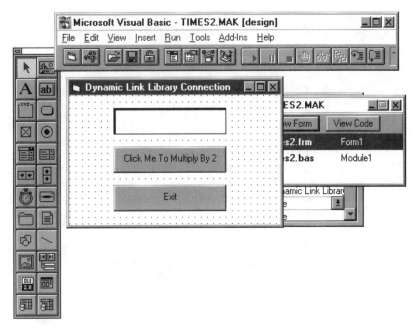

FIGURE 9.2 WE DESIGN OUR DYNAMIC LINK LIBRARY INTERFACE PROGRAM.

Now we place the text "1" into the text box when the program loads. Double-click the form to open the Form_Load() event and add this code to it (from **TIMES2.FRM**):

```
Private Sub Command2_Click()
    End
End Sub

Private Sub Form_Load()
    Text1.Text = "1"              <--
End Sub
```

When the user clicks the **Command1** button, we want to convert the text in the text box to an integer using the Visual Basic function Val(). Then we'll pass it to DLLCall(), get the resulting integer back, convert the result into text (using the Visual Basic function Str()), and display that result in the text box, Text1. We can do all that in one line in Command1_Click() (from **TIMES2.FRM**):

```
Private Sub Command2_Click()
    End
```

```
End Sub

Private Sub Form_Load()
    Text1.Text = "1"
End Sub

Private Sub Command1_Click()
    Text1.Text = Str(DLLCall(Val(Text1.Text)))          <--
End Sub
```

Now run the program. At first, the program appears with the default value, 1, in the text box, as shown in Figure 9.3. When you click the button, that value is passed to our DLL function DLLCall(), the value is doubled, and the new result is displayed, as in Figure 9.4. TIMES2 is a success, and so is our customized DLL file, **DYNAM.DLL**. In this way, we've been able to connect Visual Basic and Visual C++.

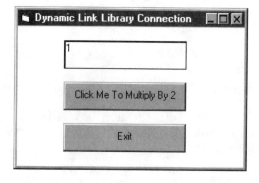

FIGURE 9.3 THE TIMES2 PROGRAM INITIALLY DISPLAYS A VALUE OF 1.

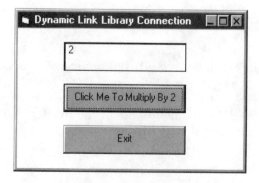

FIGURE 9.4 CLICKING THE BUTTON PASSES THE TIMES2 VALUE TO
OUR CUSTOM DYNAMIC LINK LIBRARY, DOUBLING THE VALUE.

TIMES2.FRM appears in Listing 9.15, TIMES2.BAS is in Listing 9.16, and TIMES2.VBP is in Listing 9.17.

LISTING 9.15 TIMES2.FRM

```
VERSION 4.00
Begin VB.Form Form1
    Caption         =   "Dynamic Link Library Connection"
    ClientHeight    =   2430
    ClientLeft      =   1380
    ClientTop       =   1995
    ClientWidth     =   4050
    BeginProperty Font
        name            =   "MS Sans Serif"
        charset         =   1
        weight          =   400
        size            =   8.25
        underline       =   0   'False
        italic          =   0   'False
        strikethrough   =   0   'False
    EndProperty
    Height          =   2835
    Left            =   1320
    LinkTopic       =   "Form1"
    ScaleHeight     =   2430
    ScaleWidth      =   4050
    Top             =   1650
    Width           =   4170
    Begin VB.CommandButton Command2
        Caption         =   "Exit"
        Height          =   495
        Left            =   840
        TabIndex        =   2
        Top             =   1680
        Width           =   2175
    End
    Begin VB.CommandButton Command1
        Caption         =   "Click Me To Multiply By 2"
        Height          =   495
        Left            =   840
        TabIndex        =   1
        Top             =   960
        Width           =   2175
    End
    Begin VB.TextBox Text1
        Height          =   495
        Left            =   840
        TabIndex        =   0
        Top             =   240
        Width           =   2175
    End
End
```

```
Attribute VB_Name = "Form1"
Attribute VB_Creatable = False
Attribute VB_Exposed = False

Private Sub Command1_Click()
    Text1.Text = Str(DLLCall(Val(Text1.Text)))
End Sub

Private Sub Command2_Click()
    End
End Sub

Private Sub Form_Load()
    Text1.Text = "1"
End Sub
```

LISTING 9.16 TIMES2.BAS

```
Attribute VB_Name = "Module1"
Declare Function DLLCall Lib "dynam.dll" (ByVal TheVar As Integer) As
        Integer
```

LISTING 9.17 TIMES2.VBP

```
times2.frm
times2.bas
Object={F9043C88-F6F2-101A-A3C9-08002B2F49FB}#1.0#0; COMDLG16.OCX
Object={FAEEE763-117E-101B-8933-08002B2F4F5A}#1.0#0; DBLIST16.OCX
ProjWinSize=148,427,205,115
ProjWinShow=2
IconForm="Form1"
ExeName="Project1.exe"
Path="D:\VB"
Command=""
Name="Project1"
HelpContextID="0"
StartMode=0
VersionCompatible="0"
MajorVer=1
MinorVer=0
RevisionVer=0
AutoIncrementVer=0
VersionCompanyName=" "
Reference=*\G{00025E01-0000-0000-C000-
        000000000046}#0.0#0#DAO2516.DLL#Microsoft DAO 2.5 Object
        Library
```

That completes our interface to Windows and Visual C++. As you can see, we've improved our advanced Visual Basic arsenal considerably with these techniques. In the next chapter, we'll examine two other popular topics: how to create a SETUP program and how to create Windows help files for your programs.

CHAPTER 10

CREATING WINDOWS HELP FILES AND SETUP PROGRAMS

To add more power to our Visual Basic programs, there are still two topics we should cover: creating Windows Help files and letting users install our application with a SETUP program. Windows help, which pops up when the user selects a Help menu, adds an air of professionalism to your program. Our users can benefit from our customized help just as with any other Windows program. In addition, having users install your program with a SETUP command can be useful, because SETUP creates and installs files in the appropriate directories. And, like Windows help, SETUP will give our program the feeling of a polished application. Both of these popular features are significant assets to any program. Let's dig first into customizing Windows help.

CREATING CUSTOMIZED WINDOWS HELP

To see how to add Windows help to a program, we will add it to our Visual Basic WRITER program. We begin by adding a Help menu to the menu bar of our WRITER project:

```
                            |
                            |
                            V
    -------------------------------------------------------
    |File Window Edit Help                                |
    -------------------------------------------------------|
    |  -------------    ---------                          |
    || New Document|  |  Close  |                          |
    |  -------------    ---------                          |
    |-----------------------------------------------------|
    |   --------------------------------                   |
    |  |Writer Document 1              |                   |
    |  |-------------------------------|                   |
    |  | |                           | |                   |
    |  | |                           | |                   |
    |  | |                           | |                   |
    |  | |                           | |                   |
    |  |  -----------------------------                    |
    |  -------------------------------------------------|  |
    |                                                      |
    -------------------------------------------------------
```

When the user clicks this menu, we launch Windows help, displaying our own help information. Windows provides the help program, and we provide the help data it displays:

```
    ---------------------------------------------------------
    |Writer Help                                            |
    |-------------------------------------------------------|
    |File Edit Bookmark Options Help                        |
    |-------------------------------------------------------|
    | --------   -------   -------   --------                |
    ||Contents| | Search| | Back  | | Print  |              |
    | --------   -------   -------   --------                |
    |-------------------------------------------------------|
    |   CONTENTS                                            |
    |                                                       |
    |   Welcome to Help for the Writer program. This        |
    |   help file gives you help on the menu items in       |
    |   Writer. To see help for the menu you are interested |
    |   in, click the matching topic below:                 |
    |                                                       |
    |                                                       |
    |   File Menu Items                                     |
    |   ---------------                                     |
    |                                                       |
    |   Edit Menu Items                                     |
    |   ---------------                                     |
    ---------------------------------------------------------
```

Here, we offer the user help on the File menu and the Edit menu. If the user clicks the (underlined) **File Menu Items** entry, for example, we will switch to that help topic. Then we ask the user to select from among several File menu items:

```
 ---------------------------------------------------------
|Writer Help                                              |
|--------------------------------------------------------|
|File Edit Bookmark Options Help                          |
|--------------------------------------------------------|
|  --------   -------   -------   --------                |
||Contents| | Search| | Back  | | Print  |               |
|  --------   -------   -------   --------                |
|--------------------------------------------------------|
|   Writer: File Menu Items                               |
|                                                         |
|   Select the individual item you want to get help on:   |
|                                                         |
|                                                         |
|   New Document                                          |
|   ------------                                          |
|   Open...                                               |
|   -------                                               |
|   Save As...                                            |
|   ----------                                            |
 ---------------------------------------------------------
```

If the user selects, say, **Open**, we jump to that topic, displaying the requested help:

```
 ---------------------------------------------------------
|Writer Help                                              |
|--------------------------------------------------------|
|File Edit Bookmark Options Help                          |
|--------------------------------------------------------|
|  --------   -------   -------   --------                |
||Contents| | Search| | Back  | | Print  |               |
|  --------   -------   -------   --------                |
|--------------------------------------------------------|
|   Open...                                               |
|                                                         |
|                                                         |
|   Opens a file.                                         |
|            - - -                                        |
|                                                         |
|                                                         |
 ---------------------------------------------------------
```

Note that the word *file* is underlined with a dashed underline. This means that when the user presses the mouse button on this word, an explanation (which we will have placed in our help file) will immediately appear in a box, called a help pop-up:

```
 -----------------------------------------------------------
|Writer Help                                                |
|-----------------------------------------------------------|
|File Edit Bookmark Options Help                            |
|-----------------------------------------------------------|
| --------   -------   -------   --------                    |
||Contents| | Search| | Back | | Print  |                   |
| --------   -------   -------   --------                    |
|-----------------------------------------------------------|
|  Open...                                                  |
|                                                           |
|                                                           |
|  Opens a file.                                            |
|          -----------------------------------              |
|         |A file is the same as a document. |             |
|          -----------------------------------              |
|                                                           |
|                                                           |
 -----------------------------------------------------------
```

That's how our help file will look for the Writer program. Let's put it to work.

POPPING UP WINDOWS HELP

We start by adding the Help menu to WRITER. Open the WRITER project in Visual Basic and use the Menu Editor to add that menu to the end of the menu bar. Next, open the click event associated with that menu. We display Writer help when the user clicks the Help menu (from **WRITER.FRM**):

```
Private Sub Help_Click()

End Sub
```

We will use the Windows routine WinHelp() to place our help file on the screen. The help file will have the name **WRITER.HLP**, and the call to WinHelp() looks like this:

```
Private Sub Help_Click()
--> retVal = WinHelp(Form1.hWnd, "c:\vbook\writer\writer.hlp",
        HELP_INDEX, CLng(0))
End Sub
```

459

Here, we pass the Windows handle of our window, Form1.hWnd (this handle is stored in the hWnd property of Form1), the name and path of the Windows help file, which we will name **C:\VBOOK\WRITER\WRITER.HLP**. (Use the path and drive appropriate to your system.) The other parameters indicate that we want to open the help file to the main help screen.

WinHelp() is a Windows routine, so, as we saw in the last chapter, we need to place its declaration in WRITER's module, **MODULE1.BAS**. To do that, we open the module and place this declaration there for 16-Bit windows.

```
Declare Function WinHelp Lib "User" (ByVal hWnd As Integer, ByVal
lpHelpFile As String, ByVal wCommand As Integer, dwData As Any) As Integer
```

Make sure that this code is placed at the beginning of the module (where declarations must go in Visual Basic).

The following code is the 32-bit version of this call looks like this (Use this declaration if you are using 32-Bit Visual Basic):

```
'Declare Function WinHelp Lib "User32" Alias "WinHelpA" (ByVal hWnd As Long,
ByVal lpHelpFile As String, ByVal wCommand As Long, dwData As Long) As Long
```

When the user clicks **Help**, we call WinHelp() and let Windows help take over, displaying the data in the file **WRITER.HLP**. The next step is to create **WRITER.HLP**.

The new version of **WRITER.FRM** appears in Listing 10.1, **MODULE1.BAS** is in Listing 10.2, **MDIFORM1.FRM** is in Listing 10.3, and **WRITER.MAK** is in Listing 10.4.

LISTING 10.1 WRITER.FRM

```
VERSION 4.00
Begin VB.Form Form1
    Caption         =    "Writer Document"
    ClientHeight    =    2445
    ClientLeft      =    1695
    ClientTop       =    2055
    ClientWidth     =    5475
    Height          =    3135
```

```
   Left            =    1635
   LinkTopic       =    "Form1"
   MDIChild        =    -1   'True
   ScaleHeight     =    2445
   ScaleWidth      =    5475
   Top             =    1425
   Width           =    5595
   Begin VB.TextBox Text1
      Height       =    1935
      Left         =    0
      MultiLine    =    -1   'True
      ScrollBars   =    2    'Vertical
      TabIndex     =    0
      Top          =    0
      Width        =    5055
   End
   Begin MSComDlg.CommonDialog CommonDialog1
      Left         =    3240
      Top          =    1920
      _version     =    65536
      _extentx     =    847
      _extenty     =    847
      _stockprops  =    0
   End
   Begin VB.Menu File
      Caption      =    "File"
      Begin VB.Menu New
         Caption          =    "New Document"
      End
      Begin VB.Menu Save
         Caption          =    "Save As..."
      End
      Begin VB.Menu Read
         Caption          =    "Open..."
      End
      Begin VB.Menu Font
         Caption          =    "Font..."
      End
      Begin VB.Menu Color
         Caption          =    "Color..."
      End
      Begin VB.Menu Print
         Caption          =    "Print..."
      End
      Begin VB.Menu Exit
         Caption          =    "Exit"
      End
   End
   Begin VB.Menu Window
      Caption      =    "Window"
```

```
        WindowList      =    -1   'True
     End
     Begin VB.Menu Edit
        Caption         =    "Edit"
        Begin VB.Menu Cut
           Caption      =     "Cut"
        End
     End
     Begin VB.Menu Help
        Caption         =    "Help"
     End
End
Attribute VB_Name = "Form1"
Attribute VB_Creatable = False
Attribute VB_Exposed = False
Dim MyDocumentNumber As Integer

Private Sub Color_Click()
    CommonDialog1.Color = Text1.ForeColor
    CommonDialog1.ShowColor
    Text1.ForeColor = CommonDialog1.Color
End Sub


Private Sub Exit_Click()
    End
End Sub

Private Sub Font_Click()
    CommonDialog1.FontName = Text1.FontName
    CommonDialog1.Color = Text1.ForeColor
    CommonDialog1.FontItalic = Text1.FontItalic
    CommonDialog1.FontStrikethru = Text1.FontStrikethru
    CommonDialog1.FontSize = Text1.FontSize
    CommonDialog1.FontUnderline = Text1.FontUnderline
    CommonDialog1.Flags = vbCFBoth
    CommonDialog1.ShowFont
    Text1.FontName = CommonDialog1.FontName
    Text1.FontSize = CommonDialog1.FontSize
End Sub

Private Sub Form_Load()
    MyDocumentNumber = NumberDocuments
    Text1.Height = Form1.ScaleHeight
    Text1.Width = Form1.ScaleWidth
    Caption = "Writer Document " + Str$(MyDocumentNumber)
    If NumberDocuments = 1 Then AttachWindow Me
End Sub

Private Sub Form_Resize()
    Text1.Height = Form1.ScaleHeight
```

```
    Text1.Width = Form1.ScaleWidth
End Sub

Private Sub Help_Click()
    retVal = WinHelp(Form1.hWnd, "c:\vbook\writer\writer.hlp",
        HELP_INDEX, CLng(0))
End Sub

Private Sub New_Click()
    AddADocument
End Sub

Private Sub Print_Click()
    CommonDialog1.ShowPrinter
    NumberCopies% = CommonDialog1.Copies
    For loop_index% = 1 To NumberCopies%
        Printer.Print Text1.Text
        Printer.EndDoc
    Next loop_index%
End Sub

Private Sub Read_Click()
    On Error GoTo OpenError
1   CommonDialog1.FileName = "*.*"
    CommonDialog1.CancelError = True
    CommonDialog1.ShowOpen
    Open CommonDialog1.FileName For Input As #1
    Text1.Text = Input$(LOF(1), #1)
    Close #1
    Exit Sub
OpenError:
    If Err = vbCDErrCancel Then Exit Sub
    ErrMsg$ = Error$(Err) + ". Try again?"
    'ErrMsg$ = Err.Source + " Try again?"
    Select Case Err
    Case 55
        ErrMsg$ = "File is already open. Try Again?"
    Case 57, 68, 71
        ErrMsg$ = "Check the disk. Try again?"
    End Select
    If MsgBox(ErrMsg$, 49, "Writer") = 1 Then
        Resume 1
    End If
    'MsgBox Error$(Err), 48, "Writer"
    'MsgBox "Open Error" + Str$(Err) + " in line " + Str$(Erl), 48, "Writer"
End Sub

Private Sub Save_Click()
    CommonDialog1.DefaultExt = ".txt"
```

```
        CommonDialog1.Filter = "*.txt"
        CommonDialog1.ShowSave
        Open CommonDialog1.FileName For Output As #1
        Print #1, Text1.Text
        MsgBox ("Saved")
        Close #1
    End Sub
```

LISTING 10.2 (WRITER) MODULE1.BAS

```
Attribute VB_Name = "Module1"
'   Help engine declarations.

'   Commands to pass WinHelp()
Global Const HELP_CONTEXT = &H1      ' Display topic identified by number
in Data
Global Const HELP_QUIT = &H2         ' Terminate help
Global Const HELP_INDEX = &H3        ' Display index
Global Const HELP_HELPONHELP = &H4   ' Display help on using help
Global Const HELP_SETINDEX = &H5     ' Set an alternate Index for help
file with more than one index
Global Const HELP_KEY = &H101        ' Display topic for keyword in Data
Global Const HELP_MULTIKEY = &H201   ' Lookup keyword in alternate table
and display topic

Declare Function WinHelp Lib "User" (ByVal hWnd As Integer, ByVal
lpHelpFile As String, ByVal wCommand As Integer, dwData As Any) As
Integer

Type MULTIKEYHELP
    mkSize As Integer
    mkKeylist As String * 1
    szKeyphrase As String * 253
End Type


Public NumberDocuments As Integer
Dim Documents(10) As Form

Public Sub AddADocument()
    NumberDocuments = NumberDocuments + 1
    Set Documents(NumberDocuments) = New Form1
    Documents(NumberDocuments).Show
End Sub

Public Sub AttachWindow(TheForm As Form)
    Set Documents(NumberDocuments) = TheForm
End Sub
```

LISTING 10.3 MDIFORM1.FRM

```
VERSION 4.00
Begin VB.MDIForm MDIForm1
    BackColor       =   &H8000000C&
    Caption         =   "Writer"
    ClientHeight    =   2580
    ClientLeft      =   1260
    ClientTop       =   1830
    ClientWidth     =   6495
    Height          =   3270
    Left            =   1200
    LinkTopic       =   "MDIForm1"
    Top             =   1200
    Width           =   6615
    Begin VB.PictureBox Picture2
        Align           =   2   'Align Bottom
        BeginProperty Font
            name            =   "MS Sans Serif"
            charset         =   1
            weight          =   400
            size            =   8.25
            underline       =   0   'False
            italic          =   0   'False
            strikethrough   =   0   'False
        EndProperty
        Height          =   495
        Left            =   0
        ScaleHeight     =   465
        ScaleWidth      =   6465
        TabIndex        =   3
        Top             =   2085
        Width           =   6495
    End
    Begin VB.PictureBox Picture1
        Align           =   1   'Align Top
        BeginProperty Font
            name            =   "MS Sans Serif"
            charset         =   1
            weight          =   400
            size            =   8.25
            underline       =   0   'False
            italic          =   0   'False
            strikethrough   =   0   'False
        EndProperty
        Height          =   375
        Left            =   0
        ScaleHeight     =   345
        ScaleWidth      =   6465
        TabIndex        =   0
```

```
            Top             =     0
            Width           =     6495
            Begin VB.CommandButton Command2
                Caption         =     "Close"
                BeginProperty Font
                    name            =     "MS Sans Serif"
                    charset         =     1
                    weight          =     400
                    size            =     8.25
                    underline       =     0     'False
                    italic          =     0     'False
                    strikethrough   =     0     'False
                EndProperty
                Height          =     375
                Left            =     1440
                TabIndex        =     2
                Top             =     0
                Width           =     1215
            End
            Begin VB.CommandButton Command1
                Caption         =     "New Document"
                BeginProperty Font
                    name            =     "MS Sans Serif"
                    charset         =     1
                    weight          =     400
                    size            =     8.25
                    underline       =     0     'False
                    italic          =     0     'False
                    strikethrough   =     0     'False
                EndProperty
                Height          =     375
                Left            =     0
                TabIndex        =     1
                Top             =     0
                Width           =     1335
            End
        End
        Begin VB.Menu File
            Caption         =     "File"
            Begin VB.Menu New
                Caption         =     "New Document"
            End
            Begin VB.Menu Exit
                Caption         =     "Exit"
            End
        End
    End
Attribute VB_Name = "MDIForm1"
Attribute VB_Creatable = False
Attribute VB_Exposed = False
```

```
Private Sub Command1_Click()
    AddADocument
     Picture2.Print "Ready"
End Sub

Private Sub Command2_Click()
    MDIForm1.ActiveForm.Hide
    Picture2.Print "Ready"
End Sub

Private Sub Exit_Click()
    End
End Sub

Private Sub MDIForm_Load()
    NumberDocuments = 1
End Sub

Private Sub New_Click()
    AddADocument
End Sub
```

LISTING 10.4 WRITER.MAK

```
WRITER.FRM
MODULE1.BAS
MDIFORM1.FRM
Object={F9043C88-F6F2-101A-A3C9-08002B2F49FB}#1.0#0; COMDLG16.OCX
Object={FAEEE763-117E-101B-8933-08002B2F4F5A}#1.0#0; DBLIST16.OCX
ProjWinSize=324,337,202,111
ProjWinShow=2
IconForm="MDIForm1"
HelpFile=""
ExeName="Project1.exe"
Path="D:\VB"
Name="Project1"
HelpContextID="0"
StartMode=0
VersionCompatible="0"
MajorVer=1
MinorVer=0
RevisionVer=0
AutoIncrementVer=0
VersionCompanyName=""
Reference=*\G{00025E01-0000-0000-C000-000000000046}#0.0#0#C:\WINDOWS\SYS-
TEM\dao2516.dll#Microsoft DAO 2.5 Object Library
```

We will use the help compiler, **HCW.EXE**, that comes with Visual Basic to create **WRITER.HLP**. To produce and format the data in **WRITER.HLP**, we'll need to create **WRITER.RTF**, which is a rich text format file. We'll use a word processor, such as Microsoft Word for Windows or Microsoft WordPad, that can save files in this special file format. This file, **WRITER.RTF**, will hold all the text in our help file and will indicate how the jumps will work in our help file. A *jump* occurs when the user clicks an underlined word and we jump to the matching help topic. For example, the text "File Menu Items" in our main help screen is a jump; when the user clicks that jump, we move to the help screen that displays help on that topic. We'll create **WRITER.RTF** and then use the help compiler to create **WRITER.HLP**.

Creating WRITER.RTF

The **WRITER.RTF** file holds two things: all the text we want to display in Writer help, and the information to tell the help compiler which words are associated with jumps. For example, both of the underlined items shown next—File Menu Items and Edit Menu Items—have jumps associated with them:

```
   --------------------------------------------------------------
  |Writer Help                                                   |
  |-------------------------------------------------------------|
  |File Edit Bookmark Options Help                               |
  |-------------------------------------------------------------|
  |   --------    -------    -------    --------                 |
  ||Contents|  | Search|  | Back  |  | Print  |                 |
  |   --------    -------    -------    --------                 |
  |-------------------------------------------------------------|
  |   CONTENTS                                                   |
  |                                                             |
  |   Welcome to Help for the Writer program. This              |
  |   help file gives you help on the menu items in             |
  |   Writer. To see help for the menu you are interested |
  |   in, click the matching topic below:                       |
  |                                                             |
  |                                                             |
  -->  |   File Menu Items                                      |
  |   ---------------                                           |
  |                                                             |
  -->  |   Edit Menu Items                                      |
  |   ---------------                                           |
   --------------------------------------------------------------
```

When the user clicks one of these items, we jump to the corresponding help screen. To produce **WRITER.RTF**, we'll need a word processor that can produce rich text files, and we'll use Microsoft Word for Windows 6.0. (Earlier versions can also produce **.RTF** files.) Let's start Word as shown in Figure 10.1.

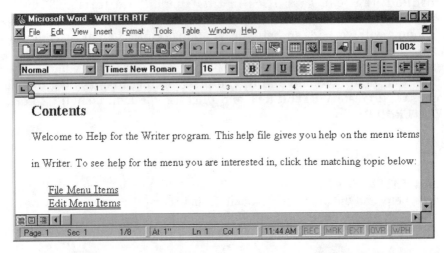

FIGURE 10.1 WE USE MICROSOFT WORD FOR WINDOWS 6.0 TO CREATE WRITER.RTF.

As you can also see in Figure 10.1, we place the first help screen—the Contents help screen—in the Word document. We make the word *Contents* the first word in the file (and Windows help will place it in its own bar). Using the Word **Format | Font** menu item, we also double-underline the two jumps: File Menu Items and Edit Menu Items. Double-underlining these items will make them into active jumps when Windows help displays them (although they will have only a single solid underline when displayed by WinHelp()).

Using Jump Tags

Now we have to associate a jump tag with each of our jumps. A *jump tag* indicates which new help screen we want to jump to when the user clicks a jump. Jump tags are stored as *hidden text* in an **.RTF** file. To display hidden text in Microsoft Word, click the paragraph button in the toolbar (the last button on the right in Figure 10.1). This shows all the paragraph marks, spaces, and hidden text, as shown in Figure 10.2.

We add a jump tag (i.e., hidden text) for the two entries File Menu Items and Edit Menu Items by placing the jump tag directly after those entries in the **.RTF** file, as shown in Figure 10.2. Place the mouse cursor after the entry you want, such as File Menu Items, and turn on hidden text by selecting the Word **Format | Font** menu item. Click the **Hidden** button in the Font dialog box's Effects box. Then type the jump tag you want to add, such as **FILE_MENU_ITEMS**. In this case, we will use the tags FILE_MENU_ITEMS for the File Menu Items jump and EDIT_MENU_ITEMS for the Edit Menu Items jump, as shown next (hidden text appears with a dotted underline):

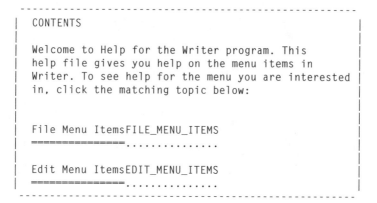

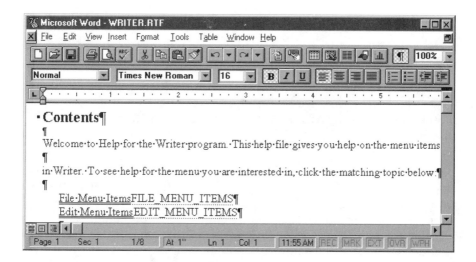

FIGURE 10.2 DISPLAYING HIDDEN TEXT IN MICROSOFT WORD.

Note that these jump tags immediately follow the jumps—leave no spaces between the jumps and the jump tags. When the user clicks the jump File Menu Items, we will jump to the page in **WRITER.RTF** labeled with the tag FILE_MENU_ITEMS.

Let's create the File Menu Items help screen next. We will jump to this page when the user clicks the File Menu Items jump in our Contents page (i.e., the first page). We want this new help screen to hold three new jumps: New Document, Open, and Save As.

```
--------------------------------------------------------------
|Writer Help                                                 |
|------------------------------------------------------------|
|File Edit Bookmark Options Help                             |
|------------------------------------------------------------|
|  --------   --------   --------   --------                 |
||Contents| | Search| | Back  | | Print  |                  |
|  --------   --------   --------   --------                 |
|------------------------------------------------------------|
|  Writer: File Menu Items                                   |
|                                                            |
|  Select the individual item you want to get help on:       |
|                                                            |
|                                                            |
|  New Document                                              |
|  ------------                                              |
|  Open...                                                   |
|  -------                                                   |
|  Save As...                                                |
|  ----------                                                |
--------------------------------------------------------------
```

In **WRITER.RTF**, separate help screens are divided from each other by page breaks. Now that we're finished with the first help screen, the Contents page, use the Word **Insert | Break** menu item to insert a page break in **WRITER.RTF** and start a new page for the File Menu Items help screen.

Start this new page in **WRITER.RTF** with the text "Writer: File Menu Items," as shown in Figure 10.3. Next, add the text we want in this new page, as also shown in Figure 10.3. We want three jumps here: New Document, Open, and Save As. Add them now and double-underline them. Give them the jump tags NEW_DOCUMENT, OPEN, and SAVE_AS by placing these tags right after the jumps as hidden text:

```
------------------------------------------------------------
|  CONTENTS                                                 |
|                                                           |
|  Welcome to Help for the Writer program. This             |
|  help file gives you help on the menu items in            |
|  Writer. To see help for the menu you are interested      |
|  in, click the matching topic below:                      |
|                                                           |
|                                                           |
|  File Menu ItemsFILE_MENU_ITEMS                            |
|  ================..............                           |
|                                                           |
|  Edit Menu ItemsEDIT_MENU_ITEMS                            |
|  ================..............                           |
|------------------Page Break-------------------------------|
|  Writer: File Menu Items                                  |
|                                                           |
|  Select the individual item you want to get help on:      |
|                                                           |
|                                                           |
-->       |  New DocumentNEW_DOCUMENT                        |
|  ============...........                                  |
-->       |  Open...OPEN                                     |
|  =======....                                              |
-->       |  Save As...SAVE_AS                               |
|  =========.......                                         |
------------------------------------------------------------
```

This new page itself is a *jump target*—we want to jump to this page when the user clicks the File Menu Items jump in the Contents page, and the jump tag for that jump is FILE_MENU_ITEMS. How do we associate that jump tag with the current page (the File Menu Items help screen) of **WRITER.RTF**?

It turns out that we connect a jump tag with a specific page through footnotes. In Word's View menu, select **Footnotes**, opening the footnote window under the main window, as shown in Figure 10.3.

Place the insertion point (the blinking cursor) at the very beginning of the new page, just before the text "Writer: File Menu Items," and select Word's **Insert | Footnote** menu item, opening the Footnote and Endnote dialog box. Click the button marked **Custom Mark** in the Number box and give this footnote the mark # (that is, type the # character in the box labeled

Custom Mark). Then click **OK**. This inserts a footnote with the text "#" and opens the footnote window at the bottom of the Word display, in case you haven't already done so. Move the insertion point to the footnote window right after the footnote mark #, and place the jump tag FILE_MENU_ITEMS there—do not make this text hidden.

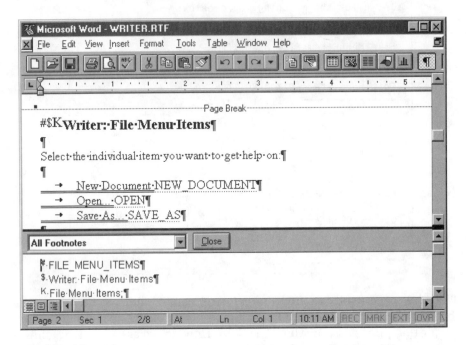

FIGURE 10.3 CREATING JUMP TAGS AND JUMP TARGETS IN MICROSOFT WORD.

That is the way we associate a jump tag—in this case, FILE_MENU_ ITEMS— with a help page: by placing a footnote with the mark # at the beginning of the page and by giving the footnote the jump tag as its text. When the user clicks **File Menu Items** in the Contents page, we will jump to the Writer: File Menu Items help page.

We can also give the current help screen a title at the top of its window. To do that, insert a new footnote using **Insert | Footnote**. Place this footnote right after the # footnote, and give it the custom mark **$**, as shown in Figure 10.3. This will give the current help screen the title corresponding to the text we will associate with this footnote—in this case, we use the title "Writer: File Menu Items." Move the insertion point to the footnote window and place the text "Writer: File Menu Items" after the $ footnote. Finally, add another footnote with the custom mark **K**, and give it the text "File

Menu Items", as shown in Figure 10.3. This will add the topic "File Menu Items" to the list of topics that the user can search through.

Now we add the next help page, which corresponds to the Edit Menu Items topic. It has one jump, corresponding to the **Cut** menu item:

```
                          .
                          .
      |                   .                              |
      |------------------Page Break----------------------|
      |   Writer: File Menu Items                         |
      |                                                   |
      |   Select the individual item you want to get help on: |
      |                                                   |
      |                                                   |
      |   New DocumentNEW_DOCUMENT                         |
      |   ===============............                     |
      |   Open...OPEN                                      |
      |   ==========....                                  |
      |   Save As...SAVE_AS                               |
      |   ==========.......                               |
      |------------------Page Break----------------------|
-->   |   Writer: Edit Menu Items                         |
      |                                                   |
-->   |   Select the individual item you want to get help on: |
      |                                                   |
      |                                                   |
-->   |   CutCUT                                           |
      |   ===...                                           |
      |                                                   |
       --------------------------------------------------
```

To add this new help page, insert a page break after the current page using **Insert | Break** and add to this new page the text shown previously. The result appears in Figure 10.4. As before, give the jump (**Cut**) a double underline, and make the jump tag (CUT) hidden text. Place three footnotes, corresponding to the custom marks #, $, and **K** as before, at the beginning of the Writer: Edit Menu Items page, and associate the text EDIT_MENU_ITEMS (i.e., the Contents page jump tag), "Writer: Edit Menu Items" (i.e., the title of this new page) and "Edit Menu Items" (i.e., this page's entry in the list of help items the user can search).

We've added four new jumps with the tags NEW_DOCUMENT, OPEN, and SAVE_AS in the File Menu Items page and CUT in the Edit Menu Items page. Now let's connect these jumps to help pages. We do that by inserting page breaks and four new pages corresponding to the jumps:

```
                              .
                              .
                              .
  |                                                           |
  |-------------------Page Break---------------------------|
  |   Writer: File Menu Items                                 |
  |                                                           |
  |   Select the individual item you want to get help on:     |
  |                                                           |
  |                                                           |
  |   New DocumentNEW_DOCUMENT                                 |
  |   ==============...........                                |
  |   Open...OPEN                                              |
  |   ========....                                            |
  |   Save As...SAVE_AS                                        |
  |   ==========.......                                        |
  |-------------------Page Break---------------------------|
  |   Writer: Edit Menu Items                                 |
  |                                                           |
  |   Select the individual item you want to get help on:     |
  |                                                           |
  |                                                           |
  |   CutCUT                                                   |
  |   ===...                                                   |
  |                                                           |
  |-------------------Page Break---------------------------|
-->   |   New Document                                           |
      |                                                         |
-->   |   Creates a new document.                               |
      |                                                         |
      |-------------------Page Break-------------------------|
-->   |   Open...                                               |
      |                                                         |
-->   |   Opens a file.                                         |
      |                                                         |
      |-------------------Page Break-------------------------|
-->   |   Save As...                                            |
      |                                                         |
-->   |   Saves a file.                                         |
      |                                                         |
      |-------------------Page Break-------------------------|
-->   |   Cut...                                                |
      |                                                         |
-->   |   Cuts selected text.                                   |
      |                                                         |
      |---------------------------------------------------------|
```

In addition, we connect the jump tags NEW_DOCUMENT, OPEN, SAVE_AS, and CUT to these new pages. As before, we start each page with a # footnote that has the jump tag as its text, as shown in Figure 10.4.

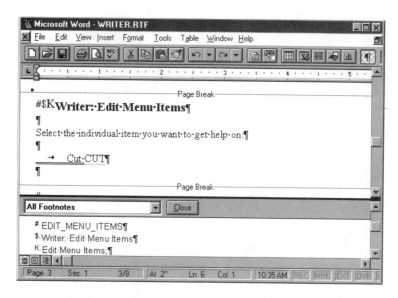

FIGURE 10.4 WE ADD THE EDIT MENU ITEMS HELP PAGE TO WRITER.RTF.

Now we've connected our jumps, and the user can search through various help topics, as we'll see. But we can do more here: we can also create help pop-ups.

Creating Help Pop-ups

As you may recall, we can pop up instant help for certain words or phrases in a help file. When the user clicks such a word or phrase—shown with a dotted underline—a help pop-up mini-window appears with more explanation. Here, we explain more about the word *file*:

```
-----------------------------------------------------------------
|Writer Help                                                     |
|-------------------------------------------------------------   |
|File Edit Bookmark Options Help                                 |
|-------------------------------------------------------------   |
| --------   -------   ------   --------                         |
||Contents| | Search| | Back  | | Print  |                      |
| --------   -------   ------   --------                         |
|-------------------------------------------------------------   |
|  Open...                                                       |
|                                                                |
|                                                                |
|  Opens a file.                                                 |
|          -------------------------------------                 |
|         |A file is the same as a document. |                  |
|          -------------------------------------                 |
|                                                                |
|                                                                |
-----------------------------------------------------------------
```

This pop-up is on our Open help page. Find that page in **WRITER.RTF**:

```
|-----------------Page Break--------------------|
|  Open...                                       |
|                                                |
|  Opens a file.                                 |
|                                                |
 ------------------------------------------------
```

To connect a pop-up to the word *file*, give it a single underline (not a double underline) and place a hidden tag with the text FILE_POPUP after it:

```
        |-----------------Page Break--------------------|
        |  Open...                                       |
        |                                                |
 -->    |  Opens a fileFILE_POPUP.                       |
        |            ----..........                      |
         ------------------------------------------------
```

The result is shown in Figure 10.5. Using a single underline in this way connects a help pop-up with the word *file* in our **WRITER.RTF** file.

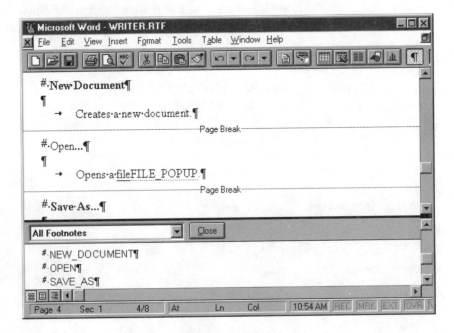

FIGURE 10.5 WE CREATE A HELP POP-UP JUMP.

Now insert a new page at the end of **WRITER.RTF** and place the pop-up text in that page:

477

```
|----------------------Page Break----------------------|
|   Open...                                            |
|                                                      |
|   Opens a fileFILE_POPUP.                            |
|           ----..........                             |
|----------------------Page Break----------------------|
|                                                      |
--> |   A file is the same as a document.              |
|                                                      |
|----------------------Page Break----------------------|
```

As before, we associate the tag FILE_POPUP with this new page using foot-notes. As shown in Figure 10.6, insert a # footnote in the beginning of the new page and give the footnote the text FILE_POPUP. Because we gave the word *file* only a single underline, the help compiler will associate its tag with a help pop-up and not a jump.

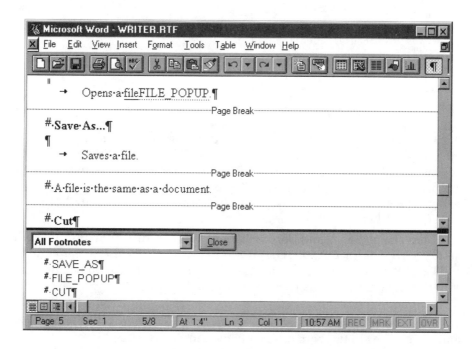

FIGURE 10.6 WE CREATE A HELP POP-UP MINI-WINDOW.

WRITER.RTF is complete. Save the file using Word's **File | Save As** menu item.

Creating WRITER.HLP

To create WRITER.HLP—the actual Windows help file that we'll load in when the user selects our Help menu in WRITER—we use the help compiler, HCW.EXE. This program comes with Visual Basic. First, in the help compiler, we have to create a new WRITER.HPJ, and we do that by selecting New in the File menu, selecting Help Project in the box labeled New, and by typing WRITER.HPJ in the File name box of the Project File Name box that opens. Close the Project File Name box by clicking OK. Next, we must add our file, WRITER.RTF to the project. To do that, just click the Files...button in the help compiler, and click the Add... button in the box that opens. This displays a box named Open; find WRITER.RTF by browsing through your disk and double-clicking WRITER.RTF when you find it, adding that file to our help project. This results in this help project file, WRITER.HPJ:

```
[OPTIONS]
HCW=0
LCID=0X409 0X0 ;English (United States)
REPORT=Yes
HLP=.\writer.hlp

[FILES]
.\Writer.rtf
```

That's all there is to it; now click the button marked Save and Compile in the help compiler. This compiles WRITER.HPJ and WRITER.RTF and creates the actual help file, WRITER.HLP. (To use the DOS version of the help compiler, HC.EXE, if you prefer to do so, you just type this: C:\.HC Writer.RTF.) That's all that was required—now we have our help file, WRITER.HLP. Let's put it to work.

Start Visual Basic and run WRITER, making sure that the new file **WRITER.HLP** is in **C:\VBOOK\WRITER** (which is where the code in **WRITER.FRM** assumes it is). Click the Help menu in the menu bar, opening Writer Help to the Contents page, as shown in Figure 10.7.

Our help file is a success so far: we see the two jumps—File Menu Items and Edit Menu Items—shown in Figure 10.7. Click the **File Menu Items** jump, moving us to the help page, as shown in Figure 10.8.

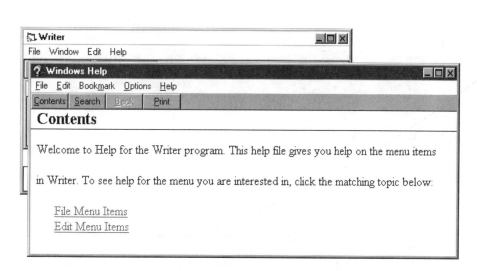

FIGURE 10.7 OUR CUSTOMIZED HELP FILE, CONTENTS PAGE.

Now we see the three jumps we've placed here—the New Document, Open, and Save As jumps—as shown in Figure 10.8. Click the **Open** jump, opening the help page, as shown in Figure 10.9.

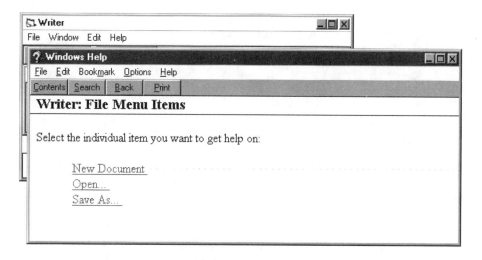

FIGURE 10.8 OUR CUSTOMIZED HELP FILE SHOWS THE FILE MENU ITEMS HELP PAGE.

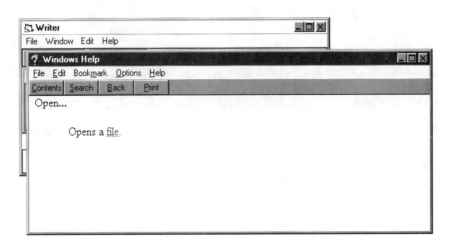

FIGURE 10.9 OUR CUSTOMIZED HELP FILE, SHOWING THE OPEN HELP PAGE.

In the Open page, note that the word *file* is underlined with a dotted under-line. That's because we've connected a help pop-up with that word. Press the mouse button when the mouser cursor is on that word, opening the pop-up as shown in Figure 10.10.

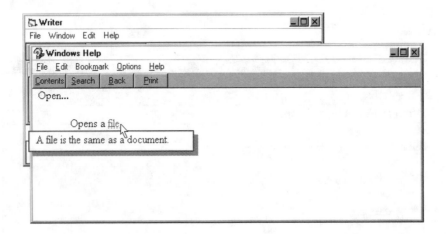

FIGURE 10.10 OUR CUSTOMIZED HELP FILE INCLUDES A HELP POP-UP WINDOW.

Finally, click the **Search** button in the help window's toolbar. The Search box opens, as shown in Figure 10.11. You can see the two entries we've added to the search box: Edit Menu Items and File Menu Items. (These items are kept alphabetized.) By clicking either of these entries, the user can jump directly to the matching help page.

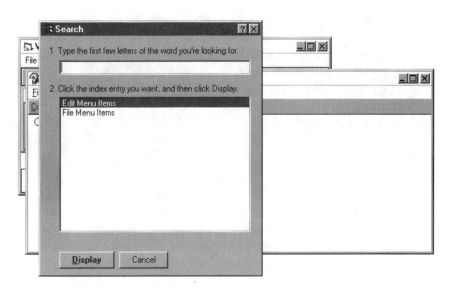

FIGURE 10.11 OUR CUSTOMIZED HELP FILE ALLOWS THE USER TO SEARCH THROUGH HELP TOPICS.

WRITER.HLP is a success. In fact, we've made quite a program of WRITER. Let's go through the final step now and create an installation program—**SETUP.EXE**—for it.

CREATING A CUSTOMIZED WINDOWS SETUP PROGRAM

Usually, writing a SETUP program so that you can distribute your application is a difficult process in Windows. For example, there are many hidden dependencies, especially in determining which supporting **.DLL** files you need to distribute. It used to be hard to make sure that you were getting everything, but it isn't difficult any more. Now you can use the Visual Basic SetupWizard, SETUPWIZ, and the whole process is automatic.

Let's see how this works with the WRITER program. Start the SetupWizard by double-clicking its icon in the Visual Basic folder. There are seven steps to create the setup program, complete all the way to producing the distribution diskettes:

1. Pass the SetupWizard the name of the application we want to distribute, WRITER, and its location. Type that into the Project File dialog box in the SetupWizard, as shown in Figure 10.12. If you want to rebuild WRITER's **.EXE** file, check the box marked **Rebuild the Project's EXE File**.

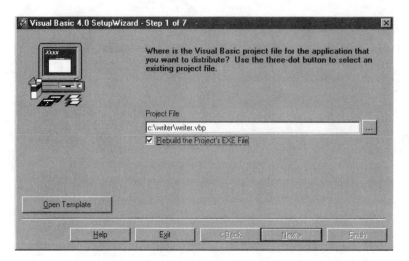

FIGURE 10.12 THE VISUAL BASIC SETUPWIZARD, STEP 1.

Now click **Next**, moving us to step 2.

2. The SetupWizard determines which Data Access Object (DAO) drivers (such as Microsoft FoxPro drivers) are needed; in our case, WRITER does not use any such drivers, so the SetupWizard automatically moves us to Step 3.

3. In this step, we indicate where we want the distribution files placed: onto diskettes or into a directory. In our case, we'll choose distribution diskettes by clicking the matching box; we also indicate a size for the diskettes, 1.44MB. Click **Next** to move to step 4.

4. In this step, the SetupWizard checks to see which OLE servers are needed and suggests that you check their license agreements before distributing them. In our case, we need no OLE servers, so we move to step 5 by clicking **Next**.

5. In this step, the SetupWizard determines which custom controls our program requires and lists the **.OCX** files it will need to place on the distribution diskettes (after compressing them). WRITER, for example, uses the Windows common dialogs **.OCX** file. After looking over this list, click **Next**.

6. In this step, SetupWizard asks you about the "deployment model." We have to specify whether our application should go into its own directory when it's installed or whether we want it installed as an OLE automation shared component. In our case, we want to install WRITER in its own directory, so we click the matching box and go to step 7.

7. In this last step, the SetupWizard lists the **.DLL** files and **.OCX** files that must be loaded onto the distribution diskettes after being compressed. The SetupWizard handles the compression automatically, and the SETUP program on the diskettes will handle the expansion of these files by itself. After looking over this list, click **Finish** to complete the process.

The SetupWizard then asks us to insert blank, formatted diskettes as it loads all the required, compressed files onto them. The process is automatic—the SetupWizard takes care of all the details.

After the diskettes are filled, you can distribute copies of them. They are fully self-contained. When users want to install WRITER, they need only run the SETUP program on the first diskette. The SETUP program takes over, as shown in Figure 10.13, asking users to load the other diskettes as required.

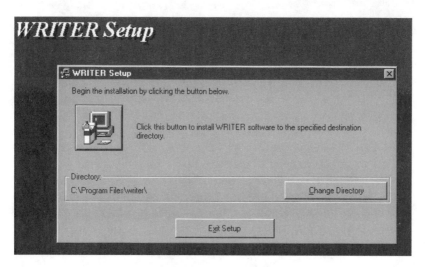

FIGURE 10.13 OUR **WRITER** SETUP PROGRAM AT WORK.

That's all there is to creating a SETUP program for WRITER. With the SetupWizard, the process has become extraordinarily easy.

And that completes this chapter. We saw how to set up a Help file for our program and how to create distribution diskettes for easy installment. In the next three chapters, we'll start working with another powerful part of Visual Basic—database programming.

CHAPTER 11

INTRODUCING DATABASES

In this chapter and the two following, we'll explore the excellent database capabilities of Visual Basic. These built-in database tools are powerful, and we will explore these popular tools in some depth. In this first chapter, we will define what a database is and how it can be useful to us. We'll explore database concepts and design and use the Visual Basic Data Manager tool to build a database. Next, we'll use the Data control in Visual Basic to connect our new database to a Visual Basic program. Inside that program, we'll use various controls, such as list boxes and text boxes, to display the data from the database. Finally, we'll see how the Visual Basic Data Form Designer allows us to create a form that we can add to our program. This form gives us easy access to the database so that we can modify the data in the database easily. In Chapter 12, we'll see how to create databases in code, setting them up as we wish without using the Visual Basic Data Manager. In Chapter 13, we'll see how to modify and work with databases in code, performing such operations as sorting, searching, and filtering. Let's start now by seeing what databases are all about and how they can be useful to us.

WHAT ARE DATABASES?

What are databases? As you might expect from the name, databases are ways of organizing data for easy handling. We're familiar with simple variables such as integers and long integers. However, data handling can be much more complex and powerful than these elementary forms. Consider, for example, a hospital that needs to maintain an inventory of thousands of supplies as well as maintain employee and patient records. It's clear that something powerful is needed, and that's what databases are all about.

To see how database methods and concepts develop, let's say that we are in charge of teaching a class on Visual Basic. At the end of the class, we are responsible for sending the students' grades to the registrar of the school. We might make a table showing the name of the students and the grade each one received:

```
Name     Grade
----------------
| Ann   |   C   |
|-------|-------|
| Mark  |   B   |
|-------|-------|
| Ed    |   A   |
|-------|-------|
| Frank |   A   |
|-------|-------|
| Ted   |   A   |
|-------|-------|
| Mabel |   B   |
|-------|-------|
| Ralph |   B   |
|-------|-------|
| Tom   |   B   |
----------------
```

This seems natural enough, and tables like this one are the foundations of databases. We've designed a database without being conscious of it, simply by making a list that has one entry for each student.

Database Design: Tables, Records, and Fields

Our table is broken into rows and columns. In database language, these are *records* and *fields*. Each row makes up a student's record, and each column makes up a field in the table (which can hold the student's name or grade):

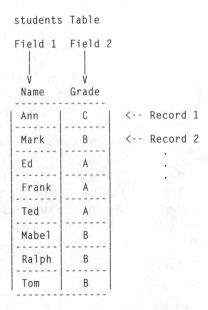

```
students Table

Field 1  Field 2
   |        |
   |        |
   V        V
 Name     Grade
 ----------------
 | Ann   |   C   |   <-- Record 1
 |-------|-------|
 | Mark  |   B   |   <-- Record 2
 |-------|-------|        .
 | Ed    |   A   |        .
 |-------|-------|        .
 | Frank |   A   |
 |-------|-------|
 | Ted   |   A   |
 |-------|-------|
 | Mabel |   B   |
 |-------|-------|
 | Ralph |   B   |
 |-------|-------|
 | Tom   |   B   |
 ----------------
```

Databases can contain several such tables. The data in each table can be related to data in other tables in various ways, such as having one or more columns, or fields, in common. This is why databases in Visual Basic are called *relational* databases. Because a database can contain several tables, we give a name to this table: students. We've designed our first database table. Now let's use the Visual Basic Data Manager tool to build it.

THE VISUAL BASIC DATA MANAGER

One of the tools that come with Visual Basic, the Data Manager allows us to create databases easily. This tool is perfect for us at this stage, because we are not yet ready for the programming details. We'll use the Data Manager to build our new database and place one table in it—students—which we'll fill with the data shown previously. We'll save our database in a file named **VBCLASS.MDB**. The **.MDB** extension is the one used by the built-in Visual Basic *database engine*, the Jet engine. We'll study the properties and methods of this engine in this and the following chapters. Databases can come in many formats—for example, dBase, Btrieve, Paradox, and those that use open database connectivity (ODBC). But when we open them in a Visual Basic program, all the properties and methods of the Jet database engine may be used regardless of the original form of the database, which is why we will study that engine here. After creating **VBCLASS.MDB**, we'll add a Visual Basic Data control to a Visual Basic program and connect the database to the control so that we can read the data from our database in the program and work with it.

Double-click the **Data Manager** icon in the Visual Basic window, opening that tool. The Data Manager presents us with a blank window at first—we have to create a new database before we can work on it. Select **New Database** in the File menu, opening the corresponding dialog box, as shown in Figure 11.1. Give this new database the name vbclass and click **OK** to create **VBCLASS.MDB**.

The Data Manager displays two windows—Tables/QueryDefs and SQL Statement—as shown in Figure 11.2.

Structured Query Language

In this first window, Tables/QueryDefs, we'll see the tables contained in this database (**VBCLASS.MDB**); in this case, our table is called students. A *QueryDef* is *query definition*, which is stored in compiled *Structured Query Language*, or SQL. There are two ways of handling databases in Visual Basic: using the methods and properties built into the Jet engine—the *native* way of handling databases in Visual Basic—and using SQL. We will mainly use the native Jet methods in our database programming. Note that if you plan to do a great deal of database work, you should buy a book on SQL programming, because it is often faster than the Jet methods. For example, an SQL query might look like the following, where we are asking for all the records in the table students that correspond to the students named Ann or Mark:

```
select * from students where name = "Ann" OR "Mark"
```

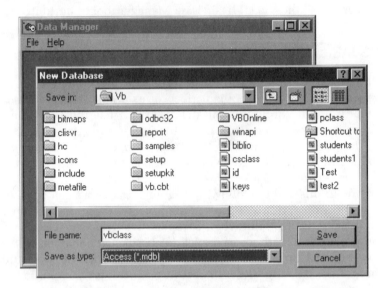

FIGURE 11.1 CREATING A DATABASE IN THE VISUAL BASIC DATA MANAGER.

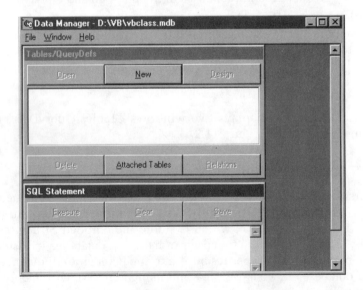

FIGURE 11.2 THE VISUAL BASIC DATA MANAGER.

When we execute this SQL query (which we could do in the SQL statement window if we had an open database), a new table is generated containing the records we have asked for. In this way, we can see that an SQL query can be thought of as defining a new table; it is for this reason that the window showing the tables in the database also lists SQL queries that we have defined, because they result in tables when executed.

At this point, we are ready to define our new table, students, and to enter the data in it:

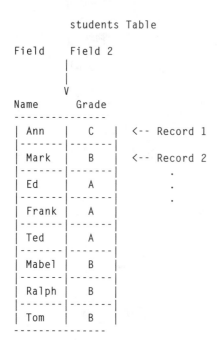

```
           students Table

Field      Field 2
             |
             |
             V
Name       Grade
---------------
| Ann   |   C   |   <-- Record 1
|-------|-------|
| Mark  |   B   |   <-- Record 2
|-------|-------|
| Ed    |   A   |      .
|-------|-------|
| Frank |   A   |      .
|-------|-------|
| Ted   |   A   |      .
|-------|-------|
| Mabel |   B   |
|-------|-------|
| Ralph |   B   |
|-------|-------|
| Tom   |   B   |
---------------
```

To create this table, click **New** in the Data Manager, opening the Add Table dialog box, as shown in Figure 11.3.

Give this new table the name **students** by entering that name in the Name box as shown in Figure 11.3. Now we are ready to define the fields (i.e., columns) in our table: Name and Grade. Enter **Name** in the Field Name box, as shown in Figure 11.3, and select **Text** in the Data Type box. To add this field to our table, click the right arrow (>) in the Add Table dialog box, adding this field to the list box as shown in Figure 11.3. Next, type the next field's name, **Grade**, into the Field Name box, selecting **Text** as its type in the Data Type box. Click the right arrow again to add this field. Now click **OK** to add this table to our database; the new table, students, appears in the Tables/QueryDefs window now, as shown in Figure 11.4.

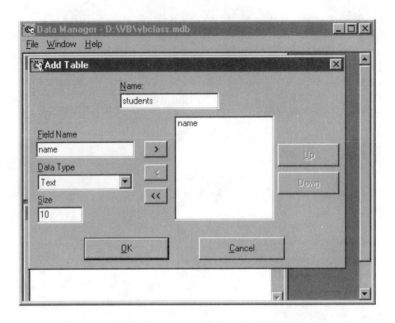

FIGURE 11.3 CREATING A NEW DATABASE TABLE.

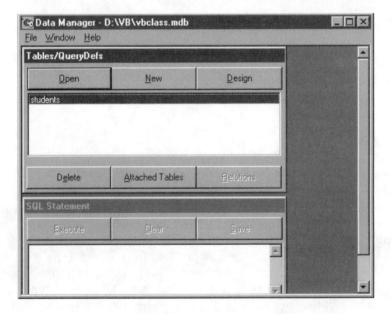

FIGURE 11.4 OUR NEW DATABASE TABLE IS CREATED.

Having created the students table, we can now add our data to it. Click **Open** in the Tables/QueryDefs window, opening the new table as shown in Figure 11.5.

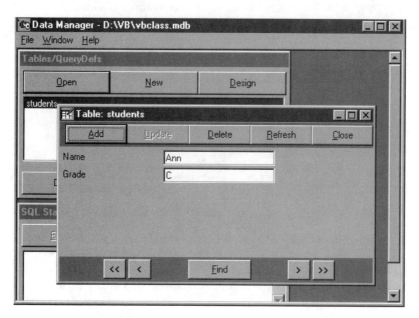

FIGURE 11.5 ADDING DATA TO THE TABLE NAMED STUDENTS.

As you can see, text boxes have been added for each of our fields, Name and Grade, making data entry easy. We will create the new records in the table and add our data, record by record. To create the first record, click **Add**. Next, type the name **Ann** and the grade, **C**, as shown in Figure 11.5. To install this new data in the record we have just created, click **Update**.

After we create our first record this way, click **Add** to add a new record to the table, and fill the Name and Grade fields with the data for the second record: **Mark** and **B**. If you want to examine the contents of the table at any time, you can use the < or > button to move back or ahead one record, or the << or >> button to move to the beginning or end of the table. If you made unintentional changes to a record, you can click **Refresh** to get a fresh copy of that record from the table. Keep going until you've entered all the data, and then click **Close**.

Now our table, students, is complete. We can examine the data in the table either by opening it and working through the records or by executing an SQL statement, such as the one we saw earlier:

```
select * from students where name = "Ann" OR "Mark"
```

Enter this SQL statement now in the SQL Statement window and click **Execute**. This causes the Data Manager to search the table students for records that match our search criteria, and to create a new table from the matches. The Data Manager opens that table for our examination, as shown in Figure 11.6.

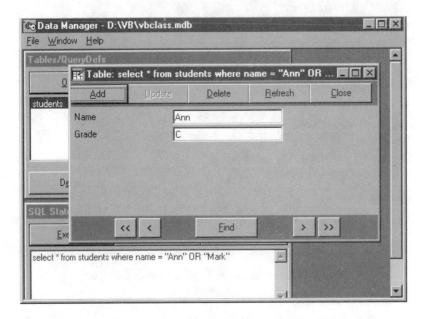

FIGURE 11.6 EXECUTING AN SQL STATEMENT.

If you are used to SQL, this is a good method of working with databases as you create them in the Data Manager.

At this point, our new students table is filled with data; exit the Data Manager now, which closes the file **VBCLASS.MDB**. Congratulations—you've just created your first database file.

THE VISUAL BASIC DATA CONTROL

Now that we have a database to work with, let's see how to handle it in Visual Basic. (Note that we didn't have to use the Data Manager to create the database. Instead, we could have used Visual Basic itself, or Microsoft

Access, or other products such as Btrieve, FoxPro, dBase, or ODBC client/server applications.) There are two main ways of interacting with databases in Visual Basic: native Jet methods/properties, and SQL. We will concentrate on the former. In addition, there are two ways of setting up databases in our programs: using the Data control, and using Data Access Objects (DAO). The easier technique is to use the Data control, and we will do so in this chapter. In the next chapter, we will see how to create Data Access Objects in code and work with them in our programs directly.

Connecting the new database to a Data control in a Visual Basic program is easy. Create a new Visual Basic project called **DATACTRL.VBP**, as shown in Figure 11.7. Next, double-click the **Data Control** tool in the toolbox (the Data Control tool is indicated in Figure 11.7); this creates a new Data control.

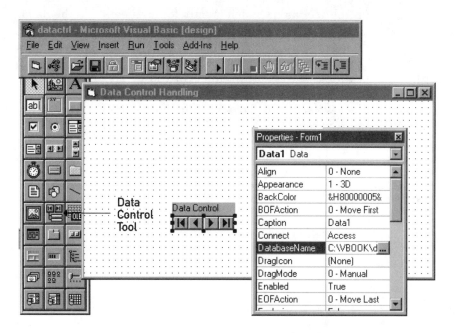

FIGURE 11.7 CREATING A NEW DATA CONTROL IN A VISUAL BASIC PROGRAM.

Now we can connect our database, **VBCLASS.MDB**, to the new Data control, Data1. To do that, simply set the Data control's DatabaseName property to the path and name of our database file, **VBCLASS.MDB**, and the RecordSource property to the table we want to look at, students. Now the Data control is connected to our database, and the data in the database is accessible to our program.

Cursored Database Access

You may be disappointed to find that the Data control is simply a short tool-bar, a few buttons, and some arrow captions, as shown here and in Figure 11.7.

Where is our data from the database? We can run the program at this point, but nothing will appear on the form beyond the Data control. The reason is that the Data control itself is responsible only for connecting to the database we've selected and setting the current record in that database. The *current record* is the one that we are currently examining—and it's possible to have only one such record. When we make changes, it's always to the current record; when we look at a record, that record is or becomes the current record. In this way, we say that access to the database is *cursored* access. For example, when we start the program as it stands, the first record in our database is the current record:

```
     Name    Grade
    ---------------
    | Ann   |  C  |     <-- Current Record
    |-------|-----|
    | Mark  |  B  |
    |-------|-----|
    | Ed    |  A  |
    |-------|-----|
    | Frank |  A  |
    |-------|-----|
    | Ted   |  A  |
    |-------|-----|
    | Mabel |  B  |
    |-------|-----|
    | Ralph |  B  |
    |-------|-----|
    | Tom   |  B  |
    ---------------
```

If we were to click the right-pointing arrow in the Data control, we would move to the next record in the database:

```
Name     Grade
---------------
| Ann   |   C   |
|-------|-------|
| Mark  |   B   |          <-- Current Record
|-------|-------|
| Ed    |   A   |
|-------|-------|
| Frank |   A   |
|-------|-------|
| Ted   |   A   |
|-------|-------|
| Mabel |   B   |
|-------|-------|
| Ralph |   B   |
|-------|-------|
| Tom   |   B   |
---------------
```

The left-pointing arrow moves us back one record. The arrow key at the far left in the Data control moves us to the beginning of the database, and the arrow key at the far right moves us to the end.

In this way, we can see that the Data control allows us to move through the database record by record. However, the question remains: how do we display our data? The answer is to use data bound controls.

DATA BOUND CONTROLS

Because there are so many ways to display data in a Visual Basic program—text boxes, picture boxes, grid controls, combo boxes, and so on—it doesn't make sense that the Data control should have only one way of displaying data. The programmer should determine how the data is displayed. In Visual Basic, that's done with controls such as the ones we've just mentioned: text boxes, picture boxes, grid controls, combo boxes, and so on. These controls are designed to work easily with a Data control.

Let's say that we had both a text box, Text1, and a Data control, Data1, in our program:

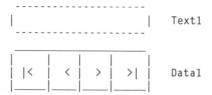

When we start our program, the Data control is connected to the students table in our database, and we can set the current record in it using the arrow buttons. We can also *display* the current record, using the text box. To do that, we set the text box's DataSource property to the name of the Data control, Data1, like this: Text1.DataSource = Data1. As we know, the current record will be made up of two fields: Name and Grade. We can display only one field in the text box. To display, say, the Name field of the current record in the database, we set the text box's DataField property to Name: Text1.DataField = Name. (We can also set the DataSource and DataField properties in the properties window at design time.)

Now when we run the program, the database is connected to the Data control—and the contents of the Name field of the current record in that database (i.e., the first record) appear in the text box:

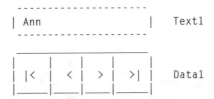

If we click the right-pointing arrow in the Data control, we move to the second record in the database, and the contents of the Name field of that record ("Mark") are displayed in the text box:

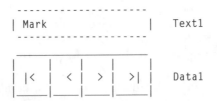

In this way, we say that the text box is *bound* to the Data control. There are 10 controls in Visual Basic that can function as bound controls: check boxes, combo boxes, DBCombo boxes, DBGrids, DBList boxes, image controls, labels, list boxes, picture boxes, and text boxes. Each control has properties that we can set to tie it to a Data control. These properties appear in Table 11.1.

TABLE 11.1 DATA BOUND CONTROLS.

Control	Properties to Set
Checkbox	DataField = desired Boolean field, DataSource = data control's name
Combo box	DataField = desired field, DataSource = data control's name
DBCombo box	BoundColumn = desired field, DataField = desired field, DataSource = data control's name, ListField = desired field, RowSource = data control's name
DBGrid	DataSource = data control's name
DBList box	DataField = desired field, DataSource = data control's name, RowSource = data control's name
Image control	DataField = desired field, DataSource = data control's name
Label	DataField = desired field, DataSource = data control's name
List box	DataField = desired field, DataSource = data control's name
Picture box	DataField = desired field, DataSource = data control's name
Text box	DataField = desired field, DataSource = data control's name

We might note the appearance of three new controls in Table 11.1 that we have not seen before: DBCombo box, DBGrid, and DBList. Although all the controls in Table 11.1 work with the Data control, these controls are specially designed to do so. Whereas the other controls work only with one field of one record at a time, the DB controls display that field of *all* the records in the database and indicate (through highlighting) which one is the current record. Suppose that we create a DBCombo box named DBCombo1 and connect it to the Data control and the Name field in our database. When we open DBCombo1 at run time, we'll see all the Name fields of all the records in the database at once, and the current record will be marked. In the same way, the DBList control displays a list of the Name field of each record, highlighting the current record. The DBGrid control is even more powerful. Because it can display both rows and columns, this control displays our entire table (Name and Grade fields) and indicates the current record by highlighting it. When you use the Data control to move to a new record, the highlighted line in a DB control also moves to match, so the current record is always highlighted.

Displaying Database Data with Bound Controls

Let's put this to work in our DATACTRL program. We can add a number of data bound controls to this program. (We won't add all of them, because some are inappropriate. For example, a data bound Image control would require a database of images and not text.) Let's add a text box, a combo box, a label, a DBList box, a DBCombo box, and a DBGrid box, as shown in Figure 11.8.

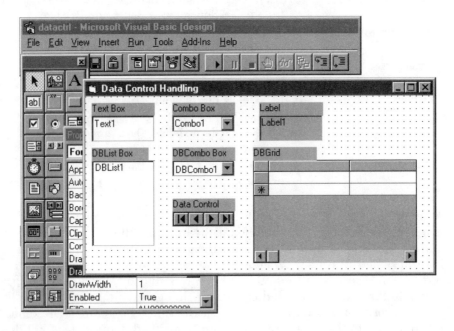

FIGURE 11.8 ADDING DATA BOUND CONTROLS TO OUR PROGRAM.

Table 11.2 shows how we set the properties of the controls in DATACTRL to connect to the Name field of our database, which is connected to the control Data1.

TABLE 11.2

Text1	DataField = Name, DataSource = Data1
Combo1	DataField = Name, DataSource = Data1
Label1	DataField = Name, DataSource = Data1
DBList1	DataField = Name, DataSource = Data1, RowSource = Data1
DBCombo1	DataField = Name, DataSource = Data1, BoundColumn = Name, ListField = Name, RowSource = Data1
DBGrid1	DataSource = Data1

Note that we have to set only one property of the DBGrid control: DataSource; we set that to Data1. Because the DBGrid displays our entire database table, there is no need to indicate a particular field to display. Now we run the program, as shown in Figure 11.9.

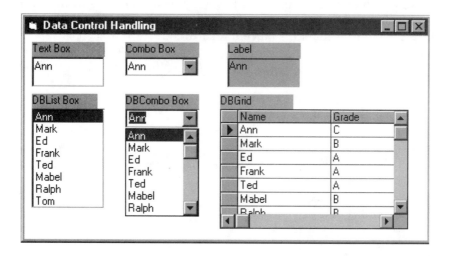

FIGURE 11.9 DISPLAYING DATABASE DATA IN A PROGRAM.

As you can see, the Name field in the first record in our student table is "Ann":

```
Name    Grade
---------------
| Ann   |  C   |      <-- Current Record
|-------|------|
| Mark  |  B   |
|-------|------|
| Ed    |  A   |
|-------|------|
| Frank |  A   |
|-------|------|
| Ted   |  A   |
|-------|------|
| Mabel |  B   |
|-------|------|
| Ralph |  B   |
|-------|------|
| Tom   |  B   |
---------------
```

This field appears in each of the data bound controls, as shown in Figure 11.9. Note also that the Name field for every record appears in the DB controls and that the DBGrid control is displaying the entire table. Also note that the DB controls mark the current record.

If we were to click the right-pointing arrow in the Data control, we would move to the next record in the database:

```
Name    Grade
---------------
| Ann   |  C   |
|-------|------|
| Mark  |  B   |      <-- Current Record
|-------|------|
| Ed    |  A   |
|-------|------|
| Frank |  A   |
|-------|------|
| Ted   |  A   |
|-------|------|
| Mabel |  B   |
|-------|------|
| Ralph |  B   |
|-------|------|
| Tom   |  B   |
---------------
```

The Name field from that record, which contains the name "Mark," now appears in each of the data bound controls, as shown in Figure 11.10. Our program is a success. **DATACTRL.VBP** appears in Listing 11.1, and **DATAC-TRL.FRM** is in Listing 11.2.

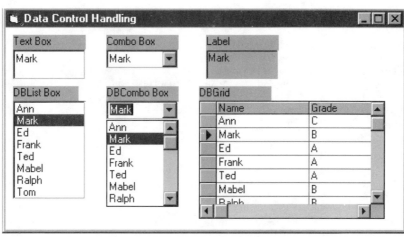

FIGURE 11.10 ACCESSING A RECORD IN A DATABASE.

LISTING 11.1 DATACTRL.VBP

```
Form=datactrl.Frm
Object={F9043C88-F6F2-101A-A3C9-08002B2F49FB}#1.0#0; COMDLG32.OCX
Object={BDC217C8-ED16-11CD-956C-0000C04E4C0A}#1.0#0; TABCTL32.OCX
Object={3B7C8863-D78F-101B-B9B5-04021C009402}#1.0#0; RICHTX32.OCX
Object={6B7E6392-850A-101B-AFC0-4210102A8DA7}#1.0#0; COMCTL32.OCX
Object={FAEEE763-117E-101B-8933-08002B2F4F5A}#1.0#0; DBLIST32.OCX
Object={00028C01-0000-0000-0000-000000000046}#1.0#0; DBGRID32.OCX
Object={F6125AB1-8AB1-11CE-A77F-08002B2F4E98}#1.0#0; MSRDC32.OCX
Reference=*\G{BEF6E001-A874-101A-8BBA-
        00AA00300CAB}#2.0#0#C:\WINDOWS\SYSTEM\OLEPRO32.DLL#Standard
        OLE Types
Reference=*\G{EE008642-64A8-11CE-920F-
        08002B369A33}#1.0#0#C:\WINDOWS\SYSTEM\MSRDO32.DLL#Microsoft
        Remote Data Object 1.0
Reference=*\G{00025E01-0000-0000-C000-000000000046}#3.0#0#C:\PROGRAM
        FILES\COMMON FILES\MICROSOFT SHARED\DAO\DAO3032.DLL#Microsoft
        DAO 3.0 Object Library
Object={A8B3B723-0B5A-101B-B22E-00AA0037B2FC}#1.0#0; GRID32.OCX
ProjWinSize=383,372,202,94
ProjWinShow=2
Name="Project1"
HelpContextID="0"
StartMode=0
VersionCompatible32="0"
MajorVer=1
MinorVer=0
RevisionVer=0
AutoIncrementVer=0
ServerSupportFiles=0
```

LISTING 11.2 DATACTRL.FRM

```
VERSION 4.00
Begin VB.Form Form1
    BackColor       =   &H00FFFFFF&
    Caption         =   "Database Control Handling"
    ClientHeight    =   3315
    ClientLeft      =   1530
    ClientTop       =   1500
    ClientWidth     =   6690
    Height          =   3720
    Left            =   1470
    LinkTopic       =   "Form1"
    ScaleHeight     =   3315
    ScaleWidth      =   6690
    Top             =   1155
    Width           =   6810
    Begin VB.ComboBox Combo1
        DataField       =   "Name"
        DataSource      =   "Data1"
        Height          =   315
        Left            =   1680
        TabIndex        =   1
        Text            =   "Combo1"
        Top             =   360
        Width           =   1215
    End
    Begin VB.TextBox Text1
        DataField       =   "Name"
        DataSource      =   "Data1"
        Height          =   495
        Left            =   120
        TabIndex        =   0
        Text            =   "Text1"
        Top             =   360
        Width           =   1215
    End
    Begin VB.Data Data1
        Caption         =   "Data1"
        Connect         =   "Access"
        DatabaseName    =   "D:\VB\vbclass.mdb"
        Exclusive       =   0   'False
        Height          =   300
        Left            =   1680
        Options         =   0
        ReadOnly        =   0   'False
        RecordsetType   =   1   'Dynaset
        RecordSource    =   "students"
        Top             =   2160
        Width           =   1215
```

```
        End
        Begin VB.Label Label8
            Caption         =   "Data Control"
            Height          =   255
            Left            =   1680
            TabIndex        =   12
            Top             =   1920
            Width           =   1215
        End
        Begin VB.Label Label7
            Caption         =   "DBGrid"
            Height          =   255
            Left            =   3240
            TabIndex        =   11
            Top             =   960
            Width           =   1215
        End
        Begin VB.Label Label6
            Caption         =   "DBCombo Box"
            Height          =   255
            Left            =   1680
            TabIndex        =   10
            Top             =   960
            Width           =   1215
        End
        Begin VB.Label Label5
            Caption         =   "DBList Box"
            Height          =   255
            Left            =   120
            TabIndex        =   9
            Top             =   960
            Width           =   1095
        End
        Begin VB.Label Label4
            Caption         =   "Label"
            Height          =   255
            Left            =   3360
            TabIndex        =   8
            Top             =   120
            Width           =   1215
        End
        Begin VB.Label Label3
            Caption         =   "Combo Box"
            Height          =   255
            Left            =   1680
            TabIndex        =   7
            Top             =   120
            Width           =   1215
        End
        Begin VB.Label Label2
```

```
      Caption          =    "Text Box"
      Height           =    255
      Left             =    120
      TabIndex         =    6
      Top              =    120
      Width            =    1215
   End
   Begin MSDBGrid.DBGrid DBGrid1
      Bindings         =    "datactrl.frx":0000
      Height           =    1935
      Left             =    3240
      OleObjectBlob    =    "datactrl.frx":000E
      TabIndex         =    5
      Top              =    1200
      Width            =    3135
   End
   Begin MSDBCtls.DBCombo DBCombo1
      Bindings         =    "datactrl.frx":0716
      DataField        =    "Name"
      DataSource       =    "Data1"
      Height           =    315
      Left             =    1680
      TabIndex         =    4
      Top              =    1200
      Width            =    1215
      _Version         =    65536
      _ExtentX         =    2143
      _ExtentY         =    556
      _StockProps      =    77
      ForeColor        =    0
      ListField        =    "Name"
      BoundColumn      =    "Name"
   End
   Begin MSDBCtls.DBList DBList1
      Bindings         =    "datactrl.frx":0724
      DataField        =    "Name"
      DataSource       =    "Data1"
      Height           =    1620
      Left             =    120
      TabIndex         =    3
      Top              =    1200
      Width            =    1215
      _Version         =    65536
      _ExtentX         =    2143
      _ExtentY         =    2858
      _StockProps      =    77
      ForeColor        =    -2147483640
      BackColor        =    -2147483643
      ListField        =    "Name"
      BoundColumn      =    "Name"
   End
```

```
    Begin VB.Label Label1
        BorderStyle    =    1   'Fixed Single
        Caption        =    "Label1"
        DataField      =    "Name"
        DataSource     =    "Data1"
        Height         =    495
        Left           =    3360
        TabIndex       =    2
        Top            =    360
        Width          =    1215
    End
End
Attribute VB_Name = "Form1"
Attribute VB_Creatable = False
Attribute VB_Exposed = False
```

In this way, you can use the data bound controls to display data from a data-base, and you can move around in that database using the arrow buttons in the Data control. This is just the beginning—you must also be able to search for and sort, to name only two common database functions—but it indicates the power of the Data control when it is coupled with bound controls. We've seen how easy it is to display our data. The next natural question is, can we modify the data in a database using the data bound controls? The answer is yes, and we'll look into that now.

Modifying Database Data with Bound Controls

Let's say that we discover a mistake in our spelling and that Ann, the first student in our database, should have her name changed to Anne:

```
       Name    Grade              Name     Grade
     - - - - - - - - - - - - -   - - - - - - - - - - - -
    |  Ann   |   C   |  ------>  |  Anne  |   C   |
    | - - - - | - - - - - |      | - - - - | - - - - - |
    |  Mark  |   B   |          |  Mark  |   B   |
    | - - - - | - - - - - |      | - - - - | - - - - - |
    |  Ed    |   A   |          |  Ed    |   A   |
    | - - - - | - - - - - |      | - - - - | - - - - - |
    |  Frank |   A   |          |  Frank |   A   |
    | - - - - | - - - - - |      | - - - - | - - - - - |
    |  Ted   |   A   |          |  Ted   |   A   |
    | - - - - | - - - - - |      | - - - - | - - - - - |
    |  Mabel |   B   |          |  Mabel |   B   |
    | - - - - | - - - - - |      | - - - - | - - - - - |
    |  Ralph |   B   |          |  Ralph |   B   |
    | - - - - | - - - - - |      | - - - - | - - - - - |
    |  Tom   |   B   |          |  Tom   |   B   |
     - - - - - - - - - - - - -   - - - - - - - - - - - -
```

We can use the Data Manager to do this: all we have to do is to open the table in the Data Manager, find the right record, edit the Name field, and then click **Update** to modify the database. That's fine as far as it goes, but how can we do the same thing in our program?

It turns out that we can use the data bound controls to modify the current record in a database table. All we have to do is to edit the displayed data and then update the database. (Note that this rules out the use of the data bound Label control, which does not allow you to edit its contents.)

Doing this is easy. After you make a change in a data bound control's contents (which sets its DataChanged property), you can update the record you've modified in the database by using the Data control's UpdateRecord method:

```
Data1.UpdateRecord
```

All we have to do is to add a new button to our program, which we label **Update Data**, as in Figure 11.11. When the user changes the contents of the current record as displayed in any of the bound controls and then presses **Update Data**, this code is executed:

```
Sub Command1_Click()
    Data1.UpdateRecord
End Sub
```

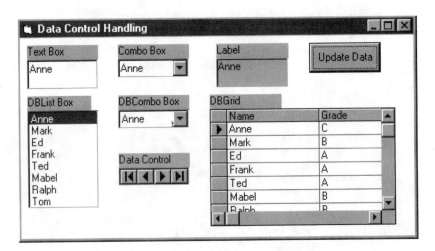

FIGURE 11.11 MODIFYING A DATABASE RECORD.

This means that we can change the name in the first record of the database from Ann to Anne using, say, the text box. When we click **Update Data**, that field is updated in the database and the new spelling appears in each of the bound controls, as shown in Figure 11.11. As we'll see in the next chapter, this is the usual way of changing fields in a record: making changes and then updating the database. In particular, we'll see that the AddNew method adds a new record to a database table, ready for us to fill with data, and the Edit method allows us to edit the current record. After we place the appropriate data into the record, we'll use the table's Update method to update the record in the table.

There are more actions we might want to take with a particular record in our program: we might want to add or delete records, as we did in the Data Manager. We can use bound controls to set up all this, or we can use the Data Form Designer, a new tool in Visual Basic that's especially designed to create a data entry form for our database.

The Data Form Designer

To use the Data Form Designer, we first use the Visual Basic Add-In Manager to add it to our program. In the Add-Ins menu, select **Add-In Manager**. When the Add-In Manager window opens, find and select the box marked **Data Form Designer**. Click **OK**, adding this tool to the Add-Ins menu. Now select the **Data Form Designer** from the Add-Ins menu, opening it as shown in Figure 11.12.

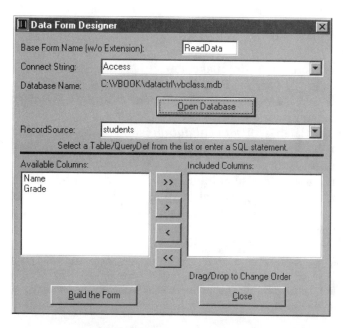

FIGURE 11.12 DESIGNING A DATA ENTRY FORM.

The Data Form Designer needs a name for the new form, so we'll call it ReadData. The name of our new form in the program will be frmReadData, and the support file will be named **READDATA.FRM**.

Next, we indicate that we want this data entry form to be designed for our **VBCLASS.MDB** database by using the Data Form Designer's **Open Database** button and selecting that file. The Data Form Designer indicates that there is one available record source—that is, table—in our database, and it is named students. The available columns in this table are Name and Grade, as shown in Figure 11.12. We want to display both fields in the new data entry form, so we select both **Name** and **Grade** and click the button marked with a right arrow (>) to move them from the Available Columns box to the Included Columns box. Now click **Build the Form** to create the new form, frmReadData. The Data Form Designer creates the form and adds it to our project automatically.

This new form will manage its own connection to our database—in fact, it has its own built-in Data control. All we have to do is to display the data entry form, frmReadData, when the user wants to use it to work with the data in the **VBCLASS.MDB** file. For that purpose, we add a button to our main form and label it with the caption **Data Entry Form**. When the user clicks this button, we display the data entry form this way:

```
Private Sub Command2_Click()
    frmReadData.Show
End Sub
```

There is one more change to make, and it is in the code that the Data Form Designer has created for us. Find **READDATA.FRM** in the Visual Basic project window and open the code corresponding to the new data entry form. Now find the subroutine Data1_Validate(), which is called just before data is updated in the database. (*Data validation* is the process of checking whether the data meets limitations and boundaries set on it before installing it in a database.) In this subroutine is one line we comment out: the line at the end where the program's mouse pointer is changed to the hourglass symbol. The mouse pointer tends to get stuck displaying the hourglass this way (even though no operation is being performed by the program), which is confusing to the user:

```
Private Sub Data1_Validate(Action As Integer, Save As Integer)
    'This is where you put validation code
    'This event gets called when the following actions occur
    Select Case Action
```

```
      Case vbDataActionMoveFirst
      Case vbDataActionMovePrevious
      Case vbDataActionMoveNext
      Case vbDataActionMoveLast
      Case vbDataActionAddNew
      Case vbDataActionUpdate
      Case vbDataActionDelete
      Case vbDataActionFind
      Case vbDataActionBookmark
      Case vbDataActionClose
    End Select
--> 'Screen.MousePointer = vbHourglass
End Sub
```

Now run the program and click **Data Entry Form**, opening the new data entry window as shown in Figure 11.13 (Note that the **Data Entry Form** button is also visible in Figure 11.13). This new window is much like the data entry window we saw in the Data Manager, and it operates the same way, with all its functionality built in. In this window, we can add, delete, and edit records in our database. (We'll see in the next chapter how this works in code.) When the user clicks **Close** in the data entry form, that form is unloaded and we return to the main window. Our program is a success. We call this modified program **DATENTRY.VBP**; the file **DATENTRY.VBP** appears in Listing 11.3, **DATENTRY.FRM** is in Listing 11.4, and **READDATA.FRM** is in Listing 11.5.

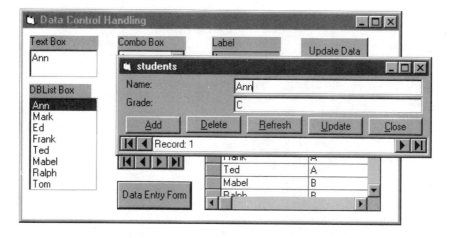

FIGURE 11.13 USING THE NEW DATA ENTRY FORM TO MODIFY THE DATABASE.

LISTING 11.3 DATENTRY.VBP

```
Form=datentry.Frm
Form=ReadData.FRM
Object={F9043C88-F6F2-101A-A3C9-08002B2F49FB}#1.0#0; COMDLG32.OCX
Object={6B7E6392-850A-101B-AFC0-4210102A8DA7}#1.0#0; COMCTL32.OCX
Object={FAEEE763-117E-101B-8933-08002B2F4F5A}#1.0#0; DBLIST32.OCX
Object={00028C01-0000-0000-0000-000000000046}#1.0#0; DBGRID32.OCX
Reference=*\G{BEF6E001-A874-101A-8BBA-
        00AA00300CAB}#2.0#0#C:\WINDOWS\SYSTEM\OLEPRO32.DLL#Standard
        OLE Types
Reference=*\G{EE008642-64A8-11CE-920F-
        08002B369A33}#1.0#0#C:\WINDOWS\SYSTEM\MSRDO32.DLL#Microsoft
        Remote Data Object 1.0
Reference=*\G{00025E01-0000-0000-C000-000000000046}#3.0#0#C:\PROGRAM
        FILES\COMMON FILES\MICROSOFT SHARED\DAO\DAO3032.DLL#Microsoft
        DAO 3.0 Object Library
ProjWinSize=356,375,217,94
ProjWinShow=2
IconForm="Form1"
Name="Project1"
HelpContextID="0"
StartMode=0
VersionCompatible32="0"
MajorVer=1
MinorVer=0
RevisionVer=0
AutoIncrementVer=0
ServerSupportFiles=0
```

LISTING 11.4 DATENTRY.FRM

```
VERSION 4.00
Begin VB.Form Form1
    BackColor       =   &H00FFFFFF&
    Caption         =   "Data Control Handling"
    ClientHeight    =   3315
    ClientLeft      =   1350
    ClientTop       =   1530
    ClientWidth     =   6690
    Height          =   3720
    Left            =   1290
    LinkTopic       =   "Form1"
    ScaleHeight     =   3315
    ScaleWidth      =   6690
    Top             =   1185
    Width           =   6810
    Begin VB.CommandButton Command2
```

```
          Caption        =    "Update Data"
          Height         =    495
          Left           =    4920
          TabIndex       =    14
          Top            =    120
          Width          =    1215
       End
       Begin VB.CommandButton Command1
          Caption        =    "Data Entry Form"
          Height         =    495
          Left           =    1680
          TabIndex       =    13
          Top            =    2640
          Width          =    1335
       End
       Begin VB.ComboBox Combo1
          DataField      =    "Name"
          DataSource     =    "Data1"
          Height         =    315
          Left           =    1680
          TabIndex       =    1
          Text           =    "Combo1"
          Top            =    360
          Width          =    1215
       End
       Begin VB.TextBox Text1
          DataField      =    "Name"
          DataSource     =    "Data1"
          Height         =    495
          Left           =    120
          TabIndex       =    0
          Text           =    "Text1"
          Top            =    360
          Width          =    1215
       End
       Begin VB.Data Data1
          Caption        =    "Data1"
          Connect        =    "Access"
          DatabaseName   =    "C:\VBOOK\datactrl\vbclass.mdb"
          Exclusive      =    0    'False
          Height         =    300
          Left           =    1680
          Options        =    0
          ReadOnly       =    0    'False
          RecordsetType  =    1    'Dynaset
          RecordSource   =    "students"
          Top            =    2160
          Width          =    1215
       End
       Begin VB.Label Label8
```

```
      Caption         =     "Data Control"
      Height          =     255
      Left            =     1680
      TabIndex        =     12
      Top             =     1920
      Width           =     1215
   End
   Begin VB.Label Label7
      Caption         =     "DBGrid"
      Height          =     255
      Left            =     3240
      TabIndex        =     11
      Top             =     960
      Width           =     1215
   End
   Begin VB.Label Label6
      Caption         =     "DBCombo Box"
      Height          =     255
      Left            =     1680
      TabIndex        =     10
      Top             =     960
      Width           =     1215
   End
   Begin VB.Label Label5
      Caption         =     "DBList Box"
      Height          =     255
      Left            =     120
      TabIndex        =     9
      Top             =     960
      Width           =     1095
   End
   Begin VB.Label Label4
      Caption         =     "Label"
      Height          =     255
      Left            =     3360
      TabIndex        =     8
      Top             =     120
      Width           =     1215
   End
   Begin VB.Label Label3
      Caption         =     "Combo Box"
      Height          =     255
      Left            =     1680
      TabIndex        =     7
      Top             =     120
      Width           =     1215
   End
   Begin VB.Label Label2
      Caption         =     "Text Box"
      Height          =     255
```

```
      Left              =      120
      TabIndex          =      6
      Top               =      120
      Width             =      1215
   End
   Begin MSDBGrid.DBGrid DBGrid1
      Bindings          =      "datentry.frx":0000
      Height            =      1935
      Left              =      3240
      OleObjectBlob     =      "datentry.frx":000E
      TabIndex          =      5
      Top               =      1200
      Width             =      3135
   End
   Begin MSDBCtls.DBCombo DBCombo1
      Bindings          =      "datentry.frx":0716
      DataField         =      "Name"
      DataSource        =      "Data1"
      Height            =      315
      Left              =      1680
      TabIndex          =      4
      Top               =      1200
      Width             =      1215
      _Version          =      65536
      _ExtentX          =      2143
      _ExtentY          =      556
      _StockProps       =      77
      ForeColor         =      0
      ListField         =      "Name"
      BoundColumn       =      "Name"
   End
   Begin MSDBCtls.DBList DBList1
      Bindings          =      "datentry.frx":0724
      DataField         =      "Name"
      DataSource        =      "Data1"
      Height            =      1620
      Left              =      120
      TabIndex          =      3
      Top               =      1200
      Width             =      1215
      _Version          =      65536
      _ExtentX          =      2143
      _ExtentY          =      2858
      _StockProps       =      77
      ForeColor         =      -2147483640
      BackColor         =      -2147483643
      ListField         =      "Name"
      BoundColumn       =      "Name"
   End
   Begin VB.Label Label1
```

```
            BorderStyle       =   1   'Fixed Single
            Caption           =   "Label1"
            DataField         =   "Name"
            DataSource        =   "Data1"
            Height            =   495
            Left              =   3360
            TabIndex          =   2
            Top               =   360
            Width             =   1215
        End
    End
End
Attribute VB_Name = "Form1"
Attribute VB_Creatable = False
Attribute VB_Exposed = False
Private Sub Command1_Click()
    frmReadData.Show
End Sub

Private Sub Command2_Click()
    Data1.UpdateRecord
End Sub
```

LISTING 11.5 READDATA.FRM

```
VERSION 4.00
Begin VB.Form frmReadData
    Caption          =   "students"
    ClientHeight     =   1350
    ClientLeft       =   1995
    ClientTop        =   1800
    ClientWidth      =   5520
    Height           =   1755
    Left             =   1935
    LinkTopic        =   "Form2"
    ScaleHeight      =   1350
    ScaleWidth       =   5520
    Top              =   1455
    Width            =   5640
    Begin VB.CommandButton cmdClose
        Caption       =   "&Close"
        Height        =   300
        Left          =   4440
        TabIndex      =   8
        Top           =   720
        Width         =   975
    End
    Begin VB.CommandButton cmdUpdate
        Caption       =   "&Update"
        Height        =   300
        Left          =   3360
        TabIndex      =   7
```

```
      Top            =    720
      Width          =    975
   End
   Begin VB.CommandButton cmdRefresh
      Caption        =    "&Refresh"
      Height         =    300
      Left           =    2280
      TabIndex       =    6
      Top            =    700
      Width          =    975
   End
   Begin VB.CommandButton cmdDelete
      Caption        =    "&Delete"
      Height         =    300
      Left           =    1200
      TabIndex       =    5
      Top            =    700
      Width          =    975
   End
   Begin VB.CommandButton cmdAdd
      Caption        =    "&Add"
      Height         =    300
      Left           =    120
      TabIndex       =    4
      Top            =    720
      Width          =    975
   End
   Begin VB.Data Data1
      Align          =    2    'Align Bottom
      Connect        =    ""
      DatabaseName   =    "C:\VBOOK\datactrl\vbclass.mdb"
      Exclusive      =    0    'False
      Height         =    300
      Left           =    0
      Options        =    0
      ReadOnly       =    0    'False
      RecordsetType  =    1    'Dynaset
      RecordSource   =    "students"
      Top            =    1050
      Width          =    5520
   End
   Begin VB.TextBox txtFields
      DataField      =    "Grade"
      DataSource     =    "Data1"
      Height         =    285
      Index          =    1
      Left           =    2040
      MaxLength      =    10
      TabIndex       =    3
      Top            =    360
      Width          =    3375
   End
```

```
    Begin VB.TextBox txtFields
        DataField       =   "Name"
        DataSource      =   "Data1"
        Height          =   285
        Index           =   0
        Left            =   2040
        MaxLength       =   10
        TabIndex        =   1
        Top             =   40
        Width           =   3375
    End
    Begin VB.Label lblLabels
        Caption         =   "Grade:"
        Height          =   255
        Index           =   1
        Left            =   120
        TabIndex        =   2
        Top             =   380
        Width           =   1815
    End
    Begin VB.Label lblLabels
        Caption         =   "Name:"
        Height          =   255
        Index           =   0
        Left            =   120
        TabIndex        =   0
        Top             =   60
        Width           =   1815
    End
End
Attribute VB_Name = "frmReadData"
Attribute VB_Creatable = False
Attribute VB_Exposed = False

Private Sub cmdAdd_Click()
  Data1.Recordset.AddNew
End Sub

Private Sub cmdDelete_Click()
  'this may produce an error if you delete the last
  'record or the only record in the recordset
  Data1.Recordset.Delete
  Data1.Recordset.MoveNext
End Sub

Private Sub cmdRefresh_Click()
  'this is really only needed for multi user apps
  Data1.Refresh
End Sub

Private Sub cmdUpdate_Click()
  Data1.UpdateRecord
```

```
    Data1.Recordset.Bookmark = Data1.Recordset.LastModified
End Sub

Private Sub cmdClose_Click()
    Unload Me
End Sub

Private Sub Data1_Error(DataErr As Integer, Response As Integer)
    'This is where you would put error handling code
    'If you want to ignore errors, comment out the next line
    'If you want to trap them, add code here to handle them
    MsgBox "Data error event hit err:" & Error$(DataErr)
    Response = 0   'throw away the error
End Sub

Private Sub Data1_Reposition()
    Screen.MousePointer = vbDefault
    On Error Resume Next
    'This will display the current record position
    'for dynasets and snapshots
    Data1.Caption = "Record: " & (Data1.Recordset.AbsolutePosition + 1)
    'for the table object you must set the index property when
    'the recordset gets created and use the following line
    'Data1.Caption = "Record: " & (Data1.Recordset.RecordCount *
    '        (Data1.Recordset.PercentPosition * 0.01)) + 1
End Sub

Private Sub Data1_Validate(Action As Integer, Save As Integer)
    'This is where you put validation code
    'This event gets called when the following actions occur
    Select Case Action
      Case vbDataActionMoveFirst
      Case vbDataActionMovePrevious
      Case vbDataActionMoveNext
      Case vbDataActionMoveLast
      Case vbDataActionAddNew
      Case vbDataActionUpdate
      Case vbDataActionDelete
      Case vbDataActionFind
      Case vbDataActionBookmark
      Case vbDataActionClose
    End Select
    'Screen.MousePointer = vbHourglass
End Sub

Private Sub Form_Unload(Cancel As Integer)
        Form1.Data1.Refresh
End Sub
```

So far we've been quite successful with our database handling, but we have just begun. Our database has been very basic, including only one simple table. A great deal more power is available in our database handling. To give you an idea of what is coming up in the next two chapters, we'll present an overview of some of those techniques now.

RELATIONAL DATABASES

So far, our database table looks like this:

```
Name    Grade
---------------
| Ann   |   C   |
|-------|-------|
| Mark  |   B   |
|-------|-------|
| Ed    |   A   |
|-------|-------|
| Frank |   A   |
|-------|-------|
| Ted   |   A   |
|-------|-------|
| Mabel |   B   |
|-------|-------|
| Ralph |   B   |
|-------|-------|
| Tom   |   B   |
---------------
```

Suppose that we bring this data to the Visual Basic school registrar, but the registrar tells us that the grade data should be indexed in terms of student ID numbers and not names. We get a new database table, which also includes phone numbers:

```
Student IDs

Name     ID      Phone
--------------------------
| Mark  |  111  | 777-1111 |
|-------|-------|----------|
| Ann   |  222  | 777-2222 |
|-------|-------|----------|
| Ted   |  333  | 777-3333 |
|-------|-------|----------|
| Ralph |  444  | 777-4444 |
|-------|-------|----------|
| Frank |  555  | 777-5555 |
|-------|-------|----------|
| Mabel |  666  | 777-6666 |
|-------|-------|----------|
| Tom   |  777  | 777-7777 |
|-------|-------|----------|
| Ed    |  888  | 777-8888 |
--------------------------
```

Using the data in this new table, we might add a new field to each record in our table and call that field ID:

```
                      |
                      V
Name      Grade      ID
-----------------------------
| Ann   |   C   |   222   |
|-------|-------|---------|
| Mark  |   B   |   111   |
|-------|-------|---------|
| Ed    |   A   |   888   |
|-------|-------|---------|
| Frank |   A   |   555   |
|-------|-------|---------|
| Ted   |   A   |   333   |
|-------|-------|---------|
| Mabel |   B   |   666   |
|-------|-------|---------|
| Ralph |   B   |   444   |
|-------|-------|---------|
| Tom   |   B   |   777   |
-----------------------------
```

Referential Integrity and Cascading Changes

Note that the data in the two tables—our table, students, and the table the registrar gave us—is related. In particular, the ID field appears in both tables:

```
                  |                        |
                  V                        V
Name    Grade    ID          Name     ID      Phone
-----------------------      --------------------------------
| Ann   |  C  |  222  |      | Mark  |  111 |  777-1111 |
|-------|-----|-------|      |-------|------|-----------|
| Mark  |  B  |  111  |      | Ann   |  222 |  777-2222 |
|-------|-----|-------|      |-------|------|-----------|
| Ed    |  A  |  888  |      | Ted   |  333 |  777-3333 |
|-------|-----|-------|      |-------|------|-----------|
| Frank |  A  |  555  |      | Ralph |  444 |  777-4444 |
|-------|-----|-------|      |-------|------|-----------|
| Ted   |  A  |  333  |      | Frank |  555 |  777-5555 |
|-------|-----|-------|      |-------|------|-----------|
| Mabel |  B  |  666  |      | Mabel |  666 |  777-6666 |
|-------|-----|-------|      |-------|------|-----------|
| Ralph |  B  |  444  |      | Tom   |  777 |  777-7777 |
|-------|-----|-------|      |-------|------|-----------|
| Tom   |  B  |  777  |      | Ed    |  888 |  777-8888 |
-----------------------      --------------------------------
```

Let's also say that the main index of the registrar's table—the field that sets the order of all the records—is the ID field. This means that the ID field is the table's *primary key*. Tables are often sorted according to their primary key.

This same field, the ID field, also appears in our students table, and we can use that field as an index into the other table. For example, if we wanted to find Frank's phone number, we would first find his ID number in our students table and then use the ID as an index in the registrar's table to find Frank's record. From Frank's record, we could find his phone number. In this way, the ID field in the students table provides us with an index into the records of the registrar's table. We call the ID field a *foreign key* in the student table, because it connects us with a *foreign table*, the registrar's table:

```
                              |                        |
                              V                        V
     Name     Grade    ID           Name     ID       Phone
     --------------------------     ----------------------------
   | Ann    |   C   |  222  |     | Mark  |  111  |  777-1111 |
   |--------|-------|-------|     |-------|-------|-----------|
   | Mark   |   B   |  111  |     | Ann   |  222  |  777-2222 |
   |--------|-------|-------|     |-------|-------|-----------|
   | Ed     |   A   |  888  |     | Ted   |  333  |  777-3333 |
   |--------|-------|-------|     |-------|-------|-----------|
   | Frank  |   A   |  555  |     | Ralph |  444  |  777-4444 |
   |--------|-------|-------|     |-------|-------|-----------|
   | Ted    |   A   |  333  |     | Frank |  555  |  777-5555 |
   |--------|-------|-------|     |-------|-------|-----------|
   | Mabel  |   B   |  666  |     | Mabel |  666  |  777-6666 |
   |--------|-------|-------|     |-------|-------|-----------|
   | Ralph  |   B   |  444  |     | Tom   |  777  |  777-7777 |
   |--------|-------|-------|     |-------|-------|-----------|
   | Tom    |   B   |  777  |     | Ed    |  888  |  777-8888 |
     --------------------------     ----------------------------
               Foreign                    Primary
               Key in this                Key in this
               table                      table
```

In this way, our two database tables are connected; the ID field in students provides us with a means of finding the record we want in the registrar's table. This is what is meant by a relational database—a database containing a number of tables that can be related in some way. Breaking a database into tables is useful in the same way that a business might keep several different books for accounting—one for accounts receivable, another for accounts payable, still another for inventory, and so on—and all these books are related, just as the tables in a database can be related.

This brings up an interesting strength of relational databases: they can maintain the connections between tables for you if you set them up accordingly. For example, let's say that Ned, a new student, wants to take our Visual Basic class. Ned's ID number is 999. We enter that value into our students table:

```
                    |                   |
                    V                   V
    Name    Grade   ID          Name    ID      Phone
    ------------------------      ------------------------
    | Ann   |  C  |  222 |       | Mark  |  111 | 777-1111 |
    |-------|-----|------|       |-------|------|----------|
    | Mark  |  B  |  111 |       | Ann   |  222 | 777-2222 |
    |-------|-----|------|       |-------|------|----------|
    | Ed    |  A  |  888 |       | Ted   |  333 | 777-3333 |
    |-------|-----|------|       |-------|------|----------|
    | Frank |  A  |  555 |       | Ralph |  444 | 777-4444 |
    |-------|-----|------|       |-------|------|----------|
    | Ted   |  A  |  333 |       | Frank |  555 | 777-5555 |
    |-------|-----|------|       |-------|------|----------|
    | Mabel |  B  |  666 |       | Mabel |  666 | 777-6666 |
    |-------|-----|------|       |-------|------|----------|
    | Ralph |  B  |  444 |       | Tom   |  777 | 777-7777 |
    |-------|-----|------|       |-------|------|----------|
    | Tom   |  B  |  777 |       | Ed    |  888 | 777-8888 |
    |-------|-----|------|       ------------------------
--> | Ned   |     |  999 |
    ------------------------
```

But note that the registrar has no record of this new student, and Ned's ID number does not appear in the registrar's table. In such a case, we could program our database to automatically create a trappable error, constraining the data we enter in our students table to only those legal values that are already in the registrar's table.

This process enforces *referential integrity*, and it's one way that relational databases work for us.

It's also possible to connect tables in such a way that if a change is made in one, the corresponding change is made in other, related tables. This is called a *cascading change*, and we'll program the above two tables to work this way. For example, if the registrar wanted to change a student's ID number in the registrar's table and to have that student's ID number automatically changed in our students table, that could be done if our tables were set up to handle cascading changes. We will work with this in the following chapters.

One other point we might note is the concept of *database renormalization*, the art of making database tables as efficient as possible. Renormalization usually consists of removing redundant fields and selecting primary keys carefully. For example, now that the registrar's table ties student names with their ID numbers, it could be considered redundant that we enter both of these in our table. From a database designer's point of view, it would be more efficient to eliminate the Name field from our table and keep the ID field as an index into the registrar's table:

```
        |                              |
        V                              V
   ID       Grade          Name       ID      Phone
 ----------------          -----------------------------
 |  111  |   B  |          | Mark  |  111  | 777-1111 |
 |-------|------|          |-------|-------|----------|
 |  222  |   C  |          | Ann   |  222  | 777-2222 |
 |-------|------|          |-------|-------|----------|
 |  333  |   A  |          | Ted   |  333  | 777-3333 |
 |-------|------|          |-------|-------|----------|
 |  444  |   B  |          | Ralph |  444  | 777-4444 |
 |-------|------|          |-------|-------|----------|
 |  555  |   A  |          | Frank |  555  | 777-5555 |
 |-------|------|          |-------|-------|----------|
 |  666  |   B  |          | Mabel |  666  | 777-6666 |
 |-------|------|          |-------|-------|----------|
 |  777  |   B  |          | Tom   |  777  | 777-7777 |
 |-------|------|          |-------|-------|----------|
 |  888  |   A  |          | Ed    |  888  | 777-8888 |
 ----------------          -----------------------------
```

We will cover these new topics in the next two chapters.

This completes our overview of and introduction to database handling, particularly using the Data control and bound data controls. In the next chapter, we'll start seeing how to create and work with databases in code. As we've just seen, there is a great deal of power to look forward to.

## CHAPTER 12

CREATING AND FILLING DATABASES

In the last chapter, we saw how to use the Data Manager tool to create and fill databases and how to use the Data control and bound controls to display their contents. In this chapter, we'll see how to perform these operations in code using Data Access Object (DAO) programming. In particular, we'll create in our Visual Basic programs the same databases we created in Chapter 11 using the Data Manager. In addition, we'll see how to create our own version of the data manager in code, allowing the user to specify both table and field names on the fly, and we'll learn how to let the user add new records and edit the old ones. Let's get started by seeing how to create our student database from last chapter in code.

CREATING A DATABASE IN CODE

Our first project is to create in code the students table we created in Chapter 11 using the Data Manager:

```
    Name     Grade
   --------------
  | Ann   |   C   |
  |-------|-------|
  | Mark  |   B   |
  |-------|-------|
  | Ed    |   A   |
  |-------|-------|
  | Frank |   A   |
  |-------|-------|
  | Ted   |   A   |
  |-------|-------|
  | Mabel |   B   |
  |-------|-------|
  | Ralph |   B   |
  |-------|-------|
  | Tom   |   B   |
   --------------
```

Create a new Visual Basic project named **CREATEDB.VBP**. Place a button on Form1 and give it the caption **Create Database**. When the user clicks this button, we can create our database, which we call **CREATED.MDB**, and display the students table in a bound Grid control:

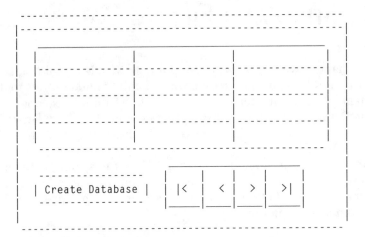

Let's start working in code. Open the click event connected to the **Create Database** button:

```
Private Sub Command1_Click()

End Sub
```

When the user clicks this button, we want to create the **CREATED.MDB** database file with the students table in it. Doing so requires more work than was evident when we used the Data Manager in the last chapter. We start by adding to our program the DAO object library. This library holds the definition of all the objects, such as database objects and table objects, that we'll need in our program. These objects form the basis of database programming in Visual Basic: to work with databases in code, we must have a database object, and that object is defined in the DAO library. Use **References** in the Visual Basic Tools menu, and click the box marked **Microsoft DAO Object Library**. Then click **OK**, adding this library's objects to our program.

Defining a Database

The first DAO object you see is the DBEngine object:

```
-----------------------
|       DBEngine       |
-----------------------
```

This object is the basis of database programming in Visual Basic. It contains a collection of workspaces. A *collection* is like an array of objects; for example, the collection of workspace objects in the DBEngine is named Workspaces, and the first workspace in Workspaces is referred to as Workspace(0). *Workspaces* are where we open and work with databases in Visual Basic, which is useful because it means that our program can have several databases open at once:

In DAO programming, collections of objects use the object name and add an *s* to the end; for example, a collection named fields contains objects of type field. One workspace already exists in this collection of workspaces: Workspace(0), the default workspace. We will create our database as an object of type Database in this workspace:

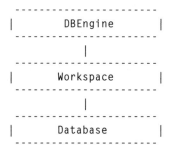

We use the CreateDatabase method of this workspace to create an object of type Database:

```
Set TheDB = Workspace.CreateDatabase(Filename, Ordering, Options)
```

Here, Filename is the name of our new database. The Ordering argument specifies how to order text records (which varies by language); the argument may be any of the constants in Table 12.1. The optional argument Options allows us to request an encrypted database or to set the version of the Microsoft Jet database engine we want. Possible values appear in Table 12.2.

TABLE 12.1 CREATEDATABASE ORDERING SELECTIONS.

Constant	Meaning
dbLangGeneral	English, German, French, Portuguese, Italian, and Modern Spanish
dbLangArabic	Arabic
dbLangCzech	Czech
dbLangCyrillic	Russian
dbLangDutch	Dutch
dbLangGreek	Greek
dbLangHebrew	Hebrew
dbLangHungarian	Hungarian
dbLangIcelandic	Icelandic
dbLangNordic	Nordic languages
dbLangNorwdan	Norwegian and Danish
dbLangPolish	Polish
dbLangSwedfin	Swedish and Finnish
dbLangSpanish	Traditional Spanish
dbLangTurkish	Turkish

TABLE 12.2 CREATEDATABASE OPTIONS.

Constant	Meaning
dbEncrypt	Create an encrypted database.
dbVersion10	Create a database that uses the Microsoft Jet database engine version 1.0.
dbVersion11	Create a database that uses the Microsoft Jet database engine version 1.1.
dbVersion25	Create a database that uses the Microsoft Jet database engine version 2.5.
dbVersion30	Create a database that uses the Microsoft Jet database engine version 3.0.

In code, we create our new database with CreateDatabase():

```
Private Sub Command1_Click()
    Dim TheDB As Database

    Set TheDB = DBEngine.Workspaces(0).CreateDatabase("CREATED.MDB",
        dbLangGeneral)
        .
        .
        .
```

At this point, we have an object of type Database named TheDB, which corresponds to our database. We are ready to set up one table in our database object, and that is our table named students:

```
       Name    Grade
      ---------------
     | Ann   |   C   |
     |-------|-------|
     | Mark  |   B   |
     |-------|-------|
     | Ed    |   A   |
     |-------|-------|
     | Frank |   A   |
     |-------|-------|
     | Ted   |   A   |
     |-------|-------|
     | Mabel |   B   |
     |-------|-------|
     | Ralph |   B   |
     |-------|-------|
     | Tom   |   B   |
      ---------------
```

We do that by *defining* a new type of table named students, using a TableDef object:

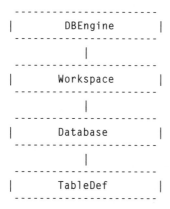

After we have designed our table definition (by specifying the fields that go into it), we will be able to create tables of that type. We begin by creating an object of type TableDef in our database object:

```
Private Sub Command1_Click()
    Dim TheDB As Database
--> Dim studentsTD As TableDef

    Set TheDB = DBEngine.Workspaces(0).CreateDatabase("CREATED.MDB",
        dbLangGeneral)

--> Set studentsTD = TheDB.CreateTableDef("students")
        .
        .
        .
```

Now the new table definition, studentsTD, is ready for us to set up as we like. In this case, we want two fields in our table: Name and Grade. Both are text fields. To create these fields and install them in our table definition, we will create new objects of type Field using the TableDef object's method named CreateField. Then we attach them to our table definition:

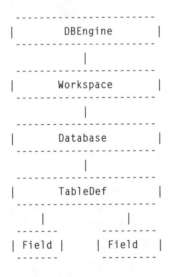

We will create two new fields, which we'll call studentsFlds(0) and studentsFlds(1), creating them and making them text fields this way:

```
     Private Sub Command1_Click()
         Dim TheDB As Database
         Dim studentsTD As TableDef
--> Dim studentsFlds(2) As Field

         Set TheDB = DBEngine.Workspaces(0).CreateDatabase("CREATED.MDB",
             dbLangGeneral)

         Set studentsTD = TheDB.CreateTableDef("students")
--> Set studentsFlds(0) = studentsTD.CreateField("Name", dbText)
--> Set studentsFlds(1) = studentsTD.CreateField("Grade", dbText)
             .
             .
             .
```

Note the keyword dbText, which indicates that these fields are text fields.
The other possibilities are dbDate, dbMemo, dbBoolean, dbInteger, dbLong,
dbCurrency, dbSingle, dbDouble, dbByte, and dbLongBinary. In addition, if
we want to specify the size of the field, such as making the Grade field only
one character long, we can do that with a third argument:

```
     Set studentsFlds(1) = studentsTD.CreateField("Grade", dbText, 1)
```

At this point, we've defined our two fields. Next, we add their definitions to
the table definition. We do that with the TableDef method Append. A
TableDef object, like our studentsTD, contains a collection of fields named
Fields, and we append the new field definitions to that collection:

```
     Private Sub Command1_Click()
         Dim TheDB As Database
         Dim studentsTD As TableDef
         Dim studentsFlds(2) As Field

         Set TheDB = DBEngine.Workspaces(0).CreateDatabase("CREATED.MDB",
             dbLangGeneral)

         Set studentsTD = TheDB.CreateTableDef("students")
         Set studentsFlds(0) = studentsTD.CreateField("Name", dbText)
         Set studentsFlds(1) = studentsTD.CreateField("Grade", dbText)
--> studentsTD.Fields.Append studentsFlds(0)
--> studentsTD.Fields.Append studentsFlds(1)
             .
             .
             .
```

Now we've defined a new type of table, students, having two text fields: Name and Grade.

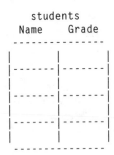

The next step is to add our completed table definition to the collection of TableDef objects (named TableDefs) in our database object. To do that, we use the Database Append method:

```
Private Sub Command1_Click()
    Dim TheDB As Database
    Dim studentsTD As TableDef
    Dim studentsFlds(2) As Field

    Set TheDB = DBEngine.Workspaces(0).CreateDatabase("CREATED.MDB",
        dbLangGeneral)

    Set studentsTD = TheDB.CreateTableDef("students")
    Set studentsFlds(0) = studentsTD.CreateField("Name", dbText)
    Set studentsFlds(1) = studentsTD.CreateField("Grade", dbText)
    studentsTD.Fields.Append studentsFlds(0)
    studentsTD.Fields.Append studentsFlds(1)
--> TheDB.TableDefs.Append studentsTD
        .
        .
        .
```

We've defined our type of database; it contains one table, students, and that table contains two fields: Name and Grade. Now that we've set up the table definition, the next step is to create an object of that type.

Creating a Table

So far, we've defined only our students table; now we need an actual object of that type to work with. In older versions of Visual Basic, we would do that by creating an object of type Table; now, however, we create an object of type RecordSet:

```
Private Sub Command1_Click()
    Dim TheDB As Database
    Dim studentsTD As TableDef
    Dim studentsFlds(2) As Field
--> Dim studentsTable As Recordset

    Set TheDB = DBEngine.Workspaces(0).CreateDatabase("CREATED.MDB",
        dbLangGeneral)

    Set studentsTD = TheDB.CreateTableDef("students")
    Set studentsFlds(0) = studentsTD.CreateField("Name", dbText)
    Set studentsFlds(1) = studentsTD.CreateField("Grade", dbText)
    studentsTD.Fields.Append studentsFlds(0)
    studentsTD.Fields.Append studentsFlds(1)
    TheDB.TableDefs.Append studentsTD

--> Set studentsTable = TheDB.OpenRecordset("students", dbOpenTable)
        .
        .
        .
```

This new recordset is what we will actually work with. We will be able to reach the Name and Grade fields in it directly and to use recordset methods such as Edit and Update. In fact, there are three types of recordsets: tables, dynasets, and snapshots.

We are already familiar with a table. To open a table-type recordset, we pass OpenRecordset() the parameter dbOpenTable. Specific methods of searching and sorting tables are discussed in the next chapter.

A *dynaset* is like a table, but a dynaset can also contain tables from other databases. In addition, it uses different methods to search and seek and can perform such operations on a number of tables at once. To open a dynaset recordset, we pass OpenRecordset() the parameter dbOpenDynaset.

A *snapshot* is like a dynaset, except that a snapshot is read-only and cannot be modified. Because it is read-only, a snapshot's operations can be much quicker than those of a dynaset or a table. To open a snapshot-type recordset, pass OpenRecordset() the parameter dbOpenSnapshot.

We will learn more about the differences among these types of recordsets in the next chapter. It's worth noting that we can reach the internal recordset of a Data control by referring to its Recordset property like this: Data1.Recordset. We can also open a recordset based on an SQL query, because such a query can return a number of records; to do so, we need only pass that query to OpenRecordset(). Here, SQLQuery is a text string holding the SQL query:

```
    Set studentsTable = TheDB.OpenRecordset(SQLQuery, dbOpenTable)
```

OpenRecordset() can also take a third argument, which sets various sharing and reading options as shown in Table 12.3.

TABLE 12.3 OPENRECORDSET OPTIONS.

Constant	Meaning
dbDenyWrite	Other users can't modify or add records.
dbDenyRead	Other users can't view records.
dbReadOnly	You can only view records; other users can modify them.
dbAppendOnly	You can only append new records (dynaset-type Recordset only).
dbInconsistent	Inconsistent updates are allowed.
dbConsistent	Only consistent updates are allowed.
dbForwardOnly	The Recordset is a forward-only scrolling snapshot.
dbSQLPassThrough	The Microsoft Jet database engine query processor is bypassed.
dbSeeChanges	Generate a run-time error if another user is changing data you are editing.

For example, we can create a table-type recordset that others are not allowed to modify or otherwise write to. Using an SQL query, we execute this line:

```
Set studentsTable = TheDB.OpenRecordset(SQLQuery, dbOpenTable,
dbDenyWrite)
```

For now, however, we open our new recordset as a table object in our program:

```
Set studentsTable = TheDB.OpenRecordset("students", dbOpenTable)
```

Our students table, studentsTable, is finally ready for use. Our first step is to add a new record to the table using the AddNew method; then we place our data in the new record. In particular, we will want to place data in the Name and Grade fields. We can reference the Name field like this: studentsTable.Fields("Name"). Visual Basic also allows us to refer to this field this way, without using the field name as an index: studentsTable.Fields!Name. In fact, the Fields collection of a recordset is considered its *default collection*, so if we want to specify an item in that collection, we can do it like this:

studentsTable!Name. The DAO library objects will assume we are referring to a field in this table. After placing the data we want in this field, we update the database with the Update method. In code, we add the first record, for the student named Ann, like this:

```
Private Sub Command1_Click()
    Dim TheDB As Database
    Dim studentsTD As TableDef
    Dim studentsFlds(2) As Field
    Dim studentsTable As Recordset
            .
            .
            .
    Set studentsTable = TheDB.OpenRecordset("students", dbOpenTable)

--> studentsTable.AddNew
--> studentsTable!Name = "Ann"
--> studentsTable!Grade = "C"
--> studentsTable.Update
            .
            .
            .
```

In this way, we fill our table in code:

```
    Set studentsTable = TheDB.OpenRecordset("students", dbOpenTable)

    studentsTable.AddNew
    studentsTable!Name = "Ann"
    studentsTable!Grade = "C"
    studentsTable.Update
    studentsTable.AddNew
    studentsTable!Name = "Mark"
    studentsTable!Grade = "B"
    studentsTable.Update
    studentsTable.AddNew
    studentsTable!Name = "Ed"
    studentsTable!Grade = "A"
    studentsTable.Update
    studentsTable.AddNew
    studentsTable!Name = "Frank"
    studentsTable!Grade = "A"
    studentsTable.Update
    studentsTable.AddNew
    studentsTable!Name = "Ted"
    studentsTable!Grade = "A"
    studentsTable.Update
    studentsTable.AddNew
    studentsTable!Name = "Mabel"
```

```
studentsTable!Grade = "B"
studentsTable.Update
studentsTable.AddNew
studentsTable!Name = "Ralph"
studentsTable!Grade = "B"
studentsTable.Update
studentsTable.AddNew
studentsTable!Name = "Tom"
studentsTable!Grade = "B"
studentsTable.Update
```

```
TheDB.Close
```

We close the database and write it to disk with this statement: TheDB.Close.
Now we've created **CREATED.MDB**. Congratulations—you've produced
your first database using Visual Basic DAO methods. To display our new
table, we add a Data control, Data1, and a DBGrid control, DBGrid1, to our
program:

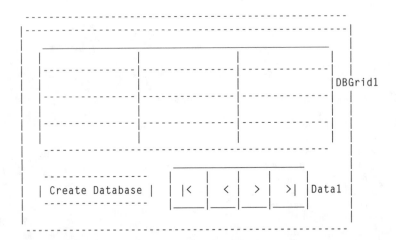

We set the Datasource property of the grid to Data1. In our program, we set
the DatabaseName ("CREATED.MDB") and RecordSource properties (the
table in our database: students) of Data1 after creating the database file.
Then we enable the Grid control and the Data control and refresh the Data
control to make it read the data from the database file:

```
Private Sub Command1_Click()
    Dim TheDB As Database
    Dim studentsTD As TableDef
        .
        .
        .
```

```
        studentsTable.AddNew
        studentsTable!Name = "Tom"
        studentsTable!Grade = "B"
        studentsTable.Update

        TheDB.Close

-->     Data1.DatabaseName = "C:\VBOOK\CREATEDB\CREATED.MDB"
-->     Data1.RecordSource = "students"
-->     Data1.Enabled = True
-->     DBGrid1.Enabled = True
-->     Data1.Refresh
End Sub
```

When the user clicks **Create Database**, our database is created and displayed, as in Figure 12.1. Our program is a success. **CREATEDB.VBP** is in Listing 12.1, and **CREATEDB.FRM** is in Listing 12.2.

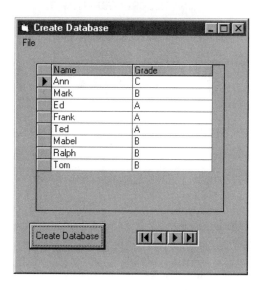

FIGURE 12.1 CREATING A DATABASE IN CODE.

LISTING 12.1 CREATEDB.VBP

```
Form=createdb.Frm
Object={F9043C88-F6F2-101A-A3C9-08002B2F49FB}#1.0#0; COMDLG32.OCX
Object={6B7E6392-850A-101B-AFC0-4210102A8DA7}#1.0#0; COMCTL32.OCX
Object={FAEEE763-117E-101B-8933-08002B2F4F5A}#1.0#0; DBLIST32.OCX
Object={00028C01-0000-0000-0000-000000000046}#1.0#0; DBGRID32.OCX
Reference=*\G{BEF6E001-A874-101A-8BBA-
```

```
            00AA00300CAB}#2.0#0#C:\WINDOWS\SYSTEM\OLEPRO32.DLL#Standard
            OLE Types
Reference=*\G{00025E01-0000-0000-C000-000000000046}#3.0#0#C:\PROGRAM
            FILES\COMMON FILES\MICROSOFT SHARED\DAO\DAO3032.DLL#Microsoft
            DAO 3.0 Object Library
ProjWinSize=356,375,217,94
ProjWinShow=2
IconForm="Form1"
Name="Project1"
HelpContextID="0"
StartMode=0
VersionCompatible32="0"
MajorVer=1
MinorVer=0
RevisionVer=0
AutoIncrementVer=0
ServerSupportFiles=0
```

LISTING 12.2 CREATEDB.FRM

```
VERSION 4.00
Begin VB.Form Form1
    Caption         =    "Create Database"
    ClientHeight    =    4140
    ClientLeft      =    2715
    ClientTop       =    1890
    ClientWidth     =    4380
    Height          =    4830
    Left            =    2655
    LinkTopic       =    "Form1"
    ScaleHeight     =    4140
    ScaleWidth      =    4380
    Top             =    1260
    Width           =    4500
    Begin VB.Data Data1
        Caption         =    "Data1"
        Connect         =    "Access"
        DatabaseName    =    ""
        Enabled         =    0      'False
        Exclusive       =    0      'False
        Height          =    300
        Left            =    2280
        Options         =    0
        ReadOnly        =    0      'False
        RecordsetType   =    1      'Dynaset
        RecordSource    =    ""
        Top             =    3360
        Width           =    1215
    End
```

```
    Begin VB.CommandButton Command1
        Caption         =   "Create Database"
        Height          =   495
        Left            =   240
        TabIndex        =   0
        Top             =   3240
        Width           =   1455
    End
    Begin MSDBGrid.DBGrid DBGrid1
        Bindings        =   "createdb.frx":0000
        Height          =   2775
        Left            =   360
        OleObjectBlob   =   "createdb.frx":000E
        TabIndex        =   1
        Top             =   240
        Width           =   3615
    End
    Begin VB.Menu File
        Caption         =   "File"
        Begin VB.Menu ExitItem
            Caption     =   "Exit"
        End
    End
End
Attribute VB_Name = "Form1"
Attribute VB_Creatable = False
Attribute VB_Exposed = False

Private Sub Command1_Click()
    Dim TheDB As Database
    Dim studentsTD As TableDef
    Dim studentsFlds(2) As Field
    Dim studentsTable As Recordset

    Set TheDB = DBEngine.Workspaces(0).CreateDatabase("CREATED.MDB",
        dbLangGeneral)

    Set studentsTD = TheDB.CreateTableDef("students")
    Set studentsFlds(0) = studentsTD.CreateField("Name", dbText)
    Set studentsFlds(1) = studentsTD.CreateField("Grade", dbText)
    studentsTD.Fields.Append studentsFlds(0)
    studentsTD.Fields.Append studentsFlds(1)
    TheDB.TableDefs.Append studentsTD

    Set studentsTable = TheDB.OpenRecordset("students", dbOpenTable)

    studentsTable.AddNew
    studentsTable!Name = "Ann"
    studentsTable!Grade = "C"
    studentsTable.Update
```

```
studentsTable.AddNew
studentsTable!Name = "Mark"
studentsTable!Grade = "B"
studentsTable.Update
studentsTable.AddNew
studentsTable!Name = "Ed"
studentsTable!Grade = "A"
studentsTable.Update
studentsTable.AddNew
studentsTable!Name = "Frank"
studentsTable!Grade = "A"
studentsTable.Update
studentsTable.AddNew
studentsTable!Name = "Ted"
studentsTable!Grade = "A"
studentsTable.Update
studentsTable.AddNew
studentsTable!Name = "Mabel"
studentsTable!Grade = "B"
studentsTable.Update
studentsTable.AddNew
studentsTable!Name = "Ralph"
studentsTable!Grade = "B"
studentsTable.Update
studentsTable.AddNew
studentsTable!Name = "Tom"
studentsTable!Grade = "B"
studentsTable.Update

TheDB.Close

Data1.DatabaseName = "C:\VBOOK\CREATEDB\CREATED.MDB"
Data1.RecordSource = "students"
Data1.Enabled = True
DBGrid1.Enabled = True
Data1.Refresh

End Sub


Private Sub ExitItem_Click()
    End
End Sub
```

What we have done so far is fine, but it's not a very true-to-life example. We knew what database we wanted to create, what table to put in it, and what the data was. In practice, this is not necessarily true; instead, the user sets the database name, what tables go into it, and what fields are in the tables. To understand database programming, we have to deal with this more general task: letting the user create and manipulate multiple-table databases. Our next project will allow us to get into the core of database programming in an application that has some real-world use. With our Database Designer program, the user can create or open databases, add tables to those databases, and set what fields are in what table and fill those fields with data. Although it sounds like a big project, the DAO methods in Visual Basic make the code quite short. We will start this program in this chapter. We'll leave part of the programming—the part where we use buttons such as >> and > to navigate through a database, as well as searching and sorting that database—to the next chapter.

OUR DATABASE DESIGNER PROGRAM

Our Database Designer program appears in Figure 12.2. With it, we'll be able to create our **VBCLASS.MDB** database and place two tables into it: students and registrar (the tables we saw in the last chapter). Writing this program is as good an introduction to database programming in Visual Basic as one can get, because much of the utility of DAO programming is represented here. Some of the code in the database designer will necessarily be similar to what we have just seen, but we will quickly pass beyond that into new material.

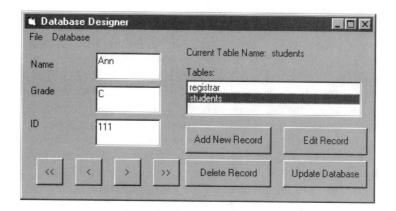

FIGURE 12.2 OUR DATABASE DESIGNER PROGRAM.

Using the Database Designer Program

Let's first summarize how the Database Designer is supposed to work from the user's point of view; refer to Figure 12.2 to see how the program's controls are arranged. Schematically, the program looks like the one shown next. We are working on the students table of our **VBCLASS.MDB** database:

```
-----------------------------------------------------------------
| Database Designer                                             |
|---------------------------------------------------------------|
| File              Database                                    |
|---------------------------------------------------------------|
|                                                               |
|                              Current Table Name:  students    |
|              --------                                         |
|   Name      |  Ann  |       Tables:                           |
|              --------        -------------------------        |
|              --------       | students                |       |
|   Grade     |  C    |       |                         |       |
|              --------       |_____|       |
|              --------                                         |
|   ID        |  111   |       ---------------  -----------      |
|              --------       |Add New Record| |Edit Record|     |
|                              ---------------  -----------      |
|   ------  ------  ------  ------   --------------  ----------------  |
|  | << |  | < |  | > |  | >> |  |Delete Record| |Update Database| |
|   ------  ------  ------  ------   --------------  ----------------  |
|                                                               |
-----------------------------------------------------------------
```

Let's look at this from the user's point of view. After starting the program, users begin by creating a new database. To create **VBCLASS.MDB**, users select **New Database** in the Database Designer's File menu and type that name as the file name of the new database. The Database Designer then creates the database. Next, it's up to users to add tables (such as students and registrar) to the new database. They do that by using **Add Table** in the Database menu (see Figure 12.2). When they select this item, a dialog box named Add Table will open, with text boxes for the new table's name and for the names of three fields. (For simplicity, we will assume that each table that we design has three fields, although you can modify the code in the Database Designer to let the user set the number of fields.)

```
-----------------------------------------------
| Add Table                                   |
|---------------------------------------------|
|                    ------------             |
|    Table Name:    |            |            |
|                    ------------             |
|                    ------------             |
|   Field 1 Name:   |            |            |
|                    ------------             |
|                    ------------             |
|   Field 2 Name:   |            |            |
|                    ------------             |
|                    ------------             |
|   Field 3 Name:   |            |            |
|                    ------------             |
|        -----------        ------------      |
|       |    OK    |       |  Cancel   |     |
|        -----------        ------------      |
|                                             |
-----------------------------------------------
```

When users specify the name of the new table and the three fields and click **OK**, the Add Table dialog box closes, and the Database Designer displays the fields for this new table (as shown in Figure 12.2).

To add a new record to the table, users click **Add New Record**, as shown in Figure 12.2, fill in the data for the three fields of this new record, and click **Update Database** (just as in the Visual Basic Data Manager). To edit a record in the table, they click **Edit**, make the changes, and click **Update Database**. To delete the current record, they click **Delete**. (In the next chapter, we will add code to the arrow buttons to make them active, allowing us to move through the database. We will also add searching and sorting capabilities.)

To add a new table to the database, users select **Add Table** in the Database menu again and specify the new table name and the names of its three fields in the Add Table dialog box as before. When they click **OK**, the new table's fields are displayed in the Database Designer and users can add data to this table. All the tables in our database are listed in the list box shown in Figure 12.2; to switch to another table (such as students or registrar), users have only to click its name in the list box.

Users can navigate through the database using the <<, <, >, and >> buttons, as well as search and sort it using the **Search** and **Sort** menu items.

When they are finished, they select **Close Database** in the File menu to close the database.

You can see that the Database Designer covers many aspects of database handling and that writing the code for this program will provide insight into many database programming techniques.

As you can see in Figure 12.2, there are a number of controls in the Database Designer, from buttons to text boxes. Because we do not want the programming details to obscure the DAO programming that we are learning, the following schematic of the program shows the controls already installed so that we can refer to them easily as we write the program. (In addition, we'll add a common dialog control, CommonDialog1, which is not shown here; we'll use it for file opening and saving operations.)

```
---------------------------------------------------------------------
| Database Designer                                                 |
|-------------------------------------------------------------------|
| File                  Database                                    |
|-  ---------------    --------------------------------------------|
|| New Database... |  | New Table... |                             |
|| Open Database...|  | Search...    |                             |
|| Close Database  |  | Sort         |                             |
|| Exit            |   -------------                               |
| ----------------              Current Table Name:  Label5        |
|               --------                                           |
| Label1       | Text1 |        Tables:                            |
|               --------                ------------------------   |
|               --------        |                             |   |
| Label2       | Text2 |        |          List1              |   |
|               --------        |_____|   |
|               --------         --------------   -----------     |
| Label3       | Text3 |        |Add New Record|  |Edit Record|    |
|               --------                                           |
|        Command5      Command7    Command1          Command2      |
|  ------ ------ ------ ------   --------------   ----------------  |
| | << | | < | | > | | >> |    |Delete Record|  |Update Database| |
|  ------ ------ ------ ------   --------------   ----------------  |
|Command4        Command6          Command8          Command3      |
|                                                                   |
---------------------------------------------------------------------
```

This, then, is Form1 for our program, ready for us to use. Let's start with the **New Database** menu item in the File menu, which is typically the first selection the user will make when running our program.

The New Database Menu Item

When users first start our Database Designer, they'll usually create a new database using the **New Database** menu item. To make that item active, we open the click event connected to it:

```
Private Sub NewDatabase_Click()

End Sub
```

Here, we want to create a new database file, using the name the user specifies. To get that name, we use the common dialog's ShowSave method to pop a Save As dialog box on the screen:

```
Private Sub NewDatabase_Click()
    CommonDialog1.ShowSave
    If CommonDialog1.filename <> "" Then
         .
         .
         .
    End If
End Sub
```

It's not hard to create a database with the file name returned to us from the Save As dialog box. We use the CreateDatabase() method, as we have seen before. Next, we use a message box to warn users that they must create a table before starting to enter data:

```
Private Sub NewDatabase_Click()
    CommonDialog1.ShowSave
    If CommonDialog1.filename <> "" Then
-->     Set TheDB =
            DBEngine.Workspaces(0).CreateDatabase(CommonDialog1.filename,
            dbLangGeneral)
-->     MsgBox ("Database created. Add a table next.")
    End If
End Sub
```

We have created the object TheDB, which corresponds to our database. So that other parts of the program can have access to TheDB, we place it in Form1's (General) object. (Click **(General)** in the code window and then declare TheDB as follows.)

```
    Dim TheDB As Database              'In Form1's (General) object
```

Now the database itself is ready to be used by our program. The next step is to create a table in the database. We do that with the **New Table** menu item in the Database menu:

```
-----------------------------------------------------------------
| Database Designer                                             |
|---------------------------------------------------------------|
| File                Database                                  |
|-          ------------    ------------------------------------|
|| New Database... | | New Table... |                           |
|| Open Database...| | Search...    |                           |
|| Close Database  | | Sort         |                           |
|| Exit            | --------------                             |
| ----------------              Current Table Name:  Label5     |
|              --------                                         |
|  Label1   | Text1  |          Tables:                         |
|              --------         ------------------------        |
|              --------         |                      |        |
|  Label2   | Text2  |          |         List1        |        |
|              --------         |_____|        |
|              --------         ---------------  -----------    |
|  Label3   | Text3  |          |Add New Record|  |Edit Record|  |
|              --------         ---------------   -----------    |
|        Command5      Command7     Command1        Command2     |
| ------  ------  ------  ------  ---------------  ----------------|
| | << |  | < |  | > |  | >> |   |Delete Record|  |Update Database| |
| ------  ------  ------  ------  ---------------  ---------------- |
|Command4        Command6            Command8        Command3     |
|                                                                |
-----------------------------------------------------------------
```

Open the click event associated with that item.

The New Table Menu Item

When users click **New Table**, they want to add a table to the database. We need four names: the name of the new table and the names of the three fields in that table. To get that information, we use a new dialog box, Add Table:

```
-----------------------------------------------
| Add Table                                   |
|---------------------------------------------|
|                  -----------                |
|   Table Name:   |   Text1   |               |
|                  -----------                |
|                  -----------                |
|  Field 1 Name:  |   Text2   |               |
|                  -----------                |
|                  -----------                |
|  Field 2 Name:  |   Text3   |               |
|                  -----------                |
|                  -----------                |
|  Field 3 Name:  |   Text4   |               |
|                  -----------                |
|     -----------         -----------         |
|    |    OK     |       |   Cancel  |        |
|     -----------         -----------         |
|      Command1            Command2           |
-----------------------------------------------
```

We add this new dialog box to our program as Form2. When the user clicks
the Database Designer's **Add Table** menu item, we clear the text boxes in
Form2 (in case we've already created a table earlier and there are still names
in the text boxes). We show this new dialog box, Form2, using this code in
the **New Table** menu item event handler:

```
Private Sub NewTable_Click()
    Form2.Text1.Text = ""        'Table name
    Form2.Text2.Text = ""        'Field 1 name
    Form2.Text3.Text = ""        'Field 2 name
    Form2.Text4.Text = ""        'Field 3 name
    Form2.Show
End Sub
```

The Add Table dialog box is used to get the name of the new table and the
new fields in that table. When it appears on the screen, users place that
information in the text boxes and click **OK** (button Command1 in Form2).
We hide this dialog box and call a subroutine named CreateTable() in Form1
to create the new table:

```
Private Sub Command1_Click()
    Form2.Hide
    Call Form1.CreateTable
End Sub
```

On the other hand, if they click **Cancel** (button Command2), we should hide the Add Table dialog box without taking further action:

```
Private Sub Command2_Click()
    Form2.Hide
End Sub
```

Now we will write the CreateTable() subroutine to create the new table and append it to our database. Open the code window in Form1, the Database Designer itself, and place the new subroutine, CreateTable(), there:

```
Sub CreateTable()

End Sub
```

The name of the new table is in Form2.Text1.Text, so we need to create a new table definition—that is, a new TableDef object—with that name. We do that with the database CreateTableDef method:

```
Sub CreateTable()
    Set TheTd = TheDB.CreateTableDef(Form2.Text1.Text)      'New table name
        .
        .
        .
End Sub
```

Our new table definition is stored in the TheTd TableDef object, and we declare that object in Form1's (General) object so that the rest of the program can have access to it:

```
    Dim TheDB As Database                    'In Form1's (General) object
--> Dim TheTd As TableDef
```

Now we have a new table definition corresponding to the table name the user gave us. The next step is to create the three fields that the user specified, and their names are in Form2.Text2.Text, Form2.Text3.Text, and Form2.Text4.Text. We can create these fields with the TableDef CreateField method. (Note that, for simplicity, we will assume that all fields are text fields.)

CHAPTER 12 ■ CREATING AND FILLING DATABASES

```
Sub CreateTable()
    Set TheTd = TheDB.CreateTableDef(Form2.Text1.Text)      'New table name
--> Set TheFlds(0) = TheTd.CreateField(Form2.Text2.Text, dbText) 'Field 1 name
--> Set TheFlds(1) = TheTd.CreateField(Form2.Text3.Text, dbText) 'Field 2 name
--> Set TheFlds(2) = TheTd.CreateField(Form2.Text4.Text, dbText) 'Field 3 name
        .
        .
        .
End Sub
```

Here, TheFlds() is an array of Field objects, and we declare it in Form1's (General) object:

```
    Dim TheDB As Database                    'In Form1's (General) object
    Dim TheTd As TableDef
--> Dim TheFlds(3) As Field
```

Next, we append the new fields to the TableDef object, TheTd, and then append the completed object TheTd to our database object TheDB to install the new table definition:

```
Sub CreateTable()
    Set TheTd = TheDB.CreateTableDef(Form2.Text1.Text)      'New table name
    Set TheFlds(0) = TheTd.CreateField(Form2.Text2.Text, dbText) 'Field 1 name
    Set TheFlds(1) = TheTd.CreateField(Form2.Text3.Text, dbText) 'Field 2 name
    Set TheFlds(2) = TheTd.CreateField(Form2.Text4.Text, dbText) 'Field 3 name
--> TheTd.Fields.Append TheFlds(0)
--> TheTd.Fields.Append TheFlds(1)
--> TheTd.Fields.Append TheFlds(2)
--> TheDB.TableDefs.Append TheTd
        .
        .
        .
End Sub
```

At this point, our new table is defined. The final step is to create a table of this new type, and we do that in the database OpenRecordset method. To create the table, we need the table name. That is still in Form2's Text1 text box, so we create our table this way:

```
Sub CreateTable()
    Set TheTd = TheDB.CreateTableDef(Form2.Text1.Text)      'New table name
    Set TheFlds(0) = TheTd.CreateField(Form2.Text2.Text, dbText) 'Field 1 name
    Set TheFlds(1) = TheTd.CreateField(Form2.Text3.Text, dbText) 'Field 2 name
    Set TheFlds(2) = TheTd.CreateField(Form2.Text4.Text, dbText) 'Field 3 name
    TheTd.Fields.Append TheFlds(0)
```

```
        TheTd.Fields.Append TheFlds(1)
        TheTd.Fields.Append TheFlds(2)
        TheDB.TableDefs.Append TheTd
```

```
--> Set TheTable = TheDB.OpenRecordset(Form2.Text1.Text, dbOpenTable)
            .
            .
            .
End Sub
```

We also declare TheTable as a Recordset object in the (General) object so that the other parts of the program can have access to it:

```
    Dim TheDB As Database                'In Form1's (General) object
    Dim TheTd As TableDef
    Dim TheFlds(3) As Field
--> Dim TheTable As Recordset
```

We've let the user define our new table, we've created it, and we've given the rest of the program access to it as the object TheTable. All that remains now is to display the table and field names in the Database Designer, preparing it for data entry. In addition, we add the new table name to the list of tables in the list box, List1:

```
Sub CreateTable()
    Set TheTd = TheDB.CreateTableDef(Form2.Text1.Text)      'New table name
    Set TheFlds(0) = TheTd.CreateField(Form2.Text2.Text, dbText) 'Field 1 name
    Set TheFlds(1) = TheTd.CreateField(Form2.Text3.Text, dbText) 'Field 2 name
    Set TheFlds(2) = TheTd.CreateField(Form2.Text4.Text, dbText) 'Field 3 name
    TheTd.Fields.Append TheFlds(0)
    TheTd.Fields.Append TheFlds(1)
    TheTd.Fields.Append TheFlds(2)
    TheDB.TableDefs.Append TheTd

    Set TheTable = TheDB.OpenRecordset(Form2.Text1.Text, dbOpenTable)

--> Label1.Caption = Form2.Text2.Text        'Field 1 name
--> Label2.Caption = Form2.Text3.Text        'Field 2 name
--> Label3.Caption = Form2.Text4.Text        'Field 3 name
--> Label5.Caption = Form2.Text1.Text        'Table name
--> Text1.Text = ""
--> Text2.Text = ""
--> Text3.Text = ""
--> List1.AddItem Form2.Text1.Text

End Sub
```

At this point, the new table has been created and we've displayed in the Database Designer the table name as well as the names of the fields in it. We're in business, and we're ready to create records in the table.

Adding a New Record

When users want to add a record to the current table, they click **Add New Record**, Command1, which is just below our list box:

```
-----------------------------------------------------------------
| Database Designer                                             |
|---------------------------------------------------------------|
| File              Database                                    |
|---------------------------------------------------------------|
|                                                               |
|                              Current Table Name:  students    |
|           --------                                            |
|   Name   |  Ann  |          Tables:                           |
|           --------          ---------------------------       |
|           --------          | students              |         |
|   Grade  |  C    |          |                       |         |
|           --------          |_____|         |
|           --------                                            |
|   ID     | 111   |          ---------------   -----------     |
|           --------          |Add New Record| |Edit Record|    |
|                             ---------------   -----------     |
| ------  ------  ------  ------   ---------------   ----------------   |
| | << | | < | | > | | >> |   |Delete Record| |Update Database| |
| ------  ------  ------  ------   ---------------   ----------------   |
|                                                               |
-----------------------------------------------------------------
```

We're familiar with the process of adding a new record to a table—we need only use the AddNew method. In this case, our open table is named TheTable, so we add a new record and clear the Database Designer's text boxes to receive the new record's data in the **Add New Record** button's event handler:

```
Private Sub Command1_Click()
    TheTable.AddNew
    Text1.Text = ""     'Clear field 1's displayed data
    Text2.Text = ""     'Clear field 2's displayed data
    Text3.Text = ""     'Clear field 3's displayed data
End Sub
```

After adding a new record to the table, users can place data in the Database Designer's text boxes, as we see in the schematics shown previously. Then users click **Update Database** to place the data in the new record's fields. Let's examine this process next.

Updating the Database

When users click **Update Database**, Command3, they want to place the data that's in the Database Designer's text boxes—Text1, Text2, and Text3—into the fields of the current record open in TheTable. When we filled fields with data before, we knew the field names (i.e., Name and Grade), but when we write the program we don't know the names of the fields we'll be filling. Instead, we reach the fields in TheTable using the Fields collection, because each field is an array member in that collection:

```
Private Sub Command3_Click()
    TheTable.Fields(0) = Text1.Text      'Field 1 data
    TheTable.Fields(1) = Text2.Text      'Field 2 data
    TheTable.Fields(2) = Text3.Text      'Field 3 data
    TheTable.Update
End Sub
```

Now we're letting users fill the table with data (even though we don't know what the names of the fields will be). At the end of this code, we use the table method Update to install our new fields into the current record.

In the same way, the user can edit the currently visible record by clicking **Edit**, making changes, and clicking **Update**. Editing a record is easy. Let's make the **Edit Record** button active now.

Editing a Record

All we have to do to set up the **Edit Record** button, Command2, is to use the table Edit method:

```
Private Sub Command2_Click()
    TheTable.Edit
End Sub
```

That's all that's required. After clicking **Edit Record** and editing a record, the user can click **Update Database** to install the changed record into the table. The user may also want to delete the current record, and that is easy to do; we only have to use the table Delete method.

Deleting a Record

To delete the current record, the user clicks **Delete Record**, Command8. We use the recordset Delete method after clearing the deleted data from the Database Designer's text boxes:

```
Private Sub Command8_Click()
    Text1.Text = ""              'Clear field text boxes
    Text2.Text = ""
    Text3.Text = ""
    TheTable.Delete
End Sub
```

(After deleting a record, the user does not have to click the **Update Database** button.) Now we've allowed the user to work with the data in the current table, including editing it, adding new records, and deleting it. We've been able to program all this without knowing the table name or the field names in advance, simply by getting that information from various DAO collections. We also have multiple tables in our databases now, and we should allow the user to choose between them.

Selecting a Table from the List Box

The Database Designer has already been filled with the names of the tables in our database (when we created each table, we added its name to the list box). To switch between tables, users should double-click the name of the table they want in the list box. To set that up, we open the list box's DblClick() event:

```
Private Sub List1_DblClick()

End Sub
```

When we enter this subroutine, users have double-clicked the name of the table they wish to open. We open that table by getting its name from the List1.Text property (the text of the selected item), and we install that table as the current table TheTable:

```
Private Sub List1_DblClick()
    Set TheTable = TheDB.OpenRecordset(List1.Text, dbOpenTable)
        .
        .
        .
End Sub
```

You may wonder why we used the name of the table, and not its location in the text box, to open it. You may assume that because we appended our new tables at the same time that we added their names to the list box, the first entry in the list box corresponds to the first table in the database, the second name in the list box to the second table, and so on. In fact, this is not true; the DAO library objects maintain a number of system tables, and you can never assume that the absolute order of tables in a database will be constant or that tables will stay where you placed them in that order (they generally will not).

Next, we display in the Database Designer the names of the newly opened table's fields, as well as the name of the table itself. (Note again that because we don't have the names of the fields when writing the program, we get the names from the Fields collection and from the Name property of the table.)

```
Private Sub List1_DblClick()
        Set TheTable = TheDB.OpenRecordset(List1.Text, dbOpenTable)
--> Label1.Caption = TheTable.Fields(0).Name
--> Label2.Caption = TheTable.Fields(1).Name
--> Label3.Caption = TheTable.Fields(2).Name
--> Label5.Caption = TheTable.Name
        .
        .
        .
End Sub
```

Finally, we display the data from the three fields of the first record of the newly opened table:

```
Private Sub List1_DblClick()
        Set TheTable = TheDB.OpenRecordset(List1.Text, dbOpenTable)
        Label1.Caption = TheTable.Fields(0).Name
        Label2.Caption = TheTable.Fields(1).Name
        Label3.Caption = TheTable.Fields(2).Name
        Label5.Caption = TheTable.Name
--> Text1.Text = TheTable.Fields(0)
--> Text2.Text = TheTable.Fields(1)
--> Text3.Text = TheTable.Fields(2)
End Sub
```

Now we've allowed the user to create a database with multiple tables, manipulate the data in those tables, and even switch between tables, all without our knowing the names of the tables or the fields within them. Our database designer is fairly powerful:

```
 ----------------------------------------------------------------------
| Database Designer                                                    |
|----------------------------------------------------------------------|
| File              Database                                           |
|----------------------------------------------------------------------|
|                                                                      |
|                              Current Table Name:  students           |
|            --------                                                  |
|  Name     |  Ann   |        Tables:                                  |
|            --------          ------------------------                |
|            --------         | students               |              |
|  Grade    |  C     |        | registrar              |              |
|            --------         |_____|              |
|            --------                                                  |
|  ID       |  111   |          --------------    ------------         |
|            --------         |Add New Record|  |Edit Record|          |
|                               --------------    ------------         |
|  ------  ------  ------  ------  --------------    ----------------   |
| | << |  | < |  | > |  | >> |  |Delete Record|  |Update Database|    |
|  ------  ------  ------  ------  --------------    ----------------   |
|                                                                      |
 ----------------------------------------------------------------------
```

At this point, we can allow the user to close the database.

The Close Database Menu Item

Closing the database is easy. We use the database Close method, which we add to the File menu's **Close Database** item:

```
Private Sub CloseDatabase_Click()
    TheDB.Close
        .
        .
        .
End Sub
```

Now that the database is closed, we also have to clear the data from the text boxes in the Database Designer, as well as clear the list box of tables and the current table name:

```
Private Sub CloseDatabase_Click()
    TheDB.Close
--> List1.Clear
--> Text1.Text = ""
--> Text2.Text = ""
--> Text3.Text = ""
--> Label1.Caption = ""
--> Label2.Caption = ""
--> Label3.Caption = ""
--> Label5.Caption = ""
End Sub
```

Now, users can close their databases, saving their work on disk. This means that we should also allow them to open a database from a file on disk. Let's look into that next.

The Open Database Menu Item

When the user selects **Open Database** in the File menu, we will be working with a database that we know nothing about. We don't know how many tables it has, or what they are called, or what the field names in the tables are. We have to get all that information from the database.

Start by opening the click event associated with the **Open Database** menu item:

```
Private Sub OpenDatabase_Click()

End Sub
```

We use the common dialog control to pop an Open File dialog box on the screen. We check that users filled in a file name by looking at the CommonDialog1.filename property when they close the dialog box:

```
Private Sub OpenDatabase_Click()
    CommonDialog1.ShowOpen
    If CommonDialog1.filename <> "" Then
        .
        .
        .
    End If
End Sub
```

If they've specified the name of a database file to open, we open it using the OpenDatabase method and place that object in our TheDB database object:

```
Private Sub OpenDatabase_Click()
    CommonDialog1.ShowOpen
    If CommonDialog1.filename <> "" Then
-->     Set TheDB =
DBEngine.Workspaces(0).OpenDatabase(CommonDialog1.filename)
           .
           .
           .
    End If
End Sub
```

Now that our database is open, we examine its tables and list them in the Database Designer's list box. We loop over the available tables in the database using the handy For Each...Next loop that is designed to work with object collections. In general, that loop looks like this:

```
For Each object in collection

Next object
```

This code loops over all the objects in the collection; in our case, we loop over all table definitions in the collection TheDB.TableDefs. Here, TheTd is our TableDef object (from Form1's (General) object):

```
Private Sub OpenDatabase_Click()
    CommonDialog1.ShowOpen
    If CommonDialog1.filename <> "" Then
        Set TheDB =
DBEngine.Workspaces(0).OpenDatabase(CommonDialog1.filename)
-->     List1.Clear
-->     For Each TheTd In TheDB.TableDefs
               .
               .
               .
-->     Next TheTd
           .
           .
           .
    End If
End Sub
```

Note that we've also cleared the list box so that it can take the new table names.

As you may recall, DAO databases maintain several "system" tables in a database, and we do not want to list them in our list box. To check whether a table is a system table, we look at the Attributes property of its TableDef. If the dbSystemObject bit is set in the Attributes property, the table is a system table and we don't want to add its name to the list box. Otherwise, the table is a user table, and we add its name to the list box:

```
Private Sub OpenDatabase_Click()
    CommonDialog1.ShowOpen
    If CommonDialog1.filename <> "" Then
        Set TheDB =
DBEngine.Workspaces(0).OpenDatabase(CommonDialog1.filename)
        List1.Clear
        For Each TheTd In TheDB.TableDefs
-->        If (TheTd.Attributes And dbSystemObject) = 0 Then
-->            List1.AddItem TheTd.Name
-->        End If
        Next TheTd
            .
            .
            .

    End If
End Sub
```

We've filled the list box with the names of user-defined tables. Now we're ready to open the first table in the database and display its data, ready for the user to work with. Once again, we have to avoid system tables, so we set up a loop to search for the first nonsystem table; after the loop is finished, the index of the first nonsystem table is in the integer named theindex:

```
Private Sub OpenDatabase_Click()
--> Dim theindex As Integer
    CommonDialog1.ShowOpen
    If CommonDialog1.filename <> "" Then
        Set TheDB =
DBEngine.Workspaces(0).OpenDatabase(CommonDialog1.filename)
        List1.Clear
        For Each TheTd In TheDB.TableDefs
            If (TheTd.Attributes And dbSystemObject) = 0 Then
                List1.AddItem TheTd.Name
            End If
        Next TheTd
-->        theindex = 0        'Find first non-system table
-->        While (TheDB.TableDefs(theindex).Attributes And dbSystemObject)
-->            theindex = theindex + 1
-->        Wend
            .
            .
            .

End Sub
```

Now that we have found the first nonsystem table and have its index in the TableDefs collection, we can open that table and place it in our TheTable object:

```
Private Sub OpenDatabase_Click()
    Dim theindex As Integer
    CommonDialog1.ShowOpen
    If CommonDialog1.filename <> "" Then
        Set TheDB =
DBEngine.Workspaces(0).OpenDatabase(CommonDialog1.filename)
        List1.Clear
        For Each TheTd In TheDB.TableDefs
            If (TheTd.Attributes And dbSystemObject) = 0 Then
                List1.AddItem TheTd.Name
            End If
        Next TheTd
        theindex = 0         'Find first non-system table
        While (TheDB.TableDefs(theindex).Attributes And dbSystemObject)
            theindex = theindex + 1
        Wend
-->     Set TheTable =
            TheDB.OpenRecordset(TheDB.TableDefs(theindex).Name,
dbOpenTable)
            .
            .
            .
    End If
End Sub
```

The final step is to open the first record in the table. We place the data from the three fields of the first record into the text boxes in the Database Designer and list them by name:

```
Private Sub OpenDatabase_Click()
    Dim theindex As Integer
    CommonDialog1.ShowOpen
    If CommonDialog1.filename <> "" Then
        Set TheDB =
DBEngine.Workspaces(0).OpenDatabase(CommonDialog1.filename)
        List1.Clear
        For Each TheTd In TheDB.TableDefs
            If (TheTd.Attributes And dbSystemObject) = 0 Then
                List1.AddItem TheTd.Name
            End If
        Next TheTd
        theindex = 0         'Find first non-system table
        While (TheDB.TableDefs(theindex).Attributes And dbSystemObject)
            theindex = theindex + 1
        Wend
```

```
      Set TheTable =
          TheDB.OpenRecordset(TheDB.TableDefs(theindex).Name,
dbOpenTable)
-->       Label1.Caption = TheTable.Fields(0).Name
-->       Label2.Caption = TheTable.Fields(1).Name
-->       Label3.Caption = TheTable.Fields(2).Name
-->       Label5.Caption = TheTable.Name
-->       Text1.Text = TheTable.Fields(0)
-->       Text2.Text = TheTable.Fields(1)
-->       Text3.Text = TheTable.Fields(2)
    End If
End Sub
```

Now we have a working program that lets the user create and fill databases with data, as shown in Figure 12.3.

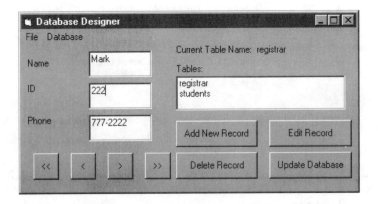

FIGURE 12.3 THE DATABASE DESIGNER PROGRAM AT WORK.

The program so far appears in Listing 12.3 (**DBDESIGN.VBP**), Listing 12.4 (**DBDESIGN.FRM**), and Listing 12.5 (**FORM2.FRM**).

LISTING 12.3 DBDESIGN.VBP

```
Form=dbdesign.Frm
Form=Form2.frm
Object={F9043C88-F6F2-101A-A3C9-08002B2F49FB}#1.0#0; COMDLG32.OCX
Object={BDC217C8-ED16-11CD-956C-0000C04E4C0A}#1.0#0; TABCTL32.OCX
Object={3B7C8863-D78F-101B-B9B5-04021C009402}#1.0#0; RICHTX32.OCX
Object={6B7E6392-850A-101B-AFC0-4210102A8DA7}#1.0#0; COMCTL32.OCX
Object={FAEEE763-117E-101B-8933-08002B2F4F5A}#1.0#0; DBLIST32.OCX
Object={00028C01-0000-0000-0000-000000000046}#1.0#0; DBGRID32.OCX
Object={F6125AB1-8AB1-11CE-A77F-08002B2F4E98}#1.0#0; MSRDC32.OCX
Reference=*\G{BEF6E001-A874-101A-8BBA-
```

```
    00AA00300CAB}#2.0#0#C:\WINDOWS\SYSTEM\OLEPRO32.DLL#Standard
    OLE Types
Reference=*\G{00025E01-0000-0000-C000-000000000046}#3.0#0#C:\PROGRAM
    FILES\COMMON FILES\MICROSOFT SHARED\DAO\DAO3032.DLL#Microsoft
    DAO 3.0 Object Library
ProjWinSize=356,375,217,94
ProjWinShow=2
Name="Project1"
HelpContextID="0"
StartMode=0
VersionCompatible32="0"
MajorVer=1
MinorVer=0
RevisionVer=0
AutoIncrementVer=0
ServerSupportFiles=0
```

```
VERSION 4.00
Begin VB.Form Form1
    Caption         =   "Database Designer"
    ClientHeight    =   2745
    ClientLeft      =   1845
    ClientTop       =   2250
    ClientWidth     =   6465
    Height          =   3435
    Left            =   1785
    LinkTopic       =   "Form1"
    ScaleHeight     =   2745
    ScaleWidth      =   6465
    Top             =   1620
    Width           =   6585
    Begin VB.ListBox List1
        Height          =   645
        Left            =   3000
        TabIndex        =   16
        Top             =   600
        Width           =   3255
    End
    Begin VB.CommandButton Command8
        Caption         =   "Delete Record"
        Height          =   495
        Left            =   3000
        TabIndex        =   15
        Top             =   2040
        Width           =   1575
    End
    Begin VB.CommandButton Command7
        Caption         =   ">>"
        Height          =   495
```

```
         Left            =    2400
         TabIndex        =    13
         Top             =    2040
         Width           =    495
      End
      Begin VB.CommandButton Command6
         Caption         =    ">"
         Height          =    495
         Left            =    1680
         TabIndex        =    12
         Top             =    2040
         Width           =    495
      End
      Begin VB.CommandButton Command5
         Caption         =    "<"
         Height          =    495
         Left            =    960
         TabIndex        =    11
         Top             =    2040
         Width           =    495
      End
      Begin VB.CommandButton Command4
         Caption         =    "<<"
         Height          =    495
         Left            =    240
         TabIndex        =    10
         Top             =    2040
         Width           =    495
      End
      Begin VB.CommandButton Command3
         Caption         =    "Update Database"
         Height          =    495
         Left            =    4800
         TabIndex        =    8
         Top             =    2040
         Width           =    1575
      End
      Begin VB.CommandButton Command2
         Caption         =    "Edit Record"
         Height          =    495
         Left            =    4800
         TabIndex        =    7
         Top             =    1440
         Width           =    1575
      End
      Begin VB.CommandButton Command1
         Caption         =    "Add New Record"
         Height          =    495
         Left            =    3000
         TabIndex        =    6
```

```
      Top             =    1440
      Width           =    1575
   End
   Begin VB.TextBox Text3
      Height          =    495
      Left            =    1320
      TabIndex        =    5
      Top             =    1320
      Width           =    1215
   End
   Begin VB.TextBox Text2
      Height          =    495
      Left            =    1320
      TabIndex        =    4
      Top             =    720
      Width           =    1215
   End
   Begin VB.TextBox Text1
      Height          =    495
      Left            =    1320
      TabIndex        =    3
      Top             =    120
      Width           =    1215
   End
   Begin VB.Label Label6
      Caption         =    "Tables:"
      Height          =    495
      Left            =    3000
      TabIndex        =    17
      Top             =    360
      Width           =    1215
   End
   Begin VB.Label Label5
      Height          =    255
      Left            =    4560
      TabIndex        =    14
      Top             =    0
      Width           =    1215
   End
   Begin VB.Label Label4
      Caption         =    "Current Table Name:"
      Height          =    375
      Left            =    3000
      TabIndex        =    9
      Top             =    0
      Width           =    1575
   End
   Begin VB.Label Label3
      Caption         =    "Field3"
      Height          =    495
```

```
            Left            =   120
            TabIndex        =   2
            Top             =   1320
            Width           =   1215
        End
        Begin VB.Label Label2
            Caption         =   "Field2"
            Height          =   495
            Left            =   120
            TabIndex        =   1
            Top             =   720
            Width           =   1215
        End
        Begin VB.Label Label1
            Caption         =   "Field1"
            Height          =   495
            Left            =   120
            TabIndex        =   0
            Top             =   240
            Width           =   1215
        End
        Begin MSComDlg.CommonDialog CommonDialog1
            Left            =   240
            Top             =   240
            _Version        =   65536
            _ExtentX        =   847
            _ExtentY        =   847
            _StockProps     =   0
        End
        Begin VB.Menu File
            Caption         =   "File"
            Begin VB.Menu NewDatabase
                Caption         =   "New Database..."
            End
            Begin VB.Menu OpenDatabase
                Caption         =   "Open Database..."
            End
            Begin VB.Menu CloseDatabase
                Caption         =   "Close Database"
            End
            Begin VB.Menu ExitItem
                Caption         =   "Exit"
            End
        End
        Begin VB.Menu DatabaseItem
            Caption         =   "Database"
            Begin VB.Menu NewTable
                Caption         =   "New Table..."
            End
        End
    End
```

```
Attribute VB_Name = "Form1"
Attribute VB_Creatable = False
Attribute VB_Exposed = False
    Dim TheDB As Database
    Dim TheTd As TableDef
    Dim TheFlds(3) As Field
    Dim TheTable As Recordset

Sub CreateTable()
    Set TheTd = TheDB.CreateTableDef(Form2.Text1.Text)
    Set TheFlds(0) = TheTd.CreateField(Form2.Text2.Text, dbText)
    Set TheFlds(1) = TheTd.CreateField(Form2.Text3.Text, dbText)
    Set TheFlds(2) = TheTd.CreateField(Form2.Text4.Text, dbText)
    TheTd.Fields.Append TheFlds(0)
    TheTd.Fields.Append TheFlds(1)
    TheTd.Fields.Append TheFlds(2)
    TheDB.TableDefs.Append TheTd

    Set TheTable = TheDB.OpenRecordset(Form2.Text1.Text, dbOpenTable)

    Label1.Caption = Form2.Text2.Text
    Label2.Caption = Form2.Text3.Text
    Label3.Caption = Form2.Text4.Text
    Label5.Caption = Form2.Text1.Text           'Display current table name
    Text1.Text = ""
    Text2.Text = ""
    Text3.Text = ""
    List1.AddItem Form2.Text1.Text

End Sub


Private Sub CloseDatabase_Click()
    TheDB.Close
    List1.Clear
    Text1.Text = ""
    Text2.Text = ""
    Text3.Text = ""
    Label1.Caption = ""
    Label2.Caption = ""
    Label3.Caption = ""
    Label5.Caption = ""
End Sub

Private Sub Command1_Click()
    TheTable.AddNew
    Text1.Text = ""
    Text2.Text = ""
    Text3.Text = ""
End Sub
```

```
Private Sub Command2_Click()
    TheTable.Edit
End Sub

Private Sub Command3_Click()
    TheTable.Fields(0) = Text1.Text
    TheTable.Fields(1) = Text2.Text
    TheTable.Fields(2) = Text3.Text
    TheTable.Update
End Sub

Private Sub Command8_Click()
    Text1.Text = ""
    Text2.Text = ""
    Text3.Text = ""
    TheTable.Delete
End Sub

Private Sub ExitItem_Click()
    End
End Sub


Private Sub List1_DblClick()
    Set TheTable = TheDB.OpenRecordset(List1.Text, dbOpenTable)
    Label1.Caption = TheTable.Fields(0).Name
    Label2.Caption = TheTable.Fields(1).Name
    Label3.Caption = TheTable.Fields(2).Name
    Label5.Caption = TheTable.Name
    Text1.Text = TheTable.Fields(0)
    Text2.Text = TheTable.Fields(1)
    Text3.Text = TheTable.Fields(2)
End Sub


Private Sub NewDatabase_Click()
    CommonDialog1.ShowSave
    If CommonDialog1.filename <> "" Then
        Set TheDB =
            DBEngine.Workspaces(0).CreateDatabase(CommonDialog1.filename,
            dbLangGeneral)
        MsgBox ("Database created. Add a table next.")
    End If
End Sub


Private Sub NewTable_Click()
    Form2.Text1.Text = ""
    Form2.Text2.Text = ""
    Form2.Text3.Text = ""
    Form2.Text4.Text = ""
```

```
    Form2.Show
End Sub


Private Sub OpenDatabase_Click()
    Dim theindex As Integer
    CommonDialog1.ShowOpen
    If CommonDialog1.filename <> "" Then
        Set TheDB =
DBEngine.Workspaces(0).OpenDatabase(CommonDialog1.filename)
        List1.Clear
        For Each TheTd In TheDB.TableDefs
            If (TheTd.Attributes And dbSystemObject) = 0 Then
                List1.AddItem TheTd.Name
            End If
        Next TheTd
        theindex = 0          'Find first non-system table While
        (TheDB.TableDefs(theindex).Attributes And dbSystemObject)
            theindex = theindex + 1
        Wend
        Set TheTable =
            TheDB.OpenRecordset(TheDB.TableDefs(theindex).Name,
dbOpenTable)
        Label1.Caption = TheTable.Fields(0).Name
        Label2.Caption = TheTable.Fields(1).Name
        Label3.Caption = TheTable.Fields(2).Name
        Label5.Caption = TheTable.Name
        Text1.Text = TheTable.Fields(0)
        Text2.Text = TheTable.Fields(1)
        Text3.Text = TheTable.Fields(2)
    End If
End Sub
```

LISTING 12.5 FORM2.FRM (DBDESIGN PROJECT)

```
VERSION 4.00
Begin VB.Form Form2
    Caption         =   "New Table"
    ClientHeight    =   2730
    ClientLeft      =   3360
    ClientTop       =   2835
    ClientWidth     =   4380
    Height          =   3135
    Left            =   3300
    LinkTopic       =   "Form2"
    ScaleHeight     =   2730
    ScaleWidth      =   4380
    Top             =   2490
    Width           =   4500
    Begin VB.TextBox Text4
```

```
      Height      =    375
      Left        =    1560
      TabIndex    =    6
      Top         =    1560
      Width       =    1215
   End
   Begin VB.TextBox Text3
      Height      =    375
      Left        =    1560
      TabIndex    =    5
      Top         =    1080
      Width       =    1215
   End
   Begin VB.TextBox Text2
      Height      =    375
      Left        =    1560
      TabIndex    =    4
      Top         =    600
      Width       =    1215
   End
   Begin VB.CommandButton Command2
      Caption     =    "Cancel"
      Height      =    495
      Left        =    2640
      TabIndex    =    3
      Top         =    2040
      Width       =    1215
   End
   Begin VB.CommandButton Command1
      Caption     =    "OK"
      Height      =    495
      Left        =    600
      TabIndex    =    2
      Top         =    2040
      Width       =    1215
   End
   Begin VB.TextBox Text1
      Height      =    375
      Left        =    1560
      TabIndex    =    0
      Top         =    120
      Width       =    1215
   End
   Begin VB.Label Label4
      Caption     =    "Field 3 Name:"
      Height      =    495
      Left        =    120
      TabIndex    =    9
      Top         =    1560
      Width       =    1215
   End
```

```
      Begin VB.Label Label3
         Caption         =    "Field 2 Name:"
         Height          =    495
         Left            =    120
         TabIndex        =    8
         Top             =    1080
         Width           =    1215
      End
      Begin VB.Label Label2
         Caption         =    "Field 1 Name:"
         Height          =    495
         Left            =    120
         TabIndex        =    7
         Top             =    600
         Width           =    1215
      End
      Begin VB.Label Label1
         Caption         =    "Table Name:"
         Height          =    495
         Left            =    120
         TabIndex        =    1
         Top             =    120
         Width           =    1215
      End
End
Attribute VB_Name = "Form2"
Attribute VB_Creatable = False
Attribute VB_Exposed = False

Private Sub Command1_Click()
    Form2.Hide
    Call Form1.CreateTable
End Sub


Private Sub Command2_Click()
    Form2.Hide
End Sub
```

We have come far with our database designer, but there is still far to go. For
example, we have not yet made the arrow buttons active to allow the user to
move through the database, and we have not allowed the user to search or
sort the database. We'll turn to that in the next chapter.

## CHAPTER 13

USING DATABASES IN CODE

So far, we have seen how to create databases in code and how to fill them with data. We've been able to create multiple-table databases and to place the records we want in them. The attraction of databases is the ease with which they let us work with that data, and although we've seen some powerful techniques, it is in this chapter that we'll examine the advanced data-handling techniques that Visual Basic gives us.

We'll start by seeing how to navigate through a database, moving record by record, as well as jumping to the beginning or end. Next, we'll see how to sort our data, search it for a particular record, and how to filter it—that is, select a subset of records that meet specific conditions that we set.

Now that we'll be moving around in recordsets and working with different recordsets at once, maintaining the integrity of the database (such as making sure that records that are supposed to be related are filled with matching data) becomes an issue. For that reason, we'll also discuss database transactions (one way of making sure that complex, multiple-record changes are not left incomplete), referential integrity (which guarantees that the relations between recordsets are maintained properly), and cascading changes (in which changing a field in one recordset also changes the same field in another recordset).

Let's start by seeing how to navigate through a database, moving from record to record.

MOVING THROUGH A DATABASE

Visual Basic databases are cursored databases—they have a current record, and operations usually take place on the current record. When we open a recordset with data in it, the first record is the current record:

```
Name    Grade    ID
----------------------------
| Ann   |   C   |  222  | <--
|-------|-------|-------|
| Mark  |   B   |  111  |
|-------|-------|-------|
| Ed    |   A   |  888  |
|-------|-------|-------|
| Frank |   A   |  555  |
|-------|-------|-------|
| Ted   |   A   |  333  |
|-------|-------|-------|
| Mabel |   B   |  666  |
|-------|-------|-------|
| Ralph |   B   |  444  |
|-------|-------|-------|
| Tom   |   B   |  777  |
----------------------------
| Ned   |       |  999  |
----------------------------
```

If we were using a Data control, we'd be able to click the right-pointing arrow button to move to the next record:

```
Name    Grade    ID
----------------------------
| Ann   |   C   |  222  |
|-------|-------|-------|
| Mark  |   B   |  111  | <--
|-------|-------|-------|
| Ed    |   A   |  888  |
|-------|-------|-------|
| Frank |   A   |  555  |
|-------|-------|-------|
| Ted   |   A   |  333  |
|-------|-------|-------|
| Mabel |   B   |  666  |
|-------|-------|-------|
| Ralph |   B   |  444  |
|-------|-------|-------|
| Tom   |   B   |  777  |
----------------------------
| Ned   |       |  999  |
----------------------------
```

We will set up our Database Designer to use the same four buttons as a Data control has (<<, <, >, and >>) for navigating through a recordset:

```
-------------------------------------------------------------------
| Database Designer                                               |
|-----------------------------------------------------------------|
| File              Database                                      |
|-----------------------------------------------------------------|
|                                                                 |
|                                      Current Table Name:  students |
|                   --------                                      |
|      Name        | Ann  |            Tables:                    |
|                   --------           ------------------------   |
|                   --------          | students              |   |
|      Grade       | C    |           |                       |   |
|                   --------          |_____|   |
|                   --------                                      |
|      ID          | 111  |            --------------   ----------- |
|                   --------          |Add New Record| |Edit Record| |
|                                      --------------   ----------- |
| ------  ------  ------  ------       --------------   --------------- |
-->|  | << |  | < |  | > |  | >> |     |Delete Record| |Update Database| |
|   ------  ------  ------  ------     --------------   --------------- |
|                                                                 |
-------------------------------------------------------------------
```

These buttons are Command4–Command7, and we will make them active. Let's start with the << button, Command4. Open that button's click event:

```
Private Sub Command4_Click()

End Sub
```

To move around in a recordset, we use the Move methods: MoveFirst (move to the first record), MoveLast (move to the last record), MoveNext (move to the next record), MovePrevious (move to the previous record), and the Move method itself (which allows us to move forward or backward the number of records we specify). In addition, recordset objects also support the AbsolutePosition property, which allows us to move to an absolute record position; but a record's positions can be changed easily, so you should not rely on this property unless you are certain of what you are doing. In addition to AbsolutePosition, we can also use the PercentPosition property to position ourselves a certain percentage of the way through a recordset.

The Database Designer's << button, Command4, is intended to move us back to the first record of the recordset. We use the recordset MoveFirst method this way:

```
Private Sub Command4_Click()
    TheTable.MoveFirst
        .
        .
        .
End Sub
```

Then we display in the Database Designer's text boxes the fields of the current (now first) record:

```
Private Sub Command4_Click()
    TheTable.MoveFirst
--> Text1.Text = TheTable.Fields(0)
--> Text2.Text = TheTable.Fields(1)
--> Text3.Text = TheTable.Fields(2)
End Sub
```

Now we're able to position ourselves at the beginning of the recordset. The >> button, Command7, which moves us to the end of the recordset, is also easy to program using the MoveLast method:

```
Private Sub Command7_Click()
--> TheTable.MoveLast
--> Text1.Text = TheTable.Fields(0)
--> Text2.Text = TheTable.Fields(1)
--> Text3.Text = TheTable.Fields(2)
End Sub
```

Now we've enabled the << and >> buttons. Next, we'll work on the < button, Command5, which moves us back one record. Here, we use the MovePrevious method:

```
Private Sub Command5_Click()
--> TheTable.MovePrevious
        .
        .
        .
End Sub
```

However, note that if we started at the first record, this will move us to a position *before* the beginning of the recordset. This means that there will be no current record, and we'll run into trouble when we try to display the current record's data, not to mention when we try to work with it.

We check to see whether we're at the beginning of the recordset (i.e., before the first record) by using the BOF property. (BOF originally stood for Beginning Of File in Basic.) If we are at the beginning of the recordset (which is before the first record and not at the first record) we have to reposition ourselves so that we are at the first record. We use MoveNext:

```
Private Sub Command5_Click()
    TheTable.MovePrevious
--> If TheTable.BOF Then
-->     TheTable.MoveNext
          .
          .
          .
End Sub
```

Otherwise, we can display the new current record's fields in the Database Designer:

```
Private Sub Command5_Click()
    TheTable.MovePrevious
    If TheTable.BOF Then
        TheTable.MoveNext
--> Else
-->     Text1.Text = TheTable.Fields(0)
-->     Text2.Text = TheTable.Fields(1)
-->     Text3.Text = TheTable.Fields(2)
--> End If
End Sub
```

Finally, let's make the > button, Command6, active. In this case, we want to move to the next record, which we do with MoveNext:

```
Private Sub Command6_Click()
    TheTable.MoveNext
          .
          .
          .
End Sub
```

As with MovePrevious, however, this raises the possibility of moving beyond the recordset's boundaries—in this case, we might move past the end of the recordset. With MovePrevious, we used the BOF property to check whether we were at the beginning of the recordset. In a similar way, we'll use EOF (which originally stood for End Of File) to check whether MoveNext has moved us past the last record. EOF is true if we are past the last record (and not true if we are at the last record). For that reason, we move back to the last record in the recordset in case we have moved past it:

```
Private Sub Command6_Click()
    TheTable.MoveNext
--> If TheTable.EOF Then
-->     TheTable.MovePrevious
            .
            .
            .
End Sub
```

Otherwise, we are ready to display the current record's fields:

```
Private Sub Command6_Click()
    TheTable.MoveNext
    If TheTable.EOF Then
        TheTable.MovePrevious
--> Else
-->     Text1.Text = TheTable.Fields(0)
-->     Text2.Text = TheTable.Fields(1)
-->     Text3.Text = TheTable.Fields(2)
--> End If
End Sub
```

That's it—we've made the Database Designer's <<, <, >, and >> buttons active. Now the user can navigate through a database, as shown in Figure 13.1.

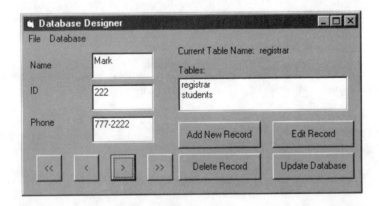

FIGURE 13.1 NAVIGATING THROUGH A DATABASE WITH OUR DATABASE DESIGNER.

Another way of navigating in a database is through the use of *bookmarks*. You can connect a bookmark to the current record by reading the recordset's

Bookmark property and storing it in a text variable. Then you are free to move around the database, adding and deleting records as you like; this process changes the record's absolute position. When you want to make the marked record the current record again, just place the stored bookmark into the recordset's Bookmark property.

Another property that is useful when you're moving through a recordset is the RecordCount property, which holds the number of records in a table-type recordset. However, this same property holds only the number of records actually "visited" in dynaset and snapshot recordsets. Unless you have moved to a particular record in these types of recordsets, it won't be counted in the RecordCount property. As you can see, there are some differences between table recordsets and dynaset and snapshot recordsets; there are also other differences, such as those that arise when we sort a recordset.

SORTING

One of the menu items in the Database Designer is **Sort**. When the user selects that menu item, we want to sort the current recordset. It turns out that we handle this operation differently for table-type recordsets than for dynaset-type and snapshot-type recordsets. For tables, we sort using the Index property, and for dynasets and snapshots, we sort using the Sort property.

Sorting a Table Recordset

Let's start by seeing how to sort a table-type recordset. We have a table available—the students table—which we can work with in the Database Designer; we'll sort it when the user clicks **Sort** in the Database menu. To sort a table, we specify which field to sort on—do we want to sort by Name, Grade, or ID?—which we make into an index. We add indices to tables to perform sorting operations as well as other operations, such as relating tables.

For the sake of simplicity, we'll make the first field of each table created into an index with the Database Designer. For our students table, that's the Name field:

```
Index
  |
  V
Name     Grade    ID
---------------------
| Ann    |  C  |  222 |
|--------|-----|------|
| Mark   |  B  |  111 |
|--------|-----|------|
| Ed     |  A  |  888 |
|--------|-----|------|
| Frank  |  A  |  555 |
|--------|-----|------|
| Ted    |  A  |  333 |
|--------|-----|------|
| Mabel  |  B  |  666 |
|--------|-----|------|
| Ralph  |  B  |  444 |
|--------|-----|------|
| Tom    |  B  |  777 |
---------------------
| Ned    |     |  999 |
---------------------
```

This means that we'll sort and search using this field. We specify that this first field become our table's index when we create the table in the CreateTable() subroutine. (Note that you can have more than one index in a table.) As you may recall, we design the fields of our table there and install them in a table definition object, TheTd:

```
Sub CreateTable()
    Set TheTd = TheDB.CreateTableDef(Form2.Text1.Text)
    Set TheFlds(0) = TheTd.CreateField(Form2.Text2.Text, dbText)
    Set TheFlds(1) = TheTd.CreateField(Form2.Text3.Text, dbText)
    Set TheFlds(2) = TheTd.CreateField(Form2.Text4.Text, dbText)
    TheTd.Fields.Append TheFlds(0)
    TheTd.Fields.Append TheFlds(1)
    TheTd.Fields.Append TheFlds(2)
        .
        .
        .
```

We also create an Index object at this time, and we call it TheIdx. Because we can have a number of indices in one table, an index can contain a number of fields, each of which corresponds to an index. Let's see this at work. We first create the Index object, using the name of the first field—which is given to us by the user in Form2.Text2.Text—and adding the word *index* to that name (creating, in our students table case, the index Nameindex):

```
Sub CreateTable()
    Set TheTd = TheDB.CreateTableDef(Form2.Text1.Text)
    Set TheFlds(0) = TheTd.CreateField(Form2.Text2.Text, dbText)
    Set TheFlds(1) = TheTd.CreateField(Form2.Text3.Text, dbText)
    Set TheFlds(2) = TheTd.CreateField(Form2.Text4.Text, dbText)
    TheTd.Fields.Append TheFlds(0)
    TheTd.Fields.Append TheFlds(1)
    TheTd.Fields.Append TheFlds(2)

--> Set TheIdx = TheTd.CreateIndex(Form2.Text2.Text + "index")
        .
        .
        .
```

Next, we indicate which field(s) we want in this index. Here, we use the first
field, whose name is in Form2.Text2.Text, as our index; we specify that field
by creating a new Field object with the Index object CreateField method:

```
Sub CreateTable()
    Set TheTd = TheDB.CreateTableDef(Form2.Text1.Text)
    Set TheFlds(0) = TheTd.CreateField(Form2.Text2.Text, dbText)
    Set TheFlds(1) = TheTd.CreateField(Form2.Text3.Text, dbText)
    Set TheFlds(2) = TheTd.CreateField(Form2.Text4.Text, dbText)
    TheTd.Fields.Append TheFlds(0)
    TheTd.Fields.Append TheFlds(1)
    TheTd.Fields.Append TheFlds(2)

--> Set TheIdx = TheTd.CreateIndex(Form2.Text2.Text + "index")
--> Set IxFlds = TheIdx.CreateField(Form2.Text2.Text)
        .
        .
        .
```

Now that we've indicated which field we want to be our index, we append
that field to the Index object TheIdx and then append the index object itself
to our table definition, TheTd:

```
Sub CreateTable()
    Set TheTd = TheDB.CreateTableDef(Form2.Text1.Text)
    Set TheFlds(0) = TheTd.CreateField(Form2.Text2.Text, dbText)
    Set TheFlds(1) = TheTd.CreateField(Form2.Text3.Text, dbText)
    Set TheFlds(2) = TheTd.CreateField(Form2.Text4.Text, dbText)
    TheTd.Fields.Append TheFlds(0)
    TheTd.Fields.Append TheFlds(1)
    TheTd.Fields.Append TheFlds(2)

--> Set TheIdx = TheTd.CreateIndex(Form2.Text2.Text + "index")
--> Set IxFlds = TheIdx.CreateField(Form2.Text2.Text)
--> TheIdx.Fields.Append IxFlds
```

```
--> TheTd.Indexes.Append TheIdx
        .
        .
        .
```

Now we've added an index to our table definition. In the case of our students table, this means that our table definition, stored in TheTd, will have the name students, the three data fields Name, Grade, and ID, and an index object named Nameindex containing an index corresponding to the Name field. In CreateTable(), we are now free to append this new TableDef object, TheTd, to the database as we did before, and to create an actual table of this type in the object TheTable:

```
Sub CreateTable()
    Set TheTd = TheDB.CreateTableDef(Form2.Text1.Text)
    Set TheFlds(0) = TheTd.CreateField(Form2.Text2.Text, dbText)
    Set TheFlds(1) = TheTd.CreateField(Form2.Text3.Text, dbText)
    Set TheFlds(2) = TheTd.CreateField(Form2.Text4.Text, dbText)
    TheTd.Fields.Append TheFlds(0)
    TheTd.Fields.Append TheFlds(1)
    TheTd.Fields.Append TheFlds(2)

    Set TheIdx = TheTd.CreateIndex(Form2.Text2.Text + "index")
    Set IxFlds = TheIdx.CreateField(Form2.Text2.Text)
    TheIdx.Fields.Append IxFlds
    TheTd.Indexes.Append TheIdx
--> TheDB.TableDefs.Append TheTd

--> Set TheTable = TheDB.OpenRecordset(Form2.Text1.Text, dbOpenTable)
        .
        .
        .
```

In addition, we add the declaration of our new index object and index field to Form1's (General) object so that we can use them in CreateTable() and other parts of the program can reach them:

```
    Dim TheDB As Database
    Dim TheTd As TableDef
--> Dim TheFlds(3) As Field, IdxFields As Field
--> Dim TheIdx As Index
    Dim TheTable As Recordset
```

Now our table definition is set up, and it's stored in the object TheTd. Our index is stored in the object TheTd.Indexes(0), where Indexes is the name of the collection of Index objects. The table corresponding to that table definition and holding its data is in the recordset object TheTable. We can sort the records in that table by placing the name of the index we want to sort by into TheTable's Index property. This code is in the Database menu's Sort event handler, where we get the name of our index from the table definition, TheTd:

```
Sub Sort_Click()
    Set TheIdx = TheTd.Indexes(0)
    TheTable.Index = TheIdx.Name
        .
        .
        .
```

(You may think that we can use a line such as TheTable.Index = TheTable .Indexes(0) to do this same task, but it turns out that TheTable's Indexes collection is inaccessible to us in Visual Basic. We must get the name of the index we want from the table definition and not from the table itself.)

At this point, the entire table is sorted according to the index field we specified. We now redisplay the current record in the newly sorted table in the **Sort** menu item's click handler:

```
Sub Sort_Click()
    Set TheIdx = TheTd.Indexes(0)
    TheTable.Index = TheIdx.Name
--> Text1.Text = TheTable.Fields(0)
--> Text2.Text = TheTable.Fields(1)
--> Text3.Text = TheTable.Fields(2)
End Sub
```

That's it—we've sorted our table. Notice that sorting a table depends on having the name of the index to sort by, and that we get that from the table definition. This arrangement has one more consequence for our program: we must keep the table definition, TheTd, up-to-date with the table definition of the current table, especially when we open a new table. We load TheTd in our CreateTable() subroutine, so the table definition is available just after we create a new table; but when we open a new database or when we switch to a new table, we should reload TheTd with the new table definition. We do that in the OpenDatabase() subroutine:

```
Private Sub OpenDatabase_Click()
    Dim theindex As Integer
    CommonDialog1.ShowOpen
    If CommonDialog1.filename <> "" Then
        Set TheDB =
DBEngine.Workspaces(0).OpenDatabase(CommonDialog1.filename)
```

```
          List1.Clear
          For Each TheTd In TheDB.TableDefs
              If (TheTd.Attributes And dbSystemObject) = 0 Then
                  List1.AddItem TheTd.Name
          Next TheTd
          theindex = 0          'Find first non-system table
          While (TheDB.TableDefs(theindex).Attributes And dbSystemObject)
              theindex = theindex + 1
          Wend
          Set TheTable =
              TheDB.OpenRecordset(TheDB.TableDefs(theindex).Name,
              dbOpenTable)
-->       Set TheTd = TheDB.TableDefs(theindex)
          Label1.Caption = TheTable.Fields(0).Name
          Label2.Caption = TheTable.Fields(1).Name
          Label3.Caption = TheTable.Fields(2).Name
          Label5.Caption = TheTable.Name
          Text1.Text = TheTable.Fields(0)
          Text2.Text = TheTable.Fields(1)
          Text3.Text = TheTable.Fields(2)
      End If
End Sub
```

We do the same thing when we switch to another table, placing the new table's definition into the variable TheTd. In OpenDatabase(), we knew we'd be using the first table in the database, but now that the user can click any table in the database, we have to make sure that we load TheTd with the new table's definition. We loop over the tables in the database and fill a new TableDef object, TempTd, until we find the one matching the one clicked by the user:

```
Private Sub List1_DblClick()
    Set TheTable = TheDB.OpenRecordset(List1.Text, dbOpenTable)
--> For Each TempTd In TheDB.TableDefs
-->     If TempTd.Name = List1.Text Then Set TheTd = TempTd
--> Next TempTd
    Label1.Caption = TheTable.Fields(0).Name
    Label2.Caption = TheTable.Fields(1).Name
    Label3.Caption = TheTable.Fields(2).Name
    Label5.Caption = TheTable.Name
    Text1.Text = TheTable.Fields(0)
    Text2.Text = TheTable.Fields(1)
    Text3.Text = TheTable.Fields(2)
End Sub
```

When we find the definition of the table we're about to open, we set TheTd from that definition. We also add TempTd, the new temporary TableDef variable, to Form1's (General) object:

```
    Dim TheDB As Database
--> Dim TheTd As TableDef, TempTd As TableDef
    Dim TheFlds(3) As Field, IdxFields As Field
    Dim TheIdx As Index
    Dim TheTable As Recordset
```

Now we've added an index to our database and have allowed the user to sort the data in any table using that index. We're ready to see this at work. We start by selecting **Sort** in the Database Designer's Database menu, as shown in Figure 13.2, to sort the registrar table by name. The Database Designer sorts the records on the Name field, and we see the resulting first record in Figure 13.3.

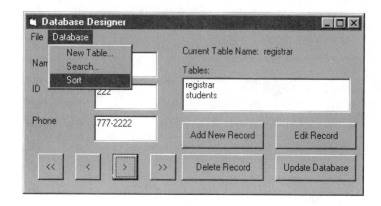

FIGURE 13.2 SELECTING THE DATABASE DESIGNER'S SORT OPERATION.

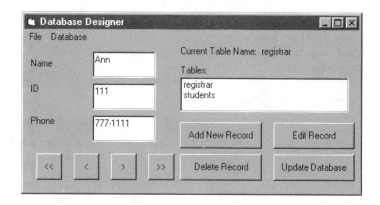

FIGURE 13.3 OUR SORTED TABLE IN THE DATABASE DESIGNER.

That's it for sorting table-type recordsets—now we can sort our data with a simple click on the Database Designer's **Sort** menu item. On the other hand, sorting a dynaset- or snapshot-type recordset is a different process, so let's look at that now.

Sorting a Dynaset or Snapshot Recordset

When we sort a dynaset or snapshot recordset, we don't use an index; instead, we create an entirely new recordset. Let's see how this works. First, we set up a database object and a recordset object:

```
Dim TheDB As Database
Dim TheDataset As Recordset
        .
        .
        .
```

Next, we open a database file, **DYNASET.MDB**, and open a dynaset-type recordset from a table we'll call Customers:

```
        Dim TheDB As Database
        Dim TheDataset As Recordset, TheSortedDataset As Recordset

-->     Set TheDB = DBEngine.Workspaces(0).OpenDatabase("DYNASET.MDB")
-->     Set TheDataset = TheDB.OpenRecordset("Customers", dbOpenDynaset)
        .
        .
        .
```

Now let's say we want to sort the TheDataset dynaset on a field named LastName. We fill the Sort property of the dynaset with the name of the field we want to sort on, and then we create an entirely new dynaset using the OpenRecordset method:

```
        Dim TheDB As Database
        Dim TheDataset As Recordset, TheSortedDataset As Recordset

        Set TheDB = DBEngine.Workspaces(0).OpenDatabase("DYNASET.MDB")
        Set TheDataset = TheDB.OpenRecordset("Customers")
-->     TheDataset.Sort = "LastName"
-->     Set TheSortedDataset = TheDataset.OpenRecordset()
```

This creates a new, sorted dynaset, TheSortedDataset, in which the records are sorted on the LastName field. That's the way to sort a dynaset or snap-shot—by producing an entirely new recordset.

In addition to sorting on a field in ascending order, we can indicate that we want the recordset sorted in descending order using the DESC keyword:

```
TheDataset.Sort = "LastName DESC"
```

We can also sort the recordset on multiple fields. Here, we sort on last name and, in case of the same last name, on first name as well:

```
TheDataset.Sort = "LastName, FirstName"
```

We've seen how to sort all three types of recordsets. Another popular opera-tion we can perform in a database is to search the database for a particular record. Let's look into that now.

SEARCHING

As with sorting, we perform different operations to search a table-type recordset than we use when searching dynaset- or snapshot-type recordsets. We'll first take a look at how to search a table-type recordset and add that capability to our Database Designer program; and when we do so, we will complete that program. Then we will look at how to find a specific record in a dynaset- or snapshot-type recordset.

Searching a Table Recordset

Like sorting, searching a table-type recordset is done with an index. We set the index property of the table to the index we want to search and then use the Seek method. In our Database Designer, we search for a particular record when the user selects **Search** in our Database menu.

When the user selects **Search**, we need to know which record to search for. In our program, we have installed an index corresponding to the first field in the table, so the user can search that index for matching records. For example, in the students table, the index field is the Name field; the user might want to search for the record that corresponds to, say, Mark. We'll need to determine which record the user wants to find, so we pop a new dialog box on the screen:

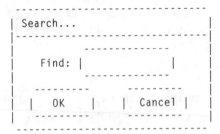

This will be Form3 in our program. (Form2 is used as the Add Table form, which gets the name and fields of new tables the user wants to design.)Add Form3 now, and add a text box (Text1) and two buttons—**OK** (Command1) and **Cancel** (Command2)—to this new form. When the user selects **Search** in the Database Designer, we will place our index in the table object TheTable's Index property and place the new form, Form3, on the screen:

```
Private Sub Search_Click()
    Set TheIdx = TheTd.Indexes(0)
    TheTable.Index = TheIdx.Name
    Form3.Show
End Sub
```

Now the user places the text to search for in the text box Form3.Text1.Text and clicks **OK**. We hide Form3 and call a new subroutine in Form1, which we name SearchTable(). (When the user clicks Form3's **Cancel** button, we hide that form without taking further action.)

```
Private Sub Command1_Click()
    Form3.Hide
    Call Form1.SearchTable
End Sub
```

At this point, we add the new subroutine SearchTable() to Form1 using the code window, and we set our table-type recordset object's Seek property to the text it is to find:

```
Sub SearchTable()
    TheTable.Seek "=", Form3.Text1.Text
         .
         .
         .
End Sub
```

This is how to search an index with table-type recordsets; in addition to the = operator, you can find records using the <, <=, >, and >= operators. Make the index the table's current index and then use the Seek method. When the appropriate record (such as the name "Mark") is found, it becomes the current record. We display it in the Database Designer:

```
Sub SearchTable()
    TheTable.Seek "=", Form3.Text1.Text
--> Text1.Text = TheTable.Fields(0)
--> Text2.Text = TheTable.Fields(1)
--> Text3.Text = TheTable.Fields(2)
End Sub
```

Now the Database Designer can search through the first field of each table. If we were to search for the record with the Name field set to Mark, we would select **Search** in our Database Designer's Database menu, as shown in Figure 13.4. The Database Designer places our new form, Form3, on the screen. We place the name **Mark** in the text box and click **OK**. The Database Designer finds the required record and displays it, as shown in Figure 13.5.

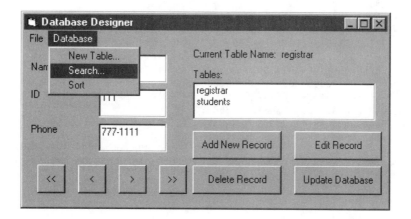

FIGURE 13.4 SELECTING THE DATABASE DESIGNER'S SEARCH MENU ITEM.

We've completed the Database Designer application, which allows us to design and create multiple-table databases as well as fill them with data, navigate through them, add or delete records, and search or sort the records. This is a powerful example of the arsenal of database tools we have available to us in DAO programming in Visual Basic, and it shows how to work with many real-world database programming techniques. The full program appears in these listings: Listing 13.1 (**DBDESIGN.VBP**), Listing 13.2 (**DBDESIGN.FRM**), Listing 13.3 (**FORM2.FRM**), and Listing 13.4 (**FORM3.FRM**).

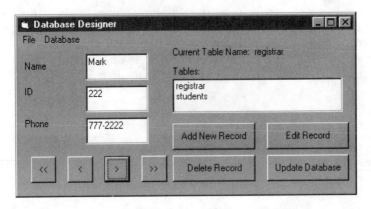

FIGURE 13.5 OUR FOUND ITEM DISPLAYED IN THE DATABASE DESIGNER.

LISTING 13.1 DBDESIGN.VBP

```
Form=dbdesign.Frm
Form=Form2.frm
Form=Form3.frm
Object={F9043C88-F6F2-101A-A3C9-08002B2F49FB}#1.0#0; COMDLG32.OCX
Object={BDC217C8-ED16-11CD-956C-0000C04E4C0A}#1.0#0; TABCTL32.OCX
Object={3B7C8863-D78F-101B-B9B5-04021C009402}#1.0#0; RICHTX32.OCX
Object={6B7E6392-850A-101B-AFC0-4210102A8DA7}#1.0#0; COMCTL32.OCX
Object={FAEEE763-117E-101B-8933-08002B2F4F5A}#1.0#0; DBLIST32.OCX
Object={00028C01-0000-0000-0000-000000000046}#1.0#0; DBGRID32.OCX
Object={F6125AB1-8AB1-11CE-A77F-08002B2F4E98}#1.0#0; MSRDC32.OCX
Reference=*\G{BEF6E001-A874-101A-8BBA-
        00AA00300CAB}#2.0#0#C:\WINDOWS\SYSTEM\OLEPRO32.DLL#Standard
        OLE Types
Reference=*\G{00025E01-0000-0000-C000-000000000046}#3.0#0#C:\PROGRAM
        FILES\COMMON FILES\MICROSOFT SHARED\DAO\DAO3032.DLL#Microsoft
        DAO 3.0 Object Library
ProjWinSize=356,375,217,94
ProjWinShow=2
IconForm="Form1"
Name="Project1"
HelpContextID="0"
StartMode=0
VersionCompatible32="0"
MajorVer=1
MinorVer=0
RevisionVer=0
AutoIncrementVer=0
ServerSupportFiles=0
```

LISTING 13.2 DBDESIGN.FRM

```
VERSION 4.00
Begin VB.Form Form1
    Caption         =   "Database Designer"
    ClientHeight    =   2745
    ClientLeft      =   1485
    ClientTop       =   1860
    ClientWidth     =   6465
    Height          =   3435
    Left            =   1425
    LinkTopic       =   "Form1"
    ScaleHeight     =   2745
    ScaleWidth      =   6465
    Top             =   1230
    Width           =   6585
    Begin VB.ListBox List1
        Height          =   645
        Left            =   3000
        TabIndex        =   16
        Top             =   600
        Width           =   3255
    End
    Begin VB.CommandButton Command8
        Caption         =   "Delete Record"
        Height          =   495
        Left            =   3000
        TabIndex        =   15
        Top             =   2040
        Width           =   1575
    End
    Begin VB.CommandButton Command7
        Caption         =   ">>"
        Height          =   495
        Left            =   2400
        TabIndex        =   13
        Top             =   2040
        Width           =   495
    End
    Begin VB.CommandButton Command6
        Caption         =   ">"
        Height          =   495
        Left            =   1680
        TabIndex        =   12
        Top             =   2040
        Width           =   495
    End
    Begin VB.CommandButton Command5
```

```
    Caption         =    "<"
    Height          =    495
    Left            =    960
    TabIndex        =    11
    Top             =    2040
    Width           =    495
End
Begin VB.CommandButton Command4
    Caption         =    "<<"
    Height          =    495
    Left            =    240
    TabIndex        =    10
    Top             =    2040
    Width           =    495
End
Begin VB.CommandButton Command3
    Caption         =    "Update Database"
    Height          =    495
    Left            =    4800
    TabIndex        =    8
    Top             =    2040
    Width           =    1575
End
Begin VB.CommandButton Command2
    Caption         =    "Edit Record"
    Height          =    495
    Left            =    4800
    TabIndex        =    7
    Top             =    1440
    Width           =    1575
End
Begin VB.CommandButton Command1
    Caption         =    "Add New Record"
    Height          =    495
    Left            =    3000
    TabIndex        =    6
    Top             =    1440
    Width           =    1575
End
Begin VB.TextBox Text3
    Height          =    495
    Left            =    1320
    TabIndex        =    5
    Top             =    1320
    Width           =    1215
End
Begin VB.TextBox Text2
    Height          =    495
    Left            =    1320
    TabIndex        =    4
```

```
      Top             =    720
      Width           =    1215
   End
   Begin VB.TextBox Text1
      Height          =    495
      Left            =    1320
      TabIndex        =    3
      Top             =    120
      Width           =    1215
   End
   Begin VB.Label Label6
      Caption         =    "Tables:"
      Height          =    495
      Left            =    3000
      TabIndex        =    17
      Top             =    360
      Width           =    1215
   End
   Begin VB.Label Label5
      Height          =    255
      Left            =    4560
      TabIndex        =    14
      Top             =    0
      Width           =    1215
   End
   Begin VB.Label Label4
      Caption         =    "Current Table Name:"
      Height          =    375
      Left            =    3000
      TabIndex        =    9
      Top             =    0
      Width           =    1575
   End
   Begin VB.Label Label3
      Caption         =    "Field3"
      Height          =    495
      Left            =    120
      TabIndex        =    2
      Top             =    1320
      Width           =    1215
   End
   Begin VB.Label Label2
      Caption         =    "Field2"
      Height          =    495
      Left            =    120
      TabIndex        =    1
      Top             =    720
      Width           =    1215
   End
   Begin VB.Label Label1
```

```
            Caption          =    "Field1"
            Height           =    495
            Left             =    120
            TabIndex         =    0
            Top              =    240
            Width            =    1215
         End
         Begin MSComDlg.CommonDialog CommonDialog1
            Left             =    240
            Top              =    240
            _Version         =    65536
            _ExtentX         =    847
            _ExtentY         =    847
            _StockProps      =    0
         End
         Begin VB.Menu File
            Caption          =    "File"
            Begin VB.Menu NewDatabase
               Caption          =    "New Database..."
            End
            Begin VB.Menu OpenDatabase
               Caption          =    "Open Database..."
            End
            Begin VB.Menu CloseDatabase
               Caption          =    "Close Database"
            End
            Begin VB.Menu ExitItem
               Caption          =    "Exit"
            End
         End
         Begin VB.Menu DatabaseItem
            Caption          =    "Database"
            Begin VB.Menu NewTable
               Caption          =    "New Table..."
            End
            Begin VB.Menu Search
               Caption          =    "Search..."
            End
            Begin VB.Menu Sort
               Caption          =    "Sort..."
            End
         End
      End
      Attribute VB_Name = "Form1"
      Attribute VB_Creatable = False
      Attribute VB_Exposed = False
         Dim TheDB As Database
         Dim TheTd As TableDef, TempTd As TableDef
         Dim TheFlds(3) As Field, IdxFields As Field
         Dim TheIdx As Index
         Dim TheTable As Recordset
```

```
Sub CreateTable()
    Set TheTd = TheDB.CreateTableDef(Form2.Text1.Text)
    Set TheFlds(0) = TheTd.CreateField(Form2.Text2.Text, dbText)
    Set TheFlds(1) = TheTd.CreateField(Form2.Text3.Text, dbText)
    Set TheFlds(2) = TheTd.CreateField(Form2.Text4.Text, dbText)
    TheTd.Fields.Append TheFlds(0)
    TheTd.Fields.Append TheFlds(1)
    TheTd.Fields.Append TheFlds(2)

    Set TheIdx = TheTd.CreateIndex(Form2.Text2.Text + "index")
    Set IxFlds = TheIdx.CreateField(Form2.Text2.Text)
    TheIdx.Fields.Append IxFlds
    TheTd.Indexes.Append TheIdx
    TheDB.TableDefs.Append TheTd

    Set TheTable = TheDB.OpenRecordset(Form2.Text1.Text, dbOpenTable)

    Label5.Caption = Form2.Text1.Text        'Display current table name
    Label1.Caption = Form2.Text2.Text
    Label2.Caption = Form2.Text3.Text
    Label3.Caption = Form2.Text4.Text
    Text1.Text = ""
    Text2.Text = ""
    Text3.Text = ""
    List1.AddItem Form2.Text1.Text

End Sub

Sub SearchTable()
    TheTable.Seek "=", Form3.Text1.Text
    Text1.Text = TheTable.Fields(0)
    Text2.Text = TheTable.Fields(1)
    Text3.Text = TheTable.Fields(2)
End Sub


Private Sub CloseDatabase_Click()
    TheDB.Close
    List1.Clear
    Text1.Text = ""
    Text2.Text = ""
    Text3.Text = ""
    Label1.Caption = ""
    Label2.Caption = ""
    Label3.Caption = ""
    Label5.Caption = ""
End Sub

Private Sub Command1_Click()
    TheTable.AddNew
    Text1.Text = ""
```

```
        Text2.Text = ""
        Text3.Text = ""
    End Sub
```

```
    Private Sub Command2_Click()
        TheTable.Edit
    End Sub

    Private Sub Command3_Click()
        TheTable.Fields(0) = Text1.Text
        TheTable.Fields(1) = Text2.Text
        TheTable.Fields(2) = Text3.Text
        TheTable.Update
    End Sub


    Private Sub Command4_Click()
        TheTable.MoveFirst
        Text1.Text = TheTable.Fields(0)
        Text2.Text = TheTable.Fields(1)
        Text3.Text = TheTable.Fields(2)
    End Sub

    Private Sub Command5_Click()
        TheTable.MovePrevious
        If TheTable.BOF Then
            TheTable.MoveNext
        Else
            Text1.Text = TheTable.Fields(0)
            Text2.Text = TheTable.Fields(1)
            Text3.Text = TheTable.Fields(2)
        End If
    End Sub

    Private Sub Command6_Click()
        TheTable.MoveNext
        If TheTable.EOF Then
            TheTable.MovePrevious
        Else
            Text1.Text = TheTable.Fields(0)
            Text2.Text = TheTable.Fields(1)
            Text3.Text = TheTable.Fields(2)
        End If
    End Sub


    Private Sub Command7_Click()
        TheTable.MoveLast
        Text1.Text = TheTable.Fields(0)
        Text2.Text = TheTable.Fields(1)
        Text3.Text = TheTable.Fields(2)
    End Sub
```

```
Private Sub Command8_Click()
    Text1.Text = ""
    Text2.Text = ""
    Text3.Text = ""
    TheTable.Delete
End Sub

Private Sub ExitItem_Click()
    End
End Sub


Private Sub List1_DblClick()
    Set TheTable = TheDB.OpenRecordset(List1.Text, dbOpenTable)
    For Each TempTd In TheDB.TableDefs
        If TempTd.Name = List1.Text Then Set TheTd = TempTd
    Next TempTd
    Label1.Caption = TheTable.Fields(0).Name
    Label2.Caption = TheTable.Fields(1).Name
    Label3.Caption = TheTable.Fields(2).Name
    Label5.Caption = TheTable.Name
    Text1.Text = TheTable.Fields(0)
    Text2.Text = TheTable.Fields(1)
    Text3.Text = TheTable.Fields(2)
End Sub


Private Sub NewDatabase_Click()
    CommonDialog1.ShowSave
    If CommonDialog1.filename <> "" Then
        Set TheDB =
            DBEngine.Workspaces(0).CreateDatabase(CommonDialog1.filename,
            dbLangGeneral)
        MsgBox ("Database created. Add a table next.")
    End If
End Sub


Private Sub NewTable_Click()
    Form2.Text1.Text = ""
    Form2.Text2.Text = ""
    Form2.Text3.Text = ""
    Form2.Text4.Text = ""
    Form2.Show
End Sub


Private Sub OpenDatabase_Click()
    Dim theindex As Integer
    CommonDialog1.ShowOpen
    If CommonDialog1.filename <> "" Then
```

```
        Set TheDB = DBEngine.Workspaces(0).OpenDatabase(CommonDialog1.
filename)
        List1.Clear
        For Each TheTd In TheDB.TableDefs
            If (TheTd.Attributes And dbSystemObject) = 0 Then
                List1.AddItem TheTd.Name
        Next TheTd
        theindex = 0        'Find first non-system table
        While (TheDB.TableDefs(theindex).Attributes And dbSystemObject)
            theindex = theindex + 1
        Wend
        Set TheTable =
            TheDB.OpenRecordset(TheDB.TableDefs(theindex).Name, dbOpenTable)
        Set TheTd = TheDB.TableDefs(theindex)
        Label1.Caption = TheTable.Fields(0).Name
        Label2.Caption = TheTable.Fields(1).Name
        Label3.Caption = TheTable.Fields(2).Name
        Label5.Caption = TheTable.Name
        Text1.Text = TheTable.Fields(0)
        Text2.Text = TheTable.Fields(1)
        Text3.Text = TheTable.Fields(2)
    End If
End Sub


Private Sub Search_Click()
    Set TheIdx = TheTd.Indexes(0)
    TheTable.Index = TheIdx.Name
    Form3.Show
End Sub


Sub Sort_Click()
    Set TheIdx = TheTd.Indexes(0)
    TheTable.Index = TheIdx.Name
    Text1.Text = TheTable.Fields(0)
    Text2.Text = TheTable.Fields(1)
    Text3.Text = TheTable.Fields(2)
End Sub
```

LISTING 13.3 FORM2.FRM (DBDESIGN PROJECT)

```
VERSION 4.00
Begin VB.Form Form2
    Caption         =   "New Table"
    ClientHeight    =   2730
    ClientLeft      =   3360
    ClientTop       =   2835
    ClientWidth     =   4380
    Height          =   3135
    Left            =   3300
```

```
LinkTopic        =    "Form2"
ScaleHeight      =    2730
ScaleWidth       =    4380
Top              =    2490
Width            =    4500
Begin VB.TextBox Text4
   Height        =    375
   Left          =    1560
   TabIndex      =    6
   Top           =    1560
   Width         =    1215
End
Begin VB.TextBox Text3
   Height        =    375
   Left          =    1560
   TabIndex      =    5
   Top           =    1080
   Width         =    1215
End
Begin VB.TextBox Text2
   Height        =    375
   Left          =    1560
   TabIndex      =    4
   Top           =    600
   Width         =    1215
End
Begin VB.CommandButton Command2
   Caption       =    "Cancel"
   Height        =    495
   Left          =    2640
   TabIndex      =    3
   Top           =    2040
   Width         =    1215
End
Begin VB.CommandButton Command1
   Caption       =    "OK"
   Height        =    495
   Left          =    600
   TabIndex      =    2
   Top           =    2040
   Width         =    1215
End
Begin VB.TextBox Text1
   Height        =    375
   Left          =    1560
   TabIndex      =    0
   Top           =    120
   Width         =    1215
End
Begin VB.Label Label4
   Caption       =    "Field 3 Name:"
   Height        =    495
```

```
         Left            =    120
         TabIndex        =    9
         Top             =    1560
         Width           =    1215
      End
      Begin VB.Label Label3
         Caption         =    "Field 2 Name:"
         Height          =    495
         Left            =    120
         TabIndex        =    8
         Top             =    1080
         Width           =    1215
      End
      Begin VB.Label Label2
         Caption         =    "Field 1 Name:"
         Height          =    495
         Left            =    120
         TabIndex        =    7
         Top             =    600
         Width           =    1215
      End
      Begin VB.Label Label1
         Caption         =    "Table Name:"
         Height          =    495
         Left            =    120
         TabIndex        =    1
         Top             =    120
         Width           =    1215
      End
End
Attribute VB_Name = "Form2"
Attribute VB_Creatable = False
Attribute VB_Exposed = False

Private Sub Command1_Click()
    Form2.Hide
    Call Form1.CreateTable
End Sub


Private Sub Command2_Click()
    Form2.Hide
End Sub
```

LISTING 13.4 FORM3.FRM (DBDESIGN PROJECT)

```
VERSION 4.00
Begin VB.Form Form3
    Caption         =    "Search..."
    ClientHeight    =    1770
    ClientLeft      =    2160
    ClientTop       =    1770
```

```
        ClientWidth     =    3435
        Height          =    2175
        Left            =    2100
        LinkTopic       =    "Form3"
        ScaleHeight     =    1770
        ScaleWidth      =    3435
        Top             =    1425
        Width           =    3555
        Begin VB.TextBox Text1
            Height          =    495
            Left            =    960
            TabIndex        =    3
            Top             =    360
            Width           =    1935
        End
        Begin VB.CommandButton Command2
            Caption         =    "Cancel"
            Height          =    495
            Left            =    1800
            TabIndex        =    2
            Top             =    1080
            Width           =    1215
        End
        Begin VB.CommandButton Command1
            Caption         =    "OK"
            Height          =    495
            Left            =    360
            TabIndex        =    1
            Top             =    1080
            Width           =    1215
        End
        Begin VB.Label Label1
            Caption         =    "Fin d :"
            Height          =    255
            Left            =    240
            TabIndex        =    0
            Top             =    360
            Width           =    615
        End
    End
End
Attribute VB_Name = "Form3"
Attribute VB_Creatable = False
Attribute VB_Exposed = False

Private Sub Command1_Click()
    Form3.Hide
    Call Form1.SearchTable
End Sub


Private Sub Command2_Click()
    Form3.Hide
End Sub
```

Now let's take a look at how to search a dynaset- or snapshot-type recordset.

Searching a Dynaset or Snapshot Recordset

Searching a dynaset-type or snapshot-type recordset is easy. All you have to do is to create a recordset as we have done before:

```
Dim TheDB As Database
Dim TheDataset As Recordset, TheSortedDataset As Recordset

Set TheDB = DBEngine.Workspaces(0).OpenDatabase("DYNASET.MDB")
Set TheDataset = TheDB.OpenRecordset("Customers", dbOpenDynaset)
    .
    .
    .
```

Then you set up the search criteria. For example, if we wanted all matches to have the last name Richardson, our search criteria would look like this:

```
        Dim TheDB As Database
        Dim TheDataset As Recordset

        Set TheDB = DBEngine.Workspaces(0).OpenDatabase("DYNASET.MDB")
        Set TheDataset = TheDB.OpenRecordset("Customers", dbOpenDynaset)

-->     MatchString = "LastName = 'Richardson'"
            .
            .
            .
```

Now we use the Find methods. There are four find methods for dynaset- and snapshot-type recordsets: FindFirst (finds the first match), FindLast (finds the last match in the recordset), FindNext (finds the next match), and FindPrevious (finds the previous match). We find the first matching record with the LastName field set to "Richardson" this way:

```
        Dim TheDB As Database
        Dim TheDataset As Recordset

        Set TheDB = DBEngine.Workspaces(0).OpenDatabase("DYNASET.MDB")
        Set TheDataset = TheDB.OpenRecordset("Customers", dbOpenDynaset)

        MatchString = "LastName = 'Richardson'"
-->     TheDataset.FindFirst = MatchString
            .
            .
            .
```

If we like, we can also find all the remaining matches in the recordset using the FindNext method and the NoMatch property. The NoMatch property becomes True when there are no more matches to our search criteria. We loop over all remaining matches using the NoMatch property and the FindNext method:

```
        Dim TheDB As Database
        Dim TheDataset As Recordset

        Set TheDB = DBEngine.Workspaces(0).OpenDatabase("DYNASET.MDB")
        Set TheDataset = TheDB.OpenRecordset("Customers", dbOpenDynaset)

        MatchString = "LastName = 'Richardson'"
        TheDataset.FindFirst = MatchString

-->     Do Until TheDataSet.NoMatch
-->         TheDataSet.FindNext
-->         MsgBox("Found next match.")
-->     Loop
```

As you can see, the Find methods make up a powerful set of tools for us to use. With them, we can search a database easily and relatively quickly (although SQL queries can be faster).

A similar operation is filtering a recordset. When we filter a recordset, we create a new recordset that is a subset of the first one. This subset contains all the records that match our filtering criteria. Let's take a look at this now.

FILTERING

We can filter only dynaset- and snapshot-type recordsets, and we do so by setting their Filter property and then creating a new, filtered, recordset. If we want a new recordset of all the records in our customers recordset whose LastName field contains "Richardson," we filter that recordset, creating a new recordset, TheFilteredRecordset, with just those records we want:

```
        Dim TheDB As Database
        Dim TheDataset As Recordset, TheFilteredDataset As Recordset

        Set TheDB = DBEngine.Workspaces(0).OpenDatabase("DYNASET.MDB")
        Set TheDataset = TheDB.OpenRecordset("Customers", dbOpenDynaset)
-->     TheDataset.Filter = "LastName = 'Richardson'"
-->     Set The FilteredDataset = TheDataset.OpenRecordset()
```

In this way, we can work with a smaller recordset. Execution time is faster, because we do not have to work with the full table of records.

In this chapter, we have seen quite a number of operations on record-sets: searching and sorting, filtering, and moving from record to record. In Chapter 12, we saw how to edit records, add new records, and delete records. All these operations can be complex, and often they are related. For example, if we want to transfer the records of five books from one wing of a library to another wing, we want to remove their records from the first wing and add them to the records of the new wing. To ensure the integrity of the database, *both* operations should be performed, or neither. To make sure that complex or multistep operations are performed properly, the DAO allows us to use database transactions, and we'll examine them now.

TRANSACTIONS

A database *transaction* usually has the effect of rolling a number of operations into one operation. If we straddle a sensitive set of operations with the BeginTrans method and the CommitTrans method (commit as in "commit the changes to the database"), we ensure that the changes are all done correctly before we allow them to occur. If we do not want the changes to take effect, we use the RollBack method to cancel all changes since the BeginTrans method was executed.

For example, we might give the user the chance to cancel changes made to the database in the Database Designer, even if he or she has already clicked **Update Database**. We execute the BeginTrans method, which is a Workspace object method, in the event handlers of both the **Add New Record** (Command1) button and the **Edit Record** (Command2) button:

```
Private Sub Command1_Click()
--> DBEngine.Workspaces(0).BeginTrans
    TheTable.AddNew
    Text1.Text = ""
    Text2.Text = ""
    Text3.Text = ""
End Sub

Private Sub Command2_Click()
--> DBEngine.Workspaces(0).BeginTrans
    TheTable.Edit
End Sub
```

After users click **Update Database** (Command3), we ask whether they really want to update the database. If they do, we execute the CommitTrans method. If they do not, we execute the Rollback method:

```
Private Sub Command3_Click()
    TheTable.Fields(0) = Text1.Text
    TheTable.Fields(1) = Text2.Text
    TheTable.Fields(2) = Text3.Text
    TheTable.Update
--> If MsgBox("Update database?", vbYesNo) = vbYes Then
-->     DBEngine.Workspaces(0).CommitTrans
--> Else
-->     DBEngine.Workspaces(0).Rollback
--> End If
End Sub
```

If the user has second thoughts, the changes do not take effect. In addition, we can perform the same operation in the **Delete Record** (Command8) button's event handler (which does not use the Update method):

```
Private Sub Command8_Click()
--> DBEngine.Workspaces(0).BeginTrans
    TheTable.Delete
--> If MsgBox("Delete record from database?", vbYesNo) = vbYes Then
-->     DBEngine.Workspaces(0).CommitTrans
-->     Text1.Text = ""
-->     Text2.Text = ""
-->     Text3.Text = ""
--> Else
-->     DBEngine.Workspaces(0).Rollback
--> End If
End Sub
```

Now our database handling is safer for the user, who can cancel changes, even at the last minute.

RELATIONAL DATABASES IN CODE

Our last database topic concerns the relational nature of databases, for this is a powerful tool. Suppose that we have two tables in our database—students and registrar—and that they have a field in common, ID:

```
                    |                           |
                    V                           V
      Name    Grade    ID            Name      ID      Phone
      - - - - - - - - - - - - - -    - - - - - - - - - - - - - - - -
    | Ann   |  C  |  111  |        | Ann   |  111  |  777-1111 |
    |-------|-----|-------|        |-------|-------|-----------|
    | Mark  |  B  |  222  |        | Mark  |  222  |  777-2222 |
    |-------|-----|-------|        |-------|-------|-----------|
    | Ed    |  A  |  333  |        | Ed    |  333  |  777-3333 |
    |-------|-----|-------|        |-------|-------|-----------|
    | Frank |  A  |  444  |        | Frank |  444  |  777-4444 |
    |-------|-----|-------|        |-------|-------|-----------|
    | Ted   |  A  |  555  |        | Ted   |  555  |  777-5555 |
    |-------|-----|-------|        |-------|-------|-----------|
    | Mabel |  B  |  666  |        | Mabel |  666  |  777-6666 |
    |-------|-----|-------|        |-------|-------|-----------|
    | Ralph |  B  |  777  |        | Ralph |  777  |  777-7777 |
    |-------|-----|-------|        |-------|-------|-----------|
    | Tom   |  B  |  888  |        | Tom   |  888  |  777-8888 |
      - - - - - - - - - - - - - -    - - - - - - - - - - - - - - - -
             students                        registrar
```

When a new student wants to be added to our database, we can set up the relations between these tables so that referential integrity ensures that we add to the students table only those records whose ID values appear in the registrar table. We cannot add a student whose ID is 999 to the students table, because such a student is unknown to the registrar. This kind of automatic check is exactly what computers are good for.

In fact, we can go farther. If the registrar makes a change in the registrar table, changing a student's ID number, our students table will be out-of-date, but we can set up the relations between these tables so that any such changes will automatically be made to the student's record in the students table. If Ann's ID is changed from 111 to 101 in the registrar table, our database will automatically change her ID in the students table as well. This is called a *cascading change*.

In this case, registrar is the primary table; we cannot add records to the students table unless a record with the same ID exists in the registrar table. But when we change a record's ID field in the registrar table, the same change is automatically made for us in the students table.

To see this at work, we'll create a new project that can display both of our tables—students and registrar—at the same time.

```
 -------------------------------------------------------
| -----------------------------------------------------  |
|                       DBGrid1                          |
|    -----------------------------------------------     |
|   | Ann            | C              | 111          |    |
|   | ---------------|----------------|--------------|    |
|   | Mark           | B              | 222          |    |
|   | ---------------|----------------|--------------|    |
|   | Ed.            | A              | 333          |    |
|   | ---------------|----------------|--------------|    |
|   |Frank           | A              | 444          |    |
|    -----------------------------------------------     |
|                      students                          |
|                         _____             |
|    -----------------    |   |   |    |    |            |
|   | Create Database |   | |< | < | > | >| |            |
|    -----------------    |___|___|____|____|            |
|        Command1              Data1                     |
|                       DBGrid2                          |
|    -----------------------------------------------     |
|   | Ann            | 111            | 777-1111     |    |
|   | ---------------|----------------|--------------|    |
|   | Mark           | 222            | 777-2222     |    |
|   | ---------------|----------------|--------------|    |
|   | Ed             | 333            | 777-3333     |    |
|   | ---------------|----------------|--------------|    |
|   | Frank          | 444            | 777-444      |    |
|    -----------------------------------------------     |
|                      registrar                         |
|                         _____             |
|    -----------------    |   |   |    |    |            |
|   | Update Database |   | |< | < | > | >| |            |
|    -----------------    |___|___|____|____|            |
|        Command2              Data2                     |
| -----------------------------------------------------  |
 -------------------------------------------------------
```

When we change Ann's ID number from 111 to 101 in the registrar table, we will be able to see the same change take place in the students table:

```
-->    | | Ann      | C       | 101       |
       | |----------|---------|-----------|
       | | Mark     | B       | 222       |
       | |----------|---------|-----------|
       | | Ed       | A       | 333       |
       | |----------|---------|-----------|
       | |Frank     | A       | 444       |
       |                      students

       | -----------------   _____
       | | Create Database | | |< | < | > | >| |
       | -----------------   |__|__|__|__|__|

-->    | | Ann      | 101     | 777-1111   |
       | |----------|---------|------------|
       | | Mark     | 222     | 777-2222   |
       | |----------|---------|------------|
       | | Ed       | 333     | 777-3333   |
       | |----------|---------|------------|
       | | Frank    | 444     | 777-444    |
       |                      registrar

       | -----------------   _____
       | | Update Database | | |< | < | > | >| |
       | -----------------   |__|__|__|__|__|
```

Let's put this to work in the new project, which we'll call **RELATION.VBP**. If you want to follow along, add the controls indicated in the schematic to Form1. When the user clicks **Create Database**, Command1, we will create the database, install the relations between our tables as we want them, and display the two tables in our DBGrid objects (by first assigning the two tables to the two Data controls, Data1 and Data2). Open the click event associated with the **Create Database** button and use CreateDatabase() to create a new database:

```
Private Sub Command1_Click()
    Dim TheDB As Database

    Set TheDB =

DBEngine.Workspaces(0).CreateDatabase("C:\VBOOK\CREATEDB\CREATED.MDB",
        dbLangGeneral)
        .
        .
        .
```

This is the database in which we will install the two tables students and registrar, as well as an index for both tables, and a *relation object* in which we will set up the relations between these two tables. We start by creating the students table, with three fields: Name, Grade, and student_ID:

```
Private Sub Command1_Click()
    Dim TheDB As Database, IxFlds As Field
--> Dim studentsTD As TableDef
--> Dim studentsFlds(3) As Field

    Set TheDB =

DBEngine.Workspaces(0).CreateDatabase("C:\VBOOK\CREATEDB\CREATED.MDB",
        dbLangGeneral)

--> Set studentsTD = TheDB.CreateTableDef("students")
--> Set studentsFlds(0) = studentsTD.CreateField("Name", dbText)
--> Set studentsFlds(1) = studentsTD.CreateField("Grade", dbText)
--> Set studentsFlds(2) = studentsTD.CreateField("student_ID", dbLong)
--> studentsTD.Fields.Append studentsFlds(0)
--> studentsTD.Fields.Append studentsFlds(1)
--> studentsTD.Fields.Append studentsFlds(2)
        .
        .
        .
```

Next, we make the student_ID field into an index for the student table, as we have done before:

```
Private Sub Command1_Click()
--> Dim TheDB As Database, IxFlds As Field
    Dim studentsTD As TableDef
    Dim studentsFlds(3) As Field
--> Dim studentsIdx As Index

    Set TheDB =

DBEngine.Workspaces(0).CreateDatabase("C:\VBOOK\CREATEDB\CREATED.MDB",
        dbLangGeneral)
        .
        .
        .
    studentsTD.Fields.Append studentsFlds(0)
    studentsTD.Fields.Append studentsFlds(1)
    studentsTD.Fields.Append studentsFlds(2)

--> Set studentsIdx = studentsTD.CreateIndex("student_ID")
--> Set IxFlds = studentsIdx.CreateField("student_ID")
--> studentsIdx.Fields.Append IxFlds
--> studentsTD.Indexes.Append studentsIdx
```

```
--> TheDB.TableDefs.Append studentsTD
        .
        .
        .
```

Now we create the registrar table, with three fields: Name, student_ID, and phone. We make the student_ID field this table's index, and we also make it the primary index by setting its Primary property to True. We also make student_ID a *unique* index, which means that every entry must have a unique student ID or a trappable error will be generated:

```
Private Sub Command1_Click()
    Dim TheDB As Database, IxFlds As Field
--> Dim studentsTD As TableDef, registrarTd As TableDef
--> Dim studentsFlds(3) As Field, registrarFlds(3) As Field
--> Dim studentsIdx As Index, registrarIdx As Index

    Set TheDB =
        DBEngine.Workspaces(0).CreateDatabase("C:\VBOOK\CREATEDB\CREATED.MDB",
        dbLangGeneral)
        .
        .
        .
--> Set registrarTd = TheDB.CreateTableDef("registrar")
--> Set registrarFlds(0) = registrarTd.CreateField("Name", dbText)
--> Set registrarFlds(1) = registrarTd.CreateField("student_ID", dbLong)
--> Set registrarFlds(2) = registrarTd.CreateField("phone", dbText)
--> registrarTd.Fields.Append registrarFlds(0)
--> registrarTd.Fields.Append registrarFlds(1)
--> registrarTd.Fields.Append registrarFlds(2)

--> Set registrarIdx = registrarTd.CreateIndex()
--> registrarIdx.Name = "student_ID"
--> registrarIdx.Primary = True
--> registrarIdx.Unique = True
--> Set IxFlds = registrarIdx.CreateField("student_ID")
--> registrarIdx.Fields.Append IxFlds
--> registrarTd.Indexes.Append registrarIdx
--> TheDB.TableDefs.Append registrarTd
        .
        .
        .
```

We have set up our two tables and have made student_ID the index in both cases. We are ready to set up the relationship between the two tables, and we do that with a Relation object. We give a name to that object: registrar_students. The registrar table is the primary table, and students is the *foreign* table:

```
Private Sub Command1_Click()
    Dim TheDB As Database, IxFlds As Field
    Dim studentsTD As TableDef, registrarTd As TableDef
    Dim studentsFlds(3) As Field, registrarFlds(3) As Field
    Dim studentsIdx As Index, registrarIdx As Index
--> Dim registrar_students As Relation

    Set TheDB =
        DBEngine.Workspaces(0).CreateDatabase("C:\VBOOK\CREATEDB\CRE-
ATED.MDB",
        dbLangGeneral)
        .
        .
        .

--> Set registrar_students = TheDB.CreateRelation("registrar_students")
--> registrar_students.Table = "registrar"
--> registrar_students.ForeignTable = "students"
        .
        .
        .
```

To make sure that changes in the registrar table are mirrored in the foreign table (students), we set the Relation object's Attribute property to dbRelationUpdateCascade, because that is how you enable cascading changes. Next, we indicate the names of the fields we want to relate in the two tables. In both cases, that field is named student_ID. We create a new field with that name and set the field's ForeignName property to the same name:

```
Private Sub Command1_Click()
    Dim TheDB As Database, IxFlds As Field
    Dim studentsTD As TableDef, registrarTd As TableDef
    Dim studentsFlds(3) As Field, registrarFlds(3) As Field
    Dim studentsIdx As Index, registrarIdx As Index
    Dim registrar_students As Relation

    Set TheDB =
        DBEngine.Workspaces(0).CreateDatabase("C:\VBOOK\CREATEDB\CRE-
ATED.MDB",
        dbLangGeneral)
        .
        .
        .

    Set registrar_students = TheDB.CreateRelation("registrar_students")
    registrar_students.Table = "registrar"
    registrar_students.ForeignTable = "students"
--> registrar_students.Attributes = dbRelationUpdateCascade
--> Set TempField = registrar_students.CreateField("student_ID")
--> TempField.ForeignName = "student_ID"
        .
        .
        .
```

Now we append this new field to the Relation object, and, finally, we append the Relation object itself to the table definition object:

```
Private Sub Command1_Click()
    Dim TheDB As Database, IxFlds As Field
    Dim studentsTD As TableDef, registrarTd As TableDef
    Dim studentsFlds(3) As Field, registrarFlds(3) As Field
    Dim studentsIdx As Index, registrarIdx As Index
    Dim registrar_students As Relation

    Set TheDB =

DBEngine.Workspaces(0).CreateDatabase("C:\VBOOK\CREATEDB\CREATED.MDB",
        dbLangGeneral)
        .
        .
        .

    Set registrar_students = TheDB.CreateRelation("registrar_students")
    registrar_students.Table = "registrar"
    registrar_students.ForeignTable = "students"
    registrar_students.Attributes = dbRelationUpdateCascade
    Set TempField = registrar_students.CreateField("student_ID")
    TempField.ForeignName = "student_ID"
--> registrar_students.Fields.Append TempField
--> TheDB.Relations.Append registrar_students
        .
        .
        .
```

We've created our relation and have added it to our table definition. The next step is to create a database with this definition and fill the two tables: students and registrar:

```
Private Sub Command1_Click()
    Dim TheDB As Database, IxFlds As Field
    Dim studentsTD As TableDef, registrarTd As TableDef
    Dim studentsFlds(3) As Field, registrarFlds(3) As Field
    Dim studentsIdx As Index, registrarIdx As Index
--> Dim studentsTable As Recordset
--> Dim registrarTable As Recordset
    Dim registrar_students As Relation
        .
        .
        .

    TheDB.Relations.Append registrar_students

--> Set registrarTable = TheDB.OpenRecordset("registrar", dbOpenTable)

--> registrarTable.AddNew
--> registrarTable!Name = "Ann"
```

```
--> registrarTable!student_ID = 111
--> registrarTable!phone = "777-1111"
--> registrarTable.Update
--> registrarTable.AddNew
--> registrarTable!Name = "Mark"
--> registrarTable!student_ID = 222
--> registrarTable!phone = "777-2222"
--> registrarTable.Update
--> registrarTable.AddNew
--> registrarTable!Name = "Ed"
--> registrarTable!student_ID = 333
--> registrarTable!phone = "777-3333"
--> registrarTable.Update
--> registrarTable.AddNew
--> registrarTable!Name = "Frank"
--> registrarTable!student_ID = 444
--> registrarTable!phone = "777-4444"
--> registrarTable.Update
--> registrarTable.AddNew
--> registrarTable!Name = "Ted"
--> registrarTable!student_ID = 555
--> registrarTable!phone = "777-5555"
--> registrarTable.Update
--> registrarTable.AddNew
--> registrarTable!Name = "Mabel"
--> registrarTable!student_ID = 666
--> registrarTable!phone = "777-6666"
--> registrarTable.Update
--> registrarTable.AddNew
--> registrarTable!Name = "Ralph"
--> registrarTable!student_ID = 777
--> registrarTable!phone = "777-7777"
--> registrarTable.Update
--> registrarTable.AddNew
--> registrarTable!Name = "Tom"
--> registrarTable!student_ID = 888
--> registrarTable!phone = "777-8888"
--> registrarTable.Update

--> Set studentsTable = TheDB.OpenRecordset("students", dbOpenTable)

--> studentsTable.AddNew
--> studentsTable!Name = "Ann"
--> studentsTable!Grade = "C"
--> studentsTable!student_ID = 111
--> studentsTable.Update
--> studentsTable.AddNew
--> studentsTable!Name = "Mark"
--> studentsTable!Grade = "B"
--> studentsTable!student_ID = 222
--> studentsTable.Update
--> studentsTable.AddNew
```

```
--> studentsTable!Name = "Ed"
--> studentsTable!Grade = "A"
--> studentsTable!student_ID = 333
--> studentsTable.Update
--> studentsTable.AddNew
--> studentsTable!Name = "Frank"
--> studentsTable!Grade = "A"
--> studentsTable!student_ID = 444
--> studentsTable.Update
--> studentsTable.AddNew
--> studentsTable!Name = "Ted"
--> studentsTable!Grade = "A"
--> studentsTable!student_ID = 555
--> studentsTable.Update
--> studentsTable.AddNew
--> studentsTable!Name = "Mabel"
--> studentsTable!Grade = "B"
--> studentsTable!student_ID = 666
--> studentsTable.Update
--> studentsTable.AddNew
--> studentsTable!Name = "Ralph"
--> studentsTable!Grade = "B"
--> studentsTable!student_ID = 777
--> studentsTable.Update
--> studentsTable.AddNew
--> studentsTable!Name = "Tom"
--> studentsTable!Grade = "B"
--> studentsTable!student_ID = 888
--> studentsTable.Update

--> TheDB.Close
            .
            .
            .
```

It's important to realize that we had to fill the registrar table before we fill the students table; before we can place a record into the students table, we need a record with the same ID number in the registrar table, because the relation object already checks that referential integrity is preserved, causing an error if it is not. After we create and fill the database, we close it to write everything to disk. Next, we reopen that database file and connect it to the two Data controls in Form1: Data1 and Data2. We connect Data1 to the students table, and Data2 to the registrar table. The next step is to display these tables in the DBGrid controls. At design time we set them up by setting the DataSource property of DBGrid1 to Data1, and we set the DataSource property of DBGrid2 to Data2. When we open the new database from disk, then, our two tables will be displayed in DBGrid1 and DBGrid2:

```
Private Sub Command1_Click()
    Dim TheDB As Database, IxFlds As Field
        .
        .
        .
    studentsTable.AddNew
    studentsTable!Name = "Tom"
    studentsTable!Grade = "B"
    studentsTable!student_ID = 888
    studentsTable.Update

    TheDB.Close
```

```
--> Data1.DatabaseName = "C:\VBOOK\CREATEDB\CREATED.MDB"
--> Data1.RecordSource = "students"
--> Data1.Enabled = True
--> DBGrid1.Enabled = True
--> Data1.Refresh
--> Data2.DatabaseName = "C:\VBOOK\CREATEDB\CREATED.MDB"
--> Data2.RecordSource = "registrar"
--> Data2.Enabled = True
--> DBGrid2.Enabled = True
--> Data2.Refresh

End Sub
```

This complete the process of creating and displaying our database and the two tables in it. After users make changes to one of the tables in its associated DBGrid control, they can update the database by clicking **Update Database**, Command2 (just as the **Create Database** button created the database). Open that button's click event:

```
Private Sub Command2_Click()

End Sub
```

We'll make changes to the registrar table as held in the Data2 control, so we update that control after we've made a change. To make sure that the new data is also displayed in the Data1 control, we use that control's Refresh method:

```
Private Sub Command2_Click()
    Data2.UpdateRecord
    Data1.Refresh
End Sub
```

Now run the program. When you click **Create Database**, the two database tables—students and registrar—are created and displayed, as shown in Figure 13.6.

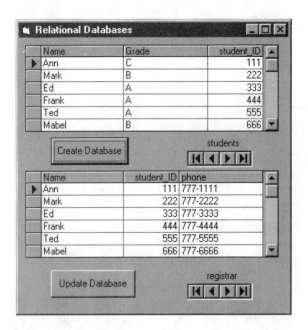

FIGURE 13.6 CREATING TWO RELATED DATABASE TABLES.

If we try to change an ID value in any record of the students table to an ID not in the registrar table, the rules of referential integrity are violated and an error occurs. On the other hand, if we change a student's ID number in the registrar table, the same change is automatically made in the students table, as shown in Figure 13.7, where we have changed the ID of the student named Ann from 111 to 101.

The program is a success; we have set up a relational database. As you can see, the potential for powerful database handling is enormous. This is what computers are best at—handling operations that would be tedious to do by hand. By working behind the scenes like this, our program takes away many of the worries associated with database handling, making it a more pleasant (and effective) task. Our program appears in Listing 13.5 (**RELATION.VBP**) and in Listing 13.6 (**RELATION.FRM**).

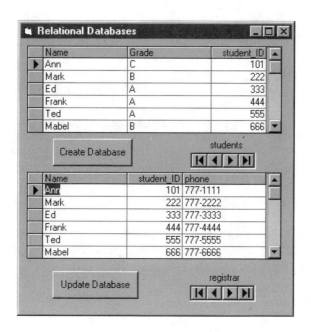

FIGURE 13.7 CHANGING A STUDENT'S ID IN THE REGISTRAR TABLE
ALSO MAKES CHANGES IN THE STUDENTS TABLE.

LISTING 13.5 RELATION.VBP

```
Form=relation.Frm
Object={F9043C88-F6F2-101A-A3C9-08002B2F49FB}#1.0#0; COMDLG32.OCX
Object={6B7E6392-850A-101B-AFC0-4210102A8DA7}#1.0#0; COMCTL32.OCX
Object={FAEEE763-117E-101B-8933-08002B2F4F5A}#1.0#0; DBLIST32.OCX
Object={00028C01-0000-0000-0000-000000000046}#1.0#0; DBGRID32.OCX
Reference=*\G{BEF6E001-A874-101A-8BBA-
        00AA00300CAB}#2.0#0#C:\WINDOWS\SYSTEM\OLEPRO32.DLL#Standard
        OLE Types
Reference=*\G{00025E01-0000-0000-C000-000000000046}#3.0#0#C:\PROGRAM
        FILES\COMMON FILES\MICROSOFT SHARED\DAO\DAO3032.DLL#Microsoft
        DAO 3.0 Object Library
ProjWinSize=356,375,217,94
ProjWinShow=2
IconForm="Form1"
Name="Project1"
HelpContextID="0"
StartMode=0
```

```
VersionCompatible32="0"
MajorVer=1
MinorVer=0
RevisionVer=0
AutoIncrementVer=0
ServerSupportFiles=0
```

LISTING 13.6 RELATION.FRM

```
VERSION 4.00
Begin VB.Form Form1
    Caption          =    "Relational Databases"
    ClientHeight     =    4950
    ClientLeft       =    1755
    ClientTop        =    1620
    ClientWidth      =    4995
    Height           =    5355
    Left             =    1695
    LinkTopic        =    "Form1"
    ScaleHeight      =    4950
    ScaleWidth       =    4995
    Top              =    1275
    Width            =    5115
    Begin VB.CommandButton Command2
        Caption      =    "Update Database"
        Height       =    495
        Left         =    600
        TabIndex     =    1
        Top          =    4200
        Width        =    1575
    End
    Begin VB.Data Data2
        Caption        =    "Data2"
        Connect        =    "Access"
        DatabaseName   =    ""
        Enabled        =    0    'False
        Exclusive      =    0    'False
        Height         =    300
        Left           =    3120
        Options        =    0
        ReadOnly       =    0    'False
        RecordsetType  =    1    'Dynaset
        RecordSource   =    ""
        Top            =    4440
        Width          =    1215
    End
    Begin VB.Data Data1
        Caption      =    "Data1"
        Connect      =    "Access"
```

```
      DatabaseName    =    ""
      Enabled         =    0    'False
      Exclusive       =    0    'False
      Height          =    300
      Left            =    3120
      Options         =    0
      ReadOnly        =    0    'False
      RecordsetType   =    1    'Dynaset
      RecordSource    =    ""
      Top             =    2040
      Width           =    1215
   End
   Begin VB.CommandButton Command1
      Caption         =    "Create Database"
      Height          =    495
      Left            =    600
      TabIndex        =    0
      Top             =    1800
      Width           =    1455
   End
   Begin VB.Label Label2
      Caption         =    "registrar"
      Height          =    255
      Left            =    3480
      TabIndex        =    5
      Top             =    4200
      Width           =    1215
   End
   Begin VB.Label Label1
      Caption         =    "students"
      Height          =    255
      Left            =    3480
      TabIndex        =    4
      Top             =    1800
      Width           =    1215
   End
   Begin MSDBGrid.DBGrid DBGrid2
      Bindings        =    "relation.frx":0000
      Height          =    1575
      Left            =    120
      OleObjectBlob   =    "relation.frx":000E
      TabIndex        =    3
      Top             =    2400
      Width           =    4695
   End
   Begin MSDBGrid.DBGrid DBGrid1
      Bindings        =    "relation.frx":0716
      Height          =    1575
      Left            =    120
      OleObjectBlob   =    "relation.frx":0724
```

```
        TabIndex       =    2
        Top            =    120
        Width          =    4695
    End
End
Attribute VB_Name = "Form1"
Attribute VB_Creatable = False
Attribute VB_Exposed = False

Private Sub Command1_Click()
    Dim TheDB As Database, IxFlds As Field
    Dim studentsTD As TableDef, registrarTd As TableDef
    Dim studentsFlds(3) As Field, registrarFlds(3) As Field
    Dim studentsIdx As Index, registrarIdx As Index
    Dim studentsTable As Recordset
    Dim registrarTable As Recordset
    Dim registrar_students As Relation

    Set TheDB =

DBEngine.Workspaces(0).CreateDatabase("C:\VBOOK\CREATEDB\CREATED.MDB",
        dbLangGeneral)

    Set studentsTD = TheDB.CreateTableDef("students")
    Set studentsFlds(0) = studentsTD.CreateField("Name", dbText)
    Set studentsFlds(1) = studentsTD.CreateField("Grade", dbText)
    Set studentsFlds(2) = studentsTD.CreateField("student_ID", dbLong)
    studentsTD.Fields.Append studentsFlds(0)
    studentsTD.Fields.Append studentsFlds(1)
    studentsTD.Fields.Append studentsFlds(2)

    Set studentsIdx = studentsTD.CreateIndex("student_ID")
    Set IxFlds = studentsIdx.CreateField("student_ID")
    studentsIdx.Fields.Append IxFlds
    studentsTD.Indexes.Append studentsIdx
    TheDB.TableDefs.Append studentsTD

    Set registrarTd = TheDB.CreateTableDef("registrar")
    Set registrarFlds(0) = registrarTd.CreateField("Name", dbText)
    Set registrarFlds(1) = registrarTd.CreateField("student_ID", dbLong)
    Set registrarFlds(2) = registrarTd.CreateField("phone", dbText)
    registrarTd.Fields.Append registrarFlds(0)
    registrarTd.Fields.Append registrarFlds(1)
    registrarTd.Fields.Append registrarFlds(2)

    Set registrarIdx = registrarTd.CreateIndex()
    registrarIdx.Name = "student_ID"
    registrarIdx.Primary = True
    registrarIdx.Unique = True
    Set IxFlds = registrarIdx.CreateField("student_ID")
```

```
registrarIdx.Fields.Append IxFlds
registrarTd.Indexes.Append registrarIdx
TheDB.TableDefs.Append registrarTd

Set registrar_students = TheDB.CreateRelation("registrar_students")
registrar_students.Table = "registrar"
registrar_students.ForeignTable = "students"
registrar_students.Attributes = dbRelationUpdateCascade
Set TempField = registrar_students.CreateField("student_ID")
TempField.ForeignName = "student_ID"
registrar_students.Fields.Append TempField
TheDB.Relations.Append registrar_students

Set registrarTable = TheDB.OpenRecordset("registrar", dbOpenTable)

registrarTable.AddNew
registrarTable!Name = "Ann"
registrarTable!student_ID = 111
registrarTable!phone = "777-1111"
registrarTable.Update
registrarTable.AddNew
registrarTable!Name = "Mark"
registrarTable!student_ID = 222
registrarTable!phone = "777-2222"
registrarTable.Update
registrarTable.AddNew
registrarTable!Name = "Ed"
registrarTable!student_ID = 333
registrarTable!phone = "777-3333"
registrarTable.Update
registrarTable.AddNew
registrarTable!Name = "Frank"
registrarTable!student_ID = 444
registrarTable!phone = "777-4444"
registrarTable.Update
registrarTable.AddNew
registrarTable!Name = "Ted"
registrarTable!student_ID = 555
registrarTable!phone = "777-5555"
registrarTable.Update
registrarTable.AddNew
registrarTable!Name = "Mabel"
registrarTable!student_ID = 666
registrarTable!phone = "777-6666"
registrarTable.Update
registrarTable.AddNew
registrarTable!Name = "Ralph"
registrarTable!student_ID = 777
registrarTable!phone = "777-7777"
registrarTable.Update
```

```
registrarTable.AddNew
registrarTable!Name = "Tom"
registrarTable!student_ID = 888
registrarTable!phone = "777-8888"
registrarTable.Update

Set studentsTable = TheDB.OpenRecordset("students", dbOpenTable)

studentsTable.AddNew
studentsTable!Name = "Ann"
studentsTable!Grade = "C"
studentsTable!student_ID = 111
studentsTable.Update
studentsTable.AddNew
studentsTable!Name = "Mark"
studentsTable!Grade = "B"
studentsTable!student_ID = 222
studentsTable.Update
studentsTable.AddNew
studentsTable!Name = "Ed"
studentsTable!Grade = "A"
studentsTable!student_ID = 333
studentsTable.Update
studentsTable.AddNew
studentsTable!Name = "Frank"
studentsTable!Grade = "A"
studentsTable!student_ID = 444
studentsTable.Update
studentsTable.AddNew
studentsTable!Name = "Ted"
studentsTable!Grade = "A"
studentsTable!student_ID = 555
studentsTable.Update
studentsTable.AddNew
studentsTable!Name = "Mabel"
studentsTable!Grade = "B"
studentsTable!student_ID = 666
studentsTable.Update
studentsTable.AddNew
studentsTable!Name = "Ralph"
studentsTable!Grade = "B"
studentsTable!student_ID = 777
studentsTable.Update
studentsTable.AddNew
studentsTable!Name = "Tom"
studentsTable!Grade = "B"
studentsTable!student_ID = 888
studentsTable.Update

TheDB.Close
```

```
    Data1.DatabaseName = "C:\VBOOK\CREATEDB\CREATED.MDB"
    Data1.RecordSource = "students"
    Data1.Enabled = True
    DBGrid1.Enabled = True
    Data1.Refresh
    Data2.DatabaseName = "C:\VBOOK\CREATEDB\CREATED.MDB"
    Data2.RecordSource = "registrar"
    Data2.Enabled = True
    DBGrid2.Enabled = True
    Data2.Refresh

End Sub

Private Sub Command2_Click()
    Data2.UpdateRecord
    Data1.Refresh
End Sub
```

AND THAT'S IT

That's it for our coverage of database programming—and that's it for our coverage of advanced Visual Basic. We've come far in this book, from the elementary to the quite advanced. We've seen how to get into Visual Basic—and get what we want out of it, including how to connect it to Windows directly, how to connect it to Visual C++, how to work with and zoom OLE items, and how to set up arrays of forms. You've learned how to work with OLE automation, and how to use advanced graphics techniques. We've covered how to create toolbars and status bars, drag graphics objects, create new controls at run time, set up MDI Visual Basic programs, handle run-time errors, use OCX controls, create help and setup files, do database programming, and much more. We've had some fun, and we've put in some hard work—all that remains now is to make use of what you've learned in your own programs!

Happy programming, and good luck.

APPENDIX A

ISSUES OF 16-BIT VS. 32-BIT PROGRAMMING

Although the developers of the 16-bit and 32-bit versions of Visual Basic have taken great pains to make the versions as compatible as possible, there are differences. For example, some newer bitmap modes were not available in Windows 3.1, and if you try to display them in Windows 3.1 you will get mixed results.

However, most of the difficulties in 16-bit vs. 32-bit programming come when you mix code between the versions. Let's look at some of the main trouble areas.

CONNECTING TO WINDOWS ROUTINES

The biggest issue in connecting to Windows routines directly is that 16-bit Windows uses 16-bit Windows handles and arguments (see Chapter 9), and 32-bit Windows uses 32-bit handles and arguments. For example, 16-bit Windows functions often return Integer arguments, whereas 32-bit functions usually return Longs. When calling Windows routines directly, you must take this into account by treating Windows handles and other arguments as either Integers (16-bit Windows) or Longs (32-bit Windows). To determine which arguments to use, you can find the declarations for 16-bit Windows functions in the file **WIN31API.TXT** (this file is not installed if you install 32-bit Visual Basic). The file **WIN32API.TXT** file contains declarations for 32-bit Windows. In addition, the **WINMMSYS.TXT** file contains declarations for Windows 3.1 multimedia functions. The API viewer included with Visual Basic allows you to work with the **WIN31API.TXT**, **WIN32API.TXT**, and **WINMMSYS.TXT** files and can be used to paste API functions into your Visual Basic programs directly.

Although character storage is accomplished differently in 16-bit Windows than in 32-bit Windows, this normally makes no difference to you because Visual Basic handles the details. However, if you explicitly handle such details—for example, passing characters to Windows library routines directly—you should know that 16-bit Visual Basic uses ANSI characters one byte long, and 32-bit Visual Basic uses two-byte Unicode characters. (32-bit OLE uses Unicode, so Visual Basic uses it for compatibility. When sending characters to either 16-bit or 32-bit Windows, it converts the Unicode into one-byte ANSI characters.) This difference is a problem only when you start accessing Windows directly and have to make the conversion yourself. This happens when you send 32-bit version Unicode (two-byte) characters to 32-bit Windows routines, which expect one-byte ANSI characters.

In general, if you are running a Windows application and call Windows library routines, you must send and receive data in the correct format. The best thing to do is to check Windows programming documentation to make sure that you know exactly what that format is. In addition, when connecting to Windows libraries, you will find Windows routines have different names in 16 bits and 32 bits; those library names will also be given in the function declarations found in **WIN31API.TXT**, **WIN32API.TXT**, and **WIN-MMSYS.TXT**. (For example, the 16-bit **USER.DLL** becomes **USER32.DLL**.)

CONNECTING TO C++ THROUGH DLLS

If you write a 16-bit program and run it as such, you will have problems connecting to a 32-bit dynamic link library file and, similarly, if you try to connect a 32-bit program to a 16-bit DLL. In general, you should make sure that the version of Visual Basic (16-bit or 32-bit) matches your DLL file or else specifically target the DLL to your version of Visual Basic. (For example, in Chapter 9 we used Visual C++ 1.5 to create 16-bit DLLs, and Visual C++ 2.0 or later to create 32-bit DLLs.)

ONE PROGRAM, TWO VERSIONS OF WINDOWS

For these or other reasons, you may have two sections of code in a Visual Basic program: one for the 16-bit version of Visual Basic and a second one for the 32-bit version. You can do that with conditional compilation:

```
#If Win32 Then
    .
    .
    .
    32-bit code goes here...
    .
    .
    .
```

```
#Else
     .
     .
     .
   16-bit code goes here...
     .
     .
     .
#End If
```

For example, here we declare the Windows Help function, WinHelp(), in a Visual Basic module:

```
#If Win32 Then
    Declare Function WinHelp Lib "User32-- Alias "WinHelpA-- (ByVal
    hWnd As Long, ByVal lpHelpFile As String, ByVal wCommand As Long,
    dwData As Long) As Long
#Else
    Declare Function WinHelp Lib "User-- (ByVal hWnd As Integer,
    ByVal lpHelpFile As String, ByVal wCommand As Integer, dwData As
    Any) As Integer
#End If
```

For the most part, 16-bit vs. 32-bit programming is not a big issue in Visual Basic 4.0. It's only when you start to mix 16-bit and 32-bit programming that you have problems.

VISUAL BASIC, ENTERPRISE EDITION

In this book, we cover many features of the Standard and Professional editions of Visual Basic. There are some features of the third, more comprehensive edition—the Enterprise edition—that aren't discussed in the main body of this book. This appendix covers these features of the Enterprise edition of Visual Basic:

- SourceSafe 4.0
- The RemoteData control
- Remote automation technology
- The Microsoft Component Manager

These features are designed to help developers working in and targeting networked environments. Briefly, SourceSafe is a programming development tool that maintains code integrity when a program is being worked on by many programmers on a network. The RemoteData control and remote data objects allow Visual Basic programs to develop database client/server relationships without using "local" query processors, resulting in improved network performance. Remote automation technology allows a program to use the OLE automation interface for network communication. The Microsoft Component Manager allows you to find and get information about OLE servers on a network. Let's review these features.

SOURCESAFE 4.0

Usually, SourceSafe is installed on a network server to which all programmers working on a piece of code have access. But now it can also be added directly to the integrated development environment (IDE) of Microsoft Visual Basic 4.0. The purpose of SourceSafe is to keep the source file(s) of a program safe by requiring that each programmer "check out" file(s) to work on, much like checking out books in a library. In addition, SourceSafe prevents deletion of files by mistake, stores all changes made to a file and creates histories of changes, allows hierarchical overviews of projects, allows documentation of changes (what you intend to do with a file or what you have done), and allows sharing of files between multiple users (as opposed to having them work on multiple copies of the same file, which can lead to version errors). SourceSafe has two levels—administrator and user—and this further permits project organization. SourceSafe is usually used for large projects with many programmers working on a network.

THE REMOTEDATA CONTROL

Remote data objects (RDOs) and the RemoteData control (RDC) allow programs to reach ODBC-accessible data sources on a network without a local query processor. This means that queries are sent on and processed remotely, which results in considerably faster response and better performance. The RemoteData control can work with any ODBC data source, but it is designed to work best with database servers, such as Oracle or Microsoft's SQL Server, that use advanced query engines.

Much like the standard Data control, then, the RemoteData control gives you an interface that works between remote data objects (nonlocal data sources in a network) and data bound controls. With the RemoteData control, you can pass to the remote data object changes made to the data, allow the user to move from record to record, and pass data to data bound controls. In other words, many of the RemoteData control's capabilities are just like the Data control's capabilities, except that with the RDC the data source is not local. RemoteData controls create *result sets* of data when you connect to the remote data object, and these sets are given the name rdoResultSet. When you set the properties of the RemoteData control to match the characteristics of the connection you want to the remote data object and use the Refresh method to create the result set, the remote data is then displayed in data bound controls. Using the mouse, you can manipulate the RemoteData control just as you would a standard (local) data control. In other words, the RemoteData control gives you much of the functionality of the Data control but allows the actual query processor to be remote. In code, you can use many of the standard RecordSet methods, such as RemoteData1.Resultset.MoveFirst, with a rdoResultSet.

REMOTE AUTOMATION TECHNOLOGY

Remote automation is the technology that allows you to use OLE automation over networks. Remote automation allows you to create shared application components that use the OLE automation interface for communication over the network.

When you use OLE automation in one computer, the method used is an OLE proxy and stub combination; the proxy is part of the controlling application, and the stub is part of the server. On the other hand, remote automation adds the Automation Manager to this connection, allowing the user to reach automation servers anywhere on a network, and replacing the local proxy and stub model.

To set up remote automation, the Automation Manager is placed on the remote computer. The Automation Manager handles requests sent from the remote automation proxy on the local machine to the corresponding remote automation stub object on the server. In this way, OLE automation becomes transparent to the programmer even though it is taking place over a network.

THE MICROSOFT COMPONENT MANAGER

The Microsoft Component Manager lets you find and categorize OLE servers in a network, get information about them, and install or register OLE servers so that you can use them in Visual Basic projects. It does this by searching a network and creating *component catalogs*, which are lists of OLE servers.

When you first start the Component Manager, it creates an empty component catalog, which appears in the Scope pane of the Component Manager. Once components are added to the catalog, they appear in the right-hand pane of the Component Manager's main window; this pane is called the Results pane. In the top pane, the Criteria pane, you can specify sorting and filtering information to find a particular component in a catalog. In addition, you can produce lists of OLE servers that are related; such lists are called *collections*. Collections of servers allow you to see immediately which servers are available and what they do. Using the Component Manager, then, you can gain an overview of the OLE servers available on an entire network, using and coordinating them as you wish.

ABOUT THE DISKETTE

Install the files on the diskette that accompanies this book to your hard disk using the **installa.bat** file if you placed the diskette in the **a:** drive, or **installb.bat** if you placed the diskette in the **b:** drive.

The installation process creates a directory named VBOOK on your **C:** drive and loads a number of projects into that directory. It is important that these projects be loaded into the directory **C:\VBOOK** because some files refer to that directory. Here is a list of the projects on the diskette:

- ANIBUTTO. Animation button example. Click the form to see the graphic of a fish move across the client area. We use an animation button control here.

- ANIMATE. Graphics animation. Click the form to see the car move off to the right. Here we use a picture box's Move method.

- CALCULAT. OLE automation example. The programmable object that comes from CALCULAT adds integers sent to it from CALCTEST. Run CALCULAT in one session of Visual Basic to make its programmable object available; start Visual Basic again, loading in CALCTEST. Add a reference to CALCULAT in CALCTEST using the **Tools | References** menu item. Run CALCTEST to see a small calculator appear. Place two integers in the text boxes above the button marked **=**, and then press that button. The integers are passed to CALCULAT, added, and passed back, and the result is displayed under the = button. In addition, CALCTEST displays the value of a property named IsFive, which is always supposed to be set to 5.

- CONTAIN. An OLE container program capable of holding multiple OLE items. Start the program, select one of the two OLE controls with the mouse, and use **Edit | Insert New Object** to place an OLE item into the control. Double-clicking the OLE item opens it for in-place editing. Clicking outside the OLE control deactivates the OLE item.

- CREATEDB. This database example creates the database **CRE-ATED.MDB** in the **C:\VBOOK\CREATEDB** directory and places one table, students, in it. The table is filled with student names and grades. The database is also displayed.

- CUSTOM. This example shows how to use various custom controls: 3-D buttons, gauge controls, and key status indicators. Click the gauge control to see its value fall from 50 to 20; change the **Num Lock**, **Caps Lock**, and **Scroll Lock** settings on your keyboard to see the corresponding changes in the key status indicators.

- DATENTRY. A data entry database program. This program expects to find the database **CREATED.MDB** in **C:\VBOOK\CREATEDB** (this file is placed there by the CREATEDB project). Many data bound controls are shown here, from text boxes to the DBGrid. You can edit the data in the database by making a change in one of the controls and clicking **Update Database**. Also, you can use the specially designed data entry form by clicking the button marked **Data Entry Form**.

- DBDESIGN. A database designer. Start by creating a new database. If you want to create, say, **VBCLASS.MDB**, select **New Database** in the Database Designer's File menu, and type that name as the file name of the new database. Next, add table(s) to the new database using **Add Table** in the Database menu. When you select this item, a dialog box named Add Table will open, with text boxes for the new table's name and for the names of three fields (for simplicity, each record has three fields here). Click **OK**. The Add Table dialog box closes, and the Database Designer displays the fields for your new table. To add a new record to the table, click **Add New Record**, fill in the data for the three fields of this new record, and click **Update Database**. To edit a record in the table, click **Edit**, make the changes, and click **Update Database**. To delete the current record, click **Delete**. All the tables in the database are listed in the list box; if you want to switch to another table, click its name in the list box. Navigate through the database using the <<, <, >, and >> buttons. You can use the **Search** and **Sort** items in the Database menu to search and sort through the first field of each record.

- FONT. This screen font example places the string "No Problem" in a window in as large a font as can fit.

- FUN. A fun graphics program. Places an interesting graphics drawing on the screen.

- GRAPH. This Graph control example shows how to use the Graph control: we draw line graphs, pie charts, 3-D pie charts, and more.

- GRAPHER. Custom scale example showing how to customize the window's scale for easy graphing of data. In this case, we set the window's internal scale to fit our data and then graph it.

- GRID. Spreadsheet example using the Grid control. In this example, we've labeled the Grid control like a true spreadsheet. Click the cell in the grid you wish to enter data into, place a positive integer in the text box marked Data, and click **Enter**. The data is entered into the grid cell you selected.

- INSIDE. "Inside" graphics lines example. In Visual Basic, thick lines are drawn straddling the line you indicate when you give drawing coordinates. This means that half of a thick line will lie outside a graphics figure. Here, we use "inside" line drawing styles to make sure that the whole thickness of the line appears inside the figure (a rectangle in this case). Run the program. A rectangle fills the upper half of the client area. If we had not used inside lines, all lines except the bottom one would have been reduced in thickness by half, because they would be outside our client area.

- LINK. OLE Link example. Start an OLE server such as Microsoft Excel, select a range of cells, save the worksheet to a file, and select **Edit | Copy**. Next, run **LINK.VBP** in Visual Basic and use **Edit | Paste Special** to paste an OLE link to the range of Excel cells you have marked.

- LOADBMP. Loading bitmaps into programs. Loads a bitmap into the form. In addition, loads an icon into a picture box and an Image control, both of which automatically resize themselves to the right size.

- MDI. MDI program showing how to create multiple document interface programs, including how to create toolbars and a status bar.

- MDIOLE. MDI OLE container program. This program shows how to support a toolbar in OLE programs. Each new MDI child window is covered with an OLE control, and you can insert items into these controls using **Edit | Insert New Object**. You can create new windows on demand.

- MULTIMED. A multimedia example using both video and CD audio. Run the program and double-click the Video Clip control at right to play the skiing video **SKIING.AVI**. (The program expects this file, which comes with Windows, to be in the **WINDOWS\MEDIA** directory.) Next, use the two multimedia controls (a bar of arrow controls): the one on top plays the skiing video in the picture box. The one under it plays a music CD if you place one in the CD-ROM drive of the computer.

- MULTVIEW. This multiview text editor allows multiple coordinated "views" into a single document (i.e., multiple windows open in the same document). When the program starts, click **New View** a few times to create new views. Next, type something in any view window and you'll see it appear in all windows. In this way, we present multiple (independently scrollable) views into the same document. We augment what is possible in Visual Basic by coordinating all views (i.e., entering text in one view enters it in all views).

- NEWCTRL. Shows how to add new controls—in this case, an **Option** button—at run time. Run the program and click the form, adding a new option button automatically.

- NOPROB. This introductory program places the string "No Problem" on the form. Click the button marked **Click me** to see the same string displayed in the text box.

- OLEPICT. OLE automation example showing how to use a form in OLE automation. Run OLEPICT in Visual Basic, start a new Visual Basic session, and load PICTTEST in that session. Add a reference to OLEPICT in PICTTEST using **Tools | References**. Click **Show Picture** in PICTTEST to pop a form from the programmable object onto the screen, displaying an icon. In this way, our OLE automation programmable objects can use forms in the same way that OLE automation controlling applications do.

- POPUP. A pop-up menu example. Run the program and click the form with the right mouse button to bring up the pop-up menu. There are two items: **Click Me** and **Exit**. Clicking **Click Me** makes the computer beep.

- PROP1. An OLE automation example. Run the PROP1 program in Visual Basic to make its programmable object—containing the Is1 property—available to controlling applications. Start a new session of Visual Basic and load **PROPTEST.VBP**. Add a reference to Prop1 using **Tools | References** in PROPTEST. Next, run PROPTEST and click the button to read the Is1 property from PROP1's programmable object and display it in a message box.

- PUZZLE. In this puzzle, a user moves the pieces around with the mouse. This example shows how to let the user drag controls. In particular, we allow the user to drag picture boxes containing various parts of a picture of a fish around until the fish is reassembled. We use the various drag and drop methods to accomplish this.

- READER. Reading keys from the keyboard. Run the program and type keys on the keyboard. As you do, we add the new character to the previous ones in a character string that grows as you type. We display the growing character string each time you type a new key.

- RELATION. A relational database program. This program creates and displays two tables in a database when you click **Create Database**. The rules of referential integrity are set up so that no entry in the students table can exist without a corresponding entry with the same ID in the registrar table. Change the ID number of a student in the registrar table and click **Update Database** to see that student's ID number changed to match in the students table—a cascading change.

- RESET. Shows how to pass controls as objects to subroutines. Start the program to see command buttons and text boxes. Select a control with the mouse and then choose **File | Reset Control** to clear the control's text.

- SCREENER. Screen capture (16-bit Windows version). Run, select the Capture menu, and press the mouse button while the mouse cursor is inside SCREENER's window. Using the mouse, outline the area on screen you wish to capture, and release the mouse button. The area of the screen you wish to capture appears in SCREENER's client area.

- SCREEN32. Screen capture (32-bit Windows version). Run, select the Capture menu, and press the mouse button while the mouse cursor is inside SCREEN32's window. Using the mouse, outline the area on screen you wish to capture, and release the mouse button. The area of the screen you wish to capture appears in SCREEN32's client area.

- SCRIBBLE. Drawing with the mouse. Start the program and draw in the client area, using the mouse. This program helps us review Visual Basic mouse events.

- TABORDER. Setting the tab order of a program (tab order sets which control the user moves to when they press the **Tab** key). In this case, the user selects one of two graphics figures to draw—a rectangle or a circle—by clicking the matching button (**Rectangle** or **Circle**). Rectangles take four parameters matching the four coordinates needed; circles need only three parameters (origin coordinates and radius). The user can tab from text box to text box, filling in the parameters and then tabbing to the final **Draw** button. (Pressing **Enter** when **Draw** is selected draws the graphics figure.) We change the tab order to skip the useless fourth parameter text box when the user draws a circle.

- TICTAC. MDI tic-tac-toe program (two-player, the computer does not play) showing more about passing controls to subroutines. Each MDI child window shows a tic-tac-toe board; when you click buttons, the whole button is passed in code to a subroutine that sets its caption to **x** or **o** as required. Add new windows using **File | New Window**.

- TILER. Multiple-window example showing how to pass windows as objects to a subroutine. In this case, click the window that appears, displaying all four windows. Each window is then passed to a subroutine that draws a tile pattern in it, tiling each window.

- TIMES2. A Visual C++ 16-bit DLL example showing how to connect Visual Basic and Visual C++. The file **DYNAM.MAK** is set up for Visual C++ 1.5 and will create **DYNAM.DLL**, a dynamic link library file containing a function named DLLCall(). Copy **DYNAM.DLL** to the **C:\WINDOWS\SYSTEM** directory and run the Visual Basic TIMES2 project. When you do, the value 1 is displayed in a text box. Each time you click the button marked **Click Me to Multiply by 2**, the value in the text box is sent to the dynamic link library **DYNAM.DLL** and multiplied by 2. The result appears in the text box, doubling each time you click the button.

- TIMES232. A Visual C++ 32-bit DLL example showing how to connect Visual Basic and Visual C++. The file **DYNAM.MAK** is set up for Visual C++ 2.0 or later and will create **DYNAM.DLL**, a dynamic link library file containing a function named DLLCall() (the 32-bit version of **DYNAM.DLL** is included on the diskette). Copy **DYNAM.DLL** to the **C:\WINDOWS\SYSTEM** directory and run the Visual Basic TIMES2 project. When you do, the value 1 is displayed in a text box. Each time you click the button marked **Click Me to Multiply by 2**, the value in the text box is sent to the dynamic link library **DYNAM.DLL** and multiplied by 2. The result appears in the text box, doubling each time you click the button.

- TIPS. How to create tooltips, the yellow prompt boxes that appear when the user places the mouse cursor over a tool in the toolbar. In this case, we have two tools in our toolbar: Draw and Erase. As the mouse cursor passes over these tools, the appropriate tooltip (reading "Draw" or "Erase") appears.

- WIN95. This program shows the use of the Windows 95 controls Toolbar, StatusBar, TabStrip, ImageList, RichTextBox, ProgressBar, Slider, ListView, and TreeView. These are 32-bit controls, and you must use the 32-bit version of Visual Basic to use them. The use of these controls is more or less self-explanatory except for the Slider control: to adjust the setting of the ProgressBar, use the Slider or click the ProgressBar itself. In addition, the RichTextBox control expects to find the rich text file **WRITER.RTF** in the **C:\VBOOK\WRITER** directory.

- WRITER. Multiple-document MDI text editor. Saves to disk, reads from disk, selects text color, scrolls through documents, and so on. Features error handling and a Windows help file, word wrap, scrolling, multiple documents, file handling on disk, and more. To create the Help file, compile **WRITER.RTF** with the help compiler, HC, which is in the directory **VB\HC**.

- XOR. Example showing how to use Xor graphics. We draw a grid of thickening lines, showing a pleasing result when the lines intersect and turn from black to white due to the Xor drawing mode.

- ZOOMER. An OLE example showing how to zoom an OLE item. This example assumes that you have Microsoft Excel. Start the program, which shows the OLE item with a particular size. Click the button marked **Zoom** to double the dimensions of the OLE item; then double-click the OLE item to open it zoomed to twice its normal height and width. Zooming OLE items can be useful, allowing you to examine them in detail.

INDEX

N